Studying Politics
An Introduction to Political Science

Edited by
Rand
Dyck
Laurentian
University

THOMSON

NELSON

Australia   Canada   Mexico   Singapore   Spain   United Kingdom   United States

THOMSON

NELSON

**Studying Politics: An Introduction to
Political Science**

Edited by Rand Dyck

Editorial Director and Publisher:
Evelyn Veitch

Executive Acquisitions Editor:
Chris Carson

Senior Marketing Manager:
Murray Moman

Senior Developmental Editor:
Rebecca Rea

Production Editor:
Tammy Scherer

Senior Production Coordinator:
Hedy Sellers

Copy Editor:
Eliza Marciniak

Proofreader:
Margaret Allen

Creative Director:
Angela Cluer

Interior Design:
Aaron Benson

Cover Design:
Ken Phipps

Cover Image:
Irving B. Haynes

Compositor:
W.G. Graphics

Printer:
Webcom

**National Library of Canada
Cataloguing in Publication Data**

Studying politics: an introduction to political science/edited by Rand Dyck.

Includes bibliographical references and index.
ISBN 0-17-616967-9

1. Political science. I. Dyck, Rand, 1943–

JA66.S84 2002   320   C2002–905407-9

Brief Contents

Contents

We dedicate this book to those who are about to experience the joys of studying politics, in the hope and expectation that they will emerge stimulated by and committed to the subject and thus become citizens capable of dealing with the domestic and global challenges of the 21st century.

Preface

Although there are many good introductory texts available in the field of political science in Canada, we feel it is time for a new one—a fresh new text for the new century. We saw the need for a text that incorporates the best of the traditional approaches and subject matter of the discipline, but at the same time acknowledges how patterns of domestic and global politics and the ways they are studied are changing at a rapid pace. The market was asking for a text designed for Canadian students, one that opens their eyes to important developments around the globe. We think this resulting work will have wide appeal among students and professors alike.

THE DEVELOPMENT OF *Studying Politics*

We canvassed a large number of professors of first-year political science courses and asked them what they wanted included in such a text. We then assembled an impressive array of leading Canadian political scientists from across the country, most of whom also teach the introductory political science course at their respective institutions, and asked each one to write a chapter in the area of his or her expertise. But we also put them together in a room and asked them to come up with common themes, common approaches, and a common format, so that their chapters would speak to each other and so that there would be a seamless transition from one to the next. Numerous political science professors were then asked to review their work and to suggest revisions.

A TEXT WRITTEN FOR STUDENTS

We believe this to be the most student-friendly text on the market today. *Studying Politics* starts out with a gentle introduction to the subject of politics and political science, conscious of the fact that many students will not have formally encountered this discipline before. Even when we get into the difficult topics and subjects, we have tried to write at an appropriate level and avoid confusing jargon. Pedagogically, basic con-

cepts are defined in definition boxes in the text and in a glossary at the end of the book. Moreover, we have integrated a large number of tables, figures, photographs, cartoons, and discussion boxes to clarify, stimulate, and amuse, and to add to the visual appeal of the book. In each chapter there is also a list of learning objectives, discussion questions, and Web links. In addition, we have provided profiles of political science graduates, illustrating how their study of politics contributed to their exciting and varied careers.

A TEXT WRITTEN FOR PROFESSORS

As for professors, *Studying Politics* provides the content and approaches that teachers of introductory political science courses are looking for. All traditional subjects are included, given substantial discussion, and organized logically. But newer concepts are also fully covered. The book has a comparative/conceptual approach, but remains Canadian. *Studying Politics* is accompanied by a wonderful array of ancillary materials, including a comprehensive Instructor's Manual, Test Banks, PowerPoint slides, and a video. The book has its own website at http://www.studyingpolitics.nelson.com, which contains a variety of other features; it is supplemented by Nelson's impressive general political science website at http://www.polisci.nelson.com.

ACKNOWLEDGMENTS

With such guidance from the political science community, with such talented, enthusiastic, and committed contributors involved, and with a top-notch publishing team at Nelson, it was not a difficult job for me to coordinate the whole project. By way of acknowledgment, I must first thank the contributors to this book. It was a joy to work with these impressive and accomplished people. Busy as they were with their teaching duties and other writing and research projects, they were all most faithful and cooperative in making this work a reality.

Then I wish to acknowledge the contributions of the many other political science professors who were asked for advice in the planning of the book or in reviewing draft chapters. Their recommendations led to many valuable changes. Among these reviewers were Christopher Dunn, Memorial University; Syed S. Islam, Lakehead University; James Kelly, Brock University; Dan W. Middlemiss, Dalhousie University; Eric Mintz, Sir Wilfred Grenfell College; Ross Rudolph, York University; David Winchester, Capilano College; and Ken Woodside, University of Guelph.

In the third place, we thank the organizations, publishers, newspapers, photographers, and cartoonists who gave us permission to reproduce their work, which has so complemented our written words.

Finally, as a veteran author attached to the Nelson Thomson publishing company, I wish to thank the wonderful people at that organization who asked me to undertake the role of general editor of this book and then gave me and the other contributors every imaginable kind of support. It could not have been done without the daily assistance, encouragement, and advice of my dear friends Rebecca Rea and Chris Carson. The specialized contributions that I am aware of and immensely grateful for are those of Murray Moman, marketeer *extraordinaire;* our copy-editor, Eliza Marciniak, who standardized the style and in the process made many substantive improvements; and the artistic people in the production department.

Rand Dyck
Laurentan University

About the Authors

Yasmeen Abu-Laban is an Associate Professor in the Department of Political Science at the University of Alberta. Her research interests centre on the Canadian and comparative dimensions of gender and ethnic politics, nationalism and globalization, immigration policies and politics, and citizenship theory. She is the co-author (with Christina Gabriel) of *Selling Diversity: Immigration, Multiculturalism, Employment Equity and Globalization* (2002). She has also published articles in *International Politics, The Canadian Journal of Political Science, Canadian Public Policy,* and *Canadian Ethnic Studies.*

Sandra Burt is a member of the Department of Political Science at the University of Waterloo, where she teaches courses on gender issues, Canadian politics, and the policy-making process. Between 1999 and 2002, she was the English co-editor of the *Canadian Journal of Political Science.* Much of her research and writing have focused on women and the policymaking process in Canada. She has recently been involved in a multidisciplinary project investigating municipal environmental tobacco smoke policies.

James Busumtwi-Sam is an Associate Professor in the Department of Political Science at Simon Fraser University, where he was a recent recipient of the Excellence in Teaching Award. He specializes in international relations and comparative development. He has published work on the politics of development finance and the role of international financial institutions; international organizations and regional security; the political economy of conflict and peacebuilding in Africa; and the politics of macroeconomic policy reform and financial liberalization in developing countries.

William D. Coleman holds the Canada Research Chair on Global Governance and Public Policy and is the director of the Institute on Globalization and the Human Condition at McMaster University. He has written four books and edited three others. Among his awards are the Konrad Adenauer Research Award from the Alexander von Humboldt-Stiftung in Bonn, the 3M Teaching Fellowship, and the Ontario Confederation of University Faculty Associations (OCUFA) Teaching Award. In 2002, he headed a team that received a Major Collaborative Research Initiatives grant from the Social Sciences and Humanities Research Council of Canada (SSHRCC) to study globalization and autonomy.

Rand Dyck is a Professor in the Department of Political Science at Laurentian University, where he won the Teaching Excellence Award along with the OCUFA Teaching Award in 2002, and where he previously served as Vice-Dean of Social Sciences and Humanities. He is the author of several widely used textbooks in Canadian political science: *Provincial Politics in Canada* (1996), *Canadian Politics: Critical Approaches* (the fourth edition of which will be published in 2003 by Nelson Thomson Learning), and *Canadian Politics,* concise second edition (2002).

Peter A. Ferguson is currently completing his Ph.D. degree at the University of British Columbia after teaching for the past three years as an Assistant Professor of Political Studies at the University of Saskatchewan. He received his previous education at prominent U.S. universities. His research focuses on questions surrounding democratization, and he is currently working on a comprehensive analysis of postwar democratic breakdowns.

Andrew Heard is an Associate Professor at Simon Fraser University and an Honourary Adjunct Professor at Dalhousie University. He was a parliamentary intern in the House of Commons before completing his graduate work. His research interests include Canadian constitutional law, parliamentary government, judicial behaviour, electoral systems, and theories of human rights. He has held a Canada Research Fellowship and is the author of *Canadian Constitutional Conventions* (1991). He has managed several political science resource websites, and he thoroughly enjoys teaching.

Heather MacIvor teaches Canadian politics and political theory at the University of Windsor. She has published books and articles about political parties, electoral systems, democratic theory, women's political participation, and party leadership selection. Her books include *Women and Politics in Canada* (1996) and *Canadian Political Parties in the Twenty-First Century* (2003). Her current research interests include the impact of the Charter of Rights on Canadian political parties, the comparative study of electoral systems, and the influence of the irrational in politics.

Kim Richard Nossal is the head of the Department of Political Studies at Queen's University, where he teaches international relations and the first-year introduction to political science. He previously spent 25 years teaching at McMaster University. He is one of the country's foremost authorities on global politics and is the author of numerous books and articles on international relations and Canadian foreign policy, including *The Politics of Canadian Foreign Policy* (1997) and *The Patterns of World Politics* (1998).

Brenda O'Neill is an Assistant Professor of Political Studies at the University of Manitoba. Her research is devoted to the study of Canadian women's political behaviour, specifically their political opinions and voting behaviour. Her recent publications include *Citizen Politics: Research and Theory in Canadian Political Behaviour* (with Joanna Everitt, 2002) and articles in the *International Journal of Canadian Studies,* the *Canadian Journal of Political Science,* and the *International Political Science Review.*

Stephen Phillips is Chair of the Political Science Department at Langara College in Vancouver. Trained in law as well as in political science, he is chiefly interested in Canadian politics and comparative government. He is a member of the advisory board of *Annual Editions: Canadian Politics* and belongs to the British Political Studies Association. In addition to academic pursuits, he is active in the New Democratic Party and currently serves on policy committees on proportional representation of the British Columbia and federal NDP.

Donald J. Savoie holds the Clement Cormier Chair in Economic Development at l'Université de Moncton. He is a past president of the Canadian Political Science Association and the author of numerous books and articles in political science and public administration. He was awarded the Vanier Gold Medal by the Institute of Public Administration of Canada; he has also been made an Officer of the Order of Canada and elected a Fellow of the Royal Society of Canada. He has been awarded four honourary degrees and several prizes for his contribution to the public administration literature.

Richard Sigurdson is an Associate Professor and Head of the Department of Political Science at the University of New Brunswick, where he teaches primarily in the fields of Canadian politics and political theory. His recent publications include "John Diefenbaker's One Canada and the Legacy of Unhyphenated Canadianism" and "Crossing Borders: Immigration, Citizenship and the Challenge to Nationality." Forthcoming are *Jacob Burckhardt's Social and Political Thought* and a book on nationalism.

Miriam Smith is a Professor in the Department of Political Science at Carleton University. She specializes in Canadian and comparative politics, especially social movements, sociology of law, and lesbian and gay politics in Canada. She is the author of *Lesbian and Gay Rights in Canada* (1999), co-author (with Charles Hauss) of *Comparative Politics: Domestic Responses to Global Challenges: A Canadian Perspective* (Nelson Thomson Learning, 2000), and co-editor of *New Trends in Canadian Federalism* (1995).

Douglas A. West is an Associate Professor and Chair in the Department of Political Science at Lakehead University in Thunder Bay, Ontario. His main research interests include Canadian political ideas, northern and Native political movements, political theory, and restorative justice. He also participates on a voluntary basis in a wide variety of community development projects, including those associated with the independent living and the social planning movements in Ontario and elsewhere.

Introduction

Career Profile: Daniel Charbonneau

Dan Charbonneau grew up in Sudbury, Ontario, and graduated with an Honours B.A. in political science from Laurentian University. While at Laurentian, Dan came across the story of how Brian Mulroney got his start in politics at the model parliament of St. Francis Xavier University in Antigonish, Nova Scotia. Being stimulated by daily political events, he decided to pursue the idea at his own school. In 1993, on his initiative, Laurentian University established an annual model parliament for students in political science. Since 1998, the proceedings have been held in the House of Commons chamber in Ottawa, and Dan has continued to help organize them, frequently serving as Speaker of the Commons.

Upon graduation, Dan was hired as a constituency assistant by Ray Bonin, the Member of Parliament for Nickel Belt, Ontario. After two years, he transferred to Mr. Bonin's Ottawa office, becoming Senior Outreach Officer. Then, in 2001, he left the partisan arena for the job of Clerk of the Standing Senate Committee on Agriculture and Forestry at Canada's Senate. As the chief administrator of the committee, Dan organizes all meetings called by the chair (many of which involve travelling across the country) and is responsible for the committee's budget. As the committee's procedural advisor, he advises the chair and committee members on all questions of parliamentary procedure relating to their work, assists in drafting motions and legislative amendments, prepares administrative reports, and works in cooperation with the Library of Parliament to prepare substantive research reports. As the committee's information officer, he handles media inquiries and information requests from the public. He also assisted the Senate Special Committee on Illegal Drugs, whose 2002 report recommended the legalization of cannabis.

Chapter 1

Studying Politics

Rand Dyck

CHAPTER OBJECTIVES

After you have completed this chapter, you should be able to

- provide several good reasons to study politics
- describe the breadth of the discipline of political science
- discuss the changing nature of studying politics
- outline the basic fields of study within political science
- define such basic concepts as politics, government, power, influence, coercion, and authority.

WHY STUDY POLITICS?

Before you commit yourself to studying politics, even in an introductory course in political science, you may well be asking the following three questions:

a) Is it interesting?

b) Is it important?

c) If I decide to major in political science, is there a job at the end of the line?

This chapter and this book seek to assure you that the answer to all three questions is an unequivocal "YES!"

Politics Is Fascinating

That politics is important is the basic reason to study it, of course, but let us start with the fact that the subject is interesting—often fascinating and even entertaining. This is partly because politics involves prominent individuals, with all their strengths, weaknesses, foibles, and idiosyncrasies, and we cannot help but be captivated by such colourful, intriguing people. A few recent examples are Jean Chrétien, Bill Clinton, Alberta's populist premier, Ralph Klein, and Toronto's frenzied mayor, Mel Lastman. Political leaders who have arguably left more meaningful legacies include Winston Churchill, in his determination to defeat the Nazi threat in World War II; Margaret Thatcher, with her "Iron Lady" determination to reduce the role of the state in the 1980s; Nelson Mandela, in his gracious stature as President of South Africa, devoid of bitterness even after having spent 27 years in prison for fighting against apartheid; Pierre Elliott Trudeau, with his stylish, debonair, and often arrogant demeanour as Canadian prime minister; Martin Luther King, whose courageous leadership of the fight for racial integration in the United States had a tremendous impact; Mahatma Gandhi, in his effective pacifist resistance to British rule in India; and even Eva Peron, immortalized in the musical *Evita*, who fought for the rights of women and the poor in Argentina, however opportunistic were her motives. One could also think of political leaders who had a devastating impact on their own countries or the world: Attila the Hun, Adolf

Hitler, Joseph Stalin, Augusto Pinochet (in Chile), and Ferdinand and Imelda Marcos (in the Philippines).

Part of the reason that the subject is so interesting is that egos and ambition abound in political life, and the leading participants are usually involved in antagonistic relationships, either with colleagues or opponents. The daily oral question period in the Canadian and British Houses of Commons and in provincial legislatures is usually a great show. The prolonged animosity between Jean Chrétien and Paul Martin, the long-standing finance minister in his cabinet, in the race for the Liberal Party leadership titillated Canadians for years. Stockwell Day's first press conference as leader of the Canadian Alliance, at which he arrived on a personal watercraft and clothed in a wet suit, attracted much attention, as did the subsequent efforts of fellow party members to bring him down.

The personal characteristics of political leaders, their personality conflicts, and the peculiarity of many of their decisions provide daily fodder for cartoonists, comedians, and satirical radio and television show hosts. Every daily newspaper features a cartoon on its editorial page, and more often than not, such cartoons reflect the humorous (or tragicomic) nature of politics. We have selected some of the best recent editorial cartoons to brighten and lighten up the material in this text. Canadians excel at political satire; two of the most popular television programs in the country are *The Royal Canadian Air Farce* and *This Hour Has 22 Minutes*. If you are not already familiar with these programs on CBC television, we strongly encourage you to give them a try.

Joe Clark with fire in his belly.
Malcolm Mayes/Artizans

While political events and personalities are interesting and often entertaining to observe, many people prefer to actively take part rather than passively follow political developments. Politics offers many exciting opportunities for participation. Joining a political party or interest group, collecting names on a petition, going to a public meeting to discuss an issue of political importance, getting involved in an election campaign at any level, or taking part in a political demonstration—all of these can be social activities that combine significance with camaraderie, excitement, and fun.

Politics Is Important

Besides being fascinating, politics is important; it has significant implications for how we live our lives. At its core, politics is about government actions and public policies that affect everyone in one way or another. When we consider water policy in Walkerton, Ontario, or mine safety policy at the Westray coal mine in Nova Scotia, for example, we can see that policies are often deadly serious. But there is even more to it than that. Because government actions and policies usually offer support for some people at the expense of others, they are normally accompanied by controversy and inevitably involve conflict. Such policy conflicts can be just as fascinating as the peculiarities of the individual policymakers involved.

There is not much dispute about the idea that government should guarantee law and order in society by passing laws to make certain types of behaviour a crime and by hiring police officers and building jails. But beyond this basic consensus, political controversies immediately begin to arise. You may well have your own opinion on these matters. Does the Canadian government's antiterrorism legislation infringe upon civil liberties? Is it a crime to kill a severely disabled daughter, as in the case of Robert Latimer, or to demonstrate against the government, as in the case of some young people at the Quebec City Summit of the Americas who spent two months in jail? You may be hoping for a career in policing, and whether the government should hire more women and visible-minority police officers may be of personal interest to you. Should private companies be given contracts to operate jails? Should the penalty for murder be capital punishment?

It is usually assumed that national governments should establish armed forces to protect the country from external threats. But how large should such armed forces be? What kinds of armaments and equipment should be provided? Should the United States build a new missile defence shield in space to protect itself and its friends from the weapons of terrorists and "rogue" states? Should a country require military training of all its citizens, especially those about the age of most readers of this book? Even in the case of internal and external security—a seemingly straightforward issue—politics becomes quite complicated because there are many different and conflicting ways of proceeding.

Beyond the commonly accepted notion of providing for law, order, and security, the question arises as to whether the government should intervene in society at all. Generally speaking, government action was limited until about 1900; the extent of government intervention then increased over the first eight decades of the 20th century, but after 1985 or so began to recede. Most governments, especially in the early part of the 21st century, continue to limit the degree of their intervention; if they must take action, they prefer to resort to symbolic acts or moral suasion. But if a government decides to get more involved, what form should such intervention take? We are all familiar with myriad government regulations that guide individual, group, and corporate behaviour, for example, and with government programs that provide many kinds of services and control money transfers to individuals, groups, communities, provinces, and corporations. In order to finance such regulation, services, and transfers, the government normally has to engage in taxation. Occasionally, though less frequently than in the past, governments go beyond regulation, services, transfers, and taxation; they actually buy or establish corporations and have them function as public-owned enterprises. In Canada, these are called crown corporations.

There is still virtual unanimity that government provision of a public education system is beneficial for society as a whole. But the consensus immediately breaks down around questions of what should be taught in such schools. For example, whether to teach evolution or creationism remains an issue for some people, including Stockwell Day, the ex-leader of the Canadian Alliance. This also leads to the question of whether there should be only one public education system or whether private institutions can be established. What about religious schools and home schooling? Should public funds be available for schools that are not part of the public system? As a recent secondary school graduate, you may well have opinions on these matters. Postsecondary education issues include the level of tuition fees, grants, and loans; the idea of private universities; and in the case of Trinity Western University in British Columbia, the question of whether the institution should teach that homosexuality is a sin.

As costs escalate, the role of government in the provision of health services has also become particularly controversial. To what extent should there be a universal, public health-care system, or what health services should people have to pay for outside that system: physiotherapy? circumcisions? eyeglasses? Should people who can afford it be allowed faster or superior service, as the proponents of the so-called two-tier system believe? Should the universal system be extended to cover pharmaceuticals and dental care? What about deterrent fees?

Education and health are the two most expensive public services provided by governments today, but the array of other social services is extensive, although far from unanimously supported. Should the government ensure that no one goes hungry, through one or more initiatives such as public pensions for the elderly and disabled, child benefits, employment insurance, or social assistance? Should the government ensure that no one is homeless? Should single mothers who want to pursue postsecondary education be provided with childcare services?

The preceding sketch of public programs leads to the question of how to finance the operations that government does decide to undertake. Who should pay what kinds of taxes? Should there be a flat rate for everyone, or should richer people pay at a higher rate? Should all forms of income be taxed equally, or should capital gains, for example, be taxed at a lower rate? What about lottery winnings? Should business people be allowed to deduct entertainment expenses from their income tax? What about charitable donations, political contributions, and interest paid on loans to buy stocks and shares?

The implications of the issues just raised are of considerable importance. Political decisions on these issues influence, if not determine, what kind of lifestyle a person or a family may possess; they can certainly make life easier or more difficult, as you yourself, as a student, can attest. While they are significant, such decisions, actions, and policies rarely constitute matters of life and death in the generally comfortable Canadian context. Canada ranked first for seven consecutive years in the United Nations **Human Development Index (HDI)** in terms of life expectancy, literacy, and income, as Prime Minister Chrétien never tired of pointing out. In 2001, however, Canada fell to third place on the general index, and in 2002 it ranked seventh on the gender empowerment index and twelfth in terms of reducing human poverty. Some of these statistics are revealed in Table 1.1.

When one looks beyond Canada and the other industrialized democracies, the decisions made by governments often have much more serious implications. Huge portions of the global population suffer from the insecurities of poverty, malnutrition, illness, and homelessness. In many cases, national governments could improve the situation with a fairer distribution of income, an internal political decision. Other situations require a helping hand from richer, industrialized countries. Many corners of the world are engaged in civil wars or military conflicts with external enemies, where government decisions or terrorist retaliations put lives in danger on a daily basis. These include Afghanistan, the Middle East (and the never-ending Israeli–Palestinian conflict), many parts of Africa, and the Balkans (Yugoslavia, Serbia, Bosnia, Kosovo, Montenegro, etc.), among others. In short, politics is a matter of life and death in a large part of the globe. The study of this important subject may serve as the first step in trying to solve such problems.

The Question of Citizenship

Another aspect of the importance of politics revolves around the obligations of citizenship. Simply put, citizens of a democracy are expected to develop the best understanding they can of the political system in which they live, in return for the right of having a say in its governance. Studying politics is hard intellectual work that will make students better thinkers and better citizens.

The concept of citizenship has changed considerably over time. In ancient Athens, for example, citizenship was severely restricted, excluding women, labourers,

---

Table 1.1 Top 15 Rankings in Various United Nations Human Development Indexes, 2002

Human Development	Gender Empowerment	Least Poverty
1. Norway	1. Norway	1. Sweden
2. Sweden	2. Iceland	2. Norway
3. Canada	3. Sweden	3. Netherlands
4. Belgium	4. Denmark	4. Finland
5. Australia	5. Finland	5. Denmark
6. United States	6. Netherlands	6. Germany
7. Iceland	7. Canada	7. Luxembourg
8. Netherlands	8. Germany	8. France
9. Japan	9. New Zealand	9. Japan
10. Finland	10. Australia	10. Spain
11. Switzerland	11. United States	11. Italy
12. France	12. Austria	12. Canada
13. United Kingdom	13. Switzerland	13. Belgium
14. Denmark	14. Belgium	14. Australia
15. Austria	15. Spain	15. United Kingdom

Source: United Nations, *Human Development Report*; cited on July 26, 2002; available at http://www.undp.org/hdr2002/indicator. Reprinted by permission of the United Nations.

slaves, and foreigners. But those propertied males who were citizens were expected to play a direct, almost full-time part in the governing of their city-state.

Early in the 20th century, in most civilized countries, women and the working class forced their way into becoming part of the electorate, and other exclusions from the right to vote were gradually eliminated. **Citizenship** became virtually universal, and it came to mean membership in a nation-state that entails rights and responsibilities within it, including that of political participation. On the other hand, a very small proportion of citizens made political life a full-time preoccupation. The direct democracy of ancient Greece evolved into a representative democracy, in which periodic elections became the main focus of political activity for the general population. In an ideal case, everyone would at least cast an informed vote in such elections.

In the period between 1945 and 1985, often called the period of the welfare state, the concept of citizenship in industrialized countries changed again. Citizens came to expect the state to provide universal programs of social security to overcome the negative effects of economic uncertainty associated with private-sector market forces. Since 1985, however, there has been an increasing consensus throughout the Western world that citizens should be more self-reliant. The balance between individual and collective responsibility underwent a major shift as governments balanced their budgets by dismantling social programs while also lowering taxes. In almost every state, the government plays a smaller role today than it did in 1985, be it in terms of regulation, ownership, taxation, or social services.

A rather dramatic development in such industrialized democracies as Canada, the United Kingdom, and the United States is the declining voter turnout rate in recent elections. Although this trend has many causes, it can be partially attributed to the fact that as the government becomes less involved in society, citizens decide that it is not as important to vote.

In this book, on the contrary, we take the position that governments continue to make a wide range of crucial decisions for society, even in the advanced, industrialized democracies such as Canada. Therefore, it is still an important obligation of citizens to cast an informed vote in elections, as well as to try to influence government decisions during the interelection period.

Studying politics is the most logical route to developing an understanding of our political system.

Moreover, besides being a citizen of a specific state, we are all now citizens of the world, and we are all subject to unprecedented global forces. The question is often raised as to whether individual states are still as capable of providing for their own citizens as in the past. We are all affected by worldwide environmental developments, massive migrations of dispossessed people, and the concentration of capital in an ever-decreasing number of rapidly expanding transnational corporations. By studying politics, global citizens can help meet their obligation to understand as much as they can about the state of the globe, and to do their part to try to improve it.

Political Science Graduates Get Jobs

But does anybody hire students who decide to study and graduate with a degree in political science? The answer is yes, and the diversity of the jobs would probably astound you. This book will introduce you to several young people who have gone beyond the introductory course to specialize in political science in Canadian universities and show you the range of their career experiences.

When you tell someone you are studying political science, chances are they will jump to the conclusion that you plan to become a politician! That may well be your intention, and a noble calling it is, however much abuse politicians take in the media and in public discussion. Many political science graduates *do* become politicians, and many politicians are political science graduates. Speaking only of Canada, many of those elected to the House of Commons, provincial legislatures, municipal councils, and other political posts have graduated in this field. We give you the example of Graham Steele on page 237.

The number of politicians is fairly limited, however, and not all political science graduates can or want to choose this option. Many are employed as assistants to politicians, be they MPs, senators, members of provincial legislatures, or cabinet ministers. Very often, a period of employment in this capacity leads people to seek political office on their own.

Another career avenue is to work for the government—federal, provincial, or municipal. These three levels of government employ over a million people, and a good proportion of these employees are political science graduates. Such graduates typically work in management positions or are involved in policy development. That is, they advise on which policies should be pursued and work to implement these policies once they are adopted. Joanne Fowler, whom we profile on page 123, is an excellent example. With government downsizing and privatization characteristic of the post-1985 period, few such positions have been available, but if you are graduating in the early years of the 21st century, your prospects are much brighter. In the next 10 years or so, governments at all levels will be replacing thousands of employees who have reached retirement age.

BOX 1.1

CIVIL SERVICE TO HIRE 12 000 A YEAR

After a decade of downsizing its workforce, the Canadian federal government expects to hire up to 12 000 new full-time workers a year for the new decade as waves of baby boomers retire and the face of the public service changes.

Treasury Board forecasts are calling for a complete rejuvenation or "renewal" of the federal public service over the next decade. With the average public servant pushing age 45, a large slice of Canada's bureaucrats will turn over by 2010, opening up job opportunities not seen since the 1970s.

Source: *Ottawa Citizen*, August 13, 2000; cited on June 28, 2001; available at http://www.ottawacitizen.com/national/000813/4579110.html.

In addition to jobs at regular government departments, there are many work opportunities at semi-independent government agencies, boards, commissions, and crown corporations, such as Elections Canada, Statistics Canada, or indeed, the House of Commons or the Senate. On page 3, we already gave you the example of Dan Charbonneau, a Senate committee clerk.

One aspect of government employment that many political science graduates find attractive is the foreign service—the diplomatic corps. Some people are particularly excited about the prospect of serving at embassies, consulates, or high commissions around the world and of advising on Canada's foreign policy. Once again, a degree in political science is the most appropriate entry to such a career, although a postgraduate degree in international relations and the ability to speak at least two languages is an additional asset. We give you the example of Roberta O. Cross, Canadian Consul and Trade Commissioner in Barcelona, Spain, on page 367. Related to this career is work for an international organization, such as the United Nations, or for a nongovernmental organization (NGO), such as Greenpeace, the Red Cross, Amnesty International, Oxfam, or others, including Third World development agencies.

In addition to NGO employees, many political science graduates prefer to work *close* to the government rather than *for* the government. They are employed by political parties, for example, as researchers, recruiters, organizers, policy advisors, and campaign managers. Political science graduates also possess the skills to seek employment in the media as radio, television, and newspaper reporters and commentators, or with polling firms, as public opinion and voting analysts. Judy Myrden, whom we profile on page 313, finds her political science degree helpful as a journalist. Another related line of work is with interest groups, pressure groups, and think-tanks. In their attempt to analyze or influence government policy, these organizations also value the knowledge and skills acquired in the course of obtaining a political science degree. Some graduates actually establish their own lobbying and consulting firms, providing policy advice for a fee.

Political science is also an appropriate background for a career in law. Although law schools welcome applicants from a wide range of disciplines, it is safe to say that they accept more applicants with political science degrees than with any other educational background. A large proportion of political science graduates from every university in Canada have gone on to law school, as did Graham Steele before he entered the political arena.

Political science graduates can also become teachers. Not all provinces hire political science graduates in their secondary schools, but all teach a certain amount of political science at the college level. Individuals dedicated to political science can also become university professors. We provide 15 examples in the form of contributing authors of this book!

So far, we have mentioned careers that put a premium on a specific *political* component, but political science is so broad in its scope and in the skills the graduates in this area develop that such a degree is valuable in a much wider range of occupations. Renny Khan, for example, whom we profile on page 27, works as the International Relations Officer at the University of Alberta. Political science graduates also find a ready market in business—in corporations of all kinds, national and multinational, from banks and insurance companies to public relations firms. Linda Coady, profiled on page 71, provides a wonderful example of a political science graduate who has made a major contribution to the environmental practices of her firm.

BOX 1.2

SKILLS ACQUIRED IN STUDYING POLITICAL SCIENCE

Thinking Skills
- The ability to think "on your feet"
- Exposure to new, unfamiliar, and alternative perspectives on issues or problems
- The ability to develop logical arguments and assess or evaluate the arguments of others

Research Skills
- Identifying and locating sources of information
- Collecting, analyzing, and interpreting data to support or refute arguments
- Critical understanding of the uses (and potential abuse) of statistics
- Computing skills

Communication Skills
- Making oral presentations and engaging in debates
- Writing reports, summaries, and essays
- Communicating ideas clearly and concisely, whether orally or in writing
- The ability to listen

Source: Department of Political Science, Brock University website; cited on June 15, 2001; available at http://www.brocku.ca/politics/whypoli.htm. Reprinted by permission of the Department of Political Science, Brock University.

The political science curriculum that you are about to embark upon, both in this book and possibly beyond, will help open your eyes to what is happening at home and abroad. You will be required to analyze public issues from a variety of points of view, and in the process you will learn to think clearly and communicate effectively. Your studies will also make you a valuable commodity to a wide range of employers whose focus is not strictly political. The Brock University Department of Political Science website is particularly helpful in identifying the skills that are acquired in pursuing a degree in political science (see Box 1.2).

You will often hear the idea that in the modern world few people will retain a job with a single employer or even have the same kind of job with different employers until retirement and that you will have to be flexible in today's labour market. That is another way of saying that employers are seeking not so much job-specific abilities as skills that allow an employee to adapt to the changing workplace and the changing world. The skills listed in Box 1.2 will be among the most valuable of all in this exciting but unpredictable environment.

THE BREADTH OF THE STUDY OF POLITICS

If we have convinced you that you are on the right track in thinking about studying politics, let us spend the rest of this chapter introducing the subject of politics. Let us show you the breadth of the field and the central concerns of the discipline, and let us provide greater proof that the subject is both interesting and important.

Political Behaviour and Participation

Voting and Elections

In part, politics is about political behaviour and participation. One main aspect of this domain of politics is voting and electing candidates to public office. Politics is also about deciding what kind of electoral system to use; nearly every country has a distinctive process to choose its politicians. Especially in countries where elections are free and fair (a characteristic of democracy), they are usually exciting, entertaining experiences. If you have not been involved in an election campaign, you might wish to track down a candidate and volunteer for action! Of course, you could even become a candidate yourself.

But elections are also very serious events, since the leader or the political party that emerges victorious can have a profound effect on the public policies that are later adopted. The winning party normally proceeds to reward its supporters, whether in the appointments it makes or in the policies it adopts. When George W. Bush succeeded Bill Clinton as president of the United States, for example, his reversal of many of his predecessor's policies had implications far beyond American borders: he reneged on the Kyoto Protocol, denied federal aid to groups that promoted abortion overseas, and generally threw American weight around throughout the world.

Since the mass media play a major role in the election campaigns in most countries, political science also studies the media. Do they give equitable coverage to all parties? Do they encourage an emphasis on image rather than substance? Does television advertising make elections too expensive and take away from their democratic character? Somewhat similarly, public opinion polls have come to feature prominently in election campaigns. Political science is interested in whether they are accurate, whether they favour one party over another, and whether they influence the results.

While being intensely interested in political participation, political science is also concerned with nonparticipation. As mentioned, the voter turnout rate in Canada, the United States, and the United Kingdom seems to be dwindling. Who is not voting, and why? Table 1.2 provides the voter turnout rates in selected countries in the 1990s.

Another method of allowing the general electorate to express itself politically is the referendum. This device is used in most political systems on an occasional basis to discover how the population feels about a specific issue. Should we go so far as to encourage e-politics, frequently referring questions of public importance to people sitting in front of their personal computers? In this book, all of these issues are addressed in Chapter 12.

Political Parties

Politics is also about political parties, which seem to crop up in virtually every political system. In most cases, candidates run for office on a party banner and as a member of a party team. Studying politics involves investigating the number of parties (one, two, three, or

---

Table 1.2 Voter Turnout Rates in 18 Countries, 1990s

Country	Percent	Country	Percent
Italy	90.2	Netherlands	75.2
Belgium	84.1	Germany	72.7
Australia	82.7	United Kingdom	72.4*
Sweden	82.6	Ireland	70.2
Denmark	81.7	France	60.6
New Zealand	80.4	Canada	60.1*
Austria	79.6	Japan	57.0
Spain	79.0	United States	44.9
Norway	75.7	Switzerland	37.7

* The Canadian figure is lower than the official figures for the 1990s because the International Institute for Democracy and Electoral Assistance uses a different methodology, comparing turnout to the census population eligible to vote rather than to the names on the voters' list. By this measure, the turnout rate in the November 2000 election would have been approximately 50 percent rather than the official 60 percent. The official turnout rate in the 2001 U.K. election was also about 60 percent.

Source: International Institute for Democracy and Electoral Assistance, *Voter Turnout: A Global Survey*, cited on September 15, 2001; available at http://www.idea.int. Reprinted by permission of International IDEA.

more) present in what is usually referred to as the party system. Political science is also interested in why established parties sometimes founder and why new parties form. In Canada, for example, we are interested in whether the Liberal Party will predominate forever and in why parties on both the left and the right of the Liberals are having so much trouble establishing themselves as an alternative.

Studying politics involves examining how democratic political parties are organized, how they choose their candidates, how they choose or get rid of their leaders, and how they develop their policies. In terms of how they are financed, is it true that "those who pay the piper call the tune"?

All of these aspects of political parties are discussed in Chapter 11 of this text. Again, most parties would welcome your own participation, and you might even want to become involved in the creation of a new one.

Interest Groups and Social Movements

Many people join together with others who share similar interests to establish organized groups. They may organize simply to promote their common interests without any thought of becoming political. But even if this is the case, such groups often find themselves drawn into the political process when they begin to see defects in government policies. Thus, countries that value freedom of association are characterized by hordes of interest groups that at least occasionally try to put pressure on the government to change public policies. Some groups may be formed with a more deliberate political purpose, and they may spend most of their time trying to influence such policies. The Canadian Federation of Students (CFS), for example, provides certain services for its members, but it is concerned primarily with influencing the policies of federal and provincial governments that affect postsecondary students. More active participation in the CFS by a greater number of students would no doubt make it a stronger political force. On the local level, the student organization at your college or university may often function as a pressure group on your own campus.

The Summit of the Americas meeting in Quebec City in April 2001 attracted thousands of protesters from both Canada and abroad—people who could be said to be part of the antiglobalization movement. Similar social movements include the women's move-ment, the environmental movement, the gay and lesbian movement, and the animal rights movement, among many others. Studying politics also means studying such social movements, whether they operate in a single country or, as is increasingly the case, they network with each other around the world. Possessing such resources as information and time, professors and students are often active in their communities in organizing demonstrations to show their opinion on contentious issues. Engaging in pressure group activity or protests can be a rather enjoyable social activity at the same time as it seriously tries to influence public policies that are felt to be detrimental. Interest groups and social movements are the subject of Chapter 13 in this book.

Political Institutions

Politics is also about the operation of the institutions of government. In fact, historically, this aspect was much more central to the study of politics than was political behaviour. Although the focus of the discipline is wider now, we must never forget that the ways in which government institutions function and the ways in which they might be reformed in order to operate more effectively are highly important topics.

Constitutions

Government institutions are normally provided for in a state's constitution, which is the subject of much study in itself. In some countries, such as the United States of America, the constitution is a single comprehensive document. In contrast, as Chapter 6 of this book shows, the Canadian constitution is an unusual combination of written and unwritten parts.

Another interesting aspect of constitutions is the ease or difficulty with which they can be amended. The process of amending the Canadian constitution is rather complex, and after the experiences of the Meech Lake and Charlottetown Accords, we know that it is almost impossible to get agreement on comprehensive changes.

Most modern constitutions also contain some kind of bill or charter of rights that prohibits the government from interfering with the basic freedoms or liberties of its citizens. Canada added the Charter of Rights and Freedoms to its Constitution in 1982, but that did not mean that Canadians had no such rights beforehand. When there is a question about whether the government has overstepped its bounds, for example in curtailing freedom of expression, it is usually up to the courts or judiciary to decide the issue.

The Political Executive

The constitution normally establishes institutions that embody four branches of government: the executive, the legislature, the bureaucracy, and the judiciary. The executive branch of government usually consists of a head of state—a president or a monarch—who may be largely ceremonial, as in Britain and Canada, or imbued with great power, as in the United States or Mexico. In the case of a country with a ceremonial head of state, there is also an effective decision-making body, often called a prime minister and cabinet. As in the case of any organization, as you may know from your own experience, the executive provides leadership and makes many of the key decisions. Studying politics includes

examining how such executive bodies function, including the question as to who *really* makes the big decisions in running a government.

The Bureaucracy

Nobody expects those politicians who make up the executive branch of government to be able to solve all of society's problems single-handed. For the most part, they are fairly ordinary mortals without a profound knowledge of the issues they are called upon to address. But in modern political systems, these politicians are assisted and advised by permanent, professional employees of the state whose job it is to be able to answer whatever questions the politicians ask. The members of the public service or bureaucracy advise the politicians on which policies to pursue and how to pursue them, and then they administer the policies adopted. The bureaucracy is the largest branch of a

The Parliament Buildings in Ottawa are the seat of the Government of Canada.

Peter Bregg/CP Picture Archive

21st-century government, and no successful politician would go very far without asking the bureaucrats for advice. Studying politics therefore means spending considerable time in assessing the role of the bureaucracy in the policy process. Chapter 7 of this book examines the political executive as well as the bureaucracy.

The Legislature

Almost every political system has a legislative chamber made up of the elected representatives of the people, variously called the House of Commons, House of Representatives, Chamber of Deputies, etc. If chosen in free and fair elections, this chamber is a defining sign of a democracy. In some countries, including Canada, the members of the executive branch also sit in the legislature, but in others, as in the United States, they are separately elected. In either case, it is essential that the legislative branch give approval to laws, whatever their origin. Many Canadian Members of Parliament, feeling that they have little influence in the making of government policies, look longingly south of the border at the real power of members of the American House of Representatives and Senate. On the other hand, American observers often envy the efficiency with which the government of Canada can make decisions. Studying politics means examining legislative chambers and assessing the functions they perform, as well as understanding the logic of single-chamber and dual-chamber legislatures. These topics will be covered in Chapter 9 of this text.

The Judiciary

Ideally, every state should have an independent judiciary, a system of courts that aim to make impartial decisions when it becomes necessary to interpret the law in cases of dispute. Studying politics has not always involved paying much attention to judicial interpretation, but this may have been a serious oversight. Nowadays, the courts seem to be making more significant decisions than previously, partly because most states have some version of a bill of rights that has to be interpreted, and partly because the judiciary has become intensely scrutinized as an integral part of the political process. Are judicial decisions impartial? How should judges be chosen? When should they be removed? Such questions are discussed in Chapter 10.

* * *

Studying politics thus includes examining how presidents, prime ministers, cabinets, councils of ministers, houses of commons or representatives, senates, bureaucracies, and courts function individually and how they interact with each other. It involves looking for the strengths and weaknesses in each national set of government institutions and tackling the question of whether what has proved successful in one country might be adopted or adapted elsewhere.

Political Values, Ideas, and Ideologies

Studying politics also means studying political values, ideas, and ideologies. These can be seen as the inspiration for much of the political behaviour and participation that we have mentioned, as well as for the decisions made by the various governmental institutions. In fact, politics is often about values, ideas, and ideologies, even when it seems to centre on more trivial issues.

Political Socialization and Political Culture

Most citizens have certain political values and ideas, whether they realize it or not. Where do these values come from? Political science uses the term *political socialization* to refer to the process of acquiring such values and ideas. Think about your own case: What are some of your own political values and ideas? Can you figure out where they came from? Common agents of political socialization are families, schools, peers, and the mass media, although there are many other sources.

Political science focuses primarily on those values and ideas that relate to the role of government in society. Figure 1.1 indicates an interesting difference of opinion on this role among Canadians of different party preferences. If we can find values and ideas that are widely held in any political system, we call such a collection the political culture. The politics of any society takes place within an often distinctive context of values and attitudes. Switzerland, for example, prefers to have citizens make many decisions by way of referendums. Chapter 4 deals with both political socialization and political culture.

Figure 1.1 Spending the Surplus: Priorities by Party Preference

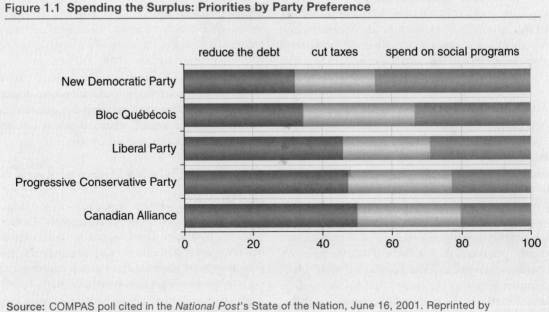

reduce the debt   cut taxes   spend on social programs

New Democratic Party

Bloc Québécois

Liberal Party

Progressive Conservative Party

Canadian Alliance

0   20   40   60   80   100

Source: COMPAS poll cited in the *National Post*'s State of the Nation, June 16, 2001. Reprinted by permission of *The National Post*.

Political Ideas and Philosophy

In the same way that we can ask where an individual's basic values and ideas came from, we can also inquire about the origins of the basic concepts in the study of politics. This inquiry usually takes us back to ancient Greece. There we find philosophers such as Socrates, Plato, and Aristotle asking the following questions: What is justice? What is the best form of the state? Who should govern? and What are the obligations of citizenship? When you start to think about them, none of these is easy to answer, but the ancient Greeks were the first ones to try.

Later on, other political philosophers added their thoughts on these and other questions. Machiavelli told us how he thought a prince should govern, and Jean-Jacques Rousseau, Thomas Hobbes, John Locke, and John Stuart Mill all contributed profound ideas about the relationship between the individual and the state and about the concepts of citizenship, equality, freedom, and liberty, among others. Even if these writers were not widely read by the general public, some of their ideas greatly influenced political developments such as the French and American Revolutions

and the evolution of democracy. Similarly, Karl Marx's call for a working-class revolution to overthrow the alleged evils of capitalism had an enormous impact on the shape of the world in the 20th century. The ideas of subsequent political philosophers also influenced the way in which that century ended, and the new century will doubtless produce political philosophers of its own.

Studying politics, therefore, includes studying the ideas of the great minds that have addressed various concepts central to political thought over the centuries. It cannot be complete without examining what these thinkers had to say, and hence some of their views are discussed in Chapter 5.

Political Ideologies

When a person or group holds a consistent set of ideas about the objectives of political life, we often call it an ideology. An ideology usually includes a collection of related thoughts on the respective roles of the individual and the government in the state. In the daily battle among politicians and among political parties, we expect their words, promises, and decisions to reflect a basic ideological framework. The labels we apply to such sets of ideas include liberalism, conservatism, socialism, communism, fascism, nationalism, individualism, collectivism, feminism, environmentalism, populism, and radicalism, among others,[1] and political scientists are always on the lookout to classify politicians and parties in terms of such ideologies.

It is often expected, for example, that democratic political systems will be characterized by two or more political parties with at least slightly different ideological orientations. In a two-party system, one party might emphasize equality and collectivism, while the other might favour individualism and privilege. In a three-party system, there might be a third party occupying a central ideological position between these two. In a multiparty system, there could be four or more parties, each claiming a narrow part of the ideological continuum: communists, socialists, social democrats, liberals, conservatives, neoconservatives, and so on. Even if such ideological clarity and consistency is often lacking in the real world, the subject remains an important part of the study of politics.

Among political values, ideas, and ideologies that are prominent in the 21st century are those of nationalism and cultural pluralism. We seem to have moved from a world made up of nation-states, in which the population was quite homogeneous, to a situation where most states are characterized by ethnic diversity. As mentioned before, there have been huge waves of migration around the world in the past 50 years, leaving few states without the problem of accommodating a variety of cultural groups within them. In many countries, Aboriginal populations have also become much more self-conscious and assertive. These cultural groups that exist within a society often wish to practise as much self-government as possible. This is true even in a traditional multiethnic state, the United Kingdom, as Scotland and Wales are granted more autonomy. The place of Quebec in the Canadian federation also comes to mind.

Whether or not multiethnic states give increasing powers to the different cultural groups within them, all states are simultaneously affected by the external forces of globalization. Thus, while many people are identifying with a small cultural group on the one hand, on the other they are increasingly conscious of being citizens of the world, subject to universalizing influences. Studying politics today includes studying the reconciliation of such seemingly opposite values. Chapter 3 focuses on such questions.

Political Development and Change

At one point in time, studying politics may have been largely confined to studying political ideas, institutions, and behaviour in the advanced, industrialized, often democratic states. But it cannot be so restricted any longer. Today, the study of politics must include what is often called the Third World or developing world, the concern of Chapter 14. Why are some countries rich and others poor? Why are some advanced and others underdeveloped? Is it a question of resources, distribution, or colonialism and exploitation? Should we expect every country to embrace the kind of democracy that we think is best? As the events of September 11, 2001, revealed, religious fundamentalism in developing countries can have dire implications for the whole world.

As for political change, we seem to be seeing a general movement from nondemocratic to democratic regimes around the world. Is this really true, and if so, what are the factors behind this fundamental transformation? How are democratic regimes consolidated in such situations, and what are the consequences? On the other hand, is there any movement in the opposite direction? Are any democracies breaking down, and if so, why? Another aspect of political change relates to questions of dissent, protest, rebellion, and violence, including terrorism and revolution. Why do some countries manage to change in a peaceful fashion, while others resort to radical, often violent change? These questions are addressed in Chapter 15.

International Politics and Globalization

So far, we have concentrated primarily on domestic politics, that is, politics within a country or state. But studying politics has always gone beyond the internal operation of individual states to include the international dimension. If we temporarily define politics as the struggle for dominance, then there is probably just as much politics involved between states as within them.

International politics has always been important, partly because conflict between states has often led to war, a dimension of violence usually much more serious than what might be experienced within a single state. Studying politics involves both examining strategies for successful military operations and searching for mechanisms to moderate or prevent international violence, such as the establishment of the United Nations. The first half of the 20th century witnessed the two most horrible wars in human history, while the second half was dominated by the Cold War between the United States and the Soviet Union, in a kind of balance of terror. But if the Cold War is over, what are the new dimensions of international security in the 21st century? Is U.S. President George W. Bush correct in proposing that an expensive new missile shield is the best way to protect peace-loving states? Or is the war against terrorism, especially after September 11, 2001, more a matter of improving intelligence capabilities? Chapter 16 addresses such questions.

Finally, as we have mentioned, individual states in the 21st century are increasingly subject to the forces of globalization (the subject of Chapter 17). That means that the global economy is increasingly dominated by huge multinational or transnational corporations. They operate around the world, have little or no allegiance to a specific state, and are often so mobile that they can move operations from one state to another. To minimize costs and maximize profits, such firms pressure the countries in which they operate to sign free trade deals with each other. Such agreements prevent the states involved from pro-

tecting their own interests and prohibit them from imposing barriers that would reduce the world-wide flow of the corporations' goods and services. Transnational companies also abhor taxation, ownership restrictions, and regulations such as environmental controls and labour standards. The 10 largest transnational corporations in the world are ranked in Table 1.3. The annual revenues of some of these equal or exceed the total value of all goods and services produced (the Gross Domestic Product) in many industrialized countries, such as Poland ($176.5 billion), Norway ($163.7 billion), Denmark ($161.5 billion), Finland ($120.9 billion), and Greece ($116.8 billion), not to mention most underdeveloped countries.[2]

Thus, pressured by such transnational corporations, organizations such as the World Trade Organization (WTO) and treaties such as the North American Free Trade Agreement (NAFTA) can force states to repeal laws and policies that favour their own companies and residents or that otherwise infringe the principles of the trade agreement. It is these aspects of globalization that are so controversial and that have led to violent clashes between demonstrators and police officers at many recent international gatherings.

Studying politics includes assessing the benefits and drawbacks of such globalizing forces, as well as inquiring about how much discretion states continue to possess in designing their own policies. Since up to now politics has been studied primarily in terms of the internal or external functioning of sovereign states, globalization

Table 1.3   The 10 Largest Transnational Corporations in the World, 2002

Corporation	Revenues in Billions of U.S.$
1. Wal-Mart Stores	219.8
2. Exxon Mobil	191.6
3. General Motors	177.3
4. BP	174.2
5. Ford Motor	162.4
6. Enron	138.7
7. DaimlerChrysler	136.9
8. Royal Dutch/Shell Group	135.2
9. General Electric	125.9
10. Toyota Motor	120.8

Source: "Fortune Global 500," *Fortune Magazine*; cited on July 26, 2002; available at http://fortune.com/lists/G500. Reprinted by permission of Fortune.© 2002 Time Inc. All rights reserved. The Global 500.

requires quite a shift in our orientation. It raises the basic question of whether electorates can still hold their governments democratically accountable.

The Changing Nature of the Study of Politics

The study of politics is now a much broader enterprise than it used to be. Today it embraces the whole world, paying attention to developing countries as well as advanced, industrialized democracies. It now must contend with multinational states, that is, states that are no longer embodiments of a single ethnic group, language, or culture, but instead are characterized by cultural pluralism. In many cases, Aboriginal peoples are part of these pluralistic states, and in almost all cases, the question of gender is of increasing significance. Studying politics now must address questions of political change, especially the general move toward democracy in the developing world. At the same time, it must examine the breakdown of former multinational states (often called state failure) and the role of rebellion, terrorism, and civil war. Finally, studying politics means coping with all the forces of globalization that impinge upon states as they try to make collective decisions for their own citizens. Who could deny that this broad undertaking is both fascinating and important?

THE FIELDS OF STUDY WITHIN POLITICAL SCIENCE

In the process of discussing the breadth of **political science**, we have, to a large extent, already outlined the subfields within the discipline. Not every university department breaks the discipline down in the same way, and many are changing their traditional organization; moreover, they sometimes call themselves "political studies" rather than "political science." At least

until recently, there has been a general consensus about the chart below. Studying politics involves examining most or all of these aspects of the subject, usually in specialized upper-year courses.

For people who are studying politics in Canada, one of the subfields of the discipline is obviously Canadian politics. If you were studying politics in another country, such as the United States or Britain, that country's politics would substitute as this first field. We have already seen the breadth of the discipline as it relates to a single state, as well as what is involved in the study of international relations. Comparative politics compares a number of states instead of concentrating on only one. Political development is essentially the study of the Third World or developing countries.

Studies in the stream called political theory begin with an examination the evolution of political philosophy or political thought, and then branch out into various aspects of modern political theory and analysis. Public administration is often separated out from a study of national politics and concentrates on the operation of the bureaucracy and the policymaking process. This is probably a sign of the significance of the bureaucracy in the making of public policy.

Political science is, of course, one of the social sciences, and it can be easily combined with any of its cognate disciplines, such as political economy, political sociology, political psychology, or political geography (or geopolitics). Of these combinations, political economy is probably most common, as it studies the close connection between the political and economic realms of life. This connection can be seen at both the national and global levels.

BASIC CONCEPTS IN THE STUDY OF POLITICS

One of the charms of the discipline of political science is that almost every concept is open to debate. Not

Political Science					
Canadian Politics	Comparative Politics	Political Development	International Relations	Public Administration	Political Theory

everyone agrees on what the basic concepts of the subject are, and not everyone agrees on how to define them. Nevertheless, we do need a common starting point.

How, then, do we define the term *politics*? One of the classic and catchy definitions is Harold Lasswell's "who gets what, when, and how?"[3] Another widely used definition is that politics is "the struggle for power"; alternatively, we could call it the struggle for dominance or advantage. Lasswell adds that "the study of politics is the study of influence and the influential," the influential being those who get the most of what there is to get. Canadian-born political scientist David Easton defined politics as "the authoritative allocation of values for a society."[4] There is a good deal of similarity among these varied definitions, although they use different terminology. For example, to talk about the allocation of values is basically to discuss the distribution of things that are valued in a society. Such desirable things include money, goods, services, health, education, security, comfort, freedom, and so on. These are the "what" of who gets what, when, and how. They are also the things of which those who are influential want to get the most.

The central concepts that emerge from these varied definitions are power, influence, and authority, so let us initially focus on these three terms. Before doing so, however, we should note that at the heart of all of these concepts is the idea that politics involves a difference of opinion, a conflict, or interests that are opposed to each other. Where there is complete harmony between two or more individuals, two or more states, or two or more actors of any kind, there is no need to think in terms of power, influence, or authority. The other unstated premise here is that there is also a desire to resolve such a conflict, as least on the part of one or some of the actors involved. Politics thus seems to arise in a situation marked by conflict, in which attempts are made to resolve that conflict.

Power is often defined as the ability of one actor to impose its will on another, to get its own way, to do or get what it wants. Such an imposition of will can be readily seen in the relations between states: for example, when Nazi Germany invaded Poland, or when Canada succumbed to American pressure to open up its magazine industry to foreign competition. Within a single state, we can witness a power relationship when a government extracts taxes from its citizens or imposes

environmental controls on corporations. In all of these cases, those in a position of power impose their will, whether on another country, on society in general, or on individuals or other entities within that society.

Definition

POWER: The ability of one actor to impose its will on another, to get its own way, to do or get what it wants.

Most political scientists are inclined to subdivide the concept of power into three parts.[5] The first kind of power is **coercion**, which involves threats of harm, penalties, violence, or punishment. This is the kind of power that Hitler used in his quest for military dominance. When the United States pressures Canada to change its policies on any matter, what is left unsaid is that economic penalties could follow if Canada resists. Coercion is also what the Canadian government does when it puts someone in jail, or what governments in the United States do when they carry out an execution. While democratic countries are entitled to use coercion in imposing their will on dissident citizens, they are expected to do so only as a last resort.

Definition

COERCION: The imposition of one's will on another by the use of penalty, force, or the threat of force.

The second kind of power is **influence**, which is usually seen as involving persuasion and voluntary compliance. One actor imposes its will on another by making arguments that the latter finds convincing. Within a single state, a bureaucrat tries to influence a minister to adopt a certain policy, a party member tries to persuade a party leader to resign, or the government pays for television advertising to try to convince smokers that it is time to quit. On the international level, the Secretary-General of the United Nations appeals to the United States to pay the arrears in its dues, for example, and states regularly try to persuade each other to change their policies.

Definition

INFLUENCE: The imposition of one's will on another through persuasion and voluntary compliance.

The third aspect of power is **authority**. This is often called legitimate power; that is, one actor imposes its will on another because the latter regards the former as legitimate, as having a right to impose its will. It is a kind of power that we have agreed to be bound by because it comes from a respected source; it stems from the acceptance of an obligation to obey. Such authority is particularly relevant to democratic governments because, having had a say (by way of elections) in who makes the decisions, citizens generally accept the decisions even when they do not entirely agree with them. When governments extract taxes, most people pay them, however reluctantly, because elected politicians have a right to make such decisions. To some extent, this kind of power is less evident at the international level, where raw coercion is more often apparent than it is in domestic politics. But even there, states have voluntarily joined a multitude of international organizations and made treaties with each other, and they usually respect the authority of such agreements.

> **Definition**
>
> **AUTHORITY:** The imposition of one's will on another by reason of legitimacy—because the subject regards the decision-maker as having a right to make such a binding decision.

We can witness power, influence, and authority in our daily lives in areas that do not necessarily involve government. The Mafia and other criminal elements, for example, are infamous for committing crimes and causing injury and death in order to impose their will. Parents sometimes resort to coercion by grounding their children in their room. Friends influence each other about what movie to see; transnational corporations try to influence what clothes we buy; and you yourself may have pleaded with someone to go out on a date. We obey our parents because we feel that they have a right to make certain decisions; we do what our bosses or union leaders demand because they are legitimately in control; and we follow the dictates of respected religious authorities. The "politics of the family," the "politics of the workplace," "corporate politics," "union politics," the "politics of religion"—all such activity involves power, influence, or authority. Politics surrounds us! Everywhere we turn we see relationships involving power, influence, and authority.

Generally speaking, however, if for no other reason than to keep the subject within manageable proportions, it is advantageous to develop a narrower concept of politics for the purposes of this book. What political science is mostly interested in are the conflicts in society that need a society-wide, authoritative resolution and that result in the authoritative distribution of valued things. That is, in fact, what we mean by public policies: an authoritative distribution of things that are valued, such as wealth, freedom, and security. Let us draw from all the definitions previously presented and say that **politics** involves that activity in which conflicting interests struggle for advantage or dominance in the making and execution of public policies.

> **Definition**
>
> **POLITICS:** That activity in which conflicting interests struggle for advantage or dominance in the making and execution of public policies.

Politics is sometimes said to be "the art of the possible," or to be marked by compromise. Regardless of whether such a description is meant as praise or criticism, it is true that the public policies adopted are frequently designed to incorporate conflicting interests or to seek a middle ground. It is not always such a bad thing to develop a compromise policy that tries to bring together as many conflicting interests as possible, and it adds to the policy's legitimacy.

The companion concept to politics, of course, is government. Political scientists also have many definitions of that term. But without further fanfare, we can simply define **government** as the set of institutions that makes and enforces collective public decisions for a society. Government is the body that decides who will get what, when, and how; government reflects the interests of the influential; government represents those who have succeeded in the struggle for power; government makes the authoritative allocation of values for a society. Chapter 2 elaborates on all aspects of government, including those that do not take the form of the government of a state.

> **Definition**
>
> **GOVERNMENT:** The set of institutions that makes and enforces collective public decisions for a society.

In making and enforcing public policies, government draws on all three aspects of power: coercion, influence, and authority. Government has the ability to impose its will by means of sanctions or penalties, relying on the armed forces, the police, and punishments such as fines or jail. Indeed, as a general rule, *only* the government is allowed to use force or coercive power in society. But, especially in democratic societies, governments try to minimize their use of coercion in seeking compliance with their decisions. They would prefer to have citizens respond voluntarily, after they have been persuaded or influenced. Merely asking citizens, corporations, or other groups to refrain from smoking, from polluting, from discriminating, or from asking for too much money may sometimes have an effect, but such voluntary compliance is not usually effective.

That leaves authority as the leading ground on which democratic governments rely to impose their will. If the citizens have had a hand in choosing the government, if the government at least appears to listen to the electorate, if the government gives the impression that it is taking all interests into account in its public policies, then the people will probably feel that the government is legitimate and that they should abide by its authority. Canadians have been seen as particularly deferential to authority and always ready to obey whatever policies the government adopts. Whether or not such deference is on the decline, as is now commonly claimed,[6] we are instinctively inclined to do what the government says because we have put it there and because we feel it has a right to make such decisions. Of course, we may also remind ourselves that if we disobey such policies, whether by speeding, stealing, or not paying taxes, the government can come down on us with coercive measures involving police, fines, and prison.

These definitions of politics and government may betray a bias in favour of peaceful, domestic, democratic political systems. When political science turns its attention to such subjects as political change, political violence, state failure, and international politics, some of the wider definitions previously outlined may be more appropriate. There are many aspects of political activity, especially in relations between states, in which authority—agreement on who has a right to make collective decisions—is severely lacking. It may sometimes be more appropriate to revert to the idea of politics as a struggle for power or dominance, but in any case, we

have now established a central focus for our study of politics in this book.

THIS BOOK

This book seeks to meet the demand for an introductory political science textbook for the new century—fresh and yet classic in its approach. It aims to be a definitive introductory text, marrying traditional and contemporary approaches and appealing directly to the learning demands of modern students.

We have already outlined the basic contents of the book. Every effort has been made to provide a solid background in the traditional subjects, while at the same time offering material that covers emerging themes and issues in political science. Chapters that deal with these issues include Chapter 3 (Cultural Pluralism, Nationalism, and Globalization), Chapter 14 (The Politics of Development and Underdevelopment), Chapter 15 (Political Change: Nondemocratic and Democratic Regime Change), and Chapter 17 (The Politics of Globalization). We wish to emphasize the cultural pluralism of most modern states; we try to promote a greater understanding of the Third World; we want to ensure that students are aware of the massive aspects of political change currently taking place around the world; and we insist that the entire study of politics be enveloped within the context of globalization. Yet, going further in unorthodox directions would probably have disturbed those who value the important material contained in the other 13 chapters. Within most of the chapters, at least wherever relevant, we have tried to mention women's issues, concerns of minority groups (including cultural pluralism), and the influences of globalization. We have tried to make the material relevant to Canadian students' lives with stimulating examples, and we are conscious of the fact that many of the students using the book will be relatively recent immigrants to Canada. We also profile a number of recent graduates in political science to show what kinds of careers they are pursuing and how their degree in this discipline got them to where they are today.

The chapters are intended to be discrete units, so professors who use this text can cover the material in a different sequence or omit certain chapters entirely.

Nevertheless, we hope that the chapters gel with each other, with certain common themes and coverage but only minimal overlap. The book might be said to have a conceptual/comparative approach, working outward from Canada to other industrialized, developed democracies, then to the developing world, and finally to the global scene.

We have put considerable effort into the visual attractiveness of this text. These visual features—photographs, cartoons, graphs, charts, and boxes of various kinds—will animate the material and allow an examination of alternative viewpoints. We have also tried to include many pedagogical features that will make the book more interesting for students to read. These include learning objectives for each chapter; definition boxes, which serve as a running glossary; discussion questions; and Web links. At the end of the book is a full-fledged glossary of all the key terms used.

For the benefit of professors selecting this text, we have also prepared an Instructor's Manual and a Test Bank, PowerPoint slides, and an accompanying video. There is also a book-specific website, supplemented by Nelson's comprehensive, general political science website.

In other words, this is a cutting-edge textbook, supplemented by helpful teaching materials and ready to meet the demands of 21st-century students and instructors.

CONCLUSION

This chapter has tried to show you that studying politics is both interesting and important, and that if you go beyond a single course, it also leads to jobs. The chapter has sketched the broad lines of the scope of the discipline of political science, outlined how the field is changing, and detailed its subfields. It concluded with definitions and explanations of some of the key concepts in political science, namely power, coercion, influence, authority, politics, and government.

DISCUSSION QUESTIONS

1. **Think about your most recent personal experiences (unrelated to government) involving relationships of power. Did they involve coercion, influence, or authority?**

2. **Think about your most recent experiences involving government. Did any of them include aspects of coercion, influence, or authority?**

3. **How would you answer the question posed in Figure 1.1: How should government divide a budget surplus among cutting taxes, reducing the debt, or spending on social programs? Why?**

4. **In what kinds of political activity have you been engaged in the past, and in what kinds do you see yourself involved in the future? Why?**

5. **What do you think are the most pressing public issues facing Canada as it enters the 21st century?**

6. **What do you think are the most pressing issues facing the rest of the world?**

w(w)w WEB LINKS

This book:
http://www.studyingpolitics.nelson.com

Thomson Nelson Political Science Resource Centre:
http://www.polisci.nelson.com

Government of Canada:
http://canada.gc.ca

Government of the United States:
http://www.firstgov.gov

Government of Mexico:
http://world.presidencia.gob.mx

Government of the United Kingdom:
http://www.open.gov.uk

The Globe and Mail:
http://www.globeandmail.com

United Nations:
http://www.un.org

World Trade Organization:
http://www.wto.org

FURTHER READING

Barber, Benjamin R. *Jihad vs. McWorld.* New York: Ballantine, 1996.

Bateman, Thomas, et al. *Braving the New World: Readings in Contemporary Politics.* Toronto: Nelson Thomson Learning, 2000.

Huntington, Samuel P. *The Third Wave: Democratization in the Late Twentieth Century.* Norman: University of Oklahoma Press, 1992.

Miliband, Ralph. *The State in Capitalist Society.* London: Weidenfeld and Nicolson, 1969.

Sens, Allen, and Peter J. Stoett. *Global Politics.* 2nd ed. Toronto: Nelson Thomson Learning, 2002.

Simpson, Jeffrey. *The Friendly Dictatorship.* Toronto: McClelland and Stewart, 2001.

ENDNOTES

1 Roger Gibbins and Loleen Youngman, *Mindscapes: Political Ideologies towards the 21st Century* (Toronto: McGraw-Hill Ryerson, 1996).

2 OECD Statistics, "Gross Domestic Product"; cited on July 26, 2002; available at http://www.oecd.org/EN/document/0,,EN-document-0-nodirectorate-no—9066-0,00.htm.

3 Harold Lasswell, *Politics: Who Gets What, When, How* (New York: Meridian Books, 1958).

4 David Easton, *The Political System: An Inquiry into the State of Political Science* (New York: Knopf, 1967).

5 Mark O. Dickerson and Thomas Flanagan, *An Introduction to Government and Politics: A Conceptual Approach,* 5th ed. (Toronto: Nelson Thomson Learning, 1998).

6 Neil Nevitte, *The Decline of Deference* (Peterborough: Broadview Press, 1996).

Governments, States, and Nations

2

Career Profile: Renny Khan

Renny Khan was born in Trinidad and became bilingual in French and English after immigrating to Canada. He graduated with a B.A. in international relations and history from McGill University in Montreal and then obtained an M.A. in political science from the University of Alberta. He began his career by working with the Alberta Ministry of International and Intergovernmental Relations in the U.S./Mexico Division.

Renny is currently employed as the Associate Director for International Relations at the University of Alberta and is responsible for the United States and Europe. As part of the international relations team, he works closely with departments, faculties, and senior administrators to assist with the development, coordination, and management of strategic partnerships, initiatives, and activities that contribute to linkages between the university and institutions in the United States and Europe. Renny liaises and networks with a host of external parties, including universities, governments, businesses, and nongovernmental organizations, to build creative institutional partnerships and to bring new opportunities to the university community.

In recognition of his successful work in facilitating partnerships between the University of Alberta and American universities, especially in linking the University of Alberta with the University of California, the U.S. State Department recently awarded Renny the International Visitorship Award.

In addition, Renny has helped develop strong, sustainable partnerships with some of the finest universities in Europe. He was part of the management team of the second Canada–U.K. Partnership for Knowledge Forum, the largest gathering ever of senior university, research, industry, and government executives from across Canada and the United Kingdom organized to discuss issues pertaining to partnerships and university–industry linkages.

Chapter 2

Governments: Power and Authority in Motion

Douglas A. West

CHAPTER OBJECTIVES

After you have completed this chapter, you should be able to

- discuss the general concept of government
- explain how classical scholars classified governments
- trace the evolution of the concepts of democracy and the state
- enumerate the principal features of the modern state
- discuss the principal features of democracy
- distinguish between authoritarian and totalitarian states
- explain and exemplify forms of non-state governments.

GOVERNMENT

Governments are key to understanding politics in any society because of their central role in regulating the population and economy. Governments have the power and authority to make and enforce collective decisions that bind a whole society. As noted in Chapter 1, the government makes decisions about who gets what, when, and how, and it settles disputes among citizens.

Governments can fine, imprison, and even kill people who refuse to obey the rules of behaviour they set. But just who controls the government and in whose interest these people govern are questions with significant consequences. Governments need not necessarily have the support of those they govern, and they certainly need not rule for the general public good. While we can identify societies with freely elected governments that rule for the greater good of all, there are also many other countries with brutally repressive governments whose prime concern is making the rulers rich and keeping them in power for as long as possible. Political science is very much concerned about studying governments and identifying the different types of governments found around the world.

This chapter examines the rise of governments, from their origins to their modern forms, in order to provide an overview of the defining characteristics of different forms of democratic and authoritarian governments. An appreciation of who controls governments and in whose interests they govern can lead to a better understanding of the desire of people around the world to have governments that they choose for themselves. One cannot separate an examination of governments from a study of the states in which they are found. It is important to understand why some people want not just to choose or control their government but also to have their own new state to set themselves apart from the ones they have lived under. This chapter concludes with a discussion of the various non-state governments to be found in today's world.

Government and governance are absolutely necessary for any society to function. As Aristotle said, if we are not political, then we are either gods or beasts. Governance, though, need not be limited in definition to the "legitimate use of force." It can be inspired by sharing and consensus, by striving for common purposes, and by making a commitment to freedom and equality, with force not really being the focal point of its operations. Governments are also responsible for the collection of taxes and the distribution and management of public funds. The management of the public purse is the task given to governments for the purpose of defining short-term and long-term goals for any society. In this context, government does not usually work alone in the development of public policy; the actions of government are intertwined with those of private interests, citizens, and other institutions— now often called "civil society"—that form the more complete fabric of society.

Gabriel Almond, a giant in the modern study of political science, proposed a checklist of functions that are performed by any government: rule-making, rule-application, and rule-adjudication.[1] Regardless of its actual form, a government must make the rules, apply, execute, or implement them, and then interpret them in case of dispute. In modern Western political systems, these three functions are usually separated into three specialized branches of government: the legislature, the executive, and the judiciary, but Almond contends that the functions are performed in all governments, even when these particular structures are not so clearly delineated.

The legislative branch of government is normally responsible for the creation of laws and regulations that respond to the demands of the population it serves. The enactment of legislation is the end product of a sometimes long and arduous process that includes a set of formal and informal procedures involving some degree of public consultation. Because of the sheer size of the public and the diversity of its interests, governments need to develop internal and external mechanisms that allow for the public's voice to be heard and for their own intentions to be understood. The role of the normally elected public representatives is to make known the wishes of their constituents while at the same time understanding the complexity of their function, which also includes loyalty to their political party and their general acceptance of the responsibility for organizing the affairs of government.

The rule-making function in many political systems is actually shared between the legislative and executive branches of government. In fact, it is the executive branch, commonly made up of elected politicians as well—called presidents, prime ministers, premiers, and cabinets—that often really sets the priorities for the public policymaking process. The political executive sometimes renders the legislative branch little more than a ratifying body or a sounding board.

But the executive branch also has another, second part, the public servants who apply or implement the rules. Known collectively as the bureaucracy, they administer the rules and perform the practical and necessary actions that are required. The word *bureaucracy* comes from the French *bureau,* which means a desk or a portfolio. In this sense, the bureaucracy represents a reservoir of expertise at the disposal of the rule-makers. The bureaucracy is theoretically distanced from the political executive by its ability to remain as governments change. Most states train their bureaucrats and elect their governments, keeping the distinction clear.

The judicial branch of government is responsible for interpreting the rules, made by the legislature or legislature and executive acting together and implemented by the bureaucracy, in case of dispute. The judiciary is often a complex set of institutions and actors who follow well-rehearsed procedures for the adjudication of the law in order to provide a sense of justice for the societies they serve. When they find that the rules have been broken, they normally have the power to penalize the infractions by means of fines, prison sentences, and sometimes death.

Although Canadians and citizens of other Western democratic societies can readily connect the rule-making, rule-application, and rule-adjudication functions with particular structures of government, it is important to realize that in many other political systems these functions may not be so clearly divided and allotted to such easily identifiable institutions. For example, in an absolute monarchy such as Swaziland, the king has complete power to make and unmake any rule and expect his orders to be implemented.

The political entities we recognize today as modern states and governments have their roots in earlier traditional forms of politics that continue to survive in many areas of the world. Whether in Asia, Africa, Europe, the Americas, or Australia and Oceania, the history of human society has common roots in small traditional communities with clear governing powers vested in a group of elders, warriors, chiefs, queens, or priests. As human communities grew in size and complexity, more rigidly defined political rules and rulers emerged to control the economy and population of the community. In a generic sense, traditional forms of ruling a community involve as much governmental power as does government in Canada or China. In traditional societies, someone or some group exercises legislative powers by making rules for a community. Someone carries these decisions out, in a form of executive power. Also, disputes are resolved and the rules are enforced in a way that is essentially judicial in character. Let us now examine how ancient scholars conceived of governments and then explore the evolution of modern political systems.

CLASSICAL FORMS OF GOVERNMENT

The study of forms of government can be traced to the work of Aristotle in ancient Greece. He classified governments in terms of who and how many people ruled and in whose interest they made their decisions. This classification is illustrated in Table 2.1.

Aristotle also judged the virtues of these different forms of government, and his assessment may surprise modern observers. He argued that the best form of government was polity, or rule by the citizens in the interest of the community. Polity was organized around the values of encouraging participation and speech, and it was restricted to those who owned property. To be members of the polity or what Plato called the *politiea* (which was translated by the Romans as the republic) people had to be able to assume the responsibility of separating their private lives from their public lives, to think and act through community while in public, leaving their own self-interest at home. In contrast, the worst form of government was tyranny, or rule by one in his or her own interest. A tyrant was one who could never be trusted and who could trust no one else. Thus, because trust was the basis for any community, polity represented the most trustworthy arrangement of equal citizens, and tyranny represented the least trustworthy. In between these extremes lay the good government model of **aristocracy**, or rule by the few (the best) in the interest of the many, and its decadent form, **oligarchy**, or rule by the few in their own interest. Finally, there

Table 2.1 **Aristotle's Classification of Forms of Government**		
	Who and How Many Rule	In Whose Interest They Rule
Kingship	one	the common good
Tyranny	one	the ruler's own good
Aristocracy	few (best)	the common good
Oligarchy	few	their own good
Polity	citizens as a whole	the common good
Democracy	citizens as a whole	their own good

was monarchy, the form of rule by one in the interest of the people, and democracy, which Aristotle believed to be a potentially dangerous form of government. Democracy means rule by the many in their own interest, which Aristotle interpreted as in the interest of the poorer classes. The other main problem with democracy was that the masses might be easily swayed by demagogues.

Definition

ARISTOCRACY: A special form of oligarchy in which "the best," which is commonly interpreted as the nobility, rule. Aristotle claimed that the best would govern in the common interest, an assumption not always shared since.

Definition

OLIGARCHY: The rule by a few; Aristotle considered that they would govern in their own interests.

The Roman equivalents of these classical Greek forms of government are virtually the same, and we derive many of our current definitions and understanding of styles of government from the Romans' experience. Modern European development echoes the three phases of Rome's political history. The first or the founding style of Roman government was based on family inheritance and was classified as monarchy. The second phase was characterized by a commitment to a system of checks and balances between the Senate, the monarchy, and the people and is known as the Republican phase. The third and final phase was the Roman Empire, during which the Romans attempted to colonize the known world.

During medieval times, the Roman Catholic Church dominated the European political landscape by creating a Holy Roman Empire that regularly installed kings and queens from noble families who could abide by the church's ultimate control of what became known as the "divine right of kings." During this time, many of the references that we have to the classical styles of governance were either lost or suppressed. The teachings of Plato, Aristotle, and other ancient Greeks came back into Europe with traders who began to interact with Rome during the Italian Renaissance around the 14th century. The revival of "classical republicanism" in the

work of Niccolò Machiavelli is testament to the power that these ideas have had in changing the nature of politics. Machiavelli made a lasting mark on European political culture with his description of how Italian princes might rule most successfully. Today his ideas are often thought of as lacking morality, or even as being immoral; for example, he said that if a prince had to make a choice, it would be better to be feared than loved by his people. However, Machiavelli was really trying to provide a dispassionate analysis of what worked and did not work for the Italian princes of his day.

Under the influence of Machiavelli's *Discourses* and *The Prince*, classical ideals again began to make their way back into the mainstream, despite the opposition of the declining church. For Machiavelli, justice was to be understood as a practical and realistic virtue, one that did not depend on the authority of access to a transcendent realm of meaning and existence, but rather relied on the will of the people and the prince to work together toward the material advancement of their society. One of the essential features of *The Prince* was that it was written entirely in Italian, rather than the Latin language favoured by the intelligentsia of the day, and was thus available to more people. To some degree, this caused a revolution in political literacy that began a process of dismantling the pervasive presence of the church as the sanctioning authority for governments.

These ancient writings on government continue to provide a useful framework for modern political scientists for analyzing how contemporary governments are functioning, especially in regard to who actually rules and in whose interests, and how to govern most effectively. For example, Aristotle's notion of an oligarchy has survived in many forms in contemporary political science. Robert Michels has argued that mass political organizations and societies cannot help but become oligarchies. A few of the most powerful people end up dominating the process, and they ensure that their interests are catered to above all else; in fact, he called this his "iron law of oligarchy." Some critics argue that even modern liberal democracies may like to portray themselves as government by and for the people, but they are all too often in fact governments controlled by a few powerful individuals who make decisions principally to maintain their hold on power and to further their own interests.

THE EVOLUTION OF MODERN FORMS OF GOVERNMENT

The modern age of democracy followed upon the increasing number of publications that were designed to revive a public debate about the good life. While not fundamentally different from ancient or medieval views, modern democracy was born in the midst of an economic revolution. As state-sponsored mercantilism became overwhelmed by the sheer volume of trade and economic development occurring around it, it was replaced by a new kind of entrepreneurial capitalism that demanded public attention and required public scrutiny. Nowhere else was this more apparent than in 17th century England. A number of ingredients came together to challenge the domination of the English political scene by the monarchy.

First, the enclosure movement produced profound changes in English society. Landlords were allowed to "enclose" or fence off lands that had been formerly available for public use, so that they could be used for increased agricultural production. This tragedy, as it is referred to by some historians, forced the displacement of people from the country to the city centres of England, providing a ready-made working class for developing industry. The corporate economic environment that these changes produced accelerated in the 17th century under the influence of certain thinkers.

Second, the new entrepreneurial or bourgeois class began to oppose the power of the monarchy to tax and to control lands at will. As their demands for the greater protection of their private property increased, so too did the tensions between them and the landed aristocracy, who had long since benefited from close proximity to the crown.

Third, religious toleration became socially and political acceptable. The liberation of England and other emerging nation-states from the power of the Catholic Church in Rome led to an increasing awareness of the power of new ideas. Along with this spiritual liberation came a scientific liberation. The burgeoning interest in a revival of classical education and a desire to improve the conditions of production created a new class of intellectuals whose interest it was to advance, as Francis Bacon put it, the state of knowledge.

These ingredients came together to form a new political culture, one that the traditional political institutions associated with the monarchy could not represent. The reforms of English parliamentary practice that were encouraged by the air of toleration and liberation went a long way in providing space for new voices in the public to be heard. The concepts of representative democracy, free speech, the right to rebel against a bad government, freedom for the accumulation of profit, human rights—all of which are now the hallmarks of our modern systems of government—were reborn in a political renaissance that owed its inspiration to the ancient thinkers and its innovation to a new intellectual class that embodied the values of the new age of democracy.

Above all, there was John Locke, philosopher and activist, who accompanied English monarchs William and Mary to London and participated in and benefited from what is known as the Glorious Revolution of 1688. In Locke's *Two Treatises on Government*, we get an introduction to human rights, a primer on how to succeed by recognizing your own self-worth, and perhaps most importantly, a justification of the right to rebel against a bad government—that is, the right of revolution.

Political revolution stands as one of the most compelling aspects of the modern age of politics because of its ability to be formed and re-formed through the eyes of different ideological persuasions. Liberalism, conservatism, and socialism, the three great ideological pillars of our modernity, each offer a revolutionary impulse. These impulses are also inspired by the ideas of progress and development, which point us firmly to the future for our political and economic salvation, and which can be formulated to fit any political situation: the revolutionary consciousness that lies beneath the expansion of capital enterprise (liberal capitalism), the liberation of the masses (socialism and social democracy), and the importance of preserving tradition in the future (conservatism).

All these social, political, and philosophical changes led to the emergence of liberal-constitutional-representative democracies. Most European and industrialized countries have made a commitment to forming governments that embody these principles. They are liberal because they allow for the increasing participation over time of more and more types of organizations of people. They are constitutional because they are founded on principles of human rights and freedoms that must be protected at all costs. They are representative because of the sheer expansion in the populations of a growing numbers of nation-states and of the need to manage that expansion for the public good. And, finally, they are democracies because they are the rule of the many.

GOVERNMENT OF MODERN STATES

Along with the evolution of modern democracy came the development of the modern state. Before examining modern democratic and nondemocratic governments, therefore, we will discuss the concept of the state. It is important to understand some basic distinctions that political scientists make when examining political systems: nation, state, and government. Nation and state both have dual meanings that can lead to some confusion. The word *nation* is often used to refer to a country; for example, "Canada is a peaceful and prosperous nation." However, it can also mean something quite different: a distinguishable cultural group with common ancestry; for example, "Most Scottish people in Great Britain believe they form a distinct nation within that country." This latter sense of the word is true to its origins in the Latin word *natio*, which means a group of people descended from a single source. The word *state* can similarly mean different things. It can refer to a geopolitical entity or country, such as the state of Egypt, or be a synonym for the whole government apparatus of a country. Although we most commonly assume that governments usually exist within states (countries), we shall see later that some governments do not take the form of a state.

As Thomas Hobbes argued, the state is the one form of organized power toward which we can all turn our loyalty because it protects us from the state of nature, a situation in which people's lives are "solitary, poor, nasty, brutish, and short."[2] The state of nature is to be replaced by the protective state, which in our instinct for survival keeps us from the "war of all against all." That state usually takes people beyond mere survival and supports the expansion of their economic, political, and cultural interests; it may at the same time

defend their right to own property, to speak, to be heard, and to be judged according to the principle of the rule of law.

The traditional definition of the **state** as a geopolitical entity includes three elements: population, territory, and a sovereign government. First, a state requires a population, which normally has some consciousness of itself as a cohesive, distinctive group. In the past, this group of people usually constituted a **nation**, giving rise to the concept of the nation-state. The idea of nation comes from the experiences that are gleaned from history of the political struggles of peoples, who by virtue of their colloquial language, their geographical proximity to each other, their family bonds, their spiritual and religious beliefs, their economy, and their cultural practices have found themselves being born, living, working, and dying together. Each of these factors gives shape to a nation, but the key ingredient is usually considered to be a common ethnicity. In the early days of statehood, most states—not only in Europe, but in other parts of the world—were composed primarily of one ethnic group. Today, however, due to massive migrations of people from one state to another, most states are characterized by cultural pluralism and are sometimes called **multination states**. This phenomenon is discussed in detail in Chapter 3.

Definition

STATE: A modern form of organizing political life that is characterized by a population, a piece of territory, and a sovereign government. The modern world is divided into nearly 200 such entities, each of which has a government that claims the power to make the ultimate decisions over its population and territory.

The second element required by the state, one that sometimes comes with the prior formation of a nation, is territory. Territory is derived from the Latin word *terra*, which literally means land. But territory is much more than land when it becomes associated with the state. Often based on history and physical features, the borders of a state become sacrosanct to its population; this population aims to control who enters their geographical space and for what purpose. Over the past 350 years, hundreds of conflicts have arisen between two or more states over their respective boundaries, and many of them have led to violent confrontations.

To people and territory, a third element is added—that of **sovereignty**. Sovereignty is derived from the Latin word *supere*, which translates roughly as "the power over." Most modern states began their existence as kingdoms, after the Treaty of Westphalia, which ended the Thirty Years War in 1648. This treaty formally recognized states in Europe as the legitimate sovereign entities that lay beyond the control and influence of the Roman Catholic Church for their authority, and beyond the natural impediments of geography for their borders. States, in the modern sense of the word, come and go. For instance, the state of Poland has expanded, diminished, disappeared from, and reappeared on European maps over the last 250 years. Thus a condition of statehood is the existence of a government with sovereignty over the people and territory it claims. This is very much a matter of the authority and capacity of the government—it should have the means to enforce its commands and carry out its decisions, as well as receive the general obedience of the population.

Definition

SOVEREIGNTY: The final or ultimate power over a population and a piece of territory, commonly claimed by the government of a state. In other contexts, sovereignty can be said to reside in the people or in parliament; in all cases, however, it has probably been eroded by global forces.

Sovereignty is not necessarily easy to achieve. It can be proclaimed, but then it must be defended and recognized as legitimate by other sovereign states. Sovereignty can be bought and sold, as in the case of Rupert's Land in Canada, or Alaska in the United States, and it can be taken away and divided, as in the case of the former state of Yugoslavia. Sovereignty is the currency of statehood, the source of any state's power, because it is through sovereignty that states act in the world at the level of diplomacy and international relations. But the state also has many internal or domestic mechanisms that help to keep it intact, such as a public education system, a public radio and television network, and a **bureaucracy**.

All states need some form of public administration to advise the decision-makers on the one hand and to implement those decisions on the other. The expansion of the idea and the territory of states since the 16th century has also meant the expansion of the bureaucracy and the extension of public administration into more and more areas of public and private life. Significant expansions have occurred during times of extreme conditions, such as war or economic disaster, or when there was a widespread desire to eradicate diseases or illiteracy. The growth of the state function has also corresponded to the growth of public awareness. As the public demands more from its elected officials, public administration responds by creating new *bureaus* or areas of activity.

A state's sovereignty is also the basis of the somewhat fictitious notion that the government of one state cannot or must not interfere in the domestic affairs of another state. Modern states are sometimes referred to as independent states, which stresses the idea that each state's government has the power, capacity, and authority to make all the decisions without any other government's involvement. However, the modern world is now very much one of inderpendence, in which all states are constrained by the actions of other states. Many states or international organizations try to directly influence or change government policies in other states. And large multinational businesses have often been described as, at best, circumventing the governments of small states, and at worst, as dictating to them.

Today there are 191 sovereign states with membership in the United Nations. Many of these recently emerged from colonial rule, and some are so tiny that they put into question the notions of population, territory, and sovereignty. In any case, Table 2.2 lists the member states of the United Nations as of 2002. Chapter 16 picks up on the importance of state sovereignty in international relations, and as mentioned, governments that do not take the form of states are discussed later in this chapter.

An extra dimension of statehood is the process by which new states are officially recognized by the governments of other states. When a government claims to have established a new state out of a part of an older, existing state, the governments of other states choose whether to recognize the new country's existence. If a new state is generally recognized, then it has the rights and responsibilities of a state under international law—it can sign treaties and agreements with other countries. At this point a state is said to exist *de jure*, as a matter of law. If, however, a group forms a government with

Table 2.2 The 191 Member States of the United Nations, 2002

Afghanistan	Cyprus	Japan	Morocco	Somalia
Albania	Czech	Jordan	Mozambique	South Africa
Algeria	Republic	Kazakhstan	Myanmar	Spain
Andorra	Democratic	Kenya	Namibia	Sri Lanka
Angola	Republic of	Kiribati	Nauru	Sudan
Antigua and	the Congo	Korea	Nepal	Suriname
Barbuda	Denmark	(Democratic	Netherlands	Swaziland
Argentina	Djibouti	People's	New Zealand	Sweden
Armenia	Dominica	Republic of)	Nicaragua	Switzerland
Australia	Dominican	Korea	Niger	Syrian Arab
Austria	Republic	(Republic of)	Nigeria	Republic
Azerbaijan	East Timor	Kuwait	Norway	Tajikistan
Bahamas	Ecuador	Kyrgyzstan	Oman	Tanzania
Bahrain	Egypt	Lao People's	Pakistan	(United
Bangladesh	El Salvador	Democratic	Palau	Republic of)
Barbados	Equatorial	Republic	Panama	Thailand
Belarus	Guinea	Latvia	Papua New	Togo
Belgium	Eritrea	Lebanon	Guinea	Tonga
Belize	Estonia	Lesotho	Paraguay	Trinidad and
Benin	Ethiopia	Liberia	Peru	Tobago
Bhutan	Fiji	Libyan Arab	Philippines	Tunisia
Bolivia	Finland	Jamahiriya	Poland	Turkey
Bosnia and	France	Liechtenstein	Portugal	Turkmenistan
Herzegovina	Gabon	Lithuania	Qatar	Tuvalu
Botswana	Gambia	Luxembourg	Romania	Uganda
Brazil	Georgia	Macedonia	Russian	Ukraine
Brunei	Germany	(former	Federation	United Arab
Darussalam	Ghana	Yugoslav	Rwanda	Emirates
Bulgaria	Greece	Republic of)	Saint Kitts and	United
Burkina Faso	Grenada	Madagascar	Nevis	Kingdom of
Burundi	Guatemala	Malawi	Saint Lucia	Great Britain
Cambodia	Guinea	Malaysia	Saint Vincent	and Northern
Cameroon	Guinea-Bissau	Maldives	and the	Ireland
Canada	Guyana	Mali	Grenadines	United States
Cape Verde	Haiti	Malta	Samoa	of America
Central African	Honduras	Marshall	San Marino	Uruguay
Republic	Hungary	Islands	Sao Tome and	Uzbekistan
Chad	Iceland	Mauritania	Principe	Vanuatu
Chile	India	Mauritius	Saudi Arabia	Venezuela
China	Indonesia	Mexico	Senegal	Viet Nam
Colombia	Iran (Islamic	Micronesia	Seychelles	Yemen
Comoros	Republic of)	(Federated	Sierra Leone	Yugoslavia
Congo	Iraq	States of)	Singapore	Zambia
Costa Rica	Ireland	Moldova	Slovakia	Zimbabwe
Côte d'Ivoire	Israel	(Republic of)	Slovenia	
Croatia	Italy	Monaco	Solomon	
Cuba	Jamaica	Mongolia	Islands	

Source: United Nations, "List of Member States"; cited on May 31, 2002, and updated by authors; available at http://www.un.org/Overview/unmember.htm

control over a given population in a defined territory but is not recognized by other states, then this government is said to be a *de facto* government; this means that there is a state as a matter of fact but not of law. An example of this situation exists when a breakaway nationalist group seeking to establish a new state for its people manages to wrest effective control over some territory from the existing state's government. Other countries can refuse to recognize that a new state has been created; the implication is that the original state's government is recognized as having a right to reassert its sovereignty over the lost territory.

The recognition of a new state thus adds a fourth element to the people, territory, and sovereign government requirements of statehood. The governments of existing states make a judgment about the legitimacy of the new state's claim to existence. Was the new state created by illegitimate means, such as a brutal civil war in which an armed group expelled the existing government's presence from the territory against the wishes of the local population? Does the new group claiming to be a government rule only by coercion? At the other extreme, a new state might be created out of a peaceful process in which the local population votes for secession and the existing state's government approves the creation of the new state. What the recognizing governments think of the reaction of the existing government to the claim of a new state can be very important. For example, the United States might be swayed by the Canadian government's stance on any government in Quebec claiming to have formed a new state. In the end, the decision to recognize or not recognize a new state may come down to a practical calculation as to whether there is more to be gained or lost by recognizing the state. A similar question of legitimacy surfaces when foreign governments decide whether to recognize a new government as the legitimate government of an existing state.

DEMOCRATIC GOVERNMENTS

Political scientists categorize governments based on the qualities of the government system. The largest distinction that can be made is between democracies and authoritarian regimes. But the mere holding of elec-

tions does not mean that a government is fully democratic. Although democracy is perhaps the single most important concept in the study of politics and government, the term is not easy to define. Thus you will find a discussion of democracy in almost every chapter of this book, each dealing with a common core of values, but each with its own nuances relevant to the subject at hand. At one end of the democratic spectrum is the **liberal democracy,** such as the type of government existing in Canada, Europe, or Japan. This type of government is based on periodically held elections in which virtually all adults are able to vote. The voters have a choice between competing parties and can support opposing political parties without fear of intimidation. Once elected, a government respects the principle of limited government by observing the rule of law and acting within constitutional limits on its power, which protect the civil rights and liberties of the population. At the other end of the democratic spectrum lie sham democracies, where showcase elections are held but there are no competing parties or candidates for the voters to choose from. Dictators like to use this ploy to dress their authoritarian regimes in the disguise of a government popularly chosen by the electorate. In between liberal and sham democracies are governments that one can term transitional democracies. These governments hold competitive elections but may still ban a range of political parties; the ruling party may physically intimidate opposition activists through goon squads or even arrests and detentions by the formal state security agencies.

Definition

LIBERAL DEMOCRACY: A form of government characterized by public participation and popular sovereignty, normally exercised in free and fair elections in which the franchise is universal, the ballot is secret, and political parties are free to organize. A liberal democracy is also marked by individual political freedoms and the absence of discrimination. Government decisions are made by majority rule but are subject to the protection of individual and minority rights. The mass media are not controlled by the government, the government observes the rule of law, and the judiciary operates independently.

Acknowledging, then, that democracy can be defined in many different ways, we will emphasize the common features of the concept here. Fundamentally, to return to its Greek origins, democracy means rule by the people, as opposed to rule by the few or rule by one. Although "rule by the people" was not completely clear-cut in ancient Greece, it is even more difficult to put into practice in large modern states.

If the people cannot rule directly on a daily basis, then they must at least be able to choose representatives to govern on their behalf, in what is now called **representative democracy**. In other words, the people are sovereign—they have the final say—and a specific requirement of democracy is popular sovereignty. Put more simply, "people have a say in decisions that affect their lives and can hold decision-makers accountable."[3] In modern states, the most common mechanism for the people to have the final say and to hold decision-makers accountable is through elections. Some people advocate other mechanisms that would permit the population at large to have a say on a more regular basis or on more specific issues, such as referendums, but as a general rule elections satisfy this first basic requirement of democracy.

To be considered democratic, elections must meet several standards. First, they must be characterized by universal suffrage—everyone must have a vote. Indeed, every vote should have equal weight, which is the principle of political equality. Second, elections must be free and fair and held at regular intervals. There are many implications of the free and fair requirement. Such elections should involve a secret ballot; any citizen should be able to seek public office; political parties should be free to organize and enter the contest; media coverage of and other public information surrounding the election should be fair; and everyone should abide by the results, which might involve a peaceful change of government. Citizens should be encouraged to exercise their opportunities for political participation, and ideally, the financing of elections should not leave political parties and candidates beholden to corporate interests.[4] Box 2.1 discusses the remarkable turnaround in the conduct of elections in Mexico in recent years.

Some of these requirements can be extended beyond the scope of the election period to the daily operation of government and society. These include the principle of political freedom: freedom from discrimination based on ethnicity, class, gender, or any other attribute, with women being "equal partners with men in private and public spheres of life and decision-making."[5] Political freedom also involves respect for people's human rights and fundamental freedoms, such as freedom of expression and freedom of assembly. While democracies operate on the general principle that the majority rules, the rights of minorities must be respected. Another important aspect of political freedom is the independence of mass media, since citizens derive so much information from these sources. In an ideal democracy, the media are the handmaiden neither of the state nor of the corporate elite.[6]

It almost goes without saying that the government in a liberal democracy will obey the rules—"the rule of law"—whether in the form of a constitution or legislation. In its Universal Declaration on Democracy, the Inter-Parliamentary Union speaks of the "primacy of the law," and the importance of "independent, impartial judicial institutions."[7] Other institutional requirements include civilian control over the security forces—the military and police. A full summary of the IPU Declaration appears in Box 2.2 on page 40.

Even in this widely accepted view of democracy, there can be a certain amount of tension between specific ingredients. For example, some analysts emphasize that democracy is characterized by majority rule and value the fact that the policies adopted by democracies are usually in the general, collective interest. For many people that is the essence of democracy. For others, however, what is even more important is the protection of individual rights. The elevation of such rights as freedom of expression and freedom of assembly to constitutional status in documents such as the Canadian Charter of Rights and Freedoms is the hallmark of democracy for such observers. Of course, the two ingredients usually coincide without too much difficulty, but there can be a conflict between doing what the majority wants and respecting individual rights. The term *liberal democracy* is often used in the context of emphasizing the restraints on government action; even in its satisfaction of majoritarian interests, a democracy must cherish individual rights and freedoms, which are often protected by an independent judiciary.[8]

To these basic requirements of electoral and governmental operation, analysts now usually add that liberal democracies are also characterized by an active **civil society**. This term refers to autonomous organizations

BOX 2.1

MEXICO'S FEDERAL ELECTION COMMISSION

Mexico's 2000 presidential elections marked a major step forward for the country's democracy. Until this point, Mexico had been governed by only one political party, the PRI. The PRI had managed to sustain its hold on power through many rules to manipulate the electoral system and even intimidating the opposition parties. However, the PRI was pressured into constitutional reforms of electoral and political systems in 1996. These changes were driven by pressure from civil society, the opposition, and the international community resulting from the controversial presidential election of 1988 and lingering questions about process in the 1994 election. The changes were also greatly helped by the efforts and growing credibility of the Federal Election Commission (Instituto Federal Electoral).

Constitutional reforms in 1990 had established the Federal Election Commission as an independent entity fully responsible for federal elections and an Electoral Court that handles appeals of election-related disputes. Later reforms in the early and mid-1990s strengthened the commission's independence and authority. The 1996 constitutional reforms, in particular, eliminated executive oversight by the Ministry of Internal Affairs and created a nonpartisan General Council of nine independent "electoral counsellors."

Mexico's other electoral innovations include creating observer committees, including judges as members of the election commission, and establishing a professional service for supervising elections that is responsible for updating voter lists every year. The election commission has also instituted campaign finance reforms, though critics argue that Congress approved a much higher ceiling than was initially proposed to benefit the wealthy PRI—the party that had been in power for more than 70 years.

These improvements contributed to the opposition winning a majority in the Chamber of Deputies in the watershed 1997 legislative elections—for the first time in Mexico's modern history—and to the 2000 presidential elections bringing an opposition candidate, Vicente Fox, to power. Electoral reforms have considerably strengthened direct democratic participation by all Mexican citizens in government institutions and processes.

Source: United Nations, *Human Development Report 2002: Deepening Democracy in a Fragmented World* (New York: UNDP and Oxford University Press, 2002); cited on August 12, 2002; available at http://www.undp.org/hdr2002, p. 73. © 2002 by the United Nations Development Programme. Used by permission of Oxford University Press, Inc.

such as interest groups, social movements, corporations, trade unions, and religious organizations. Not only does a democracy encourage the existence of such organizations to promote their own interests, but they are considered to be essential ingredients in the "capacity and willingness of citizens to influence the government."[9]

In defining democracy, many analysts talk only of procedural aspects, but another component that is often included in contemporary discussions of the term relates to the kinds of policies that are adopted. According to the 2002 United Nations *Human Development Report*, democratic policies should reflect the needs of future generations, be responsive to people's needs and aspirations, and aim at eradicating poverty and expanding the choices that all people have in their lives.[10] The Inter-Parliamentary Union adds that the policies of democratic governments should foster social justice and economic and social development.

A healthy democracy is a complex, imperfect, and delicate system of government. Since even some of the most democratic states in the world, including Canada,

BOX 2.2

THE UNIVERSAL DECLARATION ON DEMOCRACY (INTER-PARLIAMENTARY UNION, 1997)

Democracy is a universally recognized ideal, based on values common to people everywhere regardless of cultural, political, social, or economic differences. As an ideal, democracy aims to protect and promote the dignity and fundamental rights of the individual, instil social justice, and foster economic and social development. Democracy is a political system that enables people to freely choose an effective, honest, transparent, and accountable government.

Democracy is based on two core principles: participation and accountability. Everyone has the right to participate in the management of public affairs. Likewise, everyone has the right to access information on government activities, to petition government, and to seek redress through impartial administrative and judicial mechanisms.

Genuine democracy presupposes a genuine partnership between men and women in conducting the affairs of society. Democracy is also inseparable from human rights and founded on the primacy of the law, for which judicial institutions and independent, impartial, effective oversight mechanisms are the guarantors.

The declaration sets out the prerequisites for democratic government, emphasizing the need for properly structured, well-functioning institutions. These institutions must mediate tensions and preserve the equilibrium among society's competing claims.

A parliament representing all parts of society is essential. It must be endowed with institutional powers and practical means to express the will of the people by legislating and overseeing government action. A key feature of the exercise of democracy is holding free, fair, regular elections based on universal, equal, secret suffrage.

An active civil society is also essential. The capacity and willingness of citizens to influence the governance of their societies should not be taken for granted, and is necessary to develop conditions conducive to the genuine exercise of participatory rights.

Society must be committed to meeting the basic needs of the most disadvantaged groups to ensure their participation in the workings of the democracy. Indeed, the institutions and processes essential to any democracy must include the participation of all members of society. They must define diversity, pluralism, and the right to be different within a tolerant society.

Democracy must also be recognized as an international principle, applicable to international organizations and to states in their international relations.

Democracy is always a work in progress, a state or condition constantly perfectible. Sustaining democracy means nurturing and reinforcing a democratic culture through all the means that education has at its disposal.

Source: Inter-Parliamentary Union, Universal Declaration on Democracy (1997). This summary is provided in United Nations, *Human Development Report 2002: Deepening Democracy in a Fragmented World* (New York: UNDP and Oxford University Press, 2002); cited on August 12, 2002; available at http://www.undp.org/hdr2002, p. 55. © 2002 by the United Nations Development Programme. Used by permission of Oxford University Press, Inc.

exhibit serious imperfections, it is not surprising that a large proportion of those that are labelled "democracies" fall far short of the standards outlined above. As Chapter 15 points out and Figure 2.1 illustrates, however, a dramatic increase in the number of democratic regimes around the world occurred during the 1980s and 1990s. Today, for example, some 140 of 190 countries hold multiparty elections.[11]

Nevertheless, the 2002 UN *Human Development Report* is cautious about recent events:

Figure 2.1 The World Is Becoming More Democratic

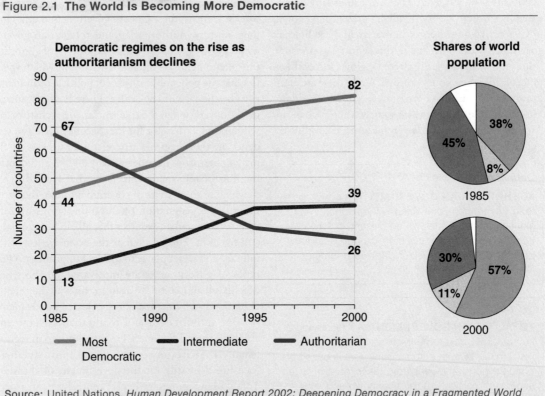

Source: United Nations, *Human Development Report 2002: Deepening Democracy in a Fragmented World* (New York: UNDP and Oxford University Press, 2002); cited on August 12, 2002; available at http://www.undp.org/hdr2002, p. 15. © 2002 by the United Nations Development Programme. Used by permission of Oxford University Press, Inc.

Several [states] that took steps towards democracy after 1980 have since returned to more authoritarian rule: either military, as in Pakistan since 1999, or pseudo-democratic, as in Zimbabwe in recent years. Many others have stalled between democracy and authoritarianism, with limited political freedoms.... Others, including such failed states as Afghanistan and Somalia, have become breeding grounds for extremism and violent conflict.

Even where democratic institutions are firmly established, citizens often feel powerless to influence national policies. They and their governments also feel more subject to international forces that they have little capacity to control.[12]

AUTHORITARIAN AND TOTALITARIAN GOVERNMENTS

Nondemocratic states are often called dictatorships and are commonly divided into **authoritarian** and **totalitarian** states. Authoritarian and totalitarian governments are equally concerned with the maintenance, at all costs, of their position of power. Both authoritarianism and totalitarianism are based on an ideology of pure and unmitigated power. There are no constitutional limitations on the government, there is no authorized process to change the government, and citizens have few (if any) rights. Both types of government have a habit of using excessive force to control the populations that they "serve." They are also usually dominated by a strong and vocal military presence. As noted in Chapter 15, however, authoritarian and totalitarian governments are in decline in this century, as pressure from more democratically elected regimes forces them to reconsider their policy options. While there are clear examples of authoritarian states, such as Saddam Hussein's Iraq, and until recently the Taliban in Afghanistan, there are few remaining examples of openly totalitarian states.

Definition

AUTHORITARIAN GOVERNMENT: A nondemocratic government that rules without public input, glorifies the leader, allows no dissent, strictly controls the mass media, relies on the police and military to root out opposition, and is dedicated to remaining in power at all costs.

Definition

TOTALITARIAN GOVERNMENT: A special kind of authoritarian government—most notably Nazism, fascism, and Soviet communism—that is based on a single party and ideology, takes control of all aspects of political, social, economic, and intellectual life, and mobilizes its mass public into active support of the government.

Because all democratic governments have tendencies to drift toward authoritarian or totalitarian options, some features of these types of government require further scrutiny. Authoritarian and totalitarian governments glorify their leadership to the point of absurdity; this phenomenon is often a written law, which specifies that the only public display of political prominence is to be the face of the leader. There is no organized, public opposition in these countries, just a charismatic, self-appointed dictator for life. Second, there is a tendency in these regimes to control all aspects of the media enterprise, in order to consolidate and control the flow of information. In fact, what has led to the downfall of these styles of government more than anything is the penetration of communications into the country from outside sources that affirm human rights and freedom. Finally, there is the extensive use of the military and secret police to root out opposition. These types of governments are motivated, in the truest Machiavellian fashion, by fear. In this way they are the exact opposite of democratically elected governments.

But authoritarian and totalitarian governments also have their differences. First, authoritarian regimes usually exercise power in a more limited sphere, focusing primarily on the government of the state. Totalitarian regimes have total control over all aspects of political, social, economic, and intellectual life; no activity is beyond the control of the government. It is partly because of developments in modern commu-

Hitler and Mussolini—two totalitarian leaders—confer with each other.

© Corbis/Magma

nications that totalitarianism is a product of the 20th century. Second, while authoritarian governments may merely want power for its own sake, totalitarian regimes are based on a single party and ideology—a mission to mould society in some way. The three most prominent totalitarian regimes in history are Nazism in Hitler's Germany, **fascism** in Mussolini's Italy, and Soviet **communism**, especially under Stalin. In each case, party had an ideology to change the society in some ideal fashion that the leadership claimed, however falsely, was in the public interest. Third, authoritarian regimes make no claim that their authority comes from the consent of the governed, and even mock elections are rare. Totalitarian regimes, on the other hand, pretend to be based on the consent of the public. They often stage manipulated single-party elections and otherwise mobilize the mass public into active support of the government.[13]

NON-STATE GOVERNMENTS

While we commonly associate government with states, whether democratic, authoritarian, or totalitarian, it is important to understand that some governments exist without being recognized as officially governing a state or being an integral part of the state's governing structure. These governments may take a variety of forms, and only some of the most common can be mentioned here.

Domestic Dependent Nations

One form of stateless government can be observed in the domestic dependent nations that were created for Indigenous peoples living within the United States. These governments are given powers to create economic opportunities for their citizens, and can enter into legally binding agreements with private companies, but they are not sovereign in the eyes of the state and federal governments of the United States. Moreover, they are also not what might be called "traditional" governments, because they exist within the institutional parameters set out in the interpretation of the American Constitution. Traditional governments are those that practice decision-making and adjudication according to the laws that their own peoples have passed down

through generations of occupation of a particular territory. Thus, while it may be said that Nunavut is a government for the Inuit people, it is not a traditional form of governance. Rather, like the domestic dependent nations in the United States, it is a hybrid of traditional and modern governmental forms.

Traditional Governments

This does not mean that traditional governments do not exist. All over the world, where Indigenous peoples have decided to apply their own laws and methods of governance to their own situations, there exist traditional governments. The Mohawk Council in Akwasasne or the Cree Grand Council in Northern Quebec are examples of traditional governmental organizations that have as their goal the discussion and creation of laws and administrative regularities for their own people. Another example is found in Pakistan, where large parts of territories are governed by the tribal authorities, which are composed of tribal chiefs ruling over their own traditional land with minimal intervention by the national government. Indigenous peoples around the world have begun to revive their traditional forms of government, some based on matrilineal succession, others based on consensus decision-making, and still others based on principles that are hard to describe because they are expressed in languages that defy effective translation into the dominant languages of the developed world. These act like governments and look like governments, but they are considered to be less sovereign than the developed world will accept; this is the legacy of colonialism that has left its mark on the Indigenous peoples of the world. There is also a world movement of Indigenous peoples that meets on a regular basis to discuss and recommend political actions that will result in the recognition of Indigenous sovereignty in various parts of the developed world.

Aboriginal Self-Government

One of the founding principles of European colonization throughout the world was the doctrine of *terra nullius*. According to this doctrine, upon encounter of any new land or people, it was assumed that there was nothing there—no language, no arts, no culture, no philosophy, no industry, and especially no government. When Indigenous peoples (people "native" to the areas under consideration for settlement) were encountered, they were considered to be living in a "state of nature" without a government, not unlike the state described by Thomas Hobbes or John Locke.

Indigenous peoples around the world have begun to revive their traditional ideas about governance and justice in a way that provides a new context for discussion of Indigenous worldviews in counterpoise to Western European worldviews. It is clear that Indigenous peoples have traditions of governance, systems of justice, methods of educating their people, health and welfare systems, and a strong sense of economy. They were never an "uncivilized" form of European, contrary to what colonizers proclaimed; they did not live in a condition of economic scarcity; and they did not occupy a territory under the principles established by the doctrine of *terra nullius*. They have extremely sophisticated language systems that perform the same functions as any others in operating as a medium to understand the world. The power of Indigenous peoples is not measured by economic advantage but by community spirit. In economic terms, wealth is not measured by commodity but by the capacity for sharing.

The licence that was taken to "civilize" Indigenous peoples through forced relocation to lands "reserved" for them by the crown or by the state, or through the development of a residential school system, or through the dispossession of territory through a process of treaty-making, has been revoked by Indigenous peoples themselves. They demand a new meaningful dialogue based on trust, respect, equality, and truth. In Canada, many Aboriginal people want to get rid of the Indian Act, which is actually a series of acts and amendments made by Parliament that identifies and organizes Indigenous peoples who happen to live within our declared sovereign territory by words that are not their own. The recent recognition of Aboriginal rights and Aboriginal title to land were steps in the right direction, but the next step is to recognize Aboriginal peoples' rights as "peoples" who have an inherent right to **Aboriginal self-government**. What forms such governments will assume and what powers they will have are currently subject to heated debate, even among well-intentioned people on both sides. At the level of international law, these rights have been affirmed by many jurists who practise within the European tradition of jurisprudence. It is up to individual nation-states to move beyond their self-interest to embrace Indigenous worldviews.

> **Definition**
>
> **ABORIGINAL SELF-GOVERNMENT:** A demand by Aboriginal or Indigenous groups that they be able to govern themselves, as they did before colonial rulers removed such power.

Territories and Protectorates

Territories and protectorates are categories of government that do not officially belong to the same class as state governments because they lack the formal sovereignty that allows them to be recognized by the world community of states. Examples of these kinds of government include Puerto Rico, which is a protectorate of the United States, or the recently created territory of Nunavut, which is considered to be a territory of the federal government of Canada. In both cases, the apparatus of government is in place; there are legislative bodies, judicial reviews of laws, and a well-developed capacity for administration of policies and procedures. The only thing that differentiates these governments from their state counterparts is the degree of sovereignty that they enjoy with regard to their "host" country. The governments of territories and protectorates have very little control over fundamental aspects of their economies and cannot engage in treaty-making with any other state or establish foreign policies. Moreover, instead of evolving into separate states in their own right, these kinds of governments will most likely develop closer ties with the federal structures that control their political destinies. Puerto Rico will most likely become the 51st state of the United States, and Nunavut may some day become a province of Canada.

Stateless Governments

Another instance of non-state governments can be found in the Palestinian experience within the state of Israel. The Palestinian people have been struggling for recognition of their statehood in the midst of Israeli policies of expansion and settlement in what are considered Palestinian lands. The government of Yasser Arafat, recognized by many states as the legitimate government of the Palestinian people, has held elections, passes laws, and administers to the people of the Palestinian territories. In addition, in the past 10 years, the state of Israel has begun to recognize this government as quasi-legitimate. Negotiations continue amidst terrorist exchanges between the two governments to formally recognize a Palestinian state.

Warlords

The warlord is a particular style of governor who takes advantage of interfactional fighting among armed militias and the lack of a recognized government to control a portion of a failing state. Such a state typically has several warlord generals competing for dominance, each supported by territorially divergent ethnic and linguistic populations. Although the result is that there is "no functioning government,"[14] it may well be in the interests of the warlords to keep the political situation as unstable as possible. This description seems applicable to earlier periods of the history of formative states, but there are recent examples, the best ones being Somalia and Afghanistan in the 1990s. Modern-day warlords are usually referred to in a disparaging manner, which may well be appropriate from a moral point of view, as they often rule through brute force. However, political scientists need to be aware that these individuals are at the top of a community grouping that is under their control and direction—in effect, many warlords actually rule over a given population in a more or less set territory. This observation is probably even more pertinent if one considers the parallels between modern warlords and the local princes and lords of Asia, Africa, and Europe who ruled over communities prior to the emergence of the larger states and empires. In other words, there may be reasons to respect such warlords because, even though they rule by force, they may be regarded as legitimate political leaders by their people.

* * *

To a large extent, it is the absence of the recognition of sovereignty, or the ability to control certain territories in the interests of the people who live there, that distinguishes non-state governments. As we have seen, sovereignty is gained in degrees by those states that consider themselves to be sovereign. There are no real mechanisms except for force and treaty that can enhance the degrees of sovereignty that these non-state governments can experience. They are, nevertheless, worthy of study as governments that challenge the status quo—as did the revolutionary governments found throughout the European and American world in the past 200 years. Many of these non-state governments also consider themselves to be governments in

The Pope kisses Palestinian soil—"That's all we have for the moment."

Serge Chapleau; Reprinted by permission of La Presse

exile, unable to serve the complete interests of their people because of the intervention in their affairs of colonial and neocolonial political and economic forces.

The European Union

An exciting new model of government exists in the form of the European Union (EU). As it evolves, the EU is developing a bureaucracy and Parliament that will serve the interests of all member countries. The EU is very careful to allow membership only to those countries that have proven and stable governing practices based on the principles of democracy and freedom. The EU is also modelled on the principle of economic, social, and political cooperation; in this way, it represents the end of ideological upheaval and centuries of warfare among its member states. Although they appreciate the advantages of belonging to the EU, most member states complain from time to time that the union is eroding their individual sovereignty.

Global Governance

The concept of **global governance** has been embodied to some extent for the past 50 years in the **United Nations (UN)**. The goals of the UN are to foster cooperation and peace among the world's nations. At the same time, the organization has been responsible for many development projects that have brought emerging countries to the point of entry into the global political economy. Although the UN is clearly the most developed international organization in existence, its effective power is challenged in a number of ways. First, the UN Security Council still maintains veto power over every decision made in the General Assembly. Therefore, as emerging countries make themselves heard, they are sometimes unable to get the body of the UN to act on their behalf. The system is too focused on the interests of the five countries that occupy permanent seats on the Security Council. Therefore, any profound political, social, and economic change that could become a part of the UN's mandate is subject to the approval by the more developed countries and their Security Council protectors. The other main limitation is that the UN is based on the recognition of the sovereignty of its member states. By acknowledging that sovereignty rests elsewhere, the UN is far short of being an international government, as noted in Chapter 16.

Globalization

In addition to the array of non-state governments discussed above, there exist informal bodies and organizations that also act like governments in certain ways. Many trade and cultural organizations have established rules of election and procedure, pass laws, and administer to their constituents, all under the watchful eyes of official state governments. These organizations are not really interested in establishing sovereignty in the traditional European and American sense, but rather seek to enhance open and uninhibited flows of trade and information among like-minded states. Nevertheless, they are often considered to challenge the traditional sovereignty of states. The **World Trade Organization (WTO)** is an informal body of states working with private corporate interests to create easier flows of capital, products of trade, and people throughout the world. Many believe that this is the essence of **globalization**: the world is reduced to a series of markets and consumer groups, and the issues of sovereignty are replaced by the goal of technical and economic efficiency orchestrated by nonelected experts. Some consider these developments as another element in the progression of the world toward a unified field of laws and human rights through the agency of an expanded economic system that rewards those who can profit. To others, they amount to a disregard for the democratic rights that are enshrined in the constitutions of democratic states in favour of accessibility to new markets. The sides have been drawn to a new kind of politics, one that sees corporate interests challenged by community development and action groups that are formed to react to the excesses of market expansion and the disregard for fundamental social, environmental, and human rights.

CONCLUSION

This chapter has provided a comprehensive discussion of the concept of government. It has examined classifications of government in the ancient world, the evolution of modern forms of government, and contemporary classifications. Today governments are usually aligned with states, which can be classified as democracies or as authoritarian or totalitarian regimes; each of these forms of government has been defined in the chapter. But the modern world also witnesses an interesting diversity of non-state governments, and a sampling of these has also been provided.

DISCUSSION QUESTIONS

1. **What do you think of Aristotle's scheme for classifying governments? Was it appropriate only for the ancient world, or is it relevant today?**

2. **What do you feel are the most important elements of a democratic government?**

3. **What are the imperfections in Canadian democracy?**

4. **What is the appeal of authoritarian and totalitarian governments?**

5. **What kind of Aboriginal self-government should Canada seek to achieve?**

WEB LINKS

Inter-Parliamentary Union:
http://www.ipu.org

United Nations' *Human Development Report 2002*:
http://www.undp.org/hdr2002

Freedom House:
http://www.freedomhouse.org

FURTHER READING

Amnesty International. *Report 2000*. London: Amnesty International Publications, 2000.

Bogdanor, Vernon, ed., *The Blackwell Encyclopaedia of Political Science*. Oxford: Blackwell Publishers, 1991.

Charlton, Mark, and Paul Barker. *Crosscurrents: Contemporary Political Issues*. 4th ed. Toronto: Nelson Thomson Learning, 2002.

United Nations. *Human Development Report 2002: Deepening Democracy in a Fragmented World*. New York: UNDP and Oxford University Press, 2002. Cited on August 12, 2002. Available at http://www.undp.org/hdr2002.

ENDNOTES

1   Gabriel A. Almond, "A Functional Approach to Comparative Politics," in Almond and James S. Coleman, eds., *The Politics of the Developing Areas* (Princeton: Princeton University Press, 1960).

2   Hobbes, *Leviathan*, ed. C.B. Macpherson (Harmondsworth: Penguin English Library, 1981), chap. 13, pp. 185–86.

3   United Nations, *Human Development Report 2002: Deepening Democracy in a Fragmented World* (New York: UNDP and Oxford University Press, 2002); cited on August 12, 2002; available at http://www.undp.org/hdr2002, p. 51.

4   Ibid., pp. 4, 68.

5   Ibid., p. 51.

6   Ibid., pp. 6, 78.

7   Inter-Parliamentary Union, Universal Declaration on Democracy (1997), quoted in United Nations, *Human Development Report 2002*, p. 55.

8   For an interesting discussion of this debate, see "Is the Canadian Charter of Rights and Freedoms Antidemocratic?" in Mark Charlton and Paul Barker, *Crosscurrents: Contemporary Political Issues*, 4th ed. (Toronto: Nelson Thomson Learning, 2002), pp. 96–108.

9   Inter-Parliamentary Union, Universal Declaration on Democracy (1997), quoted in United Nations, *Human Development Report 2002*, p. 55.

10   United Nations, *Human Development Report 2002*, p. 51.

11   Ibid., p. 1.

12   Ibid.

13   Vernon Bogdanor, ed., *The Blackwell Encyclopaedia of Political Science* (Oxford: Blackwell Publishers, 1991).

14   Amnesty International, *Report 2000* (London: Amnesty International Publications, 2000), p. 215, speaking of Somalia.

Chapter 3

Cultural Pluralism, Nationalism, and Globalization

Yasmeen Abu-Laban

CHAPTER OBJECTIVES

After you have completed this chapter, you should be able to

- define the key concepts of genocide, ethnic cleansing, nationalism, state, nation, multination state, diaspora, race, globalization, dominant conformity, and cultural pluralism
- outline and evaluate two different approaches to the study of nationalism (universalizing and individualizing comparisons)
- discuss the debate over the impact of contemporary globalization on national identity
- describe some contemporary expressions of nationalism and other identity-based claims.

WHY STUDY CULTURAL PLURALISM?

Today, cultural pluralism is a reality in most countries around the world because often a variety of different ethnic groups reside in the same geographic space. According to recent demographic statistics, only about 10 percent of countries can be said to be ethnically homogeneous.[1] Since political scientists typically study one or more countries, and since 90 percent of countries are characterized by a heterogeneous population, it is easy to see why political scientists are interested in cultural and ethnic diversity. Cultural pluralism profoundly affects people's sense of identity, as well as relations between different cultural and ethnic groups within countries.

The attempt to describe ethnic, cultural, and other forms of diversity is not merely a theoretical exercise. A better understanding of these issues has considerable practical significance, affecting people's quality of life and helping decision-makers who wish to enact effective public policies. Thus, the research findings of political and other social scientists on issues pertaining to diversity are extremely relevant. This fact has been recognized at the highest levels internationally, as exemplified by the mandate of the Management of Social Transformations (MOST) program, launched in January 1994 by the United Nations Educational, Scientific and Cultural Organization (UNESCO). MOST is an ongoing project designed to promote international comparative social science research, with the aim of transferring policy-relevant findings to governmental and nongovernmental decision-makers. A central goal of the program is to better understand multicultural and multiethnic societies, precisely because of the potential implications for a host of policy areas. Accordingly, it is argued,

the major challenge facing policy-makers in the fields of education, health, social welfare and jus-

tice is to formulate policies in such a way as to promote and sustain peaceful multi-ethnic and multi-cultural co-operation and to rebuild such co-operation in societies undergoing post-war political, social and economic reconstruction.[2]

Table 3.1 One Take on Diversity in Selected Countries

By compiling national census data and other statistical information, *The World Factbook* of the U.S. Central Intelligence Agency lists ethnic groups present in all countries of the world. Below is a selection from the 2001 edition.

Afghanistan: Pashtun 38%, Tajik 25%, Hazara 19%, minor ethnic groups (Aimaks, Turkmen, Baloch, and others) 12%, Uzbek 6%

Australia: Caucasian 92%, Asian 7%, Aboriginal and other 1%

Belgium: Fleming 58%, Walloon 31%, mixed or other 11%

Brazil: white (includes Portuguese, German, Italian, Spanish, and Polish) 55%, mixed white and Black 38%, Black 6%, other (includes Japanese, Arab, Amerindian) 1%

China: Han Chinese 91.9%, Zhuang, Uygur, Hui, Yi, Tibetan, Miao, Manchu, Mongol, Buyi, Korean, and other nationalities 8.1%

Finland: Finn 93%, Swede 6%, Sami 0.11%, Roma 0.12%, Tatar 0.02%

Germany: German 91.5%, Turkish 2.4%, other 6.1% (made up largely of Serbo-Croatian, Italian, Russian, Greek, Polish, and Spanish)

India: Indo-Aryan 72%, Dravidian 25%, Mongoloid and other 3%

Israel: Jewish 80.1% (Europe/America-born 32.1%, Israel-born 20.8%, Africa-born 14.6%, Asia-born 12.6%), non-Jewish 19.9% (mostly Arab); West Bank: Palestinian Arab and other 83%, Jewish 17%; Gaza Strip: Palestinian Arab and other 99.4%, Jewish 0.6%

Mexico: mestizo (Amerindian-Spanish) 60%, Amerindian or predominantly Amerindian 30%, white 9%, other 1%

South Africa: Black 75.2%, white 13.6%, Coloured 8.6%, Indian 2.6%

Switzerland: German 65%, French 18%, Italian 10%, Romansch 1%, other 6%

United Kingdom: English 81.5%, Scottish 9.6%, Irish 2.4%, Welsh 1.9%, Ulster 1.8%, West Indian, Indian, Pakistani, and other 2.8%

United States: white 83.5%, Black 12.4%, Asian 3.3%, Amerindian 0.8% (Note: a separate listing for Hispanic is not included because the U.S. Census Bureau considers Hispanic to mean a person of Latin American descent [especially of Cuban, Mexican, or Puerto Rican origin] living in the United States who may be of any race or ethnic group, such as white, Black, Asian, etc.)

Source: Central Intelligence Agency, *The World Factbook 2001*; cited on May 1, 2002; available at http://www.cia.gov/cia/publications/factbook.

This chapter examines the internal diversity of nation-states in light of a belief system that profoundly shaped politics and events in the 20th century: nationalism. For political scientists today, a major research question concerns the salience of nationalism in the 21st century, given contemporary patterns of globalization. The economic, cultural, and technological processes associated with globalization now seem to challenge both national identity as the only or main form of identity experienced by people and the nation-state as a form of political organization. In this chapter, it is argued that while national identity is not disappearing, its primacy is being challenged by contemporary globalization.

In the first section of this chapter, key concepts pertaining to nationalism are explained. The second section contains an overview of theories of nationalism with reference to historic nationalist liberation struggles in the developing world. In the third section, the tension between nationalism and other forms of identity (especially gender) is examined in light of recent developments in South Africa. Finally, the tension between nationalism and globalization is addressed, and contemporary expressions of nationalism and identity claims that are not based on a single national identity are explored in relation to Canada.

KEY CONCEPTS IN THE STUDY OF NATIONALISM

What comes to mind when you see the word *nationalism*? Are your reactions positive or negative? No matter how you answer these questions, you will enter into a debate that has raged among analysts and historians for two centuries. This momentous force has been viewed as the root cause of such diverse events as the emergence of the European state system, World War I, the rise of fascism in Europe, Third World anticolonial struggles, reassertions of national identity by minorities in industrialized countries (for example, in Scotland and in Quebec), and post–Cold War conflict in the former Eastern bloc countries.

Some see nationalism as a positive force. It has been suggested, for example, that the existence of nations is associated with the existence of ties of love or kinship.[3] Frequently, we may speak of nations as "motherlands"

and "fatherlands." Citizens form a national "family." Immigrants are said to "adopt" countries that are not their native homes. In the United States, the president and the president's spouse are referred to as the "First Family." In Canada, the first two lines of the national anthem (at least in English, as the Canadian anthem's meaning is different in French!) are "O Canada! Our home and native land! True patriot love in all thy sons command." When Nelson Mandela became the first president of post-apartheid South Africa, his wife at the time, Winnie Mandela, was honoured as South Africa's "Mother of the Nation."

Just as often, and probably more often, nationalism has been associated with hatred. Some have seen nationalism as the most destructive force of the 20th century—the cause of violence, atrocity, and incalculable human misery.[4] The Nazi regime in Germany and the evils of the Holocaust stood as the mid-century's horrifying example of this scourge. Responding to the tragedy of the Holocaust, Polish jurist Raphael Lemkin coined the term **genocide** (from the Greek word *genos*, meaning race, and the Latin work *caedere*, meaning to kill).[5] An international prohibition against genocide was established in 1948 when the United Nations adopted the Convention on the Prevention and Punishment of the Crime of Genocide.

Definition

GENOCIDE: The deliberate and systematic extermination of a national, ethnic, or religious group. The term was developed in response to the horrors of the Holocaust.

In the 1990s, the violence, bloodshed, and killing that occurred among rival ethnic and religious groups in the former Yugoslavia (Serbs, Croats, and Muslims) and also in Rwanda (Hutus and Tutsis) emerged as new horrors that led many to reaffirm that nationalism was one of the most destructive forces imaginable and to refocus international attention on genocide. The Rwandan genocide began on April 6, 1994, when a small group of Hutu political and military leaders targeted and began the slaughter of more than a half a million Tutsis—a group that constituted about 10 percent of the population—along with thousands of Hutus who opposed the elite in power. This genocide differed from others in its rapidity (lasting about a hundred days) and in the number of ordinary people who were mobilized by a small elite to kill.[6]

The 1992–95 war in Bosnia-Herzegovina was the most destructive segment in the dissolution of Yugoslavia, which began when the republics of Croatia and Slovenia seceded in 1991, leaving open the possibility of an independent Bosnia. There was no clear ethnic majority in Bosnia; the three constituent peoples (as defined by earlier Yugoslav constitutions) were the Muslims (most numerous at 42 percent of the population), followed by the Serbs and the Croats.[7] In this climate of uncertainty in Bosnia, President Slobodan Milosevic of Serbia used the crisis to consolidate his power by sending in his paramilitary troops bent on ethnic cleansing.[8] While the United Nations attributes violence in Bosnia-Herzegovina to all sides, the term **ethnic cleansing** was used specifically to refer to a slate of violent measures and policies designed to eliminate or dramatically reduce the Muslim and Croat populations in Serb-held territory.[9] Ethnic cleansing included the systematic rape by Serbian soldiers of Muslim and Croat women, whose captivity, torture, and forced pregnancies were designed to reproduce "Serbians."[10] The term is controversial because it is seen as somewhat euphemistic (in contrast to *genocide*) and serving to mask the impact of this nationalist violence.

Definition

ETHNIC CLEANSING: The removal of one or more ethnic groups from a society, by means of expulsion, imprisonment, or killing. The term entered the political lexicon in reference to the former Yugoslavia; it was first used to describe the violent measures and policies designed to eliminate or dramatically reduce the Muslim and Croat populations in Serb-held territory.

The travesties in both Rwanda and the former Yugoslavia, which clearly included both the direct and indirect involvement of governments, led to renewed calls within the international community for more effective means to prosecute such crimes. To this end, the United Nations convened an International Criminal Court, whose jurisdiction includes the ability to prosecute the crime of genocide, as defined in the 1948 Convention on the Prevention and Punishment of the Crime of Genocide. These tragic events of the

1990s also had an impact on the study of nationalism. Indeed, in 1993, Michael Ignatieff wrote an international bestseller, tellingly entitled *Blood and Belonging*, in which he argues that the end of the Cold War has been replaced by a new age of violence based on nationalism and ethnic particularism.[11]

While there are radically different readings of the impact of nationalism as a force, political scientists are on less contentious ground in delineating what nationalism is. At root, **nationalism** may be defined as an ideology or belief system that contains three major assumptions.[12] The first assumption is that certain identified populations contain characteristics that make them nations. The second is that the world is divided into nations. The third is that a nation should be able to establish its own institutions, laws, and government and to determine its future—this is really what lies behind the idea of self-determination. The doctrine of self-determination holds that a group of people who call themselves a nation have a right to have control over territory or domains that immediately concern them, normally through statehood. The idea of self-determination may be traced back to the emergence of the European state system in the middle of the 17th century. In the 20th century, it became enshrined in the principles of international institutions such as the United Nations, and self-determination is now considered a human right under international law.[13]

Definition

NATIONALISM: An ideology that holds that certain populations are nations, that the world is divided into nations, and that a nation should be self-determining (i.e., able to establish its own institutions, laws, and government and to determine its future).

Unpacking the ideology of nationalism requires a closer examination of several associated concepts. The first concept is that of the state. Political scientists have theorized much about the state, but there is no clear consensus about whose interests it promotes. For example, the 19th-century thinker Karl Marx (1818–83) argued that in a capitalist society the state was a class instrument that served the interests of the owners of the means of production (the bourgeoisie) over the interests of the workers (the proletariat). For Marx, the state was central in the functioning of the capitalist system and the perpetuation of class inequality. This is why Marx called on workers to unite, overthrow the state, and usher in a more egalitarian (in this case, communist) society. More recently, radical feminists have argued that the state is central in perpetuating patriarchy (the rule of males) by privileging men in law and public policy.[14] Other (mainly liberal) theorists assert that the state operates in the interests of different individuals or groups at different times.

Although there is considerable debate about whose interests are represented by the state, most political scientists do agree on what the state is and use the definition first provided by Max Weber (1864–1920). Weber argued that the "**state** is a human community that (successfully) claims the monopoly of legitimate use of physical force within a given territory."[15] For Weber, the state is characterized by territory (existing in a given geographical boundary), by sovereignty (the state is the highest authority and can back up its claims with force), and by institutions (including the bureaucracy, the military and the police, and the legislatures).

It should be noted that the way political scientists use the term *state* to refer to territory, sovereignty, and institutions is very comprehensive and precise; the term *state* is not synonymous with *country* or *government*. The term *country* describes geographical units of the globe. When you look at the divisions of the world in an atlas, you are looking at countries. As discussed in Chapters 1 and 2, the term *government* refers to the set of institutions that make and enforce collective public decisions for a society, usually a state.

The ideology of nationalism holds that territory, sovereignty, and institutions must be allocated to people of a single nation. While belonging to a state

Ottawa invests in health care…"I thought it would improve things."

Reprinted by permission of Michael Garneau

may be a simple matter of citizenship, belonging to a **nation** rests on a subjective sense of identity and of belonging to an ethnic group (usually marked by a distinct culture or language).[16] A leading theorist of nationalism, Benedict Anderson, refers to nations as "imagined communities" precisely because the idea of a nation rests on a subjective sense of belonging to a community that is neither voluntary nor organizationally defined. You might contrast being a part of a nation with joining an organization such as an undergraduate students' association (which likely holds elections for those willing to run for president, vice president, and the like). On the other hand, belonging to a nation is somewhat similar to belonging to a family—it is seemingly "natural" and involuntary.[17] For this reason, according to Anderson, dying for one's nation "assumes a moral grandeur which dying for the Labour Party, the American Medical Association, or perhaps even Amnesty International can not rival, for these are all bodies one can join or leave at easy will."[18] Undoubtedly, we could put campus student associations in this same "voluntary" category as political parties or interest groups.

> **Definition**
>
> **NATION:** A community of people, normally defined by a combination of ethnicity, language, and culture, with a subjective sense of belonging together.

Although the ideology of nationalism implies that there ought to be an easily definable correspondence between territory, a single nation, and rule, this is not the case with most countries. Some states contain more than one nation; such a state is called a **multination state**. For example, Canada has been variously described as containing two nations (the French and the British), three nations (the French, the British, and Aboriginal peoples), and even numerous nations (particularly when the multiple traditions and languages among all Aboriginal peoples in Canada are considered). This is where the problems of the doctrine of self-determination become apparent. Often, in real-world politics, the same territory is claimed by more than one group. This is especially apparent in a country such as Canada—a settler colony with an Indigenous population and a minority francophone population located primarily in Quebec. During the 1995 Quebec refer-

endum on sovereignty, separation from the rest of Canada was rejected by a very narrow margin (50.6 percent to 49.4 percent). Aboriginal peoples have land claims all over Canada, including in the province of Quebec. For this reason, when the referendum was called, some Aboriginal groups, including the Cree and the Montagnais, held their own referendums on the issue of sovereignty; the proposal was rejected by a wide margin. A prime international example of nations laying claim to the same land is the Israeli–Palestinian conflict. Both sides have insisted for decades on the legitimacy of their claim on historic grounds; a solution does not seem to be in sight.

> **Definition**
>
> **MULTINATION STATE:** A state that contains more than one nation.

A further complication to the doctrine of nationalism is the fact that nations may spill out across state boundaries—a feature encapsulated in the concept of **diaspora**. The term was originally applied to Jewish people, but today it is used to describe any ethnic group that has experienced or currently experiences dislocation across multiple states, and yet typically nurtures narratives and political projects about a "homeland" as a place of eventual return at some opportune time.[19] In contemporary usage it has been applied to such diverse groups as Palestinians, Armenians, and Cubans.[20]

> **Definition**
>
> **DIASPORA:** An ethnic group that has experienced or currently experiences dislocation across multiple states, yet typically nurtures narratives and political projects about a specific "homeland" as a place of eventual return.

Finally, it should be noted that ethnic groups can have many different political demands and points of mobilization that do not take the form of nationalism and self-determination but instead stress gaining acceptance and equality.[21] In particular, some groups may struggle against discrimination based on race.

In the past, the term **race** has been used in many different ways. During the 19th century, biologists used it to refer to different "subspecies" of humans. The inspiration behind eugenics movements—which

---

BOX 3.1

TWO NARRATIVES: "PALESTINE" AND "ISRAEL"

Both Palestinian Arabs (Muslims and Christians) and Israeli Jews lay claim to the territory of Palestine/Israel as their national home on the basis of long residence, history, and religion. The area known as Palestine was, until World War I, part of the Turkish Ottoman empire. Following the war, the League of Nations (the forerunner to the United Nations) granted Britain a mandate over Palestine. Flowing from the 1917 Balfour Declaration, the British government viewed "with favour the establishment in Palestine of a national home for the Jewish people," and promised to use immigration to support this objective.

While Palestinian Arabs remained a majority in the area until the late 1940s, the goal of creating a Jewish state in Palestine was further developed in the United Nations Partition Plan in 1947. The Partition Plan sought to divide Palestine into an Arab state and a Jewish state, with the city of Jerusalem designated as an international zone. The Partition Plan was viewed as unacceptable and unfair by Arab Palestinians, who believed it threatened the geographical integrity of Palestine and disagreed with the manner in which Palestine was divided. Hostility between Arabs and Jews mounted in Palestine, and civil war broke out. On May 14, 1948, an independent state of Israel was declared, and the British mandate came to an end. As a result, open warfare between the surrounding Arab states and Israel erupted. By the end of the war, there was more land taken by Israel than had been allotted under the Partition Plan. However, Israel rapidly gained the recognition of both the world's superpowers, the United States and the Soviet Union. Israeli leaders immediately indicated that the new state belonged to all the Jewish people around the world and invited immigration from the Jewish diaspora.

The events of 1948 are subject to very different national narratives on the parts of Palestinians and Israelis. For many Israelis, the years 1947 and 1948 are seen as a period in which the birth of a national state was made possible after the Holocaust and after what Israelis call the War of Independence of 1948. This accounts for the jubilant celebrations in Israel in 1998 of 50 years of statehood. In contrast, for most Palestinians, the year 1948 represents a disaster characterized by half of the Arab population losing homes and property and becoming stateless refugees outside of historic Palestine. Indeed, from 1949, Palestinian national identity crystallized around the loss of homeland, the longing to return, and the desire for self-determination.

A series of wars in the region (in 1956, 1967, 1973, and 1982) has served to reconfigure control of the land in favour of the state of Israel. For example, after the 1967 war, the territories of the West Bank and Gaza (known as "the occupied territories") came under Israeli control. The Oslo agreement signed in 1993 by Israel and the Palestine Liberation Organization (PLO) allows for parts of these two territories to be handed over to Palestinian rule. Nonetheless, peace remains elusive between Israelis and Palestinians, as well as in the larger region.

This case provokes the following question: Can competing claims to the same territory be adequately resolved in a framework emphasizing self-determination?

---

advocated the use of "scientific" breeding techniques to improve the genetic potential of humans—was the supposed existence of biological differences between different "racial" groups. In the early 20th century, the term *race* was often used as a synonym for *nation* and *ethnic group*. This can be seen in the metaphor of America as a "melting pot," popularized in a 1908 play "The Melting Pot" by playwright Israel Zangwill. Zangwill spoke of different "races" (by which he meant Germans, Russians, the English, the French, and the

Irish) jumping into a common melting pot and emerging as Americans.[22] By the middle of the 20th century, as a result of the atrocities of the Holocaust, the use of *race* to refer to biological differences between people was completely discredited; instead, many began to talk about "the human race" to indicate that eugenics was wrong, as all people are of the same species.

Today social scientists use the term *race* to refer to socially constructed rather than biologically inherited differences. In other words, race is viewed as significant only because of socially created beliefs about differences between people, not because biology itself determines culture or personality. In particular, social scientists are interested in how the processes of racism (or racialization) are manifested in practices and institutions to the detriment of particular groups in particular times and places. Some have advocated rejecting the term *race* altogether, or at least putting it in quotation marks to signify that there are no inherent differences between people.[23]

The idea that race and processes of racism are socially constructed and temporally specific can be readily documented. For example, historically, the Irish were held to be a separate and inferior "race" to the British; they experienced discrimination in a host of spheres in Britain, Canada, and the United States. Today groups struggling with racial discrimination include African-Americans in the United States. African-Americans overcame slavery in the 1800s, and through the civil rights movement in the 1950s and 1960s successfully challenged segregation in public schools and private establishments, yet discrimination against them remains a fact of life.

The continued inequality in employment and earnings between African-Americans and all other groups has led to public policy measures such as affirmative action. **Affirmative action** is designed to equalize the chances of members of minority groups or groups traditionally discriminated against, such as African-Americans, women, and people with disabilities, in accessing education and jobs by setting goals for ensuring the statistical representation of these groups. Affirmative action has become increasingly controversial in the United States. Critics charge that it is "reverse discrimination," while proponents argue that it helps put into practice the principle that all people are of equal worth. In the United States, affirmative action has tended to be supported by African-Americans more than by other groups.[24] Given the historical and contemporary social context of that country, categories such as "Black" and "white" (and increasingly, "mixed race") are important politically. The example of African-Americans illustrates how the mobilization and demands of groups can take forms other than national self-determination.

Indeed, political theorist Will Kymlicka suggests that in Canada and elsewhere many minority and immigrant groups have mobilized to demand **multiculturalism**. Kymlicka suggests this pursuit of multiculturalism is geared primarily to achieve inclusion in the dominant culture, rather than to attempt to live separately from it. For Kymlicka, multicultural responses to minority and immigrant group claims might involve such diverse policies as affirmative action, guaranteed seats in legislatures, curriculum changes in schools, work schedule changes to accommodate diverse religions, flexible dress codes, literacy programs in the first language of immigrants, and bilingual education programs for the children of immigrants.[25] In this way, multiculturalism may be seen as a very different kind of demand than national self-determination.

Definition

RACE: Historically, the term *race* was used to speak about differences between people that were supposedly biologically based. Today social scientists completely reject the idea that there are any significant biological differences between people which warrant the use of the term *race*. While some suggest that the term should not be used at all, many contemporary social scientists put "race" in quotation marks to refer to differences that are socially constructed and historically specific but have important consequences (e.g., racism is discrimination based on differentiating between groups).

Definition

MULTICULTURALISM: A policy sometimes adopted in a state characterized by cultural pluralism that encourages ethnic and cultural groups to maintain their customs and traditions, often with public financial assistance.

EXPLAINING NATIONALISM: NATIONAL LIBERATION MOVEMENTS AND DECOLONIZATION

So far in our discussion, two main themes have emerged. First, nationalism has been associated with many different—even opposite—phenomena in the 20th century: war, violence, hate, oppression, liberation, family, and love. Second, political scientists have defined the ideology of nationalism and related concepts in a precise way that seems to capture the essence of most if not all expressions of nationalism. The areas of agreement and disagreement help account for two very distinct approaches to studying nationalism that political scientists have used in explaining its emergence in very different times and locales.

Because the ideology of nationalism is fairly consistent across its various expressions, political scientists have tried to determine whether there is one primary factor that can explain the emergence of nationalism in so many different places. Those searching for this universal explanation have engaged in universalizing comparisons. Universalizing comparisons attempt to show how all instances of nationalism follow the same patterns. In contrast, other political scientists have postulated that, partly because of the sheer variety of phenomena associated with nationalism (from oppression to liberation), there may be many different explanations for why nationalism emerges in different locales—that is, that there is no universal explanation. Those searching to discover such differences have engaged in individualizing comparisons, which attempt to show the unique characteristics of a given instance of nationalism. To evaluate these two different approaches, it is helpful to consider how each might account for the same manifestation of nationalism.

One important manifestation of nationalism in the 20th century emerged in Third World anticolonial movements. During the 19th century, imperialism—in the form of colonization of other countries and the establishment of empires—led to the expansion of Western power over the rest of the world. However, during the 20th century, the formal control of Western states in different parts of the world largely came to an unexpected end in a relatively short period of time. Consider that in 1945, when the United Nations emerged as the primary international organization to promote peace and human rights, 51 states obtained membership. Out of these 51 states, only 3 were located in Africa (Ethiopia, Liberia, and South Africa), only 3 in Asia (of which only China was independent of colonial rule), and only 7 in the Middle East, as can be seen in Figure 3.1. Initially, then, the great majority of member states in the United Nations were the countries of North America, the Commonwealth, and Europe,

---

Figure 3.1 The Original 51 Member States of the United Nations (1945)

Argentina	Czechoslovakia	Honduras	Panama	Ukraine
Australia	Denmark	India	Paraguay	United Kingdom
Belgium	Dominican	Iran	Peru	of Great Britain
Bolivia	Republic	Iraq	Philippines	and Northern
Brazil	Ecuador	Lebanon	Poland	Ireland
Belarus	Egypt	Liberia	Russian	United States
Canada	El Salvador	Luxembourg	Federation	of America
Chile	Ethiopia	Mexico	Saudi Arabia	Uruguay
China	France	Netherlands	South Africa	Venezuela
Colombia	Greece	New Zealand	Syrian Arab	Yugoslavia
Costa Rica	Guatemala	Nicaragua	Republic	
Cuba	Haiti	Norway	Turkey	

including the former Soviet Union. Notably, most observers in the 1950s did not expect European power to end in their lifetime.[26] However, by the end of 1965, 66 new states joined the United Nations, bringing the number up to 117; in 2002, the number reached 191.

The addition of 66 new states symbolized a dramatic political change: the formal transfer of power from Europeans to non-Europeans and the liberation of some one billion people from colonial rule in Asia and Africa. The emergence and successes of Third World nationalist anticolonial movements might be explained in different ways depending on the approach one uses. Traditionally, many political scientists used universalizing comparisons to try to establish that all forms of nationalism follow the same patterns or rules. This approach was widely accepted during the 1950s, 1960s, and 1970s, and there are still people who use it today. Its popularity may be related to how political science, as a discipline, has been influenced by developments in the United States. In the United States, during the first two to three decades after World War II, political analysts were very much concerned with developing generalizations that could be applied to all societies at all times. This was part and parcel of developing a "science" of social and political life.[27]

The accounts that address nationalism from the vantage point of universalizing comparisons generally suggest that nationalism was rooted in the European experience, dating from the French Revolution and gaining speed with the unification of Germany and Italy in 1870. In this view, nationalism was somehow related to the processes of industrialization. What exactly is highlighted as important about industrialization varies in different accounts that make use of universalizing comparisons. Some have argued that technological developments in mass communication and the introduction of mass education made it possible for people to easily communicate with each other across vast distances.[28] As a result, people started to identify with one another in a new way—as part of national communities. Others have proposed that capitalism accompanied industrialization, and with capitalism came uneven development, and when there were pockets of poverty in distinct regions, expressions of nationalism emerged.[29] Both of these scenarios that use industrialization to explain nationalism have a uni-

versalizing quality to them—in both, there is a sense that the ideology of nationalism developed in Europe and was simply exported to Africa and Asia on the back of European colonialism.[30]

More recently, such universalizing explanations have been criticized for being Eurocentric, that is, focused only on the experience of Europe. Critics also argue that they are ahistorical—that is, they tend to ignore the unique historical context of different countries outside of Europe in accounting for nationalism. There is value to these criticisms, since political scientists have never been able to produce one general theory that accounts for the emergence of nationalism everywhere and for all time.

Individualizing comparisons, in contrast, take directly into account both historical and geographical specificity. They seek to uncover that which is unique about a given form or instance of nationalism. Broadly speaking, the suggestion that comes out of such accounts is that many expressions of Third World nationalism may be viewed as a political reaction against colonialism.[31] This political reaction occurs in societies where traditional modes of social and political organization have collapsed as a result of the changes introduced by colonialism.

One way to understand how Third World expressions of nationalism were a reaction against the oppressive effects of colonial rule is to consider how colonized people were treated and depicted by colonial powers. The famous lines by British poet Rudyard Kipling on "The White Man's Burden" provide a literary example of this broader phenomenon. Kipling's poem, written in 1899, describes the need for British men, and more broadly white men, to go out to the colonial world and rule the peoples there, whom Kipling describes as "half devil and half child."[32]

Unequal power relations that rested upon the dehumanized depiction of the colonized by the colonizer are key to understanding the motivation behind Third World nationalist movements for liberation. Imperialism and colonialism worked to erode the dignity of peoples of the Third World, but nationalism formed a part in the recovery of that dignity.[33] Consequently, one of the things that tends to surface in such expressions of Third World nationalism aimed at liberation is an attempt to invert and put value on the identity of the colonized. For example, Léopold Sédar Senghor, a poet who became the first president of Senegal after it achieved independence from France in 1960, is associated with a literary and political movement known as négritude. The négritude movement, which began in the 1930s and reached its zenith in the 1960s, launched a critique of Western society for suppressing Blacks and for cutting African Blacks off from their roots. Négritude aimed to rediscover ancient African values so that Africans could feel pride and dignity in their heritage and culture.

Likewise, Frantz Fanon, a West Indian–born psychoanalyst and philosopher who spent time in Algeria when it was under French colonial rule, went on to write about the necessity of creating or recreating a national cultural consciousness as a means of achieving true independence. In contrast to the négritude movement, however, Fanon saw an important, almost redemptive, role to be played by violence. He describes this idea in his famous 1963 book *The Wretched of the Earth*, which deals with the situation in Algeria. Between 1954 and 1961, there was a bitter and violent war between France and Algeria; as a result of this war Algeria gained its independence in 1962. For Fanon, the lessons of the Algerian war of independence suggest the value of violent struggle as a means to empower colonized people. Violence, he argues, is a cleansing force that "frees the native from his inferiority complex and from his despair and inaction."[34] Yet ultimately, the development of a genuine national consciousness leading to real liberation is difficult to achieve, Fanon points out, because the forces of domination are internalized by indigenous elites.[35] Even after decolonization, the unequal social and economic structures inherited from colonialism might well continue. Fanon sensed very early on that the national liberation movements in countries that experienced colonization might be successful in overthrowing foreign rulers, but that this might not necessarily in and of itself lead to an egalitarian future.

The basic idea behind individualizing comparisons is that while nationalism might be a single ideology, it contains several subvarieties.[36] From the vantage point of individualizing comparisons, manifestations of nationalism in the Third World in the context of national struggles for liberation may be seen as unique because the factors that motivated nationalism were unique. Universalizing explanations, in contrast, fail to take into account the specificity of the situation in the Third World. In an attempt to fit all manifestations of nationalism into one pattern, they fail to consider the historical effects of imperialism and colonialism in countries of the developing world. Individualizing comparisons do not have these limitations, suggesting the general necessity of attending to context when trying to understand nationalism in the contemporary period.

THE NATION VERSUS OTHER FORMS OF IDENTITY: CONSIDERING SOUTH AFRICA

The advantages of individualizing comparisons do not completely negate the need to theorize about the nation in relation to internal forces. The warnings of Frantz Fanon about the future of liberated (postcolonial) states highlight the complexities present in any nation. Any population that calls itself a nation is inevitably internally diverse and divided along some combination of class, gender, age, and rural–urban lines. As one prominent example of the relevance of this kind of internal diversity within nations, it is useful to consider the recent work of feminist scholars who have insisted on the importance of gender diversity in the study of national identity and relations of power. We have noted how nationalist discourses often make use of metaphors relating to kinship—motherlands, fatherlands, and the like. Such "familial" depictions of the nation have been the starting point for the work of these feminist scholars, who stress that nationalist movements can act to subordinate women. For example, whether women have children, how women socialize children, and even how women dress are often extremely important to most nationalist movements.[37]

Because women typically play a central role in transmitting and reflecting cultural traditions across generations, the argument has been made that it is women who play the primary role as "bearers of the nation," rather than schools or forms of mass communication (as has been suggested by some accounts focusing on explaining the rise of nationalism in relation to industrialization).[38] In this way, women can become specific targets as both the "property of men"

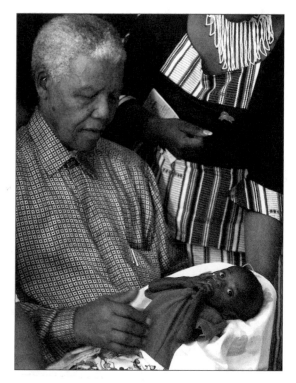

Former South African President Nelson Mandela holds a six-month-old baby infected with HIV during his visit to Beautiful Gate, a home that looks after children in Crossroads township, outside of Cape Town, South Africa; Saturday, December 1, 2001.

Obed Zilwa/CP Picture Archive

and the "embodiment of the nation," as attested to by the very systematic use of rape in the name of ethnic cleansing.[39] While, typically, nationalist movements themselves are tied to gendered relations, this does not always mean that they specifically improve the position of women. Indeed, according to feminist scholars, those who assume that nationalist movements generally improve the lot of the disadvantaged often neglect to attend to specific social and political structures and belief systems that can keep women in subordinate positions.[40]

In the context of nationalist movements aimed at liberation, South Africa provides a noteworthy recent example of a country where gender equality had to be considered explicitly. The history of the African National Congress (ANC) illustrates this point. The ANC was created in 1912 as the principal organization

reflecting Black South African interests. Although it was outlawed in 1960, the ANC was later instrumental in ending the racist policies of apartheid (or apartness) that had supported white colonial political and economic dominance. Nelson Mandela emerged from a long prison term to lead a successful anti-apartheid movement and then become the first president of post-apartheid South Africa in 1994.

The history of politics in South Africa and the reaction of Black women there to the long years of resistance and hope for liberating the country from white control demonstrate that Black women's relation to nationalism has undergone changes.[41] Initially, when the ANC was created, women were denied formal representation in the organization, yet gradually, as a result of women's own insistence, they were granted full participation. Nevertheless, calls for women's emancipation were generally seen as secondary to national revolution, sometimes even by women themselves. Over the late 1970s and 1980s, however, the issue of women's empowerment began to be raised as a project distinct from national, democratic, and social revolution. By the early 1990s, female ANC nationalists carried placards with the slogan "A nation will never be free until women are free."[42]

Such women's demonstrations were successful in leading to formal recognition of women's rights within the ANC, which in 1990 issued a Statement on the Emancipation of Women. The statement argued that the experience of other societies with successful national liberation struggles showed that the emancipation of women does not necessarily follow from national liberation. The statement asserted that, given this historical record, women's emancipation had to be addressed within the ANC, the mass democratic national movement, and society as a whole. It went as far as to say that all "laws, customs, traditions and practices which discriminate against women shall be held unconstitutional."[43] Indeed, under Nelson Mandela a new constitution that emphasized not only formal but also substantive equality for women was passed.[44] Formal equality refers to the idea that everyone has the same rights; substantive equality refers to the idea that everyone is able to actually access the same opportunities by holding and exercising those rights.

While it has been observed that no other country has a constitution with such progressive ideas to eliminate sexism,[45] constitutions do not in and of themselves necessarily guarantee all the rights they may proclaim. For this reason, gender equality in the context of national liberation in South Africa is still on the agenda for analysts to explore, and also for women's organizations to address in what is proving to be an ever-changing political environment.[46] Nevertheless, the case of South Africa and the ANC demonstrates how nationalism still matters, how nations are internally diverse, and how national movements may be affected by these phenomena.

NATIONALISM VERSUS GLOBALIZATION: THE CASE OF CANADA

Given the internal diversity of nations and the fact that what motivates nationalism might vary depending on the time period and geography, it seems clear that the idea of a universal theory of nationalism is problematic. The limitations of universalizing explanations should be kept in mind as we turn to the grand question concerning the future of national identity and nationalism in light of contemporary globalization.

In an important way, as attested to by the examples of imperialism and colonialism, **globalization** is not a completely new phenomenon. For centuries, people, money, ideas, goods, and corporations have crossed geopolitical boundaries. But the processes associated with contemporary globalization (since 1945) have some distinct features. Globalization before the end of World War II was based on imperialism, colonialism, and coercion practised by institutions of empires (such as the British empire or the French empire). Contemporary globalization processes rest on a multitude of multilateral institutions (such as the World Trade Organization and gigantic transnational corporations) and, since the collapse of the Soviet Union, the political and economic dominance of the United States.[47] As well, the contemporary economic, technological, and cultural flows associated with globalization are more intense than in earlier periods.[48] Money can flow from one country to another via e-mail and the Internet, computer technology has spread around the world, and electronic communications (including satellites) transmit popular culture to every corner of the globe. The unprecedented speed with which capital (in the form of cash, stocks, and shares, for example) can move around the world as a result of new information technologies illustrates how economic flows have changed in the past several decades. The unparalleled rapidity with which information can flow across the planet as a result of the Internet and other developments in communications (such as the advent of CNN, which is based in Atlanta in the United States but has overseas operations and services) means that information flows are not simply national but global. As well, while people may always have moved from place to place, the flows are now much more widespread and multidirectional. Currently, all regions and countries both send and receive people.[49]

> **Definition**
>
> **GLOBALIZATION:** The movement of goods, capital, ideas, and people across geopolitical boundaries today and in the past. Contemporary patterns of globalization involve a deepening constellation of economic, technological, and cultural changes that are worldwide in scope and that challenge the sovereignty of the state.

The combination of all of these developments has led some political scientists to question the future viability of the state as a form of organization. This is because one of the key aspects associated with the state (as identified by Weber) is sovereignty—the assumption that the state is the highest authority. But sovereignty may be eroding in the face of the contemporary worldwide reorganization of economic, technological, and cultural flows. For example, states have difficulty controlling the flow of information on the Internet.

Globalization also raises questions concerning national identity. Stuart Hall, a leading British analyst of culture, has argued that the developments associated with contemporary globalization that seem to challenge the state and its sovereignty also raise issues about the future of nationalism. Hall argues that the seemingly "natural" priority given to national culture (and identity) is in fact a historical phenomenon tied to the emergence of the nation-state. He suggests that contemporary globalization appears to have the effect of "contesting and dislocating the centred and 'closed' identities of a national culture."[50] Globalization raises many uncertainties about the future of national identity, not only because people who move across national boundaries may bring with them different cultural influences, but also because there are forms of culture (from Mickey Mouse to world music) that are not simply national but global. Furthermore, there are elements of identity (gender, for example) that may assume as much importance for some people as national identity has, if not more.

According to Stuart Hall, the 21st century carries three possibilities for national identity.[51] One possibility is that national identity may actually be strengthened in response to globalization. Another possibility is that national identity may be weakened. The third possibility is that new, shifting, and even hybrid forms of identity may emerge to challenge a singular national identity.

Drawing from our discussion on the advantages of individualizing comparisons, it is probably more useful to attend to specific cases when considering these propositions rather than to attempt to make universal claims. We will therefore turn our attention to the case of Canada to gain insight into the possibilities that contemporary globalization raises for the future primacy of national identity. A look at the discussion box regarding the European Union, a unique international organization consisting of 15 member states, offers another contemporary case.

In Canada, the daily news reminds us that many people of different backgrounds reside here—that is, that Canada is a country that reflects a reality of cultural pluralism, as can be seen in Table 3.2. A dominant issue that has structured Canadian electoral and other political debates revolves around the future of the province of Quebec, where many francophones (who constitute the majority of the population) are committed to the idea of sovereignty for their province. Beyond the potential secession of Quebec, other issues related to cultural

---

BOX 3.2

A NEW "EUROPEAN" IDENTITY?

The modern nation-state system arose in Europe, so it is particularly interesting to consider developments in this region when examining the question of whether national identity is weakening. The European Union (EU) is an international organization dating back to the 1950s, created with the specific goal of weakening national rivalries (especially between France and Germany) through greater economic cooperation. Over the 1980s and 1990s, economic cooperation in Europe deepened significantly, also affecting the political sphere. A European flag, anthem, and parliament were created, and in 1993 the **Maastricht Treaty** introduced a citizenship of the European Union.

Currently, there are 15 member states belonging to the EU: Austria, Belgium, Denmark, Finland, France, Germany, Greece, Ireland, Italy, Luxembourg, the Netherlands, Portugal, Spain, Sweden, and the United Kingdom. Every citizen of a member state belonging to the European Union is also considered an EU citizen and possesses certain rights. These include the right of free movement; for example, a Dutch citizen has the right to move to and work in Belgium or any other member country. EU citizens also have the right to vote and stand for elections at the local level and at the European level in any member state. Finally, EU citizenship entitles one to consular protection when abroad from any embassy of a member country.

The EU and its new citizenship raise many interesting questions. Does the new EU citizenship contribute to a new form of belonging or identity—that of being "European"? If so, how does that differ from national identity? Does EU citizenship really weaken national citizenship? Should EU citizenship be granted to any person who permanently lives in Europe regardless of citizenship (including some 12 million legally residing migrant workers and their families who have come mainly from countries of the developing world)?

Table 3.2 **Top 15 Ethnic Origins in Canada, 1996**

The following are the results of the 1996 census, based on the responses to the question "To which ethnic or cultural group(s) did [your] ancestors belong?" People were allowed to name more than one origin.

	Total Response	Single Responses	Multiple Responses
Total Population	28 528 125	18 303 625	10 224 495
Canadian	8 806 275	5 326 995	3 479 285
English	6 832 095	2 048 275	4 783 820
French	5 597 845	2 665 250	2 932 595
Scottish	4 260 840	642 970	3 617 870
Irish	3 767 610	504 030	3 263 580
German	2 757 140	726 145	2 030 990
Italian	1 207 475	729 455	478 025
Aboriginal origins	1 101 955	477 630	624 330
Ukrainian	1 026 475	331 680	694 790
Chinese	921 585	800 470	121 115
Dutch (Netherlands)	916 215	313 880	602 335
Polish	786 735	265 930	520 805
South Asian origins	723 345	590 145	133 200
Jewish	351 705	195 810	155 900
Norwegian	346 310	47 805	298 500

Source: Statistics Canada, "1996 Census: Ethnic Origin and Visible Minorities," *The Daily* (February 17, 1998): 17. Adapted from Statistics Canada website <http://www.statscan.ca/Daily/English/980217/d980217.htm>, page 17.

identity cause heated debates. For example, what about the right of francophones outside of Quebec to speak French in public institutions? What about Aboriginal peoples and their quest for self-government and cultural preservation? What about non-French or non-British immigrants and their offspring—to what extent should the maintenance of languages other than French and English be encouraged, and to what extent should Canadian institutions change to reflect and accommodate peoples of all backgrounds? And what about those who want to define themselves as simply "Canadian"—should the Canadian state foster only this kind of allegiance? All of these questions lie at the heart of the politics of multiculturalism, national recognition, and nationalism in contemporary Canada.

Diversity has been a feature of what is now Canada for a very long time. Prior to European colonization in the early 17th century, Aboriginal societies were characterized by a rich range of cultural, linguistic, social, and political practices.[52] When the French and the British established their settlements and expropriated land from Aboriginal peoples, they brought with them their own cultures and languages. Since then, there have been many waves of immigration from other European countries, and increasingly, since the late 1960s, also from countries outside of Europe.

For much of Canada's history, government policies reflected an emphasis on the model of **dominant conformity** and, specifically, Anglo conformity. The idea behind dominant conformity is that all groups should assimilate to the language, culture, and values of the dominant group, and in the case of Anglo conformity in Canada, that all groups should conform to the British group.

Waving Canadian flags, fans cheer Jeffrey Buttle of Canada as he performs in the men's short program event of the World Figure Skating Championships at the M-Wave Arena in Nagano, central Japan, on Tuesday, March 19, 2002.

Koji Sasahara/CP Picture Archive

Definition

DOMINANT CONFORMITY: A model of ethnic group integration that holds that all groups in a society should conform to the language and values of the dominant group. In the case of Canada, this is the idea behind historical policies emphasizing Anglo conformity, which aimed to have all groups assimilate by speaking English and holding the values of the dominant British-origin group.

In the last few decades, as a result of pressures from different minority groups, the Canadian state has adopted a series of public-policy measures designed to deal with diversity in a different way. In 1969, a national policy of official bilingualism (French and English) was introduced. In 1971, a national policy of official multiculturalism within a bilingual framework was established, giving recognition to the multiplicity of ethnic groups represented in the country. In recent years, both the federal and some provincial governments have been involved in discussions pertaining to settling Aboriginal land claims and fostering forms of Aboriginal self-government.

Does the shift since the 1960s suggest that national identity is weakening? If that identity is defined in terms of Anglo conformity, then the answer is yes. These kinds of initiatives reflect Canada's commitment to a variant of the model of cultural pluralism. While the term **cultural pluralism** refers to the existence of diverse ethnic groups within a country, the cultural pluralism model specifically aims at promoting peaceful cooperation and recognition among these ethnic groups. The model of cultural pluralism suggests that groups can maintain distinct features without being marginalized economically or socially. Moreover, it maintains that the cultivation of differences does not necessarily produce conflict; rather, it can produce peaceful coexistence through overarching values and institutions. Canada's official policy of multiculturalism within a bilingual framework is a variant on the model of cultural pluralism.

Definition

CULTURAL PLURALISM: The existence of many ethnic and cultural groups within a country. The model of cultural pluralism takes this reality of diversity as a starting point to argue that all groups in a society can maintain their linguistic, cultural, and religious distinctiveness without being relegated to the economic or cultural margins. This coexistence of many cultures is achieved through the creation of a common set of values and institutions.

The models of dominant conformity and cultural pluralism represent opposite methods of dealing with ethnic and cultural diversity within a country. While many federal policies in Canada today reflect the model of cultural pluralism, it should also be noted that these policies have been controversial—especially since the 1990s. For example, the Canadian Alliance (and its precursor, the Reform Party) and some intellectuals have argued that multiculturalism is leading to the fragmentation of Canada and should therefore not be publicly recognized or funded. In a related way, it has been suggested that a policy emphasis on "being Canadian" would contribute to the unity of the country and the loyalty of citizens toward the Canadian state.[53] These developments illustrate that there are those who would like to see the strengthening of a singular national identity in Canada.

Finally, there is evidence that Canadians identify in many ways that are not captured completely by the idea of belonging to any one single group, whether defined by gender, ethnicity, or other factors. For example, the National Action Committee on the Status of Women, the main umbrella association for women's groups outside Quebec, has increasingly taken the position that there is a complex heterogeneity among Canadian women along racial, ethnic, class, and other lines. Likewise, we see that Canadians self-identify in complex ways. For example, in the 1996 census, 36 percent of Canadians gave multiple responses to the ethnic origin question.[54] It is clear that many Canadians describe themselves as having multiple ethnic origins. This is also evident in some of the more popular discussions of identity. For example, writer Lawrence Hill has referred to himself as a "zebra" to describe the hybrid experience of having a white mother and a Black father.[55] It could be anticipated that such kinds of multiple and mixed identities might increase as a result of contemporary globalization, since people may migrate several times in a lifetime, and since a growing number of people appear to be at ease with multiple national attachments and fluid and shifting identities.[56]

The case of Canada therefore suggests that an argument can be made for saying that the salience of a single national identity (particularly in the form of Anglo conformity) has lessened with time. Although there are still debates about the desirability of having one dominant national identity, there is evidence that many Canadians see themselves as having multiple origins and identities. This suggests that while national identity is not about to disappear, it may be increasingly less dominant in the 21st century.

CONCLUSION

This chapter examined key terms and concepts pertaining to the politics of cultural pluralism. It surveyed different theoretical approaches to the study of nationalism, arguing that helpful insights are gleaned by attending to specific cases and using contemporary approaches that consider issues such as gender and different forms of identity. The central question raised in this chapter concerns the future of the nation-state and the salience of national identity in the era of globalization. Drawing from the work of Stuart Hall, it was suggested that there are three possibilities: national identity may be strengthened; national identity may be eroded; or new, shifting, and even hybrid forms of identity may emerge. The chapter tested these three possibilities by examining the case of Canada. The findings suggest that while national identity is not disappearing, its primacy is indeed being challenged by contemporary globalization.

Given the internal diversity of most countries around the world today, and given the fact that contemporary globalization itself may create the conditions for new and evolving forms of identity, it seems that political scientists will have much to examine in the years ahead. As well, because the already heterogeneous national populations are increasingly (and perhaps differently) affected by the larger international context, policymakers will have to think in creative ways in order to enact effective public policies.

DISCUSSION QUESTIONS

1. Is nationalism primarily a negative or a positive force? Why?

2. It has been suggested that the gendered aspects of nationalism are particularly apparent when it comes to war, the transmission of culture, and dress. Can you provide examples supporting this idea? Can you think of other ways in which men and women are called upon differently in the name of "the nation," or ways in which they are called on similarly?

3. Are people attached primarily to a singular national identity, or is there another form (or other forms) of identity to which people are attached?

4. Does contemporary globalization weaken or strengthen nationalism? What examples would you use to support your position?

5. Are the demands made by minority ethnic groups for policies such as affirmative action easier or more difficult to resolve than claims for self-determination?

WEB LINKS

UNESCO's Management of Social Transformations Programme:
http://www.unesco.org/most.

The Nationalism Project:
http://www.nationalismproject.org.

The International Forum on Globalization:
http://www.ifg.org.

Citizenship, Democracy and Ethnocultural Diversity Newsletter:
http://qsilver.queensu.ca/~philform/newsletter.html.

FURTHER READING

Abu-Laban, Yasmeen. "The Future and the Legacy: Globalization and the Canadian Settler-State." *Journal of Canadian Studies* 35 (2000–01): 262–76.

Green, Joyce. "Canaries in the Mines of Citizenship: Indian Women in Canada." *The Canadian Journal of Political Science* 34(4) (December 2001): 715–38.

Guibernau, Montserrat, and John Rex, eds. *The Ethnicity Reader: Nationalism, Multiculturalism and Migration.* Cambridge: Polity Press, 1997.

Kymlicka, Will. *Finding Our Way: Rethinking Ethnocultural Relations in Canada.* Don Mills: Oxford University Press, 1998.

McRoberts, Kenneth. *Misconceiving Canada: The Struggle for National Unity.* Don Mills: Oxford University Press, 1997.

Wilford, Rick, and Robert L. Miller, eds. *Women, Ethnicity and Nationalism.* London and New York: Routledge, 1998.

ENDNOTES

1 *MOST Newsletter* 3 (June 1995): 1; cited on August 22, 2001; available at http://www.unesco.org/most/newlet3e.htm.

2 *MOST Newsletter* 1 (December 1994): 5; cited on August 22, 2001; available at http://www.unesco.org/most/newlet1e.htm.

3 See Benedict Anderson, *Imagined Communities: Reflections on the Origin and Spread of Nationalism*, rev. ed. (London: Verso, 1991).

4 See Elie Kedourie, *Nationalism* (London: Hutchinson, 1985).

5 Danilo Türk, "Genocide," in Joel Krieger, ed., *The Oxford Companion to Politics of the World* (Oxford: Oxford University Press, 2001), p. 316.

6 Allison Des Forges, "Rwandan Genocide," in Krieger, *The Oxford Companion to Politics of the World*, p. 749.

7 Srda Trifkovic, "Bosnian War," in Krieger, *The Oxford Companion to Politics of the World*, p. 79.

8 Ibid.

9 Elizabeth Philipose, "Ethnic Cleansing," in Lorraine Code, ed., *Encyclopedia of Feminist Theories* (London: Routledge, 2001), pp. 192–93.

10 Ibid., p 193.

11 Michael Ignatieff, *Blood and Belonging: Journeys into the New Nationalism* (Toronto: Penguin Books, 1993).

12 E. Ellis Cashmore, *Dictionary of Race and Ethnic Relations* (London: Routledge and Kegan Paul, 1984), p. 182.

13 Pereket Hablte Selassie, "Self-Determination," in Krieger, *The Oxford Companion to Politics of the World*, pp. 760–61.

14 Janine Brodie, "State Theory," in Code, *Encyclopedia of Feminist Theories*, p. 462.

15 As cited in Ronald H. Chilcote, *Theories of Comparative Politics: The Search for a Paradigm Reconsidered* (Boulder: Westview Press, 1994), p. 98.

16 Sometimes the term *civic nationalism* is used to refer to an inclusive form of national belonging based on participation in a shared public sphere, as contrasted with *ethnic nationalism*, which is based on a belief in shared ethnicity or blood ties.

However, the utility of this dichotomy has been called into question on a number of grounds, including the claim that *civic nationalism* can serve to mask the power of the dominant ethnic group(s) in organizing public life in the first place. See Claude Couture, *Paddling with the Current: Pierre Elliott Trudeau, Etienne Parent, Liberalism and Nationalism in Canada* (Edmonton: University of Alberta Press, 1998), p. 112.

17 Walker Connor, "A Nation Is a Nation, Is a State Is an Ethnic Group Is A…" *Ethnic and Racial Studies* 1(4) (October 1978): 381.

18 Anderson, *Imagined Communities*, p.144.

19 James Clifford, "Diasporas," in Montserrat Guibernau and John Rex, eds., *The Ethnicity Reader: Nationalism, Multiculturalism and Migration* (Cambridge: Polity Press, 1997), pp. 283–90.

20 Ibid., p. 284.

21 Tomas Hylland Eriksen, "Ethnicity, Race and Nation," in Guibernau and Rex, *The Ethnicity Reader*, pp. 33–41.

22 Yasmeen Abu-Laban and Victoria Lamont, "Crossing Borders: Interdisciplinarity, Immigration and the Melting Pot in the American Cultural Imaginary," *Canadian Review of American Studies* 27(2) (1997): 33.

23 Robert Miles and Rudy Torres, "Does 'Race' Matter? Transatlantic Perspectives on Racism after 'Race Relations,'" in Vered Amit-Talai and Caroline Knowles, eds., *Re-Situating Identities: The Politics of Race, Ethnicity and Culture* (Peterborough: Broadview Press, 1996), pp. 25–46.

24 Lucius J. Barker and Mack H. Jones, *African Americans and the American Political System* (Englewood Cliffs: Prentice Hall, 1994), pp. 30–49.

25 Will Kymlicka, *Finding Our Way: Rethinking Ethnocultural Relations in Canada* (Don Mills: Oxford University Press, 1998), p. 42.

26 John Isbester, *Promises Not Kept: The Betrayal of Social Change in the Third World* (West Hartford: Kumarian Press, 1995), p. 109.

27 For an example, see Karl W. Deutsch, *Nationalism and Social Communication: An Inquiry into the Foundations of Nationality* (New York: John Wiley, 1953).

28 See Ernest Gellner, *Nations and Nationalism* (Oxford: Basil Blackwell, 1983) on these points, and see Anderson, *Imagined Communities,* regarding the significance of the printing press.

29 See Tom Nairn, *The Break-up of Britain* (London: NLB, 1979).

30 See especially Kedourie, *Nationalism,* p. 145.

31 Isbester, *Promises Not Kept,* p. 106.

32 Ibid., p. 102.

33 Ibid., pp. 105–48.

34 Frantz Fanon, "The Wretched of the Earth," in Omar Dahbour and Micheline R. Ishay, eds., *The Nationalism Reader* (New Jersey: Humanities Press, 1995), p. 283.

35 Ibid., pp. 274–83.

36 Anthony D. Smith, *Theories of Nationalism,* 2nd ed. (London: Gerald Duckworth, 1983), p. 193.

37 Nira Yuval-Davis and Floya Anthias, *Woman-Nation-State* (Basingstoke: Macmillan, 1989).

38 Nira Yuval-Davis, "Gender and Nation," in Rick Wilford and Robert L. Miller, eds., *Women, Ethnicity and Nationalism* (London: Routledge, 1998), pp. 23–35.

39 Elizabeth Philipose, "Ethnic Cleansing," in Code, *Encyclopedia of Feminist Theories,* p. 183.

40 For a discussion of these issues, see Deniz Kandiyoti, "Identity and Its Discontents: Women and the Nation," in Patrick Williams and Laura Chrisman, eds., *Colonial Discourse and Post-Colonial Theory: A Reader* (New York: Columbia University Press, 1994), pp. 376–91.

41 For an overview, see Sheila Meintjes, "Gender, Nationalism and Transformation: Difference and Commonality in South Africa's Past and Present," in Wilford and Miller, *Women, Ethnicity and Nationalism,* pp. 62–86.

42 This account of women's organizing and example of the placard is adapted from Anne McClintock, *Imperial Leather: Race, Gender and Sexuality in the Colonial Context* (New York: Routledge, 1995), pp. 379–86.

43 McClintock, *Imperial Leather,* p. 384.

44 Meintjes, "Gender, Nationalism and Transformation," pp. 82–83.

45 Ibid., p. 83.

46 Ibid., p. 84.

47 David Held et. al., *Global Transformations: Politics, Economics and Culture* (Stanford: Stanford University Press, 1999), pp. 425–26.

48 Ibid.

49 Ibid., p. 297.

50 Stuart Hall, "The Question of Cultural Identity," in Stuart Hall et al., eds., *Modernity: An Introduction to Modern Societies* (Cambridge: Polity Press, 1995), p. 628.

51 Ibid., pp. 596–634.

52 Olive Patricia Dickason, *Canada's First Nations: A History of Founding Peoples from Earliest Times* (Toronto: McClelland and Stewart, 1992), pp. 63–83.

53 For this position, see Rhoda Howard-Hassmann, "Canadian as an Ethnic Category: Implications for Multiculturalism and National Unity," *Canadian Public Policy* 25(4) (1999): 523–37. For a critique of this position, see Yasmeen

Abu-Laban and Daiva Stasiulis, "Constructing 'Ethnic Canadians': The Implications for Public Policy and Inclusive Citizenship," *Canadian Public Policy* 26(4) (December 2000): 477–87.

54 Yasmeen Abu-Laban, "The Politics of Race, Ethnicity and Immigration: The Contested Arena of Multiculturalism," in James P. Bickerton and Alain G. Gagnon, eds., *Canadian Politics*, 3rd ed. (Peterborough: Broadview Press, 1999), p. 478.

55 Lawrence Hill, "Zebra: Growing Up Black and White in Canada," in Carl E. James and Adrienne Shadd, eds., *Talking about Difference: Encounters in Culture, Language and Identity* (Toronto: Between the Lines, 1994), pp. 41–47.

56 See, for example, Parminder Bhachu, "The Multiple Landscapes of Transnational Asian Women in the Diaspora," in Vered Amit-Talai and Caroline Knowles, eds., *Re-situating Identities: The Politics of Race, Ethnicity and Culture* (Peterborough: Broadview Press, 1996), pp. 283–303, and Ayse S. Caglar, "Hyphenated Identities and the Limits of 'Culture,'" in Tariq Modood and Pnina Werbner, eds., *The Politics of Multiculturalism in the New Europe* (London: Zed Books, 1997), pp. 169–85.

Political Values

Career Profile: Linda Coady

Linda Coady graduated with a B.A. in political science from the University of British Columbia. She first worked as an Information Officer and Manager of Communications and Marketing at the British Columbia Federation of Agriculture, and then in a similar position at the Council of Forest Industries of British Columbia. After a stint as a self-employed consultant on public and government affairs, where her clients included forestry companies, she joined MacMillan Bloedel Ltd.

Linda was soon promoted to the position of Vice President, Environmental Affairs, and later Vice President, Environmental Enterprise, a position she retained when the company was purchased by Weyerhaeuser in 1999. In an industry in which companies are sometimes considered to be at odds with environmentalists and Aboriginal residents, Linda has gained recognition and respect for her work on environmental, Aboriginal, and trade issues in the B.C. forest industry.

Linda is a Director of Iisaak Forest Products Ltd., a joint venture in ecoforestry between Weyerhaeuser and the Nuu-chah-nulth First Nations in Clayoquot Sound. She is also a Director of the Vancouver Island Marmot Recovery Foundation and of Forest Trends, an international nonprofit organization involving forest companies, research organizations, and environmental groups interested in the development of market-based incentives for conservation and sustainable forest management.

In recognition of her commitment to collaboration and innovation in resolving conflict over forest issues, Linda recently received an Ethics in Action Award for leadership in corporate social responsibility. Similarly, the Forest Products Association of Canada gave Linda the Robert Findlay Chisholm Achievement Award in recognition of her commitment to achieving consensus among many stakeholders on conservation and management issues involving coastal old-growth forests.

Two special projects in which Linda has taken part over the past several years have also recently received recognition outside of British Columbia. The B.C. Coastal Group of Weyerhaeuser won the Ecological Society of America's 2001 Corporate Award for development and implementation of new ecosystem-based approaches to commercial forest management. Iisaak Forest Products received the World Wildlife Fund's Gift to the Earth Award in recognition of the company's efforts to create a business strategy that will support conservation-based management in coastal old-growth forests with exceptional environmental values.

Chapter 4

Political Culture, Socialization, and How We Have Been Taught to Think

Andrew Heard

CHAPTER OBJECTIVES

After completing this chapter, you should be able to

- outline the relationship between a society's culture and its politics
- discuss the nature of political culture
- explain the significance of identity politics
- describe how deep divisions between groups in a society may be handled
- understand the processes through which we acquire our political knowledge and beliefs.

WHAT IS POLITICAL CULTURE?

Politics is all about things we value and wish to see respected and protected, whether they are specific material benefits, such as health care, or higher moral principles, such as freedom of speech. What we think about the society we live in, the government that rules over us, and the other groups of people who live alongside us are all matters of personal attitude that can have profound

political effects. One will know very little indeed about politics without an appreciation of the broader cultural context within which it occurs. Ultimately, the politics of a society is a reflection of that society's culture. The depth of differences among groups within a society and the way they are dealt with can profoundly shape the nature of political discourse and conflict. For example, the difference between a stable, harmonious society and one wracked by a bloody civil war can literally flow from answers to such basic cultural questions as, "To which group do I most strongly identify myself as belonging?" and "How is my group treated by others in my country?"

Comparisons of Canadian political phenomena with those from around the world can provide an idea of the practical consequences of the cultural values people hold. A large number of francophones in Quebec supported separation throughout most of the 1990s, while there is no significant separatist movement within the United States, despite its enormous ethnic diversity. Canada does not have the death penalty, while China not only executes people but often does so in public settings. Most women have had the vote in Canadian national elections since 1918, while women in Kuwait still do not have the right to vote.[1] In the end, the differences between Canada and the other countries mentioned in these examples stem fundamentally from different values in the cultures of those societies.

Quite clearly, the variations in cultural values in societies can have a significant effect on these societies' politics. In order to understand the politics of any state or the variations and similarities between states, one has to appreciate the framing role of cultural values in political objects, principles, and processes. To understand politics, we need to grasp the essence of political culture, realize how the predominant values of that culture come to be passed on among its members, and discover whose values come to be accepted as the norm. Political scientists are interested in how deeply individuals identify with different social groups, what enduring cleavages may exist between these groups within a given society, and how political systems accommodate, foster, and suppress conflicts between them.

We all have a sense of what culture means, but the concept of culture is highly contentious; there are literally hundreds of definitions. In a general sense, culture consists of the shared values, beliefs, practices, and symbols relating to the food, clothing, social relations, language, religion, literature, music, and so on that are practised or favoured among a particular group of people. But culture in a larger sense relates to the fundamental values of communities and their beliefs about how life should be lived, how people should behave, and how society should be organized. Political culture is essentially this social phenomenon applied to politics. Indeed, political culture is really just a particular aspect of a society's broader culture.

Political culture is the collection of the understandings, values, attitudes, and principles of a community or society that relate to its political organization, processes, disputes, and public policies. Out of a society's political culture come important beliefs and values that structure the citizens' attitudes and expectations toward such basic political concepts as legitimacy, power, authority, and obedience. These attitudes play an important background role in the success and effectiveness of the government in that society. The extent to which citizens acquiesce in or defer to their political leaders has a significant bearing on

whether the government feels it necessary to use more force and coercion than influence in order to exercise authority and secure compliance with its decisions. As well, these attitudes can shape the informal processes through which a society manages to direct and settle disputes outside of the formal political institutions.

Definition

POLITICAL CULTURE: The collection of the understandings, values, attitudes, and principles of a community or society that relate to its political organization, processes, disputes, and public policies. Out of a society's political culture come important beliefs and values that structure the citizens' attitudes and expectations toward such basic political concepts as legitimacy, power, authority, and obedience.

Some powerful consequences can flow from as seemingly simple an attitude as, "We should respect and defer to the political leaders of our country." In a democracy where the culture encourages people to believe "My view is as good as the Prime Minister's (or President's)," one can expect a very different relationship between the citizens and their political leaders than in a culture that is very deferential. Imagine if most of the members of a society were to say of their political leaders, "They are the elders of our group. I do not know the things they know. I must trust and respect their opinions." This is a very different attitude about the connection between the political elite and the mass in society than one normally finds in Canada. A 1998 opinion poll found that only 4 percent of Canadians said that they have a great deal of trust in Members of Parliament; that figure compares with 5 percent who had a lot of trust in arms dealers and 50 per cent who trusted school teachers a lot.[2]

Political culture is not just about those things explicitly related to the political system; it is also about general social attitudes that can have political ramifications. For example, attitudes toward sexual practices are largely a matter of personal, private behaviour in Western countries, but they become political when issues of government censorship of pornography arise or when debates over the promotion of gay rights come up. Whether the government should ban homosexual behaviour or allow same-sex marriages has been hotly contested at different times in many countries, and an individual's attitudes toward the role of the state in this matter are deeply connected to his or her beliefs about what types of sexual behaviour are to be prohibited, tolerated, or even celebrated. The position taken by different groups on many political issues is often largely determined by their broader social beliefs and principles. The "social" becomes "political" as members of a society who hold opposing views compete over whose beliefs should be embodied in their government's laws and policies.

The values and beliefs of individuals regarding their governments and about their own sense of responsibility toward their governments can have a crucial impact on those governments' abilities to function properly. One example is people's attitudes toward paying taxes. Canadians may take taxes for granted because of a high rate of compliance; there may be a certain amount of fiddling, but only a small minority of Canadians refuse to report the bulk of their earnings and pay taxes on them.

People in different parts of the world have very different attitudes toward paying taxes to their governments; yet governments cannot function effectively without an adequate tax base. Without enough tax revenue, a government simply will not have the capacity to fulfil the functions required of it. The Swiss are the most likely to pay their taxes, with just 6 percent of the country's economic activity going untaxed. In Canada, only about 15 percent goes untaxed, compared to 27 percent in Italy.[3] The problem is chronic in many other countries. For example, Russia's uncollected tax bill was estimated at U.S.$100 billion in 1997.[4] This is a staggering figure when one realizes that the Russian government was set to collect only U.S.$26 billion in total in 1999.[5] In Kenya, almost 64 percent of the workers are estimated to be employed in the informal sector, beyond state taxation.[6] Attitudes of people in a variety of countries on questions of employment policy are another example of different values and beliefs; they are compared in Table 4.1.

Table 4.1   Attitudes toward Employment Policies

An international survey asked people if they agree with the following questions: "When jobs are scarce ..."

Country	men have more right to a job than women		people should be forced to retire early		priority should be given to "co-nationals" over immigrants	
	Agree	Disagree	Agree	Disagree	Agree	Disagree
Belgium	37.4	51.5	49.2	36.5	62.6	26.9
Britain	35.0	58.6	43.1	50.4	53.4	41.5
Denmark	10.5	86.0	24.3	66.0	52.8	37.9
France	32.9	58.9	48.9	42.7	63.0	31.2
Ireland	35.5	59.0	47.0	47.5	68.8	28.5
Italy	39.8	47.7	55.0	31.1	71.2	17.8
Netherlands	24.8	69.9	42.0	53.1	33.3	62.0
Northern Ireland	33.8	60.6	43.0	53.3	62.4	33.6
Spain	29.0	63.1	57.5	31.2	76.5	16.6
United States	23.8	71.1	15.9	79.6	52.2	42.7
West Germany	30.7	58.5	50.0	38.3	61.5	29.7
Canada	18.5	74.6	30.9	62.0	52.5	42.3
English	17.3	75.8	25.0	67.9	56.1	38.3
French	23.6	71.3	46.6	46.3	62.1	34.6
New Canadians	16.8	73.8	30.1	62.4	29.2	64.0

Source: Neil Nevitte, *The Decline of Deference* (Peterborough: Broadview Press, 1996), p. 130. Data from the 1981 and 1990 World Values Surveys. Available from the I.S.R., University of Michigan, Ann Arbor, MI. Reprinted by permission of Broadview Press.

POLITICAL SUBCULTURES AND THE POWER OF ELITES TO SHAPE IDEAS

Political cultures are almost never homogeneous or monolithic; indeed, the political cultures of most societies contain many different subgroups or **subcultures**. Even in liberal democracies, political culture is often a majoritarian phenomenon—the majority within any group essentially gets to determine and foster the views that are taken as representative of that group. As a result, it is important to keep in mind the distinction between generalization and universalization: just because most members of a society believe something does not mean that everybody believes it. It is equally important to ask whose ideas are accepted as the "norm" in a society and why. Political culture is every bit as much a creation as it is an organic phenomenon.

> **Definition**
>
> **SUBCULTURE:** A cluster of people who share some basic political values and attributes that are distinct from those of other groups in society or from the predominant values and attributes of society as a whole.

By delving more deeply into particular aspects of a society's culture, one can often find that it is not even a majority but rather a small powerful group or **elite** that is able to dominate or even totally control the values propagated publicly in that society. This is most clearly seen in states with totalitarian regimes, where ruling elites mould most aspects of the society's public values; Nazi Germany, Stalinist Russia, and China under Mao are some examples of this phenomenon. However, one can also suggest that even in liberal democratic societies, powerful cliques are able to set the tone and range of public discussion for the general community. For example, those who control the media have an enormous influence (discussed later in this chapter). Critics of Western democracies argue that even in these supposedly free cultures, dominant socioeconomic groups not only assert their preferred values as the "ideals" but also create an attitudinal environment that leads the members of the various lower strata of society to accept their exploitation. Predominant attitudes taught to the poor thus lead them away from openly questioning the distribution of benefits within their society and toward acquiescing in the prevailing order.

> **Definition**
>
> **ELITE:** A small group of individuals who have significantly more power than other members of their community. They are either in a position to make authoritative decisions or have privileged access to decision-makers.

In most societies one finds some significant distinctions between the values widely held among the elites and those held by the mass population. But because elites are the ones who make most of the public policies for a society, it is their values that are often embodied in government policies; furthermore, it is their values that are usually reflected in public descriptions of what their society believes in. Examples of the mass–elite division of values and beliefs are easy to find in Canada. For example, a majority of Canadian Members of Parliament have voted against capital punishment on three occasions: in 1967, 1976, and 1987. Opinion polls, however, have shown that a majority of the general adult population has consistently favoured the death penalty.

The **ideologies** favoured by a society's elites are usually reflected in the dominant political culture of a country as well. The elites' general understandings about how a country's economy and political system should be organized end up forming the basis of the public policies and political debate in the state. In a telling critique of human societies, Antonio Gramsci has developed an important notion of a hegemony of ideas that describes particular values and beliefs so ingrained in people that they not only do not question them but also think of them as pure common sense. Furthermore, Gramsci has argued that political rulers would succeed in the long run only to the extent to which the masses they ruled accepted the elite's worldview.[7] Perhaps the ultimate exercise of political power by elites in a society is the ability to structure the beliefs of those they rule in such ways that the masses neither question the elites' rule nor understand that their own interests may lie in a different political order or set of public policies.

> **Definition**
>
> **IDEOLOGY:** A fairly coherent set of beliefs that explains not only what may be wrong with society, but also provides a vision of what society should be like.

Michel Foucault has also argued that elites in society are able to structure even our most basic conceptions of who we are and what actions or benefits are truly in our own interest.[8] One does not have to take these perspectives to the point of asserting some deliberate conspiracy of mind control to appreciate the enormous potential that the various agents of political socialization have in shaping and moulding members of a society into sharing a vast array of common beliefs and perspectives. Furthermore, as students of politics, we can ask ourselves what interests and values particular to women, minority groups, or even the majority of "ordinary people" are not being articulated and embraced in the general political culture of a society.

POLITICAL TRUST, EFFICACY, AND ALIENATION

Several types of personal attitudes can deeply affect a political system when they are aggregated among all the members of a society. How individual members feel about their political system and even how they think about it can have very significant effects on the political culture of groups in society.

Affective attitudes and orientations are those we hold because of the way we feel about something; they are an emotional response to issues and events. Cognitive attitudes and orientations are those we hold because of what we know about the issues and events, or at least what we think we know about them. (Remember here that just because we believe something to be a fact does not mean it is true.) Evaluative attitudes and orientations are ones that combine emotion and knowledge—that is, where we combine what we know with what we feel about something to make judgments about political phenomena and events. A subtle but important part of our personal maturation process as we grow up, as well as the political socialization process in general, lies in how we learn to think about events and issues. Our behaviour in the political world will be very different depending on whether we are guided by affective, cognitive, or evaluative attitudes.

How we think is very much influenced by how we have been taught to think, by role models as well as by implicit instruction. What we believe we know about our political system and how we feel about it greatly influence our own sense of where we personally fit into our society. If we feel that we have political representatives or other leaders who generally act honestly, in good faith, and use good judgment in furthering our collective well-being, then we may have a strong sense of **political trust** in our political elites. **Political efficacy** is the belief that we as individuals can have some influence upon the decisions that affect our lives. If, however, we have a low degree of trust in our political leaders and have little sense of political efficacy, then we may well feel **political alienation**. Political trust and efficacy are essential to a political culture that can support a stable democracy, while political alienation can have very damaging effects in the long run. Low political efficacy and high alienation are likely to lead to a culture where few people actively participate in the public affairs of their community.

CIVIC CULTURE AND DEMOCRACY

Two American political scientists, Gabriel A. Almond and Sidney Verba, first coined the term *civic culture* to describe the group of attitudes and beliefs needed in a political culture in order for a stable, liberal democracy to thrive.[9] Many of Almond and Verba's views have since come under severe criticism, particularly their belief that America was an example of the virtues of a civic culture, but some of their observations have spawned a continuing debate over the cultural requirements for a peaceful, democratic society, now termed *civil society*. Not only is representative democracy predicated upon the general population having significant trust in their elected representatives, but citizens must also have a sense of efficacy in order to participate in many of the society's political processes. Thus, a stable democracy with a civic culture is most likely to be found in societies where the political culture reflects high levels of trust and efficacy but low levels of political alienation.

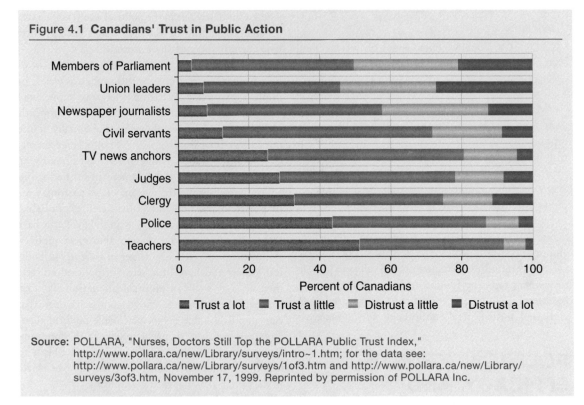

Figure 4.1 **Canadians' Trust in Public Action**

Source: POLLARA, "Nurses, Doctors Still Top the POLLARA Public Trust Index," http://www.pollara.ca/new/Library/surveys/intro~1.htm; for the data see: http://www.pollara.ca/new/Library/surveys/1of3.htm and http://www.pollara.ca/new/Library/surveys/3of3.htm, November 17, 1999. Reprinted by permission of POLLARA Inc.

Civic culture and civil society do not *cause* stable democracy, but they do appear to be an essential precondition for a stable liberal democracy.[10] A lack of a civic culture or strong civil society may explain the significant difficulties some countries have when they try to adopt a democratic form of government after many decades of a system of government that fostered political alienation and distrust of political elites. (This issue is addressed in Chapter 15.) It is also important for the political culture to embrace a spirit of genuine compromise and an ability to lose out from time to time. After all, the essence of a democracy is that different factions are willing to reach a compromise and not remain rigidly demanding that all of their claims be met; furthermore, a group has to be willing to lose in elections and allow another group to take office.

Willingness to compromise and an ability to lose may seem rather vague and distant attitudes, but they are essential cultural values for a democratic form of government to survive more than one party's term in office. Samuel P. Huntington described the fate of newly minted democracies in the late 20th century as follows:

Threats to third-wave democracies are likely to come not from generals and revolutionaries who have nothing but contempt for democracy, but rather from participants in the democratic process. These are political leaders and groups who win elections, take power, and then manipulate the mechanisms of democracy to curtail or destroy democracy.[11]

What is important, however, is that Western political scientists do not simply suppose that their own perceived virtues of Western liberal democracies are necessary for other countries to adopt in their entirety or that they are readily transferable to other, ancient cultures.

IDENTITY POLITICS

An individual's self-identification is profoundly personal and yet has enormous political relevance. How we view ourselves and who we believe ourselves to be are matters of complex psychological evolution over the course of our lives. One of the strongest human inclinations we develop is to identify ourselves with some group, or several groups, to which we feel we belong. Humans are social, gregarious animals, and most of us are naturally inclined to interact with others. Speaking in general terms, we seem to have a need to be part of a group. Most of us have many sides to our personalities and a range of interests, and as a result we associate with different groups at different times to match different aspects of our character. Some of the groups we identify ourselves with have little political significance, such as a gang of friends who share a love of snowboarding. But we may also identify ourselves with other groups that can at times have real political significance.

Identity politics draws attention to ways in which political power is structured in society. The term **identity politics** (or the politics of difference) is used to describe political activity that involves the quest by particular groups for recognition of their status and identity, as well as of ways their beliefs and value systems differ from others in any given social context. As Charles Taylor has argued, a "number of strands in contemporary politics turn on the need, sometimes demand, for *recognition*."[12] Examples include women's rights movements, minority rights groups, Aboriginal movements, movements for the rights of disabled persons, and gay and lesbian rights movements.

Of particular importance is a group's belief about how its members are treated, as a group, by the rest of society. For many groups, a prime struggle is to create and project a positive identity to counteract negative stereotypes of them created by other groups in their society. This process may involve finding ways for individual members of the group to develop a new positive self-esteem, as well as the group acting collectively to create in others a positive, respectful image of them.

For many people, group identity and membership is a precondition for meaningful choices made by an individual: who we are, the values and goals we possess, and where we stand in society are given to us by our culture and history. Culture, therefore, is not simply the aggregate of individual values. Attachments such as gender, sexual orientation, class, and ethnicity define an individual's place in society, and as such constitute part of one's culture. This is a very different view from the dominant view of culture and groups that is informed by liberalism. Liberalism separates the individual from his or her community and culture; it treats culture as an aggregate of the beliefs and values of individuals. From the perspective of liberalism, communities exist only insofar as they find expression in the values and beliefs of individuals.[13]

BOX 4.1

CLASS IDENTITY AND FALSE CONSCIOUSNESS

Class is a concept that describes the hierarchical layers within a society that result from different levels of wealth, income, occupation, and social status. Social scientists distinguish between objective class levels, which are often measured based on income levels, and subjective class, which is the class people say they identify themselves as belonging to. The difference between objective class and subjective class is striking in Canada, where there are enormous disparities in income spread across the population, but where the overwhelming majority of citizens identify themselves as "middle class." As a result, class conflict is largely absent form Canada's political scene. Countries such as France or Italy, where a significant number of people identify themselves as "working class" and possess **class consciousness**, have much more polarized political systems and much higher levels of support for left-wing political parties than in North America.

Marxists talk about "false consciousness" in situations where poor people have been socialized into believing they are middle class so that they are unlikely to organize and change the existing social and economic order. The Marxist critique is that members of the objective working class falsely identify with a higher class and therefore are not aware of the "true interests" of the group to which they really belong.

The issue of false consciousness and ignorance of one's own group's true interests is a controversial one, but it can be applied to most characteristics upon which identity is based. For example, does each group based on ethnicity, gender, sexual orientation, religion, and so on have an objective set of true interests that everyone who belongs to the group should be aware of and pursue? If so, who gets to decide what those interests are?

The politics of identity is about more than merely wanting to be valued. Achieving the respect of others is just the first step in trying to participate in the political system on a more equal basis. In many respects, identity groups are reacting against existing political structures in which a dominant culture, espousing the language of universalism, attempts to deny the importance of the particular circumstances and values—particularism—of those groups. This denial of difference is a way for the dominant culture to exercise political power and control over these groups. Identity politics and the politics of difference, in effect, represent a demand for greater political power by groups in society through the recognition of their different identities and value systems. This demand for political power is usually framed in the language of "rights."

Universalism does not recognize differences among people in the granting of rights and maintains that everyone should be treated equally and in exactly the same manner, irrespective of differences in gender, religion, sexual orientation, ethnicity, and history. The focus is on individual rights—rights that apply to all individuals equally. The purpose of these rights is to guarantee that everyone gets equal treatment in politics and in law. The particularism advocated by many identity groups, on the other hand, is based on the argument that real equality cannot be achieved without recognizing the value of differences and according differential rights on the basis of group membership. The focus here is on collective rights or group-differentiated rights. The purpose is to overcome the vulnerability and disadvantage of certain groups—to help them acquire the ability to make choices.

For example, historically marginalized groups such as African-Americans, people with disabilities, or Aboriginal people have not just striven for recognition and respect from the larger society—they also desire to be full participants in their society and to effectively pursue their own interests. The politics of identity involve groups seeking political goals related to fostering those things that give them a distinct identity. For example, francophone parents across Canada have sought the establishment of French-language schools, so that their children may learn the language and cultural heritage of their group. These parents believe that French schools will help preserve and foster the most important things that set their group apart from the rest of society.

Thus, there is a continuing controversy in modern politics about how to balance individual equality with special treatment for particular groups. Should a group receive special benefits to foster the characteristics that give its members their identity, or should all groups be treated equally? Some advocates argue that to treat different groups in very different circumstances with absolute equality only serves to perpetuate the existing inequalities between the groups. To achieve substantive equality between groups, one has to treat them in ways that account for their differences. A current example of this dilemma in Canada relates to Aboriginal self-government. Many critics of self-government argue that it offends the principle of equality by creating a particular form of government for one race when all other races in Canada belong to a common political system. (Note the discussion on the contemporary and historical usage of the term *race* in Chapter 3.)

Others counter that it is race that has created the disadvantages that so many Aboriginal people face, and a "race-based" government is actually the best solution to a cultural problem. Will Kymlicka has forcefully argued that modern liberalism can and should adapt equality to allow for special treatment that fosters a group's cultural identity.[14] This is justified on the grounds that individuals fully develop only within the context of their group memberships, and thus by providing different benefits required by the circumstances of different groups (particularly minority groups), one is fostering the development of all individuals in society. The difficulty modern politicians face in many countries is finding a way to accommodate the claims and needs of different groups while still ensuring that the common good is furthered. As Kenneth Hoover has written, "democracy becomes an exercise in balancing particular sources of distinctiveness and individual difference against the universal needs of all citizens."[15]

Many feminist writers have argued that women can be truly free only if public policies take into account the inherent differences between the genders. The social context and basic characteristics of women are said to be so different from those of men that to treat both men and women exactly the same would perpetuate the subordination of women and deny them the ability to develop. Carole Pateman puts it this way: "Women's equal standing must be accepted as an expression of the freedom of women *as women*, and not treated as an indication that women can be just like men."[16]

However, there is a lively political and academic debate over just what really are the distinguishing characteristics of women that should be accommodated. The social, economic, and political discrimination faced by women can be assessed, but it is much more difficult to determine whether there are innate attitudinal and behavioural characteristics that define women that go beyond those acquired through millennia of socialization into caregiver roles. Carol Gilligan is one feminist theorist who believes there are essential characteristics that are part of women's nature and identity.[17] Simone de Beauvoir, however, has written, "One is not born a woman, but rather becomes a woman."[18] The key point here is the enormous political significance of current debates about the identity of women.

The most potent aspect of the politics of identity and difference arises when a group believes that it is a distinct nation that needs greater political control over its own affairs. Many groups demand greater political autonomy to control matters of direct importance to them, usually because they believe their interests are continually sacrificed in favour of other, more dominant groups in their country. The drive for self-determination, and ultimately political independence, is founded on a very strong national identity and a belief that members of the nation cannot develop their group's identity, values, and needs by remaining just as one of several other groups within the existing state. Quebec nationalism is a staple of Canadian politics, and Quebec's quest for independence has become an established part of Canadian politics ever since the Parti Québécois was elected as the provincial government in 1976. Canada is lucky that most of the politics of self-determination for Quebec has played out relatively peacefully. Many civil wars have broken out across the globe as one minority group or another struggled to establish a separate state of its own. Bangladesh and Eritrea are but two examples of states that arose from civil wars aimed at the independence of a group.

While identity politics is a potent force, it is important not to overstate the phenomenon. The difficulty is that since all individuals have many characteristics

---

BOX 4.2

CHECK YOUR OWN IDENTITY

Pause a few moments and think about how you think of yourself. The questions that follow and your answers to them should give you some idea of how important your own view of yourself is—your identity. You should also have a clearer idea of the impact on you of other people's views of who you are.

Your parents gave you a name at birth. Do you like it, dislike it, or not care much? Why? Are you still called by that name, or do people call you by a short form of it (e.g., Jo instead of Joanne) or a nickname? If the name you are called has changed, did you initiate the change or have you lived with what others decided to call you? Do different groups of people call you different variations of your name? What significance would there be in that?

How many different defining characteristics do you think of yourself as having? For starters, think about religion, language, gender, sexual orientation, ethnic background(s), body size and shape, attractiveness, physical abilities, the neighbourhood or town you grew up in, how much money you have, etc.

Have you ever felt you have received privileged treatment because of who you are? Have you been singled out for poor treatment because of some personal characteristic someone else did not like?

What sorts of negative things that you have been hurt by people have said about who or what you are? How difficult has it felt to try to change other people's negative views of you?

What things about yourself would you not change, even if it meant putting up with abuse from other people?

that form their identity, they may belong to a wide variety of groups. A particular issue, such as abortion or affirmative action, may incline one to identify with the group most relevant for the moment, but another issue will find most of us identifying with a different group—or none at all. Postmodernism is a perspective on society that underlines the complexity of both individuals and society taken as a whole. In this view, it is unsound to reduce political behaviour to simple, enduring categories. Since identities are multidimensional, many people are motivated to find new ways of expressing and identifying themselves over time and across issues. Whole new social movements, such as environmentalism, are spawned as a result.

POLITICAL CLEAVAGES

Some group identities endure, and the prevailing attitudes and beliefs of that group are relevant across a wide range of public policy issues. Political **cleavages** arise in a society when there are enduring differences between groups within a society over political values, perspectives, and objectives. There are many cleavages that may occur at the same time in a society, according to gender, religion, socioeconomic class, language, ethnicity, and even ideology. Depending on what causes these cleavages, how deeply entrenched they are, and how opposed they are in outlook, a country may simply have a richly diverse political culture or be destabilized into civil war. Much also depends on the reaction to the political cleavages of political leaders of both the larger society and of the groups involved. In general, there are four broadly different strategies for reacting to political cleavages in a society.

First, there may be an attempt to actively foster a single overarching culture. While subgroups may continue to exist, their members may come to identify even more strongly with the general culture. The melting pot of the United States is one example: significant cleavages exist within American society, but they are minimized by the overarching patriotism and attachment to America as a whole. A common "American" identity is layered on top of other group identities.

A second strategy may be to recognize the cleavages and try to accommodate them by fostering mutual tolerance and respect. In essence, the multicultural policies of Canadian federal governments have successfully defused the most negative resentment toward immigration by hailing as a virtue the cultural diversity brought by immigrants to the country. This approach fosters cultural pluralism, which means that not only are there strong subcultures within a society, but that they are fostered and accommodated as a positive aspect of the political culture.

A third approach involves designing the country's political structures to accommodate the most significant cleavages within the institutional framework. In this way, the subgroups are more inclined to pursue their objectives within the existing state structure than to aim for independence and the breakup of the country. Federal systems of government are a common choice of institutional design in countries where significant cleavages coincide with geographic regions. The main idea of federations is to allow considerable variation at the regional level of the public policies most important to the different provincial or state societies. In essence, as in the case of the division of powers between the federal and provincial governments in Canada, control of issues central to the regional cultures can be given to those communities while still ensuring common national policies for other matters.

A fourth approach to political cleavages involves actively repressing the subgroups in violent or non violent ways, which means essentially trying to stamp out the cleavages. This may take the form of prohibiting the use of a language or practice of a particular religion. In Canada's history, there is a shameful reminder of this approach, where for several generations Canadian governments tried to eliminate the Aboriginal cultures by teaching Native people to behave like white people. Thousands of children where taken away from their families at a young age and taught to dress, act, and speak like those of European descent. Genocide or ethnic cleansing by forcible expulsion are the most extreme forms of dealing with cultural cleavages, aimed at simply eliminating all those who belong to the subgroup.

Another important issue arising from deep political cleavages is the question of how the groups involved respond to the approaches taken by the government. If a group believes strongly that the current situation is likely to lead to its continued subordination or even extinction by dominant groups, then a country will in all likelihood face significant political turmoil.

POLITICAL SOCIALIZATION: MOULDING THE MIND

If political cultures and identities are so important, the following questions arise: How are they formed? What processes create dominant beliefs and attitudes among large groups of people? The answers lie in one of the most important social phenomena of human existence. The sharing and propagating of attitudes, knowledge, values, and other beliefs are fundamental processes that create human societies. While the net result may be measured on a collective, group-wide level, the process occurs bit by bit on each individual member of the society. Wide ranges of influences and forces are at work throughout our lives to shape us into the people we become. The sum of those forces on all of the members of a community is what eventually creates its general culture.

Most of us would like to think of ourselves as essentially self-made individuals. We might recognize and appreciate the influence of parents and perhaps of a few key teachers and friends along the way, but overall we would like to believe that we are the people we are principally because of choices we have made for ourselves. But are we really self-made? What kinds of influences, both direct and unseen, have really moulded us and structured the range of choices that we feel we have made for ourselves? How many of our individual beliefs and attitudes are actually the product of other people's choices about what we should or should not believe? In reality, it is clear that individual members of any society are shaped by a lifelong process through which cultural, moral, and political values are shared and passed on and through which a group's culture is fostered.

Political socialization is the process through which political knowledge, attitudes, and beliefs are transmitted within a society. It is important to note that political socialization is not necessarily only about explicitly political attitudes and values, such as "capitalism is good." It also involves broader cultural and social values, such as views of the role of women, which can also have political implications. Through this process, most of us come to share certain core values and identify ourselves as members of a larger group or community. It is also through political socialization that the preferred values of particular groups and individuals within society are acquired by or even imposed on others.

> **Definition**
>
> **POLITICAL SOCIALIZATION:** The process through which attitudes toward and knowledge about political matters are passed on within a society.

The values of a political culture are passed on as new people enter the society, either as immigrants or as children born into and raised in that society. People born and raised in Argentina, China, India, Kenya, Russia, Taiwan, and Canada likely have had a different upbringing, which results in adults with many different attitudes. The whole environment and context in which we grow up has a tremendous effect on what we believe to be right and wrong and on the principles we regard highly and value above others. This socialization has its most profound impact during childhood years, but our political values and knowledge continue to be shaped throughout the rest of our lives.

Agents of Political Socialization

There are countless ways in which political socialization occurs, but there are specific **agents of political socialization** that have a particular role to play in an individual's life. It is primarily through these that an individual can acquire particular knowledge, attitudes, and beliefs about the political world. Given the potential impact on political systems, it is perhaps curious that political scientists do not undertake more serious study of the socialization process; indeed, political sociology is more usually the province of sociologists, anthropologists, and psychologists.[19] Political scientists, however, do concern themselves quite frequently with the consequences of socialization. For example, studies of voting patterns often examine whether there are correlations between the choice of political party and the specific social attributes of the voters (such as income, education, religion, or gender). A brief examination of the principal agents of political socialization, which follows below, will give you an idea of the powerful forces that can mould our views of society throughout the course of our lives, and it will illustrate how relevant political socialization can be to the study of politics.

> **Definition**
>
> **AGENTS OF POLITICAL SOCIALIZATION:** Those groups of people or institutions that convey political attitudes and values to others in society.

The Family

Undoubtedly, one of the most fundamental influences on an individual's outlook on politics is the family. Children learn all sorts of political lessons from their families in both direct and indirect ways. The most overt way in which families may act as agents of political socialization is through explicit training, when one or both parents engage in active, deliberate instruction on the political values to hold, the political parties or leaders to support, and the ways to participate in the political process. From an early age, children are aware of their parents' partisan preferences, and parents who are politically active become clear role models. Many politically active parents also take their young children along to party functions or political demonstrations. In many families, countless hours around a dining table are spent on discussing views about the political leaders and events of the day.

Children also acquire important beliefs from their families about their group identities and common enemies, both of which can have profound political implications later in life. From their family upbringing, individuals may develop strong views about the place of their group in the larger society and the wrongs their group has suffered. Nationalist movements have as their basis a commonly held belief among a large collection of individuals that they form a distinctive group; this belief is usually created and instilled on the family level. It is not an exaggeration to say that many civil wars started because of what children learned from their families.

The political socialization role of families, however, is not limited to such overt political instruction. Children also learn in subtle ways an enormous amount about how decisions are made within a group. The parental figures in the family may make authoritative decisions without consulting the children, or children may learn from an early age that they are entitled to

voice their opinion and participate in a "family conference," in which important decisions are reached collectively. In either case, the children are learning about decision-making. In countless ways, children learn from their families which social and moral principles they should value and uphold, and these in turn have many political dimensions. For example, some children may be actively taught to engage in acts of charity toward strangers; they may be given to understand that it is a good thing for those with more to share with those who have less. On the other hand, family members may believe and teach their children that it is only important to help one's relatives and close friends; they may feel they have no responsibility to help others in need, as those people must be responsible for themselves. These opposing views are examples of how children learn from their families about their relationship and responsibility to others in their community.

Everyday family dynamics also teach children a great deal about social hierarchy, deference to authority, obedience to rules, and acquiescence in judgments they do not support. There is a kernel of truth to the charge that all children are born into totalitarian regimes. Parents and other caregivers have total control over the lives of infants, and many only reluctantly and incompletely give up trying to exercise that degree of control as the children grow older. Just about every child cries out at some point in complaint against a parent's decision, "That's not fair!" And in doing so, children are expressing volumes about a conception of justice and fair process they have started to develop from a very tender age. Most children in Western families today are raised in an environment where they are encouraged, as they grow older, to voice their own opinions and question the views of their adult caregivers. Freedom of expression and a sense of personal autonomy are usually ingrained into Canadian children as a matter of course.

There is little surprise, then, that the political cultures of states such as Canada value the freedom of the individual so highly. This can be contrasted with the situation in a traditional Japanese family, for example, where the father is the source of authority and children dare not question or challenge his views. Conformity and deference to authority figures become not just domestic traits but values in the political culture as well.

Families around the world lay the foundation for different understandings of gender roles—for example, on the question of how active and vocal females should be in their society—by the role taken by the mother in relation to the father (if present in the family) or by the different opportunities given to the sons rather than daughters. Patriarchy has its social roots in the family, but those roots spread out in many ways into the political system. The Victorian-era family supposedly gave the father total final decision-making powers, and that reflected the predominant male view of the time that women were simply unsuited to vote in elections, let alone hold political office. As the patriarchal family model has begun to erode in Western countries, the place of women in society has also changed.

Educational Institutions

Usually, the next major influence on a person's development is school. Educational institutions can be very powerful agents of political socialization. In the most transparent instance of this, schools deliver a curriculum developed by the government to deliberately indoctrinate school children with a particular set of views. This is most clearly seen in communist countries, where the ruling party ensures that the official dogmas of the party are taught throughout the school years. Yet similar processes occur in democratic countries—even if the indoctrination is far less visible and not implemented to the same degree. State school authorities usually set the official curriculum guidelines for material taught in the main subjects offered in public schools—and often in private schools as well. This curriculum includes not just a sanctioned view of the society's history but also much material that has political implications, even if it is not directly political.

Students in Canada are exposed to many different messages during their school years that lead them to accept the importance of individual freedoms and personal autonomy. Tolerance of diverse cultures and religions is another social norm instilled in students that has significant implications for political culture in both Canada and the United States. Just as significant is what is not taught in school. For example, few American or Canadian secondary school graduates will have ever studied Marx and Engels's *The Communist Manifesto*; capitalist free enterprise is simply accepted as the norm in North American schools, and only a few students are exposed to teachings that seriously pose alternative forms of organizing society and the

Corporations are making inroads into schools through product placement and advertising.

Bruce MacKinnon/Halifax Herald/Artizans

economy. Instead, many corporations are making inroads into schools through product placement and advertising.

Schools have important socializing effects in many informal ways as well. The structure of classroom time and the interaction between students and their teachers can both serve as political models. A class that is structured in an informal setting, with students able to get up and move around or talk to other students provides a very different sense of liberty than does a classroom where students may never move or speak without permission. Students who use a teacher's first name will have a different notion of equality and social hierarchy than those who must call their teachers "Master," "Madam," or "Sir." The degree to which discipline is kept in the school through verbal abuse or corporal punishment can leave strong impressions on school children about the importance of deferring to or obeying authority. For that matter, however, overly strict or cruel discipline may incline students to grow up resentful of authority and make them ready to rebel.

Something as simple as teaching students to inquire and make up their own minds, rather than simply learn by rote memorization, can have consequences for the political culture. In many communist schools and universities, students have been taught from a single thick book that contains all they need to memorize about that subject. Learning becomes a matter of simply absorbing, accepting, and repeating the official position. Citizens in such countries have a very different starting point from which to assess their government's actions than do people who have grown up learning that there are many different views and interpretations on important subjects and that their own opinion is valued.

The influence of the school is so significant that across the Western industrialized world increasing education levels correlate with greater political interest and participation, as well as with more liberal attitudes on civil rights and social welfare issues.[20] However, this raises the question of whether it is education per se that has this effect, or whether these liberal values are so common among Western educators and so consistently propagated that the longer individuals are exposed to these views, the more likely they are to absorb them. Some of the most important differences in attitudes relate to the amount (if any) of postsecondary education individuals have had. This makes particular sense in Western democracies, where universities and colleges usually present quite a different style of learning and intellectual inquiry than students experienced in their earlier schooling.

The Media

The **mass media**, in their broadest sense of "the means of mass communication," include radio, television, and newspapers, as well as books, movies, music, and the Internet. Taken together, a country's media have the power to provide an important part of the cultural glue that defines that society's culture. The media provide some of the most powerful means of reinforcing common values and beliefs that create a nation's sense of identity. The media play a central role in conveying political attitudes, beliefs, and knowledge among not just the members of one society, but also across societies around the world. Whether it is news broadcasts of political developments or debates over opposing views,

much of what we come across on television, radio, and in newspapers frames what we think we know about political issues and causes. In media coverage of political issues, what is not said is just as important as what is said. An enormous amount of filtering occurs as to what issues or events are reported in the first place, as well as in the kind of coverage they receive. To understand the role of the media in modern society is to understand a lot about that society. As Marshall McLuhan (1911–80) put it, "The medium is the message."

Noam Chomsky is the best-known living critic of the media and their ability to shape a society's knowledge and understanding of political events. In a series of stinging commentaries, Chomsky has argued that one of the principal roles of the media is to manufacture consent among the masses for the existing social and political order and to control what people are told about the world around them.[21]

The power of the media to influence society's political views is most clearly demonstrated in different relationships between the media and the government found across the globe. In many countries of the world, the state actually owns and controls all media organizations, so that the only views and information that get publicly disseminated are those that the rulers of that society want people to know. In other countries, media corporations may be in private hands, but the government still exercises close supervision and censorship of the content, again to prevent the publication of facts and opinions that undermine the rulers' control of their society. At the other end of the scale is the value placed in established democracies on ensuring that the state does not censor or control the media in a general way. In these countries, because of an acceptance of the media's ability to profoundly shape people's knowledge and perceptions, freedom of expression in the media is a cornerstone of the society's culture. The more sources of information and the more perspectives citizens can draw from, the better they are able to form their own opinions on political events and issues.

Events in early 2002 show that the importance of getting the right message across in the media is not lost on either autocratic or democratic governments. Zimbabwe enacted legislation barring foreign news agencies from basing reporters in that country; in addition, local journalists are required to apply each year to the Minister of Information for a permit, which can be

Table 4.2 Ranking of Selected Countries in Terms of Press Freedom

Freedom House ranks the countries of the world according to the freedom under which the news media operate. The categories indicate the level of restrictions placed upon journalists and media companies by governments, as well as other factors, such as the concentration of ownership.

Free (1–30)		Partly Free (31–60)		Not Free (61–100)	
New Zealand	8	Brazil	32	Algeria	62
Switzerland	8	Argentina	37	Pakistan	64
Sweden	8	Mexico	40	Zambia	65
Denmark	9	India	42	Singapore	68
Norway	9	Uganda	42	Malaysia	71
Australia	10	Yugoslavia	45	Haiti	72
Germany	15	Kuwait	49	Iran	75
Canada	16	Indonesia	53	Egypt	77
United States	16	Nigeria	57	China	80
France	17	Pakistan	57	Saudi Arabia	80
Japan	17	Turkey	58	Zimbabwe	83
Spain	17	Colombia	60	Libya	88
United Kingdom	18	Jordan	60	Cuba	96
Chile	22	Russia	60	Burma	96
Philippines	30	Ukraine	60	Iraq	96

Source: Freedom House, *The Annual Survey of Press Freedom, 2002;* cited on July 17, 2002; available at http://www.freedomhouse.org/pfs2002/pfs2002.pdf. Reprinted by permission of Freedom House.

refused if the government disapproves of their work. In the United States, the Department of Defense was forced to close down its Office of Strategic Influence after only two months of operations, once it became clear that one of its prime missions was to provide disinformation to foreign news agencies as part of the campaign against terrorism.

Given the important role that the media have in informing people about political events and opinions, it is crucial to understand that the coverage of news and views that actually does occur is very incomplete, even within democracies. Only a relatively small number of stories can be covered in any one radio or TV broadcast. Newspaper editors have a finite number of column inches to devote to news items. On any given day, news editors must face choices about which stories to cover, which to ignore, and how much coverage to give to the stories they do choose to report on; they also have to find a balance between local, provincial or state, national, and international stories. Inevitably, many

stories that do get reported are greatly simplified to fit time or space constraints. The creation of news reports is far too often a matter of producers deciding what

Lloyd Robertson is probably Canada's most recognized news anchor, having presided over the CBC's *National* for six years before taking over the CTV evening news in 1976.

Courtesy of CTV; photographer Geoff George

"take" their reporters should follow on the story so that the finished report will reflect the views of those producers.

A number of studies reveal that the media consistently fail to report on certain newsworthy issues and that their coverage often favours one side of an issue over another. For example, the views of business may predominate over the views of unions. Furthermore, from time to time editors kill stories initiated by individual reporters because they cast a negative light on associates of the media corporation's owners or—more often—on those who pay for advertising. Journalists often engage in self-censorship because of a fear of repercussions, as they may become targets of intimidation or death threats if they investigate widespread corruption in the corridors of power or the activities of

organized crime. In many countries of the world, journalists are arrested, beaten, or killed by government forces if their stories become too critical of the ruling party. Self-censorship may also occur because a reporter does not want to lose important contacts and informants. Reporters who cover their local police forces are particularly vulnerable, since a negative story on some police officers' activities can quickly dry up their sources for the inside scoops they rely on when covering general criminal activity.

In many countries, the coverage of political issues is restricted by limited competition that arises from the concentration of ownership or media outlets. For example, by the late 1990s, three media chains controlled two-thirds of all daily newspaper circulation in Canada,[22] and many dailies had a complete monopoly

---

BOX 4.3

NATIONAL EDITORIALS AND FREEDOM OF THE PRESS

CanWest's Southam News created a stir when it started publishing national editorials in its major daily newspapers in late 2001 to set a common approach to major issues. One of these editorials stated, "On some national or international issues, Southam will speak with one voice across Canada, in an open and transparent manner. Its national editorials will be clearly identified. In order to be consistent within the publisher's space on editorial pages, local editorials won't contradict Southam's core positions."[23]

Many media watchers reacted with alarm that this was an assault on the freedom of the press, because it made each paper's editors subservient to their corporate owner's views. Indeed, some senior reporters at *The Gazette* in Montreal (one of the papers covered by the new policies) staged public protests. As Roger Cribb, president of the Canadian Association of Journalists, said in defense of *The Gazette* journalists, "Without diversity of voices and opinions, the marketplace of ideas is threatened, public debate is stifled and answers to impor-

tant public policy questions are hidden…. The importance of editorial independence to the credibility of journalism has always been universally accepted in the newsrooms of the nation. Weakening that independence compromises the work journalists do and the resulting public policy debates that have a direct impact on our lives."[24] The CAJ later joined with the Quebec Federation of Professional Journalists to call for a parliamentary inquiry into the matter, implying that some government regulation might be needed.

Southam's editor-in-chief, Murdoch Davis, countered forcefully that it is calls for government regulation, not national editorials, that threaten the freedom of the press: "It certainly does not mean that proprietors shouldn't have a voice in their newspapers, or in fact run their newspapers as they wish. Those freedoms are freedom from the state, from government intrusion into the editorial process, from any government role in determining or evaluating content."[25]

on local news in their communities. A significant shift in media ownership occurred in Canada in 2000, when CanWest Global bought most of the newspapers and Internet sites owned by Conrad Black's Hollinger and Southam companies, transforming itself into Canada's largest owner of daily newspapers. CanWest also owns the Global television network and other stations, which raises the spectre of one company controlling both the major TV and newspaper sources of information in many communities. Perhaps tellingly, the only government review of this media concentration centred not on the potential for one company's control over the news coverage in any particular community but instead on whether the new concentration would adversely affect the advertising market. Even where there are competing media outlets, one radio or TV station may have a crushing lead in terms of listeners and viewers. As a result, the tangible value of the freedom of the press and multiple news outlets is eroded as most citizens end up relying on only one or two sources for their news. These few sources have an enormous influence over the public.

Surveys of the public show that attitudes toward the media involve a mixture of trust and wariness and reveal that the public are more likely to believe news from some sources than from others. For example, a 1998 poll of Canadians found that only 20 percent distrusted TV news anchors to some degree, while 41 percent distrusted newspaper journalists.[26] The significance of this discrepancy is all the more important because Canadians rely far more heavily on TV than on newspapers as their primary news source. There are indications that some people are becoming more sceptical of the media over time. Gallup surveys in the United States show an increase in the number of Americans who distrust the media to report events fairly and accurately, from 26 percent in 1976 to 44 percent in 1998.[27] However, it is clear that many North Americans still have a significant trust in media sources, and this receptivity facilitates the media's ability to continue to act as effective agents of socialization.

The tremendous globalization of mass communication in the late 20th century has also created the situation where the media have a powerful role in eroding the traditional distinctiveness of some nations' cultures by spreading "alien" ideas, beliefs, and knowledge around the world. National cultures are constantly

being reshaped by the adoption of ideas spread by the media. Starting in the mid-20th century, radio was deliberately used as a **propaganda** tool by both Western and communist states to beam broadcasts to each other's citizens, all in the hopes of providing a fresh view of the world to the other side. The later growth of television has superseded the impact of shortwave radio in reaching into the homes of people around the world. CNN now provides live TV broadcasts by satellite to every continent, and countless entertainment programs are dubbed into foreign languages to be watched by global audiences.

Definition

PROPAGANDA: An organized attempt to spread beliefs through a communications campaign. It implies the use of exaggerated facts.

Television, however, is starting to be supplanted by the Internet, which has a potential for global communication that can only be described at the start of the 21st century as staggering, with 300 million users worldwide having 10 million sites to choose from. By mid-2000, 70 percent of Canadians had access to the Internet either at home, school, or work.[28] The Internet already serves as an alternative source for news and information, and there is speculation that a kind of global cyber culture is emerging that may cause us to rethink basic ideas about the territorial basis of society. The Internet also threatens to create an economic and cultural "digital divide" between those people who have ready access to information technology and those who do not.

Religious Institutions

Religious institutions may also play a important role as agents of political socialization. This idea may seem at first somewhat strange to people in Canada and the United States today, where we are used to accepting the general principle of the separation of church and state. It is generally believed in Canada that the state should not embrace one religion as the official religion of the society that is promoted above or to the exclusion of others. Furthermore, the separation of church and state means that religious institutions and leaders do not play an active role in the administration of government. Through religious teachings, however, individuals can learn about their role in society, their responsibility to others, the importance of tradition, tolerance or intolerance of other faiths, and the existence of higher duties that transcend any that secular authorities might try to impose. All of these beliefs have potential political implications. As well, followers of some religions acquire a very strong sense of group identity based on that religion, with strong cultural understandings of the history of that group and its place in the larger society. Perceived and actual wrongs inflicted by others in the same society on that religious group can have direct political consequences, including providing a basis for nationalist aspirations.

Even with the separation of church and state in North America, we still see the interplay of religion and politics. In Canada, prayers are still part of many official functions, the Christian Lord's Prayer is still recited in some public schools, and ordained ministers and priests do occasionally hold elected office. In the United States, religion is an even bigger part of everyday politics, with many organized religious groups actively funding or campaigning for their favourite candidates and against their perceived enemies. These situations are nevertheless quite different from Great Britain, where the Church of England is the official church, and where the queen or king, as head of state, is also the head of the church. Nor can the North American situation compare with Iran, where religious leaders have an official place in the constitution and are able to exercise effective political power. In some Latin American countries, social liberation theology leads many priests and their followers to expose brutal tactics of repression used by the government and wealthy landowners. As a result, some local Catholic churches become centres of political activity in ways not seen in Canada or the United States, and security forces actively target priests for intimidation or even assassination.

The power of religion has been well understood in those states where the government has tried to prohibit all organized religion. Karl Marx once said that religion is the opiate of the people; he believed that religion merely ensured that the workers of the world accepted their oppressed lot in society in anticipation of a better life after death. More practically, however, the belief in a higher divine authority may lead many devotees to disobey the laws of the state. Thus, organized religions were banned in many communist countries as insidious elements that would otherwise undermine the creation of a socialist society. After all, a quest for freedom of religion could very easily snowball into demands for other freedoms, such as freedom of expression, which have a direct bearing on the stability of the political regime.

Perhaps the most vivid example of the political impact of religious values came when Islamic extremists hijacked four planes in September 2001 and crashed two of them into the World Trade Center towers in New York City and another into the Pentagon in Washington. Although the geopolitical circumstances of the Middle East were part of the motivation behind those actions, the hijackers became a new version of suicide bombers only because of their religious conviction that they were fighting a holy war and would be rewarded in the afterlife for their martyrdom.

Peer Groups

Peer groups can be very important agents of socialization, even though they remain unorganized. Once children enter school, most of their experiences are shared by their friends. Throughout the rest of our lives, we share with our friends our thoughts and reactions, and their reactions, in turn, become an important framing for our assessment of what is right and wrong. By the late teenage and early adult years, peer groups come to play an increasingly important role in an individual's life. At election time, people end up having most of their discussions with their friends about political events and candidates. As a result, our peer groups become a crucial social context from which we learn new information about political events and where we debate political alternatives.

In our interactions with friends, we practise important political principles, such as freedom of expression, but we also practise group conformity and exclusion of "others"; we may even defer to the unofficial leader of the group. While we may have a broad collection of different types of individuals within our groups of friends, there are strong pressures on individuals with a circle of friends to "go with the flow" and do what is considered popular with the group. In addition, we tend to exclude or even ostracize individuals who "go too far" and stray beyond what the group tends to think of as acceptable attitudes and behaviour. These pressures are strongest and most visible in the teenage years, but carry on to some degree well into later life.

The Workplace

In North America, the workplace is not often thought of as being a political arena, yet there is much in our work life that has political import. Although it very much depends on the particular place of work, we can be exposed to many situations in our jobs that carry over into our political world.[29] For example, a rigidly hierarchical workplace gives individuals a very different sense of the importance of the individual, depending on whether they are at the top or at the bottom. If the lesson from work is to defer to the boss and acquiesce in authoritative decisions, we may carry this attitude with us into society in general. In contrast, based on experiences in a workplace where we are actively consulted and where we feel we can have meaningful input into collective decisions, we may be more inclined to become actively involved in the political affairs of our society.

An important minority of Canadians and Americans work in situations that are highly charged by adversarial union–employer dynamics. An active belief in the power of collective action through unions translates directly to the political world. Unions can be important sources of funds and volunteers for political parties that seek to change society and economic relations in ways that favour the workers. Pro-business parties and governments may inspire trade unions to actively support parties and governments that promise to implement policies favouring the country's workers instead of the country's industrialists. For example, there have been historically strong ties between organized labour in Canada and the New Democratic Party (NDP); indeed, trade unions even get to exercise formal votes in NDP conventions. A highly polarized workplace, that pits rich bosses against poorly paid workers may actually have a politically energizing influence on the workers; the latter may see their poverty and exploitation as resulting from a political regime that ensures the continuing dominance of business people and corporate interests. Indeed, it was the highly exploitative setting of industries in the 19th century that provided the inspiration for Karl Marx and others after him to argue that the entire political, economic, and social orders must be swept away and replaced by ones organized on socialist or communist principles.

The workplace may breed revolution, not just political activism!

State Actors

State actors can act as agents of political socialization, propagating official views of the society in the hopes of persuading the populace to support or acquiesce in government policies. Schools are one such state institution, as are state-owned media. All governments engage to some degree in publicity and propaganda, spreading their messages to the populace about what is good and proper in a political sense through pamphlets, media advertising, and public events. For example, successive Canadian governments since the 1970s have actively (and quite successfully) campaigned for Canadians to embrace multiculturalism as a central part of Canada's political culture.

A crucial part of most governments' mission is to foster—and sometimes even create—a distinct national identity for their country. An important part of this is the selection and promotion of symbols (such as flags and national anthems) and rituals (public holidays and celebrations) that promote a sense of pride in the country. American governments have been particularly successful in developing a strong sense of **patriotism**. The Canadian federal government took a series of measures in the 1960s and 1970s to develop a new set of Canadian symbols that distinguished Canada from its colonial past. In 1965, in a very controversial move at the time, the flag was changed from the one based on the British Union Jack to the current maple leaf flag. Over the next few years, the government eliminated virtually all references to "Royal" in government institutions; for instance, the Royal Mail became Canada Post. One criticism of the Canadian government is that our problems with national unity may stem in part from a failure to develop an effective sense of Canadian patriotism (which some say would be rather un-Canadian anyway).

Definition

PATRIOTISM: A sense of pride in one's country.

In some countries—democratic as well as communist—the military plays a crucial socialization role because almost every male is required to do a compulsory period of military service. In Israel, even women have to join.

The military is able to indoctrinate, in subtle and overt ways, vast numbers of citizens with views about the nature of the state, its society, and the duties of citizens to obey and defend.

Political parties also act as important agents of socialization. In communist countries in particular, where only the communist party is allowed to exist and is made a part of everyday life, the party can engage the citizens in many ways—for example, through newspapers, youth groups, neighbourhood activities, and sports clubs. In democratic countries, we do not tend to think of political parties as official state actors, and yet they are intimately tied to the political system and the process of governing. Political parties in every country can come to play central roles in the lives of those who are politically active, and these individuals acquire many beliefs and much information through party activities.

* * *

It should be clear by this point that there are many forces at work within a society that combine to mould individuals and ensure that most members of society come to accept common attitudes and beliefs. Where the same set of messages is reinforced by multiple agents—such as the family, school, friends, and the media—it is far more likely that people within a particular community will hold common attitudes and beliefs without serious questioning. Socialization may be a straightforward process of indoctrination, effectively brainwashing people to revere certain beliefs and revile others, but the socialization process that any one individual goes through usually is as much about the individual's reaction to the messages as it is about the messages themselves. This explains why members of the same family raised in much the same way and living within the same community can have very different views about political issues and principles. Nevertheless, we are all shaped by a multitude of agents of political socialization to become in some ways very much what others have wanted us to become, while still becoming in other ways what we ourselves have actually chosen to become. Political socialization is a process of absorbing information and ideas presented by others, observing role models, and internalizing our reactions to these inputs. Individuals within a group who are exposed to the same

upbringing can and do react differently, but they also share many predominant views.

THE CONSEQUENCES OF POLITICAL SOCIALIZATION

Political socialization creates a political culture. A general culture is generated and perpetuated through the accumulated effects on each individual in society. Cultures can and do change over time, but even that change occurs as new ideas spread through agents of political socialization. For example, women have struggled for political and social rights for a very long time, but feminism made significant headway only once agents of socialization in the late 20th century dealt with women's issues.

It is crucial to understand who is spreading what values and beliefs, and how easily new ideas can get circulated within an established society to spark new ways of thinking about politics. For example, research has shown very strong correlations between authoritarian views in a country's populace and the extent of authoritarian measures practised by their government. In short, authoritarian governments rely on state-orchestrated socialization to impart widespread support for the values that the government wishes to enforce and the ways in which they are enforced. By the same token, a population that strongly supports democratic values would not voluntarily tolerate authoritarian measures by their government.

A great deal depends on the type of values propagated through the various agents of socialization, on how deliberate the process of indoctrination is, and on the degree to which the various agents of political socialization reinforce the same messages. The political socialization process in the People's Republic of China, for example, involves massive, overt indoctrination that provides a stark contrast to the seemingly haphazard and uncoordinated process in Canada or the United States. However, it would be a mistake to conclude from that contrast that the Canadian or American political socialization processes are not as effective as the Chinese in instilling widespread support for and belief in the values that the most important elites in the country wish the majority of citizens to hold. Indeed, Ralph Miliband has decried the political socialization process in Western democracies as "very largely a process of mass *indoctrination*" aimed at instilling support for the existing social order and capitalist economy.[30] The belief in diversity and freedom of expression provides a more heterogeneous political culture in Canada and the United States, but that diversity and the expression of opposing points of view do not contradict the existence of many values deeply shared by most citizens that result in mass acceptance of the existing social order.

Political socialization has many important consequences for a society and for individuals and groups within a society. Essential to any stable community is a large degree of acceptance of shared values about the structure of political institutions, about the processes used to settle political disputes and issue authoritative decisions, and about the basic parameters of social and economic policies to be pursued by those who hold political office. Socialization allows the spread of beliefs, attitudes, and knowledge needed for a widespread sharing of that acceptance. In short, political socialization underlies any stable society by ensuring that enough new members who are born into or immigrate to it come to hold many values and attitudes in common with those already present. Through socialization, a society of many different subgroups can also be melded into sharing one overarching culture. The United States is often taken as a prime example of the successful creation of a single nation despite enormous regional differences in culture and ethnic background. The *melting pot* is an expression often used to describe American cultural history and socialization.

Yet the process of political socialization may have many different outcomes. Existing divisions and tensions within a society may be perpetuated and even exacerbated over time. For example, there have always been tensions between French- and English-speaking people in Quebec, but the political socialization processes in Quebec in the past four decades have amplified the nationalist sentiments that a minority had long held. By the 1990s, a large number of francophones in Quebec were in favour of separation or sovereignty association, and this growth in nationalist fervour was fostered through schools and peer groups and in the arts and the media. The growth of Quebec

nationalism can even be seen to have occurred in the workplace, through provincial legislation and policies designed to enhance the use and predominance of the French language in business.

The enduring power of political socialization is vividly highlighted in theories about the character of political cultures in societies that are largely made up of immigrant settlers. In the 1960s, Louis Hartz developed a theory of political culture known as the fragment theory, which was also explored by Seymour Lipset.[31] Hartz argued that the contemporary political culture of an immigrant society reflects the dominant views of the different groups of immigrants who settled there. Each wave of immigrants is usually recruited from a specific place in their original country and thus represents only a fragment of the original country's political culture. Each different wave of immigrants can establish an enduring set of beliefs and attitudes that will be reflected in the modern politics of the new society. Gad Horowitz adapted this theory to explain some of the most significant differences between Canadian and American political cultures, particularly the wider range of ideologies that have popular appeal in Canada, as opposed to in the United States.[32] If true, the survival of these original fragments of political culture is a testament to the political socialization process that passed the values down from generation to generation. It should be noted, however, that the contemporary values of these groups have indeed evolved significantly over time and are not simply time capsules of the values of bygone European cultures.

Further significance of political socialization lies in the ways in which political scientists study politics. For several decades, political behaviour has been studied by conducting surveys in an attempt to correlate the social background of individuals with their support for particular policies or political parties. It was thought that if religion, education, and occupation can have an impact on an individual's beliefs, one might be able to explain people's behaviour by studying their social, economic, and cultural backgrounds. This approach to studying politics first started out by trying to concentrate on developing statistical models of political behaviour. In recent years, however, an appreciation of the complexity of human behaviour and of the strong interplay of the various forces in our lives has produced serious puzzles for political scientists to unravel.

CONCLUSION

Political culture—the set of beliefs, values, attitudes, and principles that are widely held among members of a society—may be a concept formulated by academics, but it has enormous practical implications. Political culture provides the foundation upon which any political system is created and operates. The degree of consensus on fundamental values, and what those values actually are, can have a profound effect on the stability of the political order in a particular country. Identity politics, which stems from individuals' identification with groups within a society and involves those groups' pursuit of their perceived needs, has important political ramifications. The depth and causes of political cleavages and the ways in which the political elites react to accommodate or suppress members of subgroups can lead to the creation of a healthy, vibrant political pluralism or to separatist movements, civil war, and the disintegration of the state.

At the heart of understanding political culture lies our awareness of the process of political socialization, through which attitudes, knowledge, and beliefs are passed on within a society. Political socialization occurs through a variety of agents, including the family, schools, peer groups, religious institutions, the media, the workplace, and various state actors. The power of ideas is tremendous, and in every society a wide variety of groups and individuals act, sometimes in very subtle ways and other times in strikingly forceful ways, to try to ensure that others embrace their values.

DISCUSSION QUESTIONS

1. Do you think that the courts should protect citizens' rights? Try to think of all the different sources of information that have led you to give an answer to that question. Could you name several or none? Does your answer strike you simply as common sense?

2. Think of a particular issue such as clear-cut logging, strip mining, trade union rights, universal medicare, or trade between Canada and some state with an authoritarian regime. Ask yourself what your views on it are and what you think the government should do about it. Then ask yourself how you came to learn about this issue and develop an opinion—who informed and influenced you and how?

3. Think about the various agents of political socialization you have read about in this chapter. How would you rank them in order of the effects you believe each has had in forming your own political beliefs and attitudes?

4. Which agent of political socialization do you think you have reacted against the most? Have other agents positively reinforced your negative reactions?

5. How deeply divided by political cleavages do you think our society is? What do you think are the main causes of those cleavages? Do you think our political system essentially tries to accommodate subgroups or meld them into a single, national culture?

w(w)w WEB LINKS

Columbia Journalism Review: Who Owns What:
http://www.cjr.org/owners

Thomson Nelson: Political Culture:
http://polisci.nelson.com/intropc.html

The Noam Chomsky Archive:
http://zmag.org/chomsky

A Sociological Tour through Cyberspace:
http://www.trinity.edu/~mkearl

Voice of the Shuttle: Cultural Studies:
http://vos.ucsb.edu/browse.asp?id=2709

FURTHER READING

Almond, Gabriel A., and Sidney Verba. *The Civic Culture: Political Attitudes in Five Democracies*. Princeton: Princeton University Press, 1963.

Herman, Edward, and Noam Chomsky. *Manufacturing Dissent*. New York: Pantheon, 1986.

Kymlicka, Will. *Multicultural Citizenship*. Oxford: Clarendon Press, 1997.

Miliband, Ralph. *The State in Capitalist Society*. London: Weidenfeld and Nicolson, 1969.

Nevitte, Neil. *The Decline of Deference.* Peterborough: Broadview Press, 1996.

ENDNOTES

1   CNN, "Kuwaiti Women Look Forward to New Political Rights"; cited on June 4, 1999; available at http://cnn.com/WORLD/world.report/9906/04/.

2   Pollara, "Nurses, Doctors Still Top the Pollara Public Trust Index"; cited on November 17, 1999; available at http://www.pollara.ca/new/ Library/surveys/intro~1.htm. For the data, see http://www.pollara.ca/new/Library/surveys/1of3. htm and http://www.pollara.ca/new/Library/ surveys/3of3.htm.

3   The information for Canada and Italy is from Government of New Zealand, "Tax Compliance"; cited on February 27, 1999; available at http://www.executive.govt.nz/compliance/chapter 7.htm.

4   "Russia's Ever Mounting Back Taxes," *Washington Post*, December 26, 1997, p. A31; cited on July 17, 2002; available at http://www.washingtonpost.com/wp-srv/inatl/ longterm/russiagov/stories/taxes122697.htm.

5   BBC News, "Russia Cuts Taxes," November 27, 1998; cited on July 17, 2002; available at http://news.bbc.co.uk/hi/english/business/the_ economy/newsid_223000/223266.stm.

6   Hans Christiaan Haan, "Training for Work in the Informal Sector: New Evidence from Kenya, Tanzania and Uganda," International Labor Organization; cited on August 6, 2002; available at http://www.ilo.org/public/english/ employment/infeco/download/haan.pdf, p.14.

7   Antonio Gramsci, *Letters from Prison* (New York: Columbia University Press, 1994).

8   Michel Foucault, *Ethics: Subjectivity and Truth* (New York: New Press, 1997).

9   Gabriel A. Almond and Sidney Verba, *The Civic Culture: Political Attitudes in Five Democracies* (Princeton: Princeton University Press, 1963). For a more recent discussion of related issues that have since been discussed in terms of civil society, see John Keane, *Civil Society and the State* (London: Verso, 1988).

10 For a discussion of the importance of civil society, as well as the limits of its political effects, in transitions from authoritarian regimes to democratic societies, see Emmanuel Gyimah-Boadi, "Civil Society in Africa," *Journal of Democracy* 7 (1996): 118.

11 Samuel P. Huntington, "Democracy for the Long Haul," *Journal of Democracy* 7(2) (April 1996): 8.

12 Charles Taylor, "The Politics of Recognition," in Amy Gutmann, ed., *Multiculturalism and the Politics of Recognition* (Princeton: Princeton University Press, 1992).

13 Iris M. Young, *Justice and the Politics of Difference* (Princeton: Princeton University Press, 1990); Will Kymlicka, *Multicultural Citizenship* (Oxford: Clarendon Press. 1997).

14 Will Kymlicka, *Liberalism, Community and Culture* (Oxford: Oxford University Press, 1989), pp. 182–205; see also Will Kymlicka, *Finding Our War: Rethinking Ethnocultural Relations in Canada* (Toronto: Oxford University Press, 1998).

15 Kenneth Hoover, *The Power of Identity: Politics in a New Key* (Chatham: Chatham House, 1997), pp. 37–38.

16 Carole Pateman, *The Sexual Contract* (Stanford: Stanford University Press, 1988), p. 231.

17 Carol Gilligan, *In a Different Voice: Psychological Theory and Women's Development* (Cambridge, Mass.: Harvard University Press, 1982).

18 Simone de Beauvoir, *The Second Sex* (New York: Vintage Press, 1973), p. 301.

19 Richard G. Niemi and Mary A. Hepburn, "The Rebirth of Political Socialization," *Perspectives on Political Science* 24 (winter 1995): 7–16.

20 Neil Nevitte, *The Decline of Deference* (Peterborough: Broadview Press, 1996).

21 See Edward Herman and Noam Chomsky, *Manufacturing Dissent* (New York: Pantheon, 1986); Noam Chomsky and David Barsamian, *Chronicles of Dissent* (Monroe, Maine: Common Courage Press, 1992); and Noam Chomsky, "Media Control"; cited on July 17, 2002; available at http://www.zmag.org/chomsky/talks/9103-media-control.html.

22 James Winter, *Democracy's Oxygen: How Corporations Control the News* (Montreal: Black Rose Books, 1997).

23 Southam News, "About Southam Editorials"; cited on January 31, 2002; available at http://www.nationalpost.com/search/story.html?f=/stories/20020129/1269421.html&qs=national%20editorials.

24 Canadian Association of Journalists, "Canadian Association of Journalists Supports *Gazette* Reporters in Protest over Editorial Independence," December 12, 2001; cited on July 17, 2002; available at http://micro.newswire.ca/releases/December2001/12/c6426.html/42015-0.

25 Murdoch Davis, "The Facts of the Matter"; cited on January 31, 2002; available at http://www.nationalpost.com/search/story.html?f=/stories/20020131/1294847.html&qs=national%20editorials.

26 Pollara, "Public Trust Index"; cited on November 17, 1999; available at http://www.pollara.ca/new/Library/surveys/2of3.htm.

27 Gallup, "Public Trust in Federal Government Remains High"; cited on January 8, 1998; available at http://www.gallup.com/poll/releases/apr990108.asp.

28 Ipsos Reid, "Canadian Internet Access Continues to Grow, and Users Say the Net Has Had a Significant Impact on Their Lives"; cited on July 26, 2000; available at http://www.ipsosreid.com/media/content/displaypr.cfm?id_to_view=1061.

29 For an examination of the relationship between the workplace and political attitudes in America, see Steven A. Peterson, *Political Behaviour: Patterns in Everyday Life* (Newbury Park: Sage, 1990), Chapter 8.

30 Ralph Miliband, *The State in Capitalist Society* (London: Weidenfeld and Nicolson, 1969), p. 181.

31 Louis Hartz, *The Founding of New Societies* (New York: Harcourt Brace, 1964). See also Seymour Martin Lipset, "Canada and the United States: A Comparative Review," *Canadian Review of Sociology and Anthropology* 1 (1964): 173–85.

32 Gad Horowitz, "Conservatism, Liberalism, and Socialism in Canada: An Interpretation," *Canadian Journal of Economics and Political Science* 32 (1966): 143–71.

Chapter 5

Political Ideas and Ideologies

Richard Sigurdson

CHAPTER OBJECTIVES

After you have completed this chapter, you should be able to

- discuss the ways in which one's view of human nature helps determine one's attitude toward government and politics
- outline the different views on equality put forward by conservatives, liberals, and socialists
- distinguish between negative and positive concepts of freedom and discuss the relevant policy implications in emphasizing one view of freedom over another
- enumerate various answers to the question, "Who should rule?"
- differentiate between the political left and right and define the following concepts: radical, liberal, conservative, and reactionary
- define the term *ideology* and outline its functions in the contemporary world
- explain the notion of ideology as a style of thought and discuss the meaning of the term *ideologue*
- understand the "end of ideology" thesis and discuss its relevance for the contemporary world order.

INTRODUCTION

This chapter explores ideas about politics and the state and examines the ways in which political ideas come together to form ideologies. While we will necessarily deal with these notions in a somewhat abstract and academic manner, it is worth keeping in mind that ideas about politics and the ideologies they engender often determine the course of political events. For instance, the ideas of John Locke (1632–1704) and Baron de Montesquieu (1689–1755) were profoundly influential in the rise of liberalism and democracy, and are evident in such founding documents as the United States

Constitution. Jean-Jacques Rousseau's (1712–78) writings about freedom and equality inspired many of the key figures behind the French Revolution of 1789, which had as its slogan "liberté, égalité, fraternité." And the radical ideas of Karl Marx (1818–83) and Friedrich Nietzsche (1844–1900) aroused, often unwittingly, political movements, communist and fascist respectively, that had a tremendous impact on the 20th century.

In the second part of this chapter, we will look more closely at how political ideas can link together into more or less coherent worldviews or ideologies, and at how these ideologies can figure into political practice. But first we will examine some of the perennial issues and topics of political thought, organizing the material thematically in an effort to provide a broad survey of the subject. Unfortunately, this means that the specific theories of individual philosophers cannot be given the space they deserve. But we hope that you will

---

BOX 5.1

NORMATIVE VERSUS EMPIRICAL STUDIES

There are two broad paths of inquiry normally pursued by political scientists. The first is the normative approach, the other is the empirical approach. Normative studies tend to focus on political ideas, moral philosophies, and political values, as opposed to the empirical domain of facts. The most obviously normative subfield of political science is what we call political theory or political philosophy. Along with related fields in the humanities, such as ethics, political theory deals with normative issues in society, such as the nature of good and evil. Empirical studies, on the other hand, tend to rely on observation and measurement of political behaviour rather than on the analysis of the theories and norms of behaviour. In this regard, much of the work done by empirical political scientists fits in with other key disciplines in the family of the social sciences, such as sociology or economics.*

A popular way to conceive of the difference between normative and empirical studies is to think of the normative as that which seeks to discover what *should* be and the empirical as that which seeks to determine what really *is*. However, this is a bit of a superficial distinction, since not all normative political science is explicitly prescriptive. It is better to think of normative political studies as those that seek to understand, interpret, and evaluate human conduct in the light of political ideas and theories, such as the ones presented in this chapter. In addition to their attention to the abstract study of purely philosophical questions, normativists contribute to resolving matters of a more practical nature. For instance, normative studies inform us about the implications of choosing one policy over another. On the basis of a close analysis of a society's historical behaviour, political values, and cultural norms, normative studies can enlighten policymakers about what is acceptable or practicable, say in the field of education or health care.

* See Gregory S. Mahler and Donald J. Maclunis, *Comparative Politics: An Institutional and Cross-National Approach*, 1st Canadian ed. (Toronto: Prentice-Hall, 2002), p. 4.

---

be inspired by this introductory study of politics to take up the challenge of reading some of the great political thinkers in their own words. (See the accompanying box for a list of important primary texts.)

BOX 5.2

THE TOP 10 TEXTS OF POLITICAL THEORY

1. Plato, *The Republic*
2. Aristotle, *The Politics*
3. Thomas Aquinas, *Summa Theologiae*
4. Niccolò Machiavelli, *The Prince*
5. Thomas Hobbes, *Leviathan*
6. John Locke, *Second Treatise on Government*
7. Jean-Jacques Rousseau, *The Social Contract*
8. Karl Marx and Friedrich Engels, *The Communist Manifesto*
9. John Stuart Mill, *On Liberty*
10. Friedrich Nietzsche, *On the Genealogy of Morals*

PERENNIAL ISSUES IN POLITICAL THOUGHT

Human Nature and Politics

It is sometimes said that the history of political philosophy is one long meditation on the question of human nature. Indeed, whether it is acknowledged or not, the starting point for all thinking about politics is a probing into the very nature of human beingness. What does it mean to be human? What is our human essence? Are we by nature social animals, as Aristotle (384–322 B.C.) said, or are we solitary and isolated creatures, as Thomas Hobbes (1588–1679) assumed? Is the desire for power intrinsic to human nature, as Nietzsche believed, or are we by nature benign beings, capable of mutual love and cooperation, as Rousseau suggested? Our answers to these questions will determine how we approach all other aspects of political philosophizing. For instance, if we regard humans as power-hungry and self-centred by nature, as opposed to fundamentally peace-loving and cooperative, then this will very much influence our views about what form of government is necessary.

Our thinking about human nature sets the foundation upon which our political theories are constructed. One key issue at stake has already been mentioned: Are human beings estranged in essence, or are they basically united in their humanity?[1] Hobbes stands out as the most brilliant advocate of the former view. He assumed that humans are isolated, selfish creatures, driven by their "desires" and "aversions." Two basic postulates about human nature provide the foundation for Hobbes's political theory: first, that humans are inescapably engaged in a perpetual struggle for power over others that ends only in death; and second, that our strongest aversion is to violent death, which we will seek to avoid at all costs. Hobbes comes to these conclusions about human nature by imagining what people would be like if they lived in a "state of nature"—that is, in a condition free of any government or rule-making authority. While some people (e.g., anarchists) might think that such a situation would be a paradise, Hobbes concludes that this natural condition would consist of constant war "of every man against every man." Life in this state of nature, as Hobbes famously declares, would be "solitary, poor, nasty, brutish, and short."[2] What is the conclusion we are meant to draw from these Hobbesian observations about human nature? That the only rational thing for humans to do in order to avoid violence and escape anxiety is to quit the state of nature, agreeing mutually to abdicate to a single sovereign power all of one's natural rights to govern oneself. Thus, civil society is to Hobbes but an expedient. Hobbes says that while it is not natural for humans to live in society, agreeing to give up some natural freedom to live in a formally organized state allows people the security necessary to satisfy their needs.

Aristotle presents an entirely opposite point of view. For him, society is natural; humans are *by nature* social and political animals. Only a beast or a god (the subhuman or the superhuman) could live without being a member of a political community, for it is only in commune with our fellow citizens that we attain our full human potential. The political life is to Aristotle the highest form of self-actuality. We are most alive, most true to our nature, when we are participating in political activity. To many of us today, Aristotle's glorification of the political life hardly rings true. We are notoriously unwilling to become politically engaged, even though we in the Western world live in societies where virtually everyone can participate in politics. Yet not only are we uninterested in politics these days, but what little we know about the political realm turns us off. We have become cynical, distrustful, and disengaged. We seek our "true" selves in our work, our relationships, our hobbies, our identity groups, but not in our role as citizens.

One of the things that turns people away from public affairs is the incessant conflict and strife associated with the political realm. If Aristotle is correct and we are by nature social beings, then why is it so hard for us to get along? One answer, promoted by Hobbes among others, is that humans are simply avaricious and selfish by nature. Another answer comes from Rousseau. He believes that humans are essentially decent but that they were gradually led away from their natural, congenial condition toward one that is corrupt, unjust, and divisive. This misfortune occurred, Rousseau theorizes, because humans introduced into their lives private property, which led to inequality, selfishness, distrust, and the concentration of power in the hands of a few. Rousseau's thesis is that humans are basically good but have been corrupted by their sociopolitical environment. To summarize, bad institutions distort the natural goodness of humankind, but this goodness can be rediscovered if social conditions are put right. This reasoning struck a chord with utopian socialists in the 19th century, who stressed the inherent human capacity for consensus and cooperation and imagined strategies for creating a world of peace and harmony. It was also implicit in Marx's doctrine of historical materialism, with its faith in the inexorable historical progress toward the highest phase of communist society, in which there will be no classes and therefore no destructive political conflict.

In general, thinkers on the political left tend to share the fundamental belief that human nature is good, or inherently perfectible, and that humans may realize the perfection that is in them if the right environment is created. Opposing this view are those on the political right, who tend to share a belief in the imperfection of human nature, seeing in the individual varying degrees of weakness, irrationality, perfidy, and immorality. In the Western world, the conviction that humankind is morally imperfect is rooted in the Christian doctrine of original sin. According to this teaching, human beings are fallen creatures, alienated from the goodness of their Creator and divided against each other by selfishness. Most instructive on this topic is the work of St. Augustine (354–430), who regarded humans as invariably weak and helpless, driven by their most base passions to commit grievous wrongs and to suffer dearly for doing so. According to Augustine's dismal view of human nature, we are from conception wicked and dangerous creatures who need to be restrained by harsh laws, a strict education, and brutal punishment. Augustine accepted that life in this world is literally a "hell on earth." He knew that temporal institutions, as creations of a sinful humanity, would always be inherently flawed and could never bring happiness. But he insisted nonetheless that existing institutions, no matter how oppressive, must be respected, since they constitute the only earthly bulwark against disorder and violence. One should note that this general presumption is not specifically Christian or even religious, since it is shared by many secular and even atheist thinkers. For instance, we might include Sigmund Freud (1856–1939) in a list of those who agree with Augustine that humans are weak and dangerous beings, driven by unconscious, irrational, self-destructive desires and impulses.

The Augustinian penchant for established institutions shows up in later conservative political thinking as well, though conservatives base their views more on the intellectual imperfection of humanity rather than on its alleged moral imperfections.[3] That is, conservatives argue that the natural limitations of the human intellect make it futile, indeed dangerous, to attempt to improve or remake humankind according to any large-scale plans or dreams of a perfect society. Because human reason is fallible, conservatives say, we cannot expect to use our creative intellect alone to solve complex social problems. Instead, we should rely upon the accumulated wisdom of the past and the lessons from traditional life to guide our way.

Equality and Inequality

An equally pressing question about the essence of human beings is whether, or to what extent, they are equal. This question takes us to the heart of most of the political conflicts of the past two centuries. Since at least the French Revolution, equality or **egalitarianism** has been the rallying cry for those wishing to strive for political power. In domestic and international politics, in developed and developing countries alike, political struggles in the modern world are typically waged in the name of equality: of individuals, classes, religions, ethnic groups, sexes, regions, and so on.

Definition

EGALITARIANISM: The doctrine that advocates equal social and political rights for all citizens, regardless of class, sex, religion, ethnicity, etc. Reform-oriented liberals emphasize the need for an equality of opportunity, which guarantees to all the equal chance to compete for the social, economic, and political benefits available in society. Socialists often interpret egalitarianism to require an equality of condition, so that all goods and resources in a society would be distributed equally.

For political philosophy, the initial question to be determined is whether human beings are in essence equal or unequal. If the former, as egalitarians of all stripes presume, then the further question becomes whether one can justify the inevitable inequalities of wealth, rank, status, and power that seem to mark virtually every society. Clearly, our contemporary prejudice is toward the view that any apparent inequality is in reality a result of some kind of conventional or social inequality, which is then to be justified or condemned according to one theory or another. Yet the majority of political thinkers throughout history have simply denied that humans are equal at all. In ancient times, Aristotle and Plato (427–347 B.C.) presupposed a rank order of humankind according to one's capacity for reason. On this basis, Aristotle excluded from citizenship whole categories of humanity—for example, artisans, workers, women, and slaves—because they allegedly lacked the ability to reason for themselves. And Plato designed an elaborate theory to justify the rule of the naturally superior individual, the philosopher-king. More recently,

Nietzsche maintained that in virtually every way that matters humans are radically unequal. For this reason, Nietzsche was frustrated by the fact that we in the modern age increasingly promote the "slave" doctrine of equality and the values of the inferior "herd" over what he calls "master morality" and the noble doctrine of aristocracy. In his more optimistic moments, Nietzsche looked forward to the rise to power of a new breed of "supermen" who would reflect the highest potential for human creativity and vitality. Nietzsche's ideas about a new master race were subsequently misappropriated by apologists for Nazism and used to justify Hitler's racist and nationalist doctrine (in spite of the fact that Nietzsche specifically denounced racism and nationalism as perverted ideologies).

Historically, attitudes toward equality have been especially instructive of the divide between traditional conservatives and liberals. The traditional conservative position is nicely represented by the English thinker and statesman Edmund Burke (1729–97). He argued that humanity is naturally and hierarchically ordered. Like many conservatives, Burke held that the best government is an aristocracy, one in which the privileged orders, the high-born and well-bred, will rule wisely and for the good of the whole. Burke very much feared that the new egalitarian ethos arising from the French Revolution would undermine the political basis for order and stability, which are necessary for a good society. In contrast to Burke's aristocratic faith in a natural hierarchy, the liberal opinion is that humans are by nature free and equal creatures, equally in possession of their own natural rights (primarily, the right to preserve oneself, but also the right to individual freedom and private property). This view was heavily influenced by thinkers such as Hobbes, Locke, and Montesquieu, and was summed up by Thomas Jefferson (1743–1826) in the Declaration of Independence: "We hold these truths to be self-evident: that all men are created equal; that they are endowed by their Creator with certain inalienable Rights: that among these are Life, Liberty and the pursuit of Happiness."

As a statement of political ideals, these words stake out an inspiring egalitarian position. But remember that when they were written in 1776, and for almost a century thereafter, slavery was allowed in certain parts of America. To us today, it seems impossible to square the enslavement of some people on the basis of their skin colour with a belief in equality. Nor does it escape our attention that the Declaration and the rights it presumes are limited to "all men" and not to the female half of the population. We know also that the rights that were claimed by the American colonists were not extended to the Indigenous peoples of North America. Finally, equal rights to vote or to participate in government were not even enjoyed by all white men in the Thirteen Colonies, since those who did not own sufficient property were excluded. Clearly, the notion of the full legal equality of all human beings was not widely accepted in America until fairly recently. Of course, it was not only in the United States that such inequality based on race, sex, or property ownership was the norm. The right to vote in Canada did not become universal in principle until 1920. Even then, significant loopholes in Canadian electoral law allowed the exclusion of Native people and people of East Asian origin. The last of these limitations was not lifted until 1960, and it took the entrenchment of the Charter of Rights and Freedoms in 1982 to remove the final legal barriers to equality in Canada.

Now that virtually all of the formal and legal obstacles to equal participation have been dismantled in places such as the United States and Canada, have women, Black people, Aboriginal people, and the poor achieved full equality? Clearly, social or conventional inequality persists in many forms. Women and minorities suffer inequalities of income, political power, and social status. Moreover, there are significant disparities along class lines in these societies. What, if anything, should society or the state do to address the problem? This is a burning issue for contemporary political thought. For those on the political right, including those we today call conservatives in the North American context, the answer is typically that we should guarantee a formal equality of right and then rely on the free market to provide an equilibrium of societal benefits. That is, we should make sure that there is no legal or official discrimination allowed (for example, there should be no laws banning Black people from applying for medical school or women from running for office) and then accept that a fair system of competition will eventually produce equitable results. Beyond ensuring impartiality and nondiscrimination, conservatives say, the state should not be used to provide specific advantages for historically disadvantaged groups. Hence, contemporary conservatives tend to oppose measures such as **affirmative action** programs, which call for minorities and women to be given special consideration in employment, education, and government contracting decisions.

Definition

AFFIRMATIVE ACTION: The giving of preferential treatment to targeted groups in such areas as employment, promotion, housing, or education to redress the effects of past discrimination. Affirmative action began in America in the 1960s, focusing mainly on increasing opportunities for African-Americans. In the 1970s, it began to be used to increase the number of women in professional and managerial positions. Affirmative action is also used to promote hiring of ethnic minorities and Aboriginal people. While the bulk of reform-oriented liberals, feminists, and minorities support it, many conservatives claim that affirmative action amounts to reverse discrimination.

The proponents of contemporary **liberalism** (often called reform liberals) tend to go a step further. In addition to defending the equality of right, they promote the equality of opportunity. That is, they take seriously the notion that each individual should be equally free to pursue his or her own goals and desires, without discrimination based on race, sex, religion, or other identifiable characteristics. For this to be a reality, liberals believe, we must ensure that everyone can have an equal chance to compete fairly, on a level playing field with all others, for a share of the social and economic benefits that society has to offer. Judged by the results, contemporary liberals say, the playing field would appear still to be tilted very much in favour of certain individuals or groups (such as middle-class white men). So in the name of the equality of opportunity, the state must be used not only to protect individuals against discrimination, but also to provide fair chances and a minimum living standard for all. In this fashion, no one will be unduly disadvantaged when engaging in societal competition. Yet liberals fully expect that once equality of opportunity is assured—once there is an even playing field—then the striving individual should be able to

reap the rewards of his or her own competitive efforts. As a result of fair and free competition between individuals, liberals admit, there will be some winners and some losers. Social or conventional inequality will therefore exist in a liberal society, since some individuals will gain more because they will work harder or have more ability than others. However, this conventional inequality is justifiable, from the liberal point of view, so long as no one is denied a meaningful opportunity to compete and to be successful.

Definition

LIBERALISM: The ideology based on the paramount value of individual liberty. Liberals regard the individual as a rational creature who can use his or her intelligence to decide how best to live life and to maximize individual well-being. Liberalism assumes that all humans are free and equal by nature, and that society is a vehicle for the protection and enhancement of our natural rights. In its earlier form, often called classical liberalism, this ideology assumed a limited role for the state. In later years, reform liberals advocated a larger role for the state to guarantee equality and to help foster the full development of the individual.

It is at this point that **socialism** breaks with liberalism and insists that true egalitarianism demands more than equal opportunity or equal social and political rights. Socialism calls for material equality and the equal access to the resources of the community. It is often said, then, that while liberals are content with an equality of opportunity, socialist justice requires an actual equality of condition. For those on the moderate left (for example, social democrats), the equality of condition is more of an ideal than a practical goal. The objective is to narrow the gap as much as possible between rich and poor, gradually levelling out society's social and economic inequalities by raising the floor for those at the bottom and lowering the ceiling for those at the top. To achieve greater equality, the state has to intervene in the economy, adjusting the effects of the disparities that inevitably arise from market competition. Hence, social democrats promote a variety of redistributive measures, including steeply graduated income taxes, generous social welfare programs, and full employment policies.

> **Definition**
>
> **SOCIALISM:** The doctrine advocating economic equality of the classes and the use of government to serve the collective good of the whole society. Socialists value the collective good over the private interests of individuals, and thus emphasize cooperation over competition. Socialists support a positive role for government in the economy. They advocate public ownership of key industries, regulation of the market, redistribution of resources, and protection of fundamental social rights and freedoms. Although a general agreement about the goals of socialism exists, there is a wide variety of opinion on how best to achieve them. Social democrats insist on working within the parliamentary system and achieving socialism through democratic and evolutionary change. Communists and other more radical socialists believe in the need for total, revolutionary change, often through the violent overthrow of the existing regime.

For radical socialists and communists, however, these strategies are insufficient, since they can never provide for an absolute equality of condition. For justice to be achieved, it is argued, the fundamental inequality of classes—most importantly, the gap between the **bourgeoisie** and the workers—must be addressed at its root. Private ownership of property must therefore be abolished and replaced by public ownership of all of the means of production. Communists believe that to ensure that the inequalities resulting from market exchanges do not arise, **capitalism** has to be replaced by a planned economy, one in which central authority

> **Definition**
>
> **BOURGEOISIE:** In Marxist theory, the ruling class in capitalist society consisting of those who own the means of production, such as factories or mines. This capitalist class rules over the proletariat, or working people. In contemporary society, "bourgeois" has come to refer simply to the middle classes, those between the very wealthy and the working classes on the social scale. The term is often used in a derogatory fashion to refer to anything conventional and middle-of-the-road, as in "bourgeois values."

> **Definition**
>
> **CAPITALISM:** An economic system based on the operation of market forces and the profit motive, free of government intervention.

decides what is to be produced and to whom it will be distributed. At some later stage, perhaps, the state as a coercive instrument need no longer perform this planning function, and society will naturally organize itself according to the Marxian slogan, "From each according to his ability, to each according to his need." But at least for the intermediary period of postrevolutionary socialism, there would have to be a very strong state required to impose class equality.

Figures 5.1 and 5.2 reveal the inequalities in income in Canada. The first figure divides all Canadians into five groups ranging from poorest to richest, with the same number of people in each group. It shows how much income each of these fifths or quintiles of the population receives. The three columns for each quintile indicate, respectively, the amount of market income received, the total income received after government transfers, and the income left after taxes. Even after transfers and taxes, the lowest 20 percent of the population receives only about 7 percent of the income, and the top 20 percent receives nearly 50 percent. Another method of measuring economic inequality is in terms of net worth or wealth, as opposed to annual income. Figure 5.2 reveals, however, that those with the highest annual incomes also have the greatest wealth; most of it is held by those earning over $75 000 annually. Clearly, there are very real gaps between the rich and poor in advanced capitalist societies such as Canada.

While class inequality is a major source of injustice in the world, feminists point to gender inequality as another serious wrong. Unfortunately, political philosophers of the past did not spend much time debating this matter, since they assumed that men and women were by nature different and that their dissimilarities justified unequal gender roles. Aristotle epitomized this view when he said that "the relation of male to female is naturally that of the superior to the inferior—of the ruling to the ruled."[4] Women are justifiably excluded from politics, in Aristotle's estimation, since they are

Figure 5.1 Disparities by Income Quintile, 1998

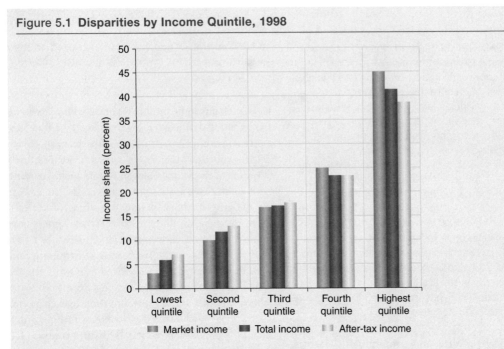

Source: Adapted from Statistics Canada, *Income in Canada,* cat. no. 75-202 (November 2001), p. 60.

Figure 5.2 Median Net Worth by Income, 1998

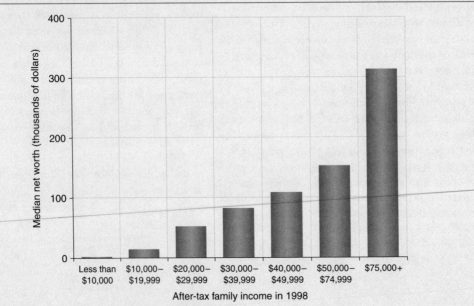

Source: Adapted from Statistics Canada, *The Assets and Debts of Canadians: An Overview of the Results of the Survey of Financial Security,* cat. no. 13-595 (March 2001), p. 10.60.

naturally unfit for rulership. In various renderings, Aristotle's position held sway among political thinkers for centuries. John Stuart Mill (1806–73) was one of the first leading philosophers to advocate the full political equality of women and to deny that there were any politically relevant differences between men and women. It is not due to nature, he said, but to social convention hardened by centuries of oppression that women are kept inferior to men. *The Subjection of Women*, published in 1869, was thought to be extremely radical in Mill's time but is now seen as a classic statement of democratic and liberal feminism. Today most people, in the West at least, agree with Mill that women should have equal rights to men. Still, disagreements rage over the sorts of public policies that might be needed to secure "real" social equality. And the nature versus convention argument is not yet finally decided. It still comes up in certain debates (e.g., over the ban on combat roles for women in the military),[5] in which one side can plausibly claim that it is not feasible to treat men and women exactly the same, since their natures are fundamentally different.

Liberty versus Authority

As the gains in the field of women's equality demonstrate, recent history has witnessed a tremendous expansion in the realm of individual liberty, with people able to expect much higher levels of personal freedom from intrusive authority than ever before. Yet almost all political thinkers agree that there is still a legitimate need for governmental authority of some kind. The exception to the rule are the proponents of **anarchism**, who hold that all hierarchical authority—be it state, church, patriarchy, or economic class—is not only unnecessary but inherently detrimental to the maximization of human potential. Anarchists believe that human beings are capable of managing their own affairs on the basis of cooperation and mutual respect. Hence, there is no need for governmental authority and state power, which anarchists fear is simply used by officials for their own purposes rather than for the good of society as a whole.

Classical liberals often share with anarchists an underlying scepticism about power, but they are not convinced that humans can do without state authority entirely. It was a liberal thinker, Lord Acton (1834–1902), who famously said that "power tends to corrupt, and absolute power corrupts absolutely." But he

did not conclude from this that there should be no state authority, that each individual should be free to do as he or she pleases. On the contrary, what Acton and others in the broad tradition of liberalism meant when they warned that power corrupts is that arbitrary power and tyranny are the likely consequences of regimes without sufficient constitutional checks and balances. The power of one individual or group needs to be held in check by countervailing powers of other individuals and groups. Moreover, individuals need to be protected, as much as possible, from arbitrary authority and from pressures to conform to the majority viewpoint.

What classical liberals tend to assume is that liberty consists essentially in the absence of coercive authority. One is free to the extent that one can live as one chooses, seeking one's own happiness, pursuing one's own self-interest, striving to fulfil one's own goals and aspirations. In economics, this translates into the principle of **laissez-faire**, the idea that the economic system works best when there is no interference from government. The virtues of this doctrine were first elaborated by the Scottish writer Adam Smith (1723–90), who argued that if government abandoned its regulatory function, leaving individuals to enter or leave economic relations as they see fit, the "invisible hand" of the market would maximize individual well-being and ensure public welfare. This principle of *laissez-faire* became the distinguishing feature of modern capitalism and remains its most sacred principle.

Definition

LAISSEZ-FAIRE: Literally "to let be" in French, this economic theory provides the intellectual foundation for the system of free-market capitalism. Following the principles of Adam Smith, proponents of *laissez-faire* believe that the economy works best when there is no government intervention. Thus, *laissez-faire* rejects state ownership or control, advocates a free market, values individualism, and promotes free trade.

Of course, even free-market liberals recognize some need for government authority. There is always a threat that unscrupulous individuals will pursue their selfish interests in ways that impinge upon the freedom of others. Consequently, the very freedoms that liberals hold most dear (i.e., the right to "life, liberty, and property") can survive only when people are defended against the violent, coercive, or fraudulent behaviour of others. Protecting people's lives and possessions by maintaining law and order is therefore a fundamental job of government. But is this all that government should do? From the classical liberal point of view, this is perhaps the *only* legitimate role for government. Such a minimalist government is often referred to as the "nightwatchman's state." That is, the state is merely a guarantor of our security and a protector of our private property. Anything beyond this limited role for government becomes a threat to liberty. But other liberals wonder, Will the nightwatchman's state serve all of us equally well? Does not freedom require more than simply being left alone to do as you please? Can people be truly free if they lack the social and economic power to exercise their freedom? These questions remind us that there are different concepts of freedom at play. The matter is not always as simple as choosing between liberty *or* authority, since a certain amount of state authority might be required to ensure that all people in society are truly free. Moreover, freedom is not just an economic issue; it encompasses a wide range of social and political relations and can be invoked to justify various individual or collective rights.

To help us clarify this issue, it is worthwhile to turn to Sir Isaiah Berlin (1909–97), who distinguishes between negative and positive concepts of freedom. The former is promoted by classical liberals and was discussed above—namely, freedom consists in the lack of external (usually governmental) restraints imposed on the individual. The latter, the concept of positive liberty, consists in there being sufficient conditions for each individual to develop to his or her full potential. A common way to express this distinction is to say that negative liberty is freedom *from*, while positive liberty is freedom *to*. Examples of negative liberty are the "fundamental freedoms" protected in **liberal democracies** through such measures as the Canadian Charter of Rights and Freedoms. Among others, negative freedoms include the freedom of religion, speech, association, and assembly, as well as such legal rights as the freedom from cruel and unusual punishment or the freedom from unlawful search and seizure. In these cases, we are free *from* the interventions by external authorities. For instance, we are free from government restrictions on where we might want to work or worship, and we are free from police officers who might

break into our homes without due cause to search for evidence against us. On the other hand, positive liberty involves the power *to* develop to the fullest of one's potential, to enjoy all opportunities for self-realization and self-fulfilment. While this might sound like a rather abstract notion, in practice positive liberty requires the removal of concrete obstacles to individual development, such as lack of adequate health care, education, social welfare, housing, and so on. If one takes seriously the right to positive liberty, one has to accept that it imposes on the state extensive obligations to provide decent conditions for all.

Not surprisingly, use of the state in the name of positive freedom is often viewed by those on the political right as a dangerous interference in private affairs. It may be fine, such critics say, to encourage everyone to realize their own goals and to achieve self-actualization, so long as they do so on their own initiative and without help from the state. The key concern here is that the pursuit of the equal right to self-realization will come at the expense of traditional liberties. In particular, since the public goods necessary to produce adequate conditions for all would have to be paid for through mandatory taxation, the pursuit of positive liberty impinges on the private right to make economic decisions for oneself in the marketplace. Without fail, fiscal conservatives will point to the deleterious consequences of high taxes and lavish public spending, which they say sap individual initiative and discourage entrepreneurial activity. For the most part, the view from the political right is that individual liberty should almost always prevail over the use of the state's authority. In particular, the free market should be allowed to organize itself, unfettered by cumbersome government control or regulation. This is at the heart of the philosophy we now call neoliberalism.

When it comes to noneconomic matters, however, the ideological dividing line over the question of liberty versus authority becomes blurry. While those on the political right, such as contemporary conservatives, usually favour less government and more individual freedom on economic matters, they do not necessarily promote this *laissez-faire* attitude when it comes to social issues. For instance, the issue of reproductive choice has become almost a litmus test of one's ideological orientation in contemporary America. For the most part, American liberals support a woman's right to choose for herself whether to have an abortion, a right which was constitutionally established by a landmark 1973 U.S. Supreme Court ruling, *Roe* v. *Wade*. American conservatives, on the contrary, overwhelmingly oppose abortion rights and make it their mission to overturn the court's decision. Likewise, North American conservatives are uncomfortable with unbridled freedom involving such matters as sexual conduct, euthanasia, drugs, homosexuality, flag burning, pornography, civil disobedience, and so on. In these cases, conservatives are usually willing to use the authority of the state to curtail the freedom of individuals to do what they want, regardless of societal values.

Liberals, on the other hand, are more likely to take their cue from John Stuart Mill when considering these matters. In his famous essay "On Liberty," Mill defended the thesis that only self-protection can justify either the state's tampering with the liberty of the individual or any personal interference with another's freedom—particularly with respect to freedom of thought and discussion. According to Mill's famous harm principle, only conduct that might do harm to others (and not action that might do harm only to oneself) is susceptible to the authority of the state or society. "In the part which merely concerns himself," Mill emphatically states, "his independence is, of right, absolute. Over himself, over his own body and mind, the individual is sovereign."[6] Mill used as an example the case of liquor prohibition, which he saw as an unwarranted infringement on liberty. In our day, we might use Mill's arguments to advocate the decriminalization of marijuana possession or to oppose censorship of sexually explicit magazines. Likewise, gambling may be one of those activities that should be free from government sanction, according to Mill's principle, even if allowing video lottery machines in public places may provoke the problem gambler into actions that are clearly harmful to himself or herself.

Mill also raised an issue that has become increasingly important in the century and half since he pondered it: the danger of the **tyranny of the majority**. Mill was alarmed that the increasing trend toward egalitarianism was placing too much power in the hands of potentially despotic majorities, who could impose their mediocre views on the minority (often through the pressure of public opinion rather than through government). The results of this situation, he argued, are a loss of individuality and freedom, a stifling social conformity, and a general levelling down to the lowest common denominator. The French writer Alexis de Tocqueville (1805–59), author of the great study *Democracy in America*, came to similar conclusions. Tocqueville found in America an impressive commitment to equality, but he was troubled by the evidence that individual liberty was often damaged by the suffocating force of public opinion. The dilemma that Mill and Tocqueville highlight is a very real one in contemporary liberal democracies. Citizens are free to pursue their own desires, to develop their own tastes, and to determine their own values and attitudes. Yet there is an amazing social and political conformity in many of these societies. This is most evident in the cultural realm—we all wear the same name brands, watch the same movies, read the same newspapers—but it is clearly present in our political lives as well, as the great bulk of the population shares a similar set of mainstream values, attitudes, perceptions, and expectations.

John Stuart Mill (1806-1873), one of the most important philosophers of liberalism.

Definition

TYRANNY OF THE MAJORITY: Abuse of the minority by the majority through excessive use of power. Many liberals believe that we have as much to fear from the oppression at the hands of unconstrained majorities as we do from the despotic rule of an all-powerful ruler. Majority tyranny was a special concern for 19th-century liberals, who distrusted the masses and feared that universal suffrage would lead to class rule of the poor over the wealthy and more refined. Today, majority tyranny is evident in the social and cultural realms, where the conformity of popular opinion runs counter to individual freedom and the right to be different. As well, ethnic and other minorities feel oppressed by the actions of majorities, who can rule through the sheer force of superior numbers.

The danger here is that societies allegedly founded upon political tolerance can become incredibly intolerant of other views or values, which are regarded as alien or otherwise perverse. At the height of the Cold War in the 1950s, for example, America was swept up in "red scare" politics, as the public became increasingly fearful of a communist threat to American liberty. Republican Senator Joseph McCarthy chaired an infamous congressional committee investigating "un-American activities." McCarthy used his position to go after anyone he deemed to be a communist sympathizer or a subversive. Using unidentified informers and passing off clearly outrageous accusations as truth, McCarthy attacked numerous individuals whose only crime was thinking thoughts that were outside of the anticommunist mainstream. His efforts left a legacy of ruined careers and broken lives. Indeed, the term *McCarthyism* is now widely used to designate the phenomenon of the political witch-hunt, characterized by sensationalist tactics and unsubstantiated accusations. Today, with the Cold War over, there are new targets for those who might exploit the public's fear of unpopular minorities. For instance, many observers are worried that the general suspicion of Islamic fundamentalism, intensified after the attack on the World Trade Center, is too easily used as an excuse to violate the rights of Muslim and Arab minorities in Western countries. In light of this danger, civil libertarians in democratic societies insist that we must redouble our efforts to protect vulnerable minorities from overly zealous majorities.

Constitutional protection and judicial intervention can sometimes be remedies.

Power and Its Use

Politics necessarily involves the use of power, and questions about power and its benefits have always been at the centre of political thinking. It should come as no surprise, from what we have seen so far, that there is a great diversity of opinion about the benefits of power. For the ancients, power was indispensable to the good life. Aristotle regarded the active exercise of political power, in common with one's fellow citizens, as the highest human activity. Plato justified power as necessary for justice, which he understood as the establishment of the proper order, both for society and the individual. For Christian thinkers, such as Thomas Aquinas (1225–74), all political authority derives from divine law. Power is sanctioned by God so that there may be peace and justice on earth. But humans use natural law (i.e., reason) to establish governments and to rule them according to their own laws. This is why the divine law is eternal and unchanging but human laws can vary and change.

BOX 5.3

WHO RULES? WHAT'S IN A NAME?

Rule of one: autocracy

Rule of the few: oligarchy

Rule of the hereditary king or queen: monarchy

Rule of the usurper of legal authority: tyranny

Rule of the best or the elite: aristocracy

Rule of the people: democracy

Rule of the wealthy: plutocracy

Rule of the masses: mobocracy

Rule of the clerics: theocracy

Rule of men: patriarchy

Rule of women: matriarchy

Rule of technical experts: technocracy

Rule of administrators: bureaucracy

Brant Parker and Johnny Hart, *The King Is a Fink.*

By permission of Johnny Hart and Creators Syndicate, Inc.

Probably the most celebrated theorist of power is Niccolò Machiavelli (1459–1527). His best-known work, *The Prince*, explains in lurid detail how a ruler should gain and maintain power. Machiavelli's ideal prince emerges from the pages of this delightfully amoral book as a ruthless yet skilful practitioner of the art of politics, one who is willing to put aside conventional morality for the sake of noble political ends. Indeed, it has become common to use the term *Machiavellianism* as a synonym for amoral political calculation and as a justification of sheer power. However, Machiavelli did not justify power for its own sake. His message was that the power of the talented ruler could serve to elevate the populace as a whole, bringing nobility and glory to the collective political enterprise. Machiavelli was a patriot who thought that bringing glory and honour to one's homeland was a noble end that justified almost any means of achieving it.

Machiavelli assumed that the best leader was a skilful prince. Many others have agreed with the notion that the "best" should rule, but they do not usually share Machiavelli's sense of what it takes to be the most excellent leader. Plato would make philosophical wisdom the sole criterion for political power, since he was convinced that knowledge equalled virtue. Nietzsche thought that the truly excellent in spirit and vitality should be free to exercise their will to power. Monarchists believe that those of royal birth and breeding should rule. Conservatives prefer aristocratic rule, which, contrary to popular belief, does not mean that the wealthy should rule (this is called *plutocracy*)

but that the truly noble should rule (*aristocracy* means literally "the rule of the best"). In fact, aristocratic thinkers often complain that newly rich entrepreneurs, who are all too often desirous of power, lack the education and sensibility required for wise rulership. Aristotle was equally dismissive of economic success as an indicator of suitability to rule. Managing a business, like running a household, was to him a banal enterprise that did not require the full range of human capabilities that have to flourish in politics. In today's capitalist liberal democracies, however, we do not usually share Aristotle's disdain for the wealthier classes. Instead, it is widely assumed that those superior in the qualities necessary to prosper in private enterprise are also superior in qualities necessary to operate a modern state. Therefore, it is often necessary for a potential candidate for high office to demonstrate his or her credentials as a competent manager by serving time in a private-sector position.

Democrats of various stripes hold simply that "the people" should rule, either directly or through their elected representatives. Debates rage among democrats about the mechanisms that are most appropriate for ensuring that the will of the people prevails. Locke and other early liberal thinkers set the groundwork for the theory that government is legitimate only if the people consent to be ruled. It is now largely assumed that full consent implies majority rule in a system of free and fair elections. For his part, Karl Marx concluded that the liberal democracies of his day were a sham, since class inequality rendered political competition meaningless.

All rule, for Marx, was rule by one class over another. In modern liberal democracies, where the capitalists own all of the means of production (the factories, mines, and so on), the working class (the proletariat) is necessarily dominated and ruled against its interests. Only when the workers rule in their own interests—a situation called the **dictatorship of the proletariat**—will power of this sort be justified, since it will serve the historical purpose of the realization of true communism and the end of class rule. Vladimir Ilyich Lenin (1870–1924), the leader of the Bolshevik Revolution, refined Marx's general thesis to make it more practical for revolutionary purposes. He feared that the working classes, left to themselves, would never become true agents of revolution. Therefore, the communist party, as the "vanguard of the proletariat," must rule autocratically, but in the name of the proletariat as a whole. The legacy of Lenin's theorizing is the one-party state, which is still in operation in Cuba, China, North Korea, and several other Third World states.

Definition

DICTATORSHIP OF THE PROLETARIAT: A Marxist concept that refers to the interim period immediately after the proletariat (the working class) has triumphed in revolutionary class war over the bourgeoisie (capitalists). The rule of the proletariat is expected to later give way to the classless society in the final stage of history, when full communism is realized.

POLITICAL IDEOLOGIES

The Political Spectrum: Right, Left, Centre

As these divergent opinions about who should rule and in whose interests demonstrate, there can be many different political views stretching across a wide range of possible ideological positions. At this stage, therefore, it might be useful to clarify some of the key concepts that are commonly used in debates about political ideas and ideologies. First, it is conventional to use the terms **right** and **left** to refer to the orientation of a person or group according to a spectrum of political positions. It is important to note, however, that these terms can be used only to designate ideas and ideologies in the modern era; they make little sense when applied to periods prior to the dawn of industrial capitalism and the rise of liberal democratic politics. So it is not very useful to speak of Plato as being on the right, for example, though it makes perfect sense to refer to Marx as a leftist thinker. Actually, many of the ideological terms we use today date from the time of the French Revolution and immediately thereafter, when people's reaction to the events of 1789 were indicative of their basic political orientation. Conservatives, like Burke, were generally opposed to the ethos of the revolution, while liberals and socialists, in varying degrees, generally approved of the spirit of the revolutionary movement.

In fact, the terms *right* and *left*, in reference to political positions, come to us from the seating arrangements in the French National Assembly of 1789, where members of the nobility, who supported the retention of substantial powers for the monarchy, were seated on the right side of the presiding officer. Seated on the left were those who wished to reduce dramatically or eliminate entirely the powers of the monarch, favouring instead a pure republic in which the elected representatives of the people would be sovereign. Apparently, those closest to the presiding officer were also moderates on this issue. Today we still say that the more conservative individuals and groups, or those who desire the least radical change to the status quo, are on the right, in contrast to the radicals on the left, who seek far-reaching and often revolutionary change, or the moderates in the centre.

The virtue of this right–left terminology is that it helps us visualize the relationships between and among

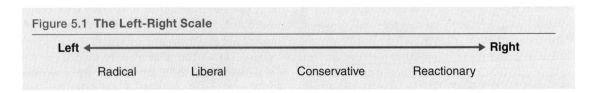

Figure 5.1 The Left-Right Scale

Left ⟵———————————————————⟶ Right

Radical   Liberal   Conservative   Reactionary

ideological perspectives. The notion of a spectrum or a continuum also helps us realize that there are overlapping values and ideals, and that being on the left or the right is very much a matter of degree. While there is more than one set of measures that can be used to place thinkers or parties along the spectrum, a popular measure of placement is attitude toward societal change, including both the degree of change deemed necessary and the direction of the change that is preferred. The key terms used here include *radical, liberal, conservative*, and *reactionary*.

On the left, radicals (anarchists, communists, socialists) tend to be discontented with the status quo and demand rapid and extensive change. The word *radical* comes from a word for root, and so in political circumstances what the radicals want to do is to get to the roots of societal injustice and, if need be, to uproot the entire economic and political system in order to remake society along more egalitarian lines. For example, radicals in capitalist societies tend to target the private ownership of the means of production as the key source of injustice. Hence, they wish to eradicate capitalism itself and replace it with some version of communal property ownership. Radicals often believe that only through violent revolutionary upheaval will society be changed in total. But not all radicals are equally keen to use revolutionary tactics or to condone violence as a strategic option for realizing radical goals. There is a range of radical beliefs, depending on the extent of change desired and the means deemed appropriate to achieve it. Hence, anarchists and communists are considered to be further to the left than socialists, and social democrats closer to the centre than others in the radical range. Radicals themselves often label their position as "progressive," since the changes they desire are forward-looking and inclusive, intended to improve the general lot of all people in society, especially the poor and disadvantaged.

We can label as liberal the more politically moderate range that covers a wide variety of different political views commonly included under the generic name of liberalism. On the left of this range one finds reform-oriented liberals who, like social democrats, favour what we just called progressive social change. That is, reform liberals share the view that government should be used to improve social and political life through various types of social planning and experimentation. As

we have already seen, reform liberals champion equality of opportunity and are willing therefore to use the state to achieve the goal of improving the lives of the less advantaged. Historically, reform liberalism was associated in the United States with proponents of President Franklin Roosevelt's New Deal legislation in the 1930s and with the civil rights movement and the "war on poverty" in the 1960s. It is also sympathetic to the goals of liberal feminism, which came to prominence in the 1970s. In Canada, and elsewhere outside of the United States, reform liberalism brings to mind the use of a mixed economy (private ownership along with some public corporations), a Keynesian approach to fiscal policy (the use of public funds to "prime the pump" of economic development), and a far-reaching **welfare state** system (characterized by old-age pensions, universal medical coverage, unemployment insurance, social assistance programs, and the like). Indeed, one will still find the term *welfare liberal* used to designate these left-of-centre liberals and to distinguish them from more business-oriented liberals. More often, however, they are simply called reform liberals, since they support extensive reforms or changes to existing institutions or practices.

Definition

WELFARE STATE: A concept that stresses the role of government as a provider and protector of individual security and well-being through the implementation of interventionist economic policies and social programs. This positive role for government stands in contrast to the minimalist government (or "nightwatchman's state") that has as its only function the protection of personal property and individual security. The welfare state is regarded as having a positive role in promoting human welfare and in shielding the individual against the economic and social consequences of unemployment, poverty, sickness, old age, disability, and so on.

More to the right within the liberal range are classical liberals (sometimes now called business liberals) who are concerned, first and foremost, with the right to private property and with the protection of individual liberty against intrusive government action. As is often noted, there is not much of a difference on economic matters between the classical liberal position and the views of those we today call conservatives. Both classical liberals and contemporary conservatives wish to "conserve" a free-market capitalist economic regime within a liberal democratic system of government. This overlap between classical liberalism and contemporary conservatism has recently caused quite a bit confusion. Again, what we call a conservative today, especially in North America, is actually a classical liberal, one who desires a limited state and a *laissez-faire* style of capitalism. Sometimes representatives of this ideology are called neoconservatives—a term that came to prominence in the 1980s as a label for the resurgence of right-wingers who challenged the values of the reform-oriented liberalism that was prominent throughout the Western world in the 1960s and 1970s. **Neoconservatism** is most often associated with Margaret Thatcher in Great Britain and Ronald Reagan in the United States, who rose to power with a promise to reduce the size and scope of government. To add further to the confusion, many social scientists now use the term **neoliberalism** to designate the system of economic policies of those who follow in the footsteps of Thatcher and Reagan by continuing to restrict public spending while encouraging global free trade. Strictly speaking, this is probably a more accurate term than *neoconservative*, since the ideas being vindicated by free-market capitalists are classical liberal notions, not traditional conservative ones.

The traditional **conservative** position dates from the backlash against the French Revolution and its promotion of liberal and egalitarian values across Europe. The true conservative is someone who does not believe in the natural equality of humankind and favours aristocracy. Conservatives place order and authority above liberty in their hierarchy of values, stressing the duties of citizenship and not just the rights of citizens. Traditional conservatives are not necessarily enamoured of the values of competitive capitalism. Instead, they have faith in the traditional ways, and trust in the notion of *noblesse oblige*—the idea that the elite of society has an obligation to help the less fortunate by ruling in the best interests of all. Today there are few (if any) such conservatives. However, conservatism as a predisposition is still very much alive. In this regard, conservatives are relatively content with the way things are, defend existing institutions against challenges from reformers, and are sceptical about our ability to improve

> ### BOX 5.4
> #### NEOLIBERALISM AND NEOCONSERVATISM
>
> **Neoliberalism** and **neoconservatism** are two terms regularly used today to refer to new trends within Western politics, especially among those on the political right. As Joyce Green explains, "neoliberalism (also known as neoclassical economics) is an economic ideology, that advocates an economic arena free of government regulation or restriction … and free of government participation in the marketplace via public ownership." Neoliberals advocate a retreat from the welfare state, and a scaling back of state commitments to programs promoting equality and social justice. In this sense, neoliberalism overlaps with neoconservatism, "a social ideology advancing a more hierarchical, patriarchal, authoritarian and inequitable society" and calling for a return to the value norms of the heterosexual family and to traditional male and female roles.
>
> **Source:** Joyce Green, "Neoliberalism and Neoonservatism," in Lorraine Code, ed., *The Encyclopedia of Feminist Theories* (New York: Routledge, 2000), p. 364.

life through social engineering. Hence, they prefer the tried and true to the new and experimental. As was discussed earlier, conservatism today is especially evident among those who decry the many "progressive" social changes that are associated with such movements as feminism, gay and lesbian rights, multiculturalism, and so on. We often refer to these people as social conservatives, since they are most concerned with preserving traditional ways and accepted social values. In contrast, fiscal conservatives are worried mainly about the growth of government and rising taxation rates, and they are indistinguishable ideologically from classical liberals. Most naturally conservative persons are relative moderates in politics. They realize that some change is inevitable, but they insist that change should be evolutionary and organic rather than revolutionary and experimental. Conservatives are comfortable with existing institutions and want primarily to hold on to those things most valued in society.

Definition

CONSERVATISM: The ideology defending the status quo against major social, economic, and political change. The classic statement of this philosophy can be found in the speeches and writing of the English statesman Edmund Burke. He argued that political order and stability will be maintained only if change is gradual and evolutionary rather than rapid and revolutionary. Today, conservatism is often used to label anyone on the political right, especially those who want to conserve the free-market capitalist system against radical demands for progressive reforms.

The political reactionary, on the other hand, is not content with the way things are and wants to return to some bygone day, real or imagined, when things were better. The level of discontent and frustration is often as high among reactionaries as it is among radicals, and they are often just as willing as their leftist colleagues to go to extremes to change things. Yet reactionaries desire changes that run in the opposite direction from those desired by radicals. Reactionaries seek retrogressive social change, one that would turn back the tide of greater egalitarianism and inclusiveness. They believe that most contemporary problems stem from an excess of democracy; they usually favour government by the elite few, preferably by military rulers. This is the ideology of the far right, and it is typically racist, xenophobic, and ultranationalist. The Nazi and fascist movements in German and Italy are examples of this sort of far-right politics. Today the reactionary position is a minority view virtually everywhere, but it has risen to significant levels in several societies. Prominent parties of the reactionary ultra-right include Jean-Marie Le Pen's National Front in France and Joerg Haider's Freedom Party in Austria. One also finds this view represented, rather less coherently, among the assorted neofascist or skinhead groups in Germany, as well as in the white supremacist or militia groups in the United States. A particularly hot topic for reactionary politicians today is the issue of immigration. Political reactionaries are often ultranationalistic and want to return to a time when each country was allegedly pure, racially and culturally. The far-right agenda normally seeks an end to foreign immigration and a denial of citizenship rights to ethnic minorities.

While the radical-to-reactionary spectrum just described can capture most of the key differences between ideologies in Western liberal democracies, it has its quirks when applied elsewhere. For instance, in the former Soviet Union or in China today, those on the political right, according to this scale, are the ones most committed to **communism**. That is, if you prefer the communist status quo and wish to conserve (or perhaps return to) the values of orthodox communism, with its highly centralized, planned economy and its dismissal of anything tinged by capitalism or Western-style political freedoms, then you would be on the right. The reformers, on the other hand, would be on the left, since

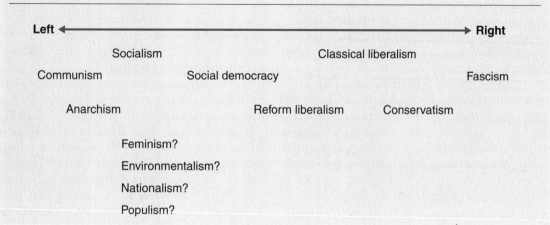

Figure 5.4 The Ideological Continuum

Left ←—————————————————————————→ Right

Socialism   Classical liberalism

Communism   Social democracy   Fascism

Anarchism   Reform liberalism   Conservatism

Feminism?

Environmentalism?

Nationalism?

Populism?

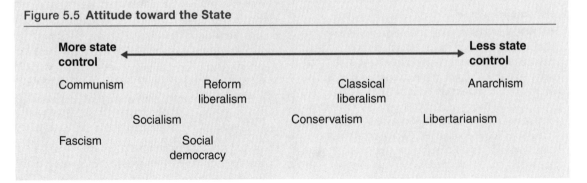

Figure 5.5 Attitude toward the State

More state control ←————————————————————————→ **Less state control**

Communism   Reform liberalism   Classical liberalism   Anarchism

Socialism   Conservatism   Libertarianism

Fascism   Social democracy

they want radical change. Yet the changes they want—the adoption of a market capitalist economy and a liberal democratic political system—are hardly what one would call radical or leftist in existing Western states.

An alternative scale for distinguishing ideologies is based strictly on one's attitude toward the use of the state as an instrument for effecting social and political policy. Today we are inclined to say that members of the political right are less comfortable with the use of state power to promote collective political purposes than are people on the left. Free-market capitalists would therefore be regarded as right-wingers, while socialists and communists would be leftists. Still, as we have already seen, there are differences of degree on each end of the spectrum. On the right, more hard-line fiscal conservatives and libertarians will oppose almost all government regulation and intervention, while more traditional conservatives will allow for a considerable degree of state control to ensure order and stability for the community as a whole. On the political left, social democrats, with their faith in a mixed economy, will be closer to the moderate centre than will those adhering to various brands of hard-line communism, which calls for total public ownership and full state control of the economy.

However, if we use attitude toward the role of the state to determine the right–left split, we have to deal with certain anomalies. First, **fascists** and communists are both, in principle, willing to use a strong state to impose their philosophical views throughout the entire society. Yet these ideologies are clearly on opposite ends of the spectrum in terms of the goals they wish to achieve. In fact, fascism first arose as an extreme reaction against socialism and communism. In particular,

fascists reject communist notions about class struggle, social equality, and internationalism. Instead, they promote racial purity, social hierarchy, and xenophobic nationalism. Likewise, libertarianism and anarchism could appear to fit on the same side of the scale, since they both stand for the maximization of individual freedom and absence of a coercive state. Yet, if one turns to the motivation for opposing state power, these ideologies clearly belong on the opposite ends of the right–left scale. Libertarianism promotes the absence of state intervention for capitalistic reasons, defending the unfettered right to acquire and enjoy personal property without interference from the community. In this regard, it is quite similar to classical liberalism or fiscal conservatism, ideologies of the political right. Take, for example, what Ronald Reagan once said about his understanding of these political terms: "If you analyze it I believe the heart and soul of conservatism is libertarianism.... The basis of conservatism is a desire for less government interference or less centralized authority or more individual freedom and this is a pretty general description also of what libertarianism is."[7] Anarchism, on the other hand, would never be allied with conservatism, nor would Ronald Reagan extol its virtues. Instead, anarchism shares many of the general values of radical socialism and communism, including the desire to free people from the constraints of the capitalist state in order to promote the collective good. Many leading anarchists, such as Mikhail Bakunin (1814–76) or Emma Goldman (1849–1940), began their political lives as communists and later broke with their comrades over the use of state power. Anarchists believe that society is natural and that humans are in essence good. There is no need to impose order, since harmony will flow naturally when free individuals participate equally in mutually beneficial decisions about how to live together in a communal environment.

Definition

FASCISM: The political system of the extreme right, based on the principles of the leader (dictator), a one-party state, nationalism, total control of social and economic activity, and arbitrary power, rather than constitutionalism. In 1922 in Italy, Benito Mussolini created the first fascist regime, emulated by Adolf Hitler in Germany. Fascist regimes also held power in Spain and Argentina. Today there are numerous neo-fascist movements advocating ultranationalist, racist, and anti-immigrant political positions.

Finally, we should note that several "isms" do not fit comfortably on the right–left spectrum at all. Nationalism, for instance, can be either a right-wing phenomenon (e.g., Nazism or today's ultranationalist parties of the right) or a left-wing movement (e.g., Quebec's radical FLQ of the 1960s). Likewise, populism—the faith in the wisdom of the common people—is neither inherently right wing nor left wing, but can complement various otherwise incompatible ideological positions. In Canada, populism of the political right expressed itself in the Alberta Social Credit Party in the 1930s, and it inspired the founders of the federal Reform Party in the 1990s. At the same time, left-wing populism was a major influence in the Co-operative Commonwealth Federation (CCF), the forerunner to today's New Democratic Party.

A prominent new ideology is environmentalism, which proudly claims to be "neither left nor right, but green." Environmentalists believe that their ideology is the only one to deny the need for humans to dominate and subdue nature. Conservatives, liberals, socialists, and communists all encourage the idea of humanity mastering nature for its own purposes, though they disagree about the ways to distribute the goods derived from the human exploitation of the environment. Environmentalists alone challenge this human-centred approach and promote an alternative, earth-centred philosophy. Likewise, **feminism** is independent of the traditional ideologies, though it can find manifestation in less radical or in more radical forms. At the most basic level, feminism assumes the equality of the sexes and

therefore decries the subjugation of women. In its less radical form (often called liberal feminism), the feminist program calls for various concrete measures aimed at producing an equality of opportunity for women—for instance, by means of affirmative action plans or pay equity legislation. In its more radical variants, feminism regards the systematic oppression of women by men through violent patriarchy as the most fundamental moral problem. From this point of view, all of the traditional ideologies are implicated, since they are inherently male-centred and therefore illegitimate. The only legitimate ideology is one that promotes a truly woman-centred approach to all things political.

The Nature and Function of Ideology

What is ideology? What does an ideology do? Ideologies are systems of thought or pictures of the world according to which we can orient ourselves politically and act accordingly. The German word *Weltanschauung* ("world-view") is sometimes used to express the total combination of ideas, values, and attitudes constituting a basic framework within which individuals understand political life and make political choices. This term, however, suggests something more personal and indefinite than the word *ideology*, which tends to refer to a coherent, specific, identifiable, and "mass" political doctrine. Put broadly, an **ideology** is a reasonably consistent system of political beliefs that aspires to explain the world, to justify certain power relationships, and to maintain or transform existing institutions. Ideologies provide a link between the world of ideas and the concrete realm of political action—for example, political parties, interest groups, mass movements, and constitutional systems.

In its philosophical aspects, the function of an ideology is to explain the key problems facing a society and to interpret key events. In this way, an ideology provides meaning for human life and history. In its policy-oriented aspects, ideology shapes the objectives and priorities of political action—it encourages the identification of specific social problems and influences the selection of the most desirable and feasible solutions. An ideology thus operates as a perceptual screen that accepts some alternatives but filters out others. Furthermore, by providing reasons for actions, ideology helps those persons holding power to gain acceptance for their deeds. Of course, ideology is also used by activists and opposition politicians who do not exercise governmental power. Ideology can challenge established authority, criticize existing policies, and offer proposals for change. Indeed, a primary function of an ideology is to mobilize human efforts behind a cause, such as ecological preservation (environmentalism) or freedom from government regulation of individual activity (libertarianism).

Ideologies are espoused by intellectuals concerned with politics—writers, teachers, politicians, journalists, lawyers, and so on. But they are necessarily mass belief systems. An ideology must be accepted by a large number of people in order to be effective. So ideological messages are formulated in a manner that can be readily understood by potential followers who do not have the ability, the interest, or the inclination to become political experts. Ideological discourse therefore seeks to simplify the inherent complexity of the world, imposing on apparent disorder a more or less systematic body of concepts and moral beliefs that can be called upon to help people make sense of the political world. In this way, ideology helps people determine how to act appropriately, how to distinguish right from wrong in political circumstances.

To a certain extent, ideology is a necessary ingredient of modern political life, since it helps individuals make their way in a complex world. In this regard, many experts follow Freud in emphasizing the psychological function of ideology as a means of equipping individuals with an appropriate set of reactions to social and political demands, in this way allowing them to cope with personal strain or anxiety. This sort of analysis would suggest that ideology is an ever-present element in political life, essential as it is to humankind's social and mental requirements.

Ideological Thought

Ideology can also be understood as a *style* of thought. Persons who think in terms of ideology tend to perceive and interpret events in the light of broad and abstract ideas, such as gender equality (feminism) or faith in the common people (populism). When we say that a particular viewpoint or line of argument is "ideological," we mean to suggest that it is based upon a general or abstract set of political principles or doctrines, rather than unique, specific, or concrete conditions. Used in

this fashion, then, ideology refers to a specific manner or style of thinking. Sometimes this will apply to patterns of thought characteristic of a whole class or group of individuals. We might say, for example, that pride in one's consumer possessions is an attribute of bourgeois ideology, since it is characteristic of the predominant ideas, values, and attitudes of the capitalist middle classes. Conversely, the principled refusal to live a life geared toward the accumulation of material wealth, on the basis that the production of unnecessary consumer goods does ecological harm, is an element of environmentalism as an ideological style.

Someone who always appears to be propagandizing in favour of a single sociopolitical program will often be called an ideologue. This term, in our society, has an unmistakably derogatory connotation. It implies that someone is narrow-minded, unduly attached to a single way of seeing the world, and given to overly simplistic explanations for complex social and political phenomena. The term is also commonly used to refer to those who voice their ideas in an uncompromising, doctrinaire manner. Political activists and people advocating fundamental changes in the existing political situation are often accused of being ideologues. For instance, it is not uncommon to hear people complain that the antiglobalization protesters who gather outside of WTO meetings are hopeless ideologues. On the other hand, leftist critics of the established order in capitalist societies are equally quick to label their opponents as ideologues.

What is often ignored by those who resort to using the term *ideologue* as a rhetorical device to undermine an opponent's intellectual or moral position is that the accusers necessarily base their own political views on grounds that are every bit as "ideological" as those they dislike. Yet so long as our political language attaches a negative connotation to the term, it will be employed as a weapon but seldom as a designation of one's own position. Few people proudly declare themselves ideologues. Yet most people obviously act ideologically when they react, either positively or negatively, to political issues or events.

As indicated in the example of the anti-WTO protesters, the charge that one is acting or thinking ideologically, rather than pragmatically, can be used quite successfully against advocates of radical change, especially those who generally lack social and economic power. Political language is not unlike other political resources in this regard—those who control it (for instance, those who own and operate major outlets of the broadcast media) will use this resource to their own advantage, in this case by branding their opponents ideologues and painting themselves and their supporters as nonideological pragmatists. The irony here is that a primary source of ideology's bad name comes from the writings of Karl Marx, the intellectual founder of revolutionary communism. To Marx, ideas and values (including ideologies) are determined by concrete material relations within society, especially class relations. When we study ideologies, we are focusing on the distorted and usually misleading reflections of real class interests. Marx also added to the debate the notion of false consciousness, which occurs when a group or class accepts an ideology that in reality is contrary to its "true"

or objective interests. Marxists use this concept to explain the fact that so many working-class individuals reject communism and instead share the ideological views of the capitalists. In this way, the workers are said to be duping themselves and helping to prop up an economic and political system that keeps them subservient.

The notion that ideology somehow hinders or obscures our ability to see the truth is a popular opinion. For instance, many commentators in the West strongly identify ideology with systems of social control, political mobilization, and manipulation—with the sort of political systems that were in place in the communist U.S.S.R., fascist Germany, and Afghanistan under the Taliban. According to this critique, ideology encourages people to abandon their reliance on individual judgment and rational choice. Instead of thinking for themselves, critics complain, ideologically minded people turn to a preordained and comprehensive vision of total societal conformity—to Marxist-Leninist doctrine, to the fascist leadership principle, to fundamentalist religion, or what have you.

It is interesting to note in this attitude, found particularly in North America, an almost blanket condemnation of states with an "official" ideology that is nonliberal in nature, since such ideology is seen to be repugnant to individual rights and freedoms. Officially sanctioned ideologies such as communism, it is said, foster an atmosphere in which individuals are discouraged from thinking freely and acting for themselves because they are indoctrinated into systems of belief rather than provided with the skills and opportunities necessary to choose for themselves. Examples easily come to mind. Chinese youth were "brainwashed" during the Cultural Revolution of 1966–76, when the Maoist government sought to restore ideological purity and combat creeping capitalism. Likewise, citizens of Islamic states are now portrayed as "fanatics" whose passions are whipped up in a frenzy of anti-Western hysteria. As valid as these concerns may be in specific circumstances, it is equally important to note the extent to which Western liberal states can privilege one ideological system over others, rendering marginal any political position that is outside of the accepted liberal democratic mainstream. Political scientists refer to **political socialization** as the process by which individuals learn about politics, establishing their individual attitudes, values, and ideals. As discussed in Chapter 4,

Karl Marx (1818-1883), the most famous philosopher of socialism.

the agents of socialization include the family, schools, religious institutions, peers, and the media—all of which serve to inculcate in the individual a given world-view or political culture that helps establish the parameters of acceptable political thinking.

The End of Ideology?

Ideology has been a very powerful force since the dawn of modernity, yet there are those who see its force waning. Indeed, commentators first suggested that political life within the major Western industrialized democracies was moving in the direction of nonideological pragmatism in the 1950s.[8] After World War II, the argument ran, economic prosperity helped to decrease the importance of historical left–right ideological cleavages throughout the Western world. The Anglo-American democracies had already been suspicious of ideology and were made more so by their exposure to the extremist ideologies of fascism and communism. Likewise, European attachment to radical politics was weakened by the shock of the consequences of ideological zealotry. Radical parties of the left and right lost supporters to the more moderate centre. Overall, the postwar industrialized world was believed to have repudiated ideology or, at a minimum, to have settled on the more moderate, pragmatic, individualistic ideologies rather than the radical, all-consuming, mass-based ideologies of the hard-line left and right.

But the 1960s—with the student protests, the race riots, the invasion of Czechoslovakia, and the escalation of the Vietnam War—were hardly a time to be talking about the end of ideology. The Cold War continued apace. The world was mythologically divided between the capitalist West (the "free world") and the communist East (the "Soviet bloc" and China), with the newly independent Third World countries providing a fertile ground for ideological competition between the two superpowers. Meanwhile, new ideologies, such as feminism and environmentalism, were coming onstream with their own versions of ideological radicalism.

As the 20th century came to a close, however, the stage was set for renewed discussion of the end-of-ideology thesis and the decline of the old left–right political animosity. The fall of communism in Russia and its former satellite states has greatly reduced the ideological disparity between East and West. Even in commu-

nist China, where state leaders remain unmoved by the democratic revolution, aspects of the capitalist system have been successfully introduced as a replacement for the failed model of Soviet-style communism, thus further reducing global ideological heterogeneity. Far-right authoritarianism has also lost some ground in places such as Latin America, Spain, and Portugal, which had remained essentially fascistic well into the 1970s. The world over, former enemies are now partners, and former pariah nations are now integrated into the international mainstream. Indeed, the degree of global integration during the past few decades—exemplified by the European Union and in free-trade agreements, such as the WTO or the NAFTA—is another indicator of increasing ideological conformity.

Certain observers, most notably American writer Francis Fukuyama, go so far as to see in this new global order "the end of history."[9] What he actually means by this provocative phrase is that we are witnessing not the end of historically significant events, but rather the end of global ideological conflict. For Fukuyama, the recent trend toward global convergence amounts to a virtual end to ideology, since the combination of a capitalist market economy and a liberal democratic political system is now the norm worldwide. Supporters of this thesis tend to regard the new world order as an unalloyed triumph for free-market capitalism, which today stands almost unchallenged.

Benjamin Barber reads the current situation somewhat differently, claiming that the post–Cold War world is characterized by a struggle between the forces of *Jihad* and McWorld.[10] Barber agrees with Fukuyama that there has been an intensification of cultural uniformity and economic integration, with nations coming together into one global network. There is, he says, one McWorld tied together by technology, ecology, information, commerce, communications, and culture. But this is not the only force in the world today. Equally powerful is what Barber calls the parochial and tribalizing force of *Jihad*, which literally means "struggle" but has come to symbolize the ethnic and religious contest of culture against culture, people against people, tribe against tribe. Barber, it is worth noting, supports neither McWorld nor *Jihad*; he says that both of these forces are essentially antidemocratic and antipolitical in nature.

Indeed, the end of the Cold War has not resulted in a net increase in democratization and peace. The breakdown of Soviet-style rule in Eastern Europe did not lead directly to increased security and prosperity for residents there, but instead ushered in a period of brutal war, with combatants divided along ethnic rather than geopolitical lines. In another disturbing trend, assorted groups on the far-right are rising in popularity within many Western societies. Extremist politics is on the rise in many other ways as well, most dangerously in the form of global terrorism. And perhaps the most obviously destabilizing ideological trend of recent years, evoked by Barber's use of the phrase *Jihad*, is the rise of extremist Islamic political movements in the Middle East, Central Asia, North Africa, and elsewhere.

This phenomenon inspired Samuel P. Huntington to argue that we have definitely moved away from old right–left ideological battles, but have entered directly into an era of clashing world civilizations, specifically involving the Western liberal democratic realm versus the non-Western, fundamentalist Islamic and Asian worlds.[11] As Huntington sees it, humanity is now divided along explosive ideological fault lines quite unlike those of Cold War days. In contrast to the old clash of right–left ideologies, where the combatants shared many of the same Western cultural assumptions but sought different paths to realize their goals, the struggle between the West and Islam, for instance, is a contest between two mutually incompatible civilizations. Though provocative, Huntington's theory fails to capture the heterogeneity of both Western and Muslim societies. For instance, it is an exaggeration to suggest that all Islamic states, or that all Muslims, share the same political values.

Moreover, even the new conflicts of the global world can be translated into disputes over fundamental political ideas. Hence, there is no end to intellectual arguments over such fundamental issues as human nature, liberty, authority, equality, power, virtue, and justice. And even though the old right–left continuum has to be readjusted in light of the decline of Soviet-style communism, it is not irrelevant to contemporary politics. As we settle into the new millennium, there are various versions of capitalism currently competing for world influence, and numerous brands of socialism have emerged out of the wreckage of communism to appeal to workers and to champion the cause of the downtrodden in countries all over the world. Within most Western-style democracies, the labels "liberal,"

"conservative," and "social democrat" are still applied to politicians and parties with the confidence that citizens will recognize these labels as designating organizations with distinctly different visions of the good society. Beyond the left–right divide, nationalism has re-emerged as an especially powerful political ideology, and it provides a strong sense of motivation for many individuals and groups. At the same time, newer ideologies—feminism, environmentalism, postmaterialism—challenge the older ones for the loyalty and trust of the people. The status quo is further upset by new configurations of older ideologies; for example, neoconservatism and populism are gaining ground among former supporters of mainstream conservatism and liberalism.

CONCLUSION

Ideology continues to play a large role in politics. Even if we do not see ourselves as ideologues, most of us have strongly held political beliefs about who should rule and what should be done by those in positions of political power. Moreover, contemporary political elites—government officials, politicians, media representatives, interest group leaders, and others active in the political process—represent ideological points of view, in spite of their frequent reluctance to be seen to do so. Ideology, then, has not come to an end—and this is probably not a bad thing. Conflicting ideologies offer us a means of understanding our society, situating ourselves in the political world, and participating in actions intended to advance our interests and those of our communities.

DISCUSSION QUESTIONS

1. **Given the nature of human beings, is it possible for all people to be united in a conflict-free society?**

2. **If human beings are equal in essence, what explains the fact that there are inequalities of rank, status, power, and wealth in virtually every society?**

3. **Should men and women always and in all ways be treated equally?**

4. In what cases are you willing to see the state interfere in society, in particular by limiting the right of individuals to live as they choose? Consider issues such as euthanasia, abortion, and pornography.

5. Are the terms *right* and *left* still relevant today?

6. How is a traditional conservative, such as Edmund Burke, different from someone we call a conservative today?

7. Is it accurate to say that only radical regimes, such as those in Nazi Germany or the communist U.S.S.R., govern ideologically?

w(w)w WEB LINKS

The Keele Guide to Political Thought and Ideology on the Internet:
http://www.keele.ac.uk/depts/por/ptbase.htm

Electronic Texts in Philosophy:
http://www.epistemelinks.com/Main/MainText.asp

Political Philosophy / Political Theory, from the University of British Columbia:
http://www.library.ubc.ca/poli/theory.html

Björn's Guide to Philosophy: The Library:
http://www.knuten.liu.se/~bjoch509/library/author_browse.html

Marxist Internet Archive:
http://www.marxists.org

Aristotle's Political Philosophy Page:
http://members.tripod.com/~batesca/aristotle.html

Peter Suber's Guide to Philosophy on the Internet:
http://www.earlham.edu/~peters/philinks.htm

Anarchy Archives:
http://dwardmac.pitzer.edu/anarchist_archives

PoliticalThought.com:
http://www.politicalthought.com

FURTHER READING

Ball, Terrence, and Richard Dagger. *Political Ideologies and the Democratic Ideal.* 4th ed. New York: Longman, 2001.

Berlin, Isaiah. *Four Essays on Liberty.* New York: Oxford University Press, 1969.

Coole, Diana. *Women in Political Theory: From Ancient Misogyny to Contemporary Feminism.* 2nd ed. Boulder, Colo.: Lynne Rienner Publishers, 1993.

Hallowell, John, and Jene M. Porter. *Political Philosophy: The Search for Humanity and Order.* Scarborough: Prentice-Hall Canada, 1997.

Kymlicka, Will. *Contemporary Political Philosophy: An Introduction.* Toronto: Oxford University Press, 2001.

Portis, Edward Bryon. *Reconstructing the Classics: Political Theory from Plato to Marx.* 2nd ed. New York: Chatham House Publishers, 1998.

Rupert, Mark. *Ideologies of Globalization: Contending Visions of a New World Order.* New York: Routledge, 2001.

Tinder, Glenn. *Political Thinking: The Perennial Questions.* 6th ed. New York: HarperCollins Publishers, 1995.

ENDNOTES

1 In formulating the question in this way, I owe a debt to Glenn Tinder, whose influential textbook (*Political Thinking: The Perennial Questions*, 6th ed. ([New York: HarperCollins, 1995]) introduces students to political philosophy by examining the great questions underlying the theory and practice of government. Students interested in exploring the full range of such questions, which is obviously beyond the scope of the present chapter, would do well to read this volume.

2 Hobbes, *Leviathan*, ed. C.B. Macpherson (Harmondsworth: Penguin English Library, 1981), chap. 13, pp. 185–86.

3   See Anthony Quinton, *The Politics of Imperfection: The Religious and Secular Traditions of Conservative Thought in England from Hooker to Oakshott* (London: Faber & Faber, 1978).

4   Aristotle, *The Politics*, trans. Ernest Barker (London: Oxford University Press, 1958), bk. I, chap. 5, para. 6.

5   For a fascinating exchange of views on this issue, see Lorry M. Fenner and Marie E. deYoung, *Women in Combat: Civic Duty or Military Liability?* (Washington, D.C.: Georgetown University Press, 2001). Fenner, a U.S. Air Force intelligence officer, calls for opening all aspects of military service to women. She contends that, historically, reasons for banning women from combat have been culturally biased. In contrast, deYoung, a former U.S. Army chaplain, argues that the different physical fitness levels of men and women would, in combat, lower morale for both sexes and put women at risk of casualty. Further, she contends that women have neither the physical nor emotional strength to endure the overall brutality of the combat experience.

6   John Stuart Mill, *On Liberty* (New York: Bobbs-Merrill, 1956), 13.

7   "Inside Ronald Reagan," *Reason*, July 1975; cited on July 18, 2002; available at http://reason.com/7507/int_reagan.shtml.

8   The best-known example of this argument is found in Daniel Bell, *The End of Ideology* (New York: Collier, 1960).

9   Francis Fukuyama, *The End of History and the Last Man* (New York: Maxwell Macmillan, 1992).

10 Benjamin R. Barber, *Jihad vs. McWorld* (New York: Ballantine, 1996).

11 Samuel P. Huntington, "The Clash of Civilizations?" *Foreign Affairs* 72(3) (summer 1993): 22–49; and *The Clash of Civilizations and the Remaking of the World Order* (New York: Simon & Shuster, 1996).

The Structure and Operation of Governments

4

Career Profile: Joanne Fowler

Joanne Fowler has an Honours B.A. in political science with specialization in public administration from the University of Waterloo. While there, she was the president of a political party campus association and coordinated a policy forum attended by students from across the province.

After receiving her B.A., she began an M.A. program at Waterloo. The program had a co-op component, and for her placement Joanne worked for the Ontario Ministry of Finance as a research assistant in labour economics. The job involved performing statistical research and analysis of labour market trends, including public policy content, options, and implications. Joanne prepared slide shows for presentations and assisted with the production of briefing notes.

Joanne left the program for a while to take a full-time position with what is now the Ministry of Community, Family and Children's Services, where she was a senior policy analyst in childcare and community services. Here, she coordinated senior management briefings and the cabinet approval process for several policy proposals. This involved writing a variety of policy materials: briefing notes, implementation guidelines, minister's speaking notes, and "Q & As". Joanne also conducted statistical analyses and worked with Legal Services to revise the Day Nurseries Act regulations.

Another aspect of her work involved developing a new administrative cost-sharing policy between the province and municipalities in this field. Joanne analyzed the financial and political impacts of several cost-sharing options and revised regulations, and she advised the deputy minister and minister on these issues. Once the policy was adopted, she developed a service planning framework for use by municipal delivery agents, conducted training sessions for regional office staff, and wrote implementation guidelines to support the implementation of decisions regarding the realignment of local services in the area of childcare. Most recently, Joanne has moved to another part of the ministry, which deals with child welfare and violence against women. She coordinated the development of a model protocol to be used between the ministry and agencies in this field, managed contracts related to training programs, and conducted evaluations of two new violence-against-women prevention programs. Meanwhile, she has re-enrolled in the co-op graduate program to complete her M.A. degree.

Chapter 6

Designing and Limiting Governments by Constitutions

Stephen Phillips

CHAPTER OBJECTIVES

After you have completed this chapter, you should be able to

- identify the main functions of constitutions
- understand the relationship between the written and unwritten rules of a constitution
- distinguish between confederal, federal, and unitary constitutions
- distinguish between parliamentary and presidential systems
- recognize the main mechanisms of constitutional change.

INTRODUCTION

For much of the past 50 years, constitutions were a neglected topic of study for political scientists, and in most states they rarely figured prominently (if at all) in national political debates. At first blush, this is hardly surprising; after all, while constitutions allocate political power to core institutions of government, such as executives, legislatures, and judiciaries, they do not state with precision the political ends to which such power is to be applied. Thus, while a constitution may assign wide powers of taxation to the national government, it does not specify how the proceeds of such taxation must be spent. Should the government provide free university tuition for qualified students or allocate more funds to

municipalities for public transport? Should it spend more money on its armed forces or increase old-age pensions? In most states, it is questions such as these, rather than questions of constitutional authority, that chiefly engage the attention of governments, political parties, pressure groups, politically attentive citizens, and the media. Moreover, for many years constitutions were thought to have no obvious effect on the policy choices of governments. Rather, such choices were presumed to hinge primarily on socioeconomic factors such as class, political culture and ideology, and the influence of organized interest groups.[1] Consequently, it is these subjects that became the principal focus of political studies, especially in the United States, while the study of constitutions was left to legal scholars.

Today there is a new interest in constitutions among political scientists, generated by two major developments. The first is a growing recognition that the design of state institutions and the allocation of power among them have an important bearing on political outcomes. In other words, what governments do, or fail to do, may be shaped to a considerable extent by their constitutional structure. This insight, developed by political scientists such as James March and

Theda Skocpol, is part of an approach to studying politics known as neoinstitutionalism.[2]

The second development sparking interest in the study of constitutions has to do with the drafting of new constitutions in many states in the past decade, such as the postcommunist states of Eastern Europe and post-apartheid South Africa. Established democracies, such as Canada, the United Kingdom, and Australia, have also undergone or debated important constitutional reforms in recent years. In addition, the continuing redesign of the European Union (EU) and its governing institutions is an ongoing exercise in constitution-making. That project, in turn, is shaping the politics of the EU's 15 member states in important ways. In short, there are sound reasons for students of politics to take a closer look at the once-neglected subject of constitutions.

WHAT IS A CONSTITUTION?

The term **constitution** has two generally accepted meanings. In its broader sense, the constitution of a state is that body of fundamental laws, rules, and practices that defines the basic structures of government, allocates power among governmental institutions, and regulates the political relationship between citizens and the state.[3] In this sense, all states have an identifiable constitution, whether they be established liberal democracies (such as Canada and the United Kingdom), communist states (such as North Korea and the People's Republic of China), or authoritarian states of various kinds (such as Nigeria, Myanmar, and Iran). In its second, narrower sense, the term *constitution* refers to a specific document or collection of documents that embody the legal rules of the constitution. Examples of such constitutional documents include the Constitution of the United States, the Basic Law of Germany, and Canada's Constitution Acts, 1867 and 1982.

In either case, constitutional rules are binding on political actors, taking precedence over nonconstitutional rules. This is made clear in Section 52 of Canada's Constitution Act, 1982, which declares the Constitution to be "the supreme law of Canada" such that any law that is inconsistent with its provisions "is, to the extent of the inconsistency, of no force or effect." Constitutions also embody norms and understandings about the appropriate exercise of political power. For example, if Canada's Governor General Adrienne Clarkson were to refuse to sign a bill duly passed by Parliament, she would assuredly be accused of acting unconstitutionally, even though, in theory, she possesses the legal authority to withhold assent to bills.

EMERGENCE OF MODERN CONSTITUTIONS

The idea that constitutions should limit the exercise of governmental power is relatively new, having been established in England in 1688, when Parliament achieved supremacy over the king, an event known as the Glorious Revolution. The principle of **constitutionalism** holds that political leaders, no matter how exalted, are bound to follow the constitution. Constitutional laws, in turn, limit government in several ways. First, by allocating power to various institutions of government, the constitution avoids an undue concentration of power in the hands of a single person or group of officeholders. After 1688, the English Constitution transferred law-making authority from the king alone to the "King-in-Parliament," meaning that laws were to be enacted with the advice and consent of the two houses of Parliament, the House of Commons and the House of Lords. Meanwhile, the power to execute laws was left to the king and his ministers, while the power to resolve disputes about the law was to be exercised by an independent judiciary.

Definition

CONSTITUTION: The body of fundamental laws, rules, and practices that defines the basic structures of government, allocates power among governmental institutions, and regulates the relationship between citizens and the state.

Definition

CONSTITUTIONALISM: The idea that the constitution should limit the state by separating powers among different branches and levels of government and protecting the rights of individuals and minorities through a bill of rights.

England's Constitution was lauded by the French political philosopher Charles Louis de Secondat, baron de la Brede et de Montesquieu, who saw in its partial separation of executive, legislative, and judicial powers an effective safeguard against tyranny. His most important work, *The Spirit of the Laws* (1748), elaborated a theory of the separation of powers that profoundly influenced the framers of the U.S. Constitution of 1787.

Constitutions may further limit government by requiring that certain procedures be followed in the making and implementing of decisions. For example, police in Canada may not ordinarily enter a private residence without a judge's warrant. Constitutions may also limit government by imposing restrictions on the content of prospective laws or executive actions through a constitutional bill of rights. Such substantive limits include the First Amendment of the U.S. Constitution, which prohibits Congress from passing laws to establish a state religion or to abridge freedom of speech. Such guarantees are designed to protect the **civil rights and liberties** of citizens.

It must be acknowledged that while all states today have a recognizable constitution, not all of them adhere to the principle of constitutionalism. Here it is useful to distinguish between two kinds that do not: nominal and façade constitutions. A nominal constitution, rather than limiting the power of the state, simply describes and legitimizes "a system of limitless, unchecked power."[4] Such a constitution would not embody the principle of constitutionalism because even the most capricious and oppressive measures of the state would always be in accordance with the constitution.[5] A façade constitution, in contrast, is one whose provisions are routinely ignored. The arbitrary arrest, torture, and extrajudicial execution of civilians that is carried out by certain regimes professing to respect the rule of law attests to the sham nature of their constitutions. The real purpose of such constitutions is to serve as window-dressing for the international community. Nevertheless, even if the constitution of a state does not accurately describe how political power is actually used in all circumstances, it may perform other functions that reveal something about the political character of the state.

FUNCTIONS OF CONSTITUTIONS

Constitutions perform a variety of functions. The most common of these functions, and the constitutional provisions associated with them, are as follows:

1. *To define the structure of major institutions of government.* Constitutions typically identify the principal offices and institutions of the state, specify who is eligible to hold office, and indicate how officeholders are to be selected—for example, by election or appointment—and for what term.

2. *To divide powers and responsibilities among the various institutions of government.* The constitutions of most states divide powers and responsibilities horizontally among the executive, legislative, and judicial branches of government. The constitutions of federal and confederal states (discussed below) also specify how powers and responsibilities are to be allocated vertically between two levels of government.

3. *To regulate relations between the citizen and the state.* Constitutions often contain rules regulating the way in which power shall be exercised by the state in relation to individual citizens or members of minority groups. These rules are usually characterized as rights and codified in a constitutional charter or bill of rights. Such rights fall into two broad categories: negative rights and positive rights. Negative rights are designed to protect the interests of individuals and minorities by restricting the scope of allowable government action. Many constitutions guarantee freedom of religion, thereby limiting the power of the state to ban or restrict unduly religious worship. Positive rights, in contrast, impose a duty on the state to provide certain benefits to citizens. For example, Canada's constitution requires the federal government to provide certain services to citizens in English and French.

4. *To serve as a political symbol.* A constitution ordinarily is expected to vest legitimacy in the state and to serve as a focus for the allegiance of its citizens. To this end, many constitutions seek to link the current constitution to values and touchstones embedded in the history of a nation or people; alternatively, they may seek to break altogether with the past and to proclaim a new political era. For example, the preamble of the Constitution of the

Republic of Ireland, adopted in 1937, pays tribute to past generations for "their heroic and unremitting struggle to regain the rightful independence of our nation."[6] The preamble of the 1954 Constitution of the People's Republic of China declared that the Communist Revolution of 1949 marked the end of "imperialism, feudalism, and bureaucratic capitalism" and the beginning of a process of social transformation leading "to the attainment of a socialist society."[7] Other constitutions emphasize order and continuity; for example, the Canadian Constitution, in its most memorable phrase, authorizes Parliament "to make laws for the Peace, Order, and Good Government of Canada."

5. *To specify a method for amending the constitution.* The procedure for amending most constitutions is more onerous than that for amending ordinary laws. Among other things, the relative difficulty of amending constitutions is designed to maintain the stability and continuity of the political order and to prevent transitory democratic majorities from abolishing too easily the constitutional rights of minorities.

TYPES OF CONSTITUTIONS

Written versus Unwritten Constitutions

A traditional basis of classifying constitutions is to distinguish between **written** and **unwritten constitutions**. A written constitution is one whose fundamental rules have been reduced to a single document or limited set of documents. An unwritten constitution, in contrast, is one whose subject matter is dispersed across a variety of statutes, court rulings, and unwritten political practices known as constitutional conventions. Though widely used, this terminology is unsatisfactory for at least two reasons. First, since the United Kingdom, New Zealand, and Israel are the only states in the world having an unwritten constitution, the overwhelming majority of constitutions cannot usefully be classified under this scheme. Second, the term *unwritten constitution* wrongly implies that most if not all of the constitutional rules of the state exist in the form of conventions. Yet much of the "unwritten" British con-

stitution exists in written form, chiefly in leading common law cases and in various acts of Parliament, such as the Bill of Rights (1689), the Act of Settlement (1701), and the Parliament Acts of 1911 and 1949. At the same time, it must be said that many of the constitutional rules of states having a written constitution exist in unwritten form.[8] It is perhaps more appropriate to distinguish between codified and uncodified constitutions. In each case, the constitution consists of both written and unwritten rules.

Definition

WRITTEN CONSTITUTION: A constitution whose fundamental provisions have been reduced to a single document or set of documents.

Definition

UNWRITTEN CONSTITUTION: A constitution whose subject matter is dispersed across a variety of statutes, court rulings, and unwritten political practices known as constitutional conventions.

As noted above, conventions are an important element of all constitutions. A **constitutional convention**, according to K.C. Wheare, is "a binding rule, a rule of behaviour accepted as obligatory by those concerned with the working of the Constitution."[9] Because these conventions are not entrenched in a constitutional document or enacted in statutory form, they lack legal status and are not enforceable by the courts. Nevertheless, they are indispensable to the operation of modern constitutions, providing "the flesh which clothes the dry bones of the law."[10] Conventions not only provide guidance where the written constitution is silent, but also specify how the legal powers set out in the written constitution are to be exercised.

Definition

CONSTITUTIONAL CONVENTION: An unwritten rule of constitutional behaviour that fills in gaps in the written constitution and conditions the exercise of legal powers under the constitution. While considered to be obligatory, they are not legally enforceable.

For example, many of the principles of parliamentary government in Canada are defined by convention, rather than by the Constitution Act, 1867. The role of the prime minister and cabinet in Canada is nowhere spelled out in the written constitution. Similarly, the Constitution Act is silent on one of the central features of parliamentary government: the obligation of the government to resign or to seek a dissolution of Parliament if it is defeated in the House of Commons on a vote of confidence. These institutions and practices were well-established conventions of British parliamentary government by the late 1700s and were well known to the Canadian politicians who drafted the British North America (BNA) Act (later called the Constitution Act, 1867) between 1864 and 1866. Accordingly, it was felt sufficient to declare in the preamble of the BNA Act Canada's desire to adopt a constitution "similar in principle to that of the United Kingdom." In this way, Canada's written constitution acknowledged and continued in force a large body of British conventions which, in any event, had been adhered to for at least 20 years by the pre-Confederation governments of Britain's North American colonies.

In addition to filling in gaps in the written constitution, conventions indicate how the legal powers of the constitution are to be exercised. For example, Section 50 of the Constitution Act, 1867, refers to the power of the governor general to dissolve the House of Commons for a general election. By convention, however, this power ordinarily is to be exercised only on the advice of the prime minister. In fact, the power of prime ministers to determine the timing of general elections (within the five-year maximum term of a Parliament) is one of the most formidable powers they have at their disposal.[11]

It should be noted that not all established political practices constitute conventions. Practices that are not generally thought to embody important constitutional principles are known as usages. Although neither conventions nor usages are legally enforceable, "there is a stronger moral obligation to follow a convention than a usage," and the breach of a convention is liable to attract louder criticism.[12] For example, in naming a chief justice of the U.S. Supreme Court, it is customary for presidents to appoint someone who has previous judicial experience. When President Eisenhower departed from this practice in 1953 by nominating Earl Warren, former Governor of California, the nomination was mildly criticized but ultimately ratified by the Senate.[13] Breach of a convention is viewed more

gravely, as proved to be the case when Franklin D. Roosevelt broke a U.S. convention limiting presidents to two terms of office by seeking (and winning) an unprecedented fourth term in 1944. Controversy about Roosevelt's breach of the term-limit convention led to its being entrenched in the U.S. Constitution in 1951 as the Twenty-Second Amendment.

Vertical Divisions of Power: Confederal, Federal, and Unitary Constitutions

Another way of classifying constitutions turns on the location of sovereignty or supreme law-making authority within the state. Here we may distinguish between three constitutional archetypes: confederal states, federal states, and unitary states.

Confederal States

A confederal state (or confederation) is one in which sovereignty is retained by numerous existing states that agree to cooperate in order to achieve certain common purposes.[14] Under a confederal constitution, the central government exercises only such powers as are delegated to it by the constituent states. That is to say, any powers transferred to the central government may be modified or revoked at any time by the subnational governments. Typically, the powers of central government are limited in number and scope. For example, the central government usually lacks the power to levy taxes and relies instead on periodic financial contributions from the constituent states. Moreover, the states may exercise a power of veto over certain decisions taken by the central government or else reserve the right to opt out of decisions with which they are unwilling to comply. Finally, states belonging to a confederation retain the right of secession.[15]

There are relatively few examples one can cite of functioning confederations today. In North America, the oldest confederal form of government is the Iroquois Confederacy, an association of various Iroquois First Nations.[16] Some confederations evolve into federations, as in the case of the 13 American states that established a confederal association under the Articles of Confederation in 1781. The chronic inability of the central government to take action in the

Figure 6.1 Confederal, Federal, and Unitary Constitutions

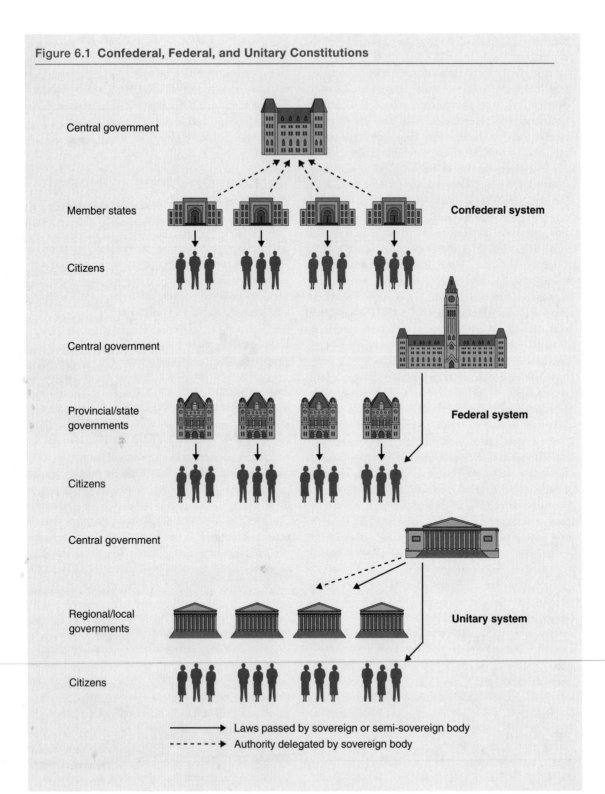

Central government

Member states · **Confederal system**

Citizens

Central government

Provincial/state governments · · · · · · · · · · **Federal system**

Citizens

Central government

Regional/local governments · · · · · · · · · · · · **Unitary system**

Citizens

→ Laws passed by sovereign or semi-sovereign body
- - - → Authority delegated by sovereign body

common interests of the states led to the drafting of a new federal constitution in 1787.

The European Union, an association of 15 sovereign states, embodies many of the characteristics of a confederation. So too does the Commonwealth of Independent States, an association of former Soviet republics established in 1991 to promote cooperation in areas of mutual interest. The confederal nature of the EU is reflected in the fact that any member state may opt out of key decisions agreed to by the others. For example, Britain, Sweden, and Denmark chose to retain their national currencies and to refrain from participating in the launching of the common EU currency, the euro, in January 2002. Similarly, in 1989, Britain's Conservative government, alone among the then 12 members of the European Community, chose to opt out of the Social Charter, a set of social and employment rights addressing such matters as the right to social assistance and equitable wages and the right to join a union.[17] Also consistent with the confederal principle is the fact that the EU does not directly tax the citizens of its member states but relies instead on revenues transferred to it by national governments. The sources and extent of these revenues are determined in multiyear agreements reached by the EU's Council of Ministers, a confederal body on which each member state has one representative.[18]

Federal States

Under a federal constitution, sovereignty is formally divided between two levels of government: a national (or central) government and a number of subnational governments. Both levels of government exercise legislative authority over the territorial units that comprise the federation, such that neither level is subordinate to the other. These territories are known variously as provinces, states, *cantons* (in Switzerland), or *Länder* (in Germany).[19]

While federal constitutions are outnumbered by unitary constitutions by a ratio of 9 to 1, it is a significant form of government nonetheless. Approximately one-half of the world's population live in federal states, and **federalism** tends to be the constitutional system of choice for geographically large countries such as Canada, Australia, Brazil, India, Russia, and the United States, as can be seen in Table 6.1.

Federal unions are formed for a variety of purposes. For small states, membership in a federation may offer the advantage of a common military defence against external threats. It may also offer economic advantages in the form of a larger internal market for trade and the building of national economic infrastructure by a central government that has superior financial resources. Both of these factors had a bearing on the decision of several of Britain's North American colonies to establish a federal union in 1867 and on that of the Australian colonies to do likewise in 1901. At the same time, federalism allows the territorial units to retain their separate identity and to continue to exercise decision-making authority over a range of local matters. Canada's adoption of a federal constitution in 1867 was, in large part, a concession made to French-

---

Table 6.1 Federations of the World

Republic of Argentina	Federal Republic of	Republic of South Africa
Commonwealth of Australia	Germany	Confederation of
Belgium	Union of India	Switzerland
Brazil	Malaysia	United Republic of Tanzania
Canada	Mexico	United Arab Emirates
Islamic Federal Republic of	Republic of Nigeria	United States of America
Comoros	Islamic Republic of Pakistan	Republic of Venezuela
	Russia	

Source: Barry Turner, ed., *The Statesman's Yearbook, 1998–99* (New York: Macmillan, 1998). Reproduced with permission of Palgrave Macmillan.

Canadian political leaders anxious to retain authority at the provincial level over matters vital to the preservation of their culture, religion, and language.

Intergovernmental Division of Powers

Under a federal form of government, the written constitution allocates authority to each level of government to pass laws in relation to particular subjects. This division of powers may be effected by enumerating separate heads of authority for the national and subnational governments. For example, the Canadian Constitution assigns to the federal Parliament the authority to pass laws in relation to such matters as national defence and marriage and divorce. It goes on to assign to the provincial legislatures, in their list of **enumerated powers**, authority over such matters as hospitals and municipal government. Other constitutions, such as those of the United States and Australia, allocate law-making power over certain subjects to the national government and declare all nonenumerated subjects to be the responsibility of the subnational governments. In either case, the constitution grants to one level of government or the other the power to deal with matters that are not clearly assigned to either level of government. These **residual powers** belong to the federal government in Canada and India and to the state governments in Germany and Switzerland.

Most of the fields of legislative authority listed in federal constitutions are to be occupied exclusively by one level of government or the other. In other words, if banking is assigned to the federal government, a provincial government may not pass laws in relation to banks. However, federal constitutions may also grant **concurrent powers**, that is, designate certain areas of jurisdiction in which both levels of government may pass laws. Where there is a conflict between a federal and a provincial law in a jointly occupied field, the Constitution specifies which law shall prevail or have paramountcy.

Responsibility for administering, enforcing, and interpreting laws does not necessarily follow the intergovernmental division of legislative powers. For example, most civil servants in Germany are employed by the *Länd* governments and are responsible for implementing both *Länd* and federal laws. In Canada, the power to enact criminal law is a federal responsibility; the provinces, however, are responsible for the administration of justice in the province, which includes the provision of police services, the handling of most criminal prosecutions, and the administration of a unitary system of courts that adjudicates disputes falling under provincial and federal jurisdiction. In the United States, in contrast, the federal principle is reflected in a dual system of state and federal courts, each of which is restricted to adjudicating cases of state law and federal law respectively.

Judicial Review

As a practical matter, no constitution divides legislative powers between the two levels of government with absolute precision. Inevitably, there is considerable functional overlap between the broad categories of federal and provincial jurisdiction. For example, in Canada, the Constitution Act, 1867, assigns responsibility for unemployment insurance to the federal Parliament (Section 91[2A]) and responsibility for education to the provincial legislatures (Section 93). Who, then, has jurisdiction to establish job training programs, involving classroom instruction, for recipients of federal Employment Insurance benefits? Similarly, does a province's jurisdiction over health and welfare allow it to apply occupational health and safety standards to industries such as national airlines, railways, and broadcasting, which are otherwise subject to federal regulation under Ottawa's power over interprovincial transportation and communications?

In federal systems, disputes of this kind typically are resolved by the courts, which are armed with the power of judicial review over law and executive action. If the courts find a particular law to be in violation of the constitutional division of powers, or in conflict with some other aspect of the written constitution, such as a bill of rights, they have the authority to declare it invalid. Germany's Basic Law explicitly establishes a Constitutional Court with the power of judicial review. In other federations, such as Canada and the United States, judicial review is not provided for in the written constitution but has come to be accepted as a legitimate power to be exercised by each country's Supreme Court.[20]

Evolution of Federal Systems

As noted above, a literal reading of the written constitution paints an incomplete and often inaccurate portrait of the real constitution of a state. This is especially true of federations, in which power may be considerably more centralized or decentralized than the written constitution would lead one to suppose. How, then, do federal constitutions evolve over time, if not by formal amendment? Three agents of change may be identified.

First, through judicial review, the courts may interpret particular fields of jurisdiction narrowly or expansively. For example, the Judicial Committee of the British Privy Council, which served as Canada's final court of appeal between 1867 and 1949, tended to give a restrictive reading to powers assigned to the federal Parliament and a comparatively wide reading to powers assigned to the provinces. In contrast, the United States Supreme Court enlarged many areas of federal jurisdiction, especially in cases decided after 1937. These divergent judicial legacies explain in part why American federalism is decidedly more centralized today than its Canadian counterpart, contrary to the intentions of each country's founders.

A second factor shaping the nature of federalism is the political legitimacy attached to the exercise of certain federal and provincial powers. In other words, is the vigorous use of certain legal powers held by one level of government or the other widely accepted as appropriate? In Canada, strong regional and provincial loyalties, overlaid by a robust defence of provincial autonomy by successive Quebec governments, has inhibited federal governments from exercising the full range of their legal powers. For example, the federal cabinet has the unrestricted legal authority to disallow any provincial law within a year of its passage.[21] However, owing to strenuous objections by the provincial premiers to the use of the disallowance power, this power has long since fallen into disuse.[22] In Australia and the United States, in contrast, there is a broader acceptance of political initiatives by the federal government.[23]

A third agent of change in federations has to do with social and economic developments and their impact on financial relations between the national and subnational governments. Federations established in the 19th century tended to assign constitutional responsibility for health and social welfare to the subnational governments. These subjects were not considered to be matters of national importance in an era in which hospitals and welfare services were largely provided by religious and private charitable institutions. By the 20th century, with the rise of the welfare state, governments began to assume responsibility for the provision of a wide array of public services and benefits. In federations, these burgeoning responsibilities often exceeded the revenue-raising capacity of the provincial or state governments, creating a problem of fiscal imbalance.

In most federations, the central government's financial resources are superior to those of the subnational governments; the national government, after all, has a broader tax base than that of any single province or state and typically has access to a wider range of tax instruments (such as customs duties, excise taxes, and corporation taxes). As a result, the problem of fiscal imbalance in federations is usually addressed through the transfer of federal funds to the subnational governments. Such transfers give the central government the potential to influence the content and administration of laws falling outside its jurisdiction. This is most obviously the case where the central government attaches conditions to funds transferred to the subnational governments. The use of such conditional grants has had the effect of centralizing power in many federations by giving the federal government leverage over the policies and programs of the subnational governments. Such grants are used extensively in the United States to ensure the compliance of state and local governments with a variety of federal laws, from civil rights legislation to environmental regulations.

Strictly speaking, conditional grants do not impair the constitutional authority of the provinces because the latter are free to decline them. Politically, however, it is difficult for the government of a province or state to refuse federal largesse; after all, its citizens have contributed to these funds through their federal taxes. Less intrusive federal fiscal transfers include unconditional grants and federal tax abatement agreements, whereby the federal government partially vacates a field of taxation jointly occupied by both levels of government in order to create additional "tax room" for the provincial or state governments. The reliance of subnational governments on fiscal transfers from the federal government is a useful benchmark for measuring the effective degree of centralization of a federation.

Intrastate Federalism

So far we have been discussing the intergovernmental division of powers. This aspect of federalism is known

Table 6.2   Conditional Grants as a Percentage of Federal Transfers to Subnational Governments in Selected Federations, 1996

Federation	Percent
United States	100.0
Switzerland	73.1
Malaysia	67.9
Germany	64.5
Australia	53.0
India	38.0
Canada	4.3*

* Canada Health and Social Transfer is treated as an unconditional grant program.

Source: Ronald L. Watts, *The Spending Power in Federal Systems: A Comparative Study* (Kingston: Institute of Intergovernmental Relations, Queen's University, 1999), p. 56. Reprinted by permission of the Institute of Intergovernmental Relations, Queen's University.

as interstate federalism. Another feature of federal systems has to do with the representation of the subnational units within the institutions of the central government. This is known as intrastate federalism, and it is typically reflected in the formal representation of states or provinces in the upper house of the national legislature. For example, in the United States Senate, each of the 50 states has two senators, who are elected to a six-year term. In Germany, the governments of each of the 16 *Länder* appoint between three and six members to the Bundesrat (or Federal Council), who act as delegates of the *Länd* governments. The *Länder* are also represented in Germany's powerful central bank, the Bundesbank.

Other forms of intrastate federalism may form part of the unwritten constitution or of established political practice. For example, in Canada, it is customary for prime ministers to ensure that their cabinet contains Members of Parliament (MPs) representing each of the 10 provinces. Similarly, when appointing judges to the Supreme Court of Canada, prime ministers strive to maintain territorial balance.[24]

The Case for and against Federalism

Leading arguments in favour of federalism include the liberal idea that federalism provides an institutional safeguard for individual liberty and minority rights by ensuring that political power is not concentrated exclusively in the hands of the central government. Indeed, by dividing political authority between two levels of government, federalism arguably acts as a second check on the potential abuse of political power, along with the constitutional separation of powers within each level of government. James Madison expressed this idea in *The Federalist Papers* as follows:

In the compound republic of America, the power surrendered by the people is first divided between two distinct governments, and then the portion allotted to each subdivided among distinct and separate departments. Hence a double security arises to the rights of the people. The different governments will control each other, at the same time that each will be controlled by itself.[25]

The interests of a national minority group are best served under a federal constitution where its members are concentrated in a particular region of the country. In that way, they may hope to have effective political influence and may even constitute a majority in the legislature and government of that region. This is the case in Canada with regard to francophones, over 80 percent of whom live in the province of Quebec. Likewise, the Sikh and Muslim populations of India constitute majorities in the states of Punjab and Kashmir respectively, while being heavily outnumbered at the national level by the majority Hindu population.

A related strength of federalism is that it permits subnational governments to adopt policies that reflect the preferences of local populations, whereas the central government may tend to reflect the interests of a dominant section of the national electorate. For example, governments of regions of the country in which conservative social values are prevalent might choose to maintain stricter liquor licensing and Sunday trading laws than those of regions in which more liberal values hold sway.

By allowing for a diversity of policies across the country in areas assigned to the subnational government, federalism may foster policy innovation. As the provinces take different approaches to addressing problems common to them all, they serve as laboratories of policy experimentation. Policies that prove to be successful and popular in one jurisdiction may then be emulated by others. For example, Saskatchewan's

CCF–NDP government pioneered Canada's first comprehensive public health insurance program in 1962 in the face of fierce opposition from the province's doctors and the Saskatchewan Liberal Party. Yet the program, once implemented, proved to be such a success that it was soon adopted by every other province and embraced by the federal government.

There are, of course, potential drawbacks to federalism. Federalism does not necessarily serve the interests of minorities that are geographically dispersed. In fact, it may be inimical to their interests by making them vulnerable to hostile local majorities. Despite the abolition of slavery in the United States in 1865, African-Americans remained subject to many forms of discrimination for decades to come. In numerous southern states, this discrimination was institutionalized in the form of racial segregation of schools and other public services and systematic efforts by state officials to thwart the registration of Black voters. In these circumstances, African-Americans applied to the national government, including the federal courts, to challenge oppressive measures in their home states.

Federalism may also give rise to intergovernmental conflicts over jurisdiction and obstruct or delay decisions requiring joint action by both levels of government. In this regard, federalism has been a factor impeding the development of social security programs.[26] On the other hand, federalism may make it equally difficult to curtail programs over which both levels of government have some say. In an era of incessant cuts to public programs in many countries, this feature of federalism is not insignificant.[27]

Finally, as an institutional response to the challenge of governing a large, culturally heterogeneous state, federalism may be a double-edged sword. Rather than merely accommodating existing territorial differences in the country, it may reinforce and even magnify them as provincial governments compete with the central government for power and prestige. "Province-building," in short, may strengthen the parochial identities of citizens at the expense of their attachment to the national political community.[28] In extreme cases, this tendency may give rise to secessionist movements.

Unitary States

Under a unitary form of government, sovereignty is vested in the central government alone. Other levels of government, such as regional, county, or municipal governments, exercise only those powers that have been delegated to them by the national government. Consequently, such powers may be modified or withdrawn as the national government sees fit. Britain, France, Japan, and New Zealand are all examples of unitary states.

By centralizing constitutional authority, a unitary state enables the national government to make decisions on a full range of matters of importance to the nation as a whole, unimpeded by the jurisdictional conflicts to which federations so often are susceptible. This capacity for decision-making at the centre offers the potential for uniformity and consistency in the design of social and economic policies. Over time, the leading role taken by the national government in public affairs may promote national unity by fostering among citizens a stronger sense of allegiance to the national political community. This was a principal aim of the Jacobin leaders of the French Revolution, as well as their heirs, who set about establishing in Paris a strong central government that would enact laws for all of France. So centralized became the French state over the following two hundred years that for a long time it was said that at any minute of any hour of the school day, the French Minister of Education knew the exact page of the national curriculum that a student in any grade should be reading!

On the other hand, an excessive centralization of authority may have undesirable consequences. The national government may be insensitive to regional differences in the country, which arise from diverse local conditions. The imposition of uniform national policies may provoke resentment and undermine the legitimacy of the national government and, ultimately, that of the constitution itself. In practice, all unitary states delegate at least some authority to subnational governments. This delegation of authority, known as **devolution**, may be broad or narrow in scope. Under administrative devolution, local authorities are responsible for delivering services and implementing policies made by the central government. Legislative devolution, also known as home rule, involves a partial transfer of law-making authority to regional governments.[29]

Unless the terms of devolution are entrenched in the written constitution, the central government may alter them by ordinary legislation. As a result, the vertical distribution of power in a unitary state may shift back and forth between periods of relative centralization and decentralization, depending on changing political conditions both locally and nationally. This point may be illustrated by reference to the politics of devolution in the United Kingdom in the past 20 years. In the 1980s, the British Conservative government of Margaret Thatcher imposed severe restrictions on local government authorities in furtherance of its program of reducing government expenditure and privatizing public services. For example, local governments were required to offer for sale government-owned council houses to their renter-occupiers and were prohibited from using the proceeds of such sales to build new public housing units. Legal restrictions were also placed on local rate (or property tax) increases in order to prevent local councils from avoiding cuts to public services made necessary by reductions in central government grants. When the Greater London Council (GLC) openly campaigned against the government's policies, the government responded by passing legislation abolishing the GLC itself.[30]

At the same time, the Conservative government was steadfastly opposed to devolving power to regional assemblies for Scotland and Wales, a long-standing demand of Scottish and Welsh nationalists and of sections of the British Labour Party. The Conservatives feared that regional devolution would open the door to a "dis–United Kingdom."

In 1997, the Labour Party, led by Tony Blair, was elected to office on a platform that included support for regional devolution and enhanced authority for local governments. After its devolution proposals were approved by voters in separate referendums held in Scotland and Wales in 1997 and in Northern Ireland in 1998, the new government proceeded to establish regional assemblies, each structured differently to reflect the unique conditions in each of the three regions. The Scottish Parliament is an example of home rule, since it has law-making powers in designated fields, including a limited power of taxation. The Welsh Assembly exemplifies administrative devolution, since it lacks the authority to pass primary legislation.[31] The Northern Ireland Assembly was established as part of a larger agreement addressing many aspects of the 30-year political conflict in Ulster. While the Assembly is intended eventually to acquire law-making authority, the British government is withholding the full transfer of such authority until stability is achieved in the power-sharing executive, which comprises members of the Protestant Unionist and Roman Catholic Nationalist parties.

Dividing Power Horizontally: Parliamentary and Presidential Government

The distinction between confederal, federal, and unitary states has to do with the vertical distribution of power between national and subnational governments. But what about the horizontal distribution of power within one level of government or the other? Here we may distinguish between parliamentary and presidential systems.

Parliamentary Systems

The parliamentary form of government, in its modern form, originated in Great Britain in the 18th century and has been widely imitated throughout the world. Countries having a parliamentary system include Canada, Australia, Germany, Japan, and Sweden. While there are important national variations in the form and function of parliamentary systems, certain essential features may be identified. First, the executive branch is divided into two components, each of which is headed by a separate officeholder. The office of head of state is held either by a monarch or an elected president. While the role of the head of state is largely ceremonial, in theory this person typically holds substantial legal powers under the constitution, including the power to sign bills into law and to appoint cabinet ministers. The second part of the parliamentary dual executive is headed by a prime minister or premier (known in Austria and Germany as the chancellor). The prime minister (PM) is appointed by the head of state, usually following a general election, and is invited to form a government by naming a cabinet. In most cases, the PM is the leader of the party having the largest number of seats in parliament. As head of government, the prime minister "advises" the head of state on the exercise of the legal powers held by the latter. Except in highly unusual circumstances, the head of state is obliged to comply with the prime minister's advice.

A second feature of parliamentary systems has to do with the relationship between the executive and the legislative branches of government. In parliamentary systems based on the British (Westminster) model, there is an overlapping of powers and personnel between the two branches, which arises from the fact that the PM and members of the cabinet simultaneously hold office in both branches. As elected members of the legislature, the PM and cabinet (usually referred to more simply as "the government") are intimately involved in parliamentary affairs, from introducing government bills to responding to questions from opposition MPs. At the same time, the PM and cabinet are responsible for discharging the executive functions of the state. As such, their duties include administering the daily operations of government departments and exercising a host of executive powers, from conducting foreign relations with other states to appointing hundreds of public officeholders, such as judges, ambassadors, senior civil servants, and the heads of various

This 1969 cartoon depicts British Prime Minister Harold Wilson "advising" the monarch on affairs of state.

Reprinted by permission of Kenneth Mahood

agencies, boards, and commissions. This intersection of the two branches of government in the PM and cabinet is known as the **fusion of powers**.

Definition

FUSION OF POWERS: In parliamentary systems, the joint exercise of legislative and executive powers by the prime minister and members of the cabinet, who simultaneously hold office in the legislative and executive branches of government.

A third feature of parliamentary systems is the doctrine of responsible government, according to which the government may hold office only as long as it maintains majority support in the legislature. If the government is defeated on a vote of confidence, it must resign or seek early elections.[32] It should be added that in most parliamentary systems, the PM exercises the power of dissolution, meaning that he or she has the discretion to request a dissolution of parliament and a general election before the government has reached the end of its term.

Political Significance of Parliamentary Government

Parliamentary systems entail an enormous concentration of power in the hands of the PM and cabinet. This is especially so in cases where the governing party has an absolute majority of seats in parliament. Moreover, political parties tend to be highly disciplined and cohesive in parliament; after all, the governing party cannot afford to lose a vote of confidence. As a result, it is customary for MPs belonging to the same party to vote as a bloc on bills and resolutions before parliament.

Parliamentary constitutions have many advantages. First, a government with a stable parliamentary majority is able to act decisively to implement its legislative program. More specifically, parliamentary governments are well equipped to adopt measures designed to serve the national interest, even if they are opposed by powerful sectional groups in the country. Indeed, disciplined parties, while disparaged by many Canadians, provide individual MPs with some measure of protection against the efforts of powerful lobby groups to influence the votes they cast in parliament.

Second, by concentrating political power in the PM and cabinet, parliamentary systems clarify political responsibility. The opposition parties in parliament hold the government to account both for its policies and its administrative competence. Equally, general elections in parliamentary systems tend to offer electors a choice between parties campaigning on national issues, rather than being a series of contests among individual candidates on local issues.

Third, the mechanism of the no-confidence vote allows for the removal of a government that has lost support in parliament. Such was the case in Britain in March 1979, when the Labour government of James Callaghan was defeated in the House of Commons and was obliged to call an early election. In Canada, a similar fate befell the Progressive Conservative government of Joe Clark in December 1979 and the Manitoba NDP government of Howard Pawley in March 1988. No less importantly, the internal rules of many parties provide for the removal of a party leader—even one who is a serving prime minister—if that leader has lost the support of his or her colleagues. In this way, Margaret Thatcher was forced to step down as British Conservative Party leader and prime minister in November 1990, to be replaced by John Major. Australian Labor Prime Minister Robert Hawke was likewise removed from office by his colleagues in December 1991 and replaced by Paul Keating.

A leading criticism of parliamentary systems is that they vest excessive power in the hands of the government. According to Lord Hailsham, a former British politician, a majority government constitutes an "elective dictatorship," since it faces no effective check on its power in parliament. This is especially true of parliamentary systems such as those of Canada and Great Britain, in which the electoral system tends to give one party an absolute majority of seats and in which the upper house of parliament lacks effective power.

Another criticism of parliamentary systems is that by engendering disciplined national parties, they leave MPs less free to represent local interests, particularly where those interests conflict with the policy of the party to which an MP belongs. MPs affiliated with the governing party are especially constrained in this regard.

Finally, parliamentary government can be unstable if no party is able to secure majority support in parliament. This has been the experience of Italy, where there have been over 50 changes of government since 1945. Governments in France during the Fourth Republic

(1946–58) were also notoriously short-lived. This condition, however, is exceptional and has more to do with such factors as the electoral system and specific design features of the parliamentary constitution. For example, governments formed under Germany's postwar constitution have been much more stable than those formed under the Constitution of the Weimar Republic (1919–33). Similarly, parliamentary government in France under the Constitution of the Fifth Republic, established in 1958, has been markedly more stable than that under the Third or Fourth Republics.

Presidential Systems

The presidential (or congressional) form of government originated in the United States in the 1780s. Although not as widely practised as its parliamentary counterpart, it has been adopted by many Central and South American states. The U.S. presidential system was designed with a view to avoiding an undue concentration of political power in any single branch of government. Consequently, there is a strict **separation of powers** among the executive, the legislature, and the judiciary. (The application of this principle to the judicial branch is discussed further in Chapter 10.)

Under a presidential system, of which the leading model is the United States, executive functions are consolidated in the president, who is both head of state and head of government (known in presidential systems as the administration). Legislative powers are assigned to the bicameral Congress, which comprises the Senate and the House of Representatives. On the relationship between the legislature and the executive, it is more accurate to say that there is a separation of personnel and a sharing, rather than a separation, of powers. For one, the president and all members of the cabinet are barred from sitting in Congress while holding executive office.[33] In addition, presidential elections are held independently from congressional elections. Thus, while the president is elected every four years, elections for the House of Representatives are held every two years; senators, meanwhile, serve six-year terms, one-third of the Senate being up for election every two years. Since both branches have fixed terms of office, the president may not dissolve Congress to hold early elections; by the same token, Congress may not remove a president in whom it no longer has confidence, except by the extraordinary procedure of impeachment.

The exercise of executive and legislative powers is subject to a complex system of **checks and balances**. Bills passed by both houses of Congress may be vetoed by the president. Congress, in turn, may override a presidential veto by a two-thirds majority vote of both houses. This sharing of legislative power by the two branches is also reflected in the joint exercise of certain executive powers—a phenomenon unknown to parliamentary systems. For example, key presidential appointments, from cabinet secretaries to federal judges to the heads of key executive agencies, must be formally confirmed by the Senate. Similarly, treaties negotiated by the president must be ratified by a minimum two-thirds majority vote of the Senate.

The Case for and against Presidential Government

Proponents of presidentialism cite various points in its favour. Among other things, it is argued that presidential executives are stable owing to their constitutionally fixed terms and to the provision made for the automatic installation of the vice president in case the president is unable to complete his or her term. At minimum, these features of presidentialism help to avoid the frequent changes of government to which parliamentary systems may be susceptible. Presidentialism also gives the legislature a more meaningful role as a law-making body by allowing members of the congress to defeat a bill sponsored by the president without automatically removing the president from office. Parliamentary executives, in contrast, too often hold the latter prospect like a hammer over the heads of MPs to cow them into supporting the government's measures. Congressional legislators therefore enjoy greater freedom from party discipline and have more scope to represent local interests. But the leading argument made in support of presidentialism is that diffusing political authority safeguards individual liberty against unreasonable encroachment by the state.

Critics of presidentialism deplore its tendency to produce deadlock between the two branches of government. This feature of presidential systems arises from the diffusion of decision-making authority and the reciprocal vetoes held by the executive and legislative branches. Moreover, being separately elected, each branch claims to have a mandate from the people and, for that reason, is often unwilling to compromise. And since the president lacks the power to dissolve the congress, there is no effective means to end the impasse. In the United States, the fragmentation of political authority arguably has helped well-funded lobby groups to block the adoption of such measures as effective gun control and universal health insurance. A related shortcoming of presidentialism is the difficulty voters face in assigning responsibility for political decisions (or political inaction) under a system of dispersed decision-making authority. This difficulty is compounded by the organizational looseness of national parties and by the tendency for congressional candidates to campaign for election on local rather than national issues.

ORIGINS OF CONSTITUTIONS

The introduction of a new constitution or the significant amendment of an existing one usually follows tumultuous and often bloody events. Such events mark the end of one chapter in the political history of a state or people and the beginning of another. Among the circumstances that give rise to new constitutions, we may count the following:

1. *Revolution.* Revolutions seek extensive political, social, and/or economic change. The American Revolution of 1774, the French Revolution of 1789, and the Bolshevik Revolution of 1917 overthrew the existing political order and ultimately produced new constitutions. More recent events include the revolutions in Eastern and Central Europe in 1989 that brought an end to Communist rule.
2. *Decolonization.* Most of the states in existence today came into being after 1945 as colonies in Asia, Africa, the Caribbean, and elsewhere gained their independence from European powers. In many cases, as in French Algeria and Portuguese Angola, independence was achieved after bloody wars of national liberation.
3. *Aftermath of war.* The defeat of a state in war may so discredit the political regime that the old constitution is scrapped and a new one adopted. In some cases, such action is driven by a new balance of domestic political forces, as occurred in 1870 when France's imminent defeat in the Franco-

Prussian War led to the downfall of the Second Empire and the establishment of the Third Republic. Similarly, Germany's defeat in World War I brought an end to the authoritarian Prussian-dominated Second Reich and led to the founding of the Weimar Republic in 1919, based on a liberal democratic constitution. In other cases, such as in Japan and in Germany following World War II, a new constitution is adopted by the defeated state at the behest of foreign military occupiers. The partitioning of Germany in 1945 into separate zones of occupation led in 1949 to the founding of two states: the Federal Republic (West Germany), under a liberal democratic constitution, and the German Democratic Republic (East Germany) under a Soviet-style communist constitution. Following the collapse of Soviet power in 1989–90, the two Germanys were reunited under the constitution of the Federal Republic.

4. *Secession.* Another occasion for the drafting of new constitutions is the breakup of a state following the secession of one or more of its constituent regions. In 1971, an uprising in East Pakistan against rule by West Pakistan led ultimately to East Pakistan's secession and the founding of the new state of Bangladesh. A more peaceable breakup occurred in Czechoslovakia in 1993, resulting in the establishment of two new states, the Czech Republic and Slovakia. Attempted secessions may also give rise to constitutional change. A case in point is the defeat in the U.S. Civil War of the Confederate States of America, which had attempted to secede from the United States. The postwar (or Reconstruction) period saw passage of the so-called Civil War amendments to the U.S. Constitution, which outlawed slavery and extended to the state governments the provisions of the U.S. Bill of Rights. In Canada, secessionist pressures in Quebec have generated several rounds of intensive constitutional debate. When Quebec voters rejected secession in a referendum held in May 1980, the federal government sought to weaken the appeal of separatism by implementing a controversial package of amendments to the Canadian constitution, key elements of which included the Charter of Rights and Freedoms and a domestic amending formula.

Not surprisingly, the circumstances in which new constitutions are adopted have a major influence on their content. The United States Constitution, for example, affirms the ideals of liberal constitutionalism that were beginning to gain ground in Europe in the late 18th century. However, so thorough was their repudiation of monarchy that the drafters of the U.S. Constitution went much further in restricting and diffusing governmental power than most other liberal democracies have thought necessary or desirable. As Harold Laski observed, "The American system, in its ultimate foundations, is built on a belief in weak government."[34]

Many national constitutions reflect an intention to remedy the perceived defects of past constitutions. Examples of such reactive constitutions include the West German Constitution of 1949 and the 1958 Constitution of France's Fifth Republic. West Germany's Constitution, known as the Basic Law, was drafted with a view to addressing the shortcomings of the Weimar Constitution of 1919 and preventing a recurrence of political extremism, which had preceded the rise to power of the Nazis. It was thought, for example, that one source of political instability in Weimar Germany was the ease with which parliament could defeat a government on a vote of no-confidence. Under the Basic Law, therefore, the Bundestag (German Parliament) may remove the chancellor only on a constructive vote of no-confidence. This requires the opposition parties simultaneously to remove the chancellor and to install his successor, a more difficult undertaking than merely bringing down the government. The Basic Law also authorizes the Federal Constitutional Court to ban political parties that seek to undermine democratic institutions.[35]

France's Constitution of 1958 reflects the accumulated experience of the many constitutions adopted and discarded since the French Revolution. The Constitution of the Fifth Republic established a mixed presidential–parliamentary system in which executive power is divided between a directly elected president and a prime minister and cabinet (who are responsible to Parliament). It is designed to avoid an excessive concentration of executive power in one person (a tendency known in France as Bonapartism) and an excessive diffusion of power among political parties and factions in the National Assembly.

CONSTITUTIONAL CHANGE

How does a constitution change over time, short of being replaced by an entirely new constitution? Under conditions of relative political stability, there are three principal mechanisms of constitutional change: evolving usages and conventions, judicial review, and formal amendment.

President Charles de Gaulle, addressing the people of France at the Place de la République on September 4, 1958, urges a yes vote for the draft Constitution of the Fifth Republic. The constitution was overwhelmingly approved in a referendum held three weeks later. The initials RF stand for République Française.

AFP

Usages and Conventions

Since all constitutions consist of both written and unwritten components, changes in the latter may transform a constitution in significant ways. For example, the role and powers of the president under France's Fifth Republic were powerfully shaped by the two longest-serving occupants of the office, Charles de Gaulle (in office from 1958 to 1969) and François Mitterrand (in office from 1981 to 1995). As president, de Gaulle established the pre-eminence of the presidency, even in areas which the written constitution appeared to assign to the prime minister and government. De Gaulle was able to enlarge the scope of presidential power as long as his political allies in Parliament commanded majority support and he was free to appoint prime ministers who would defer to him. In 1986, a Socialist president, François Mitterrand, was forced to appoint a Conservative prime minister and government when the Left lost its majority in the National Assembly. It was unclear whether the constitution could accommodate such a bifurcation of political authority; some even speculated that Mitterrand would resign and force early presidential elections. Instead, a *modus vivendi* was reached between the president and prime minister under which the former retained paramount responsibility for foreign affairs while the latter took responsibility for most aspects of domestic policy. This pattern, once established, guided subsequent "cohabitations" in the 1990s.[36]

Judicial Review

Another means by which constitutions may evolve is judicial review. Through judicial review, the words of the written constitution may be reinterpreted by the courts to reflect changing times and circumstances. This function of judicial review was memorably captured in 1930 by Britain's Lord Chancellor, Lord Sankey, who described Canada's constitution as "a living tree, capable of growth and expansion within its natural limits."[37] The particular case before the court had to do with whether women were "qualified persons" within the meaning of the British North America Act and thereby eligible for appointment to the Canadian Senate. The Supreme Court of Canada had ruled that women were not qualified persons for this purpose since the act, drafted in 1867—decades before

women acquired the right to vote—refers to Members of Parliament in masculine terms only. In overruling that judgment, the Judicial Committee of the British Privy Council said that constitutions should be interpreted in the light of contemporary circumstances rather than being frozen in time. This view is not universally accepted. For example, in the United States some conservative jurists contend that the courts should interpret the Constitution strictly in accordance with the "original intent" of its 18th-century drafters.

Constitutional Amendment

If the constitution is a framework of fundamental laws of the state, it follows that it should not be easily amendable. After all, it would be disruptive and upsetting if the rules of a hockey game could be amended by the home team in the middle of the third period, or if the bylaws of a students' council were fundamentally changed every couple of weeks. Nevertheless, there are occasions when a constitutional amendment is thought to be necessary. In most states, the constitution prescribes a special procedure for its own amendment, a procedure that requires a higher threshold of support than is required for amendments to ordinary laws. Even so, not all **amending formulas** are equally onerous; some are relatively flexible while others are relatively rigid.

Not surprisingly, the most **flexible** amending procedures are found in those states that have unwritten constitutions. Britain's constitution, for example, may be amended through ordinary legislation. Unitary states having a written constitution usually specify the need for an extraordinary parliamentary majority for constitutional amendments. For example, Article 73 of Japan's Constitution requires that proposed amendments be approved by at least two-thirds of the membership of both houses of the Diet (the Japanese Parliament).

Amending formulas employed in federal systems are among the most **rigid** because of the requirement to secure agreement both at the national level of government and among some combination of the states or provinces. For example, the United States Constitution requires that constitutional amendments be approved by two-thirds majorities of both houses of Congress and ratified by three-quarters of the states. Since the ratification of the first 10 amendments to the U.S.

Constitution in 1791 (known collectively as the Bill of Rights), only 17 amendments have been ratified.

Until 1982, the principal component of Canada's written Constitution was the British North America Act. Since it was a British statute, most parts of it could be amended only by the U.K. Parliament; but in practice, the British willingly enacted amendments requested by the Canadian federal government. Within Canada, a constitutional convention developed to the effect that the consent of a substantial number of provinces was required before the federal government could legitimately request amendments affecting the fundamental interests of the provinces. In 1982, with the patriation of its constitution, Canada acquired a revised Constitution, which included a domestic amending formula that codified the requirement for provincial ratification of key amendments.

BOX 6.1

EXCERPTS FROM PART V OF THE CONSTITUTION ACT, 1982: PROCEDURE FOR AMENDING CONSTITUTION OF CANADA

38. (1) An amendment to the Constitution of Canada may be made by proclamation issued by the Governor General under the Great Seal of Canada where so authorized by

(a) resolutions of the Senate and House of Commons; and

(b) resolutions of the legislative assemblies of at least two-thirds of the provinces that have, in the aggregate ... at least fifty per cent of the population of all the provinces.

(2) An amendment made under subsection (1) that derogates from the legislative powers, the proprietary rights or any other rights or privileges of the legislature or government of a province shall require a resolution supported by a majority of the members of each of the Senate, the House of Commons and the legislative assemblies required under subsection (1).

(3) An amendment referred to in subsection (2) shall not have effect in a province the legislative assembly of which has expressed its dissent thereto by resolution supported by a majority of its members prior to the issue of the proclamation to which the amendment relates unless that legislative assembly, subsequently, by resolution supported by a majority of its members, revokes its dissent and authorizes the amendment.

39. (2) A proclamation shall not be issued under subsection 38(1) after the expiration of three years from the adoption of the resolution initiating the amendment procedure thereunder.

40. Where an amendment is made under subsection 38(1) that transfers provincial legislative powers relating to education or other cultural matters from provincial legislatures to Parliament, Canada shall provide reasonable compensation to any province to which the amendment does not apply.

41. An amendment to the Constitution of Canada in relation to the following matters may be made ... only where authorized by resolutions of the Senate and House of Commons and of the legislative assembly of each province:

(a) the office of the Queen, the Governor General and the Lieutenant Governor of a province;

(b) the right of a province to a number of members in the House of Commons not less than the number of Senators by which the province is entitled to be represented at the time this Part comes into force;

(c) subject to Section 43, the use of the English or the French language;

(d) the composition of the Supreme Court of Canada; and

(e) an amendment to this Part....

42. (1) An amendment to the Constitution of Canada in relation to the following matters may be made only in accordance with subsection 38(1):

(a) the principle of proportionate representation of the provinces in the House of Commons prescribed by the Constitution of Canada;

(b) the powers of the Senate and the method of selecting Senators;

(c) the number of members by which a province is entitled to be represented in the Senate and the residence qualifications of Senators;

(d) subject to paragraph 41(d), the Supreme Court of Canada;

(e) the extension of existing provinces into the territories; and

(f) notwithstanding any other law or practice, the establishment of new provinces.

43. An amendment to the Constitution of Canada in relation to any provision that applies to one or more, but not all, provinces, including

(a) any alteration to boundaries between provinces, and

(b) any amendment to any provision that relates to the use of the English or the French language within a province,

may be made ... only where so authorized by resolutions of the Senate and House of Commons and of the legislative assembly of each province to which the amendment applies.

44. Subject to sections 41 and 42, Parliament may exclusively make laws amending the Constitution of Canada in relation to the executive government of Canada or the Senate and House of Commons.

45. Subject to section 41, the legislature of each province may exclusively make laws amending the constitution of the province....

47. (1) An amendment to the Constitution of Canada made by proclamation under section 38, 41, 42, or 43 may be made without a resolution of the Senate... if, within one hundred and eighty days after the adoption by the House of Commons of a resolution ... the Senate has not adopted such a resolution and if, at any time after the expiration of that period, the House of Commons again adopts the resolution.

A feature of the constitutional amending formula of some states is the requirement that amendments be ratified by citizens in a national referendum. For example, one of the two methods of amendment set out in France's Constitution of 1958 states that a proposed amendment, having been approved by both houses of Parliament, must be ratified by referendum. This procedure was employed most recently in September 2000 to reduce the term of the president from seven years to five.[38] Australia's constitution requires amendments that have been approved by Parliament to be ratified by a national majority of voters; that national majority, in turn, must consist of majority votes in at least four of the six Australian states. In November 1999, a proposal was submitted to Australian voters to establish a republic by replacing the queen with an Australian head of state. The amendment was rejected by 55 percent of voters on a national basis and defeated in all six states.[39]

Referendums are sometimes used to establish the legitimacy of controversial constitutional proposals, even where there is no constitutional requirement for a referendum. As discussed earlier, the recent devolution measures in the United Kingdom were adopted by the British Parliament only after having been approved by voters in separate referendums held in Scotland, Wales, and Northern Ireland. Though not legally binding, the national referendum held in Canada in October 1992 on a package of constitutional amendments known as the Charlottetown Accord effectively sealed its fate when the accord was decisively rejected by voters.

The Politics of Constitutional Amendment

Formal constitutional amendment in most states is not as significant an agent of constitutional change as judicial review or evolving constitutional conventions. In many states this has to do, at least in part, with the rigidity of the amending formula. A mere fraction of the thousands of proposed amendments to the U.S. Constitution has made it past the first hurdle—that of approval by Congress—while less than 20 percent of the amendments approved by the Australian Parliament since 1906 have been ratified in national referendums.[40] However, the difficulty of amending a constitution in democratic states also has to do with the fiercely contested nature of constitutional politics. After all, the stakes involved in constitutional change are often higher than those involved in the passage of ordinary legislation. Whereas a controversial law may be repealed, or an unpopular government defeated at the polls, a constitutional amendment, once adopted, is considerably more difficult to undo. Groups opposing an amendment, therefore, have a powerful incentive to campaign vigorously against it, knowing that the threshold of support needed to defeat an amendment is significantly lower than that required to reverse it once it has been ratified.

Constitutional politics also tend to arouse passions when a proposed amendment seeks to enshrine values in the constitution that are not firmly embedded or widely held within the national political culture. This was evident in Canada in the 1980s and early 1990s, when Quebec's desire for constitutional recognition as a "distinct society" was fiercely resisted by many English-speaking Canadians, who took the view that all provinces should have equal status under the Constitution. Antipathy to the distinct society clause included in the Charlottetown Accord was one of the factors contributing to the accord's defeat in the 1992 constitutional referendum.

Sometimes governments seek to entrench particular social or economic policies in the constitution so as to put such policies beyond the reach of governments of a different political stripe that may be elected in the future. For example, following the Portuguese Revolution of 1974, the left-wing provisional government proceeded to nationalize key industries and large land holdings. A new constitution, adopted in 1976, declared Portugal to be in "transition to socialism" and referred to the property nationalized since the revolution as "irreversible conquests of the working classes."[41] In the 1980s, a centre-right majority government was elected on a program that included the privatization of some state-owned industries. However, lacking the two-thirds majority in Parliament necessary to amend the constitution, the government was unable to implement these promises. It was finally able to act in 1989, when the opposition Socialist Party agreed to the necessary constitutional amendments.

Of course, conservative parties also seek the constitutional entrenchment of elements of their social and economic programs. For example, right-wing Republicans in the United States have long favoured an amendment to the Constitution that would require the federal government to maintain a balanced budget. Similarly, in 1980–81, Progressive Conservative MPs advocated the entrenchment of a property rights provision in the proposed Canadian Charter of Rights and Freedoms, to better protect the economic interests of private property owners. The Liberal government ultimately rejected inclusion of such a provision in response to opposition from New Democrat MPs, who feared that a property rights clause would be used by corporations to challenge legitimate forms of economic regulation.[42]

Nowadays, private property rights increasingly are codified in international trade and investment agreements, such as the North American Free Trade Agreement (NAFTA), and the General Agreement on Trade in Services (GATS), and in the rulings of international bodies such as the World Trade Organization (WTO). Through such agreements, states undertake to refrain from enacting laws that may be construed as interfering with international trade and investment. Are the constraints imposed on governments by these agreements analogous to constitutional limitations? Whose interests do they protect? These issues are explored in more depth in Chapter 17.

CONCLUSION

This chapter discussed the origins of modern constitutions, outlined their major political functions, and examined the relationship between written and unwritten elements of constitutions. It then described and assessed the principal types of constitutions—confederal, federal, and unitary—that allocate power on a territorial basis. The chapter also compared parliamentary and presidential systems and concluded with an examination of the major processes of constitutional change. It demonstrated that constitutions, as well as the government institutions they authorize, are an indispensable part of the larger subject of politics. In the next four chapters, we take a closer look at the core institutions of government.

DISCUSSION QUESTIONS

1. In what circumstances is federalism likely to preserve the unity of a territorially diverse state? In what circumstances is it likely to exacerbate territorial differences?

2. What is the best method for amending a constitution? Should the method used to amend the constitution of a unitary state differ from that used to amend the constitution of a federal state? Explain.

3. In your opinion, which is the superior constitutional system: a parliamentary system or a presidential system? Explain.

4. How much detail should a written constitution provide with regard to each of the following matters?

a) the structure of government institutions
b) the values and principles on which the state is based
c) the rights of citizens vis-à-vis the state
d) social and economic policies

5. Is constitutional monarchy a legitimate institution for modern parliamentary systems? If not, how should the head of state be chosen under a system of parliamentary government?

6. Are the interests of minorities better protected under federalism (or a decentralized unitary system) than under a centralized unitary state? Does the existence of a constitutionally entrenched bill of rights make a difference to your answer?

7. Which pose a greater threat to the freedom, security, and well-being of citizens today: governments or global corporations? Should constitutions in the 21st century be as preoccupied as those of the 19th and 20th centuries with restricting the power of governments?

wⓦw WEB LINKS

The International Constitutional Law Project:
http://www.uni-wuerzburg.de/law

Privy Council Office: Intergovernmental Affairs:
http://www.pco-bcp.gc.ca/aia

Inter-Parliamentary Union:
http://www.ipu.org

Institute of Intergovernmental Relations, Queen's University:
http://qsilver.queensu.ca/iigr

Centre for Constitutional Studies, University of Alberta:
http://www.law.ualberta.ca/centres/ccs

FURTHER READING

Bagehot, Walter. *The English Constitution.* Cornell: Cornell University Press, 1966.

Banting, Keith G., and Richard Simeon. *Redesigning the State: The Politics of Constitutional Change in*

Industrial Nations. Toronto: University of Toronto Press, 1985.

Bogdanor, Vernon, ed. *Constitutions in Democratic Politics.* Aldershot: Gower, 1988.

Heard, Andrew. *Canadian Constitutional Conventions: The Marriage of Law and Politics.* Toronto: Oxford University Press, 1991.

Lijphart, Arend, ed. *Parliamentary versus Presidential Government.* Oxford: Oxford University Press, 1992.

Shugart, Matthew Soberg, and John M. Carey. *Presidents and Assemblies: Constitutional Design and Electoral Dynamics.* Cambridge: Cambridge University Press, 1992.

Vile, M.J.C. *Constitutionalism and the Separation of Powers.* Oxford: Clarendon Press, 1967.

Watts, Ronald L. *Comparing Federal Systems.* 2nd ed. Montreal and Kingston: McGill-Queen's University Press, 1999.

ENDNOTES

1   Vernon Bogdanor, "Introduction," in Vernon Bogdanor, ed., *Constitutions in Democratic Politics* (Aldershot: Gower, 1988).

2   See Peter B. Evans, Dietrich Rueschmeyer, and Theda Skocpol, eds., *Bringing the State Back In* (Cambridge: Cambridge University Press, 1985); James G. March and Johan P. Olsen, *Rediscovering Institutions* (New York: Free Press, 1989); R. Kent Weaver and Bert A. Rockman, *Do Institutions Matter? Government Capabilities in the United States and Abroad* (Washington, D.C.: Brookings Institution, 1993).

3   S.E. Finer, ed., *Five Constitutions* (Harmondsworth: Penguin, 1979), p. 15.

4   Giovanni Sartori, "Constitutionalism: A Preliminary Discussion," *American Political Science Review* 56 (December 1962): 853–64.

5   From this point of view, a constitution that vested all executive, legislative, and judicial powers in an elected assembly would violate the principle of constitutionalism no less than one that vested all political power in an absolute monarch.

6   Cited in Ivo D. Duchacek, *Power Maps: Comparative Politics of Constitutions* (Santa Barbara: American Bibliographical Center, 1973), p. 18.

7   Ibid., p. 23.

8   K.C. Wheare, *Modern Constitutions*, 2nd ed. (London: Oxford University Press, 1966), p. 15.

9   Ibid., p. 122.

10   W. Ivor Jennings, *The Law and the Constitution*, 5th ed. (London: University of London Press, 1959), p. 81.

11   Ordinarily, the governor general may not refuse a prime minister's request for a dissolution. This is not to say that in appropriate circumstances the governor general would not be justified in exercising his or her prerogative to deny such a request or even to dismiss the PM. See Eugene Forsey, *Freedom and Order: Collected Essays* (Toronto: McClelland and Stewart, 1974).

12   Peter W. Hogg, *Constitutional Law of Canada*, 3rd ed. (Toronto: Carswell, 1992), p. 22.

13   The most sustained criticism of the appointment in the Senate Judiciary Committee came from southern Democrats displeased with what they took to be Warren's excessively liberal views and from a North Dakota senator who insisted that the appointment be filled by someone from his home state. Henry J. Abraham, *Justices and Presidents* (New York: Oxford University Press, 1992), pp. 257–58.

14   While Canada styles itself as a confederation, it is more accurately classified as a federation. The error stems from the fact that in the 19th century the terms *confederation* and *federation* were often used interchangeably. For example, Switzerland continued to style itself as a confederation after adopting a federal constitution in 1848.

15 Karl W. Deutsch, *Politics and Government: How People Decide Their Fate* (Boston: Houghton Mifflin, 1970), pp. 181–82.

16 Donald S. Lutz, "The Iroquois Confederation Constitution: An Analysis," *Publius* 28 (1998): 99–127.

17 Peter Coffey, *The Future of Europe* (Cheltenham: Edward Elgar, 1995), p. 129. Britain opted into the Social Charter (subject to certain conditions) following the election of a Labour government in 1997.

18 Ronald L. Watts, *The Spending Power in Federal Systems: A Comparative Study* (Kingston: Institute of Intergovernmental Relations, Queen's University, 1999), pp. 40–46.

19 Part of the land base of the federation may be under the exclusive authority of the central government. Examples include the Canadian federal government's authority over the country's three northern territories (Yukon, the Northwest Territories, and Nunavut) and the Australian Commonwealth government's authority over the Northern Territory, the Australian Capital Territory of Canberra, and the various island territories.

20 The U.S. Supreme Court asserted its authority to review the constitutionality of acts of the federal executive in 1800 in the case of *Marbury v. Madison*, [1805] 5 U.S. 137 (1 Cranch). On the origins of judicial review in Canada, see B.L. Strayer, *The Canadian Constitution and the Courts*, 3rd ed. (Toronto: Butterworths, 1988).

21 See Sections 56 and 90 of the Constitution Act, 1867.

22 The last time the disallowance power was used was in 1943, when the federal cabinet disallowed legislation relating to banking and currency passed by the Social Credit government of Alberta.

23 See Peter H. Russell, "The Supreme Court and Federal–Provincial Relations: The Political Use of Legal Resources," in R.D. Olling and M.W. Westmacott, eds., *Perspectives on Canadian Federalism* (Scarborough: Prentice-Hall, 1988).

24 The Supreme Court Act stipulates that at least one-third of the nine-person Court shall be members of the Bar of Quebec. This requirement ensures that there is a sufficient number of judges who are qualified to hear appeals arising from Quebec's Civil Code, a system of private law that differs materially from the common law legal system in force in the other provinces and territories. In practice, the remaining seats are allocated as follows: three to Ontario, two to the Western provinces, and one to the Atlantic provinces.

25 Clinton Rossiter, ed., *The Federalist Papers* (New York: Mentor, 1961), p. 323.

26 Keith G. Banting, *The Welfare State and Canadian Federalism*, 2nd ed. (Montreal and Kingston: McGill-Queen's University Press, 1987), p. 41.

27 For example, in the 1990s, the Christian Democrat government of Helmut Kohl was stymied in its efforts to curtail pension benefits because of opposition from state governments represented in the upper house of the German Parliament.

28 The term *province-building* was coined by Edwin R. Black and Alan C. Cairns in "A Different Perspective on Canadian Federalism," *Canadian Public Administration* 9 (March 1966): 27–44.

29 Andrew Heywood, *Politics*, 2nd ed. (Houndmills: Palgrave, 2002), p. 167.

30 Eric J. Evans, *Thatcher and Thatcherism* (London: Routledge, 1997).

31 Bill Jones, "Devolution," in Bill Jones et al., *Politics UK*, 4th ed. (Harlow: Pearson Education, 2001).

32 In bicameral parliamentary systems such as Canada and Britain, only the lower house, the House of Commons, is considered to be a confi-

dence chamber. The defeat of government-sponsored bills in the upper house—the Senate in Canada or the House of Lords in Britain—does not automatically bring down the government.

33 A notable exception to this rule concerns the vice president, who presides over the Senate and casts the deciding vote in the case of a tie.

34 Harold Laski, *The American Presidency: An Interpretation* (New York and London: Harper and Brothers, 1940).

35 This power was used in the 1950s to ban a neo-Nazi party and to ban the West German Communist Party.

36 David S. Bell, *Presidential Power in Fifth Republic France* (Oxford: Berg, 2000).

37 *Edwards v. A.-G. Can*, [1930] A.C. 114.

38 The reduced presidential term took effect at the beginning of the new presidential mandate in 2002.

39 Ian McAllister, "Elections without a Cue: The 1999 Australian Republic Referendum," *Australian Journal of Political Science* 36(2) (July 2001): 247–69.

40 Gwyneth Singleton et al., *Australian Political Institutions*, 5th ed. (Melbourne: Longman, 1996), p. 40.

41 Kenneth Maxwell, *The Making of Portuguese Democracy* (Cambridge: Cambridge University Press, 1995), p. 159.

42 The proposed property rights clause was also opposed by a majority of the premiers, who feared it would encroach on the legislative authority of the provinces. Alexander Alvaro, "Why Property Rights Were Excluded from the Canadian Charter of Rights and Freedoms," *Canadian Journal of Political Science* 24(2) (June 1991): 309–29.

Chapter 7

The Political Executive and Bureaucracy: On Top and on Tap

Donald J. Savoie

CHAPTER OBJECTIVES

After you have completed this chapter, you should be able to

- identify the various types of executive
- understand the basic workings of the executive in Canada
- differentiate the roles of central agencies
- compare the parliamentary and presidential executives
- describe how the executive is held accountable for its actions.

political platforms into government policy. It is also the executive that has to spring into action whenever a crisis arises because that is where both the necessary political authority and administrative capacity to deal with problems reside. It is in this sense that the executive always strives to be on top and tapping into emerging public-policy issues and administrative problems.

> Definition
>
> **EXECUTIVE:** The branch of government that is responsible for running the country and that provides leadership and makes the major decisions.

The executive has been described as the oldest and most widely adopted branch of government.[1] It dates back to when communities and nations first began to organize themselves to promote collective action or to mount a defence against outside intruders. As is well known, kings and queens in earlier times held in their own hands the power to raise revenues, spend, decide on all matters of policy and administration, and even administer justice. The monarch could legislate by royal proclamation; he or she was the supreme commander of

INTRODUCTION

Anyone setting out to determine where the action is in government needs to look no further than to the **executive**. It is here that policies are struck, programs are defined and implemented, and decisions, both large and small, are made. The executive should be of strong interest to students of political science. It is the executive that carries the bulk of the policy and administration workload in the public sector and translates the military and the "font of justice."[2] Over time, an assembly of knights met to advise the monarch, and from there the legislative branch of government developed. Today nearly all modern states have a legislative branch that is composed of elected or appointed individuals; this branch is commonly called parliament, congress, or the assembly. The role of the legislative branch and its relations to the executive are determined by the type of political system in which it operates—democratic, authoritarian, or totalitarian. In Western democracies, the legislative branch provides a forum for debating the issues confronting the nation and for holding the executive to account for its decisions and activities. But, as in earlier times, it is still the executive of government that actually runs the country.

The executive stands at the apex of power in Canadian politics. There is little in the way of institutional checks, at least within the legislative branch, to inhibit its ability to have its way. The executive sets the government's policy agenda, establishes new programs, and oversees administrative decisions. In some countries, notably the United States, the executive does not dominate the policy and decision-making process to the extent it does in Canada. Yet wherever there is government, there is an executive. This chapter explores the role and responsibilities of the executive by looking to history and by examining its functioning in various political systems. The objective is to enable readers to identify and describe the executive, explain its role and general functions, and understand the workings of the executive from a comparative perspective. For this reason, the chapter explores how the executive actually operates, how policies are struck, and how the executive relates to the legislative branch.

THE EXECUTIVE: ORIGINS AND TYPES

The basic building blocks of Canada's government executive and the working relationship between ministers and permanent officials can be found in the various government reform measures introduced even before Canada became a country, between 1841 and 1867.[3] For the most part, these building blocks were drawn from the British experience. Indeed, British practices were evident at every turn—in establishing parliamentary control of the public purse, in creating public accounts and the public accounts committee, in preparing annual estimates, in defining an audit function, and in creating the departmental structure. These measures were all designed to ensure that the executive could be held accountable for its policies and decisions.

Canada's executive was also shaped by the struggle for responsible government at home and by the desire of parliamentarians in Britain to wrest power away from the monarchy. Sir Robert Walpole is regarded by historians as the first British prime minister (in office from 1721 to 1742). It was under Walpole that the precedent was established that a minister needed the confidence of parliament no less than that of the sovereign to continue in office. Before Walpole, the government was the king's government and the ministers were the king's ministers. Accordingly, Walpole set the stage for the modern executive not only in Britain but also elsewhere, even in non–Westminster-style government.

Historians also credit William Pitt for creating the office of the prime minister, since he was the first to hold the office in a sense that would be recognized today. He became the effective head of cabinet, picked members of cabinet in consultation with the sovereign, and ensured that the policies of the government were accepted by his cabinet colleagues and were recommended to parliament.[4] The need to present a collective front in parliament and, at times, against strong public criticism, meant that the king's chief minister would wish to pick ministers with similar political views and policy preferences. For this reason, political parties grew and secured an increasingly important role throughout the 19th century, first in Britain and later in Canada.

Initially, the executive power was vested in the hands of the monarch.[5] In Westminster-style parliamentary systems, constitutional evolution has transferred this power to responsible officials, who exercise it in the name of the sovereign. Although the sovereign still remains the head of state—that is, the legal entity that embodies the government—the role of the sovereign has been relegated to what Walter Bagehot has described as "the dignified" functions of government. Today the sovereign's position is at best one of influence, not power. Accordingly, in the Canadian parliamentary system, the positions of **head of state** and

head of government are divided and held by different individuals, in what is called a **dual executive**. The ceremonial work is carried out by the head of state and the actual policy and program work by the head of government. In Canada, the head of state is the queen or king and her or his representative, the governor general. The governor general, like the sovereign in Great Britain, has the right to "be consulted, the right to encourage, the right to warn."[6] However, in Canada at least, the political executive has the option of ignoring whatever the governor general has to say.

An important function of the executive is to serve as a symbol and to provide a sense of unity and decorum for the country. The ceremonial function is largely performed by the head of state. Functions that fall under this category include reviewing military parades, receiving foreign dignitaries, and giving out honours. Apart from performing symbolic and ceremonial functions, the head of state has the political responsibility of appointing the head of government. But in virtually every instance in Canada in the past century, this has been quite a straightforward matter—the leader of the party that wins the most seats in a national election is asked to form the government.

> **Definition**
>
> **DUAL EXECUTIVE:** The executive in a political system in which the head of state and head of government functions are divided. In Canada, the head of state is the queen and her representative, the governor general, and the head of government is the prime minister.

The shift of power from king to parliament and cabinet was gradual, but it had significant implications. Ministers became part of a team and were no longer the personal choice of the sovereign. No matter how competent ministers might be and regardless of whether they enjoyed the full confidence of the king or the queen, all had to resign with the rest of the cabinet when their party lost power or the confidence of the Commons. As a result, the struggle for power took on a vastly different form than before. And leaving aside legal niceties, the fact that the monarch no longer constituted the executive meant that new relationships and new processes had to be forged.

Early British cabinets favoured the collective nature of cabinet government because it protected them against the monarch, who would otherwise pick ministers off one by one to produce a more pliant group of advisors.[7] However, in more recent years, the collective element has strengthened the position of the prime minister in that it enables him or her to force the hand of a recalcitrant minister to accept a policy or leave. In brief, it is ironic that the collective element of ministerial responsibility, established some two hundred years ago to attenuate the power of the king, today serves to strengthen the power of the prime minister.

In a presidential system, such as that of the United States, the positions of head of state and head of government are combined and occupied by one person; as a result, the executive is called a **single executive**. The American system was designed to vest the powers of the state and government in the people and only the people. That is, it was believed that there ought not to be any power beyond that of the elected representatives of the people. The Westminster parliamentary model, meanwhile, promotes the view that the power of the state is vested in the sovereign and is to be exercised by the government of the day in the sovereign's name.

> **Definition**
>
> **SINGLE EXECUTIVE:** The executive in a political system in which the head of state and head of government functions are combined and occupied by one person. In the United States, the position is filled by the president.

Because of their origins and basic differences in the structure of government, the British—and, by ricochet, the Canadian—executives have developed differently from some other executives in Western democracies. The term **cabinet**, for example, means something quite different in the American context than it does in the British and Canadian contexts. In Britain and Canada, the cabinet is collectively responsible for the policies and executive decisions of the government. Since cabinet members usually make the major political decisions together, the government in this system is a **cabinet government**. In contrast, executive authority in the United States lies with one person, the president. It is the president, not cabinet, who ultimately "shoulders responsibility individually for the executive decisions of his administration."[8] The executive in the United States is tied more closely to the president than to the cabinet. The president does chair a 14-member cabinet, but it is the president, not cabinet, that is responsible for government policy. For this reason, central agencies in the United States work for the president, not the cabinet. There is a wide variety of offices and agencies attached directly to the executive office of the president, ranging from the powerful Office of Management and Budget to the Office of Faith-Based and Community Initiatives. The vice president, meanwhile, presides over the United States Senate, carries out tasks as defined by the president, and succeeds to the presidency upon a vacancy in that office.

Definition

CABINET: The group of people chosen by the prime minister or president to provide political direction to government departments. In Canada and in Britain, the cabinet is collectively responsible for the policies and executive decisions of the government. In the United States, it is the president alone who shoulders this responsibility.

Definition

CABINET GOVERNMENT: A system of government in which the major political decisions are made by the cabinet as a whole, as opposed to one in which the prime minister or president acts with considerable autonomy.

In order to understand how the Canadian and American executives differ, one must understand the fusion of power between the executive and legislative branches in the case of Canada, Britain, Australia, and other countries with a Westminster-style parliamentary system and the separation of powers between the executive and legislature in the case of the United States. The prime minister and cabinet in a Westminster-style parliamentary system cannot function without securing the confidence of the lower house of the legislature. The prime minister and ministers also sit in parliament and are responsible to it. In the United States, the president is the chief executive officer of the government and is not dependent on Congress for his continuation in office. He is not a member of Congress at all.

The American executive branch was designed in the late 1700s as an alternative to the monarchical system. The goal was to separate powers between the legislative, executive, and judicial branches. The thinking was that one branch would act as a check against the concentration and the abuse of power by another; for example, the president can **veto** legislation passed by Congress, but Congress can override such a veto with a special majority.

Mexico looked to the United States when developing its Constitution, which provides for a federal system, a bill of rights, and the separation of powers. Mexico's president, like the American president, is both head of state and head of government. He or she appoints members of the cabinet with the consent of the Senate and is without any doubt the paramount political and policy actor in Mexico. Observers have labelled the Mexican president a "six-year monarch" because of the wide-ranging power of the position. The president appoints almost all employees of the executive; in addition, only the president may promulgate a law, and the executive can veto bills passed by the legislature. When Vicente Fox became president of Mexico in December 2000, he promised to introduce sweeping changes in the country. It was the first time in 70 years that the Partido Revolucionario Institucional (PRI) had lost a presidential election. Fox

United States President George W. Bush addresses the media alongside Canadian Prime Minister Jean Chrétien following their meeting in the Oval Office at the White House in Washington, D.C., on Monday, September 24, 2001.

Tom Hanson/CP Picture Archive

pledged to end corruption, open up the government decision-making process, and make it much more accessible to ordinary Mexicans.

As is the case with the United States and Mexico, the German chancellor is both head of state and head of government and holds in his or her own hands a great deal of political power. This power flows from provisions of the Basic Law, which limits Parliament's control over the chancellor and the cabinet. Unlike in other parliamentary systems, the lower house cannot remove the chancellor simply with a vote of no-confidence; the Bundestag, the lower house, can remove a chancellor only if it can also agree on a successor.

The Basic Law outlines three principles that define how the executive functions in Germany. First, the chancellor principle makes the chancellor responsible for all government policies. Any formal policy guidelines issued by the chancellor are legally binding directives that cabinet ministers must implement. Cabinet ministers are expected to introduce specific policies at the ministerial level that reflect the chancellor's broader guidelines. Second, the principle of ministerial autonomy entrusts each minister with the freedom to supervise departmental operations and prepare legislative proposals without cabinet interference so long as the minister's policies are consistent with the chancellor's larger guidelines. Third, the cabinet principle calls for disagreements between federal ministers over jurisdictional or budgetary matters to be settled by the cabinet. The chancellor determines the composition of the cabinet and may set the number of cabinet ministers and also dictate their specific duties.

France's Constitution provides for both a president and a prime minister; the president, however, holds the upper hand. The president is elected for a five-year term in a general election. The prime minister is nominated by the National Assembly but appointed by the president. The council of ministers is also appointed by the president on the suggestion of the prime minister. Finally, the president chairs meetings of the council of ministers.

There are still other types of executive, notably authoritarian and totalitarian executives. Authoritarian executives are often dominated by a charismatic leader; political power is highly concentrated and personalized. Supporters of authoritarianism claim that a democratic system invariably entails delays and inefficiencies and applaud the advantages of a strong central authority. Whatever the advantages of an authoritarian state, the executive dominates other branches of government, so that the power delegated to the other branches can be easily manipulated by the executive.

The most popular form of authoritarian executive is military rule. Military leaders often assume power after a successful coup d'état and rule with a firm hand, ostensibly to restore order and produce good government. In the interest of weeding out inefficiencies and corruption and to produce swift decision-making, authoritarian executives retain the ability to govern by decree, which essentially consists of issuing laws and directives, rather than having the legislature pass legislation. Authoritarian executives also reserve the right to suspend constitutional provisions, impose restrictions on the media, and if necessary, even control the administration of justice. This power extends to financial institutions of the state, which they dominate and can restructure on a moment's notice. Examples of authoritarian executives include that of Saddam Hussein in Iraq and of Muammar Qadhafi in Libya.

BOX 7.1

TYPES OF EXECUTIVES

The executive in Canada and Britain is fused with the legislative branch and is accountable to it.

The American executive is based on the premise that the legislative, executive, and judicial branches should be separated.

Other democratic executives (for example, in France and in Germany) are variations on these two types.

Authoritarian executives are often the product of military rule.

Totalitarian executives are the product of a single-party, dictatorial system.

Totalitarian executives are the product of a single-party, dictatorial system of government. A totalitarian executive extends its influence over all facets of life and commands full submission of the individual to its requirements. Though there are important exceptions, power is exercised through party channels. The term *totalitarian state* has been employed to describe the Nazi and fascist governments under Hitler and Mussolini and communist regimes in the former U.S.S.R. and its satellite states, as well as China. In such countries, state and party institutions exist alongside each other, but party leaders hold positions in both. Moreover, the constitutions of the party and the state are closely integrated, giving the party substantial authority over government organizations. Authoritarian and totalitarian states share a common characteristic—the legislative branch can be easily dominated by the party or by individuals who hold effective power. Indeed, if they so wish (and they often do), these individuals in power can ignore the legislative branch, paying it lip service only.

Some 20 years ago, China decided to decentralize economic decision-making. It has, however, continued to impose tight political controls, and it remains a communist state. China's executive is composed of the chief of state, the president, and the head of government—the premier. The cabinet or the state council is appointed by the National People's Congress (NPC). The president is elected by the NPC for a five-year term, and the premier is nominated by the president and confirmed by the NPC. The Chinese Communist Party still dominates political life in China, and the party–state relations remain strong. There are eight other small, registered parties, but all are controlled by the Communist Party.

Regardless of the type of executive in place, men have dominated the heads of government positions over the years. The table below lists prominent women who have been heads of government since 1900. It reveals that few women have occupied the position and that some have held it only briefly (for example, Kim Campbell in

Table 7.1 Prominent Female Heads of Government since 1900

Name and Country	Period in Office
Sirimavo Bandaranaike, Sri Lanka	1960–65, 1970–77, 1994–2000
Indira Gandhi, India	1966–77, 1980–84
Golda Meir, Israel	1969–74
Margaret Thatcher, United Kingdom	1979–90
Eugenia Charles, Dominica	1980–95
Gro Harlem Brundtland, Norway	1981, 1986–89, 1990–96
Corazon Aquino, Philippines	1986–92
Benazir Bhutto, Pakistan	1988–90, 1993–96
Violeta Barrios de Chamorro, Nicaragua	1990–97
Begum Khaleda Zia, Bangladesh	1991–96
Edith Cresson, France	1991–92
Tansu Ciller, Turkey	1993–96
Kim Campbell, Canada	1993
Agathe Uwilingiymana, Rwanda	1993–94
Chandrika Bandaranaike Kumaratunga, Sri Lanka	1994
Hashina Wajed, Bangladesh	1996–2001
Jenny Shipley, New Zealand	1997–99
Helen Clark, New Zealand	1999–present
Gloria Macapagal-Arroyo, Philippines	2001–present
Mame Mdior Boye, Senegal	2001–present
Megawati Sukarnoputri, Indonesia	2001–present

Canada in 1993, Edith Cresson in France in 1991–92, and Jenny Shippley in New Zealand in 1997–99).

THE HEAD OF GOVERNMENT: FIRST IN ALL THINGS

As already noted, political power is located primarily in the executive. This is true in virtually all political systems. The British, Australian, and Canadian executives, for example, have at their disposal all of the resources available to shape policy and to deliver programs. In brief, the executive holds virtually all of the cards: it proposes spending plans; it oversees program implementation; it decides which programs need to be cut back or expanded; it oversees the work of the bureaucracy; it proposes new legislation; and, when it holds a majority of seats in the Commons, it decides when a general election should be held. The legislative branch simply cannot compete with the executive when it comes to exercising political and administrative authority and, at least in the case of the Westminster (or parliamentary) model, it was never intended to do so.

The head of government occupies the highest peaks of both the political and administrative mountains, from which he or she can survey all developments. In Canada, as in other Westminster-style systems, the head of government—the **prime minister**—has in his or her hands all the important levers of political power, particularly when leading a majority government in Parliament. Indeed, all major national public-policy roads lead one way or another to the prime minister's

Jean Chrétien begins to take prime ministerial power too seriously.

Roy Peterson/Vancouver Sun/Artizans

doorstep. Before becoming the prime minister, a person must first be elected as the leader of his or her party by party members; only then can he or she succeed to this powerful position.

The prime minister has a long list of responsibilities. In Canada, he or she chairs cabinet meetings, establishes cabinet processes and procedures, sets the cabinet agenda, establishes the consensus for cabinet decisions, appoints and fires ministers and deputy ministers, and forms cabinet committees and decides on their membership. He or she exercises virtually all the powers of patronage and acts as personnel manager for thousands of government jobs. The prime minister also articulates the government's strategic direction as outlined in the **Speech from the Throne**, dictates the pace of change, and is the main salesperson promoting the achievements of the government. He or she has a hand in establishing the government's fiscal framework, represents the country abroad, establishes the proper mandate of individual ministers, decides all issues related to the machinery of government, and is the final arbiter in interdepartmental conflicts. The prime minister is the only politician with a national constituency and, unlike Members of Parliament and even cabinet ministers, need not search out publicity or national media attention, since attention is invariably focused on the PM's office and residence, 24 Sussex Drive in Ottawa (for Canadian prime ministers) or 10 Downing Street in London (for British prime ministers). In short, the prime minister is the head of government, with limited checks on his or her power within the government and in Parliament.[9]

Each of the above levers of power taken separately is a powerful instrument of public policy and public administration in its own right, but when they are all added up and placed in the hands of one individual, they constitute a veritable juggernaut of power. Other than being taken away in a general election, this power can only be stopped or slowed by the force of public opinion or by a cabinet or caucus revolt. Even then, public opinion may not be much of a force if the prime minister has already decided not to run again in the next election.

There are also plenty of subtle and not-so-subtle hints suggesting that the prime minister towers above his or her cabinet colleagues. At the cabinet table, the prime minister sits at the middle and decides which ministers sit where. The back of the PM's chair is higher than all the others. As we will see, the PM's own personal or political office is well staffed and is headed by an official of deputy minister–level status, the highest nonpolitical job in the federal government. Ministers, meanwhile, have relatively modest budgets for their own offices, which are headed by junior-level officials who are never invited to attend cabinet meetings.

CABINET AND MINISTERS

Things have changed a great deal since Sir John A. Macdonald assembled his first cabinet in 1867. The Macdonald cabinet had 13 members. Government activities have multiplied, and regions and interest groups now insist on being represented in the cabinet. The number of cabinet ministers in recent years has stood at between 23 and 40.

Today in Canada, every region and every province assumes that it should be allocated at least one cabinet minister. Even if a province does not elect a government member to the House of Commons, the prime minister is expected to appoint a senator from that province to the cabinet. The prime minister is also expected to have in the cabinet a proper mix of English- and French-speaking Canadians, women, Catholics, Protestants, Jews, Aboriginal people, francophones from outside Quebec, and anglophones from Quebec. Still, the prime minister is free to shuffle the cabinet at any moment, promoting loyal and competent ministers and discarding or demoting incompetent ones. In Britain, the prime minister has a great deal more freedom in selecting ministers than his or her Canadian counterpart. In the United States, the president has still more freedom because he or she can look outside of the legislative branch in appointing cabinet members.

What does the cabinet do? In theory, in a Westminster-style parliamentary system, the cabinet has all the power it needs to plan new policies, implement programs, and overhaul government operations. The cabinet is also responsible for guiding the work of the vast bureaucracy.

In Canada and Britain, for example, the cabinet calls the shots on matters of policy and can, if it so wishes, involve itself in the most trivial administrative matters. In theory, cabinet ministers are responsible for all policy and administrative matters, and the government is *their* government. For this reason, the nature of the cabinet is very different from that in countries such as the United States. As mentioned above, the most obvious difference is that in Canada and in Britain the cabinet is collectively responsible, so all cabinet members should be able to participate in the government's policy and program decisions. In the United States, the president is responsible for the executive, and members of his cabinet are responsible to him rather than to one another. They are also far more preoccupied with the management of their departments than with the cabinet's policy-making process.[10] But in Canada and in Britain, the cabinet, operating under the watchful eye of the prime minister and the PM's advisors, is the most important institution determining priorities and new policies. Determining priorities, however, is often a long, drawn-out process.

The first thing that is needed is an assessment of the political and public-policy environment. Public servants prepare a policy scan, reporting on the views of interest groups, political parties (in particular, the platform of the party in power), and provincial governments (in the case of Canada), as well as on the state of public finance. The purpose is not only to assist the cabinet in establishing priority areas, but also to ensure that the new policy initiative provides substantive benefits to citizens.

Because of the expansion of government activities in recent years, there is never a shortage of issues for the cabinet to consider. However, in Canada at least, the cabinet, in an effort to be representative of the regions, provinces, and various interest groups, became too large to be an effective decision-making body. For these reasons, former Prime Minister Trudeau decided to overhaul the cabinet system over thirty years ago. The broad outline of the Trudeau reforms, designed to streamline government, are still evident today in Ottawa. He established a number of cabinet committees and directed that all proposals be submitted to them before being considered by full cabinet. This means that the cabinet as a whole now mostly rubber-stamps decisions made by its committees.

The **Memorandum to Cabinet** is the key instrument by which proposals are brought forward by individual ministers for consideration by their cabinet

colleagues. Cabinet memorandums are often based on extensive research and consultations among various government departments and interest groups. They present the issues and alternatives that could be used to deal with them. They gauge how citizens will react to the proposals once they become public. In the case of Canada, they take note of federal–provincial and financial considerations and present a recommended course of action.

Definition

MEMORANDUM TO CABINET: The key instrument by which proposals are brought forward by ministers for consideration by the cabinet.

Figure 7.1 Process of Cabinet Approval

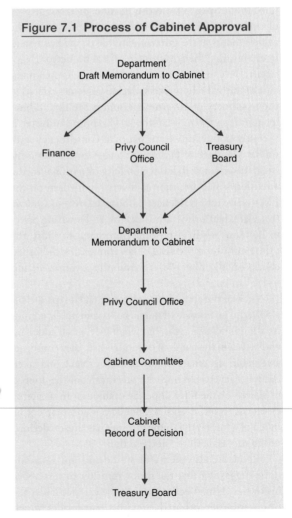

Department
Draft Memorandum to Cabinet

Finance   Privy Council Office   Treasury Board

Department
Memorandum to Cabinet

Privy Council Office

Cabinet Committee

Cabinet
Record of Decision

Treasury Board

The cabinet memorandum is first submitted to the relevant cabinet committee. Most committee recommendations are ratified by full cabinet either with very limited discussion or none at all. So what actually goes on in cabinet meetings? A typical cabinet agenda has four items. The first is General Discussion, which the prime minister opens and leads. The prime minister is free to raise any issue. Federal–provincial issues often appear on cabinet's weekly agenda under this item. The prime minister presents his or her views on the state of federal–provincial relations, on Quebec, or on a specific file that has received media attention. Ministers can then voice their opinions.

The second item on the cabinet agenda is called Presentations. Ministers, accompanied by their deputy ministers, are on occasion invited to make presentations or give briefings on various issues. The minister and deputy minister of finance might present a "deck" on the government's fiscal position. Or the minister of industry might make a presentation on Canada's productivity or competitiveness in relation to the United States. At the end of the presentation, ministers are free to raise questions and to ask for further explanation.

The third item is Nominations. Government appointments—such as the appointment of a Supreme Court judge, a senator, a deputy minister, or a member of the board of a crown corporation—require an order-in-council. There is always a list of appointments to be confirmed at every cabinet meeting; the nominations, however, have all been sorted out well in advance. Prime ministers have traditionally kept a tight control on appointments, and some positions are pretty much declared off-limits to ministers, notably the positions of Supreme Court judges and senators.

The fourth item is Cabinet Committee Decisions, presented as appendixes on the agenda. While in theory it is possible for all decisions made in cabinet committees to be reopened for discussion in cabinet, this is rarely done. The cabinet simply does not have the time to discuss cabinet committee decisions. In any event, the prime minister automatically sends a cabinet committee decision back to the committees for review whenever a minister raises questions about it in full cabinet.

Formal approval is granted in the form of a record of decision, which is circulated to all interested ministers for necessary follow-up. The record of decision is drafted by officials in the Privy Council Office—or, in the case of Great Britain, the Cabinet Office. It is important to note that the cabinet never votes on a proposal to decide if it should be accepted or rejected. Instead, the prime minister assesses the views of ministers, gauges support for a proposal, and finally calls the consensus reached by the cabinet. The consensus as defined by the prime minister forms the basis for the record of decision. In turn, the record of decision serves as the basis for ministers and their departments to prepare a Treasury Board submission to request the necessary operating budget or the financial and human resources required to implement the cabinet decision.

AGENCIES SUPPORTING THE EXECUTIVE

The prime minister and cabinet in a Westminster-style system of government have several agencies supporting their work. Table 7.2 below provides an overview of the functions of these agencies.

The cabinet and the cabinet committee system handle a great deal of business. In any given year, they meet 250 times, review over 1000 documents, produce well over 700 records of decisions, oversee several thousand Treasury Board decisions, and submit some 75 government bills to Parliament.[11] The workload is such that the prime minister and cabinet ministers need the support of central agencies. Central agencies have a link to the prime minister and the cabinet and have extremely broad and highly flexible policy advisory and coordination mandates, but they rarely have direct program responsibilities. Central agencies have been strengthened over the past 30 years to assist political executives in their efforts to control and coordinate government policies and the vast government bureaucracy. There are four central agencies that provide both policy advice and administrative support to the prime minister, the cabinet, and individual cabinet ministers: the Prime Minister's Office, the Privy Council Office, the Department of Finance, and the Treasury Board Secretariat. In the case of Great Britain, there are three main agencies: the Prime Minister's Office, the Cabinet Office, and the Treasury.

Table 7.2 **Executive Support Agencies**	
Partisan political assistants	Prime Minister's Office
	Individual ministerial staff
Policy, process, and procedure advisors	Privy Council Office (Canada)
	Cabinet Office (Britain)
	Department of the Prime Minister and Cabinet (Australia)
Economic and financial advisors	Department of Finance
	Treasury Board Secretariat
	The Treasury (Britain)

The Prime Minister's Assistants

Prime ministers do not stand alone at the apex of government. They do not rely solely on themselves in the process of dealing with incessant demands on their time, a hostile opposition in Parliament, the ever-critical media, and a large bureaucracy. PMs have political assistants and others to help them, to protect them from both internal and external threats, and to assist them in "squeezing forty-eight hours out of the Prime Minister's average day."[12] The **Prime Minister's Office (PMO)** provides partisan political advice, and for this reason it is staffed by hand-picked advisors and associates of the prime minister. The loyalty of PMO officials, who are political appointees rather than career public servants, is to the prime minister, not to the cabinet or individual cabinet ministers. The overriding concern of PMO is to safeguard the political fortunes of the prime minister. Accordingly, PMO staff ensure that the prime minister is well briefed on the political implications of major policy issues.

Table 7.3 **Workload of the Executive in a Typical Year**
250 cabinet and cabinet committee meetings
1000 documents considered
700 records of decisions
several thousand Treasury Board decisions
75 government bills submitted to Parliament

Since Pierre Trudeau, prime ministers have employed anywhere between 80 and 120 staff members in their own offices. Trudeau was the architect of the modern Prime Minister's Office. He felt that the Pearson years lacked a proper planning capacity at the centre, and as a result were marked by confusion and chaos. He resolved that things would be different in his government. He explained, "One of the reasons why I wanted this job, when I was told that it might be there, is because I felt it very important to have a strong central government, build up the executive, build up the Prime Minister's Office."[13] Trudeau considerably expanded the size of the PMO and identified specific functions and tasks for it to perform. Tom Kent, principal secretary to Prime Minister Lester B. Pearson, describes the Prime Minister's Office before Trudeau in the following way: "The PMO was then utterly different from what it became in the Trudeau era and has since remained. There was no bevy of deputies and assistants and principal this-and-that, with crowds of support staff."[14]

No prime minister since 1984 has sought to turn back the clock by trimming the size of the office or limiting its functions to what they were before Trudeau. Brian Mulroney, in fact, did the opposite. He increased the staff at the PMO by one-third, increased the office's budget by 50 percent, and added eight professional staff concerned with policy.[15] When Jean Chrétien came to office, one of the first decisions he made was to abolish the chief of staff position in ministerial offices, a position Mulroney had established. He kept a chief of staff for his own office, however, and this person is considered to be of the same rank as the deputy minister.

The PMO equivalents have also grown in both Australia and Britain in recent years. In the case of Australia, there is now a Department of the Prime Minister and Cabinet (PM & C) and a Prime Minister's

Office (PMO). The PM & C is part of the civil service, while PMO is not. The PM & C employs about 350 career officials and looks after the cabinet policymaking and decision-making processes. The PMO is a great deal smaller in Australia than in Canada, but it performs essentially the same task.[16] Britain's Cabinet Office is large (over 2500 staff members), while the PMO is smaller. Indeed, PMO consists of a handful of private or political secretaries and a principal secretary. However, the ties between the Cabinet Office and the PMO are very close.

Cabinet ministers also have their own partisan political advisors. All ministers have an executive assistant and several special assistants. They too are partisan political appointees, rather than career public servants. They do not, however, enjoy the same rank, pay, or status that their counterparts in the PMO do. The size of ministerial offices in Canada, Britain, and Australia is also a great deal smaller than the size of the PMOs. Still, ministerial assistants are often veterans of political wars and election campaigns. They are expected to quickly identify the political implications of new policy ideas emerging from the department.

The Privy Council Office and the Cabinet Office

The **Privy Council Office** (PCO) in Canada and the Cabinet Office in Britain operate at the centre of government, where they perform a variety of tasks. In both countries, there is a close working relationship between this office and the PMO, but there is an important difference between the them. PCO and Cabinet Office officials are career public servants capable of serving any prime minister and political party elected to power. Their role is to link the prime minister to the world of administration and to government departments, while the role of the PMO is to link the prime minister to the world of politics, the media, the political party, cabinet ministers, and caucus members.

The role of the PCO and the Cabinet Office has changed substantially since the late 1960s, when these offices were largely concerned with the flow of documents to cabinet and its committees. Today they perform a multitude of tasks in addition to providing major logistical and decision-making support for cabinet.

In the case of Canada, the PCO is increasingly being referred to as the prime minister's department.

The great majority of cabinet ministers have departments from which to draw policy advice and administrative support. Prime ministers have no department to call their own, but they can now turn to the PCO to secure similar support. The PCO has certain advantages that regular government departments do not have—it has no program responsibility to distract its staff, and its officials (for the most part) enjoy higher classification and pay than do their counterparts in departments.

Moreover, the prime minister, on the advice of the PCO, appoints all deputy ministers or administrative heads of government departments. The head of the PCO—the Clerk of the Privy Council Office and Secretary to the Cabinet—was designated through special legislation passed in 1992 as head of the public service. As such, the clerk can offer advice on a wide range of issues, including cabinet appointments, reorganization of government departments, the budget, and any conceivable policy issue. The only constraints are time—since the prime minister's agenda is always full—and resources. The same can be said about Britain, where the secretary to the cabinet also advises the prime minister on senior appointments in the machinery of government.

Finance and the Treasury

No government could function without an understanding of the economic forces at play in the country or without access to financial resources. In government, money steals the stage. Without money, governments cannot introduce new measures or continue to provide programs and services. All governments need strong economic and financial management advice.

The **Department of Finance** in Canada and the Treasury in Britain are often referred to as the government's chief economic advisor. These departments are responsible for overall economic management, raising revenue, preparing economic forecasts, and determining government expenditure levels. They have traditionally forged a strong working relationship with the prime minister, the Prime Minister's Office, and the Privy Council Office or the Cabinet Office.

Apart from their role as economic policy advisors to the government, they also advise the prime minister and cabinet on the impact of government policies on the economy. For this and other reasons, the minister responsible for finance or the treasury and their departments are very influential within the government. Much of their policy clout can be found in the budget process. A former senior deputy minister remarked on the influence of the Department of Finance in Canada when he observed that "through the budget, [Finance] can define the content of the entire government."[17] In government, the securing of financial resources for a department is equivalent to what a large share of the market represents to private firms.

To be sure, the ability to establish spending ceilings gives the Department of Finance and the Treasury a formidable advantage—but there is more. Imagine, for example, that the cabinet would like to launch a new program to help the homeless. In the case of Canada, the relevant government department or agency, in this case three of them—Canada Mortgage and Housing Corporation, Health Canada, and Human Resources Development Canada—together with central agency officials would review the proposal challenge and consider the alternatives. Government officials would seek to determine the level of public support for such an initiative and also explore whether provincial governments have any interest in the idea. But the critical question is whether financial resources can be made available to launch the new program. Finance holds the upper hand in this debate. Indeed, over the years the department has killed a good number of proposals by insisting that the government did not have the required resources to support an expensive new program. The point here is that the minister and Department of Finance, by virtue of the budget process, can and often do dominate the policy process.

The Treasury Board

One of Sir John A. Macdonald's first decisions on becoming Canada's first prime minister was to establish the Treasury Board. The **Treasury Board** speaks for the government on matters relating to general administrative and financial policy and personnel management. For this reason, the Treasury Board and its Secretariat are frequently described as the manager of the government. The board and its secretariat continually look for ways to improve the public service and the delivery of government programs and services. The board acts as the employer for the purpose of collective bargaining and also issues administrative directives and guidelines that can apply to all government operations.

The Treasury Board shares responsibility with the Department of Finance in managing the budget process. Finance looks after the big picture in that it estimates revenues and establishes broad spending levels. The Treasury Board looks after the smaller picture and acts as the government's accountant to ensure that departmental budgets are respected. It monitors current and projected spending plans and ensures that they stay within the spending levels established by the finance department. The board also approves operating budgets of government departments, including their employment levels.

BOX 7.2

CLASSIFYING CENTRAL AGENCIES

The Prime Minister's Office (PMO) provides political advice and is staffed by close partisan advisors and associates of the prime minister. The overriding concern of the PMO is to safeguard the political fortunes of the prime minister.

The Privy Council Office (PCO) or the Cabinet Office in Britain link the prime minister and the cabinet to the world of administration and provide logistical and decision-making support to the government. PCO and Cabinet Office officials are nonpartisan career public servants.

The Department of Finance or the Treasury in Britain are often referred to as the government's chief economic advisor. They are responsible for overall economic management, raising revenue, preparing economic forecasts, and determining government expenditure levels.

The Treasury Board and its Secretariat are described as the manager and act as the employer in government. They also act as the government's accountant and ensure that departmental budgets are respected.

THE EXECUTIVE IN NON–WESTMINSTER-STYLE GOVERNMENT

Over the years, governments in non–Westminster-style systems have also developed a capacity to strengthen the ability of their executives to plan and coordinate public policies. The United States government, for example, considerably strengthened its executive to plan and implement New Deal programs during the Great Depression and to launch its military effort during World War II. As in Canada, central agencies have grown steadily in Washington to assist political leaders, notably the president, not only with policy advice but also with coordinating more effectively a vast array of public policies and programs.

Many non–Westminster-style governments, including that of the United States, have no apex, no centre of political power where policy and decision-making are concentrated. The American system of government has coequal branches of government. The United States has built its executive around a different model—one designed to introduce checks and balances in the political system. It is for this reason that all political institutions in Washington have a large staff.

Still, the president dominates the executive, and there have been a number of efforts, starting with the Brownlow Commission in 1937, to strengthen the president and his (or, some day, her) office. Today the president can turn to a variety of agencies for support. The **Executive Office of the President** alone employs over two thousand people.[18] Whether one operates in a Westminster-style government or not, one needs to plan government-wide initiatives, prepare spending plans, develop new policies, and control government spending. The executive, even one that must share power equally with another branch, as is the case in the United States, needs a capacity to plan and coordinate activities.

The executive in the United States is much more than the White House and the Executive Office of the President. It includes the Office of Management and Budget (OMB), which performs tasks similar to those carried out by the Department of Finance and the Treasury Board in Canada. The president can also turn to a Council of Economic Advisers for advice, and many others, as seen in Figure 7.2.

In recent years, globalization has forced the hand of governments in other democracies to strengthen their executives as well. Since economic opportunities can emerge and disappear quickly, governments need to monitor them daily and have a capacity to respond quickly. Moreover, they need to keep abreast of the policies and programs of other governments, a task that legislative bodies are not well equipped to perform. Not only must governments respond quickly to emerging opportunities, but they must also be able to coordinate their policies and programs to achieve broad policy objectives. This is no small task, given the large number of departments and agencies found in modern governments.

In Germany, for example, the Chancellor's Office has grown considerably in recent years. It now employs

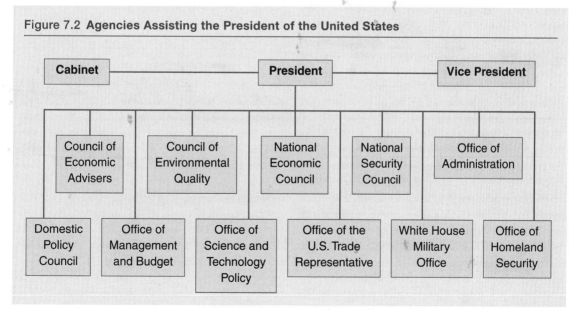

Figure 7.2 Agencies Assisting the President of the United States

about 500 people, but not more than 20 are political appointees—the rest are career civil servants. The functions of the Chancellor's Office are remarkably similar to those of the Prime Minister's Office and the Cabinet Office in a Westminster-style government. The office convenes and prepares the agenda for cabinet meetings on the chancellor's instructions. It also has a strong capacity to advise the chancellor on economic policy, foreign policy, social policy, and budget matters. The Chancellor's Office coordinates policy proposals coming from government departments and agencies. The chancellor and the cabinet review, on average, 20 proposals from departments every week.[19]

France's political system, as already noted, is semi-presidential. The country has a president, who is directly elected and who serves for a fixed five-year term, and a prime minister, who is appointed by the president. The prime minister, however, is responsible to the lower house of parliament, the National Assembly. Both the president and the prime minister have certain constitutional powers. The president is the symbol of the French state and exercises a strong influence over foreign and defence policies. The prime minister, meanwhile, represents the heart of the administrative state.

When the parliamentary majority belongs to the same political party or political camp as the president, there is a strong link and working relationship between the president and the prime minister. Things are different, however, when the president does not enjoy the support of the parliamentary majority. The situation, known in France as cohabitation, forces the president and prime minister to compromise and share the power. The president is limited in the exercise of political power because he or she was rejected by a majority of voters, who voted instead for his or her opponents in parliamentary elections.

Both the French president and the prime minister have well-staffed offices to assist them. The president has the presidential office at the Elysée Palace, with about 700 employees, nearly all of whom are employed in routine domestic and security functions. The office employs a handful of policy advisors who serve with the president and leave office when the president leaves.

The prime minister in France has access to a great deal more resources than the president to look after the machinery of government. Indeed, he or she can turn to a variety of policy and administrative units employing

about 5000 people. There are several units that provide advice on budget matters, economic circumstances, and European economic cooperation; the great majority of the staff employed in these units are career civil servants. Like the other heads of government, the prime minister also has access to staff who coordinate the activities of government departments and agencies.[20] This coordinating function is an important one because the executive has to present a sense of coherence and purpose in delivering services to citizens.

THE BUREAUCRACY

Prime ministers, presidents, cabinets, and some of the agencies that support them can be called the political executive. They are leaders of or affiliated with political parties, and are usually elected, holding office until the electorate decides that it wants to change political leaders. But every modern state also possesses an expert, permanent, nonpartisan, professional public service that is usually called the **bureaucracy** or the nonpolitical executive. In fact, the PCO, the Department of Finance, and the Treasury Board discussed above are actually important parts of the bureaucracy in Canada.

Definition

BUREAUCRACY: The expert, permanent, nonpartisan, professional officials employed by the state to advise the political executive and to implement government policies.

The bureaucracy performs two basic functions in the modern state. It advises the temporary, partisan, elected political executive, and it implements the decisions made by political leaders. Once the prime minister, president, or cabinet decide what action they wish to pursue in a policy field, the bureaucracy formulates the details of the government's policy. If these are agreeable to the political executive, then the bureaucracy carries out the new program. This may involve providing a service, regulating an activity, collecting a tax, or deciding who is eligible for a benefit. Because of this function, the bureaucracy is also referred to as **administration**.

When the extent of government operations was small, public servants could be hired on the basis of being friends or partisan supporters of the politicians in power. But as government became larger and more complex, states around the world found it necessary to move to a **merit system**, in which public officials are largely selected on the basis of their qualifications, training, and experience. Thus, each position in the vast bureaucracy is now highly specialized, and the person occupying that position is considered to be an expert. Public servants normally remain in the government's employ for their entire working life, regularly moving to a position of greater responsibility as they gain experience. The bureaucracy is organized in a hierarchical fashion, with descending levels of authority in a pyramidal shape.

DEPARTMENTS, AGENCIES, AND GOVERNMENT CORPORATIONS

As already noted, the permanent executive plans and delivers government programs and services through government departments, agencies, and state, crown or government corporations. These organizations are on the front line, delivering services, and are in daily contact with citizens. In Canada, for example, there are over 80 federal government departments and agencies. They vary considerably in size, from the Department of National Defence with 58 000 military employees to a small agency employing a dozen or so people. Each has a distinct mandate and clientele. There has been remarkable stability over the years in this area, with few departments or agencies being abolished without others being created to take their place.

In most jurisdictions, a new department can be established only with the approval of the legislative branch. Typically, however, the piece of legislation setting up a department is brief, and by design its mandate is defined in a broad fashion, the argument being that in the modern era departments and agencies must have the flexibility to respond to changing socioeconomic conditions. No longer is it possible to predict problems and situations that may crop up within six months, let alone a few years down the road. If the legislation is restrictive, the department will be unable to

deal with unanticipated issues. Going back to parliament or to congress to amend its enabling legislation is not an option, given the crowded legislative agenda.

Government departments have been classified in various fashions. The most widely employed classification divides them in terms of traditional horizontal coordinative portfolios (Finance, Foreign Affairs and International Trade), junior horizontal coordinative portfolios (Ministries of State, administrative coordinative portfolios, Public Works and Government Services), and line, or vertical, constituency portfolios (Agriculture, Fisheries and Oceans). In the United States, the machinery of government consists of a large number of fairly autonomous agencies responsible to both the president and Congress.

Although there are variations, all government departments in Westminster-style governments are organized basically along the same lines. The political head of the department is the minister, who is theoretically responsible for everything the department does. This is called the principle of **ministerial responsibility**. The permanent secretary (in Britain) or the **deputy minister** (in Canada) is the administrative head of the department. There are usually several deputy secretaries or assistant deputy ministers reporting directly to the permanent secretary or deputy minister, including one responsible for policy development and coordination; another for administrative, financial, and personnel services; and others for a geographic area or a specific program operation. Reporting to the assistant deputy minister are directors general or executive directors, and reporting to them are directors. Managers and group chiefs usually complete the departmental hierarchy.

Definition

DEPUTY MINISTER: The minister's chief policy advisor, the department's general manager, and a key participant in the collective management of the government; known in Britain as the permanent secretary.

All policy advice and all financial management issues going to the minister from the department, whether large or small, go through the permanent secretary or the deputy minister, who is the link between the political world of the minister and political advisors and the public service. The deputy minister or the permanent secretary is at once the minister's chief policy advisor, the department's general manager, and a key participant in the collective management of the government. The Privy Council Office has laid out the responsibilities of deputy ministers under three categories: "the responsibility for managing the internal operations of the department … the duty to support and participate in the collective management responsibilities of the government … [and] the duty to provide the minister and the government with policy advice."[21]

In more recent years, a development known as the agency model has been in vogue in Canada, as it has in other Western countries. Under former Prime Minister Margaret Thatcher, Britain led the way in the creation of this administrative innovation. Australia, Canada, and New Zealand quickly followed suit. The main reason for establishing an agency is to free the organization from central administrative controls, bureaucratic red tape, and partisan political considerations. Agencies are designed to operate more like private firms than typical government departments and to be more responsive to clients and more creative in dealing with problems. That said, agencies still have to report to ministers, who must answer in Parliament for their activities.

For example, the Canadian Food Inspection Agency (CFIA) was established in 1997 to regulate food safety, animal health, and plant protection. To create it, the inspection services from four federal departments (Agriculture, Fisheries and Oceans, Health, and Industry) were brought together. The government felt that a single agency would promote a more uniform and consistent approach, streamline operations, reduce costs, and provide sufficient independence from political considerations to regulate food inspection properly. The agency, unlike a regular government department, has an advisory board to provide advice on policy issues and to guide its work. It also enjoys greater management freedom in hiring staff, allocating spending, and managing financial resources than does a conventional department.[22]

State, crown, or government corporations are even further removed from day-to-day government operations and bureaucratic red tape than are agencies. They have boards of directors to guide strategic planning and oversee their operations and activities. Legislation establishing crown operations presents their *raison d'être* and outlines how they are to be governed. The role of the minister responsible for the corporation is to provide broad policy direction, table its annual report in Parliament, and answer questions (in Parliament and from the media) dealing with broad policy issues. All Anglo-American democracies, including the United States, have established corporations to take on special tasks, often ones of commercial nature.

Canada has 41 federal **crown corporations** today, down from 53 in the late 1980s. Crown corporations became a policy instrument of choice in Canada to build the national economy. Unlike our neighbour to the south, Canada has a relatively sparse population spread over a large territory. Policymakers felt that the private sector alone could not generate the kind of economic activities needed to build a strong national economy. They decided to forge new partnerships and create public enterprises to launch economic activities or provide services (for example, air transportation) that were left undeveloped by the private sector.

Crown corporations are part of the executive; they report to Parliament through a minister. They are different from government departments in that they enjoy considerable autonomy from the government decision-making process, in particular Treasury Board policies and guidelines. For the most part, crown corporations can establish their own rules and administrative guidelines for managing financial and human resources. They also enjoy a great deal of independence from ministers and even from cabinet in their day-to-day decision-making process. Examples of crown corporations include the Canadian Broadcasting Corporation (CBC) and Canada Post.

Crown corporations or public enterprises have never been popular in countries such as the United States and Japan. Britain, however, embraced the concept with enthusiasm between 1945 and the late 1970s, when it sought to develop and control its economy through public enterprises. Things changed dramatically under Margaret Thatcher; her government decided to sell or privatize a number of high-profile public corporations in the early 1980s (for example, British Gas, British Telecom, and British Petroleum). Canada also began to engage in **privatization**, that is, to sell public assets, in the 1980s and 1990s, including Air Canada, Teleglobe, Petro-Canada, and the Canadian National Railway Company.

HOLDING THE EXECUTIVE ACCOUNTABLE

The executive embodies the bulk of policy decisions and virtually every administrative decision made by government. For the most part, both the public-policy agenda and the machinery of government belong to the executive. Politicians holding power have access to the public purse and to central agencies, traditional departments, government agencies, and crown corporations to pursue their policy agenda and implement their electoral commitments. But this is not to suggest that they and public servants are left to their own devices to do as they wish. They are held to account for their decisions and activities by the legislative branch.

There are some sharp differences in how a parliamentary system and a presidential system hold the executive accountable. In the United States, the accountability of politicians and permanent officials is tied to the checks and balances of the political system. The American constitution makes it clear that executive power is vested in the president but that power "flows from the people." The emphasis is less on controlling power by making politicians and administrators accountable and more on limiting power and countervailing its operation through checks and balances. Power, as we have seen, is formally divided between the legislature, the executive, and the judiciary. Once the more senior officials in the executive are appointed by the president and confirmed by Congress, "members of the executive are formally accountable only to the president who … except in the extreme case [i.e., impeachment] is accountable not to the congress but to the people."[23] Also, because a number of senior officials in the United States are politically appointed, they have no pretensions to being politically neutral and accordingly do not enjoy permanent status. They consider themselves to be directly accountable to the president.

The president has several means by which to hold the bureaucracy and officials accountable. The president has the power to appoint and remove some 2700 senior officials who occupy key positions in the executive. Congress has delegated to the president the authority "to formulate the rules and regulations under which the bureaucracy functions." Congress, meanwhile, also has the power to hold officials accountable—notably, the "power of the purse." It has created its own office to scrutinize the budgets of government agencies. Committees of Congress can hold hearings on appropriations and launch special investigations. The Senate, meanwhile, has the authority to confirm many presidential appointments. And government agencies are legally accountable to the courts for the "administrative observance of statutes and constitutionally granted rights and liberties."[24]

Canada, Britain, and Australia have what is called **responsible government**—the sovereign or governor general acts only on the advice of the cabinet. The executive, in turn, must retain the confidence of a majority of members of the House of Commons. If defeated in a general election or in the legislature on an important matter, the prime minister submits his or her resignation or asks the crown to call an election and remains in office until it is called. If a majority of members will not support a government, a cabinet based on a minority of members is set up. This is called **minority government**. A **majority government**, on the other hand, is one backed by a majority of members in the legislature; in principle, it can last until an election is required under the constitution.

The House of Commons can hold a vote of no-confidence in the government, and if this vote is successful, the executive must resign. On the face of it, this rule provides the legislative branch with considerable power over the executive. The reality is, however, that party discipline has weakened the power of the legislative branch. There are only a few occasions when members of Parliament are allowed free votes or can vote independently of their party's position. Free votes very often involve matters of conscience or religion. For example, free votes have been allowed in Canada on questions of capital punishment and abortion.

Parliament has other means at its disposal to check and supervise the executive. Because the executive and the legislative branches are fused, the executive must continually defend its policies and activities before the legislature. The oral question period, held daily when Parliament is in session, provides opportunities for opposition parties to gain information about government actions and to embarrass ministers and score political points.

Finally, Parliament has several watchdog agencies and standing committees to assist the legislature in checking the power of the executive. The Office of the Auditor General reports directly to Parliament rather than through a minister. The office now reports regularly on whether departments have spent public funds appropriately. In addition, the mandate of the office has been expanded to report on cases when "money has been expended without due regard for economy and efficiency or when satisfactory procedures have not been established to measure and report the effectiveness of programs."[25] Thus, the office enjoys a great deal of independence and over the years has made full use of it. It continues to produce reports highly critical of the government.

There are other watchdog agencies and offices, notably the Office of the Commissioner of Official Languages and the Public Service Commission. They too enjoy considerable autonomy as they monitor and report on, respectively, the implementation of the Official Languages Act and the merit principle in staffing the government bureaucracy.

Parliamentary committees can also exercise some influence or control over the executive. In Canada, there are about 15 standing or permanent committees. These cover several departments and agencies and occupy much of their time reviewing these departments and agencies' expenditure plans. There are also a small number of special House of Commons committees, each with a specific and fairly narrow mandate (e.g., special committee on nonmedical use of drugs) and joint Commons and Senate committees (e.g., official languages committee).

It is important to highlight the work of the Public Accounts Committee (PAC). The chair of the PAC, unlike that of the other standing committees, is drawn from the opposition benches rather than from the government side of the House. The committee examines the government's year-end financial statements and the various reports produced by the Office of the Auditor General.

Finally, all Anglo-American democracies have in place or are planning to introduce **access to information** legislation. This legislation is designed to open up government and to enable citizens to gain a better understanding not only of decisions made in government, but also of the forces and conditions that led the executive to make them.

CONCLUSION

The executive is where the action is and where the great majority of public sector jobs can be found. Many students in political science who contemplate a career in government will very likely look to the executive for opportunities.

There are several types of executives. The authoritarian executive is dominated by a charismatic leader; its political power is concentrated and personalized. The totalitarian executive is the product of a single-party dictatorial system of government. In more democratic systems, political executives are usually classified as either parliamentary or presidential. Canada has a parliamentary system. In this system, the ceremonial and the political executives are separated; the political executive sits in Parliament, to which it is accountable for its actions. The United States has a presidential executive. There the ceremonial and the political functions are combined and placed in the hands of the president. The president, however, does not sit in Congress, and the political executive is accountable directly to the people.

The executive stands at the apex of power; it is the oldest branch and it has at its disposal almost all of the financial and human resources made available to the public sector. In Canada, the executive comprises the ceremonial executive—the monarch and his or her representative, the governor general—and the political, which consists of the prime minister and the cabinet. The political executive sets the policy agenda for Parliament to consider and controls the public purse. It also directs or oversees the work of all government departments, agencies, and crown corporations. It is assisted by central agencies: the Prime Minister's Office, the Privy Council Office, the Department of Finance, and the Treasury Board Secretariat. These central agencies assist the prime minister and the cabinet in formulating, implementing, and monitoring policies and programs.

In Canada and in other countries with a parliamentary system (such as Britain and Australia), the political executive must retain the confidence of a majority of members of the House of Commons. If it loses the confidence of the House, it must resign. However, because of party discipline, a party holding a majority of seats in the Commons is rarely, if ever, defeated in a confidence vote. Even though Parliament also has other means to hold the executive accountable for its policies and decisions, it is no match for the prime minister and the cabinet. The PM and the cabinet hold in their hands all the important political and policy levers; they can quickly access financial resources and tap into the vast policy and program knowledge located inside the bureaucracy. This alone gives them enormous clout and often enables the political executive to be on top of emerging policy issues, leaving Parliament on the sidelines as it tries its best to hold the government accountable.

DISCUSSION QUESTIONS

1. Where does power lie in a parliamentary system?

2. Where does power lie in a presidential system?

3. Is the executive sufficiently accountable for its actions?

4. Discuss the advantages and disadvantages of separating the head of state from the head of government.

5. How do central agencies facilitate the work of the prime minister and the cabinet? How do they facilitate the work of the president?

6. What do you consider more important to a political system—having in place checks and controls on executive power or giving the prime minister and cabinet or the president *carte blanche* power to implement a policy agenda?

 **WEB LINKS**

Parliament of Canada:
http://www.parl.gc.ca

Prime Minister's Office:
www.pm.gc.ca

Privy Council Office:
http://www.pco-bcp.gc.ca

Department of Finance:
http://www.fin.gc.ca

American Presidency:
http://www.whitehouse.gov and
http://www.americanpresidents.org

United Kingdom Prime Minister:
http://www.number-10.gov.uk

FURTHER READING

Atkinson, Michael. *Governing Canada: Institutions and Public Policy.* Toronto: Harcourt Brace, 1993.

Jones, Charles. *The Presidency in a Separated System.* Washington, D.C.: The Brookings Institution, 1994.

Lyphart, Arend, ed. *Parliamentary versus Presidential Government.* Oxford: Oxford University Press, 1992.

Peters, B. Guy. *The Politics of Bureaucracy.* White Plains, N.Y.: Longman, 1995.

Savoie, Donald J. *Governing from the Centre: The Concentration of Power in Canadian Politics.* Toronto: University of Toronto Press, 1999.

ENDNOTES

1. James J. Guy, "Executives," in *People, Politics and Government: Political Science: A Canadian Perspective*, 2nd ed. (Toronto: Maxwell Macmillan, 1990), p. 173.

2. Mark O. Dickerson and Thomas Flanagan, "Parliamentary and Presidential Systems," in *An Introduction to Government and Politics* (Scarborough: Nelson Canada, 1998).

3. J.E. Hodgetts, *Pioneer Public Service: An Administrative History of the United Canadas, 1841–1867* (Toronto: University of Toronto Press, 1955), p. 77.

4. Sir Ivor Jennings, *Cabinet Government* (Cambridge: Cambridge University Press, 1959), p. 20.

5. For an overview of the role of the "Formal Executive," see J.R. Mallory, *The Structure of Canadian Government* (Toronto: Macmillan, 1971), chap. 2.

Ibid., p. 57.

7 Sharon Sutherland, "Responsible Government and Ministerial Responsibility: Every Reform Is Its Own Problem," *Canadian Journal of Political Science* 24(1) (March 1991): 95.

8 Colin Campbell, *Government under Stress: Political Executives and Key Bureaucrats in Washington, London, and Ottawa* (Toronto: University of Toronto Press, 1983), p. 22.

9 Donald J. Savoie, *Governing from the Centre : The Concentration of Power in Canadian Politics* (Toronto: University of Toronto Press, 1999).

10 Donald J. Savoie, *Thatcher, Reagan, Mulroney: In Search of a New Bureaucracy* (Pittsburgh: University of Pittsburgh Press, 1994).

11 Savoie, *Governing from the Centre*, chap. 4.

12 A PMO official quoted in Colin Campbell and George J. Szablowski, *The Superbureaucrats: Structure and Behaviour in Central Agencies* (Toronto: Gage, 1979), p. 60.

13 Trudeau quoted in George Radwanski, *Trudeau* (Toronto: Macmillan, 1978), p. 146.

14 Tom Kent, *A Public Purpose: An Experience of Liberal Opposition and Canadian Government* (Montreal and Kingston: McGill-Queen's University Press, 1988), p. 225.

15 Peter Aucoin, "Organizational Change in the Machinery of Canadian Government: From Rational Management to Brokerage Politics," *Canadian Journal of Political Science* 19(1) (March 1986): 22.

16 See, for example, B. Guy Peters and R.A.W. Rhodes and Vincent Wright, eds., *Administering the Summit: Administration of the Core Executive in Developed Countries* (Basingstoke: Macmillan, 2000).

17 Arthur Kroeger, "A Retrospective on Policy Development in Ottawa," (Canadian Centre for Management Development, Ottawa, 1998, mimeographed), p. 2.

18 J.P. Pfiffner, *The Modern Presidency* (New York: St. Martin's Press, 1994).

19 P. Berry, "The Organization and Influence of the Chancellory during the Schmidt and Kohl Chancellorships," *Governance* 2(4) (1989): 338–54.

20 J. Massot, *Chef de l'État et chef du Gouvernement : Dyarchie et hiérarchie* (Paris: La Documentation française, 1993).

21 Canada, Privy Council Office, "The Office of Deputy Minister," June 1984, p. 1.

22 See www.inspection.gc.ca.

23 Savoie, *Thatcher, Reagan, Mulroney*, p. 37.

24 Ibid.

25 *The Auditor General Act*, 1977, c. 34, s. 7(2).

The Policy Process

Sandra Burt

WHY POLICIES MATTER

On September 11, 2001, the expectations and assumptions of citizens of the United States were shaken by the terrorist attacks on New York and Washington, in which thousands of people who happened to be in the vicinity at the time of the attack were killed. The events of September 11 led to dramatic changes in international relations and set in motion a range of reactions on both citizens' and governments' part that were based on their particular interpretations of the attacks.

The U.S. government saw the attacks as the hostile actions of religious fanatics, set to destroy the fabric of American life. American President George W. Bush quickly announced to the people of America that the world should "make no mistake, the United States will hunt down and punish those responsible for these cowardly acts."[1] With these words, Bush was signalling a new policy direction for the United States—its declared war on terrorism. But in order to place that declaration of war in its proper context, it is important to note that earlier policy decisions of the U.S. government, taken either in an effort to block the power-building efforts of the Soviet Union, or in the name of preserving the rights and freedoms of individual U.S. citizens, had contributed to the terrorists' capacity to carry out their activities.

The U.S. government gave financial support to Afghan Mujahideen groups between 1979 and 1989, and this contributed to the failure of the Soviets to maintain a presence in Afghanistan. In addition, for several years the U.S. government had resisted international efforts to impose tighter controls on bank accounts and to require more stringent security measures on all flights, both domestic and international. This resistance was consistent with the traditional policy direction of the United States—to maximize individual liberty and minimize government interference. But in an abrupt policy shift following the attacks, the U.S. government moved swiftly to tighten security measures and monitor banking activities in order to implement its declared war on terrorism. It also began to forge a stronger alliance with Russia, in an effort to defeat the Taliban government of Afghanistan.

This example of a government seeking to find a course of action that it considers appropriate in the context of particular circumstances is illustrative of the ongoing activities that are involved in making public policy. Governments are continually making choices among competing options, and the paths that they choose to follow are called public policy. For our purposes in this chapter, it is important to recognize three important aspects of the policymaking process, each of which is apparent in the September 11 example. First, the decisions taken by government have important consequences, some of which may be unintended. Second, these decisions are taken within the context of the prevailing dominant ideological perspectives that inform the government of the day. Third, the decisions are specific responses to what are seen to be policy problems. Governments may look at these problems differently than do various groups within the population; in other words, problems get represented or framed in specific ways in policy proposals.[2]

A common definition of **public policy**—that is, policy set by government—states that it can be either a course of action or of inaction that is selected by public officials,[3] usually in response to a problem or a set of problems. Because it is a general course of action, public policy usually consists of a set of laws, rather than one piece of legislation. Consider, for example, the recent law passed in Canada that requires all gun owners to register their firearms with a public agency. The firearm registration legislation is part of the Canadian government's general commitment to crime prevention. It was passed in the hope that it would make gun owners more accountable. In this example, the firearm registration law is just one part of the more general crime prevention policy direction of the federal Liberals.

Definition

PUBLIC POLICY: A course of action or inaction that is selected by public officials, usually in response to a specific problem or set of problems.

In the same way, the Canadian government's decision in 2000 to improve maternity leave provisions for Canadian women and to allow fathers to apply for leave benefits is part of its childcare policy. This policy has gradually shifted since the early 1970s from one of facilitating women's access to the paid labour force to one of facilitating the sharing of paid labour between parents. In this instance, the specific addition of fathers as beneficiaries of paid parental leave has particular significance, for it represents a change in the Canadian government's thinking of childcare as an exclusively women's issue toward regarding it as a more general parental concern. This example highlights the complexity of the relationship between specific acts or regulations of governments and their general policy directions.

It is also important to recognize that not all policies of any particular government are always consistent. For example, the Canadian government made a decision in the 1960s to improve women's access to the paid labour force. This decision has been upheld in various degrees by successive administrations. But at the same time, the government has refused to enact a national childcare strategy that would make it possible for many women (and in particular women who cannot afford private childcare services) to participate in the paid labour force. A similar confusion of policy directions can be found in the U.S. government's commitment to free trade, which culminated in the North American Free Trade Agreement and its simultaneous protectionist import policies with respect to Canadian softwood lumber. There are several possible explanations for these apparent conflicts. It may be the case that a government is highly decentralized, with multiple centres of decision-making. Alternatively, a government may have an overarching policy direction that favours one particular policy choice over another. In either case, it is the job of the policy analyst to sort through the labyrinth of government actions and try to determine a government's central focus.

In today's highly complex world, it is common to have multiple centres of power in democratic societies. The sheer volume of activity that is part of any government's mandate makes it difficult for one group or individual within government to ensure that all policies fit with one another. Indeed, it is not always desirable that there be such a concentrated coordination of activity. For example, the concept of checks and balances among competing centres of power is one of the cornerstones of U.S. democracy. Many democratic theorists (particularly pluralist theorists) subscribe to the view that the existence of several centres of decision-making makes the political system more accessible both to individual citizens and to the pressure groups to which they may belong.[4]

Most analysts of policy agree that it is useful to think in terms of collections of activity within what they call **policy networks**, rather than trying to make sense of the totality of a government's approach to issues. Much of the time, decisions about whether to take action take place within a fairly small group of people, made up of elected officials, policy advisors, and interest group or community spokespeople, although the government's final policy decisions will generally conform to its general ideological approach to issues. In other words, government departments (such as those of fisheries, justice, or the environment, for example) have ongoing relationships with a variety of individuals and groups, including interest groups, individual citizens, other government departments, and international organizations. Such a collection of groups and individuals (including both government officials and members of the public) who have a common interest in a policy area and seek to shape policy outcomes in that area can be called a **policy community**. The nature of those relationships in a policy community may vary internally within any one government, as well as between administrations. Here, too, policy analysts have the task of investigating the nature of networks within policy communities and the extent to which they shift over time and space.

Another useful concept for the policy analyst is that of a **policy cycle**. There are five stages that a government may work through in the development of a particular public policy, such as a decision to support free trade, or the setting up of a program to regulate the number and type of immigrants admitted into a country. These stages include agenda-setting, problem definition, policy design, implementation, and evaluation, as seen in Figure 8.1. While the concept of a cycle is useful to the extent that it alerts us to different stages in the policymaking process, it does have some problems. For one thing, not all policies pass through each of the five stages. In particular, governments may leave out the evaluation stage. Evaluation is certainly problematic when policies (such as the Canadian government's encouragement of smoking as a relaxation aid for soldiers in the two world wars) have delayed and long-term consequences (dramatic increases in rates of lung cancer). In addition, the cycle suggests that the policy process is very systematic and orderly, when in reality governments may simply add on to earlier policies for the sake of simplicity or may move back and forth from one stage to another. Nevertheless, it does help us "unpack" the various elements that are part of complex interactions among political parties.

Definition

POLICY CYCLE: The various stages that are part of the policymaking process of governments, including some or all of the following: agenda-setting, problem definition, policy design, implementation, and evaluation.

Definition

POLICY NETWORKS: Relationships that develop among those individuals and groups (including both government officials and members of the public) who have a common interest in a particular policy area.

Definition

POLICY COMMUNITY: A collection of groups and individuals (including both state bureaucrats and interest groups or social movement organizations) who influence each other in an effort to shape policy outcomes in their area of interest.

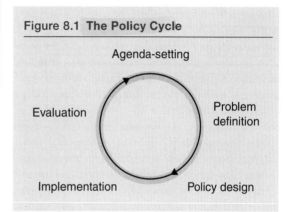

Figure 8.1 The Policy Cycle

Some analysts suggest that the agenda-setting stage is the most important one in this cycle, since it sets the stage for later events. Governments either initiate a course of action or respond to a problem within their general set of principles. Later, if their decision has been to initiate some action to resolve the problem, they will try to assess their success in matching the solution to the problem. At every step in this cycle, politicians and bureaucrats are making value judgments and deciding among alternatives.

Sometimes the process is a fairly straightforward one of building on past actions. We call this incremental policy. At other times, the process may be much more haphazard—and hard to connect to any general plan. But most of the time policies are made within the context of a general blueprint. In Canada, for example, that blueprint is set out in the Speech from the Throne that is prepared by the government and delivered by the governor general at the beginning of each new session of Parliament. Specific departments generally initiate action or respond to issues as they emerge within that blueprint, although the process is not always so straightforward.

The shape, size, and ideological colour of the agenda depend on a variety of factors. At the very core of a government's agenda is its general commitment to a set of values. Citizens often complain that it does not make much difference if they elect a Liberal or a Conservative government in Canada, or a Republican or Democratic president and/or Congress in the United States. To a certain extent, it is true that all governments are constrained by the same considerations, including the size of the government's financial coffers, the integrity of the administration, the strength of public support and/or opposition, and the conditions imposed by the institutional framework of government. But it is also generally the case that there are some differences of opinion among political parties (more apparent among some parties than others) with respect to priorities and governing styles. The governing party works within a general set of attitudes that we refer to as the prevailing political culture or the universe of discourse, which reflects commonly held beliefs among economic, political, and social elites about the appropriate role of government and the proper distribution of economic and social rewards among citizens. In the recent history (the mid-20th century) of Western industrialized societies,

those beliefs were called the welfare state because governments were prepared to take considerable responsibility for the well-being of their citizens. Since the early 1980s, there has been a gradual shift in governing values away from that welfare model to a neoliberal approach, which places much more emphasis on individual citizens' responsibilities to look after themselves and argues for a greater reliance on market forces to resolve policy problems.

In this chapter, we focus in particular on the first stage in the policy cycle—agenda-setting by governments. We will see what various factors influence governments' willingness and ability to deal with issues that affect all of us.

APPLYING CONCEPTS TO PRACTICE

The concepts of a policy network, policy communities, and the policy cycle are much easier to understand when they are applied to actual policies. In this chapter, we consider three policy areas that affect each of us in our daily lives and that have captured the attention of both citizens and governments in the past few years. These areas are health, families, and trade. Two of these policy areas (health and families) are relatively new concerns of governments. While they have always been part of the private sphere, they moved onto public agendas as recently as the 19th century in Western liberal democracies such as the United States, Britain, Australia, and Canada.

This distinction between public and private spheres of activity has always been important for understanding the policy process. In the early days of Western liberal democracies, the public sphere (which was derived from the Aristotelian notion of the *polis*) was restricted to government institutions, defence matters, and some limited regulation of trade and commerce. Family matters, health, and the economy were considered to be part of the private sphere and therefore not subject to public regulation. It was also generally thought that the public sphere was exclusively the business of men, while the private sphere was divided, with women restricted to family and men involved in business. The history of public policy has been shaped in large measure by transitions in the boundaries of these public and private spheres.

Because it was part of the public agenda as early as the 17th century, trade has a much longer policy history. Trade was the driving force behind the decision of European societies to fund the exploration and colonial settlement of North America. As Western societies moved out of the Middle Ages and into the age of capitalism and the competitive market economy, the desire to find new sources of raw materials and new markets for the finished goods produced in capitalist economies moved trade issues to the centre of public-policy debates. This policy area thus illustrates most clearly the impact of the ideological constructs of the competitive market economy on the representation of policy problems.

In each of the three policy areas that we consider in this chapter, we can discern significant patterns in the policymaking process in Western industrialized countries. We will find as well some striking comparisons between policies and the policy process in these countries and in different parts of the developing world.

HEALTH POLICIES

Agenda-Setting

Historically, health was considered to be a private issue between a patient and her or his doctor; it was exclusively a family or individual responsibility. For the most part, health was simply not on the agendas of governments, and until the middle of the 20th century Western governments devoted relatively little time and resources to health concerns. Typically, illness survival rates had at least as much to do with an individual's financial status as with the availability of a remedy. But this attitude began to change, primarily as the result of the lobbying on the part of social democratic political parties and interest groups. These parties and groups put pressure on governments to improve the terrible living and working conditions in urban centres in particular, which had developed as a result of industrial development combined with the political philosophy of *laissez-faire*.

One of the earliest markers of the movement of health onto the public agenda in Canada was the adoption of worker compensation legislation, first in Ontario in 1914 and later in the rest of the Canadian provinces. Before these worker compensation laws,

people who were injured on the job had to fend for themselves. It was only rarely that employers would offer some assistance for hospital expenses. And if the injury meant that the worker was no longer able to carry out the job, the usual outcome was unemployment. The worker compensation programs altered the discourse of disability by shifting the major responsibility for the injury from the worker to the employer.

At about the same time that provincial governments were enacting these compensation laws, women's groups, health practitioners, and the provincial government of Saskatchewan were pressuring for more substantive changes. In addition, the early 1900s saw a shift in thinking away from a minimal role for government to the welfare state. In terms of health care, this shift meant that governments were increasingly willing to take some responsibility for funding hospitals, health research, public sanitation, health education, and drugs. In Britain, the publication of the Beveridge Report in 1942 was an important catalyst for welfare state reforms. William Beveridge headed a commission of inquiry into Britain's social policy. The commission proposed sweeping changes in British social policy that included a public health insurance program. With the election of an ideologically social democratic Labour government in Britain in 1945, the implementation of the Beveridge proposals was assured.

In Canada, the legislative initiatives of the provincial Co-operative Commonwealth Federation (CCF) government in Saskatchewan were of particular significance. Tommy Douglas was the CCF premier of Saskatchewan from 1944 to 1961. The Canadian health-care system owes a great deal to his innovative policies. In the view of Douglas and his social democratic government, universal access to good health care was each citizen's public right, in sharp contrast to the prevailing notion that health was a private issue. By January 1947, Douglas had introduced a Hospital Insurance Plan for the province of Saskatchewan. Somewhat later, in 1959, he brought in medicare to that province. The Saskatchewan plan became the blueprint for the national plan, introduced by Prime Minister Lester Pearson in 1964.

Since health in Canada falls primarily within provincial jurisdiction, the federal government had to find a way to work around the constitutional rules. This has been a recurring issue in Canada, and many Canadian policies reflect the problem of the constitutional division of powers. As is often the case, beginning in 1948, the federal government used its financial clout to exercise national power over delivery of health care. Until recently, these national standards also included the principle of a single tier of service delivery, through a publicly funded and primarily nonprofit health-care system.

One measure of this federal involvement in the health-care system is the size of the federal health budget. In the estimates for 2001–02, the federal government set aside $2.7 billion for the health portfolio, in addition to the money (more than $17 billion in 2001–02) transferred to the provinces as part of the Canada Health and Social Transfer (CHST). By virtue of the division of responsibilities between the federal and provincial/territorial governments, the provinces are responsible for most of what the average citizen thinks of as health care, that is, hospitals, regulation of physicians and surgeons, and financial support to the elderly for prescription drugs. The federal health portfolio includes food, drug, and consumer product safety, health promotion, and provision of health services to First Nations and Inuit peoples.

In the United States, there is a greater mix of public and private health care that reflects the strong U.S. commitment to the free-enterprise system. While basic care is provided to those who cannot afford to pay, private clinics and hospitals are abundant, and they charge what the market will bear. But even within this more entrepreneurial system, the U.S. government spends a major portion of its budget on health-care research and provision. The budget projections for the year 2002 are $193 billion in real spending, and another $190 billion in federal tax incentives for direct health-care services, disease prevention programs, consumer and occupational safety, and research. In addition, the projected cost for medicare in 2002, which subsidizes health care for those over 65 and for people with disabilities, is $226 billion.

This can be compared with the much more modest investment in health that is possible in developing countries. In Mexico, for example, more than a decade of political and economic instability has left the rich and the poor of the country far apart in terms of economic prospects and quality of life. Health care is simply not available to most of those who are poor, and

even basic sanitation needs cannot be met. More than half of the Mexican population of about 90 million does not have access to either safe drinking water or toilets. In Africa, one of the biggest health challenges since the late 1970s has been the AIDS epidemic. At the end of 2001, 28.1 million adults and children were living with HIV/AIDS in sub-Saharan Africa. In Botswana, for example, over 35 percent of the adult population is living with AIDS. The health costs associated with the AIDS epidemic are particularly serious for African nations, since they do not have the financial capacity to support massive treatment programs. Figure 8.2 illustrates the proportion of the health and child welfare budget of Zimbabwe that is absorbed by what is in fact a fairly minimal commitment to AIDS care.

The AIDS example makes it clear that in some cases a nation's agenda-setting is influenced by circumstances beyond its control. In its HIV/AIDS strategy, the United Nations has called upon the countries most affected by this health crisis to demonstrate an ongoing commitment to reducing the impact of HIV/AIDS. But the economically poorer nations of the world do not have many policy options available to them in these health crises. The obstacles to AIDS prevention include low literacy rates, high poverty levels, weak communication links, and cultural norms that are resistant to the health message. In this policy vacuum, international organizations and in particular the United Nations have made some effort to fill the gap. One of the strategies adopted by the UN has been to negotiate with drug companies to reduce the cost of antiretroviral drugs sold to developing countries. Even with these reductions, however, the cost is prohibitive for countries with meagre budgets. In addition, the absence of a strong health infrastructure often makes the delivery of treatment impossible.

In summary, health is now a major policy issue for all countries in the world, and the programs that are developed within a health portfolio consume a major part of public funds. As we will see in the next section, spending on health also fuels a significant portion of the Western economy. But what is the main focus of these health budgets? What do governments mean when they talk about health costs? And are there any other ways to view health that could lead to different kinds of policies in the future?

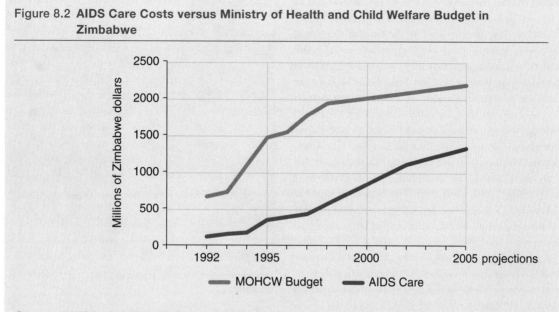

Figure 8.2 **AIDS Care Costs versus Ministry of Health and Child Welfare Budget in Zimbabwe**

Source: UNAIDS, HIV/AIDS in Zimbabwe, 1998. Reprinted by permission of UNAIDS.

The Importance of Issue Construction

When countries such as Britain and Canada first introduced public-health measures, they did so in the name of preventing rather than treating illness. The first public-health initiatives were focused on improving citizens' access to clean water and developing better cleaning practices to reduce the spread of disease. Ontario was the first province to pass a Public Health Act in 1882, and the other provinces quickly followed. The emphasis of this early initiative was on controlling the spread of germs and disease. This construction of health as sanitation can be traced back to public officials' fears as early as the 1830s that new immigrants arriving in the colonies might be spreading a European cholera epidemic to North America. Health was conceptualized as the control of disease.

Yet quickly the emphasis shifted away from control to treatment. The shift was due in part to the increasing professionalization of medical practitioners, in particular physicians and surgeons. In 1912, the Canadian

government passed the Canada Medical Act, which provided for the licensing of physicians. Around the same time, the United States government decided to standardize medical education and establish national standards of care. As Juanne Nancarrow Clarke notes in her analysis of health, illness, and medicine in Canada, "by the 1920s the hospital-based, curatively oriented, technologically sophisticated medical care system that Canadians know today was firmly established as *the* medical care system."[5]

The shift was due as well to the increasing emphasis on the need for medical insurance in the 20th century. In Canada, the first organized public initiative for such insurance was led by the Canadian Congress of Labour (which later became the Canadian Labour Congress) in 1919. In the same year, even in the United States, where national health insurance has never been adopted federally, some states began to think about having such programs. This emphasis on providing an insurance program to give citizens financial protection from high or even unaffordable health costs also naturally focused attention on treatment rather than prevention. The underlying belief that has sustained this treatment model is that illness can be cured by universal access to good health care.

However, the increased incidence of diseases such as cancer and AIDS, for which there may not be a cure, led to renewed calls in the 1970s for a return to an emphasis on prevention. In Canada, this shift to prevention was most apparent in a federal government document that was published in 1974 by the Health Ministry under Marc Lalonde.[6] The Lalonde Report listed four elements that affect the health of Canadians: human biology, the environment, lifestyle, and health-care organization. The report urged people to take more responsibility for their health by adopting healthier lifestyles. Subsequent federal government reports shifted the emphasis from the individual to the social, economic, and environmental context within which people live their lives and cemented the transition away from an exclusive focus on illness in health policy.

A good example of this return to prevention can be found in Canada at the federal level and in the United States in the states of California and Massachusetts. The health risks of smoking have been well known at least since 1964, when the U.S. Surgeon General declared that tobacco smoking may cause lung cancer. In the United States, for example, lung cancer rates had risen dramatically from only 5 to 75 cases per 100 000 between 1920 and 1970. Yet as recently as 1998, Health Canada reported that 30 percent of Canadian men and 25 percent of women aged 12 and over are daily or occasional smokers, with specific population groups having much higher smoking rates. In that same year, Health Canada estimated that 45 000 Canadians die each year as a result of the use of tobacco products. Internationally, the World Health Organization estimates that three million people die every year from tobacco-related diseases. The projected increase in smoking-related deaths in developing countries is even more striking—from one to seven million by 2030!

Governments can respond to this information in several different ways, and these differences reflect their various understandings of the problem. In North America, governments' first strategy was to simply warn people of the dangers of smoking, that is to treat smoking as an issue of individual choice. There were several reasons why governments chose a warning strategy as their first approach. Tobacco taxes provide govern-

Smoking rates are rising among children in developing countries.

Richard Vogel/CP Picture Archive

ments with revenue, although there are significant costs of treating smoking-related illnesses that are not always taken into account. In addition, the tobacco and cigarette producers have mounted effective lobby strategies over the years. On December 15, 1953, a group of senior tobacco executives meeting in New York City organized a massive and very successful "no harm from cigarettes" public relations campaign that has been referred to as the beginning of the tobacco industry conspiracy.[7] Finally, the treatment model was still the prevailing framework for health policy, and public money was directed to research on ways to treat tobacco-related diseases more effectively, rather than on smoking prevention.

But as the evidence mounted, and as opponents of the tobacco industry developed their own powerful lobby groups, government policies have shifted in Canada and the United States (although Canadian officials permitted tobacco executives to participate in a recent federally sponsored trade mission to China). In the United States, Washington and Maryland took the lead in developing policies to restrict or prohibit smoking in public places—the approach that has been favoured in Canada as well. In 1993, the Maryland Occupational Health and Safety Advisory Board proposed a smoking ban for all enclosed workplaces. A modified version of this proposal (with exemptions for the hospitality industry) was approved by the Maryland and Washington legislatures in 1994. In Canada, the federal government has focused on health and lifestyle representations of the tobacco problem, preferring to avoid a serious confrontation with the tobacco industry. The chosen policy is: smoking is legal but bad for health.

Within the more general framework of health promotion and disease prevention that has become part of the North American approach to health policy in the 21st century, governments have set up advisory committees to give suggestions on ways to improve the health status of U.S. and Canadian citizens. In 1985, the federal, provincial, and territorial ministers of health in Canada agreed to take a collaborative and comprehensive approach to reduce tobacco use. At the same time, governments have recognized that particular groups in the population respond differently to the policy approaches that the government adopts. Of particular concern are the higher-than-average smoking rates among Aboriginal peoples (62 percent for First Nations peoples and 72 percent for the Inuit in 1997, compared to 23 percent for Canadians overall).[8] In Canada, the federal government has recognized that separate strategies must be developed for Aboriginal peoples.

However, there are powerful forces at work that militate against these newer representations of the health policy problem. In the particular case of tobacco policy, they help to explain why governments took so long to move toward control of tobacco use. Public policies are developed by governments in response to what are seen to be problems in the public sphere. As noted above, the particular ways in which those problems are understood by governments are a function of many factors. In the case of health policy in general, and tobacco policy in particular, the combined influence of that industry and of the medical-industrial complex has been substantial.

The medical-industrial complex is made up of companies engaged in the business of supplying medical diagnoses and treatment for a profit. In the United States, for example, drug companies make a multibillion dollar contribution to the country's gross domestic product. In Canada, the pharmaceutical industry is one of the most profitable manufacturing sectors. The drug companies work together to mount a very powerful political lobby. In Canada, Canada's Research-Based Pharmaceutical Companies, as the association is now known, is one of the most successful lobby groups in the country, and it has a vested interest in ensuring the continued use of its products. A treatment approach to tobacco use contributes significantly to the profitability of these drug companies.

It is often the case as well that health research is funded by pharmaceutical companies, who are interested primarily in discovering new drugs that they can add to their list of products. Of course, these drugs are often important parts of illness treatment strategies. But the link between research and drug companies may mean that illness prevention, or alternative, non-drug treatments may not be given much government support. In the United States, for example, the federal government established the Office of Alternative Medicine (now called the National Center for Complementary and Alternative Medicine) within the National Institutes of Health and provided it with a $2 million research budget. In contrast, in any year the National Institutes of Health can spend $68 million on a single trial of one drug.[9]

Some recent research on tobacco control policies in two rural communities in Alberta also points to the significance of issue construction for the legislators themselves. In 1995, the town of Olds passed a moderate bylaw that prohibits smoking in the local arena, unless it is rented to a private group. In the same year, the town of Innisfail passed a comprehensive bylaw restricting smoking in a variety of public places. Both towns are similar, with populations of about 6000, and service an agricultural population. Why is there a difference in the bylaws? The researchers concluded that concerns about public and private space dictated the policy decision in Olds. Councillors decided that, when the arena was a public space used by young people, they had the right to impose restrictions. In Innisfail, the public–private debate was never resolved, so councillors held a plebiscite that supported a comprehensive bylaw.[10] The lesson here is that, even within a general approach to an issue (in this case, tobacco control), the way in which an issue is framed can have an important impact on policy outcomes.

Policy Consequences

In the case of health policy, it is particularly easy to see the consequences of constructing an issue in different ways. In the treatment model of health, the citizen becomes the patient, relying on the expertise of the medical profession and the research skills of the drug companies. The treatment model places the main responsibility for curing illness on the professionals who are part of the medical-industrial complex. In this model, the citizen as patient is primarily concerned with the availability and affordability of good health care.

When health policy is constructed according to the lifestyle model instead, as in the case of tobacco policy, the policy emphasis is placed on "denormalizing" those activities or habits that make us sick. In this case, policies developed focus on encouraging more exercise, proper diet, stress management, and cessation of smoking, for example. It is left to us, as citizens, to make healthy lifestyle choices.

A third and less common approach to health policy focuses on environmental and social factors that affect health. An environmental approach targets clean air and water as the policy goal. This approach has been relatively unsuccessful in North America, although the deaths in Walkerton, Ontario, in 2001 that resulted from *E. coli* contamination of the town's water supply have moved environmental concerns somewhat closer to the top of governments' policy agendas. Equally unpopular in North America is the social approach that draws a link between an individual's social and economic status and health. Proponents of the social approach target the elimination or removal of poverty; if governments were to adopt this approach to health, they would focus on issues such as job creation, minimum annual income guarantees, and improved social programs for the unemployed and the underemployed.

It is not quite as easy to measure the impact of different models of health care funding. It has become popular for governments to look at the experience of other countries when assessing the strengths and weaknesses of their own health care system. But comparisons are costly and complex, since health-care practices vary widely from place to place. It is, however, fairly easy to conclude that the movement away from a universal, publicly funded health-care system in Canada will increase the health-care costs that will be borne by those who use the system, since under the present system the costs are shared by all Canadians, whether they use the system or not.

FAMILY POLICIES
Agenda-Setting

In this second case study, in which we examine governments' policies for families, we need to begin with a discussion of the meanings of family. While it is still the case that most women and men throughout the world are members of monogamous, heterosexual relationships sanctioned by religious organizations or the state, other family forms abound. Sociologists see the family as one of society's basic institutions, one that carries out the functions of bearing and raising children, socializing family members within a social setting, distributing material goods and emotional support, and contributing to the social order. While we may be prepared to consider the family as "whatever people living in societies commonly think of as family,"[11] governments have been more restricted in their thinking.

In North America, the movement of family issues onto public agendas has reflected changing perceptions of the boundaries of the public and private spheres of life. But even taking into account these shifting boundaries of the public and the private, public policy has been constructed primarily within patriarchal assumptions. As Lorraine Code notes, in patriarchal societies "men have more power than women, readier access than women to what is valued in society, and, in consequence, are in control over many, if not most aspects of women's lives."[12]

These patriarchal assumptions were most apparent in the early policies made by legislators in Western industrializing societies in the 18th and 19th centuries. In Canada, at the time of Confederation, both women and men widely accepted that there was a sharp distinction between the public and private spheres and that women were suited by nature to the private sphere of the family. But while women were expected to bear and raise children and care for the household, early legislators constructed family policies that vested economic and guardianship rights in the husband/father, who was usually referred to as the head of the household. It was not until 1922 in English Canada, and 1940 in Quebec, that provincial laws were changed to permit women to purchase property in their own name. The state intervened only to the extent that it provided a meagre pension to women with small children who were widowed or deserted by their husbands. For the most part, families belonged in the private sphere and were outside the scope of public policy.

By the early 20th century, this rigid distinction between public and private had begun to break down. As women organized in feminist groups, and as they moved in ever-increasing numbers into the paid labour force, the 19th-century conceptions of women as nurturers in the home and men as wage earners and policymakers were becoming less and less accurate. Nonetheless, policymakers persisted in hanging on to their traditional view even into the years following World War II. Perhaps the most dramatic manifestation of this traditional family construct was the rapid dismantling of the childcare facilities that had been set up by the federal government of Canada to facilitate women's labour force participation during the war. The Canadian government then even went so far as to prohibit the employment of married women in the federal civil service.[13]

As legislators began to build the postwar welfare state, they did so with the notion of the male wage earner in mind. In 1944, the Canadian government introduced a national program of family allowances to supplement the haphazard and provincially run mothers' allowances that had been put in place in the early 1900s. The family allowance was paid to the mother and was put in place to help women raise healthy babies and children. Evidence from the war years had convinced policymakers that Canada's young men were not as healthy as they should be to populate the jobs emerging in the booming industrial economy. The policymakers hoped that these family allowance cheques would make it easier for women to stay at home to look after their children, in this way improving the health of the next generation. In terms of the policy cycle, the government's agenda was to improve the health of young Canadians. Its chosen policy design was a program to encourage mothers to stay at home. The family allowance cheque was the policy instrument. But by 1951, there was significant participation of women in the paid labour force (see Table 8.1), and

---

Table 8.1   Women as a Percentage of the Total Labour Force

Year	Percent*
1901	13.3
1911	13.4
1921	15.5
1931	17.0
1941	18.5
1951	22.0
1961	27.3
1971	34.4
1981	40.8
1991	44.5

* The ages of women included in these figures are: 10 years and over in 1901 and 1911; 14 years and over between 1921 and 1951, and 15 years and over between 1961 and 1991.

Sources: Canada, Women's Bureau, *Women at Work in Canada* (Ottawa: Department of Labour, 1964); Canada, Statistics Canada, Social and Economic Studies Division. *Women in Canada: A Statistical Report* (Ottawa: Statistics Canada, 1985), Catalogue No. 89-503; Canada, Statistics Canada, *Labour Force Annual Averages, 1993* (Ottawa: Statistics Canada, 1994), Catalogue No. 71-220.

---

only a slight majority (57 percent) of families had only one wage earner.

By 1971, 65 percent of Canadian families had two wage earners. Gradually, policy shifted to reflect this new reality of women's wage labour, and by the late 1970s, both provincial and federal governments developed policies to assist women to compete more equitably for positions in the paid labour force. The shift was due to several factors, but in particular the internal lobbying carried out by a relatively new group of civil servants working within the federal Department of Labour, in the newly created (in 1954) Women's Bureau. This small unit, which rarely numbered more than five members, collected information about women's labour force participation and urged the federal government to take such measures as equal pay and maternity leave legislation. The bureau met with some modest successes. For example, it was instrumental in encouraging Canada to enact **affirmative action** legislation for the first time in 1980. That early legislation applied only to the federal public service and required the setting of goals and timetables to increase the representation of women at all levels in the federal public service. It was nevertheless an important step in the recognition that there may be systemic obstacles to the equal employment of women in the paid labour force.

The U.S. path to policies on women and employment was somewhat different. In the United States, the initial impetus for employment reform emerged out of the civil rights movement. The term *affirmative action* was first used in 1965 by President Lyndon Johnson in his Executive Order 11246. It stipulated that applicants should be hired and later treated during their employment without regard to their race, creed, colour, or national origin. The list was expanded to include sex only in 1967.

The Importance of Issue Construction

Despite these measures, the old patriarchal assumptions about gender roles in the family continued to affect policymakers' construction of some of the problems emerging in this new age of women's rapidly increasing labour force participation. Nowhere is this more apparent than in the realm of childcare policies. In spite of the fact that most of the women who were part of the paid labour force were married and had children, there was little (if any) attempt to deal with the growing problem of access to safe and affordable childcare. Even though Canada had mounted a national childcare strategy funded jointly by federal and provincial governments during World War II, when women were called into industrial production to assist in the war effort, the entire system had been dismantled by 1946.[14]

Varying programs now exist across the provinces and territories, but it is most common for childcare to be unregulated and inadequate. There is a mix of commercial and nonprofit licensed centres and some government subsidies for low-income parents, and the federal government offers a modest tax refund for parents paying for childcare.[15] In spite of recurring promises for a national childcare strategy, the federal government has never considered seriously the need for public involvement in what is seen to be a private problem—of helping mothers to look after their children. Canadian governments have also justified their lack of action on the grounds that childcare crosses federal and provincial jurisdictional boundaries. But given that this obstacle has been overcome in other areas (for example, the health policies discussed above), it is clear that there are other factors at work. Annis May Timpson concludes that these include ideological factors and that "federal policies to promote gender equality in the paid workplace have failed to take sufficient account of the way that the domestic context of many women's lives impacts on their employment opportunities."[16] In other words, federal governments have constructed the problem of inadequate childcare as a primarily domestic issue.

This failure to develop policies that address childcare needs is a particularly North American phenomenon. In the United States as well, both national and state governments have tended to view childcare as a

---

Table 8.2 Marital Status of Women in the Labour Force, in Percentages

Marital Status	1931	1941	1951	1961	1971	1981	1991
Single	80.7	79.9	62.1	42.3	34.1	29.8	25.2
Married	10.0	12.7	30.0	49.8	56.9	59.9	64.4
Other	9.2	7.4	7.9	7.9	9.0	10.2	10.1

Note: Some columns do not add up to 100 percent as a result of rounding.

Source: Canada, Women's Bureau, *Women at Work in Canada* (Ottawa: Department of Labour, 1964); Canada, Women's Bureau, *Women in the Labour Force; Part 1: Participation* (Ottawa: Department of Labour, 1983), Catalogue No. 98–125; Canada, Statistics Canada, *Labour Force Annual Averages, 1991* (Ottawa: Statistics Canada, 1992), Catalogue No. 71-220.

private issue, except in the case of low-income parents. There is a Federal Child Care Bureau that keeps track of scattered childcare projects across the country. All of these projects are based on a commitment to public–private partnerships. In addition, the Child Care and Development Fund helps states, territories, and tribal organizations provide childcare to low-income families. But for the most part, childcare is unregulated, private, and inadequate. According to the 1997 National Survey of America's Families, for the 60 percent of families with children under the age of five who are using childcare, the average monthly expense is U.S.$325.[17]

Some European governments have taken a significantly different approach to childcare policies. Sweden, for example, sees a role for government in helping families. Publicly funded and regulated childcare is high on the government's agenda, since childcare is viewed as essential to the country's economic and social well-being. Likewise in France, the government provides universal access to state-run centres for all children past the toilet-training age. For younger children, there is an extensive network of nurseries run by local governments and nonprofit groups. Parents pay a small stipend that is income-related for this care. Some developing countries have also placed childcare high on their policy agenda. Even with their modest budgets, they have put in place some public programs. Cuba has a universal, publicly funded childcare program that has been used as the model for other countries. The Dominican Republic has experimented with alternative forms of service delivery. It has set up centres that are run by low-income, retired elementary school teachers. With this program, it has tried to resolve the dual problems of poverty levels of senior women and childcare needs of young children.

The main difference in the North American and other approaches to childcare lies in the way in which the policy issue or problem has been constructed. In the North American approach, the issue is seen to be one of reconciling parental needs with freedom of choice. In the Canadian case at least, this is somewhat ironic, in view of the stated commitment of the federal Liberal government led by Jean Chrétien to developing policies for Canada's children. The apparent inconsistency can be explained by the government's overarching commitment to developing a new kind of economic citi-

zenship, where the primary goal is on improving self-reliance and productivity. Within this economic model, there is little room for state-regulated and nonprofit childcare. In the Swedish model, the issue of childcare is viewed primarily from the perspective of children's needs. Swedish policies were developed within an understanding of citizenship that stresses community and shared responsibilities.

Policy Consequences

In recent years, governments throughout the world have paid lip service to the principle of concern for child welfare. Some of this concern was in response to the United Nations' declaration of 1979 as the International Year of the Child. In Canada, this concern for children has been expressed in a succession of position papers produced since 1990, the year of the World Summit for Children. Health Canada established a specialized Children's Bureau to coordinate federal policies and programs affecting children, and in 1992, the government introduced a Child Development Initiative with a five-year budget of $500 million. Yet none of these initiatives has led to better federal funding or monitoring of childcare programs. As a result, the quality of childcare is at risk. Three provincial exceptions are Quebec, Saskatchewan, and New Brunswick, each of which has some program in place that targets early childhood care; Quebec's strong program even includes a set curriculum for early childhood centres.

A weak childcare policy has particularly serious consequences for low-income single parents, most of whom are women. The increasing support for the economic citizenship model in North America has led either to recent reductions in social welfare payments or to the twinning of welfare with labour force participation. Ontario provides one of the best examples of this policy approach. When the Conservatives were elected in 1995 under the leadership of Mike Harris, they promised to reduce welfare payments while at the same time encouraging welfare recipients to make up the difference with part-time employment. This promise was followed with comprehensive welfare reforms, including the setting up of a three-tiered set of welfare assistance. This assistance ranges from workfare (unpaid work in exchange for welfare) to training initiatives, where recipients must retrain or take trial jobs in order to receive benefits. For single mothers, this means focusing on labour force participation rather than on family responsibilities, a choice that can be agonizing. Not only are the jobs available to these women frequently low paid, tenuous, and dead-end, but the absence of affordable and reliable childcare options often precludes even the least attractive employment.

FREE TRADE

Agenda-Setting

Free or freer trade moved onto the agendas of most governments throughout the world in the latter years of the 20th century, in part because the forces of globalization were at work. Although the term **globalization** can have different meanings, it generally means the integration of primarily economic forces across national boundaries. For policymakers, globalization has meant that factors from outside a nation can have an impact on domestic policies. However, questions about the movement of goods and services across national boundaries have preoccupied policymakers since the setting up of nation-states and have revolved around issues of free trade.

In Canada, for example, the topic of free trade, primarily with the United States, has been an agenda item for federal governments since the British government passed the British North America Act in 1867. Sir John A. Macdonald, Canada's first prime minister, was strongly committed to a tariff policy that would, he thought, encourage the growth of Canadian manufacturing. To this end, he devised the National Policy, which imposed customs duties on imported manufactured goods, encouraged immigration to bring new workers to Canada to populate new industrial ventures, assisted in the building of a railway across the country to permit the easy shipment of goods from east to west, and set up an Indian policy of reserves, church schools, and land appropriation.[18] Only a few years later, in 1911, the federal election was fought on the question of free trade with the United States. The free traders lost the election, but economic developments in the succeeding years gave rise to north–south trade, and a continentalist pattern was born. These continentalist sentiments became even more pronounced in the

1980s, when the U.S. government led by Ronald Reagan proposed a North American Accord, with improved economic cooperation among Canada, the United States, and Mexico. In this way, free trade was forced onto the agenda of a Canadian government that was initially hostile to the proposal. When a Conservative government led by Brian Mulroney replaced the Liberal administration of Pierre Trudeau, the stage was set for bilateral and later multilateral discussions about North American free trade.

Several explanations have been offered for the U.S. government's interest in free trade. John Warnock, a critic of free trade, argues that the United States was anxious to secure sources for strategic raw materials needed to sustain its position as defender of the "free world."[19] Other commentators have pointed to support among Western Canadian oil producers and farmers for north–south trade, since lack of trade restrictions meant for them cheaper transportation costs and bigger markets. Others argue that if the United States wanted free trade, Canada had no choice but to agree, since the bulk of Canadian exports make their way to U.S. markets; they point out that Canada thought that a formal agreement would ensure greater stability in trading relations. Ultimately, the Canada–United States Free Trade Agreement was signed in 1987. In 1994, Mexico joined as well in the refashioned North American Free Trade Agreement (NAFTA). Also in 1994, discussions were broadened to include the possibility of the creation of a Free Trade Area of the Americas (FTAA), which would include all but one (Cuba) of the 35 countries of North and South America.

In Europe, discussions about free trade began even earlier, in the 1950s. Belgium, France, Germany, Italy, Luxembourg, and the Netherlands came together in 1957 to sign the Treaty of Rome, which set up the European Economic Community. Since then, the mandate and the size of the community (now called the European Union, or EU for short) have grown significantly. In addition to the original commitment to reducing trade barriers, members of the EU now also work toward the creation of a Common Foreign and Security Policy (CFSP), as well as cooperative justice and domestic policies. The EU now numbers 15 countries, and perhaps as many as 10 more may join by 2010. In 2002, the majority of these 15 countries switched to one common currency, the euro, and agreed to operate with one central bank.

The Importance of Issue Construction

When supporters talk about free trade, they often speak in terms of creating a "level playing field." The sports analogy is apt here, since free traders see competition as a public good. They love the metaphor of a rough-and-tumble game, where only the strong survive. Such a level playing field means that small domestic producers should not be given any competitive advantage over their usually much bigger rivals from another country, even if the rival takes profits back to the country of origin or brings workers with it from that other country.

But we should be cognizant of the implications of the concept of the level playing field. Its adoption means that governments are under pressure to step back from regulations that might restrict the free flow of goods and services. Such regulations might include, for example, restrictions on the kinds of processes that can be used by pulp and paper mills to bleach the pulp. Or they might include rules restricting "subsidies" of domestic workers, such as unemployment insurance or publicly funded health care. In general, free trade agreements restrict governments from developing policies that might be viewed by other countries as affecting the profitability of corporations.

Proponents of free trade justify their position in neoliberal economic terms. In other words, they put market considerations first and stress that governments' first priority must be economic growth. At the same time, corporations argue that if they are to remain competitive and profitable, they have to reduce their input costs by seeking low-wage areas at home and abroad and searching internationally for the cheapest raw materials. The philosophical foundation of their arguments can be found in the 18th-century writings of Adam Smith, a Scottish economist whose influential *The Wealth of Nations* was published in 1776. According to Smith, a free market is the most rational use of capital and labour. Furthermore, since the functioning of the market is regulated by what Smith called an "invisible hand," a system where individuals are left free to pursue their own economic self-interest will nat-

urally produce the greatest good for the greatest number. Smith transposed these principles to his discussions of international trade and proposed that the free movement of goods and services across nations would increase the general well-being of all nations. These free trade principles have not always been popular among economists and industrialists. The most recent shift to this position began in the 1970s, when voters elected the Conservative government led by Margaret Thatcher in Britain and the Republican President Ronald Reagan in the United States. Since then, there has been a rising tide of support for free market principles among Western governments. These governments favour free trade as a way to secure markets and maintain employment levels.

Opponents of free trade counter that neoliberal economics puts business ahead of citizens. In the case of the Free Trade Area of the Americas, the protesters who gathered in Quebec City in May 2001 argued that the FTAA was an international business deal that would allow corporations to bypass environmental and worker protection laws, increase corporate power, and endanger the lives of millions, in particular women and people of colour. They constructed the issue of free trade as an attempt to further commodify citizens' lives. In the case of Canadian–U.S. trade discussions, opponents of the free trade deal charged that it would lead to a further loss of Canadian sovereignty.

Policy Consequences

The outcome of the European Union is still in question. One part of the EU framework is the European Commission, with 20 members appointed by the governments of the 15 member states (Britain, France, Germany, Italy, and Spain have two members each). The commission is charged with making EU policies, although these have to be approved by the Council of the European Union and by the European Parliament, the members of which are directly elected. Council membership shifts from issue to issue, since member states appoint one Council member each, and the person who fills this job varies, depending on the issue. This makes for a fairly cumbersome process, and it is not yet clear if a European as opposed to a set of national interests will emerge. But the EU has already had a significant impact on the policies of the countries that have applied for memberships, such as Poland, Slovenia, Romania, and the Czech Republic. These countries have had to harmonize their justice and health standards, food and drug regulations, and agricultural policies in order to qualify for membership. Policy analysts generally agree that the EU has harmonized European social and economic policies. Meanwhile, national interests and loyalties have remained more or less intact. Analysts also agree that the EU has favoured neoliberal economic policies among member states and generally contributed to economic growth.

The results also have been mixed in the case of the Canadian–U.S. free trade deal. The flow of exports from Canada to the United States has risen substantially. In 1981, 66 percent of all Canadian exports found their way to the United States. By 1998, this figure had risen to 88 percent. According to the Canadian Department of Foreign Affairs and International Trade, since 1994—when the NAFTA entered into force—"the Canadian economy has grown by an annual average of 3.8%, keeping Canada in the lead among the G-7 countries. This healthy growth has translated into the creation of close to 2.1 million jobs, representing an increase of 16% over pre-NAFTA employment levels…. Two-way merchandise trade between Canada and Mexico has doubled since 1994 and reached $14.1 billion in 2000."[20]

However, the agreement has not stopped the United States from mounting challenges to Canadian exports. Canadian supporters of free trade had argued that it would put a halt to ongoing U.S. attempts to impose countervailing tariffs, especially in the area of softwood lumber. They proposed that unless Canada made a free trade deal, these restrictive trade practices by the United States would seriously damage Canada's forest and other raw material exports, traditionally a major source of Canadian wealth. Yet as late as 1998 (just over 10 years after the deal was struck), the United States once again took measures to restrict Canadian exports of softwood lumber. In 1996, Canada and the United States entered into the Softwood Lumber Agreement, which was to have effect for five years. It allowed lumber companies in British Columbia, Alberta, Ontario, and Quebec to export specific quantities of softwood lumber to the United States without export duties. This agreement supplemented the earlier

Free Trade Agreement. Nevertheless, on July 1, 1998, and on June 9, 1999, the United States claimed that softwood lumber with drilled studs or with notches was not really softwood lumber and was therefore outside the agreement and subject to higher tariffs.

NAFTA has not proven effective against these recent U.S. protectionist policies. Following the expiration of the Canada–U.S. Softwood Lumber Agreement on April 1, 2001, the U.S. government decided in May 2002 to impose 27.2 percent countervailing duties on Canadian softwood lumber from all but the Atlantic provinces. While Canada can challenge these duties through the World Trade Organization and NAFTA, these challenges could take years.

Observers generally agree that the consequences of NAFTA and other free trade deals for Canada and the United States are mixed. The United States reports major trade gains, lower prices for consumers, and higher incomes. But Canadians have continued to feel the impact of protectionist U.S. trade policies. In addition, some critics warn that Canadian agricultural marketing boards, environmental controls, and cultural regulations are under attack as a result of free trade. Those who argue for fewer government regulations are satisfied with the trend to freer trade, but those who fear additional problems with water quality, further reductions in the size of forest reserves, and new health problems associated with recent successful challenges to controls on the use of toxic substances in industrial processes are unhappy with recent developments.

The consequences of NAFTA for Mexico have been mixed as well. Exports have increased (annually at about 18 percent with NAFTA partners between 1994 and 1999). But foreign direct investment in Mexico has risen substantially, and this has been associated with the closing of many small, local companies that are not able to compete in the new NAFTA environment. At the same time, there has been a rapid movement of U.S. media and culture into Mexico, posing yet another challenge to the survival of Mexican culture. There have been political consequences as well. NAFTA has served to "direct and limit policy changes in Mexico along neo-liberal lines; market-oriented reforms are protected and encouraged, whereas nationalist, socially oriented policies are discouraged."[21]

A free trade policy clearly has implications for much more than simply the flow of trade. It is an initiative

George W. Bush bombs the Canadian softwood industry with tariffs.

Roy Peterson/Vancouver Sun/Artizans

favoured primarily by those who argue that economic policies should drive social and cultural policy. Those who support the principle of state sovereignty and wish to see governments refocus their priorities on issues such as citizenship, human rights, and social policy argue for national controls on global capitalism.

CONCLUSION

The policy decisions taken by governments affect our lives in significant and multiple ways. Contaminated water in Walkerton, doctor shortages throughout Canada, rapidly increasing smoking rates among children in developing countries, and the presence of U.S. troops in Afghanistan are in varying degrees the conse-

quences of the courses of action (or inaction) taken by governments. These and other policy decisions form the economic, social, and cultural shape of the country in which we live and have far-reaching impacts on our individual lives.

You are probably at the beginning of your university education, and you hope to find a meaningful and well-paid job that will make it possible for you to live a happy and productive life. The shape of your future, however, has as much to do with earlier and current policy decisions of governments as with your ability to do well at school. If you are a woman and thinking about having children, your opportunities for paid employment will be affected by policies on affirmative action, maternity leave provisions, and childcare. If you are hoping to become an accountant, your career will be shaped in part by government responses to the recent Enron scandal in the United States and resulting new regulations for accounting firms. In addition, all of us pay taxes and have to balance the cost of high taxes with the reward of universal social programs such as health care.

The policy process is much more than just a contest among personalities. Recent events in both Canada and the United States have focused attention on political leaders and their actions, often at the expense of considerations of the governments' agendas. But it is the government agendas that bring politics into our daily lives and make the study of the policy process a useful and exciting exercise.

DISCUSSION QUESTIONS

1. In view of the large gap between African countries' economic capabilities and HIV/AIDS costs (see Figure 8.1), how might organizations such as the United Nations contribute to reducing the impact of HIV/AIDS?

2. North America and Europe offer two different models for childcare policies. What are the strengths and weaknesses of the two models? Discuss what you mean by strengths and weaknesses.

3. Countries such as Canada, which have small populations and are geographically close to more powerful neighbours, face some serious questions when they are developing their trade policies. What are these questions? How might they be resolved?

4. The neoliberal approach to policy is based on the proposition that what is good for the market is good for the country. How do critics challenge this argument? What criteria can we use to evaluate a country's well-being?

w(w)w WEB LINKS

Canadian Policy Research Network:
http://www.cprn.org.

NAFTA Information from the Canadian Department of Foreign Affairs and International Trade:
http://www.dfait-maeci.gc.ca/nafta-alena/menu-e.asp.

Estimates, Performance and Planning Information, from Treasury Board of Canada Secretariat:
http://www.tbs-sct.gc.ca/rma/eppi-ibdrp/eppi_e.htm

Canada's Tobacco Control Strategy, from Health Canada:
http://www.hc-sc.gc.ca/hppb/tobaccoreduction/html/table.

United Nations Battle against AIDS (Acrobat Reader is required):
http://www.unaids.org/worldaidsday/2001/Epiupdate2001/Epiupdate2001_en.pdf.

FURTHER READING

Bacchi, Carol Lee. *Women, Policy and Politics: The Construction of Policy Problems*. London: Sage, 1999.

Hauss, Charles, and Miriam Smith. *Comparative Politics: Domestic Responses to Global Challenges: A Canadian Perspective*. Scarborough: Nelson Thomson Learning, 2000.

Timpson, Annis May. *Driven Apart: Women's Employment Equality and Child Care in Canadian Public Policy*. Vancouver: UBC Press, 2001.

Urwin, Derek W. *The Community of Europe: A History of European Integration since 1945*. 2nd ed. New York: Longman, 1995.

Waring, Marilyn. *Three Masquerades: Essays on Equality, Work, and Human Rights*. Toronto: University of Toronto Press, 1997.

ENDNOTES

1 "Remarks by the President upon Arrival at Barksdale Air Force Base"; cited on January 1, 2002; available at http://www.whitehouse.gov/news/releases/2001/09/20010911-1.html.

2 For a good discussion of the process of constructing policy problems, see Carol Lee Bacchi, *Women, Policy and Politics: The Construction of Policy Problems* (London: Sage, 1999).

3 Leslie Pal, *Beyond Policy Analysis: Public Issue Management in Turbulent Times* (Scarborough: Nelson, 1997), pp. 1–2.

4 This is the view of pluralist theorists such as Robert Dahl and David Truman. For a good discussion of the weaknesses in the pluralists' approach, see E.E. Schattschneider, *The Semi-Sovereign People: A Realist's View of Democracy* (New York: Holt, Rienhart and Winston, 1960).

5 Juanne Nancarrow Clarke, *Health, Illness, and Medicine in Canada* (Toronto: McClelland and Stewart, 1990), p. 186.

6 Marc Lalonde, *A New Perspective on the Health of Canadians* (Ottawa: Minister of Supply and Services, 1972).

7 W. John Diamond, W. Lee Cowden, and Burton Goldberg, *An Alternative Medicine Definitive Guide to Cancer* (Tiburon, Calif.: Future Medicine Publishing, 1997), pp. 584–85.

8 Health Canada, "Tobacco Reduction," Preface; cited on January 1, 2002; available at http://www.tobacco-control.com.

9 Diamond, Cowden, and Goldberg, *An Alternative Medicine Definitive Guide,* p. 662.

10 Roger Gibbins et al., "Public Policies, Private Space: Tobacco Control in Rural Alberta," in W. Ramp et al., eds., *Health in Rural Settings: Contexts for Action* (Lethbridge: University of Lethbridge, 1999), pp. 85–103.

11 Susan McDaniel, "The Changing Canadian Family: Women's Roles and the Impact of Feminism," in Sandra Burt, Lorraine Code, and Lindsay Dorney, eds., *Changing Patterns: Women in Canada* (Toronto: McClelland and Stewart, 1988), p. 103.

12 Lorraine Code, "Feminist Theory," in Burt, Code, and Dorney, *Changing Patterns,* p. 18.

13 For an excellent discussion of the postwar period, see Ruth Roach Pierson, *"They're Still Women After All": The Second World War and Canadian Womanhood* (Toronto: McClelland and Stewart, 1986).

14 Annis May Timpson, *Driven Apart: Women's Equality and Child Care in Canadian Public Policy* (Vancouver: UBC Press, 2001), pp. 16–17.

15 For a comprehensive survey of the programs available across Canada, see Jane Jenson and Sherry Thompson, "Comparative Family Policy: Six Provincial Stories," *Canadian Policy Research Networks Study* F108 (Ottawa: Renouf Publishing, 1999).

16 Ibid., pp. 210–11.

17 Linda Giannarelli and James Barsimatov, "Child Care Expenses of America's Families" (Washington, D.C.: Urban Institute, 2000).

18 Joyce Green, "Towards a Detente with History," *International Journal of Canadian Studies* 12 (fall 1995): 85–105.

19 John Warnock, *Free Trade and the New Right Agenda* (Vancouver: New Star Books, 1988), p. 95.

20 Canada, Department of Foreign Affairs and International Trade, "The North American Free Trade Agreement: Overview"; cited on July 22, 2002; available at http://www.dfait-maeci.gc.ca/nafta-alena/over-e.asp.

21 Julian Castro Rea, "The North American Challenge: A Mexican Perspective," *Isuma: Canadian Journal of Policy Research* 1(1) (spring 2000): 27.

Chapter 9

Legislatures: Such Promise and Potential

Andrew Heard

CHAPTER OBJECTIVES

After you have completed this chapter, you should be able to
- understand the potential roles of a legislature in a political system
- discuss the range of actors that undermine the effectiveness of legislatures
- outline how laws are made
- differentiate among the different kinds of representation that legislators can undertake
- discuss ideas for the reform of legislatures.

WHAT ARE LEGISLATURES?

Legislatures are at once the centrepiece of democratic countries and yet at the same time are often viewed as the most visible failures of those very democracies. An elected legislature holds the promise of the people's representatives assembling together to debate, deliberate, and decide upon the nation's business. In a multiparty democracy, one would expect that significant differences of opinion would be expressed as members of the different parties listen to and weigh competing views of how best to deal with the issues of public policy under consideration. Perhaps even some visible compromises and changes of heart might be made among the parties as they try to forge a consensus on what is best for their society. The members of the legislature would be able to identify the most serious weaknesses in a proposed law, make the necessary changes, and reject any measures that proved to be profoundly unpopular with the people they represent. Unfortunately, reality often falls disappointingly short of these expectations.

> *Definition*
> **LEGISLATURE:** An institution with primary responsibility to enact laws.

This chapter explores the potential roles that legislatures might fill in any political system and then examines the practical factors that can limit that potential. The emphasis here is on balancing idealism with a fuller understanding of the limitations under which legislators do their work. It is equally important to resist the temptation to slip into cynicism and view legislatures as simply rubber stamps that blindly approve policies proposed by the executive. There are indeed a number of important and substantive functions that legislatures can undertake, and an appreciation of these can lead to useful suggestions for legislative reform. This chapter reviews legislatures generically, but also provides an opportunity to understand Canadian and other legislatures around the world. In order to assess our own legislatures, it is essential that we have a global view that allows us to appreciate what can and does occur elsewhere; with a comparative perspective, we can better understand what might be done to improve our own political institutions.

BOX 9.1

THE STRUCTURE OF LEGISLATURES

A **unicameral** legislature has only one chamber, and all members of the legislature belong to and participate in that chamber.

A **bicameral** legislature has two separate chambers (often called houses), and members of the legislature belong only to one of those chambers and have a right to participate in only their chamber's proceedings.

Example of a unicameral legislature: Israel

Knesset: 120 members

Example of a bicameral legislature: Canada

Upper house: Senate 105 appointed members

Lower house: House of Commons 301 elected members

The first task is to identify just what a legislature is. For a political institution to be called a legislature, that institution must be centrally involved in the law-making process. Moreover, the legislature must actually make law; it is not simply a consultative body that provides advice to another law-making official or institution. For example, the Shura Council in Saudi Arabia cannot be described as a legislature, since its only formal power is to offer advice on public policy to the council of ministers. However, legislatures are not the only institutions or political actors in a political system that make law. It is important to distinguish between the legislative power and the legislative branch of government—the power to make law is not restricted to just the legislative branch.

All political systems provide some legislative power to the executive branch of government; there are several possible forms this power might take. First, the constitution of a state may explicitly provide some law-making powers to the executive. For example, the president of the country may be able to make some laws by decree. Every political system also provides in some fashion that laws may be made by the ministers or cabinet who head up the executive departments of government; these laws can be called various things in different countries, such as regulations, ordinances, or orders-in-council. The law-making power of the executive is often actually power that is delegated to the executive by the legislature. In every political system, the judiciary also exercises, some law-making power in the course of interpreting and enforcing the legal rules enacted by the legislature or executive. So we find that the legislative power can actually be spread across all three branches of government.

However, the exercise of law-making by other institutions or officials in the political system does not mean that they constitute legislatures. Constitutions usually vest the prime law-making power in one particular institution, the legislature, while only limited law-making power belongs to the executive. And the law-making power of the judiciary is only an implicit power that is exercised in the course of its principal task, which is interpreting and enforcing the law.

Legislatures appear to have important symbolic cachet, judging by their proliferation over the 20th century. The vast majority of states today have a formal legislative body, 179 all told in 1998.[1] Many authoritarian regimes have legislatures in order to create a façade of democracy by holding elections and letting the people's "representatives" pass laws. In these instances, legislatures are truly rubber stamps, and any laws proposed by the rulers are dutifully passed with no criticism of the government. Only a few countries do without a legislature, reserving principal law-making power for the executive.[2] In a few of these countries, an absolute monarch stills exercises the law-making power; in Saudi Arabia, for example, the king is the sole source of formal legislative power. However, most of the states without legislatures are ones ruled by a dictator, who issues laws by personal decree.

POTENTIAL FUNCTIONS OF LEGISLATURES

In studying legislatures, political scientists have a number of concerns and interests. First and foremost, we are concerned with identifying what specific roles legislatures may fill in a political system and what factors have an impact on how effectively the legislatures carry out those roles. Legislatures can play vital informal roles in a political system, on top of the formal ones detailed in their countries' constitutions. While there may be factors specific to a particular state that have an impact on its legislature's effectiveness, a student of politics and government should always be aware of the full range of potential roles that legislatures may play in any political system, as well as the wide variety of factors that may enhance or limit the ability of a legislature to fill those roles. A deeper understanding of the functioning of any particular legislature may well arise from an appreciation of the broader contexts in which all legislatures operate in general.

One can easily identify a few key roles that legislatures perform, such as making laws, representing the people, and debating public issues. A simple reason for most legislatures' failure to fill these roles can be just as readily identified: many legislatures are effectively controlled by the executive or by the leaders of a dominating party or coalition of parties. In either case, strict discipline of the members of the legislature prevents them from taking independent positions on matters under debate and consideration. Examined in such stark terms, most legislatures around the world, whether they are part of democratic or authoritarian systems, would have to be written off as failures; they would be nothing better than symbolic ornaments in contrast to the executive's total control of the policy process. One could also argue that even in legislatures where individual members have considerable personal discretion to decide what position to take on a matter under debate, such as in the U.S. Congress, the realities are that the legislators simply choose the positions demanded by those who provide them with the financial support needed to get re-elected. On closer examination, however, such views of legislatures may prove to be more cynical than accurate.

Perhaps the best starting point for examining legislatures is to review briefly all the possible roles that legislatures can play in a political system. The great variety of functions can be surprising to many, and they give a clue to the potential value of a legislature that works well. The law-making role of legislatures is the most visible (and will be dealt with in detail in a section below), but there are many other functions that are equally important—and sometimes even more so.

The following are the potential roles of legislatures:

- to legislate
- to represent
- to debate
- to educate
- to institutionalize opposition
- to investigate issues and events
- to suggest or initiate new policies
- to scrutinize executive activities
- to legitimate the policies of the executive
- to ratify or veto executive decisions and actions
- to refine and improve policies suggested by the executive
- to decide who holds executive offices (in parliamentary systems)
- to provide alternative governments or political leaders
- to provide an ombudsman service for citizens
- to adjudicate in a judicial or quasi-judicial role.

In the process of passing new laws, legislators can actively engage in several other general functions as well. In a fully democratic system, members of the legislature debate the wisdom of any proposed law (or **bill**) and consider a variety of suggested improvements. Inevitably, such debates over the preferred policy and form in which to enact it involve a subtle but important educational role. Through listening to these debates, it is possible for those in power to learn about different perspectives on their policy proposals, and at the same time others may see the weaknesses in their own initial positions. Perhaps the most crucial part of

---

Definition

BILL: The formal text of a proposed law before it has been enacted into law. Prior to being introduced into the legislature, it is known as a draft bill. Once it has been formally introduced into the legislature for consideration, it is known as a bill. When the bill has completed all stages of the legislative process, it becomes law and is known as a statute or an act.

this educational function occurs when the media effectively report on events in the legislature and influence the views held by the general public.

In the course of these debates, members also engage in representing the interests of a wide range of groups in the general population. Depending upon the number of political parties present in the legislature and the discipline imposed on members of those parties, quite a wide range of views may be raised. This can have an important symbolic function in providing citizens with a direct and visible display of views they personally support being expressed in the legislature. As a result of these "talking" functions, legislative assemblies serve as a crucial institutional channel through which disputes get aired publicly and settled in an authoritative fashion by a majority vote.

One of the important functions of legislatures can be to institutionalize **opposition**. While we may take this for granted in a democratic society, we would soon miss the opposition if it were to be suppressed. On a broad level, people are less likely to take to the streets in violent demonstrations or start a civil war if they believe that opposition to the ruling party's policies plays some role in the legislature. Indeed, a hallmark of how democratic a country is can be seen in how free members of the legislature feel to openly criticize the government. An illustration of the importance of institutionalizing opposition came after the Liberal Party won every seat in New Brunswick's 1987 elections for the provincial legislature. Although they had no obligation to do so, the Liberals invited the leader of the Progressive Conservative Party to appear in the assembly on a regular basis to participate in the Question Period, when cabinet ministers are questioned about their conduct of public affairs. An even more striking example comes from Singapore. After the general elections in 1984 saw only two opposition members elected to the national Parliament, a constitutional amendment was passed to provide for up to six Non-Constituency Members of Parliament to be appointed, so that the opposition could participate more effectively in the legislature.[3]

Legislatures also have the potential to conduct investigations into issues and events of political importance. Committees most effectively carry out these investigations, but sometimes a series of questions on

The Nova Scotia House of Assembly is the oldest legislative building in Canada, with deliberations held here since 1819. In 1848, it was the site of the first successful passage of a no-confidence motion in any colonial legislature in the British Empire. This marked the start of responsible government in Canada.

Courtesy of Nova Scotia House of Assembly; photo by Chris Reardon

the main floor of the legislature can reveal the facts of some controversial happening. When an inquiry is held into an event, it is usually conducted as part of the legislature's role of overseeing the work of the executive branch of government, essentially to discover what government officials did or did not know or do. A committee can also hold hearings on a matter of public policy in order to make suggestions about how the policy can be improved; these can range from very focused issues, such as policies dealing with juvenile offenders, to much broader questions, such as the nation's basic foreign or defence policy. Hearings into matters of public policy are also often held as part of the process of considering legislation.

Many important functions of legislatures relate to their relationship with the executive branch of government. Briefly stated, the legislature has two sorts of functions to perform with respect to the executive. The first relates to processing and legitimating the executive's decisions concerning new policies it wants enacted into law, and the second involves performing an overseeing function to scrutinize how the executive has carried out its responsibilities. Particularly in parliamentary systems where the cabinet controls most of the policy process and proposes virtually all the bills that eventually become laws, the legislature has an important symbolic role in performing at least a ritual public debate and examination of these proposals.

Many legislatures perform a role not found in Canada, with the requirement that the legislature review and ratify any international agreements the executive has signed; for example, the United States Senate must ratify treaties. Some legislatures allow individuals and groups from the public to make presentations to the committees that study the cabinet's proposed laws and international treaties, and this public input adds another layer of democratic legitimation to the legislation. But in order for this legitimation to have substance, the scrutiny of bills must be more than just a ritual. If legislation is to be legitimate, there must be a meaningful debate of the merits and flaws of the proposals and a real possibility of amending the bills and forcing the government to withdraw the most unpopular proposals.

Similarly, legislatures can have a significant function to perform when they oversee the executive. This oversight can involve two types of activity: one is to

ensure that the government is acting acceptably and properly, in the legislature's view; the other is to ensure that the executive complies with the policies previously approved by the legislature. These oversight functions, when done well, can provide a significant check on a government that might otherwise try to cover up its misdeeds and abuses. In parliamentary systems, the legislature wields an ultimate threat over the executive: the power to cast a vote of no-confidence in the cabinet and force it to either resign or call an election. This is a powerful sanction that may be rarely exercised in countries such as Canada, where the party forming the cabinet usually controls a majority of the legislature's members in a **majority government** situation. But it is a real sanction that has brought down governments in Canada and in many other countries as well; five Canadian federal governments have either resigned or called an election as a result of a vote of no-confidence, but they were all instances of **minority governments**. The Americans' presidential system does not provide their legislatures with the power to vote no-confidence in the political executive, but Congress still has the capacity to expose and informally censure executive wrongdoing and mismanagement. Hybrid parliamentary–presidential systems like those in France and Russia put the president out of normal reach, but the prime minister and cabinet can be subject to no-confidence motions.

Definition

MAJORITY GOVERNMENT: A government in which one party holds all the seats in the cabinet and that party holds the majority of seats in the legislature (or lower house in bicameral legislatures).

Definition

MINORITY GOVERNMENT: A government in which one party holds all the seats in the cabinet but has less than 50 percent of the members in the legislature.

The most visible difference in executive oversight between the U.S. system and parliamentary government lies in the **Question Period** that just about every parliament holds. On regular occasions, members of the legislature may put direct questions to the prime minister and other cabinet ministers about their policies and the actions of their officials. While substantive answers are rare indeed, Question Periods do provide the opportunity to highlight government bungling and misdeeds, which every now and again can blow up into real political crises that eventually force the resignation of a cabinet minister or the downfall of the whole cabinet. Question Period also forces individual cabinet ministers to publicly account for their actions. The media play a crucial role in this regard by publicizing and focusing attention among the electorate on the events in the legislature; indeed, the media's role in many of the legislature's functions is important to the legislature's effectiveness.

An important function for legislatures in many countries involves selecting or confirming senior executive officials One review of constitutions found at least 19 states where members of the legislature directly choose the head of state.[4] In some cases, such as India and Germany, members of the lower house meet in a joint session with representatives of the state legislatures and collectively elect the president. In the United States and the Philippines, the legislature selects the president in the event of a tie after the general population has voted. This role is only a formal one for the U.S. House of Representatives, whose members vote to choose the president if no candidate wins a majority of votes in the electoral college convened after the general election; in almost all circumstances, the House vote simply confirms the candidate who won the most electoral college votes.

Legislatures in parliamentary systems have several roles that are not applicable to the U.S. congressional system because of the principle of **responsible government** that gives parliamentary systems their essential character. A cabinet must have the formal **confidence** of a majority in the legislature in order to govern; in legislatures with two houses, this principle usually applies just to a majority in the lower house. In a broad sense, a parliament ultimately decides whether a cabinet can stay in office; the head of state may appoint a new prime minister and cabinet, but they have to obtain and maintain the confidence of the legislature in order to govern for any period of time. Parliaments are usually organized in an adversarial fashion, in which government MPs square off against the opposition. One theoretical role of the opposition is to provide an alternative government.

Should the legislature force the resignation of the government, the head of state must be able to count on the opposition to step in and act as the new government, at least until new elections are held. But in a broader political sense, the opposition party or parties continuously act in the legislature to portray themselves to the public as an alternative to the ruling party or **coalition government**.

Definition

RESPONSIBLE GOVERNMENT: A defining principle of Westminster-style parliamentary governments, which says that the cabinet must always have majority support in the legislature (or lower house in a bicameral parliament) for votes of confidence.

Definition

CONFIDENCE (OR NO-CONFIDENCE) VOTE: There are three types of such a vote. It may be an explicitly worded motion indicating that the legislature either has or does not have confidence in the government. It may be a vote on a matter that the government has previously declared to be a matter of confidence. It may also be a vote on important measures that are central to the government's plans, such as a vote on the whole budget.

Definition

COALITION GOVERNMENT: A government that occurs when two or more parties hold seats in cabinet supported by a combination of parties that forms a majority in the legislature.

The U.S. system, however, gives the legislature another role in deciding who holds executive positions. The Senate must approve the president's nomination of individuals to the cabinet, senior levels of the civil service, the judiciary, and the armed forces. In the 105th Congress, which sat in 1998–99, the Senate considered a total of 46 053 nominations, out of which 411 were not approved for one reason or another.[5] The most visible of these nomination reviews involve hearings to scrutinize individuals who have been nominated to sit on the Supreme Court, a task that is sometimes suggested as a useful innovation for the Canadian Parliament to consider.

Loosely related to the executive oversight function, an ombudsman role is an important part of many legislatures. In this role, a legislator acts on behalf of citizens and tries to sort out troubles they may be having with the bureaucracy. This is usually known as **constituency** work (or service), and the vast bulk of it occurs outside the legislative chamber, with legislators or their staff phoning or writing to civil servants or cabinet ministers on behalf of the person involved. In a parliamentary system, MPs can raise questions during Question Period or in committee hearings about specific cases they are handling, but the sheer volume of constituency work means that only a fraction of cases are dealt with in a public forum in this manner. Despite the "invisible" nature of constituency work, it has come to be the most time-consuming task of legislators in many countries.

Two studies in the 1990s revealed that Canadian MPs devote on average over 42 percent of their time to constituency work.[6] A 1996 survey of British MPs found they spent a similar amount of time on constituency work, about 40 percent.[7] However, there is a great disparity between the Canadian public's general perception of the importance of this function compared to that of their MPs. In a 1993 Gallup poll, the public rated this the least important part of an MP's work, but when MPs were asked the same question, they rated it as their number one priority.[8] The difference might be explained by the personal satisfaction MPs feel in helping individuals, in a job that has few direct personal rewards; on the other hand, only a very small segment of the population ever turn to their MP for help, and so this work is of little consequence to most of the general public.

A limited exercise of judicial power can also be one of the functions that legislatures are expected to fill. The most important examples involve the impeachment of senior public officials. When the U.S. House of Representatives charged President Clinton in impeachment proceedings in 1998, for instance, the Senate essentially acted as a jury of a court chaired by the chief justice—and found Clinton not guilty. Brazil, India, and the Philippines are other countries whose legislatures conduct impeachment hearings of not just the president but of senior judges and other officials. In 2001, the Indonesian parliament successfully impeached President Abdurrahman Wahid on charges of extensive corruption. Another quite common exercise of judicial power is seen in the 24 countries whose legislatures act as courts to hear charges of disputed or corrupt elections; this function is a power of parliaments historically descended from the British model, but most are like Canada in delegating this function directly to the courts.

The British Parliament appears unique in the world, because the highest court in the land is technically just a committee of the House of Lords, the Appellate Committee. There are 12 members, called Law Lords, who hear cases in five-judge panels; when they are ready to pronounce judgment, they deliver a report to a full meeting of the House of Lords. The historic British model involves the principle of the High Court of Parliament, reflecting its early origins as a council that dispensed justice. However, Westminster-model legislatures today continue to retain one aspect of this principle, in acting as a court to try charges of "contempt of Parliament" that can still result in imprisonment for the guilty. The most recent Canadian example dates from 1992, when the Quebec National Assembly ordered imprisonment for someone who was found to be in contempt.[9]

FACTORS LIMITING THE EFFECTIVENESS OF LEGISLATURES

Legislatures have many functions, but just how effectively these are performed depends upon a wide range of factors. Many of them are interrelated, and attempts to reform the legislature by trying to deal with one factor may not succeed or may even exacerbate the situation, since other limiting factors are at play.

Two factors that go hand in hand in limiting a legislature's ability to fulfil its functions effectively are party discipline and the domination of the legislature by the executive. These are almost inherent problems in modern parliamentary systems, but they can play a key role in presidential systems as well. Fairly strict party discipline is needed in a parliamentary system for a variety of reasons: the cabinet must have the support of a majority in the legislature in order to remain in office; the cabinet is supposed to be the focus of the policy process and secure the passage of most of its legislation;

and cohesive party blocks are the organizational foundation of most of parliament's daily work. Indeed, parliamentary government in the modern context is really *party* government.

The following are the factors limiting the effectiveness of legislatures:

- executive dominance
- party discipline
- size
- frequency of meetings
- amount and complexity of legislation
- number, size, and membership of committees
- research and support staff
- legislators' pay
- procedural rules
- informal rewards and penalties
- electoral system
- media attention
- political culture.

Canada is typical of other parliamentary systems, with the prime minister and cabinet managing to direct almost everything that transpires. The cabinet is able to do this because of strict **party discipline**, which is the requirement that all members of a legislature belonging to the same party should normally vote according to the party's position on an issue. Each party selects one of its members of the legislature to act as an official called a whip, whose primary functions are to assign members to particular duties in the legislature and to make sure that they vote the way the party requires them to. Whips rely mainly on peer pressure and persuasion, but they also have a range of informal rewards and punishments at their disposal. In addition to the whip's rewards and penalties, the parliamentary party as a whole (known as the caucus) can impose even more severe punishments, such as temporary exile or permanent expulsion from the party's caucus. Expulsion is the ultimate punishment, since most Canadian voters—like many voters elsewhere—decide for whom to vote on the basis of a candidate's party or the party's leader.

One of many ways a Prime Minister can keep Members of Parliament subordinate and supportive.

Bruce MacKinnon/Halifax Herald/Artizans

Surveys of the past seven federal elections show that only about a quarter of Canadian voters make their voting choice primarily on the basis of the individual candidates. In the 1997 election, 58 percent made up their minds by choosing between parties and 20 percent on the basis of party leaders.[10] Members expelled from their party may "cross the floor" to join another party or try to run in the next election as an independent.

Definition

PARTY DISCIPLINE: The practice that all members in a legislature belonging to the same political party should normally vote the same way, in accordance with their party's stand on the issue at hand.

Party discipline is something of a mixed blessing in legislatures. While disciplined party blocks make the legislative process more efficient and clarify voters' choices, party discipline also seriously impedes the legislature's ability to perform many of its functions. In particular, the ruling party or coalition of parties is able to keep very tight control over the outcome of most decisions in the legislative chamber and in committees. Both at the federal and provincial levels in Canada, party discipline is very strict. This means that the cabinet will almost never lose a vote on a bill or have to face a committee report criticizing the government's policies. So long as discipline holds for a cabinet with a majority of seats, the legislature will not cast a vote of no-confidence in the government.[11] Party discipline is taken to its extreme in the Labor parties in Australia and New Zealand, which both require their MPs to sign a pledge that they will always vote according to the party position.[12] In contrast, parties in the British Parliament display a much looser discipline; one study of voting patterns in the British House of Commons found dissident votes in 20 to 28 percent of recorded votes in the three Parliaments that sat in the 1970s.[13] The American presidential system is a very different type of government, and members of Congress demonstrate a freedom to vote as they choose that would be the envy of many legislature members in parliamentary systems. However, it is a mistake to equate the relative freedom in the United States with a lack of party cohesion; in 1998, for instance, 56 percent of the votes in each of the two houses of Congress involved a majority of Democrat members voting together against a majority of Republican members.[14]

The combination of party discipline and executive dominance has a significant effect on a legislature's ability to perform a range of its potential functions. Law-making may get boiled down simply to a public debate prior to approving most of whatever the cabinet has proposed. Executive oversight can become stylized into a function of little substance, and committees are unable to produce innovative policy suggestions that run counter to the cabinet's policy agenda.

Other variables can also limit a legislature's effectiveness. Factors as basic as the size of the legislature, the number of days in the year it sits to conduct business, the research and support staff working for individual legislators, and the internal procedural rules of the legislature all can leave a legislature quite hamstrung. Most provincial legislatures in Canada have between 50 and 75 members, and this means that a cabinet of about 20 ministers necessarily includes a significant portion of the legislature's total membership and an even higher proportion of the governing party's caucus. In 1998, five provincial cabinets filled a third or more of the legislature's seats, and four cabinets constituted half or more of the ruling party's membership in the legislature. Just this simple fact of size provides a significant explanation for the high level of executive dominance of the legislative process in Canadian provincial government and weakens the legislature's ability to effectively fill several other of its potential roles. In comparison, the House of Commons in Ottawa has 301 members, and the Chrétien cabinet in 2001 constituted only about 12 percent of the total membership and 21 percent of the ruling Liberal Party caucus. The size of the Canadian House of Commons stands in stark contrast to the lower houses of Britain, with 670 members; France, with 577; Germany, 672; and the United States, with 435.

The differences in size between the provincial legislatures and the federal House of Commons also mean that, in comparison to most provincial legislatures, the House of Commons can have many more functioning committees at work because there are more than enough MPs to sit on them. Those Commons committees can be free of cabinet ministers, while many provincial legislatures may need to have cabinet ministers sitting on committees, if only because there are not enough competent government **backbenchers** to do the work. As a result, committees in Ottawa can have relatively more independence from the executive than do most provincial committees.

BOX 9.2

CAUCUS: THE LEGISLATURE'S SECRET CHAMBER?

Some of the most tangible work of legislatures occurs behind closed doors in caucus meetings. A **caucus** is a group of legislators united in a common cause. The most common kind of caucus is the party caucus, in which the members of a legislature who belong to the same party gather on a regular basis to discuss party affairs, in particular, what position the party should take on issues coming up in the legislature. These meetings are invariably confidential, although leaks to the media often occur. Some of the most heated debates in Canadian legislatures occur not in the public arena of the formal chamber itself but in the party caucuses. Here, legislators can make their most forceful arguments on behalf of the interests and constituents they represent. Once the caucus debate is over and the party's position is established, however, members are supposed to fall into line and defend that position publicly. As a result, much of the real representational function of the legislature occurs out of the public eye and usually goes unreported in the media.

Government caucuses in parliamentary systems can also serve an important function in the legislative process. In many party caucuses, committees are established to look at policy issues and suggest new laws or even changes to bills already before the legislature. Some but not all of these suggestions are taken up by the cabinet and included in the measures that are presented publicly in the legislature. In addition, many government caucuses allow the ordinary members to question cabinet ministers about their policies and conduct. Again, some of these exchanges are extremely frank and are important parts of actual oversight of the executive.

Other types of caucus meetings are organized for the members of parties from particular regions of the country or even for members of different parties who share a common interest. Each party in the Canadian Parliament has regional or provincial caucus meetings prior to its general caucus meeting, for example, while the American Congress also has bipartisan caucuses that include members from all the parties; examples include the Congressional Caucus for Women's Issues, the Congressional Black Caucus, and the Congressional Corn Caucus.

Another quite practical consideration is how much business a legislature is expected to do in a certain period of time. Table 9.1 on page 204 shows that the New Brunswick legislature had to consider 61 government bills in just 40 days, while performing many other tasks at the same time. In contrast, the House of Commons in Ottawa sat for 247 days and had to consider 87 government bills. The New Brunswick legislature could devote only a fraction of the time to each bill compared to that available to the House of Commons. It is little wonder, then, that the New Brunswick legislature amended only 23 percent of government bills while the House of Commons amended more than twice as many.

A related issue is how much legislators get paid. If they are paid only a relatively low wage, then one cannot expect the legislature to sit year-round, as many members will need to supplement their income. Furthermore, many competent professional people will not want to take a significant cut in pay in order to leave their normal jobs and run for political office. Canadian reluctance to pay much for politicians was plainly evident when the Saskatchewan government decided in 1993 to reduce the size of the provincial legislature by eight members, and Ontario in 1995 by 27 members, as part of a general cost-cutting drive. Savings continue with the research and support staff available to Canadian legislators. Many provincial legislators make do with just one or two staff members, and even MPs in Ottawa have allowances for only four staff members to serve them in Parliament and in their constituency offices. Their U.S. counterparts in

Washington have dozens of staffers, and committee chairs can have over a hundred working for them. This is not just a matter of stinginess; it has a direct impact on the kind of job legislators can do. They are simply not able to perform serious reviews of public policy without sufficient staff to provide the technical expertise needed to formulate independent policy appraisals and initiatives.

The procedural rules of a legislature can also limit its effectiveness. Whoever controls the timetable in the legislature controls what business will be considered and how much time is to be devoted to any particular measure. In most parliamentary systems, the government is able to exercise this level of control through a cabinet minister known as the House Leader. **Closure**, or time allocation, is one procedural tool available to control the amount of time spent debating any particular item on parliament's agenda. With closure, the government can cut off debate and force a vote to be held. Between 1993 and early 2002, the Chrétien government had used closure or time allocation in the House of Commons 75 times. It is the counterpart to the opposition's use of extended debates or a **filibuster**.

Definition

CLOSURE: A term used to describe procedural rules that permit the majority to put an end to debate on a motion and require that a vote on the matter be held; also known as cloture, the guillotine, and time allocation in various countries.

Definition

FILIBUSTER: A device used by a member or group of members who take advantage of the procedural rules of a legislature that allow members to speak for extended periods of time in order to stall proceedings.

While one theory of parliamentary government is that the cabinet is held "continuously" accountable to the legislature, the procedural rules may allow only limited opportunities for this to occur. In the Canadian House of Commons, every day the house is in session there is a 45-minute Question Period, but British Columbia has Question Periods that last only 15 minutes. In the United Kingdom, members can ask the prime minister questions only twice a week. Just with

these differences in the rules, one sees a significant difference in the ability of legislators to hold cabinet ministers to account.

No legislature allows business to unfold in a haphazard fashion, and someone has to decide what will be considered when. In Canadian legislatures, the Government House Leaders are in total control. They consult with house leaders from the opposition parties, but this consultation may not have any influence on what the government decides to do. Other jurisdictions avoid this problem by providing in their rules that the Speaker of the assembly can decide whether important measures should be brought forward for a vote; the Speaker of the British House of Commons, for example, has broad personal discretion to select the issues that are debated and voted upon.

Other crucial procedural rules deal with who can introduce what. In presidential systems, a great deal can change in the functioning of the legislature if the president is able to directly introduce bills into the legislature. In the United States, the president is unable to introduce bills and must negotiate with individual members of Congress to find someone who will "sponsor" the bill and actually introduce it. The situation is quite different in Mexico, however, where the president is able to introduce bills himself.

The number, size, and membership of committees can also influence a legislature's ability to perform its roles effectively in assessing and amending bills, as well as conducting investigations into events and issues. Small legislatures, such as most Canadian provincial legislatures, have few committees and make little use of even those they have. Some legislatures often funnel proposed legislation through Committee of the Whole, which is actually all the members of the legislature simply sitting as one large committee. This is a highly inefficient process, since bills can be dealt with only one at a time, and no other business can be conducted in the legislative chamber while this goes on. Legislatures that have a well-developed committee system are able to process much more business and do so in greater depth. Greater efficiency and scrutiny can occur because work can proceed in parallel in many committees at the same time, and the members of these committees can develop more expertise if these are set up to deal with specific policy areas such as transportation, health, or banking. Another related factor is whether committees are created on an ad hoc basis or standing basis. A permanent committee with stable membership is able to consider issues with considerably more expertise.

An important question is whether cabinet ministers should sit on or chair parliamentary committees. Nova Scotia and Quebec are two provinces that regularly allow both, but such a suggestion would cause outrage in the Canadian and British Parliaments. As mentioned earlier in this chapter, the presence of cabinet ministers undermines the legislature's ability to form independent judgments of the policies proposed by the executive and reduces its capacity to act as a check against the executive's power. However, the active participation of cabinet ministers in parliamentary committees can have positive effects. Since cabinet is usually the ultimate body that decides whether its caucus members should vote for an amendment, there is something to be said for cabinet ministers being present and engaged in the committee discussions so they can learn at first hand about the merits of proposed amendments.

Several sets of factors external to legislatures can also have an impact on their effectiveness. The first is the electoral system, which may produce legislative assemblies that bear little resemblance to the choices made by the voters. This is a particular problem in countries such as Canada with the first-past-the-post system. In this system, the person who gets the most votes in a riding wins the seat; as a result, candidates who have wide support but do not manage to come in first place do not get to represent the people who voted for them. The worst example of this system's potential to distort the citizens' choices was seen in the 1987 New Brunswick election, where the Liberals won about 60 percent of the votes but gained every seat in the legislature; this meant that the 40 percent of the electorate who voted for other parties were left with no one to represent them. This chapter already outlined the measures taken in New Brunswick and Singapore to provide some opposition presence in the legislature, but these hardly allowed either legislature to fill its important role of representing the people to any effective degree or to debate a full range of policy alternatives. Some countries have electoral laws that ban certain parties, or ensure that there is only one official party for all elections; again, this limits the legislature's ability to represent the people and assess policy proposals.

Another external factor is the role of the media in conveying to the public what transpires in the legislature and in covering the public's reaction. The media are known as the Fourth Estate precisely because of their crucial role as a link between political institutions and actors on the one hand and the general public on the other. In countries that control the media or where media are concentrated in a few hands, the coverage of both legislative events and public reaction can be distorted, to say the least. Even in societies with a vibrant media, there are problems, with only a few items being selected for coverage because of space and time constraints, the policy preferences of the media owners, or the public's lack of interest. Furthermore, effective coverage of legislatures requires considerable knowledge of the political system and issues, and poor coverage can often result from reporters' inexperience. Ironically, the success of legislatures that work effectively and efficiently through an extensive committee system may become a barrier to full media coverage. In the U.S. Congress, for instance, there about three hundred committees and subcommittees, and it is impossible for the media to cover the work of any but a select few.

The largest and most intangible of the external factors is the general political culture of a society. The most visible manifestation of this factor is the poor representation of women in all legislatures, since political cultures around the world continue to favour males in many subtle and not-so-subtle ways. The same absence from the legislature applies to minority groups in many societies. This underrepresentation of groups in the legislature not only undermines the representation function, but can also have an impact on the specific policies considered and on the ways they are treated. Other general cultural values come into play in the legislature as well. Whether the general public wants or tolerates very strong leadership by the executive or prefers individual members of the legislature who act independently will have an effect in the long run on the strength of party discipline in the legislature, as well as on the extent of executive domination of the legislative process. There are dozens of national parliaments across the globe modelled on the British system, yet each performs its potential functions to varying degrees.

Several countries have presidential systems modelled on the United States, but in practice none is very similar to the U.S. system. Certain differences among parliamentary and congressional legislatures can be explained by procedural rules or other specific details of the legislature, but unique political cultures remain the most important cause. The impact of political culture, at least at the elite level, is seen in quite another context in Mexico. The legal framework of its Constitution is fairly similar to the American, with a presidential system of government. But a range of cultural factors have led to a much tighter party discipline in the ruling party, which allows the president to direct the work of the legislature to such an extent that the practical workings of the Mexican legislative process bear little resemblance to its U.S. counterpart.

LAW-MAKING

Law-making is one of the most important roles of legislatures, and it is this function that sets them apart from the other branches of government. The process through which proposals must pass before they become law can give ample opportunity for them to be amended or even scrapped entirely. There is definitely the potential for new public-policy proposals to be significantly improved and for unpopular or impractical ones to be abandoned as a result of scrutiny in the legislature and subsequent public reaction. In authoritarian regimes, the legislature plays little more than a formal, ritual role in enacting into law the policies already decided upon by the political executive or ruling party. In democratic parliamentary systems, the legislature has a substantive role to play in making laws, even if the cabinet is the main source of legislative initiatives and directs much of the process in the legislature. For the most part, however, MPs focus on reviewing the cabinet's proposals rather than developing new initiatives of their own. In democratic presidential systems, the legislature can have a truly independent role to play in developing and initiating new legislation, as well as in scrutinizing proposals developed by the executive.

The law-making procedure in the legislature is only part of the whole ongoing public-policy process. Ideas for new laws are generated throughout the political system by individuals, groups, and corporations, as well as by political parties, civil servants, the cabinet, individual members of the legislature, and committees of the legislature. The ideas are then reviewed and drafted into legal language suitable for a future law; at this point, they are ready to be introduced into the legislature. The legislature then considers the proposed laws, makes any changes that the majority thinks necessary, and decides whether to enact these proposals into law. Most modern statutes passed by the legislature cannot contain all the detail necessary for their implementation, so they delegate to the executive branch the power to pass regulations filling in the details; this is known as delegated or subordinate legislation. The law and its regulations are then ready to be implemented and administered by the executive. It is at this point that the ideas for new public policies actually become reality. The new policies, in turn, generate a reaction among those in the public who are affected, which can eventually lead to ideas and demands for yet new laws. In this whole process, the legislature can potentially provide the most important public stage for formal debate and improvement of public policies.

In parliamentary systems such as Canada's, cabinet ministers propose most of the measures that are eventually enacted into law. When cabinet ministers decide to propose a change to public policy that needs to be achieved through legislation, they consult the civil servants in their department for advice on the best means to achieve that policy. The ideas are then presented to the cabinet or a cabinet committee, and if approved, the proposal is drafted into a legal document. Cabinet then reviews the matter again and makes a final decision on whether to present the measure to the legislature. When there is an opening in the work schedule in the legislature, the sponsoring cabinet minister introduces the measure as a bill (in other words, a proposed law for consideration in the legislature).

The Canadian Parliament follows a legislative process that is similar to that in most legislatures patterned after the British model, although each legislature has its own particular variations in detail. In Canada, the bill goes through three readings, or particular stages, each of which serves a specific purpose. The First Reading occurs when the bill is first introduced. It is only a formality, in that it gives everyone notice that the bill has entered the pipeline; no debate occurs at this time. The next stage, the Second Reading, is the consideration of the main principles of the bill; considerable debate can occur at this time. After Second

Figure 9.1 Legislative Process in the Canadian Parliament

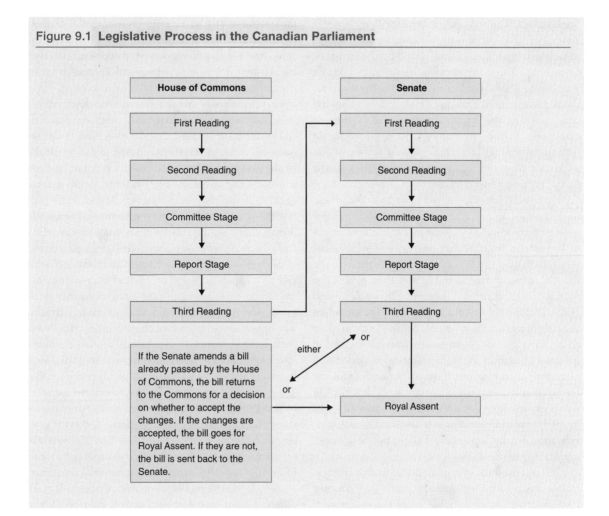

Reading, the bill usually enters the Committee Stage, where detailed examination occurs. In the Canadian Parliament, the committee usually invites interested members of the public to present their views of how the bill can be improved. While there is great potential for this public input, the sheer volume of people wanting to have their say on controversial bills means that a very deliberate and partisan process occurs within the committee to decide who will actually be allowed to give testimony. Depending on the controversy engendered by the bill and on subsequent media coverage, significant changes can be made when the governing party's members of the committee believe that it is in their best interests to do so. Often, they check informally with the minister who sponsored the bill to see

if he or she agrees to the changes, but sometimes the minister appears as a formal witness to defend the proposal and discuss potential amendments. The committee then reports back to the legislature, and all the members can debate and vote on any changes the committee proposed. After that, a debate on Third Reading is held, and members have a final opportunity to consider the bill as a whole.

Once a bill has passed Third Reading, it is sent to the other house and goes through the same stages all over again. The Canadian Parliament contains two chambers or houses, the House of Commons and the Senate, and a bill must be approved in identical form by both before it can become a law. The vast majority of bills are introduced first in the House of Commons, because the lower house is elected, while the Senate is appointed. The Senate does sometimes make changes to bills that have already been passed by the House of Commons, and then the Commons must decide whether to accept the Senate amendments or reject them. Occasionally, a bill goes back and forth several times between the Senate and House of Commons before one of them compromises, but since the Senate is an appointed body, it normally should be the one that eventually gives way.[15] Only on rare occasions does the Senate actually defeat a bill.

Once a bill has been agreed to by both the House of Commons and the Senate, it is ready for Royal Assent by the governor general and it becomes an act of Parliament. No Canadian provincial legislature has the equivalent of the Senate, so a bill goes through the three readings in the assembly and then gets Royal Assent from the lieutenant governor. The whole process of considering and passing legislation in the Canadian Parliament usually takes several months, but can often go on for a year or more; public reaction to the bill becomes crucial during such an extended period and often induces the cabinet minister responsible for the bill to accept or propose important amendments. On rare occasions, however, a bill can go through all stages in the House of Commons in a day; such speedy consideration usually occurs only if all the political parties represented in the House agree.

Perhaps the most important question that emerges from a review of the legislative process is how effective the legislature actually is. Table 9.1 gives a summary of the treatment of government bills in several Canadian legislatures, as well as in the Australian Parliament, for comparison. This information clearly demonstrates that legislatures do have a substantial role to play in reviewing the bills proposed by the cabinet. One obvious measure is that the government never gets all its bills through the legislature. Although some provincial governments come very close to achieving this on occasion, many government bills fail to pass the legislature simply because the members run out of time before the end of the session.[16] A more useful measure of the practical importance of legislatures is the percentage of government bills that get amended. Table 9.1 reveals that a significant number do. The Canadian Parliament in particular has amended a high proportion of cabinet-sponsored bills: 53 percent in the 1997–99 session. Despite the tight party discipline, governments are forced to make significant changes to their proposals when these are considered by their legislatures. The opportunities for debate on government proposals, both in the legislature and in the media, allow the interested public and the government caucus to think about the issues and to exert pressure for changes to be made. There certainly are times when a government manages to ram a measure through the legislature, whipping its troops into line to pass a bill untouched. But the government cannot do this consistently and has to relent on many occasions, allowing some changes to be made to its bills and deciding to drop other bills altogether.

The legislative process in the U.S. Congress is quite different from that described above. First of all, the

Table 9.1	**Success of Government Bills in Selected Parliamentary Systems**				
Legislature	Period	Number of Government Bills Introduced	Percent of Bills Amended	Percent of Bills Enacted	Number of Sitting Days
Australian Parliament	1998–99	266	31.6	73.7	124
Canadian Parliament	1997–99	87	52.9	82.8	247
British Columbia	1998–99	99	37.4	94.9	162
New Brunswick	1998–99	61	23.0	98.4	40
Ontario	1998–99	41	40.5	75.6	71

Note: These figures include only government public bills, and in addition, in the case of the Australian and Canadian Parliaments, bills introduced in the lower house only.

president and his cabinet cannot directly introduce bills into Congress; as a result, individual members sponsor all bills. The executive still has a strong influence on the legislative process, but this is done entirely through lobbying and negotiating with members of both the Republican and Democratic parties in both houses of Congress. Second, the vast bulk of time and attention is given to legislation in committee hearings. The only opportunity for substantial debate by all members of a house comes up at the end of the process. Third, virtually every bill is significantly altered along the way. Competing bills dealing with similar issues can be introduced by different members of both houses and are often eventually consolidated into one. Because there is much looser party discipline in the U.S. Congress, the passage of a bill depends upon a tremendous amount of negotiating among individual legislators and their staff.

Table 9.2 illustrates the enormous filtering of legislative proposals that occurs in Congress, with thousands of bills that are introduced being reduced to a few hundred that pass into law. An individual senator or representative often gives support only in exchange for an amendment that deals with one of his or her pet projects. Thus, a bill that ostensibly deals with transportation can include sections that provide meal vouchers for school children and money for pig farmers. Another major difference is that the two houses of Congress are both elected and have equal political power. As a result, an important part of the legislative process is securing eventual agreement between the two houses on identical terms for a bill; there is a joint conference committee specially charged with reconciling two versions of the same bill.

The other important difference between the U.S. and parliamentary systems arises because the president has a real veto over measures passed by Congress, while the official sanction by the head of state in a parliamentary system is always automatic. Between 1789 and 1996, presidents vetoed 1437 bills passed by Congress. The Constitution gives Congress the ability to override a presidential veto, but an override requires a two-thirds vote in both houses; as a result, only 105 vetoes were overridden during that period.[17] Many of the presidential vetoes came not because the president objected to the whole bill, but because he wanted to reject one of the particular items unrelated to the main purpose that had been added into a bill to secure its passage in Congress. In order to save so many "babies being thrown out with the bathwater," an act of Congress was passed in 1996 to give the president what is called a line-item veto. This procedure allowed the president to sign a bill into law while vetoing particular items within the bill. However, the U.S. Supreme Court struck down the line-item veto as unconstitutional in 1998.[18]

REPRESENTATION

A very important function of all democratic legislatures is to represent the citizenry in the heart of government institutions. Representation lies at the core of

---

Table 9.2   Success of Bills in the 105th U.S. Congress, 1998–99

	House of Representatives	Senate
Bills First Introduced	4874	2658
Senate Bills Passed	142	292
House Bills Passed	530	258
Bills Vetoed by President	7	n.a.*
Vetoes Overridden by Congress	2	n.a.*
Bills Enacted into Law	404	n.a.*

* The categories Bills Vetoed, Vetoes Overridden, and Bills Enacted apply jointly to both houses, since bills have been approved in identical form by both.

Source: *Congressional Record, Daily Digest,* January 19, 1999; cited on July 1, 2001; available at http://frwebgate.access.gpo.gov/cgi-bin/getpage.cgi.

the democratic mandate of a legislature to manage the affairs of a society; because of it, members of the legislature are able to perform all the other functions of the legislature. While it is easy to state this as a vital role, it is surprisingly difficult to define what representation actually entails. The difficulties emerge because there are crosscutting views of *whom* members of the legislature should represent and *how* they should represent them. Unfortunately, any given legislature at any particular time is never a mirror reflection of all the diverse segments and groups in society; in countries that use the first-past-the-post electoral system, the members of the legislature are seldom even a proper reflection of the electorate's support for the different political parties.

Someone recently elected to a seat in the legislature soon finds himself or herself torn in different directions by a wide range of groups and interests demanding that the legislator act or speak on their behalf. First, there are territorial community interests, which can be as large as the whole constituency in which the legislator ran for election or as small as a town, village, or neighbourhood. In this role, a legislator is representing all the members of the community as a collective whole. Second, there are nonterritorial sectional interests or groups that may be represented. One of the first tugs on legislators' attention is the call for special attention to be paid to those people who actually voted for them. This is a reasonable demand, since these people chose the candidate because of the policies he or she promised to pursue. However, legislators can quickly realize that the demands of the whole community can often run counter to the demands of the segment of that community who voted for them. This tension is heightened in the many constituencies where someone is declared elected with less than a majority of votes; such legislators start from a position where a majority of their constituents are opposed their policy positions.

Members of an elected legislature also wrestle with a separate responsibility to represent the political party on whose platform they ran and got elected. Another nonterritorial set of interests that legislators can represent are those relating to economic sectors or enterprises that are particularly important in the region they represent; thus, MPs can work hard on behalf of grain growers, vehicle manufacturers, a paper mill, fishers, or the high-tech service sector in their region. Finally, legislators can represent the particular social groups to

which they personally belong, be they gender, linguistic, religious, ethnic, and so on. This can be an important form of representation, given the domination of most legislatures by only one social group: males from a narrow range of professional backgrounds. The ultimate goal of this aspect of representation is that the legislature should be a microcosm or mirror of society, with members of all the significant groups present in roughly proportional numbers. When we take all these potential subjects of representation together, it should be evident that a legislator often faces competing expectations to represent groups with very different (and even opposing) interests when it comes to any specific matter of public policy under consideration.

Even if it becomes clear whom a legislator should try to represent on a particular issue, there is still controversy about how that representation should be done. There are two basic approaches to the nature of representation that can be distinguished: the delegate and the trustee. The delegate perspective requires a legislator to discern the will of the group to be represented and then to voice and pursue those interests; the delegate essentially acts in the place of those he or she represents. The delegate's own views are supposed to be set aside in favour of representing the views of the group. This perspective is based on powerful arguments of democratic theory, coming from classical liberalism, that legislative activity should always reflect the will of the people and particularly of the specific group to be affected by a piece of legislation. The difficulties with this view arise both from democratic theory and from the complicated nature of society and public policy.

Modern liberal democratic theory does not support the unflinching reign of the majority—indeed, this is sometimes called the **tyranny of the majority**. Political decision-makers are supposed to accommodate and protect minority interests as well as those of the majority. So, which group's delegate should the legislator be? Should it be the community's majority or the minority group whose interests may be significantly compromised? Furthermore, do all groups affected by legislation deserve to be represented equally? After all, a change to the criminal law equally involves the interests of both the victims of crime and the alleged criminals themselves. Even if a legislator decides which particular group he or she should speak for, it still can be difficult to discover what the preponderant view of that group really is—short of conducting ongoing opinion polls. Legislators do rely heavily on the letters and phone calls they receive, but these are always from a tiny, self-selecting group among their constituents. Sometimes petitions that are circulated in a community garner thousands of signatures, but these too are not necessarily definitive of the group's position.

The trustee view of representation suggests a very different role for legislators in acting on behalf of the groups they represent. In this view, legislators should understand the opinions and wishes of those they represent, but in the end they must use their own best judgment of what position to take on an issue. The ear-

liest proponent of this view was Edmund Burke, a Whig politician in late-18th-century Britain, but his views on this subject in particular are regarded as typical of classical Tory conservatism. Excerpts from Burke's famous speech to his voters in 1774 are reproduced below. An interesting footnote to this speech is that Burke lost the election in which he made it!

There are several justifications for this approach; they reveal a different notion of the role of the representative and of public policy than that found in arguments for the delegate model. The first principle is that people entrust their representative to act in the best interests of their overall welfare. Just what specific

---

BOX 9.3

EXCERPTS FROM EDMUND BURKE'S "SPEECH TO THE ELECTORS OF BRISTOL," 1774

Certainly, gentlemen, it ought to be the happiness and glory of a representative to live in the strictest union, the closest correspondence, and the most unreserved communication with his constituents. Their wishes ought to have great weight with him; their opinion, high respect; their business, unremitted attention.... But his unbiassed opinion, his mature judgment, his enlightened conscience, he ought not to sacrifice to you, to any man, or to any set of men living. These he does not derive from your pleasure; no, nor from the law and the constitution. They are a trust from Providence, for the abuse of which he is deeply answerable. Your representative owes you, not his industry only, but his judgment; and he betrays, instead of serving you, if he sacrifices it to your opinion.

My worthy colleague says, his will ought to be subservient to yours. If that be all, the thing is innocent. If government were a matter of will upon any side, yours, without question, ought to be superior. But government and legislation are matters of reason and judgment, and not of inclination; and what sort of reason is that, in which the determination precedes the discussion; in

which one set of men deliberate, and another decide; and where those who form the conclusion are perhaps three hundred miles distant from those who hear the arguments?

To deliver an opinion, is the right of all men; that of constituents is a weighty and respectable opinion, which a representative ought always to rejoice to hear; and which he ought always most seriously to consider. But authoritative instructions, mandates issued, which the member is bound blindly and implicitly to obey, to vote, and to argue for, though contrary to the clearest conviction of his judgment and conscience,—these are things utterly unknown to the laws of this land, and which arise from a fundamental mistake of the whole order and tenor of our constitution.

Parliament is not a congress of ambassadors from different and hostile interests ... but parliament is a deliberative assembly of one nation, with one interest, that of the whole; where, not local purposes, not local prejudices, ought to guide, but the general good, resulting from the general reason of the whole. You choose a member indeed; but when you have chosen him, he is not member of Bristol, but he is a member of parliament.

measures may favour their long-term welfare may not be immediately clear to the people, who can be motivated by individual self-interest and by the passions of the moment. It is the job of the elected representative, in this view, to ascertain all the facts and listen to the range of opinions expressed during debates in the legislature, and then come to his or her own conclusion about what should be done. In all of this, too, the legislator is viewed not simply as a representative of a particular group or community who pursues nothing but their parochial interests. The legislator is also a national (or provincial) decision-maker who must also be concerned with the welfare and interests of the whole society. Legislators have to find a balance in the conflicts of interest between what may be good for the whole nation or province against the welfare of their own constituency.

Representation is an abstract concept that carries enormous moral and philosophical weight. However, it is also something that has to operate within the real world of everyday politics. In fact, legislators usually end up living out all the different types of representation reviewed above at different times and on different issues. The real-world setting of modern legislatures also means that the fundamental principle guiding a legislator's public actions is that of party discipline. Usually the most vociferous representation of community or group interests occurs in parliamentary settings within a party's caucus, where individual legislators try to convince their colleagues that the party's policy should reflect these interests. Despite party discipline, however, individual legislators speak out in public from time to time in order to fully represent interests that are even more important to them than party loyalty. Breaking party ranks can occur for two reasons: legislators realize that the local groups feel so strongly about an issue that they may well face defeat in the next election if they do not speak out publicly, and individual legislators do from time to time simply hold extremely strong personal beliefs that a group's interests must be represented publicly regardless of the consequences.

A serious representational issue in many countries is the fact that their legislatures are so dominated by males and members of the largest ethnic groups. One of the issues that emerges from the microcosm or mirror view of representation is that legislatures do not currently reflect the composition of their societies

as a whole. There are important practical and symbolic problems with systemic underrepresentation, and these are compounded when important social groups are completely lacking from the legislature. Not only may groups feel excluded from the political process if they are not visible participants in the main political institutions, but their interests may be only weakly represented by the others present—or even not represented at all. A continued lack of participation in the legislature, and continued losing out in the decisions made there, can contribute to political alienation and eventually lead to political violence. There are many socioeconomic reasons deeply embedded in a society's political culture that combine to create conditions where women and members of minority groups do not or cannot run for office and get elected. The social groups that do participate in the legislature can make a practical difference in the legislative process. A number of studies of the American Congress and Canadian legislatures have suggested that there may be slight but discernible differences in the way members of different ethnic groups and genders vote on issues— even when other factors such as party affiliation and ideological leanings are accounted for.[19] Some researchers have even argued that women should be represented by women and ethnic minorities represented by members of their own groups, but this is a highly contested idea.[20]

UPPER HOUSES

Although a majority of the world's legislatures are unicameral, some 63 national legislatures are bicameral. In Canada, all the provincial and territorial legislatures have a single chamber, while the national Parliament in Ottawa has two. Since unicameral legislatures are inherently more efficient, with all business conducted in a single process, it may seem strange that so many countries would set up bicameral legislatures. Indeed, many Canadians have become cynical about our upper house, the Senate, and would rather scrap it than reform it. A 1998 opinion poll found that 41 percent of Canadians favoured abolishing the Senate entirely, 43 percent preferred to reform it, and only 10 percent wanted to keep it as it is.[21] The view that favours abolition, however, is probably based partly on a lack of appreciation of both what the Senate actually does and the significant roles that it could potentially play in the political system. There are two main functions for upper houses that are appealing: these houses can act as an additional check and balance in the political process, and they may provide a forum for special representation of sectional (usually based on geographic regions) interests in the country.

Perhaps the most common function is to provide "sober second thought" about measures passed without proper consideration in the lower house. This can be a very useful process in states where one party or a coalition controls a majority of members in the lower house and where party discipline can ensure that this majority approves measures without much debate or against the wishes of the general public. A second chamber can act as a brake on the legislative process, give bills closer scrutiny, and hold up approval while public reaction is gauged. The Fathers of Confederation, who designed Canada's national political institutions, reflected 19th-century British thought in choosing an appointed second chamber to act as a restraint on the "passions of the moment" to which the elected MPs in the lower house could be susceptible. Our Senate, whose members are appointed and now sit until the age of 75, was modelled on the House of Lords in Britain, whose members were hereditary and appointed aristocrats.

Just how effective a second chamber can be depends entirely upon its powers in the legislative

---

Table 9.3   Women in Selected National Legislatures around the World

The Inter-Parliamentary Union has conducted a survey of 179 national legislatures in order to determine how many women are members. Out of a total of 41 172 legislators whose gender was known, women constituted only 14.2 percent as of March 1, 2002. A sample of the percentage of women in selected countries' national legislatures (lower houses, where applicable) reveals something of the state of affairs. The 179 countries were ranked 1 to 118 because of a number of ties.

Rank	Country	Percent Women
1	Sweden	42.7
2	Denmark	38.0
3	Finland	36.5
7	Germany	31.7
10	Mozambique	30.0
13	Cuba	27.6
30	**Canada**	**20.6**
40	United Kingdom	17.9
52	United States	14.0
71	Italy	9.8
78	India	8.8
88	Japan	7.3
92	Brazil	6.8
112	Egypt	2.4
118	Kuwait	0.0

Source: Inter-Parliamentary Union, "Women in Parliaments: World and Regional Averages"; cited on July 1, 2001; available at http://www.ipu.org/wmn-e/world.htm; Inter-Parliamentary Union, "Women in Parliaments: World Classification"; cited on July 1, 2001; available at http://www.ipu.org/wmn-e/classif.htm. Reprinted by permission of the Inter-Parliamentary Union (IPU), 2002.

process and how it uses them. Essentially, it depends upon whether the consent of the upper house is actually needed before a proposal can become law or whether the upper house can merely delay the approval process. A number of upper houses possess a "suspensive veto" only. This means that if the members of the upper house vote down a measure already approved by the lower house or fail to approve it within a set period of time, the members of the lower house can pass a motion restating their approval of the bill; the bill then becomes law, regardless of its treatment in the upper house. The House of Lords in Britain has only a suspensive veto, but it serves as a useful check and balance by forcing the government to slow down and gauge public opinion before the proposals are finally enacted into law. If the House of Lords rejects a bill, the government can reintroduce it into the House of Commons a year later and pass it without the need for sending it to the House of Lords again. The waiting period forces the government to reconsider the original measure, and the government often decides to compromise by making important changes to the bill or even to scrap it entirely.

An upper house can be even more effective if the constitution provides it with an **absolute veto**. In that case, the upper house has the power to defeat a bill, and both houses must pass a bill in identical form before it can become law. In countries such as Canada, the United States, Australia, India, and Japan, the upper house has an absolute veto over all legislation.[22] In other countries, the upper house has a veto only over certain types of legislation. In Germany, for example, the upper house can veto only legislation that would affect the equivalent of provincial governments. Armed with an absolute veto, the sober second thought offered by the upper house can indeed force the government or lower house to reflect seriously on its proposals. This absolute veto is seen as an important part of the checks and balances involved in some political systems' legislative process. For this reason, almost all the American and Australian states have a bicameral legislature. An upper house may also simply amend the bill rather than veto it outright; in that case, the two houses eventually have to reach an agreement on the final form of the bill. Even in countries where the upper house has only a suspensive veto, amendments made to legislation are often voluntarily adopted by the lower house; this

may be done out of expediency to pass the bill as quickly as possible or because the amendments relate to some noncontroversial technical improvements.

An important consideration, however, is whether informal constitutional principles prevent an upper house from freely exercising its absolute veto or even from amending legislation. The Canadian Senate, for instance, is constrained by constitutional conventions from using its powers to their full extent. Still, the Senate plays a role of some substance in the legislative process in amending legislation and forcing the government to reconsider its proposals before asking the House of Commons to reaffirm its policies; occasionally, the government even agrees to amendments proposed by the Senate.[23]

BOX 9.4

THE MANY DIFFERENT WAYS TO BECOME MEMBERS OF AN UPPER HOUSE

Members of upper chambers acquire the right to sit in the house in a variety of ways, and some chambers use more than one method. In Canada, all senators are chosen by the prime minister and appointed by the governor general, and they serve until the age of 75. In the United States and Australia, all senators are directly elected by the people. In India, most members of the upper house are indirectly elected, which means they are chosen by the legislatures of each state. In Russia, each state's governor and the Speaker of the state legislature are ex-officio members of the country's upper house. Britain's House of Lords is composed of over 580 members appointed for life, 92 hereditary peers chosen either by their fellow life peers or by their political parties, 26 bishops of the Church of England, and 28 Law Lords (current and former members of Britain's final court of appeal, the House of Lords Appellate Committee).

The other principal function of an upper house is to provide special representation in the legislature for territorial or nonterritorial populations and interests that would otherwise go underrepresented or completely unrepresented. Territorial representation is very common in upper houses; for example, the French

Senate's members are chosen by the city, town, and county (*département*) councils. All federal countries have bicameral legislatures, in order to provide the provinces or states with a more equal or more effective representation than they have in the lower houses; this increased representation can come either through a more equitable distribution of seats among the regions or provinces or by having representatives of the state or provincial governments actually sit as members of the upper house. Seats in the lower house are usually distributed roughly according to population, which allows large provinces or states to swamp the smaller ones; in the United States, for example, California has 52 members in the House of Representatives, while a small state such as Rhode Island has only two. A great imbalance like this is rectified in some countries by providing each state or province equal representation in the upper house; in the United States, each state has two seats in the Senate regardless of size, and in Australia each state has 12.

Other federations do not have strict equality in the share of seats the states or provinces have in the upper house, but they do provide a more equitable distribution of seats. For instance, each of Germany's 16 states has between three and six seats in the Bundesrat, depending on its size. A few federations still have very significant disparities. Eight of India's states have only one seat in the upper house, the Rajya Sabha, while Uttar Pradesh has 34. Canada is rather odd, with a Senate that was originally designed to provide equal shares of seats for regions, not the provinces per se. The Maritime provinces, Quebec, Ontario, and the four Western provinces count as regions, with each having 24 seats.[24]

But the question remains: Is the representation of territorial interests in an upper house aimed at representing the population of the provinces or states, or is it meant to provide representation for the interests of their governments? Some countries choose to elect their upper house representatives in order to give the citizens a direct voice; Australia and the United States are examples. Others choose to provide representation for the state or provincial governments rather than the people; for example, in Germany, Russia, and South Africa, political leaders from the state or provincial governments are members of the nation's upper house, and in a sense, these chambers function like a permanent fed-eral–provincial conference. Canada is an oddity in providing neither form of representation, since the federal government appoints all the members of the Senate; as a result, neither the provincial population nor provincial governments are directly represented.

Upper houses can also provide representation of nonterritorial sections of the population. Several countries allocate some of the seats in the upper house to representatives of particular professions. In Ireland, for instance, two universities each elect three senators, and 43 other senators are elected from five occupational groups.[25] And in Pakistan, five members of each delegation chosen by the provincial legislatures to represent them in the national Senate must be members of certain religious or occupational groups.

REFORM OF LEGISLATURES

There are as many ways to reform legislatures as there are limitations on their effectiveness. Some reforms involve the internal structure and procedures of the legislature, while other changes might occur if only factors external to the legislature change, such as the electoral system, media coverage, or something as amorphous as the society's political culture. In parliamentary systems, most reforms centre on finding ways to reduce the cabinet's dominance of the legislature and on loosening party discipline. One of the most frequent suggestions is that legislatures make greater use of "free votes." Occasionally, votes in a legislature are held where the parties agree that they will not formally require their members to maintain party loyalty; the members are free to vote according to their own personal judgment. These votes usually involve matters of deep personal conscience, such as capital punishment or abortion, and the suggestion is that free votes could also be extended to matters that do not imply a vote of confidence in the government.

Another suggestion in Canada is that the political parties could adopt the British practice of notifying members of where a vote fits on a sliding scale of the degree of party cohesion expected. For example, a "three-line whip" means "You'd better get out of your hospital bed and vote for the party's position"; such votes are normally matters of confidence. This scale for votes also includes two-line and one-line whips, with decreasing requirements for party cohesion. However, extensive use of free votes would mean that MPs need to use their own personal judgment more often; in the long run, that could require a much greater support and research staff for individual MPs, so that they could form a proper assessment of the issues involved.

Other suggestions for parliaments centre on the degree of independence that legislative committees have to investigate policy issues on their own initiative, rather than requiring a cabinet-sanctioned motion in the legislature to begin the hearings. Considerable attention has also been focused in many parliamentary systems on changing the procedural rules dealing with bills introduced by private (noncabinet) members, in order to give them a better chance of actually getting passed into law. Another reform that has significant potential—but a very low political profile—is to strengthen a legislature's ability to review delegated legislation and annul the regulations passed by the executive that go beyond the policies originally envisaged by the legislature when it passed the act authorizing the delegated legislation in the first place.

The proposal for structural reform of the Canadian Parliament with the highest political profile is the idea of a Triple-E Senate: Elected, Equal, and Effective. The idea is strongly backed by the Canadian Alliance and most of the Western provinces. These senators would be elected on a province-wide basis, and the Senate would fully exercise its legislative powers to amend or defeat legislation. The scheme would also see an equal number of senators for each province, as there are in Australia and the United States. The difficulty with this proposal is twofold. First, Ontario and Quebec reject the suggestion because their level of representation would be severely reduced. Second, the result of electing senators could possibly import into that house all the problems of tight party discipline that lie at the root of many of the problems in the House of Commons that a Triple-E Senate is supposed to remedy, thereby leading to deadlock between the two chambers.

Several countries have seen debates over redressing the underrepresentation or exclusion of women and Indigenous peoples. One shortcut solution that is sometimes discussed is to set aside a certain number of seats in the legislature to ensure that at least some groups have a physical presence. For example, New Zealand has long had separate seats for the Indigenous Maori population, and a Royal Commission on Electoral Reform proposed in 1991 that Canada set aside some seats in Parliament for First Nations representatives.[26] So far, such ideas have not met with widespread support. In some countries, the idea of setting aside a specific number of seats for a group results in fierce controversy. For instance, fist fights broke out in the Indian Parliament in 1998 when it debated an amendment to the Constitution that would have required that one-third of the seats be reserved for women in the lower house of Parliament and in all the state legislatures.[27] In Canada, residents of what was to become Nunavut voted down in 1998 a referendum proposal to enact a requirement of equal representation for women and men in the new territorial legislature. Other ways to remedy these problems of underrepresentation within the legislature involve reforms outside of the legislature itself. For example, some political parties around the world voluntarily adopt policies requiring an equal number of male and female candidates and a certain number of candidates from particular ethnic groups. Other suggestions include adopting a proportional representation system, with party lists that can be deliberately constructed to provide representatives from the social groups in question.

CONCLUSION

This chapter has provided a brief examination of a range of issues related to the legislative branch of government. Legislatures are institutions with complex structures and processes, and their relationship with the rest of the political system involves many interconnected threads. Their many possible functions are all limited by a range of real-world constraints, some of which are integral to a particular system of government; executive dominance and party discipline remain both cornerstones and millstones of parliamentary government, for instance. However, this review of legislatures should open your horizons to the important contributions that most democratic legislatures do make to their political systems. These contributions can indeed be improved, but the interrelation between the structure and procedural rules on the one hand and political culture on the other mean that there are few quick fixes.

DISCUSSION QUESTIONS

1. Which form of representation do you find your-self favouring: the delegate or the trustee approach?

2. What range of social groups do you feel you belong to? If you were an MP, on what sorts of issues would you believe that you should "repre-sent" one of those groups rather than the others?

3. Imagine that you are a member of the governing party's caucus in the Canadian House of Commons who is not in cabinet. Think of what you would say in a caucus meeting about the need to loosen party discipline. Then picture yourself as the prime minister and think of what you would say in response.

4. What do you think is the single most important constraint on Canadian legislatures that stems from our political culture? Can you see any way in which the cultural values involved may change?

w(w)w WEB LINKS

Thomson Nelson: Canadian Legislatures:
http://polisci.nelson.com/legislatures.html

The Opposition in a Parliamentary System:
http://www.parl.gc.ca/information/library/PRBpubs/bp47-e.htm

Inter-Parliamentary Union:
http://www.ipu.org/

Nelson Thomson Learning: World Legislatures:
http://polisci.nelson.com/introlegs.html

FURTHER READING

Docherty, David. *Mr. Smith Goes to Ottawa.* Vancouver: UBC Press, 1997.

Franks, C.E.S. *The Parliament of Canada.* Toronto: University of Toronto Press, 1987.

Heard, Andrew. *Canadian Constitutional Conventions: The Marriage of Law and Politics.* Toronto: Oxford University Press, 1991.

Inter-Parliamentary Union. *World Directory of Parliaments.* Geneva: IPU, 1998.

ENDNOTES

1 Inter-Parliamentary Union, *World Directory of Parliaments* (Geneva: IPU, 1998).

2 It should be noted that even in countries without a legislature, the judiciary still exercises a certain amount of legislative power by interpreting and enforcing the laws passed by the executive.

3 The NCMPs have all the rights of regular MPs except they cannot vote on motions of confidence in the government, impeachment of the president, or supply and money bills. Tan Soo Khoon, "From Legislative Council to Parliament: An Overview of the History and Structure of Representative Government in Singapore," *Parliamentarian* 80(2) (supplement) (April 1999): pp. 5–6.

4 Inter-Parliamentary Union, *Parliaments of the World: A Comparative Reference Compendium*, 3rd ed., vol. 2 (Aldershot: IPU, 1986), p. 1125.

5 "Résumé of Congressional Activity," cited on August 11, 2002, available at http://thomas.loc.gov/home/resume/resume.html

6 David Docherty, *Mr. Smith Goes to Ottawa* (Vancouver: UBC Press, 1997), p. 129.

7 Philip Norton, "The United Kingdom: Restoring Confidence," *Parliamentary Affairs*, 50 (1997), p. 360.

8 Docherty, *Mr. Smith Goes to Ottawa*, pp. 190–91.

9 J.P. Joseph Maignot, *Parliamentary Privilege in Canada*, 2nd ed. (Montreal and Kingston: McGill-Queen's University Press, 1997), p. 335.

10 Jon H. Pammett, "The Voters Decide," in Alan Frizzel and Jon H. Pammett, eds., *The Canadian General Election of 1997* (Toronto: Dundurn, 1997), p. 233.

11 Louis Massicotte, "Party Cohesion in the Ontario Legislative Assembly, 1867–1990" (paper presented

at the annual meeting of the Canadian Political Science Association, Calgary, June 1994).

12 Keith Jackson, "Caucus: The Anti-Parliament System?" *Parliamentarian* 59(3) (July 1978): 160.

13 Philip Norton, *The Commons in Perspective* (Oxford: Martin Robertson, 1981), p. 227.

14 *Congressional Quarterly Almanac 1998* (Washington, D.C.: CQ Press, 1999), p. B6.

15 Andrew Heard, *Canadian Constitutional Conventions: The Marriage of Law and Politics* (Toronto: Oxford University Press, 1991), pp. 87–98.

16 Ontario Legislative Library Legislative Research Service, "The Ontario Legislature: An Overview"; cited on May 31, 2000; available at http://www.ontla.on.ca/library/c105txx.htm.

17 David V. Edwards and Alessandra Lipucci, *Practicing American Politics: An Introduction to Government*, basic ed. (New York: Worth, 1998), p. 509.

18 *Clinton v. City of New York*, [1998] 118 S. Ct. 2091.

19 For example, see Jane Arscott and Linda Trimble, eds., *In the Presence of Women* (Toronto: Harcourt Brace, 1997); Julie Dolan, "Support for Women's Interests in the 103rd Congress: The Distinct Impact of Congressional Women," *Women in Politics* 18(4) (1997): 88. Note, however, that contrary conclusions have been found with respect to African-American members of the American Congress; see Carol M. Swain, *Black Faces, Black Interests: The Representation of African*

Americans in Congress (Cambridge, Mass.: Harvard University Press, 1993).

20 Jane Mansbridge, "Should Blacks Represent Blacks and Women Represent Women? A Contingent 'Yes,'" *Journal of Politics* 61 (1999): 628. This article contains a good review of the arguments for and against mirror or descriptive representation.

21 Angus Reid, "Canadians and the Senate"; cited on May 11, 1998; available at http://www.angusreid.com/media/content/prf/pr110598.pdf.

22 Except that the Canadian Senate does not have an absolute veto over constitutional amendments.

23 Heard, *Canadian Constitutional Conventions*, pp. 87–98.

24 Quebec and Ontario each have 24 seats. The Maritime provinces' 24 seats are divided into 10 seats each for Nova Scotia and New Brunswick and four seats for PEI. The four Western provinces each have six seats. When Newfoundland entered Confederation, it was given six seats. Each of the three territories has one senator, for a grand total of 105.

25 These five occupational groups are Culture and Education, Agriculture, Labour, Industry and Commerce, and Public Administration.

26 Royal Commission on Electoral Reform and Party Financing, *Final Report*, vol. 1 (Ottawa: 1991).

27 Shri G.C. Malhotra, "Parliamentary Pandemonium: Taking Opposition Too Far," *Parliamentarian* 80(2) (April 1999).

Chapter 10

The Judiciary: The Power behind the Throne

Andrew Heard

CHAPTER OBJECTIVES

After you have completed this chapter, you should be able to

- understand the role of law and the courts in a political system
- evaluate the strengths and weakness of different methods of appointing judges
- discuss the issues involved in judicial independence and impartiality
- outline how access to the courts is restricted.

THE ROLE OF LAW AND THE JUDICIAL FUNCTION

In stable societies, law and judges play crucial roles that are not always seen or widely appreciated. Law sets the most basic rules of behaviour for all citizens and can impose fundamental limits on the power of government officials. The judicial power is an essential part of the power of governments, and through it authoritative decisions are made on disputes covering a wide range of matters. The courts have become so much a part of the fabric of our political system that they are often simply taken for granted. Yet, they are in some ways "the power behind the throne." The courts perform many vital functions and have an enormous cumulative impact, not only through the policies they enforce on behalf of the elected government but also through those they develop and implement themselves. Perhaps ironically, the power of the judiciary may be most appreciated in countries where the courts are weak, corrupt, or simply subservient to the whims of the political or military leaders of the day. There, many people long for the day when the courts will become independent developers and protectors of constitutional limits on the rulers and provide effective punishments for those who undermine basic law and order or openly terrorize people through brute force.

If you stop to think about your life, you will find that much of it depends upon laws that tell you what to do and not do, help you have what you are entitled to, protect you from false accusations, and provide you with a peaceful way to resolve disputes that arise. You also probably do many things the law requires you to do, whether you like it or not, because you believe that, in general, it is right and proper to obey the law. While we all probably break some laws some of the time, most of us still believe that we should obey most laws most of the time. In democratic countries such as Canada, obedience to the law and respect for the courts are ingrained in the general political culture.

The existence of courts to adjudicate disputes ensures that conflicts are decided by applying rules of law and not through the rule of might. If you have a dispute with your neighbour or a TV store clerk, you do not have to resort to rounding up the biggest of your friends to go and sort it out. Moreover, the courts ensure that a mere accusation is not sufficient for someone to be punished—guilt or innocence must be carefully and objectively determined. Finally, the courts can ensure that the rule of law is observed and that the government does not act outside its powers or fail to perform duties required under law.

Unfortunately, the costs of judicial proceedings raise serious questions about the equal access of all to the courts. There are also deep controversies over the extent to which judges can, or should, exercise their own discretion in interpreting the law to reflect their own personal values. Furthermore, there are important questions about how judges are appointed and removed from office, as well as the extent to which elected politicians should be involved in those decisions.

Connections between Law, Morality, and Politics

Law is not an independent force in a society, nor is it simply a set of rules of procedure. Law gives life to the policies of the government. Law may be either an instrument of justice, as is the ideal in a democratic society, or an instrument of oppression. What matters in the end is the content of the law and how it is applied and enforced. Law may be the embodiment of the noblest principles of a free democracy, or it may be the instrument used to implement torture and mass murder. Canada's legal history provides examples of the best and worst of the content of law. The law provides

---

BOX 10.1

THE LAW AND THE RIGHT TO VOTE IN CANADA

The evolution of the right to vote in Canadian federal elections is a good illustration of how laws embody prevailing values and change as those values change.

1867: Only male British subjects over the age of 21 could vote, and their right to vote depended upon owning property of a certain value (which varied from province to province).

1917: All men serving in the military were allowed to vote. Men with a son or grandson in the military were allowed to vote, regardless of property ownership. Women who had a husband, son, or brother in the military were also allowed to vote, for the first time. The right to vote was taken away from conscientious objectors and members of the Doukhobour and Mennonite religions, as well as from recent immigrants from non-English-speaking parts of the world.

1918: Women over the age of 21 were given the right to vote. Even so, only about half the Canadian population was eligible to vote because of various disqualifications.

1948: The last of the property qualifications were abandoned, and Canadians of Asian origin were allowed to vote for the first time.

1953: Inuit people were allowed to vote.

1960: Status Indians living on reserves were allowed to vote for the first time.

1970: The age for eligible voters was lowered from 21 to 18.

1988: Court rulings under the Charter of Rights gave the right to vote to federally appointed judges, people with mental disabilities, and prisoners serving less than a two-year sentence.

Source: Elections Canada, "The Evolution of the Federal Franchise," June 2000; cited on July 23, 2002; available at http://www.elections.ca/content.asp?section=gen&document=ec90785&dir=bkg&lang=e&textonly=false.

Canadians with free schooling, minimum wages, workplace safety, universal health care, and unemployment insurance; the Charter of Rights protects many rights, such as our freedom of speech and the right to vote. However, Canadian laws have also prohibited women, Chinese Canadians, and Aboriginal people from voting. Canadian laws also provided the basis for interning Canadian citizens of Japanese descent during World War II and for the complete seizure of their property and businesses.[1] There were even laws in British Columbia, Saskatchewan, Manitoba, and Ontario that prohibited white women from working for Chinese or Japanese males.

The content of law is very much a reflection of the prevailing mores and values of a society at any given time. More to the point, the law in any society embodies the prevailing moral values of the dominant elite. As times and attitudes change, so do the moral beliefs that are enacted into law and enforced by the courts. In Canada, homosexual activity was once illegal, but recently the courts have required Canadian governments to extend spousal benefits to same-sex couples. Thus the content of the law and the morality enforced change over time and vary from one country to another. While adultery was once illegal in the United States, for example, it is no longer a crime enforced by the courts; on the other hand, it is still an offence for which people are executed in Saudi Arabia and Iran. Given the intimate connection between law and politics, there are intense political conflicts involved in what gets written into law and how that law is interpreted.

Different Types of Law

There are different types of law to regulate different types of activity and disputes. The major division in law is between public and private law. **Public law** includes constitutional law, criminal law, and many aspects of international law. Public law involves the rules of how government is structured and the powers and relations between various government bodies and officials and between the government and the public. The criminal law, part of public law, is largely concerned with matters of public safety, health, and morality. Thus, it is a crime to beat or murder somebody; it is a crime to sell dangerous drugs; and it is a crime for an adult to have

sex with a child. **Private law** can be described as being principally concerned with regulating disputes between members of the public, be they individuals, groups of people, or corporations. The many different areas of private law govern contracts, corporations, inheritance, real estate, and employment.

While one might think that law is just something created by each government within a country, there is also an important body of **international law**. International law is created in many ways: formal treaties or conventions signed by the governments of the states that wish to be bound by it, declarations of the United Nations, and even the historical practice and custom of states over time. International law covers not only how the governments of different countries deal with each other, but also how business and individuals from one country are dealt with by other countries. International trade could not exist at today's levels without a strong collection of legal rules to regulate trade and settle disputes. There are even some international courts set up to deal with aspects of international law, such as the International Court of Justice and the European Court of Justice.

Definition

INTERNATIONAL LAW: A complex body of rules, derived principally from the treaties, covenants, and declarations signed by the governments of various countries. The resolutions of international organizations, the writings of academics, and rulings of domestic and international courts can also be sources of international law when the rules are not otherwise clear.

There are a number of very different legal systems around the world; the most commonly encountered ones are based on common law, a civil code, or Islamic law. The **common law** system is practised in many countries that emerged from the British Empire. Countries as diverse as Canada, India, Jamaica, and Nigeria all base their national legal systems on the common law tradition of Britain. In this system, the fundamental principle is that like cases should be decided alike and that courts are bound by the precedents of previous decisions that dealt with similar points of law and fact—the principle known as **stare decisis**. Historically, the common law also described a set of judge-made rules that British judges developed in the late Middle Ages in the absence of extensive formal legislation by Parliament. Only a small subset of these common law rules survive today; in Canada and Britain, they relate mainly to private law and some aspects of the power of the executive branch of government.

> **Definition**
>
> **COMMON LAW:** A system of law in which precedents from relevant cases in the past are applied to current ones. Judges are bound by precedent and should decide like cases alike.

> **Definition**
>
> **STARE DECISIS:** A principle of common law systems by which courts are bound to follow prior decisions that involved similar issues of law. A judgment by one member of a court binds other members, and lower courts are bound to follow the decisions of higher courts.

The civil code systems of law are found mainly in Western Europe and in newer states that emerged from the French Empire. In this system, the law is organized as a set of principles that, in theory, are applied freshly to each case. In practice, however, judges pay close attention to past decisions on the particular sections of the code involved in a case. This family of legal systems has an ancient lineage. While there are separate French, German, Dutch, and Swiss origins of the modern systems, in the French case dating from a code enacted under Napoleon Bonaparte in 1804, many principles can be traced back to the laws of the Roman Empire. It should be noted that Quebec has continued to use an updated version of the Napoleonic Code for private law matters, while the other provinces have systems based on British common law.

The most strikingly different system of law in fairly wide use today is the Islamic system of law, known as the Sharia. This system is based on a collection of ancient Islamic teachings on how people should behave and what punishments are appropriate for particular transgressions. Essentially, the Islamic holy scriptures, the Koran, and the later writings of scholars form the basis of the Sharia. Because the Sharia is based on a collection of writings, it can operate in somewhat dif-ferent ways in the countries that use it, as different aspects are emphasized. The strictest implementation of the Sharia is found in states such as Saudi Arabia and Iran, where punishments that seem cruel by Western standards are meted out: floggings, the severing of a hand for theft, and execution for adultery, either by beheading or stoning. Other states, such as Egypt, have adapted Islamic law and implemented more moderate aspects of the code. The adoption of Islamic law in the late 1990s by several of Nigeria's states caused significant controversy in that country, and a constitutional challenge to its use was started in early 2002 by activists who claim that it violates Nigeria's constitutional guarantees of equality by subjecting citizens in some parts of the country to significantly harsher penalties.

The Judicial Function

With laws comes a need to interpret and enforce them. Judicial power is exercised by those institutions and officials authorized to interpret and enforce the law. It is important to distinguish between judicial power and the courts. Although courts are usually the primary focus of judicial power, most political systems also include other officials or institutions who have an important role to play in interpreting and enforcing laws. Where judicial power is exercised by officials or bodies other than judges and the courts, it is usually known as quasi-judicial power. In all industrialized democracies and in most other states, the executive branch of government exercises a considerable amount of quasi-judicial power. For example, if you have a dispute with your landlord, you would go to a residential tenancies tribunal, where your dispute would be heard and settled according to the laws governing apartment and house rentals. Or if you felt you had been unfairly denied employment insurance or welfare benefits, you would first argue your case before tribunals composed of civil servants. Refugees in Canada have their case initially decided by a panel of officials whose job it is to determine whether someone qualifies as a refugee and may remain in the country. So important issues about whether people can stay in their apartments, have enough money to live on, or remain in the country are decided according to the relevant laws by **administrative tribunals**, which are not actual courts. However, the decisions of these tribunals can usually be appealed to the courts for a final decision.

> **Definition**
>
> **ADMINISTRATIVE TRIBUNALS:** Boards or commissions established by the government to adjudicate certain disputes by applying laws to the facts; also called quasi-judicial tribunals. These tribunals are not proper courts presided over by judges.

The judicial function can also be carried out by very different types of courts, and the legitimacy or effectiveness of judicial powers may depend on which courts deal with which matters. When political scientists and lawyers refer to "the courts," we normally mean what are properly called civil courts, which are presided over by civilian judges with some degree of independence from the other branches of government and political authorities. Military courts, in contrast, are presided over by serving members of the military; depending upon the country, the presiding officers may or may not have legal training. In Canada and Britain, for example, the lowest level of military tribunals are known as summary trials and are presided over by the normal officer commanding the unit, who could be an engineer, a pilot, or an infantry officer, as the case may be. However, there are also courts-martial that have military judges who are trained lawyers. Military courts are usually characterized by expedited processes, fewer legal protections for the accused, and harsher penalties. While most democracies restrict the jurisdiction of military courts to members of the armed forces, some countries may try the most serious offences against the state in military courts and leave more minor cases to the civil courts. And, of course, countries run by military dictators may rely exclusively on military tribunals. The use of military courts has become a political issue in the United States, as President Bush announced in 2001 that alleged terrorists captured during the war in Afghanistan would be held at a U.S. naval base in Cuba and tried before military commissions. The concern of many is that those to be tried by these tribunals will lack the constitutional rights that they would normally have if tried before the civil courts within American territory.

Some countries also have religious courts that may operate alongside civil courts or instead of them. Countries that fully implement the Islamic Sharia, such as Saudi Arabia and Iran, are most likely to empower religious courts to try cases dealing with public offences. Religious courts usually provide few if any opportunities for an accused to be properly represented by legal counsel, and the laws they enforce are interpretations of religious doctrines and decrees by religious authorities rather than individual laws passed by the legislature. Perhaps the most famous example of these in recent times were the religious courts that dished out a brutal justice under the Taliban rule of Afghanistan in the 1990s. However, much of Western Europe also experienced religious courts in the Middle Ages, when tribunals of the Roman Catholic church exercised considerable authority; the trials of the Inquisition are the most notorious examples, with thousands put to death.

THE ROLE OF COURTS

The primary function that is part of everything else performed by the **judiciary** is the interpretation and enforcement of the law. Laws are necessarily worded in ambiguous ways and cannot foresee all the future circumstances to which they must be applied. Thus, the judges must fill in the blanks and flesh out the wording of legal rules; they interpret what the laws mean. The judiciary also enforces the law by determining the guilt or innocence of those charged with an offence and by punishing those who do not obey the law. The courts do not go out and look for wrongdoers; they deal only with those who are brought before them. This role of enforcing the law ensures that there is general obedience to the rules of society and that peaceful people can be protected from wrongdoers.

> **Definition**
>
> **JUDICIARY:** The term used to refer to all the judges in a country collectively. It can also mean the whole judicial branch of government, including juries and the courts' administrative staff.

In the criminal context, the judiciary comes into play after the police or some other executive agency has discovered evidence of wrongdoing. The courts also have an important role in helping to settle private disputes (often called civil disputes) between individuals, groups, or companies. When we have a dispute over what someone has done to our property and want compensation to pay for the damages, we can go to the courts. In business, if a company does not live up to its contractual agreements or provides faulty or damaged goods, the dispute can be settled in the courts. Many disputes in our private lives can be settled in courts, according to laws that apply to everybody. Judges decide who is to blame and who violated the law; they then determine what penalty is appropriate and what compensation is due to the person or group that was wronged. Because of this, we do not have to rely on violence or vengeance to get what is owed to us. This function of the judiciary allows us to live in a peaceful society.

The courts can also act as referees that decide whether government officials are acting within their powers. The power of judicial review is the power of the courts to decide whether law authorized an action taken by a government official or body and whether a law is actually constitutional.

Courts settle disputes primarily through adjudication, which is the settling of a dispute by applying rules (laws) to the facts of a case. Adjudication is quite different from arbitration and mediation, in which one tries to find an equitable resolution to a dispute that ideally provides the best possible solution for all parties involved. Courts face a conundrum in adjudicating disputes. Although judges are supposed to apply the law to the facts of the case, the law is often ambiguous or even plagued by gaps and holes; there is not always a clear, existing law to apply. As a result, judges have an important role to play in interpreting the existing law. In the process of interpreting the law, judges sometimes actually have to make new law. Furthermore, in the process of interpreting and making new law, judges have to play a substantial policymaking role. This policymaking role is seen most clearly in interpreting con-

Figure 10.1 Canada's Court System

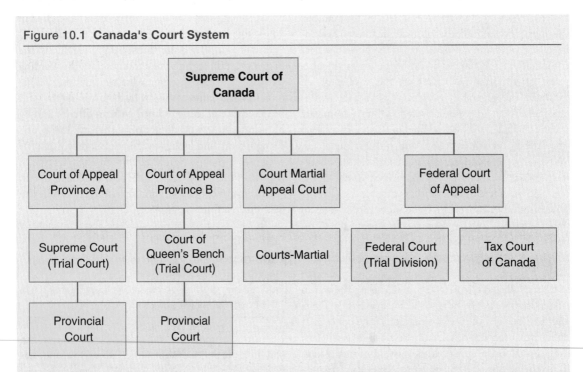

Canada has a complex court system, with some courts created by the provincial and territorial governments and others by the federal government. The Supreme Court of Canada, the federal courts, and the courts-martial (dealing with members of the Canadian Forces) are all created by the federal government. The provincial governments create the courts of appeal, trial courts, and provincial courts (they may have different names in each province). Decisions from all these courts can be appealed to the Supreme Court of Canada, which has considerable discretion over which appeals it will actually hear.

stitutional rights, but it is involved in virtually all aspects of judicial interpretation.

The courts also have an important role to play in enforcing legal limits on the powers of politicians. While this role is almost taken for granted in established democracies, it is vital in transitional democracies, where political leaders are tempted to ignore constitutional limits in trying to implement their policies. For example, judges in Zimbabwe tried for many years to restrain President Mugabe's tightening grip on that country and steer his government into respecting the country's Constitution. However, they lost their fight in 2001, when the majority of the top court resigned after the chief justice decided that he could no longer guarantee the safety of the members of that court who had stood up to Mugabe. After their resignations, Mugabe appointed new judges loyal to his policies, and they quickly set about giving the court's stamp of approval to his government's actions.[2] At least the Zimbabwean judges fared better than those in Uganda in the 1970s, some of whom were assassinated by President Idi Amin's security forces!

In enforcing limits on the powers of politicians, the courts are enforcing the rule of law. Although the rule of law is a principle that is open to many interpretations, some key aspects can be identified to reinforce the idea that law should govern all actions of governments. Laws must emanate from a known, formal institution authorized by the constitution to exercise legislative power. Citizens must be able to find out what the laws are that they are bound to obey. The law should apply to everyone in the society, including all government officials. This does not mean that the law cannot make distinctions or exceptions, just that those exceptions must be included in the law itself. And finally, the law must ultimately be enforced by proper courts of law. These aspects of the rule of law do not in themselves mean that a government is going to be democratic or benevolent; after all, even the apartheid regime in South Africa used proper laws and courts to enforce white supremacy and the brutal oppression of the nonwhite majority. However, one can say that no democratic government can function without respecting the rule of law. Thus the rule of law is a necessary but not sufficient condition for democracy.

In fulfilling their general roles, the courts may at times play a very active role in highly charged political disputes. For example, the Canadian Supreme Court has twice been asked to settle high-profile political controversies. In 1981, it had to rule on the constitutionality of Prime Minister Trudeau's plans to patriate the Canadian Constitution and introduce the Charter of Rights without gaining the consent of the provincial governments. In the *Patriation Reference* case, the Supreme Court ruled that the federal government's proposed unilateral actions were legal but contravened the informal constitutional conventions that required substantial provincial consent to changes to provincial powers. Then in 1998, the Court was asked to declare whether Quebec had a right to secede from Canada under either domestic constitutional law or international law. It ruled that Quebec did not have this right at all, but that the rest of Canada would be under a moral obligation to negotiate the terms of separation if a clear majority voted in favour on a clear question to pursue independence. In both the *Patriation Reference* case and the *Quebec Secession Reference*, the court appeared to carefully craft a decision that went beyond the strict law and to provide answers that played to both sides of the political disputes at hand.[3] In 2001, the U.S. Supreme Court became embroiled in the fallout from the unclear presidential election results that depended entirely on the outcome of voting in Florida. In a decision that generated much heated debate in the United States, the Court ruled that recounts of the votes cast in certain counties of Florida should not proceed—effectively declaring George Bush the winner and new president.[4] Decades earlier, the U.S. Supreme Court catalyzed profound social and political changes in ordering that the racially segregated school systems be integrated.[5]

Judicial Review

In democratic countries, the court's powers of **judicial review** are very important to ensuring that the principles of limited government and the rule of law are respected by government actors. If there are to be legal limits on the powers of state actors, then somebody has to review their actions to ensure that they are legal. The courts conduct several different types of judicial review with varying degrees of controversy, but they all involve the same basic role: the review of other state actors to ensure that they fulfil their duties and do not act beyond their legal powers.

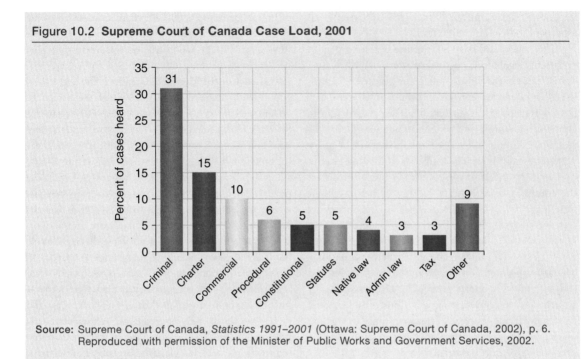

Figure 10.2 Supreme Court of Canada Case Load, 2001

Source: Supreme Court of Canada, *Statistics 1991–2001* (Ottawa: Supreme Court of Canada, 2002), p. 6. Reproduced with permission of the Minister of Public Works and Government Services, 2002.

Definition

JUDICIAL REVIEW: A function of the courts in which judges examine actions of the government to determine whether they are authorized by law. This may also include a determination as to whether statutes and regulations are contrary to the constitution.

One type of judicial review is without controversy in countries that practise the rule of law: to make sure that government officials respect the ordinary statutory provisions that govern their powers. Officials can do only what the law empowers them to do, and they must perform what the law requires them to do. Thus, teachers cannot wear army uniforms and carry guns in the classroom. School board officials must allow parents to register their children to attend school if they meet the normal requirements of age and residency. And no one can be refused a new driver's licence just because he or she has red hair; everyone must be issued a licence having completed all the forms, passed the test, and paid the fee. One example of judges conducting this type of judicial review is the writ of habeas corpus; in this process, lawyers can ask the court to determine whether their client is being lawfully held in custody. The police have to establish that the detention is justified under the law.

The second broad type of judicial review involves the courts' scrutiny of the other branches of government to ensure that their actions are within the constitution. Constitutions can limit government powers either by dividing power between different levels of government or by protecting citizens' rights. Judicial review on these grounds involves the scrutiny of the actions of specific officials, such as police and customs officers, and may also involve the review of legislation passed by municipal, provincial, or national legislatures. It should be noted that this type of judicial review can occur only in countries that have formal constitutional documents that set limits on government bodies and officials. In addition to the court-enforceable Charter of Rights, Canada's Constitution also sets limits on the powers of Parliament and provincial legislatures because of the federal–provincial division of powers. Some countries have no equivalent of the Charter of Rights or a federal system, so there is little basis for this form of judicial review.

The review of legislation on the basis of a division of powers is not inherently controversial. If there is to be a real federal system in which the national and regional governments are each given jurisdiction over specific areas of public policy, the courts have to play the role of referee. Someone has to make sure that one level of government does not try to pass laws on matters that are really in the jurisdiction of the other level of government, and the courts have that job. Controversy can occur, however, if suspicions are aroused that the courts are somehow biased in favour of one level of government. For example, Quebec nationalists have long argued that the Supreme Court of Canada has been biased because the federal government appoints all its members, although academic studies have not found any actual bias in the Court's decisions. In the process of interpreting the division of powers, the courts can profoundly transform the character of the federal system by either centralizing power in the national government or decentralizing power in the regional governments. For example, Canada's federal system has been significantly decentralized since 1867, thanks in large part to key decisions of the **Judicial Committee of the Privy Council (JCPC)**, a British body that served as Canada's final court of appeal until 1949, when the **Supreme Court of Canada** finally did become "supreme." Several key decisions of the JCPC limited the federal government's power on the one hand and expanded the authority of the provinces on the other. For one, the federal government's jurisdiction over trade and commerce has been restricted to interprovincial and international trade, while the provinces' power over property and civil rights has been interpreted to give them powers over trade within the province.

Judicial review based on a constitutionally protected set of rights can be even more controversial. The first instance of judges conducting such constitutional review came in the 1803 case *Marbury* v. *Madison*, when the U.S. Supreme Court under Chief Justice Marshall declared a law unconstitutional.[6] This case marked a watershed in judicial power, as it was the first time a court anywhere successfully claimed the power to invalidate laws passed by the legislature; it is all the more remarkable since this power is found nowhere in the text of the American Constitution. This vision of judicial review had been presaged by Lord Coke, chief justice of England's Court of Common Pleas, as early as 1610. In the famous *Dr. Bonham's Case*, Coke argued that the Parliament's law-making power should be governed by the common law to be enforced by judges: "when an act of parliament is against common right and reason, or repugnant, or impossible to be performed, the common law will controul it, and adjudge such act to be void."[7] While this task of the courts seems logical and necessary if constitutional rights are to have practical substance, critics argue that judges end up acting as policymakers. This debate is worth looking at, since important issues are raised about the powers of the different branches of government and the rights of citizens.

Those who defend judicial review on the grounds of protecting constitutional rights raise strong arguments. Just as judges must act as the referees of a federal–provincial division of powers, they also have to act as referees to sort out citizens' complaints that the government has infringed their rights in some fashion. While democratic governments do respect their citizens' rights most of the time through self-restraint, many people argue that the courts are still needed to protect the rights of individuals and minority groups, which might be sacrificed by the will of the majority. To find a Canadian example of a group who suffered at the hands of the majority, one only has to think of the thousands of Japanese Canadians who were rounded up during World War II and stripped of all their businesses and property. Little to no evidence has since surfaced to show that any of these individuals would have posed any danger to Canada by siding with Japan during the war; indeed, the vast majority were people who had lived in Canada for years, for generations in many cases, and were ready to help Canada's war effort.

The courts provide impartial referees to determine the limits of government power and to protect rights. Judges are free from the electoral pressures that politicians face to placate their supporters and can therefore act as a brake upon hasty or oppressive actions by the government. The courtroom provides a forum for the different arguments to be made and weighed and for reasoned judgments to be delivered—judgments that either uphold the government's actions or strike them down in order to defend the rights of citizens. Surveys noted below have shown that Canadians would much rather have the courts than elected politicians decide on their rights.

BOX 10.2

SELECTED SUPREME COURT OF CANADA DECISIONS ON RIGHTS ISSUES

Big M Drug Mart [1985] struck down Sunday closing mandated under the Lord's Day Act.

R. v. Oakes [1986] set out the guidelines for interpreting Section 1 and determining the "reasonable limits" that may be placed on the Charter's rights.

Dolphin Delivery [1986] decided that freedom of association does not include a right for unions to strike.

Ford v. Quebec [1988] ruled that aspects of the Quebec laws related to language used on signs were unconstitutional.

R. v. Morgentaler [1988] struck down the Criminal Code restrictions on abortions.

Andrews v. Law Society of B.C. [1989] ruled that equality should be determined among groups that are "similarly situated" and that prohibited discrimination could involve unintentional, systemic discrimination.

McKinney v. University of Guelph [1990] ruled that mandatory retirement was acceptable age discrimination.

R. v. Askov [1990] gave some limits to the "reasonable delay" allowed in bringing a matter to trial. This decision led to thousands of charges being dropped. The Court revisited the issue and gave more flexible guidelines in *R. v. Morin* [1992].

R. v. Sparrow [1990] set out important principles about the constitutional status of Aboriginal treaty rights.

Electoral Boundaries Reference [1991] decided that "the right to vote" included the right to "effective representation," and so constituencies could vary in size only according to set limits.

Delgamuukw v. British Columbia [1997] laid down principles about the nature of Aboriginal title to land, particularly in the absence of a treaty.

Vriend v. Alberta [1998] declared that the Alberta Individual Rights Protection Act must be read to extend protection against discrimination to cover sexual orientation.

M. v. H. [1999] ruled that the statutory definition of "spouse" must allow for same-sex couples.

Those who oppose judicial review of constitutional rights, however, also have substantial arguments on their side. First of all, some people have argued that a measure of a truly free society is that the people do not need to be protected from their government. Democracy means not just the rule of the majority, but also an accommodation of minority and individual interests along with the majority's. The balance between the powers of government and the liberties of citizens swings over the course of time as circumstances and public opinion change. Ideally, the politicians who make the choice of this balance are not only elected but are accountable at future elections for their actions. A

mature, established democracy such as Canada's learns from its past experience and will draw a better balance over time.

But perhaps the most telling argument is that judges are simply not the impartial referees that the public believes them to be. Moreover, their judgments do not merely set the limits of government power—they legislate on crucial areas of such public policy as abortion, mandatory retirement, sexual behaviour, pornography, and union rights. Worse still, in this view, unelected judges sit in judgment on the decisions of the elected government, and those judges enforce their own personal policy preferences in ways for which the public can never hold them accountable. Several studies have shown that individual judges develop very different patterns of support for constitutional rights, with some judges characterized as more liberal (more likely to accept rights claims) while others are more conservative (less likely to accept rights claims).[8] Indeed, one study of the Supreme Court of Canada in the 1980s found that the most liberal judge, Bertha Wilson, was more than twice as likely to accept a rights claim than the most conservative judge, William McIntyre. Furthermore, the outcomes of cases in which someone claimed their rights had been infringed were directly related to which group of judges heard the case.[9] When the personal dispositions of judges come to bear in decisions on important social questions, it is argued, judges clearly are no longer simply interpreters of constitutional texts but active policymakers substituting their policy preferences for those of elected politicians.

In the end, the debate may really be one about the degree to which judges make social policy framed by their personal views rather than over whether or not it should be done. Indeed, a policymaking role is essentially unavoidable in interpreting constitutional rights. In order to define the practical application of the constitutional right to the freedom of expression, for example, judges have to decide whether sexually explicit material is protected in general and whether certain kinds (such as violent pornography or material involving children) can be prohibited. In deciding those kinds of questions, judges have to set the bounds of social policy. However, the question is how "activist" judges become in imposing their own preferences, as opposed to deferring to some degree to the policy choices made by elected politicians. The debate over **judicial activism** is not just an academic one, but gets to the heart of the relative powers of the judiciary, the legislature, and the executive. It is an issue of who sets limits on the powers of government and how accountable to the electorate those with political power should be in a democracy.

Overall, Canadians seem quite aware of the power of the Supreme Court to set public policy priorities for the country, and most are content with the work of the court. An Ipsos-Reid poll in 2001 found that 60 percent of Canadians could name a particular Supreme Court case in the past year that stuck in their mind, and 70 percent approved of the court's work.[10] However, the Court has raised some controversies, which were revealed in a Compas poll in 2000. In that survey of public opinion, 43 percent of Canadians said they felt that the courts had taken too little power away from the elected politicians, while 28 percent said the courts had taken too much power.[11] These results are not surprising, given the high levels of trust that Canadians have in the judiciary. In a 1998 Pollara poll, 76 percent of those surveyed said that they trust judges either a little or a lot, while only 47 percent felt the same way about Members of Parliament.[12]

The Supreme Court of Canada building in Ottawa, a site of increasing significance in the Canadian political system.

Tom Hanson/CP Picture Archive

JUDICIAL APPOINTMENTS

Individuals come to office in very different ways across the world. Judges can be appointed by the executive, nominated by the executive and confirmed by the legislature, chosen by other judges, or even elected.

In Canada, the provincial and federal governments appoint judges. Traditionally, **political patronage** played an enormous role in the choice of new judges. A government was most likely to appoint lawyers who were known supporters of the political party in power. The next largest pool of candidates was drawn from lawyers who worked for the government. Lawyers who were known to be active supporters of other political parties were almost never appointed. Patronage had several negative effects because it sometimes resulted in unsuitable or even incompetent individuals being appointed simply because the party in power owed them a favour. Furthermore, highly qualified candidates could be completely overlooked simply because they belonged to opposition parties.

Definition

POLITICAL PATRONAGE: The awarding of benefits to individuals or companies based on their support for the governing political party.

Increasing resistance to political patronage grew in the early 1980s; most governments in Canada have since revised their methods of selecting judges. In many provinces, independent committees interview candidates and present the government with a ranked short list of candidates from which the government makes the appointment. While political patronage continues to a certain extent, it has been considerably reduced. Governments have been more focused on trying to appoint women and people from underrepresented ethnic or cultural groups, as support has grown for a more socially diverse judiciary. British Columbia even relies on its judicial council, composed entirely of judges, to nominate individuals for the provincial government to appoint. Although the federal government was one of the first in Canada to institute independent committees to screen candidates, it has stopped far short of the provincial reforms. The committees can only classify potential candidates into three broad groups: highly qualified, qualified, and unqualified. The government uses the results of the committee work as guidance, but it is free to select individuals from any these groups. As a result, patronage continues to flourish in federal judicial appointments.

Supreme Court of Canada judges are singular exceptions in the federal government's patronage appointments. While known partisans have been appointed, they have been the exception over the past 50 years. The federal government consults widely with bar societies and other individuals, organizations, and governments in the provinces when vacancies for the Supreme Court occur.

There are some important differences in the way in which judges come to office in the United States.[13] Federally appointed judges are nominated by the president but have to be approved by the Senate. Potential members of the Supreme Court even have to face days of questioning in a Senate committee before it decides whether or not to confirm their appointment. There have been a number of high-profile cases in which the Senate has refused to confirm the president's choice of judges. The general political and legal philosophy of the nominees is one of the prime considerations in the appointment of Supreme Court justices, as Americans use the appointment process to try to steer the policy direction of the Supreme Court. Over a period of time, a court that has been dominated by more liberal judges can be reshaped with the deliberate appointment of more conservative individuals to the court, and vice versa. This process is known as stacking the court.

It is important to note that in many of the individual U.S. states, judges are elected. Judges often run under party banners and campaign on their general ideas about how justice should be served. In some jurisdictions, judges cannot run for re-election, but in many they can. The election of judges makes quite explicit the notion discussed earlier in this chapter that judges have to enforce values that reflect the dominant beliefs in their society. While elections do provide a direct democratic mandate for judicial power, they present troubling challenges to judicial impartiality. Judges may be tempted to settle cases in a particular way in order to carry out their general election promises, and justice in individual cases may be sacrificed to the judge's determination to demonstrate a consistent pattern of sentencing. Especially where judges can·run for re-election, they need to be able to tell the voters that they acted according the promises they made in the previous election. Furthermore, there is a potential problem with the degree to which individual judges owe favours to those who financed or worked on their election campaigns.

Most countries in Western Europe take quite a different approach to the recruitment of judges. Essentially, being a judge is a professional career. Individuals interested in eventually becoming judges go to special training institutes or universities and take years of courses related to the law and the work of judges. The actual selection of new judges from these candidates is done by the judiciary itself. In addition, the judiciary is considered to be a career of advancement, in which people start on the most junior-level tribunal and, in theory, the most competent are selected by senior judges to be promoted up through levels of increasingly important courts. This model of appointment and promotion certainly avoids the problems of political patronage seen in Canada and the potential for popularity-seeking judges in American judicial elections. However, the European model is criticized for creating an insular and self-perpetuating elite.

Each of the systems of selecting and promoting judges has its strengths and weaknesses. A central concern is trying to balance the selection of suitable, competent individuals on the one hand with the means to ensure that judges reflect a society's diversity and prevailing mores on the other. Another issue is the degree to which a country's elected politicians should steer the policymaking function of the courts by deliberately choosing new judges who are sympathetic to the politicians' preferred direction of public policy. Those against such intentional policy steering through appointments argue that it can severely undermine judicial impartiality. In this view, one should simply seek intelligent and competent individuals and leave them to develop their own judicial personalities over time, settling specific cases as they think best. Those who support a more deliberate, ideological selection of new judges argue that the public must recognize the enormous role the judges have in shaping public policy. The foundation of democracy is that the will of the people should be the guiding principle of all government power. Thus, the public's elected representatives have a responsibility to choose new judges who reflect the policy directions that the public prefers.

JUDICIAL INDEPENDENCE AND IMPARTIALITY

An independent and impartial judiciary is essential to the proper functioning of a democracy. Without independence from other branches of government, judges simply become a tool for enforcing the policies of the government of the day. Judges must be impartial in order for the public to have confidence that they will decide cases on the basis of the facts of the case and the relevant law.

Judicial independence relates to the relationship of the judiciary to the legislature and the executive and means that judges can do their work without interference from politicians, bureaucrats, and other government officials, such as the police or the military. Judicial independence in the sense discussed here is unknown in communist political systems, where judges work under the supremacy of the Communist Party and are "subject to constant party control, supervision, and accountability."[14]

Definition

JUDICIAL INDEPENDENCE: A relationship between the courts and the other branches of government that allows judges to function without interference from other government officials.

The Supreme Court of Canada has laid down some important aspects of the relationship between the courts and the other branches of government that underlie judicial independence. In *R. v. Valente*, the court said that judges must have security of tenure, financial independence, and administrative independence.[15] Security of tenure means that judges cannot be removed from office simply because the government does not approve of their decisions; judges should hold office until retirement or for a set period of time and should be removed only for major misbehaviour, incompetence, or incapacity. Financial independence ensures that judges need not fear having their pay cut if the government does not like their decisions and that judges have no incentive to try to curry favour by siding with the government in the hopes that their pay will be increased. Administrative independence means that the decisions about the scheduling of cases and assignment of individual judges to particular cases is done by the judiciary itself; this prevents the government from trying to ensure a favourable outcome to a case by arranging for a "friendly" judge to hear it.

Judicial impartiality refers to a state of mind in which judges settle cases without applying their own pre-existing biases in favour of or against the people or issues involved. While impartiality is difficult to define, its essence implies that judges maintain an open mind to arguments about the facts and the proper interpretation of the law before deciding the outcome of the case. It is important to bear in mind that impartiality cannot mean a total absence of preconceived ideas or predispositions, something that is not only humanly impossible but also probably undesirable. There would be little public confidence in the judiciary if judges did not express or act on established biases against the horrors of murder and rape or the outrage of con men who defraud senior citizens of all their savings.

Definition

JUDICIAL IMPARTIALITY: A state of mind in which judges preside over and decide cases with an open mind toward the parties and issues involved.

Concerns about judicial independence and impartiality extend well beyond the relationship between the courts and the other branches of government. Judges must also be protected from pressures from the general public, interest groups, unions, and business. If judges bow to pressures not to decide a case the "wrong" way, or anticipate rewards if they decide a case the "right" way, then there can be no assurance that judges will act impartially. At the same time, the requirements of judicial impartiality also place restrictions on how judges behave on and off the bench. Canadian judges have been forced to resign because they openly socialized with figures known in organized crime circles, because they have donated money to support the election of particular politicians or political parties, or because they themselves have been convicted of a criminal offence. In these instances, the public could not have confidence that the judges would be free from major biases.

Threats to judicial impartiality and independence come in many forms. Controversy has been stirred several times by cabinet ministers talking to judges about cases the judges have under consideration. For example,

Jean Charest resigned from Brian Mulroney's government in 1990 after it became known that he had telephoned a judge. As serious as such direct attempts to influence judges may be in Canada, they pale in comparison to other examples from around the world. Judges in Colombia and Italy live with constant police escorts because of threats to their lives from organized crime. And Italian judges have fought an ongoing battle with Prime Minister Silvio Berlusconi, who was under investigation and was convicted on corruption charges several times, only to have his convictions overturned on appeal. Berlusconi has claimed that left-wing judges are persecuting him and declared he would remove police protection for judges. Hundreds of Italy's judges went on a brief strike in late 2001 to protest against a move they believed was intended to bully them into leaving Berlusconi and his associates alone. A more graphic example of intimidation of judges occurred in Indonesia, where former President Suharto's son, Tommy, was sentenced in 2001—a couple of years after his father was forced from office—to 18 months in jail on corruption charges. Shortly afterward, the judge who upheld the sentence was gunned down; unsurprisingly, perhaps, the Indonesian Supreme Court acquitted Tommy Suharto of the original charges three months after the murder. However, Suharto was charged in early 2002 with contracting the judge's murder, in a move that was widely seen as a test of the success of new President Megawati Sukarnoputri's ability to restore confidence in the country's judicial system.

Judicial impartiality and independence are not only intended to protect judges from outside interference, but also require judges to distance themselves from becoming involved in political debates and activities outside of the courtroom. In a famous case in Canada, the Canadian Judicial Council reprimanded Judge Thomas Berger for having made a public speech criticising Prime Minister Trudeau's constitutional reform package that led to the Constitution Act, 1982. Berger had complained that the constitutional reforms were put together without consultation with the Aboriginal leaders and without any attempt to redress their many grievances. Judges have to walk a fine line in commenting on issues of public interest without compromising the public's perception that they can still rule impartially on related issues, should these end up in their own courtroom.

As important as judicial independence and impartiality are, however, these are principles that still operate within limits. Although an important aspect of judicial independence and impartiality holds that judges should be able to decide cases without fear that they may lose their jobs, it is also clear that there are limits on what the public and the government will tolerate in judicial decisions. Judge Raymond Bartlett was removed from the Nova Scotia Family Court in 1987 because he frequently quoted from the Bible in court and told women appearing before him that they should be subservient to their husbands. Neither of these actions would have been all that remarkable a hundred years ago, but they were considered to be unacceptable in the late 20th century. While judges are supposedly free to behave as they think best and decide a case for the reasons they think best, they cannot simply follow their personal views regardless of how out of the step they are with prevailing values in their society. In the end, judges may lead or lag behind public opinion to a certain extent, but they will face pressures to resign or be removed if they act too far beyond prevailing mores—even in democratic countries that espouse judicial independence and impartiality.

The Personal Values of Judges Can Shape Their Decisions

While good judges can deliberately set aside many of their personal views in any particular decision, it is all but impossible to set aside all of their basic beliefs on an ongoing basis. As a result, judges tend to develop distinctive patterns in their handling of cases that reflect their own underlying personal values. Like everybody else, judges are products of the socialization processes in their own upbringing. While the settled aspects of the law provide boundaries in many cases, judges have to exercise their personal discretion in many ways as they hear and decide a case before them. Questions of credibility—whose story a judge believes—are entirely discretionary and can be influenced in many subconscious ways by each judge's personal beliefs, likes, and dislikes. Judges often have considerable leeway in deciding what penalty or settlement to impose, and

BOX 10.3

YOU JUDGE THE JUDGES

What limits would you place on judicial impartiality and the ability of judges to settle cases as they see best? In theory, judges should feel free to express themselves and decide cases without fearing that they will lose their jobs simply because their decisions are unpopular. However, consider the following hypothetical case and ask yourself if you believe the judge should be removed from office.

Judge Smith hears a case in which a person is accused under Canada's Anti-Terrorism Act of having plotted to blow up the pipeline carrying oil to the United States; the man was arrested before the attack was carried out. At his trial, the accused states that he was motivated to do this because U.S. corporations are raping the environment in many developing countries. He wanted to strike a blow against U.S. capitalism by trying to cut off some of their oil.

The judge acquits the man on the grounds that he was exercising his rights under the Canadian Charter of Rights to the freedom of conscience and expression. The judge notes that no actual attack had occurred. But Judge Smith then goes on to say that the accused had been justified in highlighting the fact that the U.S. economy is dripping with the blood of poor people around the world, whose virtual slavery is essential to providing cheap goods for American consumers.

inevitably these decisions hinge to some extent on a judge's personal belief in what is right and appropriate.

Because of the potential for personal background to play a role in judicial decision-making, concern has arisen about the social composition of the judiciary. The historical pattern in all countries has been for males of the dominant social classes and ethnic groups to fill the bench. Academics and social activists have long been concerned that this leads to an institution that embodies and enforces the values of the predominant group or groups. As a result, there have been strong calls in recent decades for the judiciary to become more socially diverse. In established liberal democracies such as Canada, there has been a deliberate policy in the past two decades to try and appoint more women and people of underrepresented social groups to the bench. Even so, critics argue that the underrepresentation of women and ethnic minorities in Canadian courts creates a "democratic deficit."[16]

Social and gender diversity among judges is important at least symbolically in a modern democracy that espouses women's equality and multiculturalism. But does or should this diversity make a practical difference to the kinds of decisions made by the courts and the values they enforce? There are many who say a socially diverse judiciary does act differently from an exclusively white middle-class one, and they would add that this is a good thing. Modern democratic societies should not have paternalistic and ethnocentric values perpetuated by the courts, as they had in the past. Cultural sensitivity must be embodied in judicial decisions, and what better way for that to occur than to have members from different cultural groups both deciding cases directly and acting as an educational influence on their fellow judges? Furthermore, the diverse groups within a society will have more confidence in the quality of justice delivered by the courts if members of their own groups are judges too. In fact, there have been a number of academic studies that reveal measurable differences, although not large ones, between male and female judges, and between African-American and Caucasian judges.

However, the degree to which individual judges may decide cases differently because of their sex and cultural or social background poses a challenge for those who believe that law should be interpreted and enforced as impartially as possible. In theory at least, justice can be properly served only if there is a general uniformity in the ways in which judges apply the law to similar cases.

An important point related to the personal discretion of judges is their fallibility—they can make wrong decisions. In Canada, at least seven people in the past 20 years have been finally exonerated after spending many years in jail for rapes or murders they did not commit. In the United States, eight people have been freed from death row since the early 1970s after DNA evidence played a crucial role in establishing their innocence.[17] The police occasionally mismanage an investigation, discriminate, lie, or encourage other witnesses to lie, but judges ultimately have to decide for themselves who is telling the truth. Sometimes judges simply believe the wrong person.

Discipline and Removal of Judges

The discipline and removal of judges from office raises a number of complex issues. While there can be no independence for judges if they can be fired simply for offending other political actors, there also has to be some way to remove judges who engage in criminal acts or otherwise bring the administration of justice into fundamental disrepute. Both the grounds for removal and the process to be followed can have profound impacts on the independence of the judiciary and the quality of justice in a society.

Who gets to remove judges from office, and for what reasons, varies a great deal around the world. In military regimes, where the military command or president can remove judges for almost any reason, there is no protection for judges who displease powerful authorities on policy grounds. At the other end of the spectrum is France, where all matters of judicial discipline are handled within the judiciary and there is no role for either the executive or legislature to play at all. Many countries fall somewhere in the middle, with a mixture of involvement by the three branches of government.

Historically in Britain, the monarchs could remove judges from office whenever they felt offended by what a judge said or did. To protect the judges from such arbitrary removal by the monarch, the British Parliament passed the Act of Settlement in 1701; after this date, judges could be removed from office only after a parliamentary resolution. The Act of Settlement established the principle, since followed in most common law systems founded on the British model, that judges hold office during "good behaviour," which actually means that judges can be removed for "misbehaviour." The act also ensured the supremacy of Parliament over the other branches of government and protected judges from being removed on the whim of the executive. The specific grounds for removal, however, are open to considerable interpretation. In general, judges can be removed for failing to perform their duties or behaving in a way that fundamentally undermines the public's confidence in their ability to perform their duties. Those judges who frequently fail to appear for their court sessions or behave completely irrationally in the courtroom can be removed. But there are also wide grounds for removal for behaving in ways that are incompatible with being a judge. For example, Robert Flahiff was forced to resign from the Quebec Superior Court after being convicted of money laundering, and Ronald MacDonald had to resign from the Nova Scotia Provincial Court after being convicted of assaulting his wife.

Canada inherited the British process, and federally appointed judges can be removed from office only by the governor general with the approval of both houses of parliament.[18] A trend has emerged in recent decades to distance elected politicians from both the formulation of codes of judicial conduct and the actual removal process. The tendency has been to give judges increasing control over the discipline of their colleagues. This distancing is based on a concern for the independence of judges and the belief that politics should not play a role in the disciplinary process. In all Canadian jurisdictions, complaints about judges are first dealt with either by the normal courts or by an independent judicial council. While this may be viewed as a positive development in general, it does raise the possible problem of a public perception that judges might either "protect their own" or enforce a set of values that are not in step with the prevailing public beliefs. In stark terms, the judges' "old boys' club" might protect its members from the outside world. For this reason, several provinces have included lay members from the public on their judicial councils. However, the Canadian Judicial Council that oversees federally appointed judges is composed entirely of judges.

The United States has moved away from the involvement of the legislature in judicial removal proceedings as well. Although the U.S. Constitution states that Congress can impeach judges, a new process was developed in 1980 to provide for a judicial commission to investigate and rule on judicial misbehaviour. This model is also widespread at the state level in the United States. These judicial commissions have been quite active, with New York's removing 60 of its 3500 state judges between 1979 and 1985.[19]

While there is no controversy in removing judges who commit criminal offences, much more debate arises when judges make controversial statements that enrage or offend the public. For example, the Canadian Judicial Council recommended the removal of Justice Jean Bienvenue in 1996 when it found that the "judge's remarks about women and his deep-seated ideas behind those remarks legitimately cast doubt on his impartiality in the execution of his judicial office."[20] However, seven of the 29 members of the council voted against removal on the grounds that Bienvenue's comments were simply reflective of a bygone era and that sensitivity training would be a more appropriate remedy. A central issue is whether judicial independence should protect judges from being removed because they offend contemporary social mores.

In the end, the limits on judicial behaviour are as difficult to define as they are important to a healthy system of government. The crucial role that judges play is founded upon the general authority they have in the public eye, which in turn is based on the belief that judges act impartially to enforce the values of their society. Failure to remove individual judges can erode the public's deference to the courts' authority. In some respects, there is real merit in the elected representatives of the public having a substantive role to play in at least setting the grounds for removing judges, as the limits on judicial behaviour are then set by people who are both representative of and accountable to the general public. In Canada, a compromise has been reached on the removal process of superior court judges. The Canadian Judicial Council, composed of senior judges across the country, must first investigate complaints about judicial behaviour. If it deems the situation serious enough, it can recommend to Parliament that a judge be removed. As judges play a more visible policymaking role, however, they have come under increasing pressures to be held accountable for their judgments and speeches. There is a danger that the discipline process is used to remove or pressure judges simply because their actions or words are politically unpalatable. And the essence of judicial independence is that judges should be free to make the decision they feel is best without fear of recriminations as a result of its unpopularity.

ACCESS TO THE COURTS

The effectiveness of the courts in their various roles can depend to a large degree on how courts function and who has access to them in practice. There are several ongoing weaknesses that can be identified with the courts that undermine the potential they have in a society. First and foremost, the courts are essentially passive institutions. Judges do not go out and seek legal problems to solve or disputes to settle. Instead, judges have to wait for someone to decide to take an issue to the courts. Significant disputes may go unresolved because those involved either cannot or do not want to go to court. This inability or unwillingness to take a dispute to court may arise from the prohibitive costs of a court case, or it may be based on a belief that disputes should be settled outside the formal court setting. Just

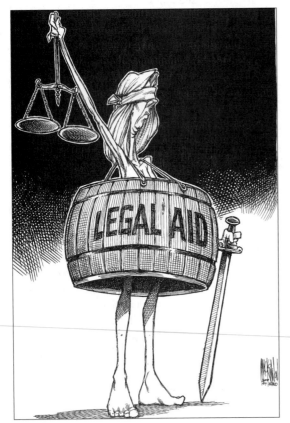

Legal aid programs are starved for funds.

Bruce MacKinnon/Halifax Herald/Artizans

how equal the access to the courts is for all segments of a society has a great bearing on the kind of justice the courts can provide.

The cost barrier is a central weakness of courts as social and political institutions. The legal system and judicial processes are complex, and anyone involved in a court case should really have a professional lawyer to conduct his or her case. In Canada, a relatively short and simple criminal case can cost several hundred to several thousand dollars, so it may cost less to plead guilty than to fight the charges through a full trial. Parties who fail to win their case in the first instance have to decide whether to appeal. But the cost of a case before a provincial court of appeal starts at around $25 000 to $50 000. Parties determined to take their case to the Supreme Court of Canada for final resolution can expect to spend at least $150 000, but cases often run well over $1 million. Clearly, these are costs that cannot be afforded by the average person. Governments in most liberal democracies have legal aid programs in place to help pay for the cases of the poorest members of their society. However, the limited budgets and personnel available significantly undermine the quality of representation a person can expect. Only some people benefit from paid legal counsel, and a lucky few have their cases appealed to the final court. The rich, of course, can afford to hire the most expensive legal teams and carry their cases up to the top court. In the middle are many people who either have to use up their savings or decide that, while they can finance the first court hearing, they cannot afford to appeal if they lose. A question then arises about how many innocent people are jailed simply because they could not afford a good lawyer or enough of the lawyer's time to mount a proper defence, or because they were not able to appeal an initial trial that found them guilty.

The problem is even worse outside of the criminal law. Private cases are notorious for lengthy delays and high costs; the time and costs involved in suing a neighbour, a relative, or a business may be prohibitive. This is a particular issue in countries where losers in a private court case have to pay for the legal fees of the person they sued, in addition to their own. The quality of legal services to people of poor and modest incomes is a special concern in family law cases. When couples part or divorce, they need to divide the matrimonial property and decide on their access to and financial obligations for child and spousal support. High-quality legal representation is crucial in these proceedings, as the outcome of these cases can have repercussions for years. One strong criticism of the cost of court access is that it unfairly affects women in family law disputes. Usually the men involved have higher incomes and more assets at the time of the marital breakup and can therefore afford better lawyers and more of the lawyer's time than can women. As a result, men generally have much higher living standards several years after a divorce than do women, who more often than not have to care for their children. In 2002, British Columbia's attorney general, Geoff Plant, was formally censured by the Law Society of British Columbia because of dramatic cutbacks to legal aid services. Earlier in the year, he had announced that legal aid would no longer be available for most family law disputes, including divorce. Legal aid can now be used only if there is a question of physical danger, or in cases where children are taken into protective custody.

Justice is supposed to be blind to the participants, and the rich and poor are supposed to have equal consideration in the courts. However, the reality of the judicial process is that justice often falls very short of the mark. As legal aid programs are squeezed by government cutbacks and as court costs escalate, many people are left without fully prepared lawyers to argue their cases. Legal aid is seldom available for serious civil cases beyond family matters.

CONCLUSION

All states rely on law to structure their societies, with the policies and mores of the dominant elite groups embodied within them. The courts have a crucial role to play, particularly in democratic countries, in interpreting and enforcing the law. Democratic regimes require independent and impartial courts to act as fair adjudicators of disputes and gain public support and deference. In practice, however, both the institutional independence and personal impartiality of judges are limited. The selection and appointment of judges can be done in several different ways, and a country's choice of a particular process can provide the elected politicians with an opportunity to steer the general policy direction of the courts. Control over the discipline and removal of judges provide, firm limits on the behaviour of judges, and there is controversy over the role that politicians should play both in setting the rules for judges and in effecting their removal. Judges inevitably have an important policymaking role to play in interpreting laws and in their exercise of the powers of judicial review.

DISCUSSION QUESTIONS

1. **Do you believe that it is important to have all the major social and ethnic groups represented in a country's judiciary? If so, do you believe it is because members of these groups will decide cases differently?**

2. **Do you trust judges to enforce your rights more than you trust politicians to respect them? What is the basis for your answer—is it just a gut feeling, or do you have specific reasons?**

3. **What limits, if any, would you place on the independence and impartiality of judges?**

4. **Do you think judges should be elected, so that they have a democratic mandate to conduct their work?**

5. **Would you be prepared to sell everything you own in order to afford a lawyer to defend you against a criminal charge that you know you are not guilty of? Does it matter how serious the charge is?**

WEB LINKS

Thomson Nelson: The Canadian Legal System:
http://polisci.nelson.com/legal.html

European Court of Justice:
http://europa.eu.int/cj/en/index.htm

Federal Courts of the United States:
http://www.uscourts.gov

International Court of Justice:
http://www.icj-cij.org/icjwww/icj002.htm

Thomson Nelson: Introduction to Judicial Systems:
http://polisci.nelson.com/introcourts.html

The Supreme Court of Canada:
http://www.scc-csc.gc.ca

FURTHER READING

Devlin, Patrick. *Judges*. Oxford: Oxford University Press, 1988.

Gall, Gerald L. *The Canadian Legal System*. 4th ed. Toronto: Carswell, 1995.

Manfredi, Christopher P. *Judicial Power and the Charter: Canada and the Paradox of Liberal Constitutionalism*. 2nd ed. Don Mills: Oxford University Press, 2001.

Morton, F.L., and Rainer Knopff. *The Charter Revolution and the Court Party*. Peterborough: Broadview Press, 2000.

Russell, Peter H. *The Judiciary in Canada: The Third Branch of Government*. Toronto: McGraw-Hill Ryerson, 1987.

Waddams, S.M. *Introduction to the Study of Law*. 5th ed. Scarborough: Carswell, 1997.

ENDNOTES

1 During World War II, all Japanese Canadians were interned and had their property disposed of; many German and Italian Canadians were also interned, as were German and Ukrainian Canadians during World War I.

2 Peta Thornycroft, "Pro-Mugabe Judges Rule Land Grabs Are Legal," *National Post*, October, 2001, p. A15. For more background, see also Angus Shaw, "Zimbabwe Court Allows Land Seizures," *The Independent*, October 3, 2001; cited on July 24, 2002; available at http://www.independent.co.uk/story.jsp?story=97309; Andrew Meldrum, "Supreme Court Justice Defies Mugabe Threat," *The Guardian*, February 10, 2001; cited on July 24, 2002; available at http://www.guardian.co.uk/international/story/0,3604,436086,00.html; British Broadcasting Corporation, "Mugabe Challenges Supreme Court," February 8, 1999;

cited on July 24, 2002; available at http://news.bbc.co.uk/hi/english/world/africa/newsid_274000/274262.stm.

3 *Reference re Resolution to Amend the Constitution*, [1981] 1 S.C.R. 753; *Reference re Secession of Quebec*, [1998] 2 S.C.R. 217.

4 *Bush v. Gore*, [2000] 531 U.S. 98.

5 *Brown v. Board of Education*, [1954] 347 U.S. 493; *Baker v. Carr*, [1962] 369 U.S. 186.

6 This case is discussed in Henry J. Abraham, *The Judiciary: The Supreme Court in the Governmental Process*, 8th ed. (Dubuque: Wm. C. Brown, 1991), pp. 59–62.

7 8 Co. Rep. 107a, 114a C.P. 1610; also available at http://press-pubs.uchicago.edu/founders/documents/amendV_due_process1.html. Lord Coke's notion was never acted upon by British judges, and Coke himself was removed from the bench by King Charles I in 1616.

8 For example, see F.L. Morton, Peter H. Russell, and Troy Riddell, "The Canadian Charter of Rights and Freedoms: A Descriptive Analysis of the First Decade, 1982–1992," *National Journal of Constitutional Law* 5 (1994): 1.

9 Andrew Heard, "The Charter in the Supreme Court of Canada: The Importance of Which Judges Hear an Appeal," *Canadian Journal of Political Science* 24 (1991): 289.

10 Ipsos-Reid, "Canadian Supreme Decisions: Public's View of the Supreme Court," July 4, 2001; cited on July 24, 2002; available at http://www.ipsos-reid.com/media/content/displaypr.cfm?id_to_view=1257.

11 Compas, "The Power of Judges," February 18, 2000; cited on July 1, 2001; available at http://www.compas.ca/html/archives/powerjudges_surv.html.

12 Pollara, "Public Trust Index," May 29, 1998; cited on July 24, 2002; available at

http://www.pollara.ca/new/Library/surveys/1of3.htm and http://www.pollara.ca/new/Library/surveys/3of3.htm.

13 For a discussion of the American system, see Henry J. Abraham, *Justices and Presidents: A Political History of Appointments to the Supreme Court*, 3rd ed. (New York: Oxford University Press, 1992).

14 Konrad Zweigert and Hien Kotz, *Introduction to Comparative Law*, vol. 1 (Oxford: Clarendon Press, 1987), p. 324.

15 *R. v. Valente*, [1985] 2 S.C.R. 673.

16 R. Devlin, A. Wayne MacKay, and Natasha Kim, "Reducing the Democractic Deficit: Representation, Diversity and the Canadian Judiciary, or Towards a 'Triple P' Judiciary," *Alberta Law Review* 38 (2000): 752.

17 No judge has actually been removed by a vote of the two houses of the Canadian Parliament, although several have resigned when it became apparent that removal procedures would have been undertaken.

18 Martin L. Friedland, *A Place Apart: Judicial Independence and Accountability in Canada* (Ottawa: Canadian Judicial Council, 1995), p.123.

19 Raju Chebium, "Reports of a Flawed Legal System Push Death Penalty Debate into High Gear," March 19, 2002; cited on July 24, 2002; available at http://www.cnn.com/LAW/trials.and.cases/case.files/0006/deathpenalty/overview.html.

20 Canadian Judicial Council, *Annual Report 1996–1997*, Appendix G (Ottawa: CJC, 1997), p. 70. This document is also available at http://www.cjc-ccm.gc.ca/english/annual_reports/1996-1997_append.htm.

Political Participation

5

Career Profile: Graham Steele

Graham Steele graduated with a political science degree from the University of Manitoba. He then studied at Oxford University as a Rhodes Scholar and returned to Canada to take a law degree at Dalhousie University. After doing a clerkship at the Federal Court of Canada, Graham got a job as the lawyer for the Nova Scotia Workers' Compensation Board. Like so many lawyers, he then entered the political arena, first as a research director for the Nova Scotia NDP caucus. In 2001, he got himself elected to the Nova Scotia House of Assembly. He is the member for Halifax Fairview and the party's critic responsible for finance and human rights.

When Graham studied law, the field that interested him most was administrative law, that is, the law of government. Working for a government agency, he became fascinated with the question of how government *really* works, and he tried to learn as much as possible about the psychology and sociology of people in bureaucratic organizations.

Graham thinks that the best part of being an elected politician is the tremendous variety. Every day is different because his constituents are as varied and interesting as people can be. He says, "I've been a student of government, a lawyer around government, a civil servant in government, and now an elected official. What I've learned, and am still learning, is how much of a 'people' business it is. It's important though to have a good grounding in the history, structure, and process of government." The worst part is knowing that any mistakes one makes are public. For many politicians, another drawback is being away from their family.

Chapter 11

Political Parties

Heather MacIvor

CHAPTER OBJECTIVES

After you have completed this chapter, you should be able to

- define the key terms in your own words, providing examples to illustrate your definitions
- explain the major elements of party organization and identify the primary relationships among them
- identify the institutional factors that shape party structures and explain how they operate
- identify the major party functions and explain their importance
- explain the role of parties in government
- identify and explain the major party ideologies in democratic states
- distinguish among party systems according to at least four major criteria.

INTRODUCTION

Political parties have long been considered to be essential to representative democracy: they give voters a choice of governments; they recruit and select the candidates and leaders who run for public office; and they organize the relationship between the various political institutions within governments—the legislative and executive branches, especially in parliamentary systems, and the national and subnational governments. But do **political parties** still matter? By the end of the 20th century, many citizens of Western democracies would have said no. While parties continue to nominate candidates for public office and to orchestrate their campaigns, once the winning party takes office, it may fail to keep its election promises. Although such reversals are often forced upon governments by external factors, such as globalization or fiscal constraints, they may be perceived as evidence of dishonesty and manipulation. Public policies are devised not by party members, but by public servants, think-tanks, and interest groups. Voters are increasingly fickle, floating from party to party at each election instead of forming enduring ties to one political organization. Party memberships are shrinking, partly as a consequence of voter apathy and partly because of competing demands on citizens' time and energy. Growing populist movements across the developed world portray parties as corrupt, unrepresentative, and a barrier to genuine democracy. More and more voters are simply staying home on election day, especially in Canada; this drop in voter turnout is widely interpreted as a sign of the parties' failure to inspire public enthusiasm and loyalty. As the parties have declined, according to their critics, the links between citizens and their political institutions have eroded. Democracy is weakened, together with the legitimacy on which effective government depends.

> **Definition**
>
> **POLITICAL PARTY:** An organization of members, mostly volunteers, who work together to achieve common goals. For most parties, the primary goal is to win seats in the national legislature.

This is a serious indictment indeed. If parties have truly become irrelevant, the implications are worrisome. Representative democracy depends on the opportunity for voters to make an informed choice among competing visions for the future. In the absence of such choices, no government can claim a mandate to make binding decisions on behalf of the electorate. Parliamentary government—the system used in most Western democracies, with the obvious exception of the United States and other presidential countries—requires disciplined party caucuses. Legitimate political institutions rest on active and engaged citizens, who express their support for the political system by participating in elections. In sum, the health of political parties in Canada and elsewhere is more than just an academic question; it is central to the present and future viability of democratic government.

This chapter argues that, despite the problems just listed, political parties are neither irrelevant nor doomed. In most democracies, regardless of the level of economic development, government is still party government. It is certainly true that individual parties and the national party systems to which they belong are responding to dramatic changes in their environments. These changes include

- the declining power of the nation-state, relative to both international organizations (such as the United Nations and the World Trade Organization) and subnational units within state boundaries (e.g., provinces or regional governments)
- the rapid and widespread adoption of new information and communication technologies, particularly the Internet
- significant social changes, including rising levels of education, less deferential cultural values, and the declining influence of class and religion as motivating forces in political behaviour.

It is also true that party responses to external challenge do not always succeed. Some existing parties will survive, while others will succumb. But the important point is that political parties are not passive victims of external change. Those parties that can adapt will do so, however slowly and painfully. New parties will replace those that cannot adjust to a new political environment. In their modern form, political parties have existed for well over a century. Their structures and activities have evolved over time, and they will continue to do so into the foreseeable future.

To understand political parties, we must answer four questions, to which the rest of this chapter is devoted:

- What do parties do?
- How are they organized?
- What is their role in government?
- How do the parties in each country interact with each other?

PARTY FUNCTIONS

To understand what parties do, we must first determine why they exist.[1] There have been political factions—distinct groups dedicated to promoting a particular point of view—at least since the golden age of Athenian democracy around 500 B.C.

> Parties are universal because in politics men act for motives which can be and are stated in opinions. Opinions are disputable, especially opinions about the most important topics, opinions on which citizens and regimes stake their lives. Being disputable, such opinions attract and repel; they create partisans. Politics seems to be essentially partisan.[2]

Until fairly recently, "factions" have been generally perceived as a danger to the body politic. The drafters of the 1787 American Constitution warned that differences of political opinion "lessen the respectability, weaken the authority, and distract the plans and operations of those whom they divide."[3]

Despite these fears, political parties had become an indispensable part of parliamentary government in Britain by the beginning of the 19th century. The first organized parties formed within Parliament, as cliques who coalesced around a leader and/or a set of principles. These "cadre parties"[4] were consumed by the struggle for control over the executive branch of government, which could be secured and maintained only with a majority of the seats in Parliament. They did not establish organizations outside the legislature, principally because relatively few citizens had the right to vote, so there was no need for electoral machinery. Gradually, as the franchise was widened during the late 19th and early 20th centuries, cadre parties in parliamentary democracies created party "clubs" or associations in the electoral districts where they ran candidates for Parliament. While the cadre parties' structures changed, the leader and his legislative supporters continued to dominate the party organization. Although the methods were now different, the cadre party's goal remained the same: to win a majority of the seats in the legislature and, thereby, to control the government.

Beginning in the late 19th century, mass parties emerged to challenge the power of the cadre parties. Most of these new parties emerged outside Parliament, to represent social groups that were not represented by the wealthy politicians who occupied the government. Social democratic, labour, and communist parties sought to mobilize newly enfranchised working men (women were not allowed to vote until after 1918 in most countries), and to use their numerical power at the ballot box to transform the political and economic systems of Europe, Australia, and New Zealand. While their goal was the same as that of the cadre parties—to win enough seats to control the government—they pursued that goal by recruiting mass memberships and continually educating the public, whereas the cadre parties had small memberships and only intermittent contact with voters.

By the late 20th century, the distinction between cadre and mass parties had been replaced by a new categorization: **electoral-professional parties** versus **mass-bureaucratic parties**.[5] Both share one primary goal: to win public office. The differences between them arise from the relative strength of their secondary goals and their motivations for pursuing power. Mass-bureaucratic parties are more dedicated to ideology and principle, as well as to promoting the political involvement of their members. It would be wrong to suggest that electoral-professional parties are devoid of principle, because they may use policy and claims of

internal democracy as means to the end of attracting voters. Table 11.1 summarizes the major differences between the two types. (Terms such as *party in central office* are defined in the next section of the chapter.)

Definition

ELECTORAL-PROFESSIONAL PARTY: A political party with a small membership that is more concerned with electoral success than principle and tends to be dominated by professional consultants and strategists. Such parties appeal to floating voters and seek the financial support of corporations and wealthy individuals.

Definition

MASS-BUREAUCRATIC PARTY: A political party with a large membership that is dedicated to ideology and principle and to promoting the involvement of its members. Such parties tend to target a particular class of voters and are generally dependent on party members and trade unions for financial support.

Among its various advantages, this distinction between party types reminds us of the *raison d'être* of political parties: to run candidates for public office. This shared goal shapes the activities of all party organizations, regardless of country, ideology, and size. Not surprisingly, therefore, all political parties perform a standard set of functions in pursuit of that goal. We will focus here on three of those functions: leadership selection, candidate recruitment and nomination, and electoral campaigning.

Leadership Selection

A party leader must be selected according to a clear and consistent set of rules. The choice of leader is a crucial decision for a party, for at least four reasons. First, the leader is the public face of the party. He or she features prominently in media coverage of the party's activities, both inside and outside the legislature. Therefore, the leader must be an effective communicator in person and through the news media. Second, the leader has enormous influence over party policy. Even in a mass-bureaucratic party with clear and consistent principles, the leader usually has the final word on the party's

Table 11.1   Two Types of Party Structure

Characteristic	Mass-Bureaucratic	Electoral-Professional
Locus of Decision-Making	The permanent party bureaucracy in central office	A shifting team of professional consultants: media spin-doctors, advertising experts, pollsters, and political strategists
Primary Task of Party Organization	Recruiting and educating members; appealing to like-minded voters	Winning or retaining power through electoral victory; appealing to "soft" or "floating" voters
Dominant Element of Party Structure	Party in central office	Party in public office
Sources of Finance	Party members; affiliated organizations (e.g., trade unions)	Public funds; large corporations and wealthy individuals
Rhetorical Emphasis and Electoral Strategy	Ideology; particular policies supported by shared principles; targeting one or more distinct groups within the electorate (e.g., the working class)	Short-term issues; leadership; appealing to the broad "middle" of the political and economic spectrum
Relationship between National and Regional Organizations	Integrated	Truncated or confederal
Examples	Britain's Labour Party; Germany's Social Democratic Party (SPD); Australia's Labor Party; the former communist parties of France and Italy	The Democratic and Republican parties in the United States; Mexico's Institutional Revolutionary Party (PRI); Japan's Liberal Democratic Party; Canada's Liberal and Progressive Conservative parties

election platform. According to Jean Charest, former leader of the Progressive Conservative Party of Canada, the leader must have the final word on the platform because he or she has to "carry it in his [or her] heart and soul."[6]

Third, in parliamentary systems, the leader is the party's general in the daily legislative battle. He or she must be able to rally the troops in caucus, keep their fighting spirit up, and unite them against the slings and arrows of the competing parties. In a single-party government, the leader is the prime minister. In a coalition cabinet made up of two or more parties, the prime minister is the leader of the largest party, and the leader of the junior party is normally a senior minister.[7] On the opposition side, the leader of the largest party is designated as the Leader of the Official Opposition (at least in British-style parliamentary systems). He or she leads the verbal assault on the government, while simultaneously trying to act as a prime-minister-in-waiting. The leaders of the smaller opposition parties have more freedom to attack the government aggressively, without worrying about providing a "constructive alternative." The ability to keep a caucus united under intense political pressure is one of the most important skills a party leader can demonstrate. It requires an intimate knowledge of parliamentary procedure and the ability to build and maintain strong personal relationships with fellow legislators.

Fourth, the leader is ultimately responsible for keeping the party organization in a state of election readiness. He or she must be able to inspire the volunteers in the local party organizations, motivating them to devote their time and energy to party tasks. The leader must also be an effective fundraiser, both in public (for example, by giving speeches at party dinners) and in private (persuading business and interest-group leaders to support the party's efforts). In some cases, the leader is also the chief inducement for prospective candidates; if he or she can persuade prominent local or national figures to run for office under the party banner, the party's prospects in the next election may be enhanced.

To summarize, the party leader must be an excellent communicator and a compelling symbol of the party. He or she must be well versed in the policy issues of the day and in the imperatives of party organization. Because political parties are largely volunteer organizations, built on strong personal bonds of loyalty and affection, the leader must also take the time to "stroke" the members and make them feel important. Finally, the leader must project an aura of competence and optimism at all times; a consistent failure to do so alienates voters, party workers, and potential donors.

It should now be clear that choosing a party leader is a matter of great importance. The methods for selecting leaders vary from party to party and from country to country. Electoral-professional parties have tended to leave the choice of leader to the parliamentary wing, which generally selects one of its own members. There are at least two advantages to this caucus selection system. First, the men and women who work closely with the leader every day possess the necessary knowledge—both of the political system and of the various contenders—to choose wisely. Second, a candidate with extensive parliamentary experience is better qualified for the job than one who has never held public office, particularly when the party is in government. In recent years, however, there has been a trend in most Western democracies away from closed, exclusive party leadership contests to open and "democratic" races.[8] Most parties have now switched to either leadership conventions or universal membership voting (UMV).[9] In a leadership convention system, delegates elected (or appointed) to represent various elements in the

Boxer Jean Chrétien controls all aspects of the fight.

Bado/Artizans

party organization gather to choose among the various candidates by voting on successive ballots. In UMV, each party member has the right to vote directly for the candidate of his or her choice. Popular UMV methods include telephone voting, mail-in ballots, and voting in person at a local polling place. The causes and implications of the UMV trend are explored in the accompanying box.

BOX 11.1

UNIVERSAL MEMBERSHIP VOTING

The recent popularity of UMV leadership-selection systems highlights some of the differences between the electoral-professional and mass-bureaucratic party models. Although some electoral-professional parties were initially reluctant to take the power to choose the leader away from the caucus, the relative informality and simplicity of their internal structures makes such changes relatively easy to implement once the decision has been taken by the party elite.

For some mass-bureaucratic parties, UMV is more difficult to put into practice, despite its greater ideological appeal for a left-wing political organization. The British Labour Party, like the Canadian New Democratic Party, consists of three separate sections: the parliamentary wing, the constituency associations, and the affiliated labour unions. The latter have long been guaranteed a fixed percentage of the votes at party conventions, reflecting the importance of the labour movement as a source of policy ideas, campaign volunteers, and financial support. Because UMV treats all voters equally, it eliminates labour's "block vote" in the selection of a new party leader. The reluctance of the affiliated unions to give up this "block vote" helps explain why the New Democrats were the last major federal party in Canada to adopt UMV.

There are at least three reasons why UMV has rapidly become the standard method for choosing party leaders. First, it appears to be more "democratic" than the older caucus and convention models. Anyone who is eligible for party membership can vote for the leader with a minimum of effort and expense, instead of having to pay hundreds of dollars to attend a convention. Second, parties that have recently lost power are often pressured by their members to grant them more influence in internal decision-making. As we have already seen, power tends to shift from the parliamentary to the extra-parliamentary wing of a party when it moves from government to opposition. (See page 247 for a discussion of these two wings of a party.) Third, the competitive dynamics of party systems often produce a "contagion" effect. Once a UMV contest has taken place in a particular country, the other parties in the system may feel pressured to make a similar change. That pressure may arise from their members, who envy the new privilege extended to their counterparts in the UMV party, or from party elites, who fear that the leadership will be perceived by the public as "undemocratic" if they stick with their old method of selecting a leader. Either way, a major innovation in one party's internal structure or procedures often creates a copycat effect among its rivals.

However compelling the reasons for its widespread adoption in recent years, UMV does have its drawbacks. First, different methods of party leadership selection tend to favour different types of candidates. Caucus selection emphasizes legislative skill and experience—valuable qualities indeed, given our earlier comments about the importance of parliamentary leadership. Because conventions and UMV appear to favour novelty and charisma over experience and substance,[10] they may choose leaders who lack the background and the skills to lead a party effectively.

Second, the more people who are involved in choosing a party leader, the more difficult it becomes to hold that leader accountable. A comparison of two case studies illustrates the point. In 1990, British Prime Minister Margaret Thatcher was quickly and unceremoniously removed as the leader of the Conservative Party. She had been chosen in a caucus vote in 1975 and lost her position 15 years later, when her MPs decided that she had become a political liability. Contrast her experience with that of Canadian Alliance leader Stockwell Day, who faced an unprecedented caucus revolt in the summer of 2001. Thirteen of his 66 MPs quit the caucus in protest over his leadership, and there was enormous pressure from inside and outside the party organization for Day to step down. But there was nothing that anyone could do to force him out; the Alliance constitution provides for a cumbersome and lengthy process to trigger a leadership review, which Day's opponents thought would take too long. His defenders made it clear that they would oppose any attempt to organize a review at the grassroots level, effectively insulating the leader against internal accountability. The difficulty of removing a leader chosen by the party on the ground—that is, by members in the local party associations—despite the problems that he or she may pose for the party in central or public office underlines the earlier point: choosing a party leader is a crucial process, which must not be undertaken without solid information and a clear sense of the skills required to do the job effectively.

Third, a shift from caucus selection to conventions and UMV alters the balance of power among the various elements of the party organization in subtle but important ways. The legislators lose some of their influence when they are deprived of the power to fire the leader. The party on the ground is too large and dispersed to hold the leader accountable, which leaves him or her—and the party in central office—in an even stronger position than before.

Candidate Nomination

The second party function is the recruitment and nomination of candidates, which is directly affected by the electoral system that operates in each country. Single-member districts tend to decentralize control of nominations to the local party associations on the ground; multimember districts in which the legislators are chosen from party lists tend to centralize power in the central office. When the central office nominates party candidates, the leader has more control over who is chosen. Leaving candidate selection in the hands of the party on the ground effectively prevents the leader from handpicking the men and women who will make up the party caucus.[11]

In general, parties look for "star" candidates: men and (increasingly) women with professional qualifications, high public profiles, good communication skills, and clean personal reputations. They may also seek out candidates who fulfil particular representational criteria, such as ethnicity, gender, or class. Parties that are expected to do well in the next election usually find it easier to recruit strong candidates than those that are likely to win few legislative seats. The quality of the candidates may be less important in multimember electoral systems, where voters cast their ballots for a party list rather than for individual standard-bearers. Under such conditions, aspiring candidates who have worked their way up through the party ranks have an advantage over newcomers with strong local ties. The reverse is true in Canadian parties, where the single-member system and the relative autonomy of the constituency associations favour the recruitment of local notables who may have little, if any, experience in the party. In the United States, where candidates for public office are often chosen by primary elections of voters, the parties have even less control over the nomination process.

Election Campaigns

The third and final function of parties is the orchestration of election campaigns. The nature of party campaigns has changed dramatically in the past 40 years, partly because of the growing importance of television in national politics. In the first half of the 20th century, election campaigns were very labour-intensive: volunteers went door to door, speaking directly to the voters on behalf of their parties and candidates. Since the 1960s, campaigns have become increasingly capital-intensive: parties hire experts to craft sophisticated advertising campaigns, relying on analyses of opinion data gathered by pollsters and interpreted by political strategists.[12] The high cost of polling, professional expertise, and broadcast advertising has pushed election spending into the stratosphere. Party members still go door to door in some places, but the emphasis has shifted from local mobilization to national persuasion. This shift is both cause and consequence of shrinking party memberships and the growing dependence of parties on public resources.

In principle, party campaigns provide important cues to voters. Party leaders try to win over the public, selling their platforms on the nightly news. Strategists identify groups of voters that might be predisposed to support their party, working to solidify that support by crafting narrowly targeted appeals. For example, labour and social democratic parties often use the rhetoric and symbols of class struggle to mobilize their target audience: they speak of "working people" and "average citizens," implicitly contrasting "their" voters to the "elites" or the "fat cats" who support the more conservative parties. The U.S. Democratic Party strives to maximize its support base among African-Americans by encouraging them to register to vote and by highlighting prominent figures (for example, the Reverend Jesse Jackson) at their presidential nominating conventions.

In practice, parties in many Western states appear to be losing their capacity to mobilize voters. Turnout levels in Canada and Britain have fallen sharply in recent elections, while fewer than half of all American voters routinely participate in the choice of their national leaders. This disturbing trend may reflect the weakening of parties on the ground; it may also demonstrate the erosion of long-standing ties between parties and their particular subcultures. Labour parties have been hurt by the waning of working-class consciousness in much of Western Europe, as an ever-increasing proportion of the workforce moves from the manufacturing sector to the service sector of the economy.[13] Catholic, Protestant, and Christian Democratic parties have suffered from the decline of religious observance in industrial democracies. In all of these cases,

older parties have been forced to change their structures and strategies in an effort to preserve their status in the party system. Mass-bureaucratic parties, including the British Labour Party, have adopted a more professional approach to campaigning, while existing electoral-professional parties (including Canada's older parties) have become even more dependent on public resources to sustain their organizations.

While the older parties have tried to adapt to social change, new parties have sprung up to fill an apparent political vacuum. The left–right ideological division on which 20th-century party systems were based appears to be giving way to "new politics," in which personal identity and values outweigh economic self-interest in the minds of some voters.[14] In the 1970s and 1980s, minority language groups, disaffected regions, and environmental activists in many Western European states created political parties to press their demands for change. Typically, these new parties—often called antiparty parties because of their contempt for the "old politics" in their respective countries—are neither mass-bureaucratic nor electoral-professional. At least initially, their structures are looser and less hierarchical, emphasizing grassroots consensus instead of leader domination. Most discover rather quickly that such informal structures hinder their efforts to organize election campaigns and to present unified policies to the electorate. Consequently, those that do manage to win seats in the legislature—thus qualifying for public subsidies and ensuring their survival at least in the short term—usually acquire some of the characteristics of mass-bureaucratic parties. The German Greens, which have participated in the national governing coalition since 1999, are a good example of this trend. Despite their determination to preserve their integrity as an internally democratic antiparty party, the realities of competing for power in order to carry out their policies forced them to adapt their structures to the institutional demands of parliamentary government.[15] This example illustrates the central theme of the next section of the chapter: regardless of their other characteristics, political parties must perform certain key functions in similar ways if they are to achieve their electoral goals. Therefore, their organizations share certain universal features, regardless of country or ideology. In politics as in engineering, form follows function.

PARTIES AS ORGANIZATIONS

There are at least three universal features of party structure. For one, parties have written constitutions, which set out the formal division of powers and responsibilities among the various groups and individuals involved in party activities. These constitutions typically include a statement of party principles, job descriptions for the different party offices, rules for electing the leader and other officials, and criteria for membership in the party. Most party constitutions formally locate power within the organization at the grassroots level—in the members on the ground, either in the mass (through internal referendums) or as delegates to a party convention. These claims of internal democracy are almost always exaggerated, as we will see below.

Second, parties that elect candidates to public office are divided into **parliamentary** and **extra-parliamentary wings**. The parliamentary wing includes the leader, the elected legislators, and the people who work in their offices. (In Canadian and British parties, it also includes appointed senators and lords respectively.) The parliamentary wing is often called the **caucus**. More generally, it is referred to as the party in public office.[16] The extra-parliamentary organization (literally, "outside Parliament") is divided into two sections. The smaller of these is the party in central office: the permanent paid staff in the national headquarters (and any regional offices), together with the professional consultants—spin-doctors, advertising experts, pollsters, and political strategists—who work on contract before and during election campaigns. By far, the biggest section of the extra-parliamentary party is the party on the ground: the members in the local party associations. They are responsible for electing delegates to party conventions, nominating candidates and electing party leaders (in some parties), and organizing campaigns for individual candidates or groups of candidates. In theory, they also make party policy and hold the party leadership accountable; in practice, they have less power within party structures than the rhetoric of internal democracy would suggest.

> ### Definition
> **PARLIAMENTARY WING:** That wing of a political party that includes the leader, the elected legislators, and the people who work in their offices. It is also called the caucus or the party in public office.

> ### Definition
> **EXTRA-PARLIAMENTARY WING:** That wing of a political party that consists of the members of local party associations and the permanent paid staff in the party headquarters; in other words, the party organization outside the legislature.

Finally, all parties are dominated by their leaders, who are supported by the party in public office and the party in central office. This Iron Law of Oligarchy[17] cannot be broken, despite the best efforts of the party on the ground to exert control over party elites. (Recall the earlier discussion of the German Greens.) The relative power of the three elements in the party structure varies, to a degree, with the position of the party in the national legislature. In other words, power within a party is more tightly centralized in government than in opposition.[18] The relationship among the three elements may also vary, at least in formal terms, with the ideology of the party. Socialist and green parties tend to establish internal mechanisms for the members to

Figure 11.1 Major Elements of Party Organization

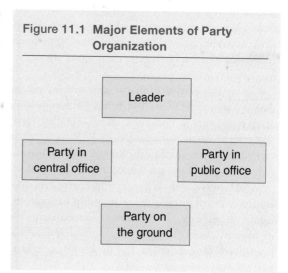

hold the caucus accountable; conservative and liberal parties are less likely to do so. Even where such mechanisms exist, they are rarely effective. After all, it is no easy matter for thousands of scattered party members to control a relatively small and tightly knit party caucus or staff, whose control of the resources required for the survival of the party organization is absolute (at least in the short term). Because all political parties pursue public office, the dominance of the elected legislators and the experts in campaign techniques cannot be broken. It is a fact of life within party organizations.

It should be noted that the leader may or may not be responsible for hiring the staff who work in the central office. In mass-bureaucratic parties, the employees in central office are usually permanent and unionized. Their loyalty is to the party, not to a particular leader. They cannot be fired when a new leader takes over the party. In electoral-professional parties, the leader normally has the power to staff the central office with people who are personal loyalists. The central office typically expands shortly before an election campaign, as professional political operatives on short-term contracts arrive to orchestrate the campaign strategy. The party in public office is directed by the leader, but his or her competing responsibilities often prevent the leader (especially in a governing party) from making the day-to-day decisions about caucus management. Therefore, the leader is assisted by other senior legislators: a house leader (also called a majority or minority leader, or a caucus leader), a whip (who makes sure that caucus members carry out their legislative responsibilities in the house and on committees), and often a caucus chair to run the regular meetings of the parliamentary wing.

To say that party organizations are roughly similar does not mean that they are identical. Within the universal framework just outlined, there are endless variations in the detail of party structures. Some of these variations are produced by the unique political institutions that operate in each democratic state. The institutional factors that most directly affect party structures are the electoral system, the relationship between the legislative and executive branches of government, the division of powers between the national and subnational levels of government, and the laws that regulate party competition.

Electoral Systems

An electoral system that divides the country into single-member districts tends to decentralize the party on the ground. In Canada, for example, every national party must maintain 301 separate constituency associations (or, failing that, as many as it possibly can). Each constituency association is responsible for nominating one candidate in each general election and orchestrating his or her campaign for Parliament. To do this effectively, the association must raise funds and recruit members both during and between elections. The health of a national party organization depends, in large measure, on the size and vigour of its local clubs.[19] By contrast, electoral systems in which parties run lists of candidates in large multimember districts tend to concentrate power in the central office.[20] Because the nomination of candidates for public office is such a crucial task of party organizations, the locus of nomination reflects the general distribution of power and influence within party organizations.

The Relationship between the Legislative and Executive Branches

Political systems in which the legislative and executive branches are fused—as they are in most parliamentary democracies—tend to reinforce the dominance of the parliamentary wing over the party membership. Responsible cabinet government requires a disciplined majority in Parliament, which in turn requires that the parliamentary wing be relatively autonomous from the more diverse interests that make up the party on the ground. On the other hand, the separation of legislative and executive powers (as in the presidential-congressional systems of the United States and Mexico) permits a looser, less coherent party organization.

In the United States, for example, the president is elected by the voters.[21] He is guaranteed a four-year term in office, whether or not his party controls a majority of the seats in the House of Representatives and the Senate. Partly for this reason, American parties are highly decentralized.[22] Each candidate campaigns independently of the others. Nor are American candidates dependent on local party associations for their nominations; as we have seen, candidates for Congress (and for executive offices, including governorships and the presidency) are nominated by the voters in primary elections (as opposed to local party members in nominating conventions). The cumulative result is that American parties are less cohesive organizations than those in parliamentary systems such as those of Canada, Britain, or Australia. The party in public office is divided between the executive branch (the White House) and the legislative branch (Congress). The party in central office is similarly divided, as is the party on the ground.

Where the authority of the executive branch depends on the cohesion of the legislative wing(s) of the party or parties in the cabinet, the incentives for party unity are much greater. The leader of the (senior) governing party is simultaneously the head of the political executive (the cabinet) and the dominant figure in the legislature. Because the effectiveness of the government depends, in part, on the qualities of the men and women in the parliamentary caucus, the leader has good reason to encourage the nomination of capable candidates (although, as we have just seen, he or she may be prevented from direct intervention by a decentralized electoral system). The party in public office is united behind a single leader, as is the party in central office. The party on the ground can focus its efforts on one goal—the election of as many MPs as possible, ideally a majority of the legislature—instead of dividing its scarce resources between separate presidential and congressional campaigns.

Federal versus Unitary States

In most constitutional democracies, powers are divided between as well as within governments. Chapter 6, on constitutions, explains the concept of federalism, and it is easy to understand how federalism shapes party structures. The presence of separate state or provincial governments requires political parties to establish distinct national and subnational organizations to contest power at both levels. In the United States, for example, the Democratic and Republican parties monopolize the executive branches (and, for the most part, the legislative branches) in Washington and in the 50 state capi-

tals. This does not mean, however, that all federal parties have the same structure. We can distinguish among three models of party organization in federations:[23]

- *Integrated* parties are electorally competitive at both levels of government, and relations between the two levels of the party are generally close.
- *Confederal* parties are present at both levels of government, but the links between the national party and one or more of its subnational organizations are strained (and sometimes openly hostile).
- *Truncated* parties operate only at one level of government, in whole or in part. For example, the Progressive Conservative Party has no provincial organization in British Columbia and Quebec, and the Bloc Québécois does not exist outside Quebec.

The degree to which a particular party resembles one of these three models depends on at least three factors: the nature of the party itself, the degree of centralization in federal institutions, and the intensity of

Alberta PC Premier Ralph Klein (left) and federal PC leader Joe Clark share a laugh at Klein's annual Calgary Stampede breakfast in July 2001. Klein's provincial party was of limited help to Clark's federal party in Alberta.

Adrian Wyld/CP Picture Archive

conflict among the component parts of the federation. A mass-bureaucratic party seeks to maintain a unified organization across the two levels of government. Its national and subnational organizations are tightly integrated, and its ideology may provide the glue that holds the various local associations together. An electoral-professional party is more likely to be confederal or truncated. Each separate wing of the party is dominated by its leader. Its ideology is rarely a sufficient unifying force to hold the party together. In regions where it cannot compete effectively, it may fade away entirely. Personal or political clashes between national and subnational leaders may provoke splits between the two levels of party organization, as the members on the ground choose sides in the dispute. A prolonged failure to win power at one level of government may induce party officials and members to concentrate on the other, more promising level. For example, the defeat of the Liberal Party of Canada in 1984 was followed, one year later, by the formation of a Liberal minority government in the province of Ontario. Senior Liberal strategists and fundraisers flocked to Toronto, abandoning the national party in its hour of greatest need.

The impact of different federal systems on party structures is illustrated by comparing Canada and Germany. Canada has a highly decentralized federal system, in which the two levels of government pursue distinct (though generally coordinated) policy agendas. Most aspiring politicians devote their efforts to either federal or provincial politics.[24] It is relatively rare for Canadian legislators to serve at both levels of government, although there are important exceptions: federal cabinet minister Sheila Copps was a member of the Ontario legislature before her election to Parliament in 1984, and former Canadian Alliance leader Stockwell Day was Treasurer of Alberta before he entered federal politics in 2000. Nonetheless, the fact that most politicians lack experience at both levels of government may exacerbate the political divisions within the federation.

The German federal system is considerably more centralized, and the two levels of government—the national government, or *Bund*, and the states, or *Länder*—are tightly integrated. The upper house of the national parliament is the Bundesrat, which is composed of delegations from the *Länd* governments. All national legislation that directly affects the *Länder* must be passed by a majority of the state delegations in the

Bundesrat. The state governments are responsible for implementing much of the legislation passed by the national legislature, in addition to executing their own local laws. The design of Germany's federal institutions creates strong incentives for the national and *Länd* party organizations to work closely together, and for individual politicians to move back and forth between the two levels of government. Hence, "In sharp contrast to Canada or the United States, [Germany] can be said to have nationally integrated party organizations."[25]

Intense or prolonged conflict within the federation can turn an integrated party into a confederal party, or even a truncated party. When the national government enacts policies that arouse anger and hostility in a particular region, its party organization in that region suffers the political consequences. For example, the Liberal governments of Lester Pearson (1963–68) and Pierre Trudeau (1968–84) pursued a centralizing agenda that alienated the party's Alberta and Quebec wings.[26] Those provincial Liberal organizations are formally separate from the national party, with distinct personnel, central offices, and memberships. The alienation of a particular region from a national party is intensified by Canada's electoral system, which distorts the translation of each party's vote share into its share of seats in the House of Commons. The Liberals have elected few MPs from the four Western provinces since 1972, despite winning respectable shares of the regional vote in most elections; consequently, national policies have not always been sensitive to Western concerns, which further alienates voters in that region. Our electoral system also encourages each party to focus its campaign in areas where it expects to do well,[27] which exacerbates feelings of resentment in the "neglected" provinces. Over time, provincial wings that cannot rely on organizational support from the federal party either disappear or separate themselves from a national organization that to them has become a political liability.

Election Laws

Finally, the legal regime that regulates party activity can affect the ways in which parties compete for power, thus shaping their internal structures. Most democratic states provide some form of assistance to party organizations, ranging from financial subsidies to free airtime on government-regulated broadcast networks.[28] In recent years, as their memberships have shrunk and the costs of campaigning have soared, parties have become increasingly dependent on these public-sector resources.[29] Because the subsidies and the broadcast provisions are provided to (and used by) the party in central office, they increase the power of the party bureaucrats at the expense of the volunteers on the ground. (Note, however, that Canada's rules regarding election finances also provide direct financial subsidies to local candidates, who are reimbursed for a portion of their campaign expenses.[30] Those reimbursements are normally turned over to the local constituency association. The result is that some local party clubs amass huge bank accounts, while the national party struggles to pay off its campaign debt after each general election.)[31]

* * *

To summarize, while political parties in Western democracies are organized along broadly similar lines—largely because all parties pursue the goal of winning public office—there are some structural variations. Those variations are imposed by the varying political institutions in each country and by the relative positions of each party within Parliament. In other words, while the party in public office and the party in central office dominate the party on the ground in all cases, the degree of that dominance in any given party depends on external factors.

This discussion of party organization provides a different perspective on the claims of party decline that we sketched at the beginning of this chapter:

> it is really only the party on the ground which is in decline, whereas the resources of the party in central office, and especially those of the party in public office, have in fact been strengthened.... the emphasis on party decline *tout court* may be misplaced.[32]

In other words, parties continue to control governments, to organize legislatures, and to run election campaigns, despite shrinking memberships and weakening ties to distinct groups within their electorates. We turn now to a discussion of parties that have achieved their primary goal—winning power—and the restrictions on their exercise of that power within the institutional structures of government.

PARTIES IN GOVERNMENT

As we have already seen, governing parties tend to concentrate power in their parliamentary wings and, more particularly, in their leaders. Beyond these universal claims, the ways in which governing parties operate vary according to three institutional factors:

- the number of parties in the cabinet
- the relationship between the legislative and executive branches
- the extent to which that particular government is constrained by external forces, including constitutional rules and globalization.

The Number of Parties in the Cabinet

The number of parties in a given cabinet is determined partly by the electoral system and partly by the voting patterns in each national electorate. The combination of a proportional representation system—in which each party receives a share of legislative seats roughly proportionate to its share of the vote—and a fragmented voting pattern, in which votes are divided among several parties, tends to produce parliaments in which no party holds a majority of the seats. Under such conditions, a stable political executive requires the creation of a parliamentary majority by combining two or more parties in government. The leaders of those parties are included in a coalition cabinet, whose legislative program is constructed through negotiations among the various party leaders. Most coalitions are dominated by a single party, which holds a majority of the cabinet posts, with the remaining ministries assigned to the "junior partner(s)." Examples include the pre-1994 Italian coalitions, which were anchored by the Christian Democratic Party, and the Christian Democrat–Free Democrat coalition that governed Germany from 1949 until 1969. In a single-member electoral system, which tends to give the largest party a majority of the seats in parliament (usually with less than half the vote), coalitions are rarely required. Even when the largest party fails to win a majority, it usually governs alone as a minority government with informal support from one or more opposition parties (e.g., Canada's Liberal minorities of

1963–68 and 1972–74). While a single-party majority government has the greatest freedom to enact policies that reflect its stated principles and priorities, that does not translate into absolute partisan control over the legislative agenda.

The Relationship between the Legislative and Executive Branches

The behaviour of governing parties is directly affected by the relationship between the legislative and executive branches. As we have already seen, party structures are looser and less cohesive in congressional systems than they are in British-style parliamentary systems. In the United States, the president may find it easier to work with a Congress in which his party holds a majority; this is not always the case, however, because of persistent ideological and regional factions within American congressional caucuses. Because the authority of the executive branch does not rest on the maintenance of a stable legislative majority, there is little incentive for congressional caucuses to form disciplined units. In contrast, the executive branch in a parliamentary system can lose power if its caucus refuses to support its spending plans or, in rare cases, its policy initiatives. So in Canada, as in Britain, Australia, and other parliamentary democracies, the power of the prime minister rests on his or her ability to retain the loyalty of the government MPs. The result is a strong tradition of party discipline, which restricts the freedom of individual legislators to vote according to their consciences or the priorities of their local constituents.

External Constraints

Finally, the policy choices of governing parties are constrained by external factors, including fiscal conditions, global forces, and domestic constitutions. A party that promised to spend lavishly on social programs may find, soon after taking office, that it lacks the financial resources to do so. If its economic policies conflict with those of other Western states—for example, if it lowers interest rates below those of its counterparts in the G8—it could provoke an invest-

ment exodus that sends the economy into a recession. If the national government in a federal state seeks to legislate in policy fields that properly belong to another level of government (for example, education is a provincial responsibility in Canada), its laws may be declared null and void by the courts. So there are important restrictions on the power of national governments, which translate into reduced freedom of choice for the parties that control them. In particular, globalization and fiscal constraints can prevent a party from keeping its policy promises and thus imperil its chances for winning re-election.

Parties and Public Policy

It is often assumed that parties create public policy. Most parties claim that their election platforms—the collection of specific promises that they issue during campaigns, also called manifestoes—are based on resolutions passed by their members. The truth is often rather different. We have already seen that party leaders enjoy considerable influence over policy and principle, and that election campaigns are crafted by the permanent staff and contract consultants who work in central office. More often than not, parties rely for policy innovation on interest groups, think-tanks, public servants, and other external sources. Even if governing parties did have a free hand in making policy, in other words, their policies would not necessarily reflect the priorities of their members. In this sense, the constraints on governing parties reinforce the structural characteristics that concentrate power in the leader's office and the permanent party staff.

PARTY SYSTEMS

The previous sections of this chapter have treated parties as individual organizations with a degree of autonomy in their internal decision-making. While this portrait is accurate, it does not reveal the whole picture. Each political party belongs to a **party system**: an interconnected set of parties that compete for legislative office and other scarce resources (such as money and votes). When one party in a given country makes a significant change in its structures or policies, its competitors may feel compelled to follow suit.

Comparative studies of party systems often focus on three particular variables: the number of parties, the pattern of competition among the parties (voting patterns, social cleavages), and the ideological composition of the party system as a whole.

The Number of Parties

The number of parties in a party system, like the number of parties in a government, is determined by the electoral system and the voting patterns in the electorate. All other things being equal, a more proportional electoral system permits the translation of all major social **cleavages** into individual parties in the legislature.

In other words, in a proportional electoral system, smaller parties can win enough seats in parliament to satisfy their members and voters that their views are being expressed in national politics. A single dominant cleavage—for example, the class cleavage in Austria—will translate into two large parties in parliament; a more complex cleavage structure, such as that in Belgium, will produce several parties (regional, linguistic, working-class, religious, and Green). A disproportional electoral system, such as that in Canada, the United States, and Britain, makes it difficult for smaller parties to win seats in parliament (with one notable exception: regional parties, such as the Bloc Québécois and the Scottish National Party, tend to do very well under such systems). Over time, the supporters of smaller parties become discouraged by their failure to gain parliamentary representation, and these parties gradually fade away, leaving one or two large parties to contend for power.

The Pattern of Party Competition

The pattern of party competition comprises three elements: the frequency with which parties alternate in government, the consistency of government composition, and the openness of access to government.[33] If we combine the two characteristics of party systems mentioned so far—the number of parties and the structure of competition—we come up with four major categories, namely **two-party system**, two-and-a-half party system, and two types of **multiparty systems**. Some multiparty systems include a number of parties, none of which could govern on their own, whereas other multiparty systems are dominated by a single party and can also be called **one-party dominant systems**. Table 11.2 lists these types of party system, together with examples of each.

As Table 11.2 reveals, the concept of party competition brings together several key concepts: the number of parties in the system, the relative size of the parties (in terms of both voting support and legislative representation), the willingness of the parties to overcome their differences when required (e.g., to create and sustain a coalition cabinet), and the degree of competitiveness among the parties. Table 11.3 provides actual statistics on one example in each category.

Table 11.2 Four Types of Party Systems

Type of Party System	Description	Examples
Two-Party	Two major parties compete for power; they alternate in government more or less frequently	United States; New Zealand (pre-1996)
Two-and-a-Half Party	In addition to the two parties described above, there is a third party, which rarely challenges for power but which may support one of the major parties during periods of minority government	Canada (1963–93); Britain
Multiparty System with a Dominant Party	Four or more parties contest national elections, only one of which has a realistic chance either to form a single-party majority government or to become the senior partner in a coalition	Italy (pre-1994); Canada (post-1993); Japan (pre-1993); India (pre-1977); Mexico (pre-2000); West Germany (1949–69)
Multiparty System with No Dominant Party	Four or more parties compete for inclusion in governing coalitions, with fairly regular alternation in power; after each election, the composition of the new government depends on bargaining among all of the parties, not just the incumbents	The Netherlands; Italy (post-1994); Norway

Source: Based on Peter Mair, "Party Systems and Structures of Competition," in Lawrence LeDuc, Richard G. Niemi, and Pippa Norris, eds., *Comparing Democracies: Elections and Voting in Global Perspective* (Thousand Oaks: Sage, 1996), pp. 86–92.

It should now be clear that the number of parties, by itself, tells us little about the politics and government of a particular country. When we combine the number of parties with the other factors just mentioned, the result is a useful categorization of party systems. Systems in which one party remains in power for long periods of time—either alone, or with one or more junior coalition partners—produce different patterns of government and politics from highly competitive systems, which feature two major parties or two (or more) possible coalitions that regularly alternate in power. At the very least, the possibility of a meaningful choice between alternative governments implies a more vibrant and engaging democracy than one that exists in a state where the outcome of an election is predetermined well before voters go to the polls. Public policy may also be affected by the type of party system. Significant changes in the party composition of a government may produce major changes in policy direction, at least in those fields (such as law and order) that are least affected by globalization and fiscal constraints.

Ideology and Party Systems

As Chapter 5 demonstrates, ideologies play an important role in democratic politics. An electorate that is divided into several ideological factions tends to produce multiple **ideological parties**, at least under a

Table 11.3   An Example of Each Type of Party System

(a) The United States as a Two-Party System

Party Standings in the 107th Congress, 2001–03

	Republicans	Democrats	Others
House of Representatives	221	212	2
Senate (as of June 6, 2001)	49	50	1

Results of the 2000 Presidential Election

	George W. Bush	Al Gore	Others
Popular Vote	50 456 062	50 996 582	3 910 654
Electoral College	271	266	0

(b) The United Kingdom as a Two-and-a-Half Party System, 2001 General Election

	Seats	Percent of Votes
Labour	412	40.7
Conservatives	166	31.7
Liberal Democrats	52	18.3
Other	29	9.3

(c) Canada as a Multiparty System with a Dominant Party, 2000 General Election

	Seats	Percent of Votes
Liberal Party	172	40.8
Canadian Alliance	66	25.5
Bloc Québécois	38	10.7
Progressive Conservative Party	12	12.2
New Democratic Party	13	8.5

(d) The Netherlands as a Multiparty System with No Dominant Party, 2002 Election

	Seats	Percent of Votes
Christian Democratic Appeal	43	27.9
List Pim Fortuyn	26	17.0
People's Party for Freedom and Democracy	24	15.4
Labour Party	23	15.1
Green Party	10	7.0
Socialist Party	9	5.9
Democrats 66	7	5.1
Christian Union	4	2.5
Political Reform Party	2	1.7
Livable Netherlands	2	1.6

Sources: a) House of Representatives, Office of the Clerk; cited on May 22, 2002; available at http://clerkweb.house.gov/histrecs/househis/lists/divisionh.htm; "Senate Statistics," cited on May 22, 2002; available at http://www.senate.gov/learning/stat_13.html; National Archives and Records Administration, Federal Register, cited on May 22, 2002; available at http://www.nara.gov/fedreg/elctcoll/2000map.html; b) *The Times Guide to the House of Commons, June 2001* (London: Times Books, 2001), p. 296; c) Elections Canada, *Report of the Chief Electoral Officer of Canada* (Ottawa: Elections Canada, 2000); d) "Elections in the Netherlands"; cited on May 22, 2002; available at http://www.electionworld.org/election/netherlands.htm.

proportional electoral system. But the number of ideologies reflected in a particular party system is only part of the story. To fully understand the party system in a given country, we must also determine how strongly the parties differ from each other in their principles and beliefs. In other words, two party systems might reflect the same number of ideologies, but if one is fairly moderate and consensual (that is, if some or all of the parties agree on basic political values and could work together when necessary) and the other is deeply divided and conflictual, the two systems will operate very differently. For example, until recently, the party systems of Sweden and Italy revolved around a single major cleavage: the division between the working class and the middle class. But whereas Swedish politics was very stable, with long-lived social democratic governments, Italian politics was bitterly polarized and often chaotic. The Communist Party (PCI) was perceived as beyond the pale by the Christian Democrats and their coalition allies; although it was the second-largest party in the Italian Parliament, the PCI was never included in government. Instead, the Christian Democrats cobbled together diverse and often short-lived coalitions of smaller parties to ensure that the communists would never attain power. A party system that cannot build and maintain stable governments poses a serious threat to democracy; the collapse of democratic government in the German Weimar Republic, which brought Adolf Hitler to power in 1933, is a case in point.

When democracy was restored in Western Europe in the late 1940s, political leaders in most states sought to overcome the bitterness of the left-right ideological divisions of the 1920s and 1930s by establishing catch-all parties.[34] These were electoral-professional parties, geared to achieving and retaining power by appealing to a large proportion of the electorate. Unlike the mass-bureaucratic parties that had refused (or had been unable) to compromise their ideological demands, catch-all parties sought to bridge the class cleavage and stabilize their party systems. The German Christian Democrats were the most successful example; they have governed the Federal Republic of Germany (West Germany before 1990) for most of its history. Their electoral success forced the Social Democratic Party

(SPD) to adopt the catch-all model, watering down its ideology and replacing some of its mass-bureaucratic structures in favour of the electoral-professional approach.

The party systems in Canada and the United States needed no such renovation after World War II because they were already stable and ideologically moderate. Although both societies are divided by a class cleavage, class exerts an unusually weak influence on voting behaviour in both countries.[35] Consequently, all of the major parties in both countries belong to the electoral-professional category; the mass-bureaucratic party requires a strong working-class vote in order to survive. In effect, Canadian and American parties began as cadres and quickly became catch-all or **brokerage parties**.

The primary goal of brokerage parties is to win enough parliamentary seats to form a government; to achieve this goal, these parties attempt to appeal to a broad spectrum of the electorate. Canada's Liberal and Progressive Conservative parties are classic brokers, building coalitions of voters at each election in an attempt to control a majority of the seats in Parliament. This brokerage strategy is primarily regional; to win a majority in Canada, a party must target its campaign to voters in the heavily populated central and Western provinces. Brokerage parties may try to downplay ideological divisions in the electorate, although this does not mean that they are entirely devoid of principle. The members of a brokerage party are united and motivated by its ideology,[36] which differs in subtle but significant ways from those of its competitors.[37] Nonetheless, the efforts of North America's brokerage parties—like those of electoral-professional parties in other democracies—to overcome ideological divisions in the electorate do not always succeed. Groups that perceive that their particular values and interests are ignored by the major parties may establish their own parties in order to challenge the dominance of the established brokers. This impulse explains the emergence of the Reform parties in Canada and the United States, as well as the German Greens, New Zealand First, and other "insurgent" parties that rapidly achieved political prominence over the past two decades.

Definition
BROKERAGE PARTY: A party that seeks power by appealing to a broad spectrum of the electorate, in an attempt to win enough parliamentary seats to form a government. A brokerage party avoids clear and potentially divisive ideologies, preferring to attract voters from a wide range of perspectives and cleavages. Canada's Liberal and Progressive Conservative parties are prime examples of brokerage parties.

In general, parties in Western party systems work together fairly harmoniously, despite the furor of parliamentary debate and the intensity of partisan competition in elections. A party system that reflects all of the major political viewpoints in its electorate is an important ingredient in democratic legitimacy. It is sometimes argued, however, that globalization is narrowing the ideological spectrum of national party systems, forcing all parties to adopt similar policies. If true, this occurrence poses worrisome questions about the future vitality of party politics in both developed and developing countries. When important ideological groups within a national electorate perceive that the party system does not reflect their priorities, they may turn to alternative political agencies (such as new social movements) or turn away from political institutions altogether.

Nor is the risk of political disengagement confined to ideological minorities. We have seen that new politics, in which ideologies are replaced by identities, can prompt the formation of new parties. However, voters inspired by new politics are at least as likely to withdraw from the party system altogether, devoting their energies instead to new social movements (for example, the antiglobalization movement discussed in Chapter 13). Identity politics often rests on irreconcilable rights claims, which cannot be solved as easily as ideological conflicts over the distribution of resources among competing social classes. Although the new politics values of direct participation and commitment may turn out to be a vital source of democratic energy in the long run,[38] in the short run they represent the most perplexing challenge facing political parties in Western democracies.

CONCLUSION

This chapter argues that political parties remain central to democratic politics and government, despite the problems they have faced in recent decades. While parties may be less effective in mobilizing the electorate and linking citizens to their governments, their organizational capacities have been enhanced by growing public subsidies and the increasing professionalization of their personnel. Nonetheless, neither we nor the parties that serve us can afford to be complacent. As the power of the nation-state shrinks relative to global economic forces and supranational institutions, the prize for which parties compete loses some of its value. External constraints on governing parties are likely to become stronger, not weaker, in the coming years. Meanwhile, voters in most Western states are less engaged in party activity and less likely to follow campaign cues than they were half a century ago. As the power of the party in central office and the party in public office grows at the expense of the party on the ground, "the gap between the citizenry and the established political class" grows wider:

> the problem is not one of party decline per se, as is often imputed to be the case; rather, it appears to be one in which the parties are at once stronger, but also more remote; at once more in control, but also less powerful; and at once more privileged, but also less legitimate.[39]

In response to these challenges, parties are changing their internal structures—the shift to UMV is a good example—and using new technologies to reach out to voters. Most parties have experimented with the Internet and interactive broadcasting as a way to communicate their policies and attract the attention of younger voters. But these tools are also available to other political organizations, including antiparty parties and the new social movements, which are drawing many younger voters away from party organizations.

It may not be possible to return to the days when parties commanded the loyalty of cohesive political subcultures, voters flocked to the polling booths, and local party associations mobilized large numbers of citizens into participating in the political process. All we can know for sure is that parties and party systems in democratic states will continue to confront the challenges identified in this chapter, as well as new challenges that are as yet unforeseen. Some of today's parties will thrive in a changing world, perhaps rebuilding the links between citizens and states, while others will fall by the wayside. But political parties as organizations—and the party systems to which they belong—will persist as long as there are differences of political opinion and elective institutions through which to express them.

DISCUSSION QUESTIONS

1. Do you pay close attention to national and/or provincial party politics? Why or why not?

2. If you wanted to influence public policy on a particular issue, which do you think would be more effective: joining a political party or participating in a public protest? Explain your choice.

3. Do you plan to vote in the next federal or provincial election? Why or why not?

4. Should a party in government keep all of its election promises? Why or why not?

w(w)w WEB LINKS

Bloc Québécois:
http://blocquebecois.org

Canadian Alliance:
http://www.canadianalliance.ca

Green Party of Canada:
http://www.green.ca

Liberal Party of Canada:
http://www.liberal.ca

New Democratic Party:
http://www.ndp.ca

Progressive Conservative Party of Canada:
http://www.pcparty.ca

U.K. Conservative Party:
http://www.conservatives.com

U.K. Labour Party:
http://www.labour.org.uk

U.S. Democratic Party:
http://www.democrats.org

U.S. Republican Party:
http://www.rnc.org

International Foundation for Electoral Systems:
http://www.ifes.org

International Institute for Democracy and Electoral Assistance:
http://www.idea.int

Elections, Political Parties and Parliaments, from the University of British Columbia Library:
http://www.library.ubc.ca/poli/electoral.html

FURTHER READING

Bakvis, Herman, ed. *Canadian Political Parties: Leaders, Candidates and Organization.* Vol. 13 of the collected research studies for the Royal Commission on Electoral Reform and Party Financing. Toronto: Dundurn, 1991.

Carty, R. Kenneth. *Canadian Political Parties in the Constituencies.* Vol. 23 of the collected research studies for the Royal Commission on Electoral Reform and Party Financing. Toronto: Dundurn, 1991.

Harmel, Robert, and Kenneth Janda. "An Integrated Theory of Party Goals and Party Change." *Journal of Theoretical Politics* 6(3) (July 1994): 259–87.

Katz, Richard S., and Peter Mair, eds. *How Parties Organize: Change and Adaptation in Party Organizations in Western Democracies.* London: Sage, 1994.

Lawson, Kay, and Peter H. Merkl, eds. *When Parties Fail: Emerging Alternative Organizations.* Princeton: Princeton University Press, 1988.

LeDuc, Lawrence, Richard G. Niemi, and Pippa Norris, eds. *Comparing Democracies: Elections and Voting in Global Perspective.* Thousand Oaks: Sage, 1996.

Maor, Moshe. *Political Parties and Party Systems: Comparative Approaches and the British Experience.* London: Routledge, 1997.

Panebianco, Angelo. *Political Parties: Organization and Power.* Cambridge: Cambridge University Press, 1988.

Punnett, R.M. *Selecting the Party Leader: Britain in Comparative Perspective.* London: Harvester Wheatsheaf, 1992.

ENDNOTES

1   For a thorough discussion of party goals, see Robert Harmel and Kenneth Janda, "An Integrated Theory of Party Goals and Party Change" *Journal of Theoretical Politics* 6(3) (July 1994): 259–87.

2   Harvey C. Mansfield, Jr., *Statesmanship and Party Government: A Study of Burke and Bolingbroke* (Chicago: University of Chicago Press, 1965), p. 1

3   James Madison, Alexander Hamilton, and John Jay, *The Federalist Papers* (London: Penguin, 1987 [1788]), p. 404.

4   Maurice Duverger, *Political Parties: Their Organization and Activity in the Modern State* (London: Methuen, 1964), pp. xxiv–xxx, 63–67.

5   This terminology is taken from Angelo Panebianco, *Political Parties: Organization and Power* (Cambridge: Cambridge University Press, 1988), p. 264. See also Moshe Maor, *Political Parties and Party Systems: Comparative Approaches and the British Experience* (London: Routledge, 1997), pp. 105–07.

6   Hon. Jean Charest, telephone conversation with author, April 4, 1998.

7   For example, in the SPD–Green coalition that took power in Germany in 1999, SPD leader Gerhard Schroeder is the chancellor (the equivalent of prime minister), while Joschka Fischer, the Green leader, is the foreign minister.

8   See the *European Journal of Political Research* 24(3) (special issue on party leadership selection) (October 1993).

9   R.M. Punnett, *Selecting the Party Leader: Britain in Comparative Perspective* (London: Harvester Wheatsheaf, 1992), p. 18; Heather MacIvor, "From Emergence to Electronics: Explaining the Changes in Canadian Party Leadership Selection, 1919–1995," *National History* (1995), pp. 173–85.

10   John C. Courtney, *The Selection of National Party Leaders in Canada* (Toronto: Macmillan, 1973), p. 137. See also R. Kenneth Carty and Peter James, "Changing the Rules of the Game: Do Conventions and Caucuses Choose Different Leaders?" in R. Kenneth Carty et al., eds. *Leaders and Parties in Canadian Politics: Experiences of the Provinces* (Toronto: HBJ Canada, 1992), p. 29. Carty and James argue that the differences in legislative experience between leaders chosen in caucus and those chosen by conventions are more apparent than real.

11   There are exceptions, however. The Liberal Party of Canada gives its leader the right to appoint candidates where this is necessary to ensure a reasonable percentage of female nominees or to smooth the way for a "star" candidate.

12   This distinction between capital-intensive and labour-intensive campaigning is taken from David M. Farrell, "Campaign Strategies and Tactics," in Lawrence LeDuc, Richard G. Niemi, and Pippa Norris, eds., *Comparing Democracies: Elections and Voting in Global Perspective* (Thousand Oaks: Sage, 1996), pp. 160–83.

13   For a discussion of the British case, in which the decline of class voting has been particularly marked, see Anthony King, "The New Electoral Battleground," in Anthony King et al., eds., *New Labour Triumphs: Britain at the Polls* (Chatham, N.J.: Chatham House, 1998), pp. 219–23; Richard Rose and Ian McAllister, *Voters Begin to Choose: From Closed-Class to Open Elections in Britain* (London: Sage, 1986). On the general decline of cleavage voting in Western democracies,

see Russell J. Dalton, *Citizen Politics: Public Opinion and Political Parties in Advanced Western Democracies*, 2nd ed. (Chatham, N.J.: Chatham House, 1996), chap. 8.

14 See, for example, Ronald Inglehard, *Modernization and Postmodernization: Cultural, Economic, and Political Change in 43 Societies* (Princeton: Princeton University Press, 1997); Russell J. Dalton, "Value Change and Democracy," in Susan J. Pharr and Robert D. Putnam, eds., *Disaffected Democracies: What's Troubling the Trilateral Countries?* (Princeton: Princeton University Press, 2000).

15 See Alan Ware, *Political Parties and Party Systems* (Oxford: Oxford University Press, 1996), pp. 109–10; Thomas Poguntke, "Parties in a Legalistic Culture: The Case of Germany," in Richard S. Katz and Peter Mair, eds., *How Parties Organize: Change and Adaptation in Party Organizations in Western Democracies* (London: Sage, 1994).

16 The names for the sections of the party organization are taken from Peter Mair, "Party Organizations: From Civil Society to the State," in Katz and Mair, *How Parties Organize*, p. 4.

17 Robert Michels, *Political Parties: A Sociological Study of the Oligarchical Tendencies of Modern Democracy* (New York: Free Press, 1962 [1911]).

18 Réjean Pelletier, with François Bundock and Michel Sarra-Bournet, "The Structures of Canadian Political Parties: How They Operate," in Herman Bakvis, ed., *Canadian Political Parties: Leaders, Candidates and Organization*, vol. 13 of the collected research studies for the Royal Commission on Electoral Reform and Party Financing (Toronto: Dundurn, 1991), p. 271.

19 R. Kenneth Carty, *Canadian Political Parties in the Constituencies*, vol. 23 of the collected research studies for the Royal Commission on Electoral Reform and Party Financing (Toronto: Dundurn, 1991); Anthony M. Sayers, *Parties, Candidates,*

and Constituency Campaigns in Canadian Elections (Vancouver: UBC Press, 1999).

20 Pippa Norris, "Legislative Recruitment," in LeDuc, Niemi, and Norris, *Comparing Democracies*, p. 199.

21 Note, however, that the president is not directly elected by the voters; he (someday she) is chosen by the Electoral College, made up of delegates from the various states.

22 Richard S. Katz, "Party Organization as an Empty Vessel: Parties in American Politics," in Katz and Mair, *How Parties Organize*, pp. 28–29.

23 Rand Dyck, "Links between Federal and Provincial Parties and Party Systems," in Herman Bakvis, ed., *Representation, Integration, and Political Parties in Canada*, vol. 14 of the collected research studies for the Royal Commission on Electoral Reform and Party Financing (Toronto: Dundurn, 1991), pp. 129–32.

24 Dyck, p. 155.

25 William M. Chandler, "Federalism and Political Parties," in Herman Bakvis and William M. Chandler, eds., *Federalism and the Role of the State* (Toronto: University of Toronto Press, 1987), p. 160.

26 Dyck, pp. 138–39.

27 Alan C. Cairns, "The Electoral System and the Party System in Canada, 1921–1965," in Douglas E. Williams, ed., *Constitution, Government, and Society in Canada: Selected Essays by Alan C. Cairns* (Toronto: McClelland and Stewart, 1988), pp. 111–38.

28 Comparative data concerning public support for parties can be found in LeDuc, Niemi, and Norris, "Introduction: The Present and Future of Democratic Elections," in LeDuc, Niemi, and Norris, *Comparing Democracies*, Table 1.5.

29 Maor, *Political Parties and Party Systems*, pp. 110–13.

30 Canada Elections Act, 48–49 Elizabeth II, c. 9, s. 464–70.

31 John Laschinger and Geoffrey Stevens, *Leaders and Lesser Mortals: Backroom Politics in Canada* (Toronto: Key Porter, 1992), pp. 146–48.

32 Mair, "Party Organizations: From Civil Society to the State," p. 4.

33 Mair, "Party Systems and Structures of Competition," in LeDuc, Niemi, and Norris, *Comparing Democracies*, p. 90.

34 Otto Kirchheimer, "The Transformation of the Western European Party Systems," in Joseph LaPalombara and Myron Weiner, eds., *Political Parties and Political Development* (Princeton: Princeton University Press, 1966).

35 Russell J. Dalton, "Political Cleavages, Issues, and Electoral Change," in LeDuc, Niemi, and Norris, *Comparing Democracies*, p. 325.

36 A. Brian Tanguay, "Canadian Party Ideologies in the Electronic Age," in Alain Gagnon and James P. Bickerton, eds., *Canadian Politics: An Introduction to the Discipline* (Peterborough: Broadview, 1990), p. 134.

37 See Keith Archer and Alan Whitehorn, "Opinion Structure Among Party Activists: A Comparison of New Democrats, Liberals and Conservatives," in Hugh Thorburn and Alan Whitehorn, eds., *Party Politics in Canada*, 8th ed. (Toronto: Prentice-Hall, 2001).

38 Sidney Tarrow, "Mad Cows and Social Activists: Contentious Politics in the Trilateral Democracies," in Pharr and Putnam, *Disaffected Democracies*, pp. 270–71.

39 Mair, "Party Organizations: From Civil Society to the State," p. 19.

Chapter 12

Democracy in Action: Elections, Referendums, and Citizens' Power

Brenda O'Neill

CHAPTER OBJECTIVES

After you have completed this chapter, you should be able to
- describe the difference between direct democracy and representative democracy
- describe the functions of elections
- compare plurality, majoritarian, and proportional representation electoral systems
- explain why voters vote the way they do
- describe the many forms of political participation and explain what influences the decision to participate in politics
- explain the use of tools of direct democracy for increasing citizens' political power.

POPULAR PERCEPTIONS OF DEMOCRACY

Press coverage of the March 2002 elections in Zimbabwe was fairly unanimous in condemning its outcome. Elections are meant to be a key mechanism for granting citizens a measure of power in democracies. The United States denounced the elections in Zimbabwe for being "fundamentally flawed" and lacking in "democratic legitimacy." Similarly, Britain decried President Mugabe's "systematic campaign of violence and intimidation." In the end, Zimbabwe was suspended for a year from Commonwealth meetings for the manner in which its elections were conducted. But how many of us know what criteria make for democratic elections that are acceptable to the international community? Why were Zimbabwe's elections so roundly condemned? And why is democracy valued so highly?

This chapter hopes to help answer these questions and more. Many of us employ the word *democracy* in everyday conversation, but the term is often ill defined or misunderstood. Few citizens in Western states are fully aware of the underlying assumptions, goals, and mechanisms required for the successful adoption and implementation of democracy.

Although there exist many academic definitions, most agree that democracy is something close to "the rule of the people." The main principle is that political power should originate with the people rather than with those who rule. Modern democracy argues that the government's authority rests on the free and fair participation of all who are subject to its rule. Zimbabwe's elections were criticized for failing to meet the "free and fair" criteria on a number of counts.

Western states and their citizens rarely challenge the normative superiority of democracies. Democracy is without question the *best* form of government. Unlike authoritarian systems, democracies provide opportunities for citizens to make decisions about the state, its citizens, and its relationship with other states, because ultimately those very citizens will have to live with the consequences of those decisions. Citizens, that is, are politically powerful. Citizen participation is assumed to lead to *better* decisions than any alternative system.

The study of politics requires us to challenge popular perceptions in an effort to better understand the use and distribution of political power. Important questions include: What are the requirements of a democratic political system? Do democracies actually provide citizens with such opportunities? Are modern democracies successful? Answering such questions requires a basic understanding of the structures, procedures, and requirements adopted by modern democratic states in an attempt to meet the "democratic ideal." It is not an ideal that is easily met by those regimes that have only recently adopted the democratic system—sometimes called fledgling democracies. But more established democracies, while undoubtedly more successful at the democratic challenge, are not without their own weaknesses. Few offer many opportunities for direct rule. Citizens get to vote in regular elections to select representatives in a number of legislative and executive bodies. Citizens might have an opportunity to vote in referendums on whether or not they support particular pieces of legislation or constitutional changes. They may also be given the opportunity to initiate their own pieces of legislation. But most democratic opportunities provide little in the way of direct control over the day-to-day workings of the state. Instead of citizen rule, we have something closer to citizen choice over who will rule. For some, this is an unacceptable alternative. For others, the opportunities afforded by democracies

for decision-making are quite acceptable. One goal in this chapter is to explore the bases for such contradictory conclusions.

CITIZEN POWER

In a majority of the world's states, citizens are granted a measure of power to make public decisions. The ideal of democratic governance is to ensure that citizens "enjoy an equal ability to participate meaningfully in the decisions that closely affect their common lives as individuals in communities."[1] In other words, democracy advocates that the ultimate source of political power is the people, and that the best method for deciding upon questions that affect the community is to allow its members to debate alternatives freely and openly and to select the option that receives support from more than half of those affected.

The ideal of democratic governance, however, is rarely met. Modern democracies provide citizens with only an indirect ability to influence public decisions, and not all citizens enjoy equal ability to participate effectively in politics. The lack of formal restrictions on participation is very different from the existence of equal means and skills for participation purposes. What sets democracies apart is the belief that vesting political power in citizens is a laudable goal.

In the fifth century B.C. in the city-state of Athens in ancient Greece, citizens were more intimately involved in the day-to-day decision-making required for the community.[2] Given a marked commitment to civic virtue, politics played a part in everyday life. In this version of democracy, called **direct democracy**, citizen power came from participation in popular assemblies—the equivalent of modern-day legislatures. Citizens, not politicians, were responsible for making key political decisions. Consensus was preferred, but the support of a majority of those assembled could also decide on the alternatives. A key difference from today's legislatures is that *all* citizens were meant to participate in these assemblies, not only a smaller number of elected representatives. Democracy, rule of the people, was direct: the people sitting in the assemblies debated and ruled on community questions. And the debate that took place in these assemblies was crucial; if citizens were made aware of alternatives, were allowed to voice their own concerns, and could hear the concerns of others, the outcome of the deliberation was believed to be *better* than those potentially offered by some smaller select group of individuals.

> **Definition**
>
> **DIRECT DEMOCRACY:** A political system in which citizens hold power directly rather than through elected or appointed representatives.

Before concluding that this is a system on which to pattern modern democracy, make note of the fact that the ability to meet in assembly requires a limited number of citizens. Gathering thousands of people together anywhere to debate and render decisions is unlikely to be easy or successful; indeed, think about how hard it is to get a group of friends to agree on which restaurant to choose for a dinner out. Direct democracy in ancient Greece worked because the city-state was small (an average of 2000 to 3000 of the approximately 50 000 citizens would attend an assembly) and citizenship was not extended to slaves, women, and children. These exclusions effectively meant that the men sitting in these assemblies constituted a minority of the population. This minority imposed its will on the majority. It also worked because slavery provided Athenian citizens with plenty of free time. While this application of direct democracy is likely to leave us uncomfortable, the ideal of all citizens having an equal and direct say in public decisions remains an important standard by which to judge modern democracies.

Few modern democracies are able to employ the model of direct democracy of ancient Greece. Indeed, even among ancient political systems, the Athenian model was atypical. Democracy has evolved in response to the requirements of modern living, and representative assemblies have replaced Athenian popular assemblies as a compromise. Instead of making public decisions directly on a regular basis, citizens vote for individuals who will act as their representatives in these assemblies.

Representative democracies retain the important deliberative element of earlier assemblies—decision-makers must be able to gather and debate options before coming to any conclusions—but not the popular basis for filling these assemblies. The considerable time requirement imposed by politics on Athenian citizens is made today only of citizens who choose to stand for public office. The compromise works, however, only if representatives are conscious of the needs, desires, and concerns of the people they are elected to represent; that is, citizens are powerful only if their representatives act in ways that correspond with the desires of the represented. Most modern democracies attempt to ensure this consciousness by requiring periodic elections. Elections mean that representatives must present themselves regularly before those who selected them to defend their actions and to receive the privilege of continuing on in their role. What is often overlooked in this process is each citizen's responsibility in this compromise. To keep modern democracies from degenerating into elite rule, citizens must stay informed, active, and committed to the public project to ensure the accountability of elected representatives. Thus elections assume a crucial role in the maintenance of modern democracies. According to Schumpeter, democracy is the "competitive struggle for the people's vote."[3] Because elections have degenerated to a degree into negative ad campaigns, leader image contests, and fundraising competitions, many challenge the degree to which the democratic ideal is currently being met in modern democracies. Indeed, in the Athenian system, appointment to offices and executives occurred by lot, in an effort to avoid the problems that accompanied direct election.

> **Definition**
>
> **REPRESENTATIVE DEMOCRACY:** A political system in which citizens hold power indirectly by selecting representatives who render public decisions on their behalf in popular assemblies.

Technological innovation provides the potential for allowing modern democracies to incorporate the popular participation found in direct democracy and perhaps to counter the excesses of elections. E-democracy and **digital democracy** have been championed by many who consider communications technology the perfect vehicle for allowing citizens to regain some of the direct political power lost under representative systems. One estimate suggests that, as of February 2002, over 500 million users around the world were connected to the Internet.[4] Given the ease of access to and the wealth of information available on the Internet, this medium provides the potential for citizens to become proactive democratic participants. Citizens can be tremendously empowered by communicating directly and instantly with each other, with elected representatives, and with the government. Wisconsin's state assembly and Belgium's parliament are already wired.[5] The protests surrounding the 2001 Summit of the Americas in Quebec City were organized in part through the Internet; using discussion lists and e-mail, organizers were able to communicate with potential protesters at the click of a button and were able to organize the protest at relatively little cost.[6] Another option rests in the possibility for completing political transactions online, for example by televoting. In one experiment in the Arizona Democratic primary in March of 2000, 4000 people voted online, a 600 percent increase in total turnout over the election of 1996.[7] Similar experiments have been conducted in a number of party leadership races in Canada.[8] Technological innovation provides the potential for getting many more citizens to discuss, get information about, and participate in politics.

Definition

DIGITAL DEMOCRACY: A broad term meant to encompass the application of technological innovations to politics and political participation; also called e-democracy or e-politics.

The potential that exists in digital democracy is mitigated, however, by a number of difficulties. Televoting experiments have had their share of technological problems: lost PINs (personal identification numbers), computer incompatibilities, site crashes, software glitches, and security breaches. Such concerns are at least as troubling as the problems encountered with the traditional technology of the "butterfly ballot" employed in the 2000 American elections. The ballot used in Palm Beach, Florida, had two vertical columns listing candidates and parties (resembling the wings of the butterfly), and voters punched a hole in the centre to indicate their preference. Unfortunately, the holes were not well aligned with the party and candidate names, and the resulting confusion probably cost the Democrats enough votes to lose the presidency.

Yet there are bigger issues than simply getting the systems to work properly and securely. There is a "dig-ital divide," that is, a vast gulf separating the rich and the poor with respect to accessing this technology. Remember for a moment that the democratic ideal is to allow citizens *equal ability* to participate meaningfully in public decision-making. There is little doubt that if democracy embraces technology, a number of citizens will be left behind. Democracies such as Norway, the United States, Sweden, and Canada boast that over 40 percent of their populations have Internet access in the home.[9] Read differently, that means that about 60 percent do not. And those without access are disproportionately made up of the poor, the uneducated and illiterate, and ethnic minorities. Estimates suggest that the Middle East and Africa make up less than 2 percent of those having access to the Internet.[10] Unequal access translates into unequal ability. Greater access, however, is not enough to breach the divide. Broadband access in every city may provide greater access, but it cannot guarantee ability—citizens must possess the requisite skills to employ this technology successfully. If this fact is overlooked, our democracies might eventually consist of two groups: the powerful and the increasingly powerless. As some point out, however, this would not be very different from the current state of affairs.

One difficulty with which modern democracies grapple is the conflicting desire to increase citizen power while at the same time ensuring that those very citizens respect the rights and obligations of others.[11] Historically, majorities have sometimes voted to remove the freedoms of minorities. While citizens in modern democracies are quick to assert the rights owed them by virtue of their citizenship, fewer acknowledge the obligations that come from being a member of a larger community, especially the obligations for greater responsibility for public decision-making. Increasing citizens' political power could result in greater rates of participation, but only if the citizens have both the capacity and the desire to participate. Creating civic capacity by increasing skills and means is partly the responsibility of government, and governments could increase the desire to participate if political systems, structures, and processes were modified to create more effective citizen power. Technology may well provide one potential mechanism for increasing this power.

A further challenge for modern democracy is globalization.[12] Globalization has served to erode state sovereignty in such a way that modern democratic institutions may no longer be effective. If important political decisions are being made by nongovernmental organizations (NGOs) or by international political organizations, rather than by democratically elected governments, then increasing citizen political power might ultimately be in vain. Democracy is meant to provide a mechanism by which a community can render decisions on how it will be governed. If institutions and groups outside the community are making such decisions, then existing democratic structures are inadequate.

ELECTIONS

Without question, one of the key democratic instruments is the **election**. Elections are the primary mechanism through which citizens in democratic states participate in the political system. And in terms of citizen power, citizen political decision-making takes place mainly through elections. Elections can provide much information about the condition of democracy in a country. When Canadians went to the polls in the 2000 general election, only 61.2 percent of registered voters bothered to take advantage of their civic right (see Figure 12.1).[13] The turnout rate has been declining in Canada, and many take this to indicate that Canadians are dissatisfied with—rather than merely apathetic about—their governments, politics, and democracy.

> *Definition*
>
> **ELECTION:** A mechanism by which the expressed preferences of citizens in democratic states are aggregated into a decision regarding who will govern.

Elections provide the prime mechanism in representative democracies for holding governments accountable. Governments are made up of representatives belonging to various political parties who are often selected on the basis of territory. Voters are provided an opportunity for retrospective evaluation—they can render a decision on whether or not they believe that the government has done a good job while in office and whether it should be returned to power. At the same time, voters have an opportunity to assess the alternative parties and their platforms to see whether another party might not deserve a shot at governing based on the platform that it put forward. Elections also occur within a reasonable time frame to ensure that representatives

Figure 12.1 Turnout in Federal Elections, 1968–2000

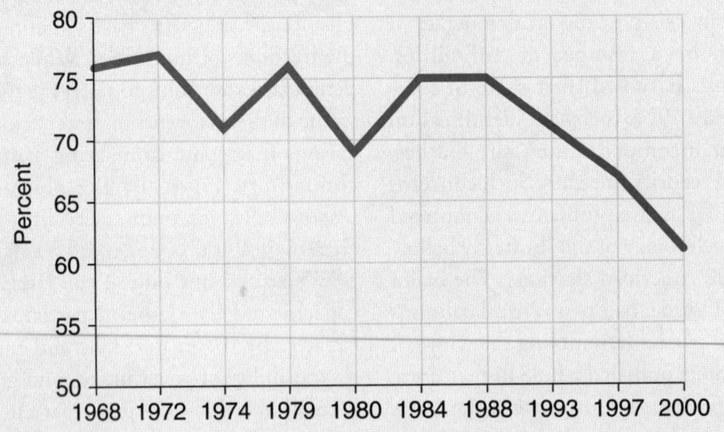
80
75
70
65
60
55
50
Percent
1968 1972 1974 1979 1980 1984 1988 1993 1997 2000

Source: CRIC, *Voter Participation in Canada*, CRIC Paper No. 3, October 2001. Available online at www.cric.ca. Reprinted by permission of the Centre for Research and Information on Canada (CRIC).

and governments are continually reminded of the need to "face the voters." Competitive (or effective) elections, then, determine—either directly or indirectly—the composition of the government and attempt to ensure government accountability to citizens.[14]

Competitive elections can perhaps be better understood by examining what they should be like.[15] Elections should not restrict citizens' right to vote—called the **franchise**—unnecessarily, and most modern democracies have relatively few limitations on the franchise. The removal of property qualifications, the extension of the right to vote to women and Aboriginal people, and the lowering of the voting age greatly increased the number of voters in Canada. Free and fair elections require at the very least that political parties be relatively free to assemble and put forward candidates (see Table 12.1). Citizens must be presented with alternatives at elections; if they are not, the process is

---

Table 12.1   Criteria of Free and Fair Elections

	Free	**Fair**
Campaign Period	• freedom of expression • freedom of assembly • freedom of association • universal suffrage • right to stand for office	• transparent election process • equality of political parties and groups • equal access to public media by parties, candidates • impartial, independent electoral commission • no impediments to voter registration • equal access to party information by voters
Election Day	• opportunity to vote • secret ballot • absence of intimidation of voters • accessible polling stations	• access to polling stations for party representatives, media, and election observers • impartial ballots • tamper-resistant ballot boxes • effective and transparent ballot counting procedures • effective and transparent procedures for determining invalid ballots • security measures for the transportation of ballot boxes • protection of polling stations
After Election Day	• ability to legally contest election results	• impartial and prompt treatment of election complaints • official and timely announcement of election results • unbiased media reporting of results • acceptance of results by all involved • installation in office of winners of the election

Source: Adapted from Richard Rose, ed., *The International Encyclopedia of Elections* (Washington, D.C.: CQ Press, 2000), p. 133. Reprinted by permission of CQ Press.

A demonstrator dressed as Uncle Sam holds up a sign rejecting Governor George W. Bush as president during a rally in support of Vice President Al Gore in Tallahassee, Florida, on Wednesday, December 13, 2000.

Dave Martin/CP Picture Archive

devoid of meaning. Not all groups, however, are given the freedom to associate and contest elections. In the Federal Republic of Germany, for example, "parties which, by reason of their aims or the behaviour of their adherents, seek to impair or destroy the free democratic basic order or to endanger the existence of the Federal Republic of Germany" are deemed unconstitutional, with the Federal Constitutional Court having the ultimate authority to decide on the question of unconstitutionality.[16] German history makes it clear why such restrictions are in place.

Definition
FRANCHISE: The right to vote in public elections.

Intimidation, violence, threats, and bribes should occur neither during election campaigns nor at the polls. The use of the secret ballot was adopted in part to curtail such practices. Finally, the administration of elections should be fair; the counting and reporting of votes cast, for example, should occur in an honest, fair, and consistent manner. The recent election ballot reform adopted in Florida came in response to the difficulties encountered in the 2000 presidential election. Optical scan ballots have replaced the butterfly ballot punch card system in the hope of preventing a repeat of that fiasco; counting votes fairly should not require that individual vote counters attempt to "guess" voter intent according to the depth of a dimpled chad on a punch card.

What are the effects of competitive elections, and what exactly do elections do?[17] There are two contradictory views on the main function of elections in competitive democracies. The first, called the bottom-up view, suggests that elections are mechanisms for allowing citizens to select their governments, to influence public policies, and to be represented. The alternative top-down view emphasizes the controlling elements of elections. Competitive elections provide mechanisms for governments to control the democratic process—by focusing dissent, by limiting political participation primarily to elections, and by legitimizing a system in which citizens have little effective power. Most people accept a middle ground between these two positions; elections provide opportunities for exchange between governments and citizens. This conclusion sets the stage for assessing how well elections perform their purported functions.

A key function of elections is to decide who will govern. In many liberal democracies, however, this is true only to a degree. Elections normally allow citizens to choose members of the legislature, but legislatures rarely govern (the American Congress being an exception). The formation of a government in parliamentary systems results from bargaining among the parties represented in the legislature or from some long-standing convention rather than from direct election. More importantly, perhaps, parliamentary governments can change between elections. A majority of presidential systems, on the other hand, allow for direct election of the president.[18] Yet the American president, contrary to popular belief, is not directly elected. When American voters cast a vote for president, they are actually voting for a slate of electors called the Electoral College; these electors pledge to vote for the winning candidate in their state when they formally elect the president roughly a month later. Electoral College votes are distributed on a state-by-state basis, equal to the number of members sent from the state to the two houses of Congress, making them roughly proportional to each state's population. Because most states' college electors vote as a block, it is possible for the college to elect a candidate who lost the nationwide popular vote, as was the case in the 2000 American presidential election: Al Gore won 48.4 percent of the popular vote but only 267 of the 537 Electoral College votes. George W. Bush, on the other hand, won only 47.9 percent of the popular vote but captured 271 Electoral College votes to win the presidency.[19] Finally, the public service, courts, and military play an important role in helping the executive to govern, although executive appointment rather than election is normally the rule employed to fill the vast majority of these positions. Accordingly, "competitive elections play an important part in government formation but the relationship is less tight, less strict than many people imagine."[20]

Elections are also mechanisms designed to ensure government accountability. This claim may seem suspect, given the fact that elections do not always directly determine the government. They can, however, force a change in government, particularly if the people are especially unhappy with decisions made during the government's tenure and if a clear alternative party exists. Democratic governments understand that at some point they must face the electorate, a knowledge that can constrain their behaviour to some degree. It cannot guarantee, however, that all government decisions will be popular: the Mulroney government, for example, imposed the Goods and Services Tax (GST) despite widespread public hostility.

Elections allow citizens to choose their political representatives; they necessarily determine who serves as the representative or representatives of individual territorial districts. But the concept of representation is a difficult one to pin down. What does it mean to represent others politically? One common interpretation emphasizes three styles of electoral representation: trustee, party, and constituency.[21] The trustee model emphasizes that

although representatives take the interests and concerns of their electors into account, decisions are ultimately made according to the representative's own judgment. Citizens should, the argument goes, trust their judgment. Such an argument might seem immediately unacceptable, but democracy emphasizes the importance of debate and the articulation of alternative viewpoints for political decision-making—and this is exactly what is supposed to take place in the legislature. Few ordinary citizens have the information, expertise, and awareness of consequences that would allow them to render reasonable judgments on many current political questions.

The party model, on the other hand, emphasizes that legislators are chosen on the basis of their party membership—very few independents ever get elected—and as a result their responsibility is to support the party position in the legislature. This argument focuses on the fact that many people vote according to party rather than individual candidate; once elected, legislators should be bound to support that party's platform. Such an argument is often heard in Canada to criticize MPs who "cross the floor" to join another political party or to sit as independents.

Finally, the constituency model emphasizes the role that representatives play in supporting the interests of their constituents by helping them to deal with the large government bureaucracy, promoting government spending in the constituency, and in some cases, generating employment opportunities. For many Canadian backbench MPs, this casework can take up a significant portion of their time.

Elections are also the mechanism through which governments are granted a measure of **legitimacy**. As a key element of democratic systems, fair and free elections provide a chance for citizens to participate in politics and to decide who will hold political power. With this opportunity, however, comes the expectation that the people will comply with government decisions. The opportunity to choose the rulers in a fair and legitimate manner obliges citizens to obey the decisions of that popularly elected government. The legitimacy of the electoral process provides the government with political authority, but an obligation to obey does not remove the right to political dissent and the opportunity to change such policies.

Elections are also meant to provide governments with a specific policy mandate for their tenure in office.

Understanding the nature of elections provides insight into why this function is rarely fulfilled. Political parties offer specific campaign platforms, filled with a number of policy prescriptions. One might, then, conclude that the winning party has been given a vote of support for its specific policy proposals. In order for this to occur, however, voters must be voting for the party *because* of its specific policy positions and for no other reason, which is not often the case. It must also be true that a majority of the electorate support the party and its platform; this, too, is not always the case. Although Brian Mulroney claimed that the election of the Progressive Conservative Party in 1988 indicated that Canadians wished to go forward with the Canada–U.S. Free Trade Agreement, he failed to mention that the party had won only 43 percent of the popular vote. One cannot make the claim that elections determine public policy if more people vote against than for the positions ultimately adopted. In addition, once parties have formed the government, they can drop key elements of their electoral platforms without major repercussions. This seriously weakens the argument that elections shape public policy. In 1993, the Liberals promised in their Red Book to replace the GST upon assuming office. However, only cabinet minister Sheila Copps was inconvenienced by the failure of the party to meet its promise: she resigned in principle over the issue, only to be re-elected in a by-election soon afterward.

Finally, elections provide opportunities for political education, mobilization, and socialization. Elections allow for the political education of both voters and members of political parties. Voters can learn about political campaigns, candidates and party leaders, and the major issues facing the government. Parties and candidates have an opportunity to find out what the people are thinking and also to shape their opinions. Such education can provide an incentive for people to get out and vote and possibly become politically involved in additional ways. Elections can also socialize citizens regarding the requirements of democracy and the importance assigned to politics within a particular country. If such learning is to occur, however, citizens must already be interested enough in politics to pay attention to the media coverage of campaigns. The most recent Canadian election study reveals that on a scale of 0 (not at all interested) to 10 (extremely interested), Canadians possess an average interest of 5.4 for politics in general. This average jumps to 6.3, however, when asked more specifically about their interest in the federal election.[22]

ELECTIONS AND THE MEDIA

Any discussion of elections in modern democracies must address the role played by the **mass media**. Television, radio, and newspapers provide an important source of information for voters, a point that is not lost on politicians and campaign managers. On the one hand, more often than not, the media present the electoral contest as a "horserace." The focus is on which party and leader are ahead on any particular day, rather than on more substantive policy issues or the parties' platforms. This sensational treatment makes for entertaining reading; it does little, however, to advance the political education of voters or the message that politics and elections are more than contests. On the other hand, parties and candidates, especially party leaders, have learned to speak in sound bites, since the media like answers in the form of 10-second clips. Not all political questions, however, can be reasonably answered in so short a time period.

Definition

MASS MEDIA: The methods of communication, such as television, radio, and newspapers, designed to reach large numbers of people.

This focus on style, often over substance, leads politicians to hire professional image consultants and speech specialists. The transformation of Preston Manning during his tenure as leader of the Reform Party in Canada suggests the importance assigned to image: a change from glasses to contact lenses, a change in hairstyle (and colour?), a serious overhaul of his wardrobe, and voice lessons. Selecting the proper media image is not always easy. Most political analysts agreed that the support generated for selecting Stockwell Day as leader of the newly formed Canadian Alliance in 2000 was his younger, more energetic image. But his decision to ride in on a personal watercraft wearing a wetsuit for his first media interview after his election to the House of Commons went over about as well as a wet balloon.

Tighter regulation might be the solution to ensuring more realistic, informative, and substance-driven media coverage of politics, but the media's portrayal of politics and politicians would be extremely difficult to control. Although there exist public broadcasters (CBC Radio and Television in Canada, for example), much of the industry is dominated by commercial (private) broadcasters and publishers, whose bottom line is either circulation numbers or size of the audience. Selling papers or attracting that audience would prove difficult if the media were forced to provide in-depth and substantial coverage of politics and elections. And while regulation might prove successful in altering coverage, the cost to political freedom, namely freedom of expression, would certainly prove to be too high.

A further concern is the growing concentration of mass media ownership and its increased commercialization. Giants such as AOL Time Warner and Viacom increasingly dominate all forms of mass communication, driven by a set of values that is not always in line with journalistic ones.[23] The rise in commercialization has meant a simultaneous decrease in the importance of public broadcasting based on a greater sense of public

purpose and responsibility. Public broadcasters offer more current affairs and political news programs than commercial broadcasters; public broadcasters, then, help to produce a politically informed and aware citizenry. Increased concentration also raises concerns about the responsiveness of media empires to local political concerns and issues, as exemplified by concerns in Canada over CanWest Global's decisions to adopt common editorials for various newspapers across the country and to refocus journalists' stories that were at odds with the views of the owners.

ELECTORAL SYSTEMS

In each country, the conduct of elections is governed by a set of rules and regulations. These rules and regulations cover a number of elements within elections: the offices that will be filled by the election; requirements for candidates and parties that wish to run in the contest; voting eligibility requirements; regulations concerning the drawing of electoral boundaries; and even the requirements for the ballot, such as the order of candidates' names.

BOX 12.1

HOW THE CANADIAN ELECTORAL SYSTEM DISCOURAGES WOMEN'S PARTICIPATION

The Royal Commission on Electoral Reform and Party Financing reported in 1991 on its findings concerning the principles and processes governing elections to the House of Commons. In setting out the objectives of Canadian electoral democracy, the study suggested that one objective must be to ensure equitable access to candidacy. And while few formal restrictions exist, the commission noted that women have been greatly underrepresented among those running as candidates for and those elected to the House. It highlighted that in 1988 women made up only 19 percent of candidates and only 13 percent of those elected. This virtual exclusion of women, it argued, was no longer acceptable. According to the report,

It is not merely a matter of political symbolism; elected representatives will not and cannot effectively represent the full range of Canada's interests if they do not reasonably reflect its society. To this extent, the electoral system fails to secure the best persons to sit in the House of Commons (p. 8).

Two of the key barriers for women's entry into the House of Commons are the nomination process and the inattention of political parties. The nomination process presents a particular financial barrier to women, whose earnings continue to be less than those of men. First, women are more likely to find themselves in expensive contested nominations rather than in acclamations to run as the party's candidate. And second, they receive fewer and smaller donations than men, in part due to their different social and professional contacts.

To deal with these problems, the report recommended the imposition of spending limits on nomination contest campaigns and the issuing of tax receipts to those who donate money toward nomination contests. The report also highlighted the role played by political parties in increasing the representation of women in the House. Although it noted that the major parties at the federal level had measures designed to assist prospective women candidates (especially the New Democratic Party), progress had been slow. Women continued to be underrepresented in "safe" ridings, which decreased their chances of getting elected. They also continued to work in "pink-collar" positions within party hierarchies (for example, as constituency association secretaries),

rarely stepping stones to political office. The report recommended "the by-laws and constitutions of registered political parties require the establishment of formal search committees and commit the parties to processes that demonstrably promote the identification and nomination of broadly representative candidates" (p. 121).

Have we made any progress in the 10 years since the report came out? In the 2000 federal election, women made up 21 percent of all candidates and 21 percent of those elected to the House of Commons. Is this enough? What do you think?

Source: Canada, Royal Commission on Electoral Reform and Party Financing (Lortie Commission), *Final Report*, vol. 1 (Ottawa: Minister of Supply and Services Canada, 1991). Reproduced with permission of the Minister of Public Works and Government Services, 2002, and courtesy of the Privy Council Office.

Key among this set of rules are those surrounding party and election finance. These regulations can cover a number of areas, including the amount and sources of party funds, party and candidate spending, and third-party advertising, a term encompassing spending by organizations other than political parties during elections.[24] The need for financial regulation stems from a concern for equity and fairness among those contesting elections: regulating how money is raised and spent during elections can help to "level the playing field" and to limit the degree to which money influences electoral outcomes and ultimately government decisions. Britain and France, for example, have laws on how political parties can spend money, limiting their ability to use television and radio advertisements during election campaigns.[25] Restricting the ways in which parties can spend money diminishes their need for raising funds, levelling the playing field and reducing candidates' and parties' obligations to those donating the funds.

The government of Manitoba recently brought forward legislation designed to address concerns regarding the perception that money unduly influences politics and elections. This legislation bans contributions from corporations and unions to political parties, limits individual contributions to $3000 per year, limits third-

party spending during election periods to $5000, and reinstates limits on political party advertising during elections. Similar legislation has existed in Quebec since the late 1970s. The National Citizens' Coalition, a right-wing nonprofit organization in Canada, has fought hard against restrictions on third-party election advertising, which it calls "gag laws." On three separate occasions, Alberta courts have agreed with the organization's argument that the rules represent an unreasonable violation of the right of freedom of expression. The challenge is to balance the desire for a level playing field with the desire for ensuring free and open debate during elections.

Another key set of electoral rules governs electoral districting and apportionment, particularly in electoral systems based on territorial representation, such as those of Canada and the United States. *Districting* refers to the drawing of electoral boundaries in order to establish territorial districts or constituencies from which one or more representatives will be sent to the legislature. The manipulation of district boundary lines to advantage a particular group (or to disadvantage another) is referred to as gerrymandering. In an effort to reduce the likelihood of such manipulation, the responsibility for the drawing of electoral boundaries has been placed in the hands of independent bodies, rather than in the hands of the sitting government.

The principle of **representation by population** advocates that electoral districts should be roughly equal in population in order to ensure that individuals receive a proportionate share of representation in government, so that each vote is of equal weight. *Apportionment*—the determination of representative seats according to population—should occur on a regular basis, normally after the taking of a census, in order to account for shifting population bases. The rep by pop principle, however, recognizes that other considerations can come into play in the drawing of boundaries, including a desire to keep the geographic expanse of a district to a manageable size and to ensure that minority groups are not scattered across several districts (which would minimize their electoral influence). In federal states, such as Canada and the United States, the rep by pop principle is adopted for the lower house at the national level but not for the upper house. In the United States, representation in the Senate occurs on a state basis (two representatives per state). In Canada, representation occurs on a more complicated regional basis. In both instances, however, population size is not a consideration in the apportioning of seats to the upper house.

> **Definition**
>
> **REPRESENTATION BY POPULATION:** The principle suggesting that the allocation of seats in assemblies should occur in a manner that encourages an equal division of the population across electoral districts, so that each vote is of equal weight.

The rules employed to translate votes into seats have been the subject of great debate in many countries.[26] New Zealand, Japan, and Italy have recently changed their electoral systems in an attempt to address various concerns. Such changes reflect the importance of electoral systems—these systems set the rules for determining how individual votes are translated into legislative seats. To better understand the importance of rules for outcomes, let us employ an academic analogy. Imagine your response if a professor decided to change the format of an exam from multiple choice to essay questions one day before you were scheduled to write the exam. Rules (in this example, the format of the exam—multiple choice or essay questions) determine

how you will study for the exam and possibly the grade you will receive. Electoral systems are no different—they shape electoral strategies, electoral outcomes, and voter behaviour. Because of this, students of politics require a basic understanding of the various electoral systems in use in today's democracies.

One common method for distinguishing electoral systems focuses on the electoral formula employed, that is, the rule for determining how many votes are required to earn a seat. Two main types of electoral systems based on an electoral formula are proportional and nonproportional systems (see Table 12.2). The nonproportional type includes the electoral system most familiar to North Americans: the plurality system. The requirement for winning in a plurality system is to earn more votes than any other candidate—hence its more common name, **first-past-the-post (FPP)**. In elections to the Canadian House of Commons, for example, the country is divided into single-member districts: one representative is selected from each territorially defined district. A number of political parties nominate a single candidate to run in each district, and since the winner needs to earn only more votes than the other candidates, it is usually the case that he or she does not earn a majority of the votes cast. The cumulative effect of this "wasting of votes" can lead to serious distortions in the vote share to seat share ratio at the national level. Such distortions have led to demands to change Canada's electoral system, a concern that will be returned to below. Since the governing parties often achieve power as a direct result of this distortion, however, one can understand why they might be hesitant to change the system. The failure to address these demands in recent years has undoubtedly increased the level of cynicism and lack of deference that Canadians exhibit toward their political institutions.

> **Definition**
>
> **FIRST-PAST-THE-POST (FPP):** An electoral system that requires the winning candidate to receive more votes than any other in order to win the seat—that is, to receive a plurality of votes. The majority of first-past-the-post systems employ single-member electoral districts.

An additional but less common nonproportional electoral system is the **majoritarian system**. The distinction between such systems and FPP is that the winning

Table 12.2   Electoral Systems

Nonproportional Systems	Proportional Systems (All in Multimember Districts)
a) Plurality (First-Past-the-Post [FPP]) Candidate who wins more votes than any other (i.e., wins the plurality of votes) is awarded the seat. This method is used most often in combination with single-member districts. Examples: Canada (House of Commons); United States (House of Representatives).	**a) List System** Seats are awarded to parties that meet or exceed an electoral quota. In a closed-list system, voters choose a party, and candidates from that party's list are elected in the order they appear on the list. In an open-list system, voters can select specific candidates from the available party lists. Examples: Israel; Switzerland.
b) Majority Candidate must win a majority of votes (50 percent + 1) in order to win the seat. Majority is achieved by employing one of three methods: *Runoff:* Second ballot lists only the top two candidates from the first ballot round. This method is used most often in combination with single-member districts. Example: French presidential elections. *Plurality:* Second ballot is also employed, but winner needs to obtain only a plurality of votes. There is no significant reduction in the number of candidates on the second ballot, although a threshold may be imposed. Example: French legislative elections. *Alternative:* Single election occurs, but voters rank the candidates in order of preference. Winner must obtain a majority of first preferences. If no candidate earns a majority of first preferences, the second preferences of the last-place candidate are transferred to the remaining candidates until one candidate achieves a majority. Example: Australia (House of Representatives).	**b) Single Transferable Vote (STV)** Voters rank their candidate choices across parties. Candidates meeting a quota are awarded a seat. Initial counting looks at first preferences only; any candidate meeting the quota is elected. Second preferences of any surplus votes (in excess of the quota) are then transferred to any remaining candidates. Again, the candidates who meet the quota after the second preferences have been transferred are elected. If seats are still vacant, the weakest candidate is eliminated and the second preferences from those ballots are allocated to the remaining candidates until the quota is met and all seats are allocated. Examples: Ireland; Australia (Senate). **Mixed Systems** Such systems combine elements of nonproportional and proportional electoral systems. The mixed member proportional (MPP) system is an example. Voters have two votes: one for the constituency representative and a second for a party. A share of seats are allocated through single-member districts, while the remaining seats are allocated in order to bring each party's seat share in line with the party's popular vote share. Examples: Germany (Bundestag); New Zealand.

Source: Adapted from André Blais and Louis Massicotte, "Electoral Systems," in Lawrence LeDuc, Richard G. Niemi, and Pippa Norris, eds., *Comparing Democracies: Elections and Voting in Global Perspective* (Thousand Oaks: Sage, 1996). Reprinted by permission of Sage Publications, Inc.

candidate is required to earn a majority of votes in order to be declared the winner (a majority being 50 percent plus 1). This requirement often means that one election will not produce a winner, since elections normally involve more than two candidates. As a result, majoritarian systems employ one of three mechanisms for producing a winner. The majority runoff requires that a second election be held after the first but that the second ballot include only the top two finishers in the first race. In majority plurality systems, the winner in the second election is required to achieve only a plurality of votes on the second ballot. The alternative vote system, on the other hand, requires only one election: voters are asked to rank the candidates listed on the ballot in order of preference, and the winner is the candidate earning a majority of first preferences. If no such majority is achieved, the second preferences of the candidate with the fewest number of first preferences are then transferred to the remaining candidates. If a majority is still not achieved, the process continues until transferred preferences provide a majority.

Definition

MAJORITARIAN SYSTEM: An electoral system that requires the winning candidate to receive a majority of votes to win the seat. The majority is normally achieved through a second ballot or by an alternative voting system.

Proportional representation (PR) systems use a different measure for determining seat allocation; the priority lies in awarding seats to parties in rough proportion to the share of votes earned rather than in awarding the seat to a single candidate from each district. All PR systems use multimember districts because it is impossible to divide a single seat among several candidates. The higher the number of members elected per district (that is, the bigger the district magnitude), the more proportional the system is likely to be. In Israel, the entire country serves as a single constituency, allowing for a large degree of proportionality in seat allocation. Most PR systems use a **list system** that requires voters to choose from among the complete lists of candidates prepared by the parties. In a closed-list system, candidates are elected according to their order on that list. An open-list system allows voters to choose specific candidates from among the

party lists, thereby weakening the power of the party officials who create the list.

Definition

PROPORTIONAL REPRESENTATION (PR): An electoral system that attempts to award seats to parties in proportion to the share of votes earned. Such systems must be combined with multimember constituencies.

Definition

LIST SYSTEM: The most commonly adopted form of proportional representation, employing relatively large electoral districts and a ballot that requires voters to choose from among party lists or candidates on party lists.

The procedure employed for allocating seats in proportional systems varies, but it normally involves dividing the number of votes cast for the party by a quota or divisor. Seats are allocated to the parties according to the resulting figure. The end result is that the "cost" for each seat (in terms of votes) is roughly equal. Some PR systems also adopt thresholds that deny seats to parties that receive very small shares of the vote, normally around 5 to 6 percent of the vote share. The argument for adopting thresholds is that it keeps extremist parties from gaining a measure of legitimacy, at least that afforded by a legislative seat. Such thresholds necessarily introduce distortion in the seat-to-vote ratio, however, a criticism often aimed at nonproportional systems.

An alternative to the list system is the single transferable vote (STV), which requires voters to rank their candidate preferences on the ballot, in a manner similar to the method employed in the alternative vote system. Voters can select from across party lists, which provides them with a greater measure of freedom than some other PR systems. Voters' first preferences are counted, and candidates who meet the required quota gain a seat in the district. Any surplus or remaining votes for these elected candidates are transferred proportionately to the second-preference candidates on the ballot. Second-preference votes are then added to the remaining first-preference votes; the candidates who meet the quota are awarded any remaining seats. If seats remain unallocated at this point, the bottom candidate is eliminated, and the second preferences listed on those ballots are transferred to the remaining candidates. The process continues until all seats are allocated.

Several countries have adopted an electoral system that combines elements of the proportional and non-proportional electoral systems into mixed systems. Japan, for example, elects 300 members of its House of Representatives using a first-past-the-post system combined with single-member constituencies. An additional 200 members are elected from 11 regional multimember constituencies through a PR system.

New Zealand is another country that many are watching closely since it moved from FPP to a mixed member proportional (MMP) system.[27] The 1996 election in New Zealand was the first test of the new system, which was adopted following a series of referendums. The adopted system is modelled on Germany's, and the New Zealand experience is instructive because it mirrors the Canadian debate on the merits of adopting some form of PR. The existence of FPP in combination with the Westminster-style parliamentary system encourages single-party majority governments, in part because of the distortion that occurs in the translation of votes into seats (see Table 12.3 for the distortion in Canada's 2000 federal election). The "unfairness" of this electoral distortion was argued to have fed the increased political cynicism of New Zealand voters, leading to drops in voter turnout. The election of only one representative per district

means that votes for all but the winning candidate are essentially wasted, encouraging voters to support parties that are likely to win, rather than parties that might more closely reflect the voters' ideological positions but that possess relatively little chance of winning the seat. FPP encourages a two-party system, since minor parties whose electoral support is evenly dispersed across constituencies are unlikely to earn a significant number of legislative seats (the Canadian examples are the Progressive Conservatives and the New Democratic Party at the federal level). Minorities, such as New Zealand's Maori population, or particular groups, such as women, have a more difficult time gaining representation under a nonproportional system. This results in a questioning of the overall fairness and representativeness of the assembly elected under such systems.

Such arguments were instrumental for the adoption of electoral reform in New Zealand. The MMP system now in place creates two sets of elected members: those elected under the traditional FPP system in 65 single-member districts and another 55 elected under a PR closed-list system. The 55 members are awarded to the parties in order to "top up" the seat shares awarded by the single-member districts to ensure proportionality of all seats with party vote shares cast under the list system. Since FPP overrewards larger parties, the PR seat allocation corrects this distortion. The adoption of a 5 percent vote threshold for the awarding of seats in the national assembly prevents the proliferation of a high number of small parties. This system was argued to pro-

---

Table 12.3   Distorting Effects of the Canadian Electoral System, 2000

Party	Seats	Seat Share (Percent)	Vote Share (Percent)	Seat-to-Vote (Ratio)
Liberal Party	172	57.10	40.80	1.40
Canadian Alliance	66	21.90	25.50	0.86
Bloc Québécois	38	12.60	10.70	1.18
New Democratic Party	13	4.30	8.50	0.51
Progressive Conservative Party	12	4.00	12.20	0.33
Total Seats	301			

Note: If the seat-to-vote ratio is greater than one, the party has been awarded more seats than it deserved based on its vote share. If the ratio is less than one, the party has been underrewarded.

Source: Elections Canada, "Percentage of Valid Votes, by Political Affiliation"; cited on August 16, 2002; available at http://www.elections.ca/gen/rep/37g/table9_e.html.

vide for a more accurate and thus fairer representation of the vote in the legislature (both women and the Maori population increased their representation under MMP), to maintain direct electoral representation through the 65 district seats, and to increase voter satisfaction and, as a result, turnout (which remained relatively stable in the 1996 election at 79 percent). The greatest concern with the new electoral system appears to be that the selection of government has been removed from the hands of the electors and awarded to parties which enter into negotiation at the conclusion of the election to decide on a governing coalition. It was a full two months following the 1996 New Zealand election before voters knew the composition of the governing coalition. At first polls showed that voters were dissatisfied with the newly adopted MMP electoral reform, but by 2002 they were more supportive.

It is worth noting the debate between those who advocate PR and those who favour maintaining FPP in Canada.[28] Advocates of PR stress that the current system unnecessarily exaggerates electoral regionalism by rewarding parties whose support is concentrated (such as the Bloc Québécois and, to a lesser extent, the Canadian Alliance) and by allowing governing parties to come to power with little or no support from some parts of the country. Perhaps the strongest argument in favour of the adoption of PR lies in the distortions that can occur under FPP. The electoral boost awarded to the leading party can result in majority governments that earned much less than majority support—and even at times less electoral support than other parties. In 1996, the NDP came to power in British Columbia with 52 percent of the seats in the legislature, having earned only 39.45 percent of the popular vote. The British Columbia Liberal Party, on the other hand, formed the official opposition despite having earned 41.82 percent of the popular vote. Similarly, the boost can result in unusual and, many would argue, undesirable results, such as the Liberals' sweep of the New Brunswick legislature in 1987. A number of the arguments voiced in support of a move to PR in New Zealand have been made in Canada as well, including the likelihood of increased representation for minority and other groups and the potential for increased electoral turnout. Proponents of maintaining the current FPP system emphasize, however, the potential difficulties resulting

from the adoption of PR in Canada, including the increased political fragmentation of the party system, the greater likelihood of coalition governments requiring consensus on issues that present the possibility for moving away from campaign promises, weakened government accountability, and the weakening of the traditional MP–constituency relationship. Electoral change seems unlikely, however, since the power to initiate it lies in the hands of the very body that benefits the most from FPP—the executive.

VOTING

If elections are a key element of democratic systems, then without a doubt elections are the primary mechanism for engaging the people in democracies. And without question, the study of voting behaviour and the way voters decide has preoccupied political scientists for quite some time, especially since the advent of public opinion polling in the 1940s.

Why do people vote the way they do? Three theories of voting can be identified that together provide a fairly complete answer to a rather complex question.[29] The first theory, the sociological theory, explains voting by identifying the social forces that determine individual values and beliefs. People make their decisions based on such things as their place of residence, the religious group to which they belong (if any), their ethnic background, their class, their age, and their gender. The social groups based on these characteristics shape their members' interests in ways that are important for the voting decision. Such an explanation takes us only so far, however, as people belong to many groups, often with conflicting interests, and although group memberships are fairly stable, voters often change their vote from one election to another.

The second model, the sociopsychological model, casts a wider net in the search for an explanation of vote decisions. The focus in this model is on the psychological process of voting—on how people come to make their individual choices. The result is a much more complex model of the various factors influencing voters. One group of influences mirrors the social group influences identified in the sociological model. Friends and family, ethnic groups, and social cleavages are likely to shape the interests and values that voters bring to

The NDP performed so poorly in the last British Columbia election that it wondered if Florida-style chads might have helped.

Reprinted with permission from The Globe and Mail

their vote decisions. But more important are the personal and political factors that often occur closer in time to the vote decision itself. Key among these is **party identification**—the long-standing psychological attachment or loyalty to a party that can directly influence where one is likely to draw one's X on the ballot. Party identification acts a filter through which individuals interpret election issues, candidates, parties, and leaders; it can serve as a shortcut in what can be the daunting process of gathering the information necessary to make a rational voting choice. But if the explanation for why a person voted for the Progressive Conservative Party, for example, is "because they always vote that way," the result is that we really have not

explained all that much. Moreover, evidence suggests that the importance of party identification is decreasing; younger and more educated voters are less likely to defer to partisan loyalties at the ballot box.

The third model of voting stresses the actual calculus that voters employ. According to this model, voting is a rational decision rather than one based on social ties or partisan identification. The **rational voting** model assumes that, in deciding how to cast their ballot, voters employ a process of evaluation, involving the important issues in the campaign, their assessment of the candidates and the parties' platforms, and their evaluations of party leaders. This process might compare the alternatives in the search for the right choice or it might simply involve an evaluation of the sitting government in an attempt to determine whether a change is needed. This retrospective element to voting is assumed in campaign slogans that emphasize "a time for change" and helps to explain why voters often punish governments for periods of economic downturn that are at least partly beyond their control. Recent research suggests, however, that campaigns and campaign strategies set the stage for or frame the evaluations that individuals undertake in elections.[30] A party's ability to remain in government is not, then, completely outside its control. An opposition party's ability to become the government is similarly dependent on its ability to shape the electoral agenda. The rational model also helps explain the current preoccupation with party image and the attention directed to leaders.

Definition

RATIONAL VOTING: A model that seeks to explain voting decisions by emphasizing the rational evaluation of alternatives (parties and candidates) and the retrospective assessment of the governing party.

The important part played by **public opinion polling** in modern elections should also not be overlooked.[31] Modern polling techniques allow parties to quickly and accurately gauge public opinion and potential reaction. Such information has implications for the timing of elections, the selection of leaders, and campaign strategies, tactics, and slogans. Published polls can also influence voter behaviour, in deterring them from voting for "lost causes" or in providing them with the information necessary for casting a strategic vote. Their importance in elections is underscored by the adoption of restrictions on the publication of polls at certain times during election campaigns. The degree to which such restrictions unnecessarily restrict freedom of expression continues to be debated.

Definition

PUBLIC OPINION POLLING: The use of survey interviews, often conducted over the telephone, with a representative, randomly selected sample of people, providing an accurate description of the attitudes, beliefs, and behaviour of the population from which the sample was drawn.

POLITICAL PARTICIPATION

A young mother joins a parent–teacher organization to try to change school policy. A university student jumps on a bus to attend a rally in another city to protest against increasing corporate power. A senior citizen attends a political party's constituency meeting to help select the party's candidate in the next election. Each is an example of **political participation**. And each provides a measure of political power to the citizens who employ it. If democracy is supposed to afford political power to the people, then one could make the claim that healthy democracies are those with high rates of political participation among their citizens.

Definition

POLITICAL PARTICIPATION: actions taken by individuals and groups in an attempt to influence political decisions and political decision-makers.

The avenues available to citizens in liberal democracies for influencing political decisions are many, ranging from the most simple act of voting to more involved acts such as running for political office or organizing a petition-signing campaign. Participation can occur on several different levels: individual (for example, voting or attending a rally), organizational (for example, volunteering time to an interest or community group or donating money to a political candidate's campaign), and professional (for example, working as a paid lobbyist or a political appointee). More often than not, such action is undertaken in an effort to bring about some kind of political change (including a return to the status quo), directly by influencing decision-makers or indirectly by gaining sympathetic media coverage or public support for the cause. Participation can also occur for purely expressive rather than instrumental reasons, that is, one may participate to feel a sense of belonging with the community as much as to influence political decisions, although the former reason has attracted the attention of fewer researchers than the latter.[32]

Most liberal democracies make participation voluntary, except for the few that legally require citizens to vote, such as Australia. Note that while a failure to vote in Australia may be illegal, the penalty is minor: only

$20.[33] The objective of such laws is to instil a belief in the importance of political participation, which can result in higher rates of participation than one finds in countries such as Canada and the United States. Some have suggested that such a law should be adopted in Canada in order to increase the rate of participation in elections—a rate that has been steadily dropping. While the adoption of such a law would no doubt increase the number of Canadians who vote, it would do little to change the underlying causes of low voter turnout.

The vast majority of political acts in liberal democracies are legal, but some actors choose other means to affect political decisions. Civil disobedience, that is, breaking laws in a nonviolent fashion to increase public awareness of their injustice, can often be successful. Recent examples in Canada include blockades of logging roads by environmentalists and of public highways by Native groups. The emphasis on nonviolent protest and on accepting punishment willingly helps generate support for the cause. **Terrorism**, on the other hand, is a more violent but less effective technique sometimes employed by marginal groups in an effort to dramatically focus attention on their cause. The Front de Libération du Québec (FLQ) kidnapped British Trade Commissioner James Cross in Montreal in 1970 in an attempt to pressure the federal government to release 23 members of the group imprisoned for terrorist acts. The group, committed to Quebec independence, resorted to the murder of Quebec cabinet minister Pierre Laporte in response to the invoking of the War Measures Act by Prime Minister Pierre Trudeau. While dramatic, the events did little to increase public support for the group's cause. The terrorist acts committed on September 11, 2001, in the United States are a vivid reminder that the use of illegal acts for political purposes continues.

Early studies of political participation constructed a hierarchy of political activity in the shape of a triangle, with simple activities such as voting at the base and more demanding activities such as running for office at its peak. The width of the base of the hierarchy meant that a good portion of the population were engaged in the simple activities; the narrowness of the top of the hierarchy meant that relatively few were involved in the more demanding ones. Early researchers also assumed that citizens in democracies naturally progressed from simple activities to more demanding ones—from

voting to canvassing for a political party to running for office, for example.[34] And in an example of the traditional domination of male thinking in the study of politics, the most active participants were labelled "gladiators," the less active "spectators," and the uninvolved "apathetics." The general conclusion was that many democracies did not meet the level of participation one would expect in a healthy democratic system.

Early research also suggested that those who could afford to participate and those who had the time to participate made up the largest share of the politically active.[35] This included men and those from historically dominant groups, such as the British and to a lesser extent the French in Canada.[36] More recent studies point to the importance of the definition of politics one employs in determining whether certain groups can be considered to be politically active. Immigrant women, for example, have organized immigrant and ethnocultural associations in response to the lack of attention from the women's movement and minority organizations.[37] Such associations have not traditionally been defined as political, however, and as such, immigrant women's level of political participation has been underestimated. More recent studies have also abandoned the conclusion that citizens progress from simple to more demanding political activities. Data suggest that people's political activity tends to cluster into types; the three most common types are voting, campaign activity, and community activity.[38] People choose political activity partly on the basis of the amount of effort required, the degree of cooperation needed among a number of people, the degree of potential conflict involved, and the nature of the issue addressed.

Without a doubt, one of the most striking findings regarding political participation is how few people actually participate in traditional activities. A comparison of average turnout rates between 1960 and 1995 in free elections in 37 democracies suggests that where you live determines in large measure the likelihood that you vote; while only 51 percent of eligible voters cast their ballots in Poland, 95 percent do in Australia.[39] The rates of participation are much lower for activities that require greater time commitments and resources. Evidence from Great Britain gives a sense of how dramatically the rates drop as the demands of the activity increase; while voting turnout in the 1990s fell to just under 80 percent, only 9 percent of the population belonged to a political party, and only 2 percent worked or canvassed for a candidate.[40]

The rate of participation in various political activities varies by country depending on whether the culture encourages participation and whether the institutional structure makes it easy. Electoral turnout in the United States is relatively low, partly due to the fact that electoral registration depends on individual effort. Some estimates suggest that the rate could increase by up to 10 percent if a centralized and less demanding system of registration was adopted.[41]

Participation also varies according to the characteristics of individuals, regardless of geography. If those who participate are not drawn equally from all groups in society, then government decision-making may not accurately reflect the desires of the population. Age is an important predictor of political activity (see Box 12.2). So too are gender, class, and attitudes. Women are significantly underrepresented in elite political activity, constituting only 14 percent of members of national parliaments around the world.[42] The poor and those of lower social classes are less likely to engage in political activity than those with greater access to resources. Political dissatisfaction, political apathy, and political cynicism are likely to lead people to turn away from the political system.

BOX 12.2

WHY DON'T YOUNG CANADIANS PARTICIPATE MORE IN POLITICS?

How closely do you follow politics? Have you voted every time the opportunity was available to you? You have much in common with your peers if your answers are "not very closely" and "not always." Research tells us that young Canadians are less likely to vote than older Canadians. It also reveals that they are less interested in politics but are also happier with democracy and government (see Table 12.4).

Life cycle explanations for this pattern suggest that young people are not participating at high rates because their interests are such that politics is not a priority. Once they start paying taxes, acquire a mortgage, and start to think about public school for their children, however, they will naturally become more interested in politics. Evidence from a Canadian poll taken in the spring of 2000 by the Institute for Research on Public Policy suggests that the life cycle explanation can help us understand this pattern in opinion and behaviour. Today's young Canadians will be participating at higher rates in 10 years' time. The study also reveals, however, that if we compare the participation rates of today's young Canadians to those of Canadians of the same group in 1990, the results are discouraging. Today's youth are participating at lower levels than young people were only 10 years ago, and although they will become more politically active as they age, they are unlikely to catch up to the rates exhibited by the previous generation. Can you think of an explanation for why today's young people are less politically active than in previous generations?

Source: *IRPP Policy Matters*, Vol. 2 No. 5, October 2001. Reprinted by permission of IRPP.

Another striking finding is the degree of change taking place in the kind of political activity that citizens are willing to engage in. Evidence suggests that there has been a rise in the numbers willing to engage in protest behaviour in democracies, both lawful (signing petitions and joining a boycott) and unlawful (attending unlawful demonstrations and occupying buildings), especially in Canada and among younger citizens.[43] Protest activity can be explained by deprivation—political alienation and frustration with the system can lead individuals to pursue unconventional modes of political activity. Alternatively, the resource model stresses that protest behaviour is merely an alternative mechanism for drawing attention to a cause; those with the political skills and resources are more likely to undertake such activity.

Explanations for the changing nature of political participation in modern democracies point to the changing nature of civil society or of overall patterns of social interaction (sometimes called social capital) and the increasing dissatisfaction with politics and governments. Robert Putnam's work suggests that citizens in the United States are less engaged at the civic level than they were previously and that this has important implications for the health of that democracy.[44] Community activities, ranging from bowling leagues to parent–teacher associations, provide opportunities for community members to build the social trust and social capital necessary for democratic government. There is debate, however, over whether social capital has indeed declined, or whether it simply may be manifesting itself in different ways, such as recycling (a community-minded event), and in different forums, such as the Internet (through discussion lists and zines).

Neil Nevitte, on the other hand, suggests that participation rates have changed due to increased education, the expansion of mass communications, and the rise of a knowledge-based economy. Today people are smarter and can access information much more easily than previous generations. Combine this with a loss of confidence in traditional political institutions, and the result is a shift from traditional to nontraditional forms of participation, including protest (see Figure 12.2).[45]

Is there such a thing as too much democratic participation?[46] Some argue that effective political decision-making requires that leaders enjoy a degree of freedom from democratic demands. Decision-makers are better informed than ordinary citizens and are more likely to be able to make decisions in the general public interest. Individual citizens are more likely to think about the costs and benefits to their own neighbourhoods and groups, for example, and are less likely to have as much information or expertise as political elites. Besides, the argument goes, people are generally politically apathetic. The participation of apathetic citizens leads to uninformed decision-making. To this way of thinking, too much democracy is definitely a bad thing.

For others, however, full participation by an informed and rational citizenry is a necessary and crucial condition for democracy. Such an argument rests on the assumption that the pursuit of individual truths—a goal of liberalism—can and will lead to conflicting interests. The mechanism for controlling such disputes is to establish laws on the basis of popular consent. Popular consent, the argument continues, can be established only through full political participation. Without it, the legitimacy of political authority is in doubt. Participation also helps citizens learn greater tolerance and greater rationality and develop an appreciation for civic activism.

TOOLS OF DIRECT DEMOCRACY

A number of devices have the potential for increasing direct citizen political power in representative democracies. The three most common are the referendum, the initiative, and the recall. Despite their potential, they are not immune from manipulation by governments

Table 12.4 Generational Patterns in Canadian Political Opinion and Behaviour, 2000	18–27	28–37	38–47	48–57	Over 57
	(Percent)	(Percent)	(Percent)	(Percent)	(Percent)
Attention to Politics: Not Very Closely or Not At All	59	41	42	36	32
Voted in the 1997 Election	66	69	85	92	91
Very or Fairly Satisfied with Democracy	82	75	74	70	65
Total Number of Respondents	271	268	281	224	211

Source: Brenda O'Neill, "Generational Patterns in Political Opinions and Behaviour of Canadians," *Policy Matters* 2(5) (October 2001): 11–12, 16.

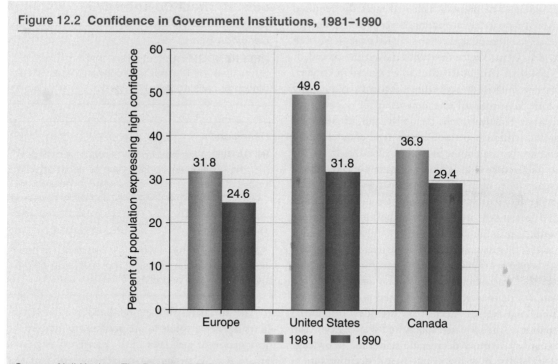

Figure 12.2 Confidence in Government Institutions, 1981–1990

Source: Neil Nevitte, *The Decline of Deference* (Peterborough: Broadview Press, 1996), p. 56. World Value Surveys 1981 and 1990. Available from the I.S.R., University of Michigan, Ann Arbor, MI. Reprinted by permission of Broadview Press.

and powerful groups of citizens alike. The result is that few governments have adopted such mechanisms wholeheartedly; most employ them on occasion, where there is the desire and the will to do so. Others have employed them in some degree in an attempt to manipulate the political outcome.

Referendums provide opportunities for citizens to vote directly on pieces of legislation or on constitutional questions. The binding referendum requires that the government act on the result of the referendum and thus provides the greatest potential for citizen power. Such referendums are employed in Australia for constitutional change. Nonbinding referendums (sometimes referred to as plebiscites) do not tie a government's hands in the way that binding referendums do. In democracies with politically interested, informed, and active populations, however, the reality is that the results of nonbinding referendums would be hard for any government to ignore. In 1992, Canada employed a referendum to determine whether citizens accepted the constitutional changes that the prime minister and premiers had set out in the Charlottetown Accord. The results of that vote were surprising, in that a majority of citizens voted to defeat a constitutional package that had been the result of intense and protracted negotiations between the federal and provincial governments and leaders of Aboriginal communities in Canada. While this was only the third referendum used at the national level, thousands have been used at the municipal level and over 60 at the provincial level, most notably within Quebec regarding seccession.[47]

Government-initiated referendums can take place whenever governments believe that there is a need for public consultation.[48] Obligatory referendums, on the other hand, are held when the government is required by law or custom to consult the public on a particular issue. Both Australia and Ireland require constitutional amendments to be ratified by a referendum. In 1999, Australia held a referendum to replace the queen and governor general as head of state with an elected president. The proposal failed to meet the required level of support for ratification. Several referendums on access to abortion services and related issues have been held in Ireland since the 1980s. Given the precedent established with the Charlottetown Accord in Canada, it seems unlikely that governments could avoid putting future constitutional amendments up for popular ratification. Finally, citizens themselves can initiate referendums through petitions. This type of referendum will be discussed in the section on initiatives.

Referendums have both advantages and disadvantages. One advantage is that public decisions are arrived at in a public manner—through free and open public debate.[49] Such debate leads to political education: people are more likely to inform themselves about issues if they have a direct say in the outcome. A second advantage lies in allowing the people to voice their own interests, rather than having those interests filtered through political representatives and political parties. This empowering mechanism provides a potential counter to the increased apathy and growing cynicism occurring in many democratic states; the knowledge that one has an ability to take part in deciding fundamental public questions is likely to increase satisfaction with democracy and the political system. But perhaps most importantly, the use of referendums, especially on divisive issues, can provide a measure of legitimacy to the outcome, since it can be said that "the people have spoken." But such a result is likely only if the public believes that the process was conducted fairly.

The use of referendums can also be problematic. Opponents highlight the fact that referendums can be employed strategically by the political elite for purposes other than to solicit the people's views on the issue. Such concerns were raised in the referendums on sovereignty held in Quebec regarding the wording of the question; the way the question is phrased can encourage, although rarely guarantee, a particular outcome. Second, referendums do not provide the public with a mechanism for shaping the policy agenda; instead, the people are provided with an opportunity merely to veto a government's proposal.[50] Some observers have also questioned the capacity of the general public to deal with complex issues. Finally, referendums can be highly divisive when the issue is a salient one and if it engenders strong opposing positions in various groups in society.

Tools of Direct Democracy

Definition

REFERENDUM: A mechanism that provides citizens with the ability to vote directly on pieces of legislation or constitutional changes.

Definition

INITIATIVE: A mechanism that allows citizens to petition the government to introduce or adopt specific pieces of legislation or force a referendum on an issue.

Definition

RECALL: A mechanism that allows citizens to petition to remove their political representative before the next election period.

The **initiative**, on the other hand, is a device that allows registered voters to use petitions to propose the introduction of new laws or to change existing laws. Initiatives were meant to complement representative democracy by providing citizens with a populist mechanism for introducing laws that the government might be avoiding, for whatever reason. One possibility is that a successful petition can force a referendum on the proposed bill, and if sufficient support is achieved, the bill automatically becomes law. Alternatively, a successful petition can result in the bill being introduced into the legislature, where it follows the normal legislative process.

A successful initiative process must set the requirements fairly high to ensure that minority interests do not hijack the democratic process. In 23 of the 50 U.S. states, initiatives appear on the election ballot if a previously circulated petition receives a small proportion of the population's signatures; voters then have the opportunity to agree or disagree with the initiative. But the process can be taken over by wealthy interest groups and industries that hire professional signature gatherers to collect the signatures at $1.50 each.[51] Once on the ballot, many of these initiatives pass, even though a majority of the state's population opposes the measure. If only a small proportion of the population actually votes, a minority of dedicated voters can wield tremendous but unrepresentative influence. In some cases, the proposed legislation is even inconsistent with existing laws or constitutional requirements. In others, it dangerously ties the legislature's hands. Proposition 13, for example, which passed in California in 1978, prohibited the state's government from ever increasing property taxes (one can imagine that it was not too difficult to gather support for this proposal!). The result, however unintended, is one of the worst public school systems in the nation. Minority interests do not always correspond with those of the greater public good.

The initiative process is in place in two Canadian provinces: British Columbia and Saskatchewan.[52] In British Columbia, the requirements for a successful petition are fairly stringent: organizers have 90 days to collect the signatures of 10 percent of registered voters in each electoral district in the province. Importantly, the legislation forbids canvassers from offering any payment for the signatures they gather. If sufficient support is received in an initiative petition, the bill is forwarded to the Select Standing Committee on Legislative Initiatives that decides either to introduce the bill into the legislature or to hold an initiative vote. A successful initiative vote requires the support of more than 50 percent of the total number of the registered voters in the province *and* more than 50 percent of the total number of registered voters in at least two-thirds of the electoral districts. Since the introduction of the initiative, a handful of petitions have been undertaken but none has progressed beyond the petition stage of the process. Most recently, a petition to establish a proportional representation electoral system (MMP) in the province was accepted and began to circulate in May 2002.

The third mechanism of direct democracy employed in representative democracies is the recall. The **recall** allows registered voters to petition to remove a member of the representative assembly between elections. The mechanism is intended to increase representative accountability by providing a direct means for unhappy electors to "de-elect" their representative without having to wait for the next general election. The same concerns that exist for the initiative exist with the use of the recall. The number of signatures required on the petition to trigger the recall of an elected member should not be so low that the process can be hijacked by a small group of disgruntled voters, for elections are costly affairs in terms of both time and money. But neither should the number be so high as to render the recall process meaningless. Just what is the right number of signatures to require, however, is up for debate.

Canada's experience with the recall is limited. In 1936, Alberta's Social Credit Party passed a recall measure that provided for the triggering of a special election in the event of a successful recall petition signed by two-thirds of eligible voters.[53] Despite this seemingly high hurdle, it appeared as though voters in the premier's own riding would successfully petition for his recall, and he responded by repealing the legislation and killing the petition.

The recall currently exists only in British Columbia. The legislation provides 60 days for the collection of signatures in support of the recall from 40 percent of voters in the member's riding. By May 1999, 11 petitions had been initiated to recall a member of the legislative assembly, but most failed to receive the required number of signatures in the allotted time period or were withdrawn. One petition, however, was successful. In 1998, Liberal MLA Paul Reitsma was found to have written under a pseudonym letters to the editors of local newspapers that criticized his opponents and praised his own work. It was only after a recall petition was initiated and when it was clear that sufficient signatures had been collected that Reitsma resigned. The petition was undoubtedly successful because of the media coverage generated by the incident and the overwhelming hostility created by the MLA's dishonesty.

Recall provisions are in place in 15 U.S. states for elected state officials and in a majority of states for the recall of municipal officials.[54] Although most of the states require 15 percent of registered voters' signatures for a successful petition, the number varies between 10 and 40 percent. As in Canada, however, the success rate of recall petitions is not very high.

Recall provides an important mechanism for ensuring that representatives keep the interests of their constituents in mind. At the same time, however, the parliamentary system makes it particularly difficult for representatives to always act according to the wishes of constituencies (assuming for the moment that such wishes are easily determined). Party discipline, for instance, requires that the interests of the party determine the actions of each representative, given the requirements of responsible government. In addition, representatives may be provided with information that makes it clear that constituents' interests may be best served in a manner that contradicts their own wishes.

CONCLUSION

Democracy is based on instilling a certain measure of political power in the hands of the people. Modern representative democracies provide only a few mechanisms by which citizens are able to influence government policy. Encouraging the use of the referendum, the initiative, and the recall for increasing citizen power rests on the presumption that the citizenry desires to participate more fully in democratic decision-making. Declining voter turnout in Western states and increased political cynicism suggest that attention should be focused on problems other than simply the lack of opportunity for political participation. Successful democracy requires above all else that citizen participation is effective—citizens must believe that legitimate political action will result in clear and understandable initiatives that respond to that action. The most fundamental of democratic institutions, the election, provides the clearest mechanism for instilling that belief. In too many instances, however, electoral results are ambiguous, do not directly reflect the choices made by the voters, and appear to shut out a number of groups and interests whose chances are directly dependent on achieving electoral success. The democratic ideal will remain an elusive goal until citizens believe they are powerful, regardless of whether or not they choose to act on that power.

DISCUSSION QUESTIONS

1. What factors do you consciously consider when you are deciding how to cast a vote in a general election? Can you think of any factors that might affect your decision unconsciously?

2. When should referendums be used? For what issues? Can you think of any occasions or reasons when the use of a referendum might be ill advised?

3. Explain why students' participation in university politics is so low. Does your answer help explain participation in politics more broadly?

4. Should recall be adopted at the federal level in Canada? What might be the benefits? What might be the costs?

5. What do you consider to be the greatest challenge facing modern democracies? Why?

www **WEB LINKS**

Elections Canada:
http://www.elections.ca

The U.S. Federal Elections Commission:
http://www.fec.gov

Stanford University's Comparative Democratization Project:
http://democracy.stanford.edu

CNN's Elections Around the World:
http://www.cnn.com/WORLD/election.watch

International Institute for Democracy and Electoral Assistance:
http://www.idea.int

Fair Vote Canada:
http://www.fairvotecanada.org

Canadian Election Study:
http://www.fas.umontreal.ca/pol/ces-eec/index.html

FURTHER READING

Butler, David, and Austin Ranney, eds. *Referendums around the World: The Growing Use of Direct Democracy.* Washington, D.C.: American Enterprise Institute, 1994.

Centre for Research and Information on Canada. *Voter Participation in Canada: Is Canadian Democracy in Crisis?* Research paper no. 3, October 2001. Available online at http://www.cric.ca/en_html/publications/cahiers_cric.html.

Dalton, Russell J. *Citizen Politics: Public Opinion and Political Parties in Advanced Western Democracies.* 2nd ed. Chatham, N.J.: Chatham House, 1996.

Everitt, Joanna, and Brenda O'Neill, eds. *Citizen Politics: Research and Theory in Canadian Political Behaviour*. Don Mills: Oxford University Press, 2002.

Harrop, Martin, and William L. Miller. *Elections and Voters: A Comparative Introduction*. Houndmills: Macmillan, 1987.

LeDuc, Lawrence, Richard G. Niemi, and Pippa Norris, eds. *Comparing Democracies: Elections and Voting in Global Perspective*. Thousand Oaks: Sage, 1996.

ENDNOTES

1 Darin Barney, *Prometheus Wired: The Hope for Democracy in the Age of Network Technology* (Chicago: University of Chicago Press, 2000), p. 22.

2 This section relies heavily on David Held, *Models of Democracy*, 2nd ed. (Stanford: Stanford University Press, 1996), chap. 1.

3 Joseph Schumpeter, *Capitalism, Socialism and Democracy* (New York: Harper, 1942), p. 265.

4 NUA Internet Surveys, "How Many Online?"; cited on March 23, 2002; available at http://www.nua.com/surveys/how_many_online/index.htm.

5 Matthew Symonds, "Digital Democracy," *Economist.com,* June 22, 2000; cited on July 1, 2001; available at http://www.economist.com.

6 See, for example, http://www.grassroots.com.

7 Symonds, "Digital Democracy."

8 See David Stewart and Keith Archer, *Quasi-Democracy? Parties and Leaders in Alberta* (Vancouver: UBC Press, 2000).

9 Symonds, "Digital Democracy."

10 See NUA Internet Surveys, "How Many Online?"

11 Held, *Models of Democracy,* p. 317.

12 Ibid., pp. 353–60.

13 See the Elections Canada website at http://www.elections.ca for information on the 2000 and previous general elections.

14 In most parliamentary systems, voters choose the members of the legislature, and the share of seats held by parties within that body determines the government. Hence, voters only indirectly determine which party forms the government.

15 These requirements follow those laid out by David Butler, Howard Penniman, and Austin Ranney, eds., *Democracy at the Polls: A Comparative Study of Competitive National Elections* (Washington, D.C.: American Enterprise Institute, 1981), p. 4.

16 See "The Basic Law for the Federal Republic of Germany," September 23, 1990; cited on July 29, 2002; available at http://www.psr.keele.ac.uk/docs/german.htm.

17 See Martin Harrop and William L. Miller, *Elections and Voters: A Comparative Introduction* (Houndmills: Macmillan, 1987), chap. 9.

18 André Blais, Louis Massicotte, and Agnieszka Dobrzynska, "Direct Presidential Elections: A World Summary," Electoral Studies 16 (1997): 441–55.

19 See "2000 Presidential Electoral and Popular Vote," The U.S. Federal Election Commission; cited on March 23, 2002; available at http://www.fec.gov/pubrec/fe2000/elecpop.htm.

20 Blais, Massicotte, and Dobrzynska, "Direct Presidential Elections," p. 251.

21 Hanna Pitkin, *The Concept of Representation* (Los Angeles: University of California Press, 1967).

22 The 2000 Canadian Election Study is available at http://www.fas.umontreal.ca/pol/ces-eec/index.html. André Blais, Elisabeth Gidengil, Richard Nadeau, and Neil Nevitte are the study's coinvestigators. The survey was conducted by the

Institute for Social Research at York University and Jolicoeur & Associés (Quebec). The study was funded by the Social Sciences and Humanities Research Council of Canada, Elections Canada, and the Institute for Research on Public Policy.

23 Peter Dahlgren, "The Transformation of Democracy?" in Barrie Axford and Richard Huggins, eds., *New Media and Politics* (Thousand Oaks: Sage Publications, 2001), pp. 69-70.

24 See Donald Blake, "Electoral Democracy in the Provinces," *Choices: Strengthening Canadian Democracy* 7(2) (2001).

25 "You Pays Your Money," *Economist.com,* July 29, 1999; cited on August 11, 2002; available at http://www.economist.com.

26 This section closely follows André Blais and Louis Massicotte, "Electoral Systems," in Lawrence LeDuc, Richard G. Niemi, and Pippa Norris, eds., *Comparing Democracies: Elections and Voting in Global Perspective* (Thousand Oaks: Sage, 1996), pp. 49–81.

27 See J. Volwes, Peter Aimer, Susan Banducci, and Jeffrey Karp, "Expectations of Change," in J. Volwes et al., *Voters' Victory? New Zealand's First Election under Proportional Representation* (Welington: Auckland University Press, 1998).

28 Louis Massicotte, "Changing the Canadian Electoral System," *Choices: Strengthening Canadian Democracy* 7(1) (2001).

29 See Mebs Kanji and Keith Archer, "The Theories of Voting and Their Applicability in Canada," in Joanna Everitt and Brenda O'Neill, eds., *Citizen Politics: Research and Theory in Canadian Political Behaviour* (Don Mills: Oxford University Press, 2002), pp. 160–83.

30 Richard Johnston, André Blais, Henry Brady, and Jean Crête, *Letting the People Decide: Dynamics of a Canadian Election* (Montreal and Kingston: McGill-Queen's University Press, 1992).

31 See David Butler, "Polls and Elections," in LeDuc, Niemi, and Norris, *Comparing Democracies,* pp. 236–53.

32 Sandra Burt, "The Concept of Political Participation," in Everitt and O'Neill, *Citizen Politics,* pp. 232–46.

33 Australian Electoral Commission; cited on July 1, 2001; available at http://www.aec.gov.au/pubs/electoral_procedures/offences.htm.

34 Lester Milbraith, *Political Participation: How and Why Do People Get Involved in Politics?* (Chicago: Rand McNally, 1965).

35 Sidney Verba and Norman H. Nie, *Participation in America: Democracy and Social Equality* (New York: Harper & Row, 1972).

36 John Porter, *The Vertical Mosaic: An Analysis of Class and Power in Canada* (Toronto: University of Toronto Press, 1965).

37 Yasmeen Abu-Laban, "Challenging the Gendered Vertical Mosaic: Immigrants, Ethnic Minorities, Gender and Political Participation," in Everitt and O'Neill, *Citizen Politics,* pp. 268–83.

38 Russell J. Dalton, *Citizen Politics: Public Opinion and Political Parties in Advanced Western Democracies,* 2nd ed. (Chatham: Chatham House, 1996), p. 41.

39 Mark Franklin, "Electoral Participation," in LeDuc, Niemi, and Norris, *Comparing Democracies,* pp. 216–35.

40 Dalton, *Citizen Politics,* chap. 3.

41 Ibid., p. 44.

42 Inter-Parliamentary Union, "Women in National Parliaments"; cited on March 23, 2002; available at http://www.ipu.org/wmn-e/world.htm.

43 Neil Nevitte, *The Decline of Deference* (Peterborough: Broadview Press, 1996).

44 Robert Putnam, "Bowling Alone: America's Declining Social Capital," *Journal of Democracy* 6 (1995): 65–78.

45 Nevitte, *The Decline of Deference.*

46 See the discussion in William Mishler, *Participation in Canada* (Toronto: Macmillan, 1979).

47 Patrick Boyer, *Direct Democracy in Canada: The History and Future of Referendums* (Toronto: Dundurn Press, 1992).

48 See Matthew Mendelsohn and Andrew Parkin, "Introducing Direct Democracy in Canada," *Choices: Strengthening Canadian Democracy* 7(5) (2001).

49 This section relies heavily on David Butler and Austin Ranney, eds., *Referendums: A Comparative Study of Practice and Theory* (Washington, D.C. and London: American Enterprise Institute for Public Policy Research, 1978) and Patrick Boyer, *The People's Mandate: Referendums and a More Democratic Canada* (Toronto: Dundurn Press, 1992).

50 Mendelsohn and Parkin, "Introducing Direct Democracy in Canada," p. 7.

51 Doug Sanders, "Practical Pitfalls of the Plebiscite," *The Globe and Mail,* October 24, 2000, p. A3.

52 For information on British Columbia's initiative and recall processes, see http://www.elections.bc.ca.

53 Peter McCormick, "Democratic Practice in Canada and the United States," in David Thomas, ed., *Canada and the United States: Differences That Count* (Peterborough: Broadview, 1993), pp. 185–86.

54 Ibid., pp. 184–85.

Chapter 13

Civil Society: Interest Groups and Social Movements in Politics

Miriam Smith

CHAPTER OBJECTIVES

After you have completed this chapter, you should be able to

- understand what interest groups and social movements are
- enumerate the differences among the major subtypes of interest groups and social movements
- discuss the most common ways in which such groups influence the political system
- engage in the debate over whether or not such groups are too powerful.

INTRODUCTION

Antiglobalization protesters take to the streets of Quebec City to demonstrate against the Summit of the Americas. Farmers in Britain object to the British government's policies on foot-and-mouth disease. Russian pensioners picket to protest the government's failure to pay their pensions. Students at the National Autonomous University of Mexico (UNAM) go on strike against privatization and budget cuts. Business groups in the United States argue for lower tax rates. Pro-life groups appear before the Supreme Court to

claim that life begins at conception. What all these incidents have in common is that they are expressions of protest based on nonterritorial interests, identities, and values: students, business, pensioners, farmers, and pro-life groups.

Much of our everyday discussion of politics is defined by territory. Government and the state are ideas that are based on the assumption of a certain geographical region. When we think of Canada or China, we are thinking of a defined geographical territory around which politics is organized. In democratic political systems, voting is often organized around constituencies or districts in which voters elect a representative.

While the electoral system provides for the territorial representation of citizens, groups and movements organize citizens according to nonterritorial interests and identities. In the electoral system, voters choose a representative of the geographical area in which they live. In group and movement politics, citizens join together with like-minded citizens to form a group or movement that reflects political cleavages such as economic interests, gender, language, or simply political opinions.[1]

Democratic freedoms are very important for the organization of movements and groups. Without freedom to assemble, freedom of the press, and freedom of expression, it is very difficult for citizens to form groups and movements. Yet, even in nondemocratic systems, group politics may operate. Authoritarian states may permit certain types of political groups to continue to exist, or they may not be able to expend the resources necessary to stop such groups from forming. And movements of political protest may bring people into the streets, leading to the downfall of an authoritarian regime and the transition to democracy.

WHAT ARE INTEREST GROUPS AND SOCIAL MOVEMENTS?

Interest groups and **social movements** bring together people with common interests and/or a common sense of identity for the purpose of influencing the political process. Groups and movements are not part of the state, although in some cases, they may have very close relationships with the state. Groups and movements are different from political parties because they do not seek public office. They may seek to influence public policy or they may primarily aim to influence the beliefs and values of their fellow citizens.

Definition

INTEREST GROUP: A group that brings together people with common interests and/or a common sense of identity for the purpose of influencing the political process.

Definition

SOCIAL MOVEMENT: An informal network of activists who seek to transform the values of society.

Groups and movements form part of **civil society**, that is, social institutions and organizations that are independent of the state and in which citizens pursue their interests, express their beliefs, and live in communities. Examples of institutions of civil society are churches, schools, professional associations, trade unions, companies, and families.

Definition

CIVIL SOCIETY: Social institutions and organizations that are independent of the state and in which citizens pursue their interests, express their beliefs, and live in communities.

This chapter discusses both interest groups and social movements. Interest groups are formally organized, while social movements function as informal networks of activists. Further, social movements often engage in **contentious politics**, that is, strikes and demonstrations, as a means of achieving their goals, while interest groups usually pursue their goals through conventional means such as lobbying.[2]

Definition

CONTENTIOUS POLITICS: Protests that take the form of disruption of the normal activities of society, such as demonstrations and civil disobedience.

An example of social movement politics is provided by the student movement at the Autonomous University of Mexico, mentioned at the beginning of the chapter. Students were initially brought together simply by having a common sense of identity as students and common interests in trying to fight tuition hikes. The university imposed tuition fees that have ended free universal university education in Mexico. The protest spread by word of mouth and the Internet through networks of students. These developments are typical of an informally organized social movement, in which networks of activism create protests and demonstrations that are intended to change public policies. In this case, the students brought the university to a halt by not attending classes.

The fate of the UNAM strike also shows that social movement tactics of striking and demonstrating can provoke a violent response from the state. Although Mexico has made strides toward democracy in recent years, the legacy of authoritarian rule can still be seen in the fact that in February 2000, the military and the police forcibly occupied the UNAM campus in order to end the strike. Six hundred students were arrested, and student groups alleged that students were tortured by police.[3]

In the spring and early summer of 1999, thousands of students, labour unionists, parents, teachers, and others marched half a dozen times to the Zócalo in Mexico City, the main square and the political heart of Mexico, to demand a fair resolution to the conflict over tuition fee hikes, privatization, and budget cuts.

Courtesy of Jeremy Simer

The social movement politics of the UNAM student strikers can be contrasted with interest group politics, for example, the politics of the National Rifle Association (NRA) in the United States. This group is well organized and has thousands of members, a large budget, and spinoff organizations, such as organizations that fund litigation in gun control cases, a charitable organization in defense of shooting sports, and a special organization for legislative action, which alerts members to upcoming legislation in Congress. The NRA has been heavily involved in lobbying members of Congress on gun control legislation. Moreover, the organization is well known to the public and has a high media profile. It is said that it is almost impossible to change gun control legislation in the United States because of the influence of the NRA on Congress.[4]

The politics of interest groups and social movements can also be distinguished from the activities of lobbying or consulting, in which groups or companies hire professionals to contact and influence government on their behalf. For example, tobacco companies might hire professional lobbyists to influence legislators' and public servants' views on the relation of tobacco products and tobacco advertising. Typically, lobbyists and consultants are paid well to protect the interests of their clients in government policy. This type of activity is common in most democratic countries; it is a very sizable industry in the United States and increasingly so in Canada.

Interest groups and social movements are sometimes called **nongovernmental organizations (NGOs)**. This term is particularly common in the fields of international relations and development, where it draws attention to the fact that such organizations are neither part of the state nor part of international organizations such as the United Nations (UN). These organizations are active in both international and domestic politics. In addition to targeting states and aiming to influence domestic politics, they also aim to influence international organizations, for example the UN and the World Trade Organization (WTO).

Definition

NONGOVERNMENTAL ORGANIZATION (NGO):
A nonprofit organization that is not part of the state and is not a private corporation. Usually, this term is used to describe organizations that operate across borders in areas such as peace, development, human rights, and international affairs.

FUNCTIONS OF INTEREST GROUPS AND SOCIAL MOVEMENTS

Interest groups and social movements serve a number of functions in the political system. The four main types of functions of interest groups and social movements are:

- to provide a means for citizens to express their views to government and to participate in the political system
- to influence the policies followed by governments, international organizations, and corporations
- to influence views held in society
- to provide information and legitimacy to governments and to international organizations.

First of all, group and movement politics provide a link between citizens and government and allow citizens an alternative means of expressing their views to government. Group and movement organizations allow for the expression of political opinions that are much more specific than those that can be expressed through voting periodically in an election or even by actively participating in party politics. Some voters may feel that none of the political parties represents their views on issues that are important to them.

Environmentalists, for example, might feel that party politics is a waste of time and that their political activism would be more effectively channelled through participation in the environmental movement. People who support the pro-life side of the abortion debate may join a pro-life organization that reflects their specific viewpoint. People may belong to religious and cultural organizations; while these organizations do not exist primarily to influence government, they may from time to time involve themselves in politics and aim to influence government policy. Some citizens may feel that government is not serving their interests and may organize in their own communities to provide services that they feel are needed. Many women's organizations such as rape crisis lines and battered women's shelters started out as community-based organizations that were intended to fill gaps in public services. In this sense, then, group and movement politics provide a means for citizens to express their views to government and to participate in the political system.

In authoritarian systems, some forms of group political activity may be permitted and may provide a vehicle for some citizens to express their views to government in a limited fashion. In Box 13.1, you can see an example of the range of interest groups that currently exists in China, an authoritarian regime.

Second, group and movement politics influence the policies followed by governments, international organizations, and even in some cases, corporations. Citizens banding together may convince government to follow one course of action rather than another. Protesters against the Multilateral Agreement on Investment (MAI) had some effect on causing the Organisation for Economic Co-operation and Development (OECD) and the WTO not to go ahead with the treaty. Farmers in Britain who banded together managed to influence the British government's stance on the treatment of the foot-and-mouth disease affecting British cattle.

Third, groups may aim to influence society as much as or more than they may aim to influence the state. For certain types of groups, it may be more important to change what citizens believe about an issue or to change the core political values of citizens than to change public policy. For example, business groups may attempt to use the media to put forth the point of view that free-market policies are superior to state intervention as a means of ensuring economic development and growth. For business groups, it may be just as important to convince citizens to believe in a free-market perspective as to convince governments to

---

BOX 13.1

INTEREST GROUPS IN NONDEMOCRATIC SYSTEMS: THE EXAMPLE OF CHINA

According to Chinese politics experts George Gilboy and Eric Heginbotham, the following important interest groups exist in China, despite the fact that it is not a democratic country:

* * *

Farmers. With increasing frequency, Chinese farmers are organizing to protest corrupt local officials, onerous and arbitrary taxes, and extreme poverty. In recent months, farmers have attacked tax collectors, blocked roads, and fought with officials and police.

The unemployed. As economic reform continues, millions of Chinese workers are being laid off each year with little hope of re-employment or adequate social welfare support. In some cities, unemployed workers are now joining together in large-scale protests, involving as many as 20 000 people at a time.

Consumers. Today's Chinese consumers frequently speak out and organize against defective products, financial scams, and official corruption.

Industry associations. Because China's official industry associations are weak and dominated by the Communist Party, they are unable to mediate effectively between industry and government. Yet some industry leaders have coalesced to force the central government to change policies on taxes, international trade, and price reforms.

Religious and spiritual movements. The rise of Falun Gong is only the most visible indication of resurgent spiritualism in China. Traditional religions, mystical movements, and cults have attracted millions of followers in recent years.

Special-interest groups. A variety of nascent special-interest groups, ranging from environmental and animal-rights organizations to regional soccer clubs now place new demands on the state for resources and attention. For example, environmental groups—some with nationwide reach—have sponsored direct actions such as tree-planting programs and petitions calling for better municipal waste management.

Source: Excerpted from George Gilboy and Eric Heginbotham, "China's Coming Transformation," *Foreign Affairs* 80(4) (July/August 2001): 31–33. Reprinted by permission of FOREIGN AFFAIRS (2001). Copyright 2001 by the Council on Foreign Relations, Inc.

---

undertake a certain policy decision. This is increasingly the case as certain types of decisions by corporations are subject to democratic scrutiny. Whether in the economic or environmental areas, corporations may be scrutinized by groups of citizens and may find it more productive and useful to expend their "political" resources in media and public relations strategies.

Similarly, social movements may also find it more important to influence society than to influence the state per se. The women's movement in many countries has fought for women's equality with men, a battle that is very far from over, especially in certain areas of the world. While the state's actions are important in this respect, the women's movement has also aimed to change public opinion on this issue in order to ensure greater social equality. Governments may mandate equality between the sexes, but legal rules and regula-

tions are unlikely to make a difference unless citizens believe in them.

Finally, group and movement organizations may provide information and legitimacy to governments and to international organizations. Government may encourage the formation and establishment of groups and movements. Even where governments and organizations have not actually encouraged the establishment of groups or movements, they may promote their involvement in the policy process.

Why? There are two main reasons that governments and international organizations may actually welcome input and even pressure from group and movement organizations. First, in both democratic and nondemocratic states, governments need to know what their citizens think. Groups may provide a barometer of public opinion to government. Further, precisely because interest groups and social movements bring together citizens with a sense of common interests or a common identity, they are in a position to provide targeted information to governments or international organizations regarding the views of their constituencies on given policies or issues. Governments may wish to know what a given group thinks about a particular issue. If a government wished to know farmers' views on an international trade agreement that was under negotiation, the fastest way to find out would be to ask farmers' groups.

Group and movement organizations may also provide technical information to government and international organizations. In some cases, it may be cheaper for governments and organizations to obtain information from groups and movement organizations than to collect the data themselves. While such data might be tainted by the groups' own biases and interests in putting their own collective claims in the best possible light, nonetheless, governments and international organizations may still find such information useful.

For example, if the government of Botswana wanted to update its information about water availability and quality in villages, it could send out its own inspectors to obtain this data. One could imagine that the task of sending out such inspectors to villages would be a very expensive and labour-intensive task. So instead, the government might seek out this information from farmers' organizations and from traditional village leaders. Such civil society organizations and networks would have access to excellent information on water availability and quality, as might NGOs working in the field of development. An NGO that had worked in many parts of the country at the village level might be able to give the government updated information on water. Although NGOs, farmers' groups, or village leaders might provide information that reflects their interests and experience, it might be cheaper and more efficient for government to use the information provided by these interest groups rather than to collect the information from scratch.

A second reason that governments and international organizations might encourage the formation and participation of group and movement organizations in the policy process is because such participation may enhance the **legitimacy** of governments or international organizations. When group or movement organizations participate in the process of policy for-

mation, they send the message that the governments or international organizations with whom they are collaborating are legitimate political actors. If governments can secure the agreement of group or movement organizations to particular policies, it is more likely that those policies will be viewed positively by the public. For example, in almost any democratic system, a government that brings down a budget or economic plan will provoke reactions from economic groups such as business, labour, and farmer groups, as well as from others. If every economic group in the country, from farmers to business, condemns the government's economic plan, it is unlikely that the public will support it. The same phenomenon exists in other policy areas. President George W. Bush's plan to open up the Arctic Wildlife Reserve to drilling has been condemned by environmental groups, undermining Bush's support among Americans who care about the environment.

> *Definition*
>
> **LEGITIMACY:** The degree to which citizens accept and tolerate the actions and decisions of social and political actors such as states, international organizations, and civil society groups themselves, usually based on the notion that the decision-makers have a right to such power.

These dynamics are reinforced by the media, which tend to seek out groups and movement organizations that can give reactions to government initiatives. In this process, the interests and identities of some groups may be privileged over others. Those with economic and media expertise and resources are better able to exert influence in this way. The media tend to reinforce existing definitions and concepts of the interests and identities that are at stake in any given area of policy. For example, economic policy is defined as something that is of interest to groups that are clearly economic, such as business, labour, and farmers. However, development NGOs, antipoverty groups, and women's groups might all argue that they have a stake in economic policy as well.

Furthermore, how well a particular group or movement organization can lend legitimacy to government depends in turn on its own legitimacy. The legitimacy and visibility of a group or movement organization in the public eye are two of its key resources. Such legitimacy and visibility depend on the characteristics of the group and the characteristics of the political, social, and economic context in which the group or movement organization operates. In a given context, opponents of the group or movement may attempt to delegitimate or undermine it through a wide variety of tactics, ranging from questioning how well it represents the constituency it purports to represent to accusing its leaders of political corruption.

TYPES OF INTEREST GROUPS AND SOCIAL MOVEMENTS

Interest groups and social movements may be classified into types. When considering these, it is important to remember that such typologies are approximations of the complex and rich reality of group politics in diverse political contexts.

At the beginning of the chapter, we saw that interest groups are more organized than social movements and tend to use more conventional means to achieve their goals; social movements are less organized networks of activists who may use unconventional means of influence, such as demonstrations. One way to imagine the variety of groups and movements is to use a continuum, with social movements on one end and interest groups on the other end.

Interest Groups

The continuum is based on the degree of organization of a group or movement. At one end of the continuum, we have groups that have no formal organization whatsoever. For example, if we consider all taxpayers as a group of people, there is no organization that represents "all taxpayers." There may be organizations that claim to represent the interests of taxpayers and to put forth goals and values that are in the interests of "all taxpayers." However, "all taxpayers" are not, as such, organized into a formal group in any country. Hence, the category "all taxpayers" is a latent group, that is, a group that is not organized. Other important latent groups include consumers and the unemployed. Both of these groups have important interests in common, yet neither of them is organized.

In contrast, some groups are highly organized. In most countries, people that have a stake in business, farming, or labour are organized into **institutionalized groups**, which represent the interests of their members and attempt to influence government policies. In democratic countries, such groups may have very long histories of organization. In many European countries, the employers' federations (or business groups) date back to the late 19th century.

Institutionalized groups are characterized by the development of a permanent organization for the group. This means that the group has the economic and other resources necessary to sustain ongoing organization. In many cases, institutionalized groups employ

Table 13.1 **Types of Groups and Movements**	
Institutionalized Groups	Social Movement Organizations
General Features	
Division of labour	Networked
Narrow goals	Broad goals
Well organized	Loosely organized
Formal structure	Informal structure
Many resources	Few resources
State-oriented	Society-oriented
Examples	
Canadian Federation of Agriculture	Egale (gay and lesbian rights)
Canadian Council of Chief Executives (formerly BCNI)	National Action Committee on the Status of Women (NAC)

professionals to carry out some of the work of the group. In some instutionalized groups, political goals may be secondary to the primary function of the group. For example, religious organizations may have as their first purpose spiritual or religious goals. Yet they may also have political goals, such as to protect the status of their religion within the state, to pursue particular tax or legal advantages in the education system, or to promote strong views on family and gender-related policies such as abortion and birth control or strong preferences in foreign policy. Institutionalized groups also tend to use conventional means to achieve their goals, for example lobbying politicians or entering into consultations with governments. At times, groups may press their case through legal action or by joining forces with political parties.

The more institutionalized interest groups are also characterized by the nature of their goals. Because these groups use conventional strategies, their goals also tend to follow a certain pattern. In general, institutionalized groups pursue goals that are easily negotiable. For example, an institutionalized group might attempt to pressure the state to follow a particular regulatory or tax policy that will benefit the group. Regulation and tax policies are divisible and hence negotiable. If the group is demanding that certain types of taxes be lowered, taxes can be lowered by a greater or lesser amount. Governments can go part of the way toward meeting the goals of the group, if not all the way. In this sense, the goals of the group fit in with the language and assumptions of government and can be dealt with by politicians and by civil servants.

In order to support all of this organization, institutionalized groups tend to have access to a stable base of economic resources. Business and professional groups charge their members a fee to join and are able to sustain themselves in this manner. Groups that represent constituencies that are less affluent may also charge dues. In this case, the group may create a stable base of funding by charging a large group of members small membership dues. Farmers' groups and trade unions are good examples of groups that have often organized themselves in this manner.

In some cases, groups may receive funding from governments interested in the creation and maintenance of organizations representing certain societal interests. In many European countries, for example, governments fund community groups at the local level in hopes that such local groups will help spark urban renewal in areas with social problems and high crime rates. These community organizations become part of consultative processes with governments over urban policy and problems. In other cases, government funding may be withdrawn from groups that disagree with governments. For interest groups and social movement organizations, government funding may be a double-edged sword. Although such funding may provide a stable base for the organizations' work, it may also hinder their ability to speak freely and to influence government policy in the best interests of their members.

In Canada, there has been a lively debate over whether or not the federal government should fund groups that disagree with it.[5] The Canadian Alliance and Progressive Conservative politicians have both argued that government should not fund interest groups that are critics of the government. In this view, government funding to groups only gives the governments' critics more ammunition to disagree with and undermine government policy. On the other hand, the Canadian government under the leadership of the Liberal Party has recently become interested in the idea of institutionalizing links with certain civil society groups with the aim of strengthening Canadian society. During a period in which government has been expected to do less, not more, and in which large-scale state intervention is out of favour, government may benefit from downloading tasks to interest groups and from developing a consultative partnership with such groups. In Canada, Australia, and most of the European democracies, state funding of group life is practised to some extent. In the United States, in contrast, groups do not benefit from such systematic state funding.

Social Movements

Moving to the other end of our continuum, social movements tend to be less organized, to use less conventional means, and to have less easily negotiable goals than institutionalized groups. In place of the permanent and professional organization of the institutionalized group, social movements are often composed of networks of activists. These networks may be linked in part by informal ties rather than by large professional organizations.

Social movements often begin life with very broad goals, which may be based on assumptions that are very different from the assumptions of policymakers and power holders. Movements may demand democracy from authoritarian regimes (for example, democracy movements in the former Eastern bloc and across many developing countries during the 1980s and 1990s), an end to foreign occupation and domination (for example, anticolonial movements and the Palestinian intifada), an end to race-based laws (the South African anti-apartheid movement), an end to rampant economic growth (the deep ecology and radical environmental movements in industrialized countries), or peace in a time of war (the Israeli peace movement, the U.S. anti–Vietnam War movement). In these cases, the goals are often not easily negotiable with governments or elites. Even in stable democracies, demands for human rights (for example, made by the women's movement) or environmental protection may be difficult to negotiate with governments and power holders. In many cases, the goals sought are not easily divisible.

Social movements may have goals that differ profoundly from those of governments. In particular, social movements commonly aim to influence society as well as the state. For example, the women's movement has been concerned with influencing social attitudes as much as it has been concerned with changing government policy. Further, some social movement organizations have goals that reach beyond the borders of the nation-state—they may aim to influence the policies of other states. Human rights groups such as Amnesty International aim to change the behaviour of other states and organize themselves across borders in order to do so. Other groups may try to influence the policies of international organizations. The antiglobalization movement has had an effect on opening up the WTO and the International Monetary Fund (IMF) to greater involvement by NGOs. These are all cases in which the movement is not simply trying to change the policy of a government but, more broadly, is trying to change the policies of many governments or is trying to influence social mores and values or international organizations. As politics increasingly moves out to the global level, however, many groups, including institutionalized interests groups, are reaching beyond borders in ways that were once the preserve of the social movement organizations. Once again, it is important to note that the continuum described here is an approximation of the real-world complexities of group and movement behaviour.

Over time, social movements may be tempted to moderate their goals in order to obtain influence with states and international organizations. Some environmental groups may even choose to try to find common ground with government in order to influence environmental policy. Of course, in addition to influencing states or international organizations, social movements may also aim to influence civil society. For example, some environmental groups might choose to try to change consumer or corporate behaviour directly rather than to influence government policies.

Social movement organizations often use unconventional means to achieve their goals. These means may include demonstrations, such as those that have occurred in recent years in the antiglobalization movement. The civil rights movement in the United States, drawing its inspiration in part from the anticolonial struggles in India and elsewhere, used the strategies of nonviolence to achieve its goals. Civil disobedience, sit-ins, and marches were used to dramatize and challenge the segregationist laws of the southern U.S. states during the 1950s and 1960s. At times, governments may react with violence to such protest, as when state authorities in the United States attacked civil rights protesters in southern cities or police forces used tear gas and arrests against antiglobalization protesters.

Another means of influence that may be employed by social movements is direct action. The technique of direct action is based on the assumption that changing government policies may not be the most efficient way to achieve a political goal. Direct action has been common in the environmental movement over the last 30 years and, as a strategy, has been publicized best by Greenpeace. Greenpeace has intervened directly to stop environmental damage. For example, it sent its ships, such as its famous *Rainbow Warrior*, to stop French nuclear testing in the South Pacific and was successful in achieving this goal in 1996. Other environmental organizations, such as Earth First!, have engaged in tree spiking, that is, placing a spike in a tree and then marking the tree to prevent it from being cut. At times, such tactics can veer into the realm of violence. Most commentators agree that social movement organizations that systematically engage in violence to achieve their goals do not belong in the category of social movements but in the category of those engaged in armed struggles.

Social movements are also organized differently from institutionalized interest groups. Social movements tend to function as networks of activists, who may be brought together by shared interests, identities, and values, but who may not actually belong to formal organizations. Where organizations form, their members may overlap with informal networks. Social movement organizations are typically smaller than the organizations of institutionalized interest groups and have fewer economic resources.

* * *

The two ends of our continuum of group and movement organizations represent different **organizational cultures**. Social movements and their attendant social movement organizations springs from a political culture that is populist, emphasizing democratic participation in the decisions and actions of the group or network. An important and sizable sector of social movement organizations springs from progressive or left-wing politics; as a result, they share the political cultural heritage of such politics. For example, social movement organizations may make decisions by consensus, allowing each member of the group or each member of the decision-making group to approve or veto decisions of the group.

Definition

ORGANIZATIONAL CULTURE: Clusters of beliefs about the way groups should be organized. Examples are a belief in hierarchy and a belief in internal democracy.

In contrast, some institutionalized groups share an organizational culture that is markedly different in many ways from the social movement culture. This culture emphasizes majoritarian decision-making rather than consensus decision-making; that is, decisions are made by majority rule rather than by consensus. Further, institutionalized groups, by their very nature, embrace the division of labour. Members may play a passive rather than a participatory role, and professionals often dominate the organization.

The differences between institutionalized interest groups and the social movements that have been high-lighted on our continuum represent generalizations about the real-world shape and behaviour of civil society actors. The reality of associational life is much more complex. For example, over time, social movement organizations may take on some of the characteristics of the institutionalized interest group. Some environmental groups have been involved in extensive consultation with government and have developed many of the professional attributes of the institutionalized group, despite their origins in social movement organizing. At times, institutionalized groups may even deploy the tactics of the social movement. Farmers' organizations, for example, have been known to engage in direct action, demonstrations, and occupations in pursuit of their goals. This last example shows the importance of viewing civil society actors in historical context. In most countries, farmers' organizations began as social movements. Similarly, trade unions, which are usually defined as part of the universe of the stable, institutionalized groups, began as social movements and often deploy the ultimate weapon of direct action—the strike—in pursuit of their goals.

GROUPS AND MOVEMENTS IN PUBLIC POLICY

It is now time to discuss more systematically the means used by groups and movements to achieve their goals. Groups and social movements have a number of means at their disposal to influence government and society.

Influencing Politicians

Perhaps the most obvious and visible way in which groups may influence the shaping of public policy in democratic systems is through bringing pressure to bear on politicians. In most democratic countries, the legislature is by definition the key forum for law-making; hence, it might seem natural for groups to seek out politicians to champion their views.

However, the influence that groups are able to exercise through the legislature depends on the role played by the legislature within the political institutions of the country. In some democratic systems, legislatures play a more important role than in others. In parliamentary systems, which are common in much of the democratic political world, legislative and executive power are fused, in the sense that the executive (prime minister and his or her cabinet) is responsible to the legislature and must have the support of the legislature in order to govern. In practice, however, the members of the legislature are loyal to their political parties. The political party that wins the general election forms the government, and for most of the duration of the government's term in office, the prime minister and the cabinet are able to dominate the business of the legislature.

The extent to which prime ministers and their cabinets dominate legislatures in parliamentary systems does vary. In some cases, such as Britain, MPs tend to serve long terms in office and to develop policy expertise. Parties allow their MPs some latitude, so that the MP can actually play an independent role in law-making. In other systems, such as Canada, there is a higher turnover of MPs and a great concentration of power in the hands of the prime minister and the cabinet. In the Canadian system, MPs do not have much influence in law-making.

Yet another important difference among parliamentary systems is the type of electoral system used. In the first-past-the-post system, used in Canada and Britain, the candidate with the most votes wins the election, which tends to favour one-party majority governments, such as the current Liberal government in Canada and the Labour government in Britain. In Germany, Italy, and many of the northern European democracies, the system of proportional representation allocates seats in the legislature in part based on the proportion of votes received by each party or candidate. In this system, it is rare for one party to have a majority on its own; most of the time, these countries are governed by coalitions of parties.

In presidential systems, such as that of the United States, there is a separation of powers between the legislature and the executive. In contrast to the parliamentary model, the president and the congress are elected independently of each other, and the tenure of the president does not rest on his party's dominance of the congress. President Bill Clinton, a Democrat, ruled with a Republican-dominated Congress, while President George W. Bush governs with a Republican House of Representatives and a Senate dominated by a

bare majority of Democrats. This system of divided government means that party discipline is not as strong as in parliamentary systems. Cross-party coalitions between Democrats and Republicans often form, and individual members of Congress have much more latitude to make their own decisions about law-making.

These political institutional differences play a very important role in determining how interest groups and social movement organizations lobby members of the legislature or the executive. In first-past-the-post parliamentary systems, such as the British and Canadian systems, attempting to influence the legislature is not a very effective strategy for interest group and social movement organizations, since MPs do not have much independence in the development of public policy. In the proportional representation system, similarly, lobbying individual MPs is not likely to have a direct influence on policy formation. In such a system, the parties reach agreement by negotiating among themselves behind closed doors, which tends to decrease the possibility of direct group influence on individual members of the legislature.

In the presidential system, such as the U.S. system with its separation of powers, the situation is quite different. Because of the freedom from party discipline of the individual members of Congress, the Congress is ripe for group influence. Indeed, the United States is the home of pressure group politics, as groups and organizations vie with each other to exercise influence in the Congress.

Another means by which interest groups and social movement organizations may influence politicians is through exerting pressure in electoral politics. In the U.S. system, there is a lack of regulation of campaign finances, which means that groups and social movement organizations can influence the political process by giving money to politicians for their re-election campaigns. Groups often do this through the formation of **political action committees (PACs)**, whose express purpose is to donate to political campaigns and to influence the views of parties and politicians on issues of import to the group. Such a system obviously favours groups that have plenty of resources.

Because of the influence wielded by groups in election campaigns, campaign finance reform is a major issue in U.S. politics. There have been lively debates about the selling of access to decision-makers, as you

Figure 13.1 U.S. Political Action Committees, 1977–1998

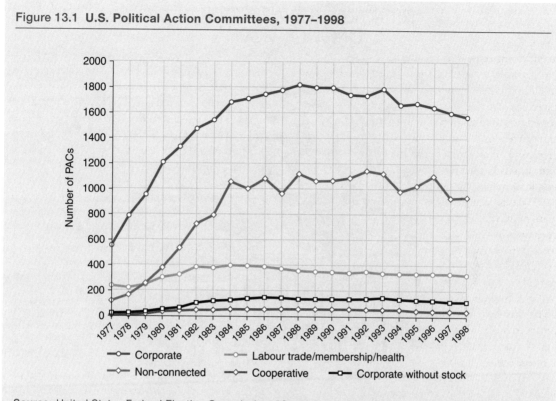

Source: United States Federal Election Commission, "Campaign Finance Reports and Data"; cited on July 12, 2002; available at http://www.fec.gov/press/paccnt_grph.html.

can see in the cartoon about party fundraising. President Clinton was accused of selling off guest invitations for overnight visits to the White House (in the Lincoln bedroom, for example) in return for donations from groups that contributed to his campaigns, while President Bush was beholden to a variety of corporate interests.

In parliamentary systems, influence through the electoral system takes different forms. In some cases, groups have formed parties to put forth their views. Trade unions in many countries played an important role in the creation of socialist and social democratic parties such as the British Labour Party. Business groups often have close but informal ties with right-of-centre political parties. Green parties have been formed in many democracies to put forth the environmental point of view, and in some countries (for example, Germany), these parties have been quite successful. In Iceland, the Women's Party was formed to advocate feminist views. Groups may also attempt to gain influence within an existing political party. Pro-life and evangelical Christians play an important role in the Republican party in the United States and to some extent in the Canadian Alliance.

Influencing the Bureaucracy

In most societies, **bureaucracy** plays a very important role in the formation and implementation of public policy. Civil servants often wield a decisive influence over government action, partly because civil servants in many states are experts in their fields. Even in democracies in which civil servants are expected to be accountable to democratically elected politicians, they may still wield much influence because of their expertise, stability, and longevity in government positions. This is

"BUT NOTICE — NOT ONE OF THEM IN THE LINCOLN BEDROOM"

Regardless of the party in power in the White House, election contributions are always a priority.

Copyright 2001 by Herblock in The Washington Post

particularly true of the merit-based bureaucracy, in which civil servants are selected for their positions based on their merits, rather than on their political connections. In authoritarian systems, civil servants may be chosen in part for their political connections, particularly their connections to the party in power.

In any case, in most contexts, influencing the bureaucracy is one of the most effective means for groups to influence public policy. It is important to note that this is a strategy that works best for institutionalized groups, which have the resources, the money, and the expertise to develop stable relationships over time with government bureaucrats. In both democratic and authoritarian systems, governments may cultivate these relationships for the reasons outlined earlier, namely in order to obtain valuable political or technical information from these groups and to use the groups to legitimate the policies of government.

In many democratic systems such as Canada, the United States, and Britain, relationships between interest groups and bureaucrats are so close that these groups and the bureaucracy are involved in institutionalized patterns of relationships and form what scholars call a **policy community**. Groups and the bureaucracy mutually influence each other and collaborate in the formation of public policy. This does not necessarily mean that groups dictate public policy; in some cases, groups may be dominated by government priorities, while in others groups may indeed play an influential part in policy formation.

Definition

POLICY COMMUNITY: A collection of groups and individuals (including both state bureaucrats and interest groups or social movement organizations) who influence each other in an effort to shape policy outcomes in their area of interest.

The pattern of relationships between groups and the civil service varies depending on the type of regime and the type of political institutions in place. In authoritarian political systems and in new and fragile democracies, such as Russia, the civil service may be weakened or even corrupted by links to organized crime, making institutionalized group relationships of the type described here impossible. Access may depend solely upon elite connections. In other cases, the civil service may be dominated by appointees of a particular political party, as was the case in Mexico with the dominant party prior to the election of Vicente Fox in 2000. In this case, social groups were institutionalized within the party and dominated by party elites.

Influence through Lobbying

Those who wish to influence government may choose to do so by hiring professional **lobbyists** to do the job on their behalf. Interest groups may choose this approach if they feel that they are unlikely on their own to secure access to the relevant department of government or to the policies that will shape legisla-

tion. Corporations or groups of corporations with similar interests may choose this approach because they can afford to pay for lobbying by professionals. Ottawa-based Hillwatch Inc., for example, provides a list of its current and past clients, as well as samples of its work, on its website at http://www.hillwatch.com/inc/hillincclientshome.htm. This list gives us a view of the type of work that is undertaken by lobbyists. The list of clients includes different levels of government (such as the City of Ottawa), utilities from outside of Canada (such as the New York Power Authority), embassies of foreign governments (such as the Embassy of Japan), interest groups that represent particular economic sectors (such as the Ontario Lumber Manufacturers' Association), and large corporations (such as Nestlé, Paramount, and Honeywell Canada).

Lobbying is effective for those who have relatively narrow and well-defined goals with respect to specific issues that affect a particular industry, such as levels of taxation or regulations. Tobacco companies hired professional lobbyists to influence the Canadian government on tobacco advertising. At the same time, tobacco companies also hired lawyers to pursue their interests through the courts, arguing that restrictions on tobacco advertising constituted an unconstitutional limit on free expression under the Charter of Rights and Freedoms. Lobbying and the use of courts to advance policy goals are similar in that professionals (lobbyists, lawyers, or both) are hired for the express purpose of securing political influence.

Many countries have recognized that lobbyists pose a threat to the democratic process. Because lobbyists are hired by those with money, they may give corporations and well-funded interest groups an advantage in the political process. In recognition of this, some countries have regulated paid lobbying. In Canada, lobbying is regulated by the 1989 Lobbyists Registration Act. Lobbyists must register and state the general areas in which they are undertaking to influence government. The act does not have much in the way of enforcement mechanisms, although the federal ethics counsellor may report on breaches of the code. However, the current ethics counsellor, who is appointed by the prime minister, has been under fire for failure to stand up to the government.

Influencing the Courts

In democratic societies, the courts also provide a venue for interest groups to exert influence. As in the case of politicians and the bureaucracy, the opportunities for influencing the courts depend on the specific shape of political institutions and the role that courts play in the political system. In Britain, for example, groups traditionally have not had much influence on public policy through the courts. Without a written Constitution and judicial review, groups did not have strong legal tools to force changes in government policies. Britain's membership in the European Union is changing the role of courts in the British political system, however. Increasingly, groups are turning to European courts, such as the European Court of Human Rights and the European Court of Justice, to influence the British political system. Recent issues in which British laws have

been influenced by European court decisions include assisted suicide for the terminally ill and equality of the sexes in entitlement for government benefits.[6]

In the United States, judicial review has formed part of the Constitution from an early period. Groups and social movement organizations in the United States often turn to the courts to influence public policies. There are many examples of such influence. Two of the most well-known are the use of the courts by the women's movement to secure the right to abortion in *Roe* v. *Wade* in 1973 and the African-American civil rights movement's use of the courts to end segregation of the school system in *Brown* v. *Board of Education* in 1954.[7]

In Canada, venues for group influence through the courts were weak before the entrenchment of the Charter of Rights and Freedoms in the Canadian Constitution in 1982. Since then, many groups have turned to the courts, using the Charter's rights guarantees and other provisions of the 1982 Constitution (such as Aboriginal rights' guarantees in section 35) to achieve important policy objectives. Political scientist Gregory Hein has studied these group efforts to influence public policy through the courts, and his tabulation of frequency of recourse to the courts by different groups in society appears in Figure 13.2. His data show that recourse to the courts has increased across different groups in society, although corporations use the courts far more frequently than other groups. Hein concludes that "interest group litigation is ... an established form of collective action"[8] in Canada.

Influencing the Media

The success of collective actors in challenging government policy or seeking to influence social norms and values may be greatly enhanced through the skilful use of the media. In particular, when groups seek to influence politicians and elections, the media provide a vehicle for drawing public attention to the groups' point of view. In the cases of gun control, abortion, and lesbian and gay rights, supporters and opponents on each issue attempted to capture the media's attention as a way of bringing pressure to bear on MPs. Because media such as television tend to focus on dramatic conflicts within a limited time frame, groups that can successfully produce quick sound bites tend to receive more attention than collective actors who are attempting to call

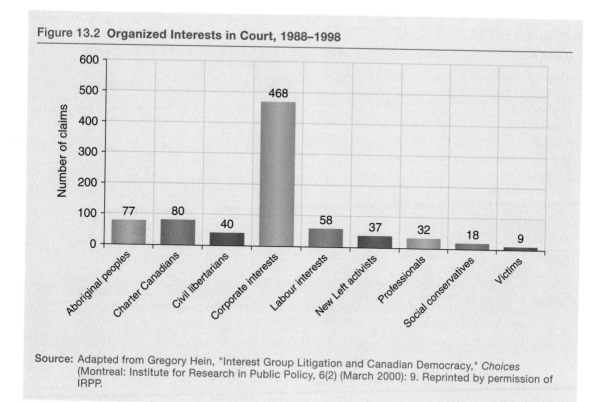

Figure 13.2 Organized Interests in Court, 1988–1998

Source: Adapted from Gregory Hein, "Interest Group Litigation and Canadian Democracy," *Choices* (Montreal: Institute for Research in Public Policy, 6(2) (March 2000): 9. Reprinted by permission of IRPP.

attention to the structural forces that shape government policy or societal norms. In the case of environmentalism, for example, there are a wide variety of deep ecology perspectives emphasizing that economic development in many parts of the world threatens humanity's survival. However, complex scientific and philosophical arguments about deep ecology are unlikely to produce the quick media sound bites that television demands. Hence, successful environmental groups have often sought to dramatize environmental issues in ways that can be captured easily for global media consumption. As Stephen Dale has pointed out, Greenpeace is a master of media tactics. By sailing into the U.S. nuclear test site in the Aleutian Islands in 1971, a tiny band of Greenpeace protesters were able to draw worldwide media attention to the nuclear test. This was Greenpeace's start as an environmental organization. From a few protesters in an old fishing boat, Greenpeace has grown to an international organization with a budget of U.S.$28.3 million in 1994.[9]

Influence at the Transnational Level

Globalization has had important effects on the mobilization of groups and movements. More than ever, public policy is subject to pressures from beyond the borders of one country. Enhanced communications technology facilitates links between groups across borders. International organizations ranging from the WTO to the UN play an increased role in the making of policy decisions. Regional economic and political integration, as in the European Union, create new transborder policies. Trade agreements, such as the North American Free Trade Agreement (NAFTA), limit the range of policy choices that are open to governments. This process of "decentring" the state, as Warren Magnusson has termed it, has been characterized by a marked increase in **transnational group** activity in recent years, as shown in Table 13.2.[10] The table shows the extent to which various types of

Table 13.2   **International Nongovernmental Social Change Organizations**

Issue Area	1953		1963		1973		1983		1993	
	Number	Percent	Number	Percent	Number	Percent	Number	Percent	Number	Percent
Human Rights	33	30.0	38	27.0	41	22.4	79	22.7	168	26.6
World Order	8	7.3	4	2.8	12	6.6	31	8.9	48	7.6
International Law	14	12.7	19	13.4	25	13.7	26	7.4	26	4.1
Peace	11	10.0	20	14.2	14	7.7	22	6.3	59	9.4
Women's Rights	10	9.1	14	9.9	16	8.7	25	7.2	61	9.7
Environment	2	1.8	5	3.5	10	5.5	26	7.5	90	14.3
Development	3	2.7	3	2.1	7	3.8	13	3.7	34	5.4
Ethnic Unity/ Group Rights	10	9.1	122	8.5	18	9.8	37	10.6	29	4.6
Esperanto	11	10.0	18	12.8	28	15.3	41	11.8	54	8.6

Note: The percentages in any one decade do not add up to 100 because groups that champion other causes have not been included.

Source: Adapted from Margaret E. Keck and Kathryn Sikkink, eds., *Activists beyond Borders: Advocacy Networks in International Politics* (Ithaca and London: Cornell University Press, 1998), p. 11. Used by permission of the publisher, Cornell University Press.

transnational advocacy groups have grown over the past few decades.

Definition

TRANSNATIONAL GROUP: A group that organizes across the borders of nation-states with the aim of influencing national governments, international organizations, or public opinion.

Interest groups and social movement organizations may appeal to international organizations to pressure their own state, or they may form alliances with other groups outside of their own state. This may occur in cases in which groups have failed in their efforts to achieve positive results through domestic strategies alone. For example, pro-democracy and human rights activists in South Africa were successful in mobilizing international organizations and public opinion to overthrow the apartheid regime. In the last 20 years, First Nations in Canada have developed links with Indigenous peoples around the world, especially through the World Council of Indigenous Peoples. Another example of transnational linkages is the campaign to stop the OECD's Multilateral Agreement on Investment (MAI), a proposed investment treaty. Over

500 NGOs from 67 countries signed a joint statement condemning the MAI; this concentrated effort was widely credited with delaying the ratification of the accord in 1997.[11] Christina Gabriel and Laura Macdonald have demonstrated that, in the wake of NAFTA, incipient linkages are developing between feminist activists in Canada and Mexico, as women attempt to deal with the economic, social, and political consequences of North American economic restructuring.[12]

Interest groups and social movement organizations within one country may mobilize to influence politics elsewhere in the world, targeting foreign states or international organizations in an effort to influence the behaviour, policies, and practices of foreign states and international actors. One of the best examples of this type of activity occurred during the campaign against South Africa's apartheid regime. Anti-apartheid activists within South Africa appealed to NGOs and human rights groups outside of the country for support. Many solidarity groups sprang up in developed democracies. The campaign against apartheid targeted the South African regime through pressure put on the government by other states, international organizations, private companies, and other social institutions. For example, the divestment campaign in North America and Europe pressured social institutions such as universities to cancel their investments in companies doing business with South Africa. International pressure played a key role in instituting change in South Africa.[13]

The antiglobalization protests of the last few years have had important effects on the ways in which multilateral economic institutions function. According to Robert O'Brien and his colleagues, the labour, women's, and environmental movements have all had very important impacts on the way in which international institutions function. Organizations such as the

IMF, the WTO, and the World Bank have all responded to pressure from the transnational social movements. These scholars argue that transnational social movement advocacy is creating a new and complex form of global governance as political issues move from the domestic to the international and global levels.[14] In this sense, the contestation and social movement tactics we have seen on television at protests such as those Seattle and Quebec City are counterbalanced by the actions of more institutionalized groups, which serve some of the same functions for international institutions and for multilateral economic organizations as

---

BOX 13.3

NATIONAL SECURITY AND INTEREST GROUP POLITICS

Following the September 11, 2001, attack on the World Trade Centre and other U.S. targets, interest groups in the United States began to back off from the business-as–usual approach, as the following article shows.

* * *

Several influential U.S. environment groups have silenced their criticism of the U.S. government and stopped lobbying for conservation measures because of the terrorist attacks on New York and Washington.

The Sierra Club, one of the largest U.S. environmental groups, last week dropped all of its work challenging Bush administration policies. Greenpeace, known for its high-profile environmental campaigns using civil disobedience, has also decided to take a lower profile.

The terrorist attacks have rattled the leaders of environmental organizations and made them wary of being viewed as divisive and unpatriotic while the country faces a national trauma.

As well, the attacks have swept environmental issues off the political agenda.

"We lost the stomach, both personally and individually, for some of the fights we had been engaged in prior to that," Craig Culp, a spokesman for Greenpeace in the United States, said.

The decision by the groups to play down activism could have implications on a number of pressing public-policy issues, including the U.S. response to global warming, the opening up of Alaska's Arctic wildlife reserve to oil drilling and the development of the Star Wars missile-defence system.

Until the attacks, environmentalists had been on a roll. They had launched highly effective attacks on the Bush administration on issues ranging from the higher arsenic levels allowed in drinking water to the government's failure to endorse the Kyoto pact on global warming.

The administration had inadvertently become a boon to conservation groups, which were successfully using the government's anti-environmental policies as tools to raise funds and to mobilize their members.

But with the terrorism crisis, those campaigns became unexpected collateral damage.

The head of the Sierra Club, Carl Pope, issued a statement shortly after the attacks saying his group was going to pause because of the country's national-security crisis and unsettled public mood.

Source: Martin Mittelstaedt, "Environmental Groups Drop Campaign Criticizing Bush," *The Globe and Mail*, September 21, 2001, p. A8. Reprinted with permission from *The Globe and Mail*.

we have already identified at the domestic level. While the social movements protest in the streets and put pressure on such organizations through the media, the more organized groups are developing institutionalized relationships with these international and transnational organizations. As on the domestic level, interest groups at the international level provide international organizations and institutions with information about complex areas of public policy. Also at the domestic level, transnational advocacy groups lend legitimacy to the actions of international organizations such as the World Bank and the IMF. In an era of heightened and increasingly competitive and globalized media scrutiny, special-interest social movement groups are valuable potential allies for such international organizations.

ARE INTEREST GROUPS TOO POWERFUL?

Are interest groups and social movement organizations too powerful? In the media, one often hears the view that special-interest groups should not be able to dominate policymaking. This holds true at both the domestic and international levels. This debate revolves around the question of democratic legitimacy. Are groups and social movements legitimate representatives of citizens? Or do interest groups and social movement organizations pervert and distort the democratic process by using money and other illegitimate means to pursue their interests? Do such groups and movements reflect or impede the spirit and practice of democracy? The cartoon of President Clinton allegedly selling off the Lincoln bedroom to the highest bidder while President Bush responded to various corporate interests would seem to encapsulate one side of this debate; the sight of the Mexican students pursuing their interests against an undemocratic government would seem to embody the other. In the first case, interest groups appear to be "special interests" (in the vocabulary of U.S. politics) that are corrupting the political process. In the other case, the students are pushing forward the process of democratization in Mexico.

Which side we take on this question may well depend upon the context. In an undemocratic system such as Mexico's before the Fox election, we might favour the mobilization of societal interests in order to facilitate the transition to democracy. In recent years, we have seen many social movement mobilizations that have pushed forward democratic transitions, as noted in Chapter 15. In Eastern Europe's struggle against communism, in the Philippines' "people power" movement, and in South Africa's anti-apartheid movement, we see examples in which street power, demonstrations, and other tactics of social movement protest have brought about democracy. Even in existing authoritarian regimes, groups may play an important role in permitting channels for the expression of public opinion between citizens and the state. Such channels, although they are likely to be narrow and circumscribed, are even more important when citizens do not have access to free elections.

Furthermore, many scholars believe that interest groups and social movement organizations are essential to the healthy functioning of democratic political institutions, and a prerequisite to the establishment of democracy. In the 19th century, observers such as Alexis de Tocqueville (in his famous book *Democracy in America*) and French sociologist Emile Durkheim argued that democratic political institutions required the healthy soil of associational and group life in order to flourish. Some scholars have argued that societies in which interest groups and social movements do not exist or where they have been weakened by a strong and repressive state, as in Russia, may have difficulties in making democracy work.[15]

On the other hand, in capitalist democracies, the power of groups and movements may in part depend upon their access to money. Left-wing and populist critiques of group involvement in democratic politics emphasize the way in which business groups may use their financial resources to access and influence political elites. In this view, the playing field for interest group and social movement activity in a market society is not level. Certain groups have more power than others because of their ability to mobilize economic resources. Many argue that interest group activity during election campaigns should be limited because of the fact that monied groups (such as the PACs in the United States) can circumvent election spending laws and influence election outcomes. From a right-wing perspective, it is sometimes argued that certain minority groups have too much power and have been able to influence public policy against the interests of the democratic majority.

Right-wing critics of interest group and social movement activism often point to feminism as an example of a negative identity politics that has produced public policy outcomes that ignore the wishes of the majority.

CONCLUSION

Debates over the power of groups and movements as political actors go to the heart of debates about the nature of political power itself. How is political power exercised? Who has power and who doesn't? Who should have power? Should politics be limited to politicians? How can citizens engage in democratic deliberation, and how can group politics and associational life facilitate citizen engagement? There are no easy answers to these questions. They are questions that extend from the realm of political debates in any one country into the international arena as groups increasingly overlap across borders in the new political spaces of our globalized world.

DISCUSSION QUESTIONS

1. **Choose one social movement organization or interest group. Trace its attempts to influence public policy.**

2. **Are demonstrations and civil disobedience a legitimate means of influencing public opinion and public policy?**

3. **Should interest groups and social movement organizations have the right to spend money during election campaigns?**

4. **What are the main similarities and differences between institutionalized interest groups and social movement networks?**

wᴡᴡ WEB LINKS

The U.S. Civil Rights Movement:
http://www.msnbc.com/onair/modules/selma.asp

Greenpeace:
http://www.greenpeace.org

The Confederation of British Industry (CBI):
http://www.cbi.org.uk/home.html

An American-style Interest Group:
http://www.mynra.com

Mexico Solidarity Network:
http://www.mexicosolidarity.org

Political Action Committees in U.S. Electoral Politics:
http://www.opensecrets.org/pubs/bigpicture2000/pac/index.ihtml

FURTHER READING

Broder, David S. *Democracy Derailed: Initiative Campaigns and the Power of Money.* New York: Harcourt Brace, 2000.

Della Porta, Donatalla, and Mario Diani. *Social Movements: An Introduction.* Oxford: Blackwell, 1999.

Graziano, Luigi. *Lobbying, Pluralism and Democracy.* London: St. Martin's Press, 2001.

Keck, Margaret E., and Kathryn Sikkink. *Activists Beyond Borders: Advocacy Networks in International Politics.* New York: Cornell University Press, 1998.

Pross, A. Paul. *Group Politics and Public Policy.* Toronto: Oxford University Press, 1993.

Ruffin, M. Hold, ed. *The Post-Soviet Handbook: A Guide to Grassroots Organizations and Internet Resources.* Seattle: University of Washington Press, 1999.

Schwartz, Frank J. *Advice and Consent: The Politics of Consultation in Japan.* Cambridge: Cambridge University Press, 1998.

ENDNOTES

1   John Agnew, *Geopolitics: Re-visioning World Politics* (London and New York: Routledge, 1998).

2   Sydney Tarrow, *Power in Movement: Social Movements, Collective Action and Politics* (Cambridge: Cambridge University Press, 1994).

3   "UNAM Students Arrested: Appeal for Solidarity!"; cited on July1, 2001; available at http://www.newyouth.com/archives/campaigns/mexico/unam_students_arrested_appeal_20000222.asp.

4   Osha Gray Davidson, *Under Fire: The NRA and the Battle for Gun Control* (Iowa City: University of Iowa Press, 1998).

5   Leslie A. Pal, *Interests of State: The Politics of Language, Multiculturalism and Feminism in Canada* (Montreal and Kingston: McGill-Queen's University Press, 1993).

6   *Pretty v. the United Kingdom* (European Court of Human Rights, January 18, 2002); *Fielding v. the United Kingdom* (European Court of Human Rights, January 29, 2002).

7   Charles Epp, *The Rights Revolution* (Chicago: University of Chicago Press, 1998).

8   Gregory Hein, "Interest Group Litigation and Canadian Democracy," *Choices* (Montreal: Institute for Research in Public Policy) 6(2) (March 2000): 9.

9   Stephen Dale, *McLuhan's Children: The Greenpeace Message and the Media* (Toronto: Between the Lines, 1996), pp. 4, 15ff.

10 Warren Magnusson, "Decentring the State," in James Bickerton and Alain G. Gagnon, eds., *Canadian Politics* (Peterborough: Broadview Press, 1994).

11 Council of Canadians, "Joint NGO Statement on the Multilateral Agreement on Investment (MAI) to the Organization for Economic Cooperation and Development"; cited on July 1, 2001; available at http://www.canadians.org/ngostatement.html.

12 Christina Gabriel and Laura Macdonald, "NAFTA, Women and Organizing in Canada and Mexico: Forging a Feminist Internationality?" *Millennium* 23(3) (winter 1994): 535–62.

13 Audie J. Klotz, *Norms in International Relations: The Struggle Against Apartheid* (New York: Cornell University Press, 1996).

14 Robert O'Brien, Anne Marie Goetz, Jan Aart Scholte, and Marc Williams, *Contesting Global Governance: Multilateral Economic Institutions and Global Social Movements* (Cambridge: Cambridge University Press, 2000).

15 Robert Putnam, *Making Democracy Work* (Princeton: Princeton University Press, 1994), pp. 163–86.

Political Development and Change

6

Career Profile: Judy Myrden

Judy was born in Halifax and took a four-year honours degree in political science and economics at Dalhousie University. After graduation, she went to the London School of Economics in London, England, to study for an M.Sc. degree in the politics and government of Western Europe.

After a year, she returned to Halifax and was hired by The Halifax Herald Ltd., publishers of *The Chronicle-Herald/The Mail Star*, one of the last independent newspapers in Canada. Judy has worked as a reporter at the newspaper since 1985, at first in the newsroom, where she covered judicial issues and politics. She has also written freelance articles for *Time* magazine and *Lawyers Weekly*.

For the past five years, Judy has worked in the business section of the newspaper, covering the emerging offshore oil and gas industry in the province of Nova Scotia. While working this beat, she has travelled across the country to gain an understanding of the development of the East Coast's first natural project—the $2 billion Sable Island natural gas project and the connecting Maritime and Northeast Pipeline. She reported on the regulatory hearings both in Canada and in Washington, D.C. In 1997, she was going to Aberdeen, Scotland, to cover the impact of the oil and gas industry on that country, but was rerouted to London to cover Princess Diana's funeral.

More recently, Judy covered a federal arbitration hearing between Nova Scotia and Newfoundland over the potentially rich in oil and gas Laurentian subbasin. This was an excellent opportunity to use her education because the hearings focused heavily on intergovernmental relations during the 1960s and 1970s and the possible economic ramifications if one province won out over the other. In the end, Nova Scotia lost, as the international arbitration panel gave the lion's share of the ocean floor in question to Newfoundland.

Judy enjoys playing tennis and squash, is treasurer of the newsroom local of the Newspaper Guild of Canada, and is married to a political reporter for Halifax CBC television.

Chapter 14

The Politics of Development and Underdevelopment

James Busumtwi-Sam

CHAPTER OBJECTIVES

After you have completed this chapter, you should be able to

- identify some of the dimensions of global inequality, including inequality between men and women

- discuss the history and sources of development as a global issue and the evolution of the dialogue between rich and poor countries over how best to achieve development

- identify some of the main explanations offered for patterns of development and underdevelopment

- outline the contemporary issues and debates that arise from processes of development and change.

INTRODUCTION

Economic growth and industrialization, as well as advances in science and technology, have resulted in a level of prosperity and material well-being unparalleled in human history. But these very same forces of development and change have generated deepening imbalances among countries, individuals, and groups; between men and women; and between human civilization and the natural environment. These imbalances have been a source of past and continuing political conflict and disagreement. In this chapter, we examine development as an international issue and discuss some key questions arising from processes of development and change. What does development entail? Why do some countries and peoples enjoy very high standards of living while others live in poverty? What are the consequences of underdevelopment, and what prescriptions are available for addressing these consequences? The phrase "politics of development and underdevelopment" in the title of this chapter draws attention to the fact that the answers to these questions are not straightforward but have been and continue to be highly contentious.

We begin with an overview of some key challenges to development globally, highlighting the dimensions of the gap between the haves and the have-nots of the world. We then proceed to examine the question of what development entails by highlighting the different circumstances of countries classified as developing. Having a good sense of the relevant history helps our understanding of the present, and so the next section discusses the history and legacy of colonialism in Africa, Asia, and Latin America. The countries in these regions were subject to European colonial expansion between the 17th and early 20th centuries; in the contemporary period, as a group, they generally fall into the have-nots category. The efforts by these countries to effect change in international economic and political relations are examined in the following section. Next, we consider the difficulties in and controversies surrounding the measurement and explanation of patterns of development and underdevelopment. Here we examine different ways of looking at development—political, economic, and social—as well as some of the theories and explanations offered for development and the lack thereof. Worldwide, women fare comparatively worse than men on various indicators of development, so we also examine aspects of the debate over women in development, highlighting the gender dimensions of global inequality.

The final sections explore some contemporary issues and debates arising from processes of development and change, including the debate over the role of foreign aid in development and the debate over the environment and development captured by the term *sustainable development*. Also examined are the role of democracy and

civil society in development, as well as problems of political violence and civil strife in many poorer countries.

CHALLENGES OF GLOBAL DEVELOPMENT[1]

Challenges to global development are manifold, but they can be usefully grouped into three broad categories: challenges arising from global poverty and inequality, challenges in the area of human security, and challenges arising from environmental stress and degradation.

Global Poverty and Inequality

Since the early 1960s, considerable advances have been made in improving living standards for people around the world. On the global scale, overall production of wealth has increased sevenfold since the early 1960s. However, out of an estimated world population of about 6 billion, approximately 1.2 billion people lived in absolute poverty—that is, on an income of less than U.S.$1 per day. While the proportion of the world's population living in poverty has decreased (down from about 28 percent in 1987 to about 26 percent in 1998), the number of poor people has actually increased in many regions of the world, particularly in Africa and in parts of Latin America and Asia (see Table 14.1 below). The majority are women and children. Income disparities between the richest 20 percent

Table 14.1 **Population Living on Less than $1 a Day**				
Region	Population (Millions)		Share of Population (Percent)	
	1987	1998	1987	1998
East Asia/Pacific	415.5	278.3	26.6	15.3
Eastern Europe/Central Asia	1.1	24.0	0.2	5.1
Latin America/Caribbean	63.7	78.2	15.3	15.6
Middle East/North Africa	9.3	5.5	4.3	1.9
South Asia	474.4	522.0	44.9	40.0
Sub-Saharan Africa	217.2	290.9	48.5	46.3
Totals	1183.8	1198.9	28.3	26.2

Source: World Bank, *World Development Report 2000/01* (New York: Oxford University Press, 1999; 2001), table 1.1, p. 23. Reprinted by permission of the International Bank for Reconstruction and Development/The World Bank.

and the poorest 20 percent have also more than doubled since the early 1960s. The ratio of income of the top 20 percent to the poorest 20 percent stood at 78 to 1 in 1997, having risen from 30 to 1 in 1960.

Human Security

Another major challenge to global development lies in the insecurities faced by large numbers of individuals and groups around the world. Traditional interstate wars affected the security of states and nations, but modern forms of warfare and political violence largely affect the security of individuals and communities. Many recent armed conflicts, the majority of which have occurred in poorer developing countries, were accompanied by some of the most gruesome violations of human rights and humanitarian law, including the use of child soldiers and the direct targeting of civilian populations. The proportion of civilian casualties soared from 5 percent of total casualties in World War I to 80 percent in armed conflicts that occurred during the 1990s.

The concept of **human security** was first introduced through a publication of the United Nations Development Programme (UNDP) in 1994 and has since become a central theme in discussions of international development and international security. The evolving discourse on human security, in which Canada has played a leading role, represents an attempt to focus attention on threats to the safety of individuals and groups and to link insecurity to problems of underdevelopment. Factors such as political repression and violence, abuse of human rights, extreme poverty and deprivation, lack of food and health security, and environmental degradation are seen as prime sources of the fragmentation of a large number of political and social systems around the world. Human security is said to have two main components: *safety* (of individuals and groups) from such chronic threats as hunger, disease, and repression; and *protection* from sudden and hurtful disruptions in patterns of daily life. More than half of the 35 poorest countries have experienced a major armed conflict in the past 15 years. The 1990s also saw a dramatic increase in displaced persons (internal refugees) and international refugees—over 70 million people. Mass migrations of people across borders seeking better economic conditions can also be a source of conflict. Also on the increase is the incidence of violent crime, within nations as well as internationally. This increase has led to recognition of the phenomena of transnational organized crime and terrorism as global issues. The issue of political violence and warfare is discussed later on in this chapter as well as in Chapters 15 and 16.

> **Definition**
>
> **HUMAN SECURITY:** A broadened concept of security focusing not just on national security and interstate war but on threats to the safety of individuals and groups.

Environmental Stress and Degradation

Challenges to development are also evident in the area of increased pressure on the earth's natural environment. Only 1.7 million out of an estimated 30 million species living on the planet have been identified. However, natural habitats, including forests and wetlands, where many of the unidentified species live are disappearing at a rate of 0.5 to 1 percent per year. The world's population is increasing by approximately 800 million people per decade; by 2030, it is expected to reach an estimated 8.5 billion. To keep pace with this growth, world food production will need to double in the next 30 years. Approximately 1.3 billion people worldwide have no access to safe drinking water or basic sanitation; 800 million people (200 million of them children) are at risk of disease and malnourishment. Resource scarcity, including declines in arable land and shortages of fresh water supplies, compound the insecurities faced by individuals and groups around the world and can contribute to the incidence of violent conflict, both within nations as well as between them.

DEVELOPMENT AND UNDERDEVELOPMENT: PROBLEMS OF CLASSIFICATION

Considerable differences exist among the 192 sovereign states in the world today in terms of their levels of development. Generally, international discussions of development have focused on how to improve the conditions or circumstances of people living in a group of countries variously described as developing countries, less developed countries, underdeveloped countries, the Third World, or the South. This group is said to include all countries in Central and South America, the Caribbean, Africa, Asia (excluding Japan), the Middle East, and the Pacific islands (excluding Australia and New Zealand). In all, over 120 countries are included in this group (see Figure 14.1). These terms are used to differentiate this group from the developed countries (also called the North), which include Canada, the United States, Europe, Australia, New Zealand, and Japan.

Some analysts question whether such classifications and generalizations are still relevant today.[2] They point to the fact that the term *Third World* was originally a political classification describing one of the "three worlds" that existed during the Cold War: the "first world" of Western industrialized states; the "second world" comprising the Soviet Union and its allies in Eastern Europe, and a "third world" that included all other countries that were not aligned with either of these groups. Now that the Cold War is over, the argument goes, this classification is no longer relevant.

Others point to the increased diversity within the group of developing nations. For example, the group includes countries such as Singapore and South Korea, which are among the fastest-growing economies in the world. On some economic indicators of development, these countries outperform many developed Western states. Singapore, for example, had a higher average national income (U.S.$32 940) than Canada (U.S.$19 290) in 1997.[3] While these criticisms have merit, the fact remains that diversity within the group of developing countries tends to be exaggerated when the focus is mainly on economic indicators of development. When the concept of development is disaggregated into its economic, social, and political dimensions, on the other hand, it becomes evident that the developing countries as a whole tend to score lower on all three dimensions when compared to developed countries. (These three dimensions of development are explored in greater detail later in this chapter.)

Figure 14.1 The North and the South

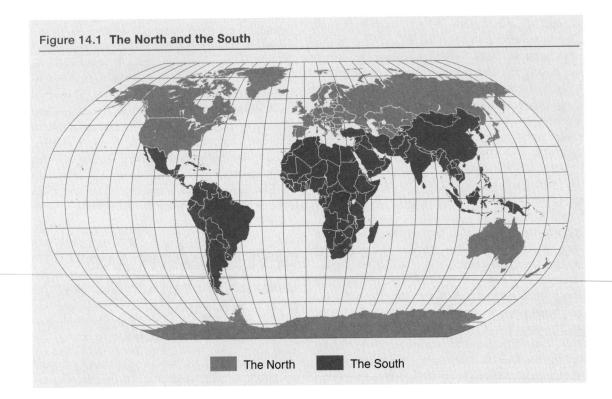

The North   The South

Other critics object to the terms *underdeveloped* and *less developed* on normative grounds. These are essentially negative concepts that describe and classify a group of countries and people by what they do not have in comparison to what another group of countries has (i.e., "not developed").[4] To minimize some of these negative connotations, the subsequent discussion in this chapter will use the terms *the South* or *developing countries* interchangeably. As the map in Figure 14.1 indicates, most of the countries that comprise the developing world are located in the southern hemisphere or to the south of the developed countries. Most developed states, with the notable exceptions of Australia and New Zealand, are located in the northern hemisphere.

Another important factor that unites the developing countries of the South vis-à-vis the developed North is a technological gap or dependence. The term *technology* as it is used here does not simply mean machines and physical tools but rather applied knowledge—the instruments and processes used to solve social, economic, and political problems. For much of the post–World War II period, development in practice has been virtually synonymous with modernization and westernization—the adoption of Western forms of social, political, and economic organization. Even non-Western developed countries such as Japan owe their success in part to their ability to adapt their practices to Western forms of technology and organization.

For example, although bureaucracy may have originated in China, the modern bureaucracy—based on rational-legal authority and an efficient technocracy—is very much a Western invention. As the discussion in one of the sections below shows, the emergence of such rational-legal authority is seen by some as a key to successful political development. Furthermore, the most dominant form of political organization in the world today, the sovereign territorial state, is also a Western invention. Almost all present-day developing countries in Africa, Asia, and the Americas were once colonies of European states, and all of them are the product of a process that began in the late 15th century in Europe, through which scattered peoples throughout the world were brought together into single societies of sovereign states and a single global economy.[5] The history and legacy of colonialism is examined below.

COLONIALISM IN THE AMERICAS, ASIA, AND AFRICA[6]

By far the greater part of what is currently the South was at one time or another subjected to formal colonial rule by European states. Even those non-Western societies that retained their independence, such as Japan and China, were forced to come to terms with a world in which European technology and influence were dominant and to adapt their own domestic political structures to meet the European prerequisites of statehood. European **colonialism** took different forms depending on the colonizing state itself, the reasons for which it undertook colonialism, and especially the sociopolitical organization and response of the colonized peoples. In many cases, this domination was characterized by the establishment of great European empires in the process of **imperialism**.

Definition

COLONIALISM: The ownership and administration of one territory and people by another as if the former were part of the latter.

Definition

IMPERIALISM: The domination of one country by another with the aim of controlling and/or exploiting the latter; this domination can be economic, political, social, or cultural. Imperialism literally means "empire building."

Colonialism in the Americas

European colonialism in the Americas was distinguished from that in Africa and Asia by the thoroughness with which it displaced existing societies. In the islands of the Caribbean, the first point of contact in the Americas, Indigenous populations almost entirely disappeared within a few generations. In Central and South America, strong Indigenous empires, such as the Aztec and the Inca, could not resist European expansion. However, the extent to which Indigenous populations were displaced varied in the Americas. In the northwest portion of the South American continent and in Central America, Indigenous populations still constitute a significant proportion of the total population: 70 percent in Bolivia, 46 percent in Peru, 39 percent in Ecuador, and 30 percent in Mexico. In the southern part of South America and the Caribbean islands, however, they have all but disappeared. Although substantial Indigenous populations still exist in Canada and the United States, they remain socially, politically, and economically peripheral.

The displacement of local populations in the Americas was due to a variety of factors. Many of the territories that had a temperate climate similar to that in Europe were designated "white settler" lands—especially in Canada, the United States, Argentina, and Chile. The more tropical areas of the Americas (the Caribbean, Brazil, southern United States, etc.) were designated for the production of cash crops for the European market: sugar, cotton, tobacco, and coffee. For various reasons, the Indigenous populations were deemed "unsuitable" for work in the production of cash crops, and the solution was the importation of people from the African continent to work as slaves. This led to the transatlantic slave trade, which began in the mid-16th century and continued for 300 years. Millions of Africans were brought to the Americas, some estimates putting the figure as high as 100 million people. A renewed demand for plantation labour in the 19th century after the demise of the slave trade led to the importation of indentured labourers from India and China.

Colonialism in Asia

What distinguished colonialism in Asia from that in the Americas was the comparative strength and resistance of its Indigenous cultures and societies. In no case (except for small islands in the Indian Ocean, such as Mauritius) could these be destroyed or completely subordinated to a predominantly European settler society. Even though Asia had been the prime target for European mercantilist expansion even prior to the "discovery" of the Americas in the late 15th century, the cohesiveness of Asian societies restricted European incursions to coastal trading posts. The formal imposition of colonial rule in Asia occurred mainly in the 19th century and was made possible by European technological advances. A number of political entities, however, such as Iran, Afghanistan, and Thailand never became subject to formal colonial rule.

European colonialism in Asia proceeded by taking over existing political systems, including preserving local political leaders (for example, in India). Societies were taken over in their entirety, and the new fixed colonial territorial frontiers roughly coincided with the undemarcated boundaries within which the precolonial rulers had ruled. The Middle East also experienced a unique brand of colonialism. This region had been subject to European expansion since the time of the crusades (5th century to 10th century), and by the mid-17th century had come under the control of the Ottoman Empire. At the end of World War I, European powers such as France and the United Kingdom ruled (under the League of Nations Mandate system) most of these former Ottoman territories in conjunction with local dynasties. The impact of European incursions here was limited by the strength of the local dynasties and by the force of pan-Arabism that produced a very strong sense of regional identity.

Colonialism in Africa

Unlike Asia, Africa was initially perceived to have little economic worth (except for its people, who could be exported as slaves); it had an interior that was difficult to penetrate, and it was considered to have a climate inhospitable for European settlement. Thus, except for a few coastal trading forts and settlements that were used primarily for slave raids and the storage of slaves for export, formal imposition of colonial rule did not occur until the end of the 19th century (except for Algeria, colonized by France in 1830). By the time Africa began to be formally colonized in the late 1800s, most colonies in the Americas (except in the Caribbean) had already become independent states.

Colonialism in Africa, like that in Asia but unlike the Americas, did not involve the displacement of Indigenous peoples. But unlike in Asia, no attempt was made to create colonial boundaries that broadly coincided with existing cultures and political systems. Instead, colonial boundaries in Africa were demarcated by European powers at the Berlin Conference of 1884–85. Only one existing African state—Ethiopia—retained its independence for much of the colonial period (save for a brief period in the 1930s when Mussolini attempted to colonize it). By 1914, all of

Africa was made up of colonies of the European powers—except for Liberia, created in 1822 as an independent state for freed slaves from the United States, Lesotho, Ethiopia, and South Africa.

DECOLONIZATION AND THE POLITICS OF NORTH–SOUTH RELATIONS, 1950–2000

The collapse of European colonialism was rapid, and with very few exceptions, it is virtually complete today. **Decolonization** began in Central and South America in the 1820s with the independence of Brazil and Mexico. The relative decline of Spain and Portugal—the main colonizers of the region—as major European powers contributed to this early start of the process. In most of Africa and Asia, however, decolonization did not begin until after World War II, starting with the independence of India and Pakistan in 1947. (As a result, the term *post-colonial era* usually refers to the period after 1945.) A number of factors contributed to decolonization on these continents, including the weakening of European colonial powers as a result of the war, the rise of nationalist movements in the colonies demanding political independence, and the emergence and institutionalization of new norms in international relations that delegitimized colonialism.[7] These norms centred on a new interpretation of the principle of self-determination.

> **Definition**
>
> **DECOLONIZATION:** The process through which a population and territory formerly under colonial domination achieve formal political independence and become a sovereign state.

The resolution adopted by the United Nations General Assembly in 1960, called the Declaration on the Granting of Independence to Colonial Countries and Peoples, sums up the new views on self-determination: "All peoples have the right to self-determination; by virtue of that right they freely determine their political status and freely pursue their economic, social and cultural development.... Any attempt aimed at the partial or total disruption of the national unity and the

territorial integrity of a country is incompatible with the purposes and principles of the Charter of the United Nations" (UN General Assembly Resolution 1514-XV, December 14, 1960).

> **Definition**
>
> **SELF-DETERMINATION:** A principle of international law that grants all peoples/nations the right to determine their political status and pursue their economic, social, and cultural development free from external domination or interference.

Prior to 1945, the European state system dominated the international arena (with countries such as the United States and Japan emerging in the early 20th century). The founding of the United Nations in 1945 involved only 51 states as members. By the year 2002, the UN had a total of 191 member states. This phenomenal growth is largely due to decolonization. Once political independence was attained, the countries of the South, through a series of international conferences and negotiations beginning in the mid-1950s, sought to achieve changes in the international political and economic order. These demands often brought the interests of the South into conflict with the interests of the North. Four stages or phases can be discerned in the evolution of the dialogue between the North and the South.

Phase One: The 1950s and 1960s

The first phase of decolonization, which occurred in the 1950s and 1960s, was characterized by the South's attempt to carve out a separate identity in world politics. Two international conferences served to highlight these efforts: the Afro-Asian Conference, held in Bandung (Indonesia) in 1955, and the first meeting of the Non-Aligned Movement (NAM), held in Belgrade (Yugoslavia) in 1961.

By the early 1960s, a more focused strategy to influence international events began to emerge on the part of the South. It involved an attempt to extend the international normative consensus that had emerged in favour of decolonization and political independence into international support for development. Prior to the 1960s, the issue of development assistance—the notion that resources should be mobilized internationally to help poorer nations develop—was not on the international agenda. Through the UN system and the creation of new institutional frameworks, such as the United Nations Conference on Trade and Develop-ment (UNCTAD), the countries of the South were successful in bringing the issue of development onto the international agenda. Their objectives during this period were defined mainly in terms of "closing the gap" with the North.

Phase Two: The 1970s

At the beginning of the 1970s, a series of events occurred that produced a change in strategy on the part of the South. These events included the quadru-pling of oil prices by the Organization of the Petroleum Exporting Countries (OPEC) after the 1973 Middle East war. This new strategy was more explicitly redistributive and combined the threat of negative sanctions (on the North) with the promise of mutual gains for both the North and the South. This strategy, known as the **New International Economic Order (NIEO)**, represented an attempt by the South to affirm a "right to development" and to convince the North that reform of existing institutions and practices in the global political economy was needed (see Box 14.1 below).[8] The call for the NIEO, however, failed to produce the results that developing countries expected.

BOX 14.1
_____

THE NEW INTERNATIONAL ECONOMIC ORDER (NIEO)

The New International Economic Order refers to a set of proposals made by the South for reform of the international economic order. The idea for the NIEO took shape first within the Non-Aligned Movement and subsequently in the United Nations. Two Resolutions adopted by the UN General Assembly (UNGA) in 1974 launched a series of global negotiations between the North and the South. These were UNGA Resolution 3202 (The Programme of Action on the Establishment of the New International Economic Order) and Resolution 3281 (The Charter of Economic Rights and Duties of States). Three sets of reforms were proposed:

- the self-reliance reforms, designed to increase the control of developing countries over their natural resources

- the resource transfer reforms, designed to achieve greater and more regular flows of financial resources from the developed coun-tries to the developing countries (e.g., an increase in grants and concessional foreign aid)

- the international influence reforms, designed to increase the participation of developing countries in the central institutions that regu-lated international economic and political interactions.

Some modest changes occurred as a result of these negotiations, but the fundamental reforms sought by the South did not occur. By the early 1980s, negotiations for the NIEO were effectively over.

Phase Three: The 1980s

During the 1980s, several events displaced the NIEO from the top of the international agenda. These included the international recession of the early 1980s, precipitated by a second round of oil price increases in 1979, and the emergence of the first developing country debt crisis in 1982, which saw the collapse of the markets for exports from the South and a sharp increase in interest rates. These events undermined the unity of the South and weakened its bargaining posi-tion vis-à-vis the North.

In view of these developments, a new strategy began to emerge in North–South relations. This strategy de-emphasized redistribution and focused on common problems and on the interdependence between North and South. The premise was that the development problems of the South and their political, social, and environmental consequences were very much a concern for the North, and hence the efficient working of the international system as a whole required cooperation between North and South. This new emphasis on interdependence and multilateralism was articulated through a series of reports commissioned by the UN.[9]

Phase Four: The 1990s and Onward

For most of the 1980s, issues arising from the management of the 1982 debt crisis dominated North–South relations. Debt problems of developing countries continued into the 1990s with a number of currency and financial crises, including the Mexican peso crisis in 1994 and the Asian financial crisis that began in 1997. However, a number of other significant issues were added to the agenda of North–South relations, aided by the end of the Cold War in 1990, which created the space for these newer issues to emerge.

One of the most prominent of these was the increased concern with the relationship between development and the natural environment, encapsulated in the concept of sustainable development. Other debates arose on the role of foreign aid and on democracy, human rights, and development. Also in the 1990s, increased attention was paid to the role of women in development. In addition, the end of the Cold War focused attention on problems of human security in the context of civil war, state failure, and ethnic conflict in various regions of the world. Each of these contemporary issues is explored in more detail later in this chapter.

Assessing Outcomes of the 50-Year North–South Dialogue

At the beginning of the new millennium, assessing the outcomes of the 50-year dialogue between the North and the South is difficult. On the whole, the fundamental changes in international political and economic relations that the South wanted have not been achieved. Nevertheless, some changes have occurred. Perhaps the most visible impact of the South has been normative

and institutional. In normative terms, countries of the South have been successful to a degree in placing issues on the international agenda that, arguably, would not be there otherwise, such as the very notion of development as an international issue. Even more important was the impact of the South on international institutionalization, especially within the United Nations system.

MEASURING DEVELOPMENT: ECONOMIC, SOCIAL, AND POLITICAL DIMENSIONS

The synopsis of North–South relations shows that the question of development is a highly contentious one. Defining exactly what development entails is, as with many other concepts in the study of politics, subject to much debate. While analysts agree that development involves processes of change, considerable discussion has revolved around specifying what the target or object of development is, exactly what these processes of change involve, and what the desirable goals of such development processes are. Despite these disagreements, the practice of development as it has evolved over the past 50 years has generally included economic, social, and political dimensions. These three aspects of development are analyzed below.

Economic Development[10]

The economic dimension of development refers to the production and distribution of wealth and income in a country. Perhaps the most widely used measure of the production of wealth in a country is the Gross Domestic Product (GDP) or Gross National Product (GNP).[11] The GDP/GNP can also be expressed as a ratio of a country's population to provide a representation of that country's average national income— GDP/GNP per capita. Less economically developed countries tend to produce less wealth and income than do more economically developed countries. For example, in 1998, the per capita GDP for the United States, one of the wealthiest countries in the world, was U.S.$28 000. In comparison, Ethiopia, one of the poorest countries, had a per capita GDP of only U.S.$450. The 18 richest countries in the world—the United States and Canada plus the 15 countries of the European Union (EU) and Japan—account for 47 percent of total global GDP.

In addition to GDP per capita and GDP growth, levels of economic development are also measured by how that wealth and income are distributed. Developing countries tend not only to produce less wealth and income—but frequently whatever they do produce is poorly distributed. For example, in the United States, the poorest 40 percent of the population earn about 15.7 percent of the national income and the richest 20 percent earn 41.9 percent of the national income. Most developed states have comparable income distributions, and while many observers would not call these figures very equitable, they are more impressive than in many countries in the South. In Mexico (and also in places such as South Africa, Brazil, and Kenya), the richest 20 percent of the population earn over 60 percent of the national income while the poorest 40 percent earn less than 15 percent—a highly skewed and inequitable income distribution.

The World Bank, the leading institution charged with promoting development internationally, has developed a four-fold classification of countries to distinguish their level of economic growth. This classification is reproduced in Table 14.2.

Social Development[12]

The social dimension refers to the development of a country's human resources. Indicators such as levels of education, school enrolments, literacy rates, life expectancy, and levels of nutrition are often used as measures of the level of a country's social development. The United Nations Development Program (UNDP), an agency of the UN, has developed a **Human Development Index (HDI)**, a composite index that contains three variables: longevity (measured by average life expectancy), knowledge (measured by adult literacy and combined enrolment in primary, secondary, and tertiary education), and standard of living (measured by the real GDP per capita).

Definition

HUMAN DEVELOPMENT INDEX (HDI): A composite index measuring longevity, knowledge, and standard of living, designed to give an indication of and a basis for comparing the quality of life in various countries.

The HDI is calculated for each country and is expressed on a scale between 0 and 1 to allow for comparisons. A score of 1 indicates that a country has attained the highest possible quality of life for its citizens. HDI scores of less than 1 indicate how far a country must go to reach this ideal. All countries are ranked from high (scores of 0.81 and above) to medium (0.51 to 0.80) and low HDI (0.50 and below). Since the HDI was introduced in 1990, no state has ever scored perfect. Generally, developed countries of the North tend to score higher than developing countries of the South. For example, in 1998 Canada achieved the highest HDI score of any country: 0.960. The lowest was Sierra Leone, with a HDI of 0.185. In effect, Canada was rated the best country in the world to live in, while Sierra Leone—a country afflicted with civil war and extreme poverty—was the worst. In 2001,

---

Table 14.2 The World Bank's Classification of Levels of Economic Growth

Classification	GNP Per Capita, in U.S.$	Example
Low Income	785 or less	India (U.S.$390)
Lower Middle Income	786–3125	Indonesia (U.S.$1110)
Upper Middle Income	3126–9655	Brazil (U.S.$4720)
High Income	9656 and above	Canada (U.S.$19 290)

Source: World Bank, *World Development Report, 1998/99* (New York: Oxford University Press, 1999), annex table 1, p. 187. Reprinted by permission of the International Bank for Reconstruction and Development/The World Bank.

however, Canada slipped from first to third place in the HDI rankings, as mentioned in Chapter 1; it maintained this position in 2002.

Political Development[13]

Measuring **political development** is far more difficult than measuring economic and social development. Because no widespread agreement on suitable indicators of political development exists, political variables—dealing with values and beliefs, institutions, and power—cannot be quantified as readily as economic and social variables. Ideological and cultural differences also further complicate the debate. Despite these disagreements within the literature, several influential views on measures of political development may be discerned. These include the degree of state capacity and the degree of political stability. More recently, issues of governmental responsiveness and representation have been added as criteria of political development.

Definition

POLITICAL DEVELOPMENT: A concept that describes how well a society has developed politically, usually measured by the degree of state capacity to effectively carry out the legislative, executive, and judicial functions of government; the degree of political stability, or ability to resolve political conflicts in a peaceful manner; and the degree of governmental responsiveness to public demands and respect for fundamental rights.

Degree of State Capacity

Political development involves the creation of specialized and differentiated government institutions that have the capacity to effectively carry out the functions of government—making (legislative functions), implementing (executive functions), and adjudicating (judicial functions) public policy and laws. The idea here is that political development entails the institutionalization of rational-legal authority and the establishment of an effective state bureaucracy. Although they possess all the attributes of statehood, such as population, demarcated territories, and so on, many states in the South do not have governments that can discharge these functions effectively. In some extreme cases—in what are known as failed states—govern-

ment capacity is virtually nonexistent. Examples include Somalia and Afghanistan.

Degree of Political Stability

Countries that are politically developed enjoy a degree of political stability. The notion of political stability addresses the issue of how political conflicts and disputes are resolved. Stable polities are those where political conflicts can be resolved in a peaceful manner without recourse to widespread violence. In contrast, less developed polities are plagued by instability—civil strife, communal violence, military coups, and sometimes outright civil war. Generally, developed countries of the North tend to be more stable than those of the South. Indeed, since 1945, almost all major armed conflicts in the world have been located in the South.

Degree of Governmental Responsiveness and Representation

In addition to state capacity and political stability, some observers include the degree of governmental responsiveness and representation as indicators of political development. The idea here is that politically developed countries have governments that are responsive to broad segments of society and show respect for the population's fundamental rights and freedoms. Representative governments reflect the wishes of their populations and govern with the consent, or at least the acquiescence, of that population. Responsive and representative governments enjoy a high degree of legitimacy. They allow their citizens to pursue their values, interests, and goals peacefully; they have mechanisms and procedures in place to prevent the abuse of power; and they allow for a peaceful change in government.

The criteria of responsive and representative government sound similar to criteria associated with the form of government known as democracy. Does this mean that political development is synonymous with democratization? Early works on political development gave ambiguous answers to this question in order to avoid the accusation that they were attempting to impose Western values. Today, however, the widespread view is that political development does entail the emergence and consolidation of some type of democratic political institutions and procedures. Democratic governments tend to have greater political capacity, tend to be more stable, and are more responsive and representative than authoritarian governments. This issue of democracy and development is examined in greater detail later in this chapter and in Chapter 15.

Using the three broad measures of economic, social, and political development, we can generally say that more developed societies have higher levels of economic growth with a degree of equity in their income distribution, a relatively high level of social development, and a higher degree of state capacity and political stability, with governments that are responsive to and representative of their populations.

BOX 14.2

GHANA: DEVELOPMENT DECAY AND RECOVERY

Ghana is a relatively small country located on the west coast of Africa; its population is about 18 million. It was one of the first sub-Saharan African countries to achieve political independence (from Britain) in 1957. In the immediate post-independence period, Ghana's development prospects looked bright. The country was relatively well endowed with natural resources (gold, manganese, timber, bauxite) and by the standards of colonial Africa at the time (which were generally very low), it had a relatively well educated population. In 1960, Ghana had a GNP per capita that was similar to that of South Korea. But in 1998, the GNP per capita of South Korea (U.S.$10 550) was more than 20 times greater than that of Ghana (U.S.$400). South Korea is generally seen as a success story of development (see Box 14.3 for more information), having achieved marked improvements in the economic, social, and political dimensions of development. The experience of Ghana between 1960 and the early 1980s, on the other hand, appeared to demonstrate everything that could go wrong in the development of a country.

For example, between 1970 and 1982, GNP per capita in Ghana fell by 20 percent, and almost every social indicator of development, including school enrolments, declined. Politically, Ghana's post-independence history has been unstable, having experienced five successful military coups d'état, in which incumbent governments were violently overthrown. The country has also experimented with a wide range of governments, civilian and military-authoritarian. By the early 1980s, the central institutions of the state were near collapse. However, at the end of 1981, an authoritarian military leader who took power was determined to break the cycle of economic, social, and political decay and to set the country on a path to development. He rigorously implemented policy reforms. These reforms appear to have reversed the cycle of decline and resulted in improvements in economic, social, and political development.

From the mid-1980s and throughout the 1990s, for example, the rate of GNP growth in Ghana exceeded the average for sub-Saharan Africa (about 5 percent per annum compared to the continental average of about 2 percent). Ghana has also shown signs of political development. In 1992, it made a transition from authoritarian to democratic government. Since then, a degree of political stability has been achieved, and the capacity of state institutions has been strengthened. Three successful rounds of democratic elections have been held (in 1992, 1996, and 2000), the latest resulting in a peaceful transfer of power. This was one of the few instances in Africa where an incumbent government has accepted defeat in an election. As a result of the dramatic turnaround in the country's political, economic, and social development, Ghana today is considered to be one of the countries in sub-Saharan Africa that is on a road to recovery and development.

POLITICAL, ECONOMIC, AND SOCIAL DEVELOPMENT: ISSUES OF DEBATE

The relationship among the three dimensions of development has generated considerable debate as to whether they could be achieved simultaneously. Influential works identified important tradeoffs and tensions within and between the economic, political, and social dimensions of development. In terms of political development, for example, some analysts argued that to achieve the goal of political stability, a country in the early stages of development has to forego a degree of political participation and representation. This argument stated that for many of the new countries in the South, democracy was incompatible with order and stability and that premature democratization created political instability. From this perspective, priority was to be given to stability at the expense of democracy.[14]

Some versions of this argument went further to posit a tension between political and economic development, stating that premature creation of democratic governments in developing societies would impede economic growth. Put another way, it said that strong authoritarian government was necessary to achieve economic growth. Only a strong authoritarian government, free from particular interests in society, could take the necessary measures to foster economic growth. This was the so-called tradeoff between liberty and growth. To support their position, the proponents of this view pointed to the successes of the Asian Newly Industrialized Countries (NICs)—Singapore, South Korea, and Taiwan—each of which achieved impressive rates of economic growth in the 1970s and 1980s under authoritarian governments. More recently, China has adopted elements of this approach and is also recording impressive rates of economic growth (see Box 14.3). However, the empirical record supporting a direct correlation between type of government and economic growth is mixed. While the Asian NICs did achieve impressive rates of economic growth under authoritarian governments, they were the exception, not the rule. The majority of authoritarian governments elsewhere in the South—in most Latin American and where in the South—in most Latin American and

African countries—have failed to achieve sustained economic growth. With respect to democratic government, the historical record is also mixed. While some democratic governments (such as Botswana) have been able to manage impressive rates of economic growth, others (such as Bolivia) have not.

Another important tension that has been identified is between economic growth and equity. Some analysts have argued that economic growth should be accorded priority over income distribution and equity. One influential theory that became known as the trickle-down doctrine posited that income inequality was indeed necessary to provide incentives for investment. If investors were allowed to reap differential rewards for their entrepreneurial efforts, total societal income would be maximized, and the benefits would eventually trickle down to those less well-off in that society. However, here again the empirical record is mixed. For example, rapid economic growth in South Korea and Singapore was achieved together with a marked reduction in levels of poverty and income inequality. In contrast, other countries that pursued growth-first strategies, such as Mexico and Brazil, did so at the cost of widening income disparities and of increased inequality. Furthermore, countries such as Cuba and Costa Rica, which recorded comparatively slow rates of economic growth, nevertheless recorded impressive gains in the area of social development, including marked improvements in literacy, school enrolments, and the reduction of infant mortality rates.

The relationship among the three dimensions of development (especially between political and economic development) is very complex and continues to be the subject of much debate. Such debate, in turn, has been influenced by strong disagreements among analysts on the causes of development and underdevelopment.

THE CAUSES OF DEVELOPMENT AND UNDERDEVELOPMENT

Debates over development have not only revolved around how best to measure levels of development, but have also centred on how to understand and explain the present condition of poorer countries and societies, as well as on how to possibly shape and predict the future

BOX 14.3

THE EAST ASIAN EXPORT-ORIENTED DEVELOPMENT STATE APPROACH

For much of the early postcolonial period in the 1950s and 1960s, there was little variation in the domestic economic structures throughout the South. The period from the 1970s onward, however, began to see significant variations in domestic economic performance, especially between those in East Asia (and a few Latin American states) on the one hand and the rest of the South on the other. Observers have argued that the explanation of these differences lies in a particular model of development adopted by the East Asian countries—the development state model.

The success of the east Asian Newly Industrialized Countries, including Singapore, South Korea, and Taiwan, is attributed to an outward-oriented growth strategy based on export growth and a strong private sector. Centralized and authoritarian economic management was a major ingredient in this model. In each of these NICs, state agents and administrators, backed by government-financed think-tanks, played a key role in the direction of economic policy, with little public debate and input. Government intervention was directed at ensuring an efficiently working market economy, including policies of trade liberalization, currency devaluations, reductions in wasteful government spending, and the reduction of barriers to foreign investment. In contrast to this outward-oriented set of policies, the majority of countries in Latin America, Africa, and the rest of Asia pursued inward-oriented growth strategies involving extensive state interventions, economic nationalism, and import substitution, which distorted markets and discouraged production.

In summary, the three key ingredients of the development state model, first developed by Japan and subsequently adopted by East Asian NICs, involve

- strong centralized economic management. This is essentially a market economy, but the government intervenes in and controls the operation of the economy in the areas of finance, foreign investment, and industrial and export development;

- emphasis on the promotion of exports, with preferential access to credit for exporters, investment incentives, and other trade interventions (for example, the use of trade tariffs);

- emphasis on industrialization and export valorization, but also support for more efficient agricultural production.

Much debate continues as to whether the success of the East Asian countries can be replicated elsewhere in the South. Those who question the transferability of this model point to the changed international environment of today compared to that of the late 1960s and 1970s, when these NICs began their phenomenal growth. They note, for example, that the NICs received large amounts of foreign aid, particularly from the United States and Japan, which assisted in their economic growth. Foreign aid to many other countries in the South declined considerably in the 1990s. Also, the financial crises that hit several East Asian countries in 1997 have led to questions about the durability of this model.

direction of change. The kinds of answers to these questions depended on the type of theoretical framework or paradigm employed. A paradigm is a model or a world-view from which springs a coherent tradition of research. Paradigms include collections of theories that share a common set of assumptions and a common set of questions and methodological tools that shape the way a problem to be investigated is diagnosed, as well as the types of solutions or prescriptions that are offered. We will first examine early views on development provided by modernization theories; then we will explore the dependency and world system theories, which provided an alternative explanation of development. We will end this discussion by looking at a view of development that became dominant in the 1990s—the Washington consensus on international development—as well as at some of the critical perspectives on gender and development.

The Modernization Paradigm

As the name implies, theories within the **modernization** paradigm—which emerged in the 1950s and 1960s—saw development as a process of progressive transformation, in which societies moved from "traditional" through a series of stages to "modern" (see Box 14.4).[15] Developing countries were thought to be at an earlier stage in the historical trajectory of development through which all states had to pass. The obstacles to development thus lay within the countries of the South—in the nature and operation of their political institutions and processes, as well as in their economic and social systems. These political institutions were still steeped in ancient traditions and cultures and had not yet acquired the rational institutions and processes found in the North.[16]

In their prescriptions for change, modernization theories placed emphasis on the creation of institutions and processes within poorer countries that would allow for more rational and efficient public policymaking and administration, by doing away with practices such as nepotism and corruption. A more efficient system for allocating and distributing economic resources (the operation of competitive market forces) was needed to allow economic growth to occur. The diffusion of technology, skills, capital, and other values from North to South, through trade and other international transactions, was also seen as a key instrument of change. In this respect, modernization theories drew on the works of Max Weber (1864–1920) on political organization, authority, and bureaucratic rationalization, as well as the ideas of classical economists such as Adam Smith (1723–90), who championed *laissez-faire* economics, in which the "invisible hand" of the market was the best mechanism to allocate economic resources for development.

Modernization theories were criticized on a number of fronts, including their view of what development entailed, their diagnosis of development problems, and

their prescriptions for change. With respect to the first, modernization theories were accused of being ethnocentric because of the notion that development was synonymous with westernization. Their view of history was also criticized for being linear—they assumed there was only one path to development, and that path was the one followed by the present-day developed states. Modernization theories also came under criticism for, in effect, blaming the poor for their poverty. They implied that the poor were poor because they were inefficient. In addition, these theories were criticized for placing too much emphasis on domestic changes within developing countries and ignoring the international aspects of the problem, such as the protectionist practices of developed countries in international trade relations that discriminated against exports from the South. In response to these criticisms, various attempts were made to modify modernization theories by rejecting the linear view of history, identifying important tradeoffs in the development process, and attempting to acknowledge the special political and historical circumstances of developing countries.[17]

Dependency and the World System Paradigm

By the beginning of the 1970s, the influence of modernization theories began to wane. The initial optimism that countries in the South recently emerged from colonialism would rapidly modernize was soon replaced by pessimism. This pessimism in part reflected world events, such as the adoption of various types of military and authoritarian governments by a majority of states in Africa, Asia, and Latin America. Another factor was the fact that although some economic growth had been achieved throughout the developing world, less progress had been made in reducing poverty.

The most serious challenge to the modernization paradigm came from theories in an alternative paradigm of development—theories of **dependency** and the world system—that provided a very different explanation of problems of poverty and underdevelopment in the South. World system theories were broader in scope. They provided an explanation of the evolution and impact of imperialism and capitalism on political and economic organization throughout the globe since the 16th century. Dependency theories had a narrower

---

BOX 14.4

WALT W. ROSTOW'S FIVE STAGES OF ECONOMIC GROWTH (1960)

The work of Walt W. Rostow is considered to be a classic in the modernization paradigm. Rostow identified five stages through which all countries had to pass on the path to modernization and development.

- *Traditional Society*: This stage is characterized by an agrarian economy, the existence of traditional authority structures, a high level of subsistence, and low levels of technological and scientific knowledge.

- *The Preconditions for Takeoff*: This is a period of transition from tradition to modernity and is characterized by the development of new ideas and processes, as well as advances in education. A change occurs in the balance of social forces—away from traditional authority structures toward new elites. This period also sees the creation of a centralized state.

- *The Takeoff*: This is the stage where the traditional, premodern ways of doing things are finally overcome. Technology plays a key role.

Rapid increases in agricultural productivity and industrialization occur, together with the emergence of elites who champion modernization of the economy.

- *The Drive to Maturity*: This is a period of fluctuating but sustained progress. Here a society and economy demonstrate the ability to move beyond the original industries that fuelled takeoff. Rostow argued it took roughly 60 years from the stage of takeoff for an economy to reach maturity.

- *The High Mass-Consumption Society*: At this stage the society and economy move toward the production of consumer goods and provision of services and away from a reliance on heavy industry. This period is characterized by a rapid rise in per capita income and overall living standards. Also at this stage we see the development of social welfare programs.

Source: Walt W. Rostow, *The Stages of Growth: A Non-Communist Manifesto* (Cambridge: Cambridge University Press, 1960).

---

focus. They examined the consequences of imperialism, colonialism, and global capitalism for the development of countries in the South.[18] Dependency theories may thus be seen as a subset of world system theories.

Theories of dependency and the world system, despite considerable differences among them, saw a causal relationship between the historical expansion of Western European political and economic influence (beginning with the Industrial Revolution and the expansion of European colonial empires) and the progressive impoverishment of countries in Africa, Asia, and the Americas. Unlike modernization theories, which saw underdevelopment as a natural stage or condition on a linear process of development, for theorists of dependency there was nothing natural about underdevelopment. It was a specific historical creation, a product of unequal political and economic relations between developed countries located at the core of the

world system and underdeveloped countries located at its periphery. In the words of one prominent dependency theorist, "underdevelopment was developed."[19]

The central concern for dependency theories in their diagnoses of the problems of underdevelopment was an analysis of how power was used to allocate and distribute resources, especially economic resources. Two broad positions emerged, the neo-Marxist view and the structuralist view. The neo-Marxists, who drew on the works of Karl Marx (1818–83), focused on the internal class structure within countries on the periphery. While acknowledging the exploitative international linkages between rich and poor countries, the neo-Marxists diagnosed the problem of underdevelopment primarily in terms of the weaknesses of domestic classes within poor states and their failure to play their "historic role" of overturning traditional elites and practices and spearheading economic and political development.

The structuralists, on the other hand, focused on the international linkages between core and periphery. The structuralists described the unequal relationships between core and periphery in terms of an "international division of labour" created by core states. This international division of labour was the prime determinant of economic and political outcomes in the developing countries. In effect, the poor were poor not because they were inefficient, but because they were exploited by the rich and powerful. Such dependency relationships were maintained by the cooperation of classes and elites in the periphery who profited from their economic links with the core and whose common identity and survival as a class derived from subordination to the international economy. In effect, although formal political independence had been achieved, exploitative economic relationships were maintained by former colonial and imperial powers—a situation described by some analysts as neocolonialism.

Theories of dependency and the world system were criticized for being too deterministic by overemphasizing the role of international and global forces on countries in the South. Other critics rejected them as little more than conspiracy theories for implying that rich countries deliberately kept the poor impoverished. One of the most serious criticisms was that dependency theories were better at explaining why countries did not develop rather than how countries actually did develop. In other words, unlike modernization theories, dependency theories had no explanation of how development occurred—they had no vision of the future. In response to these criticisms, a "soft" variant of dependency emerged. It argued that dependent capitalist development—a form of development that did not fundamentally alter the unequal relationship between core and periphery—was possible, but only when it was in the interests of the developed core states.[20]

The ideas developed by dependency and world system theories were embraced by many developing countries. It was a paradigm that had been developed in large part by scholars from developing countries themselves, and one that reflected their sense of exploitation going back to the era of European colonialism. Indeed, the demands by the South for the NIEO that were outlined above were strongly influenced by theories of dependency and the world system.

The Washington Consensus on International Development

The influence of dependency theories was relatively short-lived. By the mid-1980s a newer perspective on development called the Washington consensus began to take hold.[21] In part, the shift occurred in response to the series of international crises during the 1970s and 1980s that produced important changes within the South and in these countries' relations with the North. They included the oil crises of 1973 and 1979, the international recession of the early 1980s, and the debt crisis that emerged in 1982.

The Washington consensus is so named because it was strongly endorsed by agencies within the United States government and by the two central institutions of the global economy, the **International Monetary Fund (IMF)** and the **World Bank**, both with their headquarters in the capital of the United States, Washington, D.C. This view is based on the classical economic principles developed by Adam Smith, which place emphasis on a free and competitive market in which rational economic agents can make choices to overcome scarcity and efficiently utilize productive resources. Government intervention in the economy is to be minimal (*laissez-faire*), and is to focus on stimulating savings, investment, and production by the private sector. This ensures that the economy produces those goods that are desired and that it does so in the most efficient manner. Market instruments are supposed to encourage greater allocative efficiency, increased investment, faster economic growth, and increased standard of living. From this perspective, the obstacles to development in the South lie in government interventions into the market, which result in an inefficient allocation of resources.

In some respects, then, the Washington consensus can be seen as a contemporary restatement of some of the ideas that informed modernization theory. The influence of the Washington consensus has been extended in part through the lending conditions of the IMF and the World Bank to countries in the South that required assistance in managing their debts. These loans come with a package of conditions linked to specific economic and institutional reforms known as structural adjustment. The neoclassical economic principles on which the Washington consensus is based have also become an integral part of the contemporary phenomenon known as globalization. This issue is explored in greater detail in Chapter 17.

Perspectives on Women and Gender in Development

For most of the post–World War II period, scholars and policymakers were largely oblivious to the role of women in development. In the last two decades, however, the emergence of gender-related social science research and recognition of the role of women in development processes led to the emergence of Women in Development (WID) and Gender and Development (GAD) perspectives. The inclusion of gender-related issues in the study of development draws attention to the sources and dimensions of gender inequality and the victimization of women, the analysis of structures of power and patriarchy, and ways to empower women and increase their participation in development processes.[22]

For example, with respect to the dimensions of women's inequality and victimization, women tend to be relegated to particular occupations. In Africa and South Asia, women dominate in the informal sector and in agricultural labour. In Southeast Asia and parts of Central and South America, women (and children) are largely found in low-wage labour-intensive industries. Even in developed countries, a gendered division of labour is evident in the overrepresentation of women in the so-called nurturing professions, such as teaching, nursing, social work, and so on. Furthermore, women tend to be underrepresented in the public sphere of politics and business. With a few notable exceptions, throughout the developing world, women hold fewer government positions and their representation decreases as one moves up the ladder of political power. In addition, women worldwide are subject to a wide range of abuses, injustices, and acts of violence.

Most official statistics on economic activity have tended to overlook women's participation and contribution. Informal sector activities and production for

How the IMF helps the Third World.

household consumption, where women tend to dominate, for example, are not normally included in official GDP accounts. The UNDP has created a Gender Development Index (GDI) to complement the HDI. The GDI measures the gap between scores obtained by women and men on the HDI. In 1998, the country with the highest GDI (i.e., the lowest gap between men and women) was Norway, followed closely by other Scandinavian countries. In general, countries of the North score higher on the GDI than countries of the South. The highest-rated country in the South in 1998 was South Korea (at number 36). However, in every country in the world, developed and developing, women generally fare worse than men in virtually all indicators of development.

Sources of women's inequality in the South include traditional beliefs and cultural practices, such as the preference in many parts of Africa and Asia for male children over female ones. Colonialism also compounded women's inequality by changing some traditional patterns of authority and economic activity. In some West African societies, for example, matrilineal patterns of lineage enabled women to play important political roles as clan elders, as decision-makers in the selection of traditional chiefs and kings, and even as chiefs. This system was eroded under British colonialism. Other factors affecting women's inequality include social class, ethnicity, religion, urbanization, and levels of education.

Studies on women in development identify ways to enhance women's participation in development processes and focus on the issue of women's empowerment. The premise here is that rights are not given, but are won through political action. Greater equality for women will come about only through mobilization, activism, and participation.

CONTEMPORARY ISSUES AND DEBATES

A number of issues and debates arising from processes of development and change have become prominent in the contemporary period. These include debates over the role of foreign aid and over the impact of globalization on national development, sustainable develop-

ment, democratization and development, and the management of political violence and war.

Foreign Aid, Globalization, and Development[23]

Foreign aid may be defined as the administered transfer of resources from rich to poor countries, ostensibly to promote the latter's welfare and development. The term *foreign aid* is usually reserved for official (i.e., government-to-government) transfers and resource flows, as distinct from private resource flows. Foreign aid is also known as official development assistance (ODA). ODA is provided as bilateral aid (assistance that flows directly from a donor to a recipient government) and as multilateral aid (assistance that flows from donor governments through international organizations, such as the World Bank, to recipients). The largest source of bilateral ODA comes from the 21 member states of the Development Assistance Committee of the Organization for Economic Cooperation and Development (DAC-OECD).

The practice of giving aid emerged mainly in the post–World War II era and was driven by a mixture of self-interest and altruism on the part of donors. Aid was used to promote the strategic and political interests of donors (for example, to counter the threat of communism), as well as to promote long-term growth of countries in the South. The amount of foreign aid increased steadily from the 1960s, peaking in 1991 at U.S.$69 billion, but declined during the 1990s. Table 14.3 provides a summary of foreign aid as a percentage of the GNPs of some of the major donor countries in the North. In 1974, the UN recommended that donor countries devote a minimum of 0.7 percent of their GNPs to development assistance. As the table indicates, however, most of the major aid donors, including Canada, have not met this target, and some of the richest countries in the world, including the United States and Japan, devoted a smaller proportion of their GNPs to development assistance in 1997 than in 1960.

The reasons for the decline in foreign aid include the end of the Cold War, which reduced the strategic importance of the South to donors, and the emergence of unfavourable public attitudes within donor countries to foreign aid, reinforced by the perception that

Table 14.3   Some of the Major Donors of Official Development Assistance (ODA)

	ODA as Percentage of GNP				
Country	1960	1970	1980	1990	1997
Canada	0.19	0.43	0.43	0.44	0.31
Denmark	0.09	0.38	0.74	0.94	0.97
Germany	0.31	0.32	0.44	0.42	0.28
Japan	0.24	0.23	0.32	0.31	0.22
Netherlands	0.31	0.63	0.97	0.92	0.81
Sweden	0.05	0.37	0.78	0.91	0.76
United Kingdom	0.56	0.37	0.35	0.27	0.26
United States	0.53	0.31	0.27	0.21	0.08

Source: Organisation for Economic Co-operation and Development, annual reports on development cooperation, various years.

aid was wasted and supported corrupt regimes in the South. Other important factors that contributed to the decline in ODA included the emergence of the Washington consensus, the expansion and integration of global financial markets, and the increase in private capital flows. Worldwide, private capital invests about U.S.$4 trillion annually, of which about U.S.$1.5 trillion is invested in developing countries. This figure is six times greater than the amount invested by governments. These factors have led to serious questions about the relevance of foreign aid in a globalized world. The new slogan is "trade, not aid."

Indeed, some have characterized the contemporary period as a post-aid world, claiming that globalization has rendered the kinds of official financial transfers between governments that we call foreign aid redundant. Supporters of this view argue that instead of receiving aid from donor governments in the North, countries in the South should adopt the policy prescriptions of the Washington consensus, "get their houses in order," and thereby attract foreign private capital investment. Such private investment, together with increased trade opportunities, they argue, are more effective avenues for achieving development than official government-to-government aid transfers.

Supporters of increased foreign aid take a very different view. They point out that aid played a large role in the successful development of many countries in the post-1945 era. For example, the Marshall Plan (named after U.S. Secretary of State George C. Marshall), through which the U.S. government provided aid to

Western Europe, played a significant role in European reconstruction and development after World War II. At its peak, the Marshall Plan represented about 2.0 percent of U.S. GNP; in 1997, however, U.S. aid was only about 0.08 percent of its GNP. Another good example of the success of foreign aid is more recent; as noted in Box 14.3, foreign aid was a key ingredient in the development of some of the East Asian NICs.

Supporters of foreign aid also point to the paradox of "globalizing poverty amidst global prosperity," evident in the increased levels of poverty and inequality around the world. They also question the ability of private capital to foster stable development. For example, they note the volatility and instability of such investment, as seen in the major financial and debt crises that occurred in the South in the 1980s and 1990s. At the end of the 1990s and into the year 2000, levels of foreign aid from the major donors appeared to be on the increase. However, debates about the role of foreign aid in development are likely to continue as processes of globalization intensify and as global inequities widen.

Sustainable Development

The concept of **sustainable development** emerged in the 1980s and was popularized through the publication of a report titled *Our Common Future* by the World Commission on Environment and Development (WCED) in 1987.[24] According to the WCED report, sustainable development is "development that meets the needs of the present without compromising the ability of future generations to meet their needs." It is "a process of change in which the exploitation of natural resources, the direction of investments, the orientation of technical development, and institutional change are all in harmony and enhance both current and future potential to meet human needs and aspirations." Since the publication of the report, the concept of sustainable development has become a central feature in discussions of development. The key premise underlying the concept is that a healthy natural environment is the lifeblood of successful development. Many contemporary development practices, however, are unsustainable because they create numerous environmental problems, including the depletion of natural resources, destruction of ecosystems, and air and water pollution. In the quest for economic growth, the environment had traditionally been seen as little more than a resource to be used and exploited. When environmental problems arose, they were seen as discrete technical problems requiring technical solutions, rather than as interconnected problems producing wide-ranging and often unforeseen consequences that required political as well as technical solutions.

Definition

SUSTAINABLE DEVELOPMENT: An approach to development that makes environmental protection an integral part of the development process, in order to enhance the ability of current and future generations to meet their needs.

Sustainable development attempts to redirect the way people and governments think about and approach development. It counters two set ways of thinking about environment: the tendency to focus on the effects of environmental problems rather than on the causes and the tendency to separate environmental issues from development issues. Sustainable development treats environmental issues and development issues as a unity rather than as two separate spheres, and it strives to prevent environmental problems.

Since the late 1980s, international conferences have been convened (and agreements signed) with the objective of planning and implementing sustainable development programs worldwide. These include the United Nations Conference on the Environment and Development (UNCED), also known as the Earth Summit, held for the first time in 1992 in Rio de

Janeiro in Brazil. The second conference was held at UN headquarters in 1997. The third Earth Summit was held in Johannesburg in 2002. While a measure of international agreement exists on the desirability of environmentally sound development, there are considerable disagreements on how to implement sustainable development programs. These disagreements have assumed a distinct North–South dimension and revolve around questions of who should bear the costs of cleaner and more environmentally friendly products and development processes.

For example, many countries in the South take the position that the North has contributed disproportionately to global environmental degradation. The North produces a disproportionate amount (relative to its population) of pollutants and consumes a disproportionate amount of global resources. At the 1992 summit, concerns were expressed that the focus on sustainable development may place too strong an emphasis on the environment at the expense of development in the South. Furthermore, some of the issues at the core of the environment–development debate, such as population growth, are among the most divisive political issues. They reflect the differences between North and South and between the "neomalthusians," who see dire negative consequences arising from unchecked population growth, and "cornucopians," who look to technology, increased production, and economic growth to meet demands of increased populations. Issues arising from women's rights and reproductive health are also at the centre of the debate. Matters of national power and prestige, culture, race, and religion further complicate the debate over population growth.

Democracy, Civil Society, and Development

The term **democratization** describes the processes involved in the creation of democratic governments. Democratization entails the relaxation of authoritarian political control by political leaders, the expansion of political and civil liberties, and the creation of institutional mechanisms that open up a political system to greater representation and participation. Based on this definition, analysts have identified three waves of democratization.[25] The first wave occurred between the 1820s and the 1920s and involved the expansion of the franchise and the creation of universal adult suffrage. The second wave occurred between 1945 and the early 1960s and was largely due to decolonization in Asia and Africa. By the end of the 1960s, however, the trend toward democratization was reversed. Many of the newly emerged democratically elected governments in the decolonized countries were replaced by military dictatorships and single-party authoritarian systems. The current or third wave of democratization began in the mid-1970s, continued in the 1980s with democratic transitions in South and Central America, and intensified in the 1990s with the collapse of authoritarian communist governments in the Soviet Union and Eastern Europe and the emergence of democratic forms of government in Africa and Asia.

Democracy and democratization have become important issues in discussions of development, generating many interesting debates. One of these debates centres on identifying the conditions that promote democratic transitions and the consolidation of democratic systems of government. One of the factors identified as playing a central role in processes of democratization is the role of **civil society**. Civil society is seen as the realm of organized private social life, represented by nongovernmental actors and associations, that emerges through the organization of individuals and groups in society in pursuit of their interests.

Another aspect of the debate centres on the role of democracy in development. Some of the key issues informing this debate were outlined earlier in this chapter, when we discussed the relationship between political and economic development. While the empirical record does present inconclusive results, the widely held view today, influenced in part by the Washington consensus, is that some form of democratic government is conducive to economic growth, if not an essential prerequisite for such growth. The reason is that the procedural aspects of democratic government are more likely to produce "good governance"—upholding the rule of law, ensuring transparency in the administration of justice, and allowing for citizen participation in decision-making. These are seen as essential for private capital investment and market-driven economic growth.

The issue of democracy is important in discussions of development for yet another reason—the apparent relationship between democracy and peace and stability. This idea is captured in the notion of democratic

peace, which suggests that democratic governments tend to be more peaceful because they have institutional and procedural safeguards that make it difficult to go to war, and because democratic norms encourage negotiation, compromise, and the peaceful settlement of disputes. This issue is of particular importance in view of the problems of civil war and state failure in many regions of the developing world, examined briefly below and in more detail in the following chapter.

State Failure, Political Violence, and Civil Strife

While the incidence of interstate war (that is, war between two or more states) has declined since the end of World War II, the incidence of various types of intrastate war and other forms of organized group political violence within states has increased. Almost all the major wars since 1945 have been in the developing world, with the exception of the wars that erupted in Central and Eastern Europe following the breakup of Yugoslavia and the U.S.S.R. in the early 1990s. That decade saw an average of 30 ongoing civil wars per year, most of which were in developing countries, especially in Africa, South and Central America, and South Asia. Many of these wars have had devastating consequences for the political, economic, and social development of the affected countries. Table 14.4 provides a list of countries that have experienced major armed conflicts in the last 30 years.

Thus, one key debate has focused on identifying the factors that lead to civil war and other forms of political violence. Some have sought the sources of war in economic factors, while others have looked to social factors, such as ethnic, cultural, and religious differences; yet others examine the political sources of war. Here, the concept of **state failure**—a situation that arises when central governmental authority breaks down—has emerged as a key variable in the study of war.[26] Other aspects of the debate have centred on how best to manage, resolve, and prevent various types of armed conflicts. As noted in the first section of this chapter, the concept of human security involves searching out the sources of and possible solutions to insecurity, state failure, and political violence in processes of development and change.

Table 14.4   Countries Experiencing Major Armed Conflicts, 1970–1999

Africa	The Americas	Asia/Middle East	Europe
Algeria	Colombia	Afghanistan	Armenia
Angola	El Salvador	Burma (Myanmar)	Azerbaijan
Burundi	Guatemala	Cambodia	Bosnia and
Central African Republic	Haiti	Indonesia	Herzegovina
Chad	Nicaragua	Iraq	Croatia
Congo, Democratic	Peru	Israel/Occupied	Georgia
Republic		Territories	Russia
Congo, Republic		Lebanon	(Chechnya)
Djibouti		Sri Lanka	Yugoslavia
Eritrea		Tajikistan	(Kosovo)
Ethiopia		Yemen	
Guinea Bissau			
Liberia			
Mali			
Mozambique			
Namibia			
Niger			
Rwanda			
Sierra Leone			
Somalia			
South Africa			
Sudan			
Uganda			

Source: Carter Center, *State of World Conflict Report*, 2000. Reprinted by permission of The Carter Center.

CONCLUSION

The comparative study of development is a broad subfield within the discipline of political science, and as a result a single chapter cannot cover all of the topics, issues, themes, approaches, and methods that make up this vibrant area of study. Nevertheless, this chapter has provided an introduction to the main issues that arise from the politics of development and underdevelopment. It has outlined various dimensions of global inequality, introduced key concepts, provided a brief history of the evolution of the dialogue between the rich countries of the North and the poorer countries of the South, offered some of the major explanations for patterns of development and underdevelopment, and discussed the contemporary issues and debates that arise from ongoing processes of development and change.

DISCUSSION QUESTIONS

1. Why has democracy become important in the study of development?

2. Are the explanations offered for development and underdevelopment by modernization and dependency theories still relevant today? Why or why not?

3. Should rich countries provide more aid to poorer countries?

4. In what ways does the inclusion of gender-related issues alter the way we think about development?

5. Why have issues of development generated conflict between the rich countries of the North and the poorer countries of the South?

 **WEB LINKS**

The World Bank:
http://www.worldbank.org

The United Nations Development Programme:
http://www.undp.org

World Trade Organization:
http://www.wto.org

International Development Research Centre (Ottawa):
http://www.idrc.ca

International Monetary Fund:
http://www.imf.org

FURTHER READING

Chilcote, Ronald H. *Theories of Development and Underdevelopment*. Boulder: Westview Press, 1984.

Handelman, Howard. *The Challenge of Third World Development*. 2nd ed. New York: Prentice Hall, 2000.

Huntington, Samuel P. *The Third Wave: Democratization in the Late Twentieth Century*. Norman: University of Oklahoma Press, 1992.

Kiely, Ray, and Phil Marfleet, eds. *Globalization and the Third World*. London: Routledge, 1998.

Moser, Caroline. *Gender Planning and Development: Theory, Practice and Training*. New York: Routledge, 1993.

Rostow, Walt W. *The Stages of Growth: A Non-Communist Manifesto*. Cambridge: Cambridge University Press, 1960.

Sen, Armatya. *Development as Freedom*. New York: Alfred Knopf, 1999.

Weatherby, Joseph N., et. al, eds. *The Other World: Issues and Politics of the Developing World*. New York: Addison Wesley Longman, 2000.

Weiner, Myron, and Samuel P. Huntington, eds. *Understanding Political Development*. Boston: Little, Brown & Co., 1987.

World Commission on the Environment and Development. *Our Common Future*. New York: Oxford University Press, 1987.

ENDNOTES

1 Statistical information in this section is drawn from the following sources: World Bank, *World Development Report, 1998/99* and *World Development Report 2000/01* (New York: Oxford University Press, 1999; 2001); World Bank, *Advancing Sustainable Development: The World Bank and Agenda 21* (Washington, D.C.: World Bank, 1997); United Nations Development Program (UNDP), *Human Development Report* (New York: Oxford University Press, various years).

2 See, for example, Allen H. Meriam, "What Does 'Third World' Mean?" in J. Norwine and A. Gonzalez, *The Third World: States of Mind and Being* (Boston: Unwin Hyman, 1988); and Richard E. Bissell, "Who Killed the Third World?" *The Washington Quarterly* 13(4) (autumn 1990): 23–32.

3 World Bank, *World Development Report, 1998/99*, table 9.

4 See, for example, Meriam, "What Does 'Third World' Mean?"

5 See Christopher Clapham, *Third World Politics* (London: Croom Helm, 1985).

6 For more information on colonialism in the Americas, Africa, and Asia, see Clapham, *Third World Politics*; Joseph N. Weatherby et al., eds., *The Other World: Issues and Politics of the Developing World* (New York: Addison Wesley Longman, 2000), pp. 113–25.

7 See Robert H. Jackson, *Quasi-States: Sovereignty International Relations and the Third World* (Cambridge: Cambridge University Press, 1990).

8 For more on the NIEO, see Jagdish Baghwati and John Ruggie, *Power, Passions and Purpose: Prospects for the North-South Negotiations* (Cambridge: Cambridge University Press, 1984).

9 These included the Independent Commission on International Development Issues (Brandt Commission, 1980); the Independent Commission on Disarmament and Security Issues (Palme Commission, 1982); the World Commission on Environment and Development (Brundtland Commission, 1987); the South Commission (1990); and the Commission on Global Governance (1995).

10 Statistical information in this section is from the World Bank, *World Development Report, 1998/99*.

11 GDP measures the total economic output of a country for a given period (usually a year); this figure is then divided by the total population to obtain the GDP per capita. Production of wealth is also sometimes expressed as the Gross National Product (GNP). The GDP excludes net income earned from abroad, while the GNP includes this income. Of the two, the GDP is more commonly used to compare economic production across countries.

12 Statistical information in this section is from the UNDP, *Human Development Report 1998* (New York: Oxford University Press, 1998).

13 For more on political development, see Myron Weiner and Samuel P. Huntington, eds., *Understanding Political Development* (Boston: Little, Brown & Co., 1987); and Howard Handelman, *The Challenge of Third World Development*, 2nd ed. (New York: Prentice Hall, 2000).

14 See, for example, Samuel P. Huntington, *Political Order in Changing Societies* (New Haven: Yale University Press, 1968).

15 See Walt W. Rostow, *The Stages of Growth: A Non-Communist Manifesto* (Cambridge: Cambridge University Press, 1960).

16 Notable works on modernization include Clifford Geertz, *Old Societies, New States: The Quest for Modernity in Asia and Africa* (New York: Free Press, 1963); Gabriel A. Almond and James S. Coleman, *The Politics of Developing Areas* (Princeton: Princeton University Press, 1960); Edward Shils, *Political Development in the New States* (The Hague: Mouton, 1966); David Apter, *The Politics of Modernization* (Chicago: University of Chicago Press, 1965); and A.F.K. Organski, *Stages of Political Development* (New York: Knopf, 1965). For a recent discussion of modernization theory, see Huntington and Weiner, *Understanding Political Development*.

17 See for example, Samuel P. Huntington, *Political Order in Changing Societies*.

18 Prominent works in the dependency tradition include A.G. Frank, *Capitalism and Underdevelopment in Latin America* (New York: Monthly Review Press, 1966); Samir Amin, *Accumulation on a World Scale* (New York: Monthly Review Press, 1975); Ronald H. Chilcote, *Theories of Development and Underdevelopment* (Boulder: Westview Press, 1984); F. Cardoso and E. Falletto, *Dependency and Development in Latin America* (Berkeley: University of California Press, 1979); Walter Rodney, *How Europe Underdeveloped Africa* (London and Dar-es-Salaam: Bogle L'overture and Tanzania Publishing House, 1972); and Immanuel Wallerstein, *The Modern World System* (New York: Academic Press, 1974).

19 Gunder Frank, *Capitalism and Underdevelopment in Latin America* (New York: Monthly Review Press, 1966).

20 See for example, F. Cardoso, "Dependent Capitalist Development in Latin America," *New Left Review* 74 (1972); and Peter Evans, *Dependent Development: The Alliance of*

Multinational, State and Local Capital in Brazil (Princeton: Princeton University Press, 1979).

21 For more on the Washington consensus, see John Williamson, "What Washington Means by Policy Reform," in John Williamson, ed., *Latin American Adjustment: How Much Has Happened?* (Washington, D.C.: Institute for International Economics, 1990); and Charles Gore, "The Rise and Fall of the Washington Consensus as a Paradigm for Developing Countries," *World Development* 28(5) (2000): 789–804.

22 See Caroline Moser, *Gender Planning and Development: Theory, Practice and Training* (New York: Routledge, 1993).

23 See Ray Kiely and Phil Marfleet, eds., *Globalization and the Third World* (London: Routledge, 1998).

24 World Commission on the Environment and Development, *Our Common Future* (New York: Oxford University Press, 1987).

25 See Samuel P. Huntington, *The Third Wave: Democratization in the Late Twentieth Century* (Norman: University of Oklahoma Press, 1992). This subject is examined in more detail in Chapter 15.

26 Michael Brown, ed., *Ethnic Conflict and International Security* (Princeton: Princeton University Press, 1993), pp. 103–24; I. William Zartman, ed., *Collapsed States: The Disintegration and Restoration of Legitimate Authority* (Boulder: Lynne Rienner Publishers, 1995).

Political Change: Nondemocratic and Democratic Regime Change

Peter A. Ferguson

CHAPTER OBJECTIVES

After you have completed this chapter, you should be able to
- describe how the state of global democracy has changed over the past 30 years
- explain the causes and consequences of the regime breakdown process
- discuss the implications of a democratic transition
- discuss the impediments to and the consequences of democratic consolidation.

WHY STUDY NONDEMOCRATIC AND DEMOCRATIC REGIME CHANGE?

During your lifetime, the world has experienced a dramatic transformation in the way most people are governed. The number of democratic governments worldwide has surged over the past 30 years to the point that there are many more countries with democratic governments than with nondemocratic ones. This wave of democracy has extended across the globe from southern Europe to Latin America, Southeast Asia, Eastern Europe, and Africa. The implications of this change can be seen from things as simple as where

you are now able to travel to where you may end up doing business when you graduate from school. On a national level, the countries with which Canada interacts have radically changed. Recent negotiations dealing with expanding the North American Free Trade Agreement (NAFTA) to include all the Americas—the Free Trade Area of the Americas (FTAA)—for example, included discussions about the importance of maintaining democracy throughout the Americas. On an international level, as the forces of globalization and interdependence "shrink" the size of the world we live in, the scope of incentives (and disincentives) for these new democracies to avoid nondemocratic change has greatly increased. Table 15.1 tracks the increase in democratic states between 1900 and 2000.

Why, then, should you be interested in the global democratic transformation? The answers are the same as the ones found in Chapter 1 when we discussed the reasons to study politics. Global democratization is fascinating—there are colourful characters and interesting stories about faraway places. Beyond that, democratization is very important. It has serious implications not only for the people who live in countries that experience such transitions, but also for people who come into contact with those countries, whether through family,

Table 15.1 Tracking Polity in the 20th Century

| | Sovereign States and Colonial Units | | | | | | Population | | | | | |
| | 2000 | | 1950 | | 1900 | | 2000 | | 1950 | | 1900 | |
	Total Units	Percentage of World Total	Total Units	Percentage of World Total	Total Units	Percentage of World Total	Total Population (millions)	Percentage of World Population	Total Population (millions)	Percentage of World Population	Total Population (milliions)	Percengae of World Population
DEM	120	62.5	22	14.3	0	0.0	3439.4	58.2	743.2	31.0	0	0.0
RDP	16	8.3	21	13.6	25	19.2	297.6	5.0	285.9	11.9	206.6	12.4
CM	0	0.0	9	5.8	19	14.6	0	0.0	77.9	3.2	299.3	17.9
TM	10	5.2	4	2.6	6	4.6	58.2	1.0	16.4	0.7	22.5	1.3
AM	0	0.0	2	1.3	5	3.8	0	0.0	12.5	0.5	610.0	36.6
AR	39	20.3	10	6.5	0	0.0	1967.7	33.3	122.0	5.1	0	0.0
TOT	5	2.6	12	7.8	0	0.0	141.9	2.4	816.7	34.1	0	0.0
C	0	0.0	43	27.9	55	42.3	0	0.0	118.4	4.9	503.1	30.2
P	2	1.0	31	20.1	20	15.4	4.8	0.1	203.3	8.5	26.5	1.6
TOTAL	192	100.0	154	100.0	130	100.0	5909.6	100.0	2396.3	100.0	1668.0	100.0

DEM = Democracy
RDP = Restricted Democratic Practice
CM = Constitutional Monarchy
TM = Traditional Monarchy
AM = Absolute Monarchy

AR = Authoritarian Regime
TOT = Totalitarian Regime
C = Colonial Dependency
P = Protectorate

Source: Adapted from Freedom House, *Democracy's Century: A Survey of Global Political Change in the 20th Century* (New York: Freedom House, 1999); cited on August 1, 2002; available at http://www.freedomhouse.org/reports/century.html#table1. Reprinted by permission of Freedom House.

business, or travel. The issues surrounding the questions of citizenship are galvanized around democratization. At a time when many Canadians no longer care about politics, reading a story about people waiting in lines for eight or nine hours while facing military forces bent on intimidation—simply to be able to exercise their right to vote—should help us all appreciate the importance of democratic citizenship. Finally, the wave of democracy that has transformed the world we live in holds great opportunities for political science graduates. In this era of globalization, companies, governments, and all sorts of organizations need to hire people who are knowledgeable about this expanding list of democratic countries—about which they lack a real understanding but are now forced to interact with on a variety of levels. Understanding the material in this chapter could lay the foundation for you to take one of these exciting jobs.

REGIME BREAKDOWN

Change is the one constant in politics, and this is especially evident in the examination of political regimes. Throughout history, one can witness the rise and fall of regimes. Some persist longer than others, but change is the one thing they all have in common. This section examines issues surrounding regime breakdown. Why should we be interested in such breakdowns? If we are to understand why some countries become democracies and others do not and why democracy persists in some countries and not in others, we must first understand the roots of such change. These are found in an examination of the breakdown of the prior nondemocratic regimes. One thing that is important to understand from the beginning is that the collapse of a nondemocratic regime does not necessarily result in a democratic regime coming to power. Throughout history, the most likely result of a nondemocratic regime breakdown has been the institution of another nondemocratic regime, not the establishment of a democratic regime. In order to understand why this is the case, we must first look at the various trigger events or causes of breakdown and then examine the various actors that play a part in such breakdowns. Once we have been introduced to the potential trigger events and arrive at an understanding as to what the interests and concerns of the important actors are, we can then turn our attention to the various consequences of such breakdowns.

Breakdown Causes

What are the events or situations that raise the possibility of regime breakdown? There is a wide assortment of potential explanations. This chapter argues that the causes of breakdowns interact with the actors in a particular country to lay the foundation for breakdown. These causes set the table for change. Once the table has been set, we need to examine the various actors to determine not only if the regime will break down but also what outcome will be produced. For ease of understanding, the trigger events are divided into economic, social, and political explanations. The theories found in each of these three areas should be seen as representative of each division, rather than an exhaustive listing.

Economic Causes

One of the most widely studied concepts in political science is the idea of modernization. Seymour Martin Lipset advanced the argument that socioeconomic development is a prerequisite for democracy. In order for nondemocratic countries to become democratic, they must achieve a certain level of development. The idea is that as a country modernizes, its social structures become increasingly complex, and a variety of new groups emerge; this produces a system that can no longer be effectively governed by command and thus democracy emerges.[1] This theory makes sense in that poor countries tend to be nondemocratic, whereas rich countries tend to be democratic. The fate of middle-income countries, however, varies widely. The search for an economic threshold for democracy continues to be a highly contested idea in political science.

A second potential economic explanation examines the economic performance of regimes. Unlike the modernization theory, this approach argues that enduring levels of poor economic performance trigger regime changes. As the economy in a country deteriorates, the resources available are reduced, making it harder to maintain the regime's bases of support. One way of thinking about this is that political regimes usually have a group of allies. The regime receives support from its allies, which allows it to continue to run the country. In exchange for this support, the regime's allies receive benefits, many of which cost the regime money (tax breaks, subsidies, and so on). As the economy deteriorates, the amount of money available to the regime is reduced, resulting in a reduction of the regime's ability to deliver benefits to its supporters. At some point, benefits are reduced to such an extent that support is withdrawn and the regime collapses.[2]

Social Causes

There are a variety of explanations for regime breakdown that revolve around social (and psychological) issues in a country. The theory of rising expectations recognizes that people have a set of expectations about their future and that significant events, such as a regime change, can cause people to raise their expectations. These expectations are commonly economic in nature but can also include things such as human rights. The difficulty with such expectations arises when they go unmet, causing people to agitate for change. When a new regime comes to power, such as when Nelson Mandela was elected in South Africa, people expect that their economic situation will improve. In this case, as in others, they expected that jobs would be more plentiful, that they would earn more money, and that they would be able to buy more goods. As the euphoria surrounding the demise of apartheid and Mandela's election began to fade from memory, the people of South Africa started asking themselves if they were, in fact, better off than they had been before these changes. Many observers of South Africa believe these unmet expectations hold the seeds for significant tensions in the future.

A second theory, that of relative deprivation, looks at situations in which the conditions people have come to understand as normal change for the worse. Unlike the rising expectations theory, this theory examines the circumstance where people have a relatively stable set of expectations that have been met over time. When these expectations are no longer met, people begin to support systemic change. A number of Eastern European countries saw communist parties return to power in the second round of elections following the demise of the Soviet Union. A number of observers have argued that some of this shifting support can be explained by the idea that the initial post-Soviet regimes were forced to cut back on commodity price supports and to slash the size of the public sector. As a result, concerns and expectations that people had regarding issues ranging from the price of food to job security significantly worsened and caused them to throw their support behind parties that had maintained acceptable levels of these values in the past. Such a shifting of support back to past non-democratic actors increases the chances of regime change.

A third set of theories relevant to regime breakdown surrounds the issue of ethnic conflict. Many countries throughout the world are now home to numerous ethnic groups. In some places, two main groups vie for power. In India, for example, the Hindu majority makes up more than 80 percent of the population, while the Muslim minority makes up a little more than 10 percent. Other countries face more severe cleavages. Nigeria contains people of more than 250 languages and tribes, of which the three main groups make up two-thirds of the population. Such cleavages do not always trigger problems, however. Canada and the United States both have populations consisting of a wide variety of ethnic groups. Donald Horowitz argues that ethnic divisions threaten regimes due to problems with inclusion and exclusion. Those included in power structures receive certain privileges, while those excluded from power receive penalties. The difficulty arises when groups begin to feel that the exclusions from power are permanent. If groups foresee that there is no possibility for them to receive the privileges of power, they may begin to cause problems for the regimes, especially through violent actions. The groups in power, likewise, feel the need to protect their power and often resort to violence in order to do so.[3] The postcolonial histories of the Central African countries of Burundi and Rwanda demonstrate that when ethnic divisions explode, in this case between the Hutu and the Tutsi, hundreds of thousands can die in the subsequent fighting.

Political Causes

One of the most common explanations of regime breakdown is corruption. While a certain level of corruption is found in every country, the level in some countries is extremely high. As you can imagine, higher levels of corruption are generally found in developing countries. Almost without fail, when a regime is overthrown, the victors point to the endemic levels of corruption found in the old regime as a justification for taking power. Their argument is that such corruption creates economic inefficiencies that make it impossible for the country to develop. They also point out that it becomes increasingly difficult for the mass public to trust political leaders who are seen as personally benefiting from the fruits of corruption. Transparency International is an international nongovernmental organization devoted to studying the causes and consequences of and cures for corruption. Their website, located at http://www.transparency.org, contains a wealth of information on this issue.

A second set of political explanations can be found in the idea of institutional failure. When the institutions of government cease to function, it becomes increasingly difficult for a regime to sustain itself. Legislative assemblies that can no longer pass legislation because of fractionalized party systems make it virtually impossible for a regime to solve the problems it faces. Bureaucracies that have extensively relied on patronage appointments may no longer be capable of administering the country. This is especially problematic when the effectiveness of the tax (revenue) agency is compromised. The problems a regime faces when institutional failure begins to occur are manifold. In Turkey, for example, the military has intervened at least three times since independence because of institutional failure. In 1980, the situation reached such an extreme point that the military argued the government could no longer control the spread of violence across the country, so they took control of the government. Each time the Turkish military stepped into power, they vowed to return power to civilian governments as soon as they got the situation under control. And each time they did—something that cannot be said of many other military regimes.

A final political explanation can be found in war. History is replete with examples of defeated regimes breaking down and being replaced by new ones. If a regime cannot maintain the integrity of its borders, it has little hope of surviving. Following World War II, political regimes in defeated Germany and Japan had new democratic regimes imposed on them. Shortly after losing the Falklands War to England, the military regime governing Argentina collapsed. It is not always the case, however, that military defeat signals the demise of a regime. Most would argue that the Gulf War coalition led by the United States defeated Iraq, yet if anything, the regime led by Saddam Hussein emerged more fully entrenched in power. In general, though, military defeat signals to regime opponents that there is a vulnerability that can be exploited, thus raising the risk of regime breakdown.

Breakdown Actors

There are a variety of actors and groups involved in and affected by any type of political regime. We will discuss here five sets of actors: political elites, business elites, the military, the mass public, and the international community. These are obviously rather large groupings that are not necessarily mutually exclusive—a member of the military could also belong to the political elite, for example. Nor do these groups function as a unified whole; there is certainly no agreement within any one group across all issues and concerns. Such a basic division of actors, however, will provide us with an understanding of the set of players within a regime and help us explain why one or more of these groups might seek to change the regime.

Political Elite

The political elite is obviously a group that is interested in the functioning and overall success of any regime. This group consists of more than just the political leader and his or her immediate advisors. Also included is the upper echelon of the various departments of the bureaucracy, members of the legislature, the leadership of any recognized "loyal" opposition, important regional and local leaders, and a variety of civilian leaders who play a vital role in the support and operation of the government. These people are powerful players in the country because of their ability not only to influence government policy but also to distribute

the benefits of such policy. These benefits may include such disparate things as providing family and friends with jobs, securing public works projects for one's home region, and getting a tax policy approved to benefit an important domestic industry.

If these people are most directly responsible for the functioning of politics in a country, why would they ever take part in its demise? As in most sporting events, politics creates winners and losers. The winners seek to maintain or augment their power. If, for example, the finance minister in a country feels that he has reached the apex of his power under the current regime but has aspirations to be the leader himself, it is conceivable that he may support change, anticipating that he will become the leader of the new regime. If someone at such a high level in government could defect (withdraw support from the existing regime), then it should be fairly easy to understand why those within the political elite who have not attained such powerful positions might also withdraw their support. Beyond the desire to improve personal or group position and power, there could also be a concern about the direction in which important policy is heading or a concern for the overall welfare of the country. Likely, there is some combination of all of these factors at play.

Business Elite

The second important group of actors is the business elite. This group consists of the people outside of government involved in the functioning of the country's economy, including the leaders of the country's largest corporations, key associational groups (for example, lawyers or engineers), and trade groups (such as major unions). These people and groups are important players in that they are responsible in large part for the health and direction of the country's economy: they provide people with jobs, government with tax revenues, and the country with regional or global prestige. Most obviously, the business elite may withdraw their support from a regime if the economy is performing poorly or if it is in the midst of a severe crisis. However, it may happen that regimes also break down during relatively stable or prosperous economic times. Why? It could be that certain groups feel left out of the political process (for example, labour unions). Others may feel that while the economy is in good shape, in order for the country to experience real success, the policies of the government must be changed (such as opening the country to more global trade or restricting the flow of goods entering the country). The point is not the particular policy or problem; it is that sometimes the economic losers are willing to gamble to improve their position, while the winners feel they could do even better under a new regime.

The Military

The group most often considered when examining regime change is the military. It is the military that executes coups and crushes rebellions. If, as Mao said, power grows out of the barrel of a gun, then surely the military will always be a key actor in regime breakdown. Unlike in Western democracies, the military in most nondemocratic regimes plays an important role in both external and internal security. Political leaders rely on the support of the military for their survival. There are numerous explanations as to why the military might withdraw its support from a regime. It is useful to divide such explanations into internal and external rationales. Internally, the military is usually concerned, first and foremost, with its institutional survival. Actions, events, and circumstances that the military perceives as threats to its survival can include things such as the dismissal of popular or powerful military figures, the undermining of military discipline, and severe budget cuts. Additionally, internal conflicts can arise within the military when junior officers see no room for promotion, or when traditional elements perceive the institution as becoming too politicized. External rationales can include, for example, a perception that the civilian government is corrupt or unable to deal with economic or political crises, and the desire on the part of the military to seek a stronger role in influencing the direction the country is taking. Most often there are a variety of reasons; they interact with one another and serve as justification for military intervention.

Mass Public

The mass public also has a role to play in the breakdown of nondemocratic regimes. Too often people think of such regime change as an elite-driven process, but as events from the fall of the Berlin Wall to the "people power" movement in the Philippines demon-strate, the power of the mass public should not be ignored. The mass public consists of all the people in a country not included in the first three groups—the "regular" citizens. The raw numbers of people involved is what makes this group powerful. Nothing makes elite groups sit up and pay attention as do a hundred thousand people—normally only marginally involved in politics—marching in the streets. As a result, the public holds a lot of potential power. It also represents a significant source of potential power for other groups to use or threaten to use. Groups perceived to have the support of the masses can often increase their power simply by threatening to mobilize mass demonstrations. Likewise, groups occasionally may set out to mobilize the masses to push for reforms, but end up frightening other actors (such as the military) into much more extensive responses because of these actors' fear of such mobilization.

The public may withdraw its support for the old regime for a variety of reasons. Economic reasons span a wide spectrum, which includes factors such as poor economic performance, the onset of economic crisis, the failure to meet expectations raised by initial successes, and a lack of hope for the future among the rising middle classes. Political reasons can range from scandals involving key leaders to extensive levels of corruption to assassinations of sympathetic or popular figures. That said, it is important to remember that there is a normal level of public activity in most countries that is usually not exceeded. It is rare for the public to be mobilized to an extent necessary to trigger regime change. While it does happen, the role the public more often plays is in the credible threat that another actor may gain its support and mobilize it.

International Community

The final player in regime change is the international community. This group includes any actors not resident in the country in question; it may include actors in neighbouring countries, in countries with economic or political involvement in the country, and in regional and international organizations. During the Cold War, the role of the international community was defined more by strategic interests than by other considerations. The international influence on regime breakdown was more a function of who the regime (or its opponents) supported at the global level and how important its strategic position was to the superpowers. Since the end of the Cold War, the international community has become much more involved in expressing its support for or opposition to both certain types of regimes and certain specific regimes. Basically, the international community, owing in significant part to the influence of the United States and its closest allies, has become decidedly more active and aggressive in the promotion of global democracy.

Of the variety of tools available to this set of actors, aid and trade are the most important. Countries desiring aid from the West and from international organizations such as the **World Bank** and the **International Monetary Fund (IMF)** are much more likely to receive that aid if they are democratic or if they undertake democratic reforms than if they operate in a nondemocratic fashion. Increasingly, democratic reforms are one of the main preconditions for such countries to receive economic assistance. Countries experiencing democratic reversals are much more likely to come under pressure to return to democracy or face the prospect of losing access to such assistance. Likewise, trade relations are increasingly becoming tied to democracy and democratic reform. Western countries have become more reluctant to trade with countries that are not democracies; when they do trade with such countries, they often attempt to use the expansion (or restriction) of trade as a tool to encourage democracy. An example of this can be seen in the debates surrounding the expansion of NAFTA to include all of the Americas: the proposed FTAA treaty text includes provisions for the exclusion of countries that experience democratic reversals. Economic assistance and trade relations have, in short, become a powerful tool used to push for democratic reform in nondemocratic countries and to prevent democratic breakdown in existing democracies.

Breakdown Consequences

Having outlined the major actors in the regime breakdown process, we can now turn our attention to the consequences of such breakdowns. This section will address three basic consequences: nondemocratic change, liberalization, and democratization. As previously stated, the most common result of the breakdown of a nondemocratic regime is its replacement with another nondemocratic regime: one military government replaces another or one dictator replaces another. If one is able to identify the key actors and their interests, it is not difficult to see why they may not favour a democratic outcome. If the goal is to get rid of the old regime in order to take power, there is no real desire for open competition. In certain cases, however, regime breakdown holds the potential to start the democratization process.

A second potential outcome is liberalization. Liberalization occurs when a regime significantly expands civil and political liberties in the country or opens itself up, at some level, to more meaningful competition from opposition forces. This does not mean that it becomes a democracy, but rather that it takes on some of the trappings of democracy. Why would a regime do such a thing? First, a regime that finds itself in trouble may seek to stave off radical change and total loss of power by agreeing to ease off some of the restrictions it has in place. It may attempt to address problems of human rights violations; allow increased group formation (for example, labour organizations); ease restrictions on freedom of the press, religion, association, or speech; or allow opposition parties to compete in a more meaningful fashion at the local, regional, or national level. It takes these actions not to begin the process of democratic change but rather to stave it off. The idea is to change certain policies to address the concerns of powerful opposition forces in order to guarantee the survival of the regime.

Second, regimes may pursue liberalization because they seek to expand their power and influence. Occasionally, very stable nondemocratic regimes pursue liberalization exactly because they feel secure and powerful. As the above discussion about the international community points out, there are a number of advantages (such as access to aid and trade) available to regimes that undertake some type of democratic reform that are not available to nondemocratic regimes. Therefore, regimes that feel they can undertake some democratic reforms while continuing to maintain their control and power liberalize in an attempt to receive these extra benefits.

In both cases, the difficulty is that, once started, liberalization is difficult to control. As the different actors begin to get a taste of the advantages of change, they are often tempted to push for even more change. Such reforms also send unintended signals to opponents of the regime. Rather than seeing such reforms as a decision made from a position of strength, opponents often interpret them as a sign of weakness and redouble their efforts to overthrow the regime. This is especially true in regimes attempting to save themselves from mounting problems. Opponents see such reforms as signals that the regime is on its last legs and that now is the time to act. Finally, almost all nondemocratic regimes overestimate their power and popularity. When the means to express dissatisfaction with the system are restricted long enough, leaders often (incorrectly) take silent acquiescence as a positive sign of support for the regime. This combination produces a situation where the regime overestimates its power while signalling to the opposition that it is vulnerable and at the same time providing an opportunity for all the actors (both its supporters and its opponents) to experience the benefits of reform. This creates fertile ground for the newly emboldened opposition to sow the seeds of the regime's demise. The bottom line is that while liberalization often seems to be a sound strategy for a regime to maintain its control over a country, it proves difficult to control in the end.

The final potential outcome of regime breakdown is some form of transition to democracy. Most often, this involves the announcement that democratic elections will be held at some future date. Depending on the circumstances and the degree of power that the old regime still holds, several events follow from such an announcement. One has to do with the country's constitution. In order to accommodate democracy, countries often have to write an entirely new constitution or radically overhaul the old one. The terms of such constitutional reforms are a function of the power and desires of the old regime and the opposition. A second issue arises from the fact that the old regime has to make political room for the opposition, usually in the form of political parties. Again, the strength of the old regime dictates its ability to control this process. Outgoing regimes that maintain a significant power base often attempt to exclude popular leaders or parties that might threaten the success of their preferred candidate or party. Regimes with little power may attempt to exclude only antisystem parties, such as rebel groups or communists. A final issue surrounds the election itself. Regimes attempt to control a variety of things,

including the timing of the election, voter eligibility and registration, access to the media, the runoff process, and the transparency of tabulating the results. As with the other issues, the ability to control the election is a function of the distribution of power of the players and their various objectives.

* * *

This section examined the breakdown of nondemocratic regimes. There are three types of explanations for the causes of regime breakdown: economic, social, and political. There are five main actors in this process: the political elite, the business elite, the military, the mass public, and the international community. Each set of actors draws its power from different sources, has its own set of interests, and possesses different potential reasons to withdraw its support from the old regime. Once regime breakdown has begun, these different players and concerns combine to produce three possible outcomes: nondemocratic change, liberalization, or transition to democracy. To understand regime change in general and transitions to democracy in particular, it is essential to understand the actors, causes, and consequences of the breakdown of nondemocratic regimes.

NONDEMOCRATIC REGIME CHANGE

The most common historical outcome of regime breakdown is nondemocratic change, of which there are three main forms. The first involves political dissent. Such dissent can range from protest to domestic violence to international terror. The second involves rebellion. For the purposes of this section, rebellion involves military coups and autogolpes (that is, leaders' coups against themselves). The final form involves state failure. Such failure is illustrated by examining civil war and social breakdown.

Political Dissent

Political dissent involves some form of action taken to indicate a rejection of the existing order. Protest is one aspect of dissent that is both widespread and accepted throughout the world. People who feel they are unable to effect change through the mechanisms of government turn instead to protest. When groups feel that government is no longer paying attention, one option they have is to expand the scope of the conflict. By organizing rallies and demonstrations, they hope to inform a greater portion of the population about their cause and thus force the government to act. It is important to remember that protest can produce results ranging from no change to wider recognition of the issues to the initiation of regime change. The world has recently seen a variety of protests surrounding the issues of globalization. The first major action in this regard took place in November 1999, when protesters attempted to disrupt the World Trade Organization's meetings in Seattle, Washington. One of the major difficulties with protest is that it may turn violent. While many protesters look to the likes of Gandhi and Martin Luther King for examples of nonviolent protest, others believe the only way to galvanize opinion (and media coverage) is through violent protest. Students protesting economic and human rights conditions in South Korea during the late 1980s routinely hurled rocks, bottles,

and Molotov cocktails at the police. Anyone following the protests of Palestinian youths against Israel has probably seen similar pictures. The point here is that protest is undertaken for a wide variety of reasons, can take many forms, and can have a variety of effects. The importance of protest for our purposes is that it can signal that there is a potential for regime change.

A second form of political dissent can be found in domestic violence and terror. Groups seeking systemic change in a country sometimes turn to organized violence in an attempt to force change. The battle between the Irish Republican Army (IRA) and the British government is a prime example. Feeling that the British had no legitimate claim to rule Northern Ireland, the IRA, which was formed following the Easter Rebellion in 1916, undertook a sustained campaign of terrorism in both Ireland and England. The aim was to force change by constantly reminding the people of the IRA's cause and making them doubt their personal security. In December 1999, the political arm of the IRA (Sinn

During the WTO summit meeting in Seattle in late 1999, protesters stood in silent confrontation with a line of police officers who had closed the intersection after a demonstration at McDonald's.

Eric Draper/CP Picture Archive

Fein) formally entered into the governing process in Northern Ireland in exchange for the disarmament of the IRA. Another example of domestic terror involves the Shining Path (Sendero Luminoso) in Peru. This group was a communist guerrilla force that turned to domestic violence in the 1980s. By the late 1980s, the Shining Path found a great deal of success in targeting urban infrastructure so as to disrupt the lives of Peruvian citizens. The democratic regime broke down in 1992, when President Alberto Fujimori suspended the Constitution, one of his justifications being the need to defeat the Shining Path and capture its leader, Abimael Guzmán Reynoso. Guzmán was captured within six months, which greatly diminished the activities of the organization. Once Fujimori fled the country in 2000, a fragile democracy was restored, but during 15 years of terror in Peru, more than 25 000 people (mostly civilians) died. The examples of both the IRA and the Shining Path should point to the potential importance of domestic terror in the regime change process.

The Grim Reaper taken on the United States and Afghanistan.

(Carlucho), Cartoonists & Writers Syndicate//cartoonweb.com

A third form of political dissent can be found in international **terrorism**. The events of September 11, 2001, drove home the relevance of this phenomenon. The actions of the United States and its coalition partners in response to what came to be known as 9/11 aptly demonstrate the linkage between international terrorism and regime change. The ramifications of this act of terror went far beyond the deaths and injuries of a single day. For example, the global economy was seriously damaged. Demonstrating the effects of interdependence, economies from Europe to Asia to North America turned down. Contrary to the intentions of the initiators of this act, at least one country, Afghanistan, experienced a regime change in the subsequent U.S.-led war on terrorism. While 9/11 certainly was not the first example of international terrorism, it demonstrated the vulnerability of even the United States, and it serves as a primary example of how such events can play a role in regime change.

> **Definition**
>
> **TERRORISM:** The threat or use of violence, usually directed at civilian populations in order to effect some form of political change.

Rebellion

The most common form of regime failure involves some form of rebellion. The two most salient examples of rebellion are military coups and autogolpes. A **coup d'état** is the mechanism which most people understand as the cause of nondemocratic regime change; it is defined as the overthrow of a political regime or leader by military force.

> **Definition**
>
> **COUP D'ÉTAT:** The overthrow of a political regime or leader by military force.

A quick reference to the motivations of the military as an actor in the regime change process should indicate why the military may step in and overthrow a regime. While a variety of motivations may appear reasonable, there are two basic sets of theories explaining why militaries seize power. The first revolves around the national interest of the country. This view sees the military as the nonpartisan adjudicator of politics in the country. As such, the military will seek power when the existing government has lost legitimacy and can no longer govern effectively. When exactly this point is reached is the subject of much debate. Typically, the military will point to economic crisis, a deadlocked or ineffective legislature, or widespread governmental corruption to indicate that the current regime has put the national interest at risk. The Turkish military is a prime example of this approach, having executed military coups in 1960, 1971, and 1980. Each time the military has stepped into politics, in the form of bloodless coups, they have pointed to the idea that legislative deadlock had left the country unable to confront serious crises it faced. In the case of the Turkish military, they established control over the country, made a series of constitutional changes, and then withdrew from power in favour of an elected civilian government. This end result, however, is certainly not the norm.

The second theory explaining military motivation examines the idea of the corporate interest of the military. From this perspective, the military undertakes a coup when the interests of the military as an institution are threatened. If the military feels that its very existence is put at risk by the current regime, then it fights to defend itself. What types of actions or events trigger such a feeling? For one, they may concern money. From this perspective, the chief corporate concern of the military is its budgetary support. If the institution's funds are put at risk (or significantly reduced), the military may feel it can no longer meet its obligations to its members (because, for example, it cannot pay them) or its obligations to the nation (because, for example, it lacks equipment or training). Another triggering factor has to do with the autonomy of the military. Threats to this autonomy can be found when the existing regime attempts to interfere in the internal affairs of the military. Such interference may cover issues such as the education and training curriculum, the assignment of posts, the promotion of all but the most senior officers, and the crafting of national defence strategy. Militaries express concerns that such interference puts the chain of command at risk and thus threatens the entire institution.[4] When the Goulart regime in Brazil changed promotion patterns and then proclaimed amnesty for all involved in a sailors' revolt, the military took control of the country via a coup.

A second example of rebellion is the autogolpe. An **autogolpe** is a self-coup perpetrated by the leader of the country. It occurs when the leader (usually elected) decides to rule by decree. Such events normally happen in countries with ambitious leaders when the country faces an economic crisis at the same time as the leader experiences institutional gridlock. The primary example of the autogolpe occurred under Alberto Fujimori in Peru. In April 1992, President Fujimori forcibly closed the Congress and suspended the country's Constitution. This action was greeted with massive public support because of Peruvians' weariness with the corrupt and incompetent Congress. The international community, on the other hand, overwhelmingly opposed this seizure of power by the democratically elected leader and moved to isolate Peru, in an attempt to force it to return to democracy. Fujimori's success in dealing with the economic problems and defeating the Shining Path gained him re-election in 1995.[5] It wasn't until his right-hand man was caught on video bribing a member of Congress that events commenced that eventually forced him to flee to Japan, ending his rule in Peru.

State Failure

The third form of nondemocratic regime change involves **state failure**. Such failure involves more than simply rebellion, coups, or riots. State failure refers to "a situation where the structure, authority (legitimate power), law, and political order have fallen apart and must be reconstituted in some form, old or new."[6]

> *Definition*
>
> **STATE FAILURE:** A situation in which the structure, authority, law, and political order have fallen apart and must be reconstituted in some form.

The first example of such failure is civil war. When two or more factions within a country take up armed struggle against one another, it puts the state at risk. History is replete with examples of civil war and the threats they posed to regimes. The civil war in the United States threatened to tear the country apart and throw it into chaos. John A. Macdonald drew on the lessons learned from watching those events in arguing that Canada should not provide too much power to the provinces. The bloody civil war fought in El Salvador in the 1980s can be understood in light of the Cold War politics of the times. The civil war fought in Ethiopia really began after World War II as a result of the unification of two historically distinct groups by European powers. The effects of civil wars extend well beyond body counts. The death and destruction caused by such events are truly awful, but civil wars have other important effects: they serve to divide the loyalties of citizens and place the very existence of the state in question.

A second example of state failure is total social breakdown. Occasionally, events in a state reach such a point that the state basically ceases to exist. It is under these circumstances that humans find themselves closest to a Hobbesian state of nature, where life is "solitary, poor, nasty, brutish and short." In 1991, the leader of Somalia was ousted from power, which plunged the country into civil war. A significant portion of northern Somalia announced it had seceded. A devastating famine the following year killed an estimated 300 000 people, triggering an attempt by the United Nations to broker a truce that would allow peacekeepers and famine relief workers and supplies into the country. For all practical purposes, the truce was ignored. Attempts by the international community to prevent looting only served to draw it into the burgeoning tribal conflict. The escalating fighting, which resulted in deaths and casualties among the international peacekeeping forces, led to in the departure of the UN by 1995. In the period that followed, the country was ruled by tribal warlords. There was no central government, and all services usually carried out by a state ceased to function. At this point, Somalia was literally close to anarchy. Since that time, a ray of hope has emerged, as by 2000 an attempt to establish a central government began to take root in the capital.

THE TRANSITION TO DEMOCRACY

The world has seen a remarkable wave of **democratic transitions** over the last three decades. Thus, it is important to have a more complete understanding of the issues surrounding the democratic transition itself. In order to more fully understand democratic transitions, we must first define what is meant by democracy.

Without agreement on such a definition, we have no hope of identifying transitions, much less discussing and studying them. While it is possible to define democracy in terms of the roots of authority and the ideal outputs of democratic regimes, this chapter defines it in terms of the procedures for constituting government and therefore focuses on free and fair elections. Having defined democracy, we then try to understand the background to such transitional elections by examining the conditions under which the nondemocratic regime left power. By looking at the strengths and interests of both the old, nondemocratic regime and the opposition forces in the country, we can arrive at an understanding of who sets the rules for the transition and what effects such rules can have. Finally, we turn our attention to the defining event of the transition—the election. In order for the election to be considered as the end of a transition to democracy, it must be seen as free and fair. We therefore examine what is meant by free and what is meant by fair in the context of elections and explore the limitations of the groups that arrive at such judgments—election observers.

> **Definition**
>
> **DEMOCRATIC TRANSITION:** The change from nondemocratic to democratic government, usually indicated by the existence of at least one free and fair election.

Defining Democracy

The idea of democracy has meant different things to different people over the ages. One approach is to focus on the source of authority. From this point of view, democracy means government by the people. We could debate the question of whether history has ever witnessed a regime that has operated as a true direct democracy, where the people really govern. Certainly women and other people not offered the advantages of citizenship would disagree with even the "best" cases of ancient democracy. In the modern age, there are no examples of the people directly governing. Such a solution is simply not practical. So while this approach offers interesting food for thought, it does not provide guidance for discriminating between democratic and nondemocratic cases in today's world.

Figure 15.1 The Map of Freedom 2001

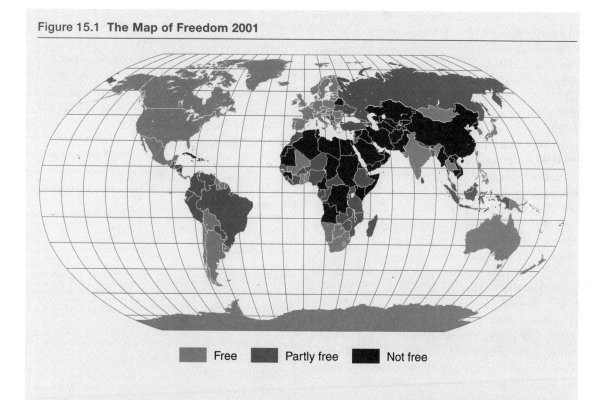

Free   Partly free   Not free

One Method of Measuring Democracy. Freedom in the World is an evaluation of political rights and civil liberties in the world provided by Freedom House on an annual basis since 1973. (Established in New York in 1941, Freedom House is a nonprofit organization that monitors political rights and civil liberties around the world.) The survey assesses a country's freedom by examining its record in these two areas: A country grants its citizens political rights when it permits them to form political parties that represent a significant range of voter choice and whose leaders can openly compete for and be elected to positions of power in government. A country upholds its citizens' civil liberties when it respects and protects their religious, ethnic, economic, linguistic, and other rights, including gender and family rights, personal freedoms, and freedoms of the press, belief, and association. The survey rates each country on a seven-point scale for both political rights and civil liberties (1 representing the most free and 7 the least free) and then divides the world into three broad categories: "Free" (countries whose ratings average 1-3), "Partly Free" (countries whose ratings average 3-5.5), and "Not Free" (countries whose ratings average 5.5-7).

Source: Reprinted by permission of Freedom House.

Another approach is to focus on the outputs of government. We all know that democracies are supposed to protect the common good: safeguard individual rights, provide equality, and guard against tyranny. We could no doubt come up with a more extensive list. The question that must be asked is whether these are defining features of democracy as a form of government or whether they are objectives that democracies are supposed to strive to accomplish. Put another way, if a regime must accomplish the objectives set out in our list before being considered to be a democracy, then how many democracies actually exist in the world? Surely we could come up with examples where even Canada and the United States violate some of these requirements, such as their early treatment of women, their dealings with Aboriginal peoples, etc. If we can use the terms of the definition to question even the most well-established democracies in the world, how useful is the definition in examining newly formed democracies? While this approach provides us with a useful method to examine the accomplishments of democracies, it does not allow us to distinguish between democracies and nondemocracies in the countries we are interested in during the post–World War II period.

The third approach is much more limited. It focuses on the procedures for constituting the government, arguing that we must examine the method of leadership selection. This definition, first advanced by Joseph Schumpeter in *Capitalism, Socialism, and Democracy* (1942), argues that democracy is "that institutional arrangement for arriving at political decisions in which individuals acquire the power to decide by means of a competitive struggle for the people's vote."[7] Several scholars have pointed out additional elements necessary to improve on this definition. Robert Dahl argued that democracy requires contestation, participation, and civil and political liberties. There must be meaningful competition (also called contestation) for the effective positions of power in government. This is accomplished through regular elections. These elections must allow for a highly inclusive level of political participation that excludes no major social group. In order to carry out such elections, a minimum level of civil and political liberties (such as those of speech, press, and association) is necessary.[8] This definition allows for the inclusion of newly formed democracies and provides us with a reasonable list of factors to examine when determining whether or not a country is a democracy.

The State of Global Democracy

Samuel P. Huntington argues that there is an observable historical pattern of global political change. He refers to the patterns of change as waves. It is important to recognize that history is not unidirectional: countries can experience transitions *to* democracy but they can also experience transitions *away* from democracy. Transitions away from democracy are referred to as reverse waves. While recognizing that history is messy and, as a result, it is difficult to sort historical

Table 15.2	Huntington's Waves of Democratization	
First Wave of Democratization	1828–1926
First Reverse Wave	1922–1942
Second Wave of Democratization	1943–1962
Second Reverse Wave	1958–1975
Third Wave of Democratization	1974–present

Source: Samuel P. Huntington, *The Third Wave* (Norman: University of Oklahoma Press, 1990), p. 16.

events into nice, neat boxes, Huntington argues that in modern history there have been three waves of **democratization** and two reverse waves.[9] Table 15.2 shows when these waves occurred.

Definition

DEMOCRATIZATION: A group of transitions from nondemocratic to democratic regimes, involving the relaxation of authoritarian political control by political leaders, the expansion of political and civil liberties, and the creation of institutional mechanisms that open up a political system to greater representation and participation. Democratization can be seen to occur in waves. A reverse wave occurs when some of the countries that had previously made the transition to democracy revert to nondemocratic forms of government.

Even a cursory examination of these dates reveals that the waves overlap; for example, the first wave did not end until 1926, but the first reverse wave began in 1922. This should reinforce the inexact nature of attempting to divide history into neat groupings. Nevertheless, Huntington's classification provides an easy way to conceptualize the ebb and flow of democracy over time.

The first wave is rooted in the American and French Revolutions. Exactly when these countries became democratic is a subject of ongoing debate. Nevertheless, when we employ even a basic democratic qualification of 50 percent adult male suffrage and some type of responsible executive (either through parliamentary support or periodic election), we can see that the United States began this wave with the 1828 presidential election. By the end of the first wave, 33 countries, including Canada and most of Europe, experienced some form of democratic transition. The first reverse wave began in 1922, with Mussolini's rise to power in Italy, and continued with Hitler's rise to power in Germany. During this period, military coups resulted in the overthrow of democracy in numerous places across the globe, ranging from the Baltic states to a number of South American countries.

The second, short wave of democratization began during World War II but lasted only through the early 1960s. A number of countries, such as West Germany and Japan, adopted democratic forms of government following occupation by Allied forces. Others, such as a number of Latin American states, seemed to follow the lead of the Allied democracies, which facilitated improved aid and trade relations. In addition, a number of countries "created" during this period due to the decline of Western colonial rule began as democracies. Most of these postcolonial democratic experiments, however, were short-lived. The second reverse wave saw a return to nondemocratic regimes across the globe. From Latin America to Asia to southern Europe, democratic governments were swept from power through military force.

The third wave of democratization began in southern Europe with the end of dictatorial rule in Portugal, followed quickly by a return to democracy in Greece and Spain. This wave picked up steam during the late 1970s in Latin America. Ecuador, Peru, and Bolivia all saw military governments attempting to withdraw from power. The movement to democracy subsequently spread throughout Latin America. At the same time, beginning with India and continuing from the Philippines to South Korea, Taiwan, and Pakistan, the democratic wave also spread throughout Asia. The collapse of the Soviet Union triggered a surge of democracy across Eastern Europe. Beginning with Hungary in 1988, the world witnessed a rapid and dramatic spread of democracy across the countries formerly behind the Iron Curtain. The 1990s have seen the third wave spread into Africa, leaving no major region of the world untouched by this substantial democratic movement.

Transition Modes

Having defined democracy and examined its spread, we turn our attention to the terms under which the old regimes lost their power, so that we can understand the manner in which the transition to democracy occurs. The most straightforward way to analyze this transition is to examine the situation of the old regime as compared to that of the opposition (even though we have already recognized that there are a number of groups that exist under both of these umbrellas, each with its own interests and concerns).

The first potential method of the old regime's exit is one in which that regime controls the process. In this situation, the old regime still maintains a significant amount of power. The opposition is weak or divided, which allows the old regime to control the rules under which it will exit. If the constitution needs to be redrafted, this will be done on terms favourable to the old regime. Such provisions could include guarantees for representation in the legislature, protections against prosecution for past human rights violations, and electoral rules favourable to the regime's candidates. It is in this last set of provisions that the old regime is most likely to assert itself. In setting up the electoral rules, the regime will attempt, for example, to exclude parties it does not favour, restrict the opposition's access to the media, and control the eligibility or registration process. The objective is to make certain that their preferred candidate and party win the election. In the end, this may result in a free and fair election and thus a transition to democracy, but it also serves to limit the long-term viability of such a transition.

In a situation where the old regime maintains a good degree of power but the opposition is also considered to be powerful, **pacted transitions** are more likely. Both sides are willing to enter into such arrangements because these offer guaranteed outcomes. When both sides hold considerable power, neither can be certain that the process leading up to the election will produce favourable results. The outgoing regime risks losing control of the process, whereas the opposition risks having the transition process shut down by the government. Beyond that, neither side has a good idea as to who will ultimately win the election. As a result, both sides are willing to accept less than their most preferred outcome (total power) so as to protect against the possibility of their least preferred outcome (total loss of power). Pacted transitions usually create more post-transition stability because rules and/or outcomes are agreed on in advance. In the long run, such transitions may experience difficulty because at some point the agreements will no longer reflect the distribution of power in society. When countries attempt to undo pacts, they often experience instability.

Definition

PACTED TRANSITION: A regime transition that involves a set of agreements (or pacts) between the outgoing regime and the opposition as to the terms of the transition. Pacts usually include agreements on some of the following issues: election rules, exclusion of antisystem parties, prosecution for past human rights violations, and guarantees of representation levels under the new regime.

The third manner of transition is one in which the opposition controls the process. In this situation, the old regime no longer maintains a credible power base and is therefore not an active player. This usually occurs when the old regime has experienced a major economic crisis, a significant military defeat, or some type of major scandal that has undercut the regime's legitimacy or forced it to withdraw.

The fourth method of exit occurs in situations in which the distribution of power is much less clear and more fluid. This type of transition usually involves a liberalization process that has gone beyond the regime's ability to assert control. As described above, under these conditions, the regime is unable to stop the process, which results in an election where the procedures and outcomes are not fixed or negotiated in advance.

Free and Fair Elections

The defining moment of the democratic transition is the initial election. Whether the regime is ultimately viewed as a democracy or not comes down to a judgment as to whether the transition election is seen as free and fair. This is the litmus test for whether the international community considers a regime to be democratic. In this context, the word *free* gets at the element of participation, whereas the word *fair* refers to contestation. The idea of civil and political liberties underpins both the free and fair aspects of an election. Therefore, the first question we must ask is how is it determined if an election is free and fair?

Whether an election is free usually comes down to the issues of suffrage and coercion. Is there universal suffrage? To determine this, we examine whether virtually all of the adult citizens in the country are eligible to vote. Are women excluded? Are significant minority groups—especially ethnic and religious—excluded? If there is universal suffrage, then the question of whether the election was also generally free from coercion must be examined. To determine this, we usually ask whether voters were intimidated, either when registering or when actually voting. A certain degree of intimidation is allowed for; however, turning large numbers of voters away from polling stations or widespread, especially targeted, violence during the election period is usually grounds for declaring an election to have been not free.

Whether an election is fair usually comes down to restrictions placed on candidates and parties, as well as to the level of corruption throughout the process, especially in the tabulation of votes. While some restrictions on contestation are accepted, for example, excluding antisystem and communist parties, we have to examine whether the major opposition leaders and parties were, in general, allowed to have candidates run in the election in an open fashion. If they were, then we turn to the issue of corruption. It is widely recognized that no election is totally free from corruption. The questions become how pervasive was the corruption and whether it affected the outcome. While minor indiscretions during the campaign may be tolerable, stuffing the ballot box or not counting ballots from opposition strongholds is usually not. Of course, out-and-out fraud in the reporting of election results—assuming such fraud can be identified—results in a declaration that the election was not fair.

The issue of civil and political liberties, while recognized as important to the definition of democracy, does not extensively come into play when examining the issue of free and fair elections. It is generally accepted that significant restrictions on such liberties will exist. As long as the outgoing regime loosens its restrictions to some extent, such restrictions rarely result in a declaration that the election was not free or fair. Aside from the elements of the free and fair determination that overlap with such liberties, the main focus usually comes down to media access. In most countries experiencing transition elections, the major media in the country are state-owned and thus dominated by those loyal to the old regime. If the opposition forces are excluded from all media access, then the election risks losing the free and fair determination. But as long as they have some degree of access, issues such as the state media's bias against the opposition are generally ignored.

There is one outcome that always results in a declaration that the election was free and fair: if the opposition wins the election. Regardless of any violations mentioned above, such a victory is seen as prima facie evidence that it was a democratic election. If the opposition does not win, analysts examine whether the opposition forces were provided with a chance to win. They may not take advantage of such opportunities, of course, and even if they do, they still may not win. In the end, the real question is simply the existence of such opportunities.

An important question to keep in mind when considering the issue of free and fair elections is, Who decides? The problem with making such a determination is that it is almost entirely subjective. Elections are inherently imperfect, even in developed democracies. Answering questions dealing with the allowable degree of exclusions, intimidation, and corruption is ultimately a judgment call. Who then is making this call? The answer varies over time and across countries. As the third wave of democratization has matured, a system of international election observers has developed. Such observer missions operate under the umbrella of international organizations, such as the United Nations or the Organization of American States; think-tanks, such as the Carter Center at Emory University (operated by former U.S. President Jimmy Carter) and the National Endowment for Democracy; and individual countries, such as Canada and the United States.

While generally well intentioned, election observation missions face numerous difficulties. The first is the issue of access. Will the government allow observers access to the entire country during both the campaign and the election itself? If so, can these observers be offered a reasonable guarantee of safety? Will the government allow access to party officials, candidates, party headquarters, and domestic media? What about outside observation of the vote count? The second is the issue of money. Assuming reasonable access is granted, can observer missions afford to take advantage of it? This is usually a function of the size of the country, its location, the infrastructure (travel and telecommunications), and the importance that the international community attaches to the election. The bigger, the farther away from the West, the poorer, and the less important a country is, the harder it is to gather even minimally sufficient funds to observe the election. Finally, there is the question of timing. As the world has moved to real-time communications, people have become much less patient about receiving judgments on international events. If missions wait several weeks to gather all the data they believe to be necessary to judge the election, the media have either already passed judgment without their input or are no longer interested in the story. On the other hand, if observer missions attempt to make judgments according to the news cycle of the Western media, how informed can such decisions actually be? The best that most missions can usually hope for is to have people covering a small sample of the important or controversial polling stations, some form of limited access to the vote count, and enough clear information to make their best guess in time to receive international media attention. These are important yet difficult tasks indeed.

* * *

In summary, Huntington's third wave discussion points to the importance of understanding democratic transitions. In order to have an informed discussion about such transitions, it is necessary to first arrive at a definition of democracy. To this end, the democratization literature has adopted a minimalist definition that relies on the procedures for constituting regimes and focuses on the idea of free and fair elections. The rules and conditions for such elections are a function of the interaction between the forces of the old regime and the opposition groups. Once the rules have been established and the election takes place, teams of election observers attempt to judge whether the election should be deemed free and fair. If it is, the international community considers the country to be a democracy.

DEMOCRATIC CONSOLIDATION

Once an election that is certified as free and fair occurs, does the world have another democracy? Is that the end of the story? No. At this point, all that has happened is this: the nondemocratic regime experienced a breakdown, and subsequently there was a democratic election. If you compare a country that has just gone through this process to Canada, it is difficult to make the case that they are the same in terms of democracy. Canada has well-developed democratic political institutions, a vibrant democratic political culture, and minimal prospects of reverting to a nondemocratic form of government in the foreseeable future. The only thing that the new democracy has under its belt is a single free and fair election. Rather than indicating an attainment of the democratic condition, such an event is really indicative of the beginning of a long challenge. In political science, the issues surrounding this challenge are known as **democratic consolidation**.

Consolidation Definition

Democratic consolidation gets at the "what next" question. Now that a fledgling democracy has been put in place, what needs to happen for that country to remove the "fledgling" tag? This is what the study of democratic consolidation is concerned with. Democratic consolidation exists when none of the major political actors, parties, organized interests, forces, or institutions consider that there is any alternative to democratic processes to gain power, and when no political institution or group has a claim to veto the action of democratically elected decision-makers.[10]

> **Definition**
>
> **DEMOCRATIC CONSOLIDATION:** The achievement of a situation in which none of the major political actors, parties, organized interests, forces, or institutions consider that there is any alternative to democratic processes to gain power, and in which no political institution or group has a claim to veto the action of democratically elected decision-makers.

A consolidated democracy may have small antidemocratic actors and groups. The important idea here is that the major actors in the regime, especially in times of crisis, do not turn to such groups for assistance. Rather than seeking such support, groups embrace the uncertainty of democracy—the idea that winners and losers are temporary and prone to change from election to election. It is this uncertainty that tempers the interactions and competition of groups both in and out of power. Out-of-power groups recognize that the uncertainty of democracy guarantees them a chance to regain power during the next election; rather than attempting to take power by force, they put their energies into attempting to turn this uncertainty to their advantage. Likewise, groups in power recognize that the uncertainty of democracy means they may lose the next election; rather than planning to stay in power by force, they plan for how to maintain their power through elections—and if they lose, how to regain it the next time. Because of this ebb and flow of groups in power and the likelihood that even though a party is a winner today, it may not be a winner after the next election, it behooves each group to treat its opposition with some level of respect at all times. The objective of the post-transition period is to get actors to embrace the advantages of uncertainty. Thus, as Juan J. Linz put it, a democracy is consolidated when democracy becomes "the only game in town."[11]

Consolidation Challenges

How do democracies become consolidated? While it must be understood that there is no simple checklist for new democratic regimes that want to consolidate, such regimes face at least four common challenges. One of these concerns the relationship between the civilian government and the military. Asserting civilian control over the military is likely the most important challenge confronting a new democratic regime. In most cases, the military was either in direct control of the prior regime or provided significant support to that regime. Even in a case where the military has been discredited or finds itself in poor fighting condition, it is still the institution most capable of wielding force in the country. Actors in disagreement with the new regime are therefore likely to try to get the military to side with them prior to any attempt to oust the regime from power. Given that new regimes often face numerous threats and contenders for power, they actually require more from the military than simply a return to the barracks. Newly formed democracies often find themselves turning to the military to actively assist them in defeating challengers, so that democratic regime may survive.

Thus, for consolidation to take place, the civilian government has to achieve control over the military. A number of problems stand in the way of such control. The first is the issue of what to do about past human rights violations. A significant portion of nondemocratic regimes that experience a democratic transition have a history of human rights abuses. The military has almost always played a critical role in such abuses. One of the first things that the public demands in a new democracy is some form of response to past violations. Accurate information on past government abuses is sought and trials are demanded. While it is difficult to disagree with the desire for justice, these demands put a transitional government in an awkward position. If it openly confronts the military (especially high-ranking military figures) with accusations of past violations, the military may feel it has nothing to lose by supporting the opposition. The government is left in a no-win situation: if it prosecutes the military it greatly increases the risk of a coup, but if it ignores past violations it may anger the mass public. Countries such as South Africa have tried to deal with this problem via Truth and Reconciliation commissions. Such commissions attempt to uncover information about past injustices, but they do not aim to prosecute the people behind the acts. While this is an interesting solution, and one to which many countries have turned, it usually ends up satisfying no one. As the South African case demonstrates, though, it may be enough to diffuse the issue and allow the new regime to move on.

Another issue confronting civil–military relations in new democracies revolves around the military's budget. Most third-wave democracies have sprung up in relatively poor countries, which face severe budget problems. This is especially true in cases where international actors such as the IMF and the World Bank come into play, as one of the first things they call for is widespread budget cuts. Before regime change, when the military was in power (or supporting the regime in power), its budget was a top priority. In most cases, the military was consuming an inordinate percentage of the government's budget. Now the government not

only has to redistribute the budget, reducing the percentage received by the military, but at the same time cut the overall amount of money it spends. Like any organization, the military is not happy with such cuts. Generally speaking, governments can cut military budgets in countries where the military has lost a significant amount of prestige and influence, but they try to insulate the military from cuts where it still retains significant power. However, it may be that just the opposite should occur. Powerful militaries should be confronted if the civilian government ever hopes to gain dominance, while defeated militaries should not be pushed into a corner where they feel they have nothing else to lose. Obviously, such decisions are very tricky and are fraught with danger.

Given these and other challenges, how should the new regime respond to the military? The overarching object must be democracy's survival. In the short term, this may require the regime to appease the military. In the long run, however, the civilian regime must assert its control over the military. Democracies must figure out how to send the military back to the barracks and how to keep them there. What this means is that military professionalism must be increased. The military must come to understand that its job exists in the military realm, not in the political or economic realms. Probably the most common suggestion for accomplishing this objective is to put a civilian directly in charge of the military. The idea is to create a defence minister or a secretary of defence who will be in overall charge of the military. He or she oversees everything from budget requests and expenditures to force deployments and promotions. Obviously, the minister relies heavily on the input of high-ranking military officers, but in the end, the civilian makes the call, not a military officer. The military is supposed to take its orders from the civilian government in any democracy, but in practice this has often proved harder to accomplish than it sounds.

A second major challenge that transitional democracies face is how to build and reform the democratic institutions of government. The most obvious elements that need to be looked at here are the legislature, the courts, and the bureaucracy. Outside of the executive, these three institutions are most responsible for the functioning of government—for making, enforcing, and carrying out the law—and are crucial to the government's ability to operate as a democracy. The obvious problem is that these same institutions were also responsible, in some manner, for the operation of the previous, nondemocratic regime. As such, we should expect them to experience difficulties in operating under a completely new set of rules. Specifically, these institutions must somehow confront issues surrounding responsiveness and corruption.

Assuming that electoral rules have been put into place to constitute the legislature, that institution must now learn how to function under a democracy. Since it is unable to rely on most of its old norms, new rules must be established for institutional processes to allow the legislature to legislate. This demands attention to everything from how to form committees to how question period will work. There are also a variety of challenges surrounding funding. For example, while staff may have previously been in place to deal with constituency demands, they are now needed to assist in many aspects of the legislative process, from research to communications. In addition, the legacy of corruption must be confronted. This extends from the undemocratic selection of members to issues of unequal access to perverted delivery of public projects (often called pork barrelling or pork). The list of necessary reforms is almost endless, but this sample makes the point that the legislature has to undergo a radical makeover before the people come to see it as a democratic institution.

Similar challenges are found when examining the courts. For a consolidated democracy to function properly, the courts must be able, at minimum, to check abuses that occur in the rest of the government. For this reason, rules that allow the courts to operate as a separate branch of government are required. This is not to say that the courts are above the law, but rather that they must be free to enforce the law. Instead of relying on the desires of the executive, the courts have to be put in a position to rely on the law. Here, too, the legacy of corruption must be overcome. To accomplish this, the courts will require additional funding for the recruitment of new judges and staff members. The corrupt judges of the old regime must be retrained or retired. This task is something that is not easily accomplished and that quite often sets off a long war between supporters of the new and old regimes, threatening the viability of the entire institution.

Finally, the bureaucracy also faces challenges. Citizens are much more likely to have direct interactions with the bureaucracy than with the legislature or the courts, so reforms in this sector are no less important. While the bureaucracy is much more likely to be properly staffed than either of the other two institutions, the staffing rules under the old regime have undoubtedly created corruption and inefficiencies. One of the toughest tasks in reforming the bureaucracy is the implementation of merit-based hiring practices. In most nondemocratic (and even many democratic) regimes, staffing in the bureaucracy is used as a way to reward followers. An important job allows one to employ family and friends, regardless of qualifications. This is the reason that high-level bureaucratic jobs are often more desirable than similar jobs in the private sector in such regimes. The higher up one goes in public service, the more people one is able to take care of, and the more people who in some way became beholden. In other words, such jobs are powerful, not because of the missions or objectives of the position but rather as a function of their ability to deliver goods. The most straightforward solution to the problem is to hire civil servants based on merit. As with the courts, however, this reform is widely resisted within the institution and is thus not easily implemented.

Having examined the military and other institutions of government, we turn our attention to a third element—**civil society**. The proper functioning of government is not enough to push a democracy toward consolidation; democracy also requires a functioning civil society. Civil society refers to nongovernmental groups in society, but in nondemocratic political systems, the term goes beyond the definition provided in Chapter 13. Civil society in this context is

a set or system of self-organized intermediary groups that: 1) are relatively independent of both public authorities and private units of production and reproduction, that is of firms and families; 2) are capable of deliberating about and taking collective actions in defense or promotion of their interests or passions; 3) do not seek to replace either state agents or private (re)producers or to accept responsibility for governing the polity as a whole; and 4) agree to act within pre-established rules of a civil nature, that is, conveying mutual respect."[12]

The idea is that as more groups are created and as more people join them, the chances of democratic consolidation increase. At an individual level, membership in such groups helps develop people's understanding of the way democracy functions and therefore serves as an incubator for democratic political culture in the country. At a group level, such organizations offer a check against the abuse of power and a backstop support for democracy. These two points make it clear that democratic consolidation is not just dependent on the groups that make up civil society, but also on the ways these groups interact with their members, each other, the business sector, and the government. While such groups are more likely to form spontaneously in a democracy, anything transitional governments can do to foster their formation and survival will assist in the consolidation process.

A final element that should be considered when examining democratic consolidation is the international community. As the forces of the Cold War have faded and the forces of globalization have spread around the world, the role that the international community plays in democratic consolidation has greatly increased. During the 1990s it became clear that the international community, especially the Western world, favours democracy and actively works to foster and maintain it. The West relies on economic tools to accomplish its objectives. Western-backed international organizations, such as the World Bank and the International Monetary Fund, condition aid packages to new democracies on a set of economic reforms, which are aimed at making these fledgling democracies more competitive. Individual donor countries often tie aid not only to meeting conditions set out by the World Bank and the IMF but also to consistent progress toward democratic consolidation. The effectiveness of conditioning aid on the achievement of democracy (or democratic progress) remains very controversial.

The other tool employed in this respect is international trade. Given that the world is becoming more interdependent, countries that desire economic success must become more open and active in the realm of international trade. Aid and trade are also used to foster consolidation by delivering needed short-term assistance, which helps countries get their economic house in order, and then to offer these new democracies prospects for long-term success by putting them in a position where they can take advantage of globalization and world markets. The existence of a controversy regarding if and how democratization is related to economic development has been previously addressed. That said, in the short term, opponents of democracy must confront the potential loss of such benefits when considering withdrawing their support from the regime. In the longer term, the idea is for the various players to learn that these benefits are tied to the democratic regime and are so extensive that there is no reason to consider nondemocratic alternatives.

Unconsolidated Democracy

An understanding of the challenges facing countries during the consolidation period should lead one to understand that consolidation is not easily achieved. In fact, depending on the way one defines and measures democratic consolidation, it is more typical for a country that experiences a democratic transition *not* to achieve consolidation. Throughout Latin America and Asia, countries that experienced democratic transitions have more often than not found a sort of semi-democracy persisting in their country, rather than experiencing a move to the eventual state of consolidation. One way of looking at this is to consider such states as so-called electoral democracies. These states have experienced one or more free and fair elections but have failed to consolidate. There are still serious nondemocratic actors in the country, and the levels of civil and political freedoms common in Western democracies have not materialized. This is not to say that electoral democracies can never consolidate. Rather, their condition should serve as a reminder that there is no natural pattern of regime evolution. Not only is it possible for countries to experience a democratic transition that never results in democratic consolidation—it is also important to remember that democracies can and do break down.

Consolidation Consequences

Having laid out the issues surrounding the challenge of democratic consolidation, we will now consider its consequences. What are the practical effects of consolidation? Life in a country that has experienced a nondemocratic regime breakdown, an initial democratic transition, and the successful completion of the democratic consolidation will be much different at the end of the process. The domestic and international implications vary among individual countries and across time, but it is possible to isolate some common consequences of a successful democratic consolidation. Political rights, including things such as the right to vote, the fairness of electoral rules, the principle that votes endow actual power, the ability to organize political parties, and the existence of meaningful opposition are the norm and are almost taken for granted. Civil liberties, encompassing the freedoms to hold views, maintain institutions, and possess personal autonomy apart from the state, are widespread.[13] While they may come under attack from time to time, society recognizes their importance and strives to protect the core set of liberties. The political elite sees democracy as the only possible regime and spends its time trying to take advantage of the rules in order to gain power. The military takes its orders from the civilian government and is now considered to be professional and divorced from politics. Civil society has blossomed as people are more engaged in group activities and government is more responsive to and inclusive of outside groups' views. The socioeconomic situation of the country has gradually improved and gross distributional problems such as famine have become much less frequent. On the international level, the country is much more fully involved in the globalized world. Aid donors and trade partners no longer question whether they should be engaged with the country. While there may be disagreements as to the degree or type of engagement, the regime is no longer questioned over democratic legitimacy. While this is obviously an idealized picture, and even consolidated democracies will have trouble achieving all of the benefits just described, it does provide the end-results rationale for attempting the consolidation process.

In summary, having experienced the breakdown of nondemocracy and successfully navigated the transition to democracy, countries are faced with the challenges of democratic consolidation. The democratization process does not end with an initial free and fair election. After this initial success, the regime must strive to make democracy the only alternative acceptable in that society. In order to accomplish this, the regime must establish civilian control over the military; reform the

central institutions of government, such as the courts, the legislature, and the bureaucracy; foster the development of civil society, and integrate itself into the globalized world. In short, the regime must endeavour to sell to its citizens the advantages of democracy, including its uncertainties. In confronting these challenges, it is much more typical for a country to fail to consolidate. During the third wave of democratization, the world has witnessed an unprecedented number of transitions to democracy, but most of these transitions have resulted in unconsolidated, electoral democracies. However, in countries where all the major actors embrace the advantages of democratic uncertainty, consolidation has been achieved.

CONCLUSION

During the past three decades, the world has undergone a radical transformation toward democracy. The third wave of democratization began in the early 1970s and continues today. For this reason, the study of democratization has never been more important. In order to understand this process, it is essential to begin with an examination of the key actors: political elites, business elites, the military, the mass public, and the international community. With an understanding of their interests and strengths, the reasons why some of these groups may withdraw their support from nondemocratic regimes and thus break those regimes down become more apparent.

It is important to remember that the consequence of such breakdowns is, more often than not, the installation of another nondemocratic regime. Sometimes, however, the result is a transition to democracy. But what exactly is democracy? In this chapter, democracy is defined in terms of the procedures employed to constitute a government. By examining the key actors in the breakdown of the nondemocratic regime, it is possible to outline different modes of transitions. It is in these different modes that the rules for democratic transitions are set. The defining moment of any transition is the election itself. In the end, whether a country is considered by the international community to be democratic depends on the judgment of election-monitoring teams as to whether the election was free and fair. Having completed a free and fair election, the democratic regime enters into the consolidation phase of democratization, where the objective is to make democracy the only game in town. Once this is accomplished, a country can expect the benefits of democracy to take on a more permanent status.

DISCUSSION QUESTIONS

1. Identify and discuss the importance of the different actors in the democratization process.

2. Identify and discuss the importance of the different consequences of the breakdown of nondemocratic regimes.

3. Compare and contrast the different approaches to defining democracy.

4. What is meant by free and fair elections?

5. Discuss the challenges regimes face during the democratic consolidation process.

www WEB LINKS

Freedom House:
http://www.freedomhouse.org/index.htm

World Audit:
http://www.worldaudit.org

Election World:
http://www.electionworld.org

International Foundation for Election Systems:
http://www.ifes.org

The National Endowment for Democracy:
http://www.ned.org

International Institute for Democracy and Electoral Assistance:
http://www.idea.int

National Democratic Institute for International Affairs:
http://www.ndi.org

Transparency International:
http://www.transparency.org

Stanford University's Comparative Democratization Project:
http://democracy.stanford.edu

World Forum on Democracy Resource Page:
http://www.fordemocracy.net/resource.shtml

FURTHER READING

Diamond, Larry. *Developing Democracy: Toward Consolidation.* Baltimore: Johns Hopkins University Press, 1999.

Haggard, Stephan, and Robert R. Kaufman. *The Political Economy of Democratic Transitions.* Princeton: Princeton University Press, 1995.

Huntington, Samuel P. *The Third Wave.* Norman: University of Oklahoma Press, 1990.

Mainwaring, Scott, Guillermo O'Donnell, and J. Samuel Valenzuela, eds. *Issues in Democratic Consolidation: The New South American Democracies in Comparative Perspective.* Notre Dame: Notre Dame University Press, 1992.

Przeworski, Adam, et al. *Democracy and Development: Political Institutions and Material Well-Being in the World, 1950–1990.* Cambridge: Cambridge University Press, 2000.

ENDNOTES

1 Seymour Martin Lipset, "Some Social Requisites of Democracy," *American Political Science Review* 53 (1959): 69–105; Adam Przeworski, et al., *Democracy and Development: Political Institutions and Material Well-Being in the World, 1950–1990* (Cambridge: Cambridge University Press, 2000), pp. 78–80.

2 Stephan Haggard and Robert R. Kaufman, *The Political Economy of Democratic Transitions* (Princeton: Princeton University Press, 1995), pp. 25–32.

3 Donald Horowitz, *Ethnic Groups in Conflict* (Berkeley: University of California Press, 1985).

4   Eric A. Nordlinger, *Soldiers in Politics: Military Coups and Governments* (Englewood Cliffs: Prentice-Hall, 1977).

5   Maxwell A. Cameron and Philip Mauceri, eds., *The Peruvian Labyrinth: Polity, Society, Economy* (University Park: Pennsylvania State University Press, 1997).

6   I. William Zartman, "Introduction: Posing the Problem of State Collapse," in I. William Zartman, ed., *Collapsed States: The Disintegration and Restoration of Legitimate Authority* (Boulder: Lynne Rienner Publishers, 1995), pp. 1–11.

7   Joseph Schumpeter, *Capitalism, Socialism, and Democracy,* 2nd ed. (New York: Harper, 1947), p. 269.

8   Adapted from Samuel P. Huntington, *The Third Wave* (Norman: University of Oklahoma Press, 1990), p. 6; and Georg Sorensen, *Democracy and Democratization* (Boulder: Westview Press, 1993), pp. 12–13.

9   Huntington, *The Third Wave*, pp. 15–26.

10 Juan J. Linz, "Transitions to Democracy," *Washington Quarterly* 13(3) (1990): 158.

11 Ibid.

12 Philippe C. Schmitter, "Civil Society East and West," in Larry Diamond, Marc F. Plattner, Yun-han Chu, and Hung-mao Tien, eds., *Consolidating the Third Wave Democracies: Themes and Perspectives* (Baltimore: The Johns Hopkins University Press, 1997), p. 240.

13 See the checklist of political rights and civil liberties employed by Freedom House for their Freedom in the World reports, available at http://www.freedomhouse.org.

International Politics

7

Roberta Cross speaking at the official inauguration of the Canadian consulate in Barcelona, attended by Minister for International Trade Pierre Pettigrew; Ambassador of Canada to the Kingdom of Spain Alain Dudoit; and Catalan Minister of Industry, Trade and Tourism Antoni Subirà i Claus.

Career Profile: Roberta O. Cross

Before undertaking her political studies degree at the University of Saskatchewan, Roberta O. Cross spent one year as a Rotary Exchange Student in Sydney, Australia, and finished the year with a heavy accent and a passion for understanding people of different cultures, origins, and languages. She returned home to Saskatoon to focus on international studies and be inspired by courses in political philosophy. She graduated in 1992 with the Robert Lawson Elliot International Relations Book Prize and top honours in the Department of Political Studies and the Department of International Studies.

Following graduation, Roberta was self-employed as a public relations consultant until she was invited to join the Department of Foreign Affairs and International Trade (DFAIT) as a trade commissioner in 1993. After an initial stint in the Middle East Trade Development Division, she became the junior departmental assistant in the office of the Minister for International Trade. In 1995, a junior trade commissioner position opened up at the Canadian Embassy in Cuba because of growing Canadian commercial interest in the market, and after two months of language training, Roberta was relocated to Havana for a three-year posting. She eventually became responsible for the trade and investment program during the time of the deliberations surrounding the anti-Cuba Helms-Burton Bill and dramatic increases in Canada–Cuba trade.

Upon her return to Canada, Roberta was involved in improving trade commissioner services for businesswomen seeking to increase export sales of their goods and services. In 1999, she was assigned to the Communications and Media Relations division of the Hemisphere Summit Office, responsible for communicating to Canadians the importance of Canada's growing relationship with the Americas. Roberta worked on the first ministers' meeting of the Free Trade Area of the Americas (FTAA) negotiations in 1999 and the General Assembly of the Organization of American States (OAS) held in Windsor, Ontario, in 2000. She was responsible for representing DFAIT to the Windsor community, which included politicians, business people, students, and antiglobalization demonstrators.

Roberta is currently posted to Barcelona, Spain, where she has been responsible for the opening of the new Canadian consulate, established to promote trade and investment links with the economically and culturally dynamic region of Catalonia. She speaks English, French, and Spanish and struggles daily with Catalan.

Chapter 16

World Politics: Global Anarchy, Global Governance

Kim Richard Nossal

CHAPTER OBJECTIVES

After you have completed this chapter, you should be able to

- discuss the nature and scope of world politics
- put contemporary global politics into broader historical perspective
- discuss the impact of anarchy on the nature of politics at a global level
- understand the nature and limitations of global governance.

INTRODUCTION

The deaths of just under 3000 people on the morning of September 11, 2001, at the hands of radical Islamist terrorists provided a grim and deadly reminder of the ways in which world politics intrudes on our lives. The attacks on the twin towers of the World Trade Center in New York City and on the Pentagon in Washington, D.C., might have come as a complete surprise to those who found themselves on the four hijacked aircraft or to those caught in the destruction on the ground. But these attacks did not come out of the blue. Rather, they were part of a larger war that the United States and Islamist radicals had been fighting for over two decades. What was different about September 11 was the audacity of the attacks, the scale of death and destruction, the highly symbolic nature of the targets—symbols of both global capitalism and American military might—and the fact that the war had finally made

its way to American soil in an unambiguous way. Likewise, what was different about the response of Americans after September 11 was the willingness to engage in all-out military action against those who were engaged in open warfare against the United States.

It is precisely because war usually seems so remote and distant from the daily reality of North Americans that we tend to forget that it is one of the central problems of politics. Indeed, the foremost challenge of all political communities is how to create structures and processes that will allow people to live out their lives without having to go to war against other members of their political community—and thus avoid the fate of the United States in the 1860s, China in the 1940s, Lebanon in the 1970s, Yugoslavia in the 1990s, and Afghanistan in late 2001. The civil wars in those countries not only killed huge numbers of people, but made normal life impossible for those left behind. However, such disintegrative civil wars are the exception rather than the rule; most political communities have managed to create the conditions of peace—more or less. Indeed, it is a testament to the widespread existence of essentially peaceful political communities that most of the other chapters in this book explore facets of

New York City, Tuesday, September 11, 2001.

In a horrific sequence of destruction, terrorists hijacked two airliners and crashed them into the World Trade Center in a coordinated series of attacks that brought down the twin 110-storey towers.

Todd Hollis/CP Picture Archive

a mini-text on international relations that seeks to provide a capsule summary of that rich field of scholarly enquiry; most students will be more fully introduced to international relations (or IR, as it is commonly known) in their second year. (For those interested in a preview of what they are likely to find in an introductory course in international relations, several IR textbooks are cited in the Further Reading section at the end of the chapter.) Rather, the purpose of this chapter is to provide an overview of the nature of world politics and in particular the primary problems of politics at a world level: the causes of war, the conditions of peace, and the difficulties of governance in an anarchical world.

THE NATURE OF WORLD POLITICS

Many people, when they think about politics at a global level, use the term international relations or international politics. However, when taken literally, the etymology of this word—*inter* + *nation*—suggests that we are interested only in the politics (or relations) between nations. But in fact we are interested in more than the politics between *nations;* and we are interested in more than the politics *between* nations.

First, we do not want to restrict our attention merely to the nation. Rather, we are interested in looking at politics involving a much wider range of actors and agents. Moreover, using *inter* + *national* could refer as reasonably to "domestic" politics as to "international" politics. After all, the politics between the Scottish and English *nations*, the Québécois and Canadian *nations*, or the Catalan and Spanish *nations* could be considered *inter* + *national*—even though these politics are not normally considered "international," since they occur within the boundaries of Britain, Canada, and Spain.

However, trying to find a more apt generic description leads one into the jargonistic or simply the bizarre. Using the word *polity* (a political community) is one possibility, though "interpolity politics" does not exactly roll smoothly off the tongue. Nor do generic synonyms work any better: intergroup, intercountry, or interunit. "Independent political community" is a reasonably accurate generic descriptor for all the polit-

politics and governments within the different political communities in which we live that are essentially peaceful in nature. But there is one realm of politics where war has not been banished: the global realm.

This chapter focuses on politics at this broader and wider political level. Its purpose is not to serve as

ical formations mentioned above—and more besides. However, while it might be somewhat more accurate, "interindependent-political-community politics" is unlikely to find a place in common usage.

Second, the *inter* in "international" is also problematic. We should be interested in more than simply how independent political entities—be they empires, states, nations, fiefdoms, kingdoms, chiefdoms, tribes, or villages—interact politically *between* each other. The relationships between different countries today are all *international* and often highly *political*, but international politics is more than simply the sum of the 18 000 possible bilateral relationships between the 191 states in the world today. While we are interested in the bilateral relationships of different countries, we are also interested in looking at much broader political processes.

That is why modifying the word *politics* by specifying the domain with which we are concerned is useful. We all have a sense of "politics by domain" that can begin with units as small as the family, the clan, or the tribe. As the aperture widens, the domain expands: for example, urban politics is about the politics of the city, both inside the city and outside, in its relations with a broader sociopolitical environment. National politics includes all the lower layers, as well as the relations between the nation-state and the outside—or what is usually called foreign policy. And beyond the nation are two further levels of politics. The next step is **supranational** politics, where a separate and independent political community exists "above" the nation-state. At present, there is only one active site of supranational politics: the European Union (EU). It is a supranational community of 15 European nation-states that have joined together to create a higher level of government in Brussels. Consequently, the politics of the EU is a mixture of national and international politics, similar to the politics one finds in a federal state, where different levels of government share political authority over the same territory and the same people.

Definition

SUPRANATIONAL: A sphere of politics and political institutions that exists "above" the nation-state but usually "below" the global level. The only supranational polity in the world is the European Union.

The next step up from supranational politics is politics at the level of the whole world. We could call this global politics, planetary politics, or Earth politics, but world politics is both a common and a commonsense way of naming this level. By its very nature, then, world politics seeks to provide an account of politics at a global level, which is the broadest domain of politics. (Unless, of course, the truth really *is* out there, and in that case we will get to open the aperture wider still. In the meantime, we will have to leave imaginings on galactic politics to Hollywood film studios.)

We also need to focus on the noun and ask: What is the *politics* of the world? For some, politics is the pursuit of the good. For others, politics is the struggle for power; for others still, politics is the art and science of governing. For yet others, politics is, to use Harold Lasswell's classic definition, about who gets what, when, and how (and why).[1] Although it might be tantalizing to be able to capture the essence of a huge sphere of human activity in a single phrase, such simple definitions unfortunately cannot convey the multifaceted nature of the political realm. One can count at least five related facets of politics at a global level: community, economic structures, interests, power, and governance.

Community

Politics is first and foremost about the communities into which human beings have always organized themselves. Political communities come in markedly different shapes, sizes, and types, and they exist for varying amounts of time: tiny clan-based hunter-gatherer bands, small agricultural villages, the small *poleis* (or city-states) of ancient Greece, the vast empires of antiquity, nomadic tribes such as the Vandals or the Mongols, the feudal fiefdoms of medieval Europe, the kingdoms of West Africa, the continental-sized contemporary states with hundreds of millions of members, or the supranational community of the European Union. As the other chapters in this book make so clear, politics always focuses on the community and its nature, as well as the relationship of individuals and groups to the community.

But people are also capable of conceptualizing the existence of community at a level above their own political community and of seeing their polity as part of a broader community. For example, ancient Greeks believed that they constituted a single community—the Hellenes. Although divided into various *poleis*, they saw themselves as a united singularity against others, particularly Persians, and developed numerous community institutions. These included common spiritual institutions, such as the oracle at Delphi; the inter-*polis* games, held in four-year cycles; and a system of lawsuits for settling contractual disputes. *Poleis* would even hold civilized debates with one another about inter-*polis* affairs—before engaging each other in brutal and bloody wars. Likewise, as Kalevi J. Holsti points out, we can point to Christendom in Europe during the feudal period or the conceptualization of "Europe" in the 17th century, when phrases such as "the tranquillity of Europe," "the health of the European community," and "*le repos général de la Chrétienté*" (the general repose of Christendom) dotted the discourse of international politics—at the same time that the armies of European kings and princes were fighting a series of destructive wars.[2] And in the contemporary period, we conceptualize the world in community terms with the widespread use of the phrase "the international community." This phrase is invariably used in a way that means much more than "190 governments and what they are doing." Rather, it usually refers to an inchoate unity—*all-governments-and-peoples-in-the-world*.

While world politics is about the capacity of humans to conceive of some kind of community at a global level, it is also about the boundaries that human beings have always erected to divide themselves from one another, boundaries that intensify the physical distances created by geography and the cultural distance created by language. From the earliest civilizations to the contemporary nation-state, humans have divided themselves on the basis of language, race, class, tribe, religion, gender, culture, nationality, ideology, and wealth. And division may also come simply from the heavy hand of history—that which has gone before but which is remembered and passed down, reinforcing patterns of difference, and perhaps even enmity and hatred.

Economic Structures

Politics also focuses on the economic structures that each political community creates for itself. These structures do not just spontaneously occur, but are heavily dependent on ways of thinking—and acting—about economic exchange: what is of value, what is treated as a commodity, what money is, and how property is to be regarded. Economies are *determined*: for example, political ideas and political activity determine whether the economy is barter-based or monetarized, or whether land and labour are commodified (that is, treated as commodities that can be bought and sold). Ideas and actions govern how markets within communities operate, if they operate at all; they determine how wealth is generated and distributed and how much of the production or labour of individuals and groups is appropriated by the community as taxation.

And just as political communities have economic structures that are determined by ideas and political decisions, the larger world has certain economic structures that operate on a wider scale. These differ considerably depending on time, place, level of technological development, and ideas about wealth and how it should be organized, created, and distributed. For example, before 1500, the world was marked by a large number of different localized economies, largely self-contained systems of barter exchange that involved localities such as villages, towns, and even larger political units. Local economies were almost always nested within a broader economic structure. Thus, for example, each Greek *polis* had its own economy, but all *poleis* were intimately connected in a broader system of economic exchange. Moreover, economic exchange between Greeks occurred in the context of a broader economic relationship that existed between the Greeks and their neighbours around the Mediterranean and the Aegean Seas.

Beginning around 1500, we see the emergence of an internationalized economy—a single international marketplace connecting the different local economies of the world. European states expanded out into the world during the eras of mercantile imperialism and nationalist imperialism, fuelled by the technological innovations of the Industrial Revolution. European expansion consolidated regional economies into a single global economy that linked the centre, in Europe and the United States, with a vast periphery that extended around the world. The descent of the world into a prolonged period of general conflict—marked by two world wars and an interwar period of economic and political crisis—strained the European-dominated international economy.

In the half-century after the end of World War II, the international economy enjoyed a period of considerable growth. There were dramatic increases in trade in goods and services, investment, finance, agriculture, and other primary products. The changes in the international economy during the last quarter of the 20th century formed the beginnings of what some have called a globalized economy. As William D. Coleman demonstrates in the next chapter, no longer is the economy at the world level merely a marketplace for the exchange of goods and services between local economies; rather, all of the elements of wealth creation—finance, investment, production, distribution, marketing—are beginning to be organized on a global scale.

Like economic structures within different countries, economic structures at the global level are determined by ideas about the economy and the way economic exchange should be organized. Through the ages, those who wielded political power and authority have sought to use the marketplace for political purposes. The shape of the international marketplace and how it operates, the nature of wealth creation, and the complexity and dynamism of international exchange are all determined by the various communities that operate in the global arena. As James Busumtwi-Sam shows in Chapter 14, political decisions determine the global distribution of wealth and thus determine who is rich, who is poor, who lives a marginal existence, who lives in luxury and plenty.

Interests

Human beings have the capacity to know what they like, what they want, what they think is good and righteous and just, and what they think is bad and unjust; in other words, to know what their interests are. Political philosophers have long sought to identify universal political interests—what humans seek at all times and in all places. The Greek historian Thucydides identified a classic trio: safety (security), gain (possessions or wealth), and reputation (honour and standing). He put the following words into the mouths of some Athenians who happened to be in Sparta in 432 B.C. when that *polis* was debating whether to declare war against Athens. The Athenians sought to defend their *polis* against charges that they were being too aggressive. "We have done nothing

extraordinary," Thucydides had the Athenians say, "nothing contrary to human nature in accepting an empire when it was offered to us and then in refusing to give it up. Three very powerful motives prevent us from doing so—security, honour, and self-interest."[3] Such a trio of goals was echoed some 2000 years later in *Leviathan*, the book in which the English philosopher Thomas Hobbes sought to explain the logical consequences of the natural equality of humankind. Arguing that there were three principal causes of quarrel between humans—competition, diffidence (or insecurity), and glory—Hobbes suggested that

> The first, maketh men invade for Gain; the second, for Safety; and the third, for Reputation. The first use Violence, to make themselves Masters of other mens persons, wives, children, and cattell; the second, to defend them; the third, for trifles, as a word, a smile, a different opinion, and any other signe of undervalue.[4]

One can usefully apply this classic trio of interests to actors in world politics. **Security** is that peace of mind that comes with a sense of safety, a freedom from threats of harm to all that one values; insecurity is one's fear that harm will come to that which one values. Gain is the desire of humans to possess and control. It can refer to the desire to own things of value and to accumulate desirable possessions (wealth); efforts to provide safety through gain can also be characterized as efforts to provide welfare, an objective that overlaps with both security and wealth. Welfare normally refers to a sense of well-being, including the sense of well-being that comes from freedom from threats to one's security (economic, physical, environmental). Honour, reputation, or prestige involve the desire of actors in global politics to be well regarded by others and seen as legitimate, valued members of the international community. They tend not to take kindly to characterizations of themselves by others that are contemptuous or "undervaluing." They dislike being described in negative terms, and they generally respond defensively to criticisms or insults levelled against them.

While much of the activity of global actors can be understood by reference to safety, gain, and reputation, one other universal interest can also be identified—**independence**. Actors in world politics have always demonstrated an interest in seeking autonomy, or

BOX 16.1

THE NATURE OF SECURITY

Students of security remind us that we have to specify (a) *what* is to be made safe, (b) against *what threat*, and (c) *for whom* the security is to be provided.

These different facets of security and insecurity must be analyzed on the individual level. Individuals have markedly different conceptions of their own security, even when they occupy the same space at the same time. While individual definitions of security vary considerably, we can generalize about what is likely to create peace of mind in individuals. First, security begins with a sense of personal safety: in other words, the ability to live in and move around one's own community without fear of being interfered with, mocked, hassled, robbed, assaulted, raped, taken away, imprisoned, expelled, "ethnically cleansed," or killed; as well, one must be assured that no one is going to break into one's home and do the occupants harm. Security is also concerned with a sense of community safety—a sense that some other group is not going to try to seize the community's land, occupy its property, or imprison or harm the community in which one lives. Security involves a sense that one's property is safe against robbery, seizure, and destruction. Finally, security is a sense of well-being that can have economic, environmental, social, linguistic, and cultural dimensions.

Threats to security come in a wide variety of forms—some natural, some as the consequence of human agency. Living on a geological fault line, in the shadow of a volcano, in a frequently deluged river delta, or at the fringe of a desert subject to desertification are examples of sources of natural insecurity. Insecurity can also result from the consequences of human action: not knowing where the next meal will come from; worrying whether one will be infected with HIV; living near a rickety Soviet-era nuclear power plant; or not knowing whether the fish stocks, on which one relies for a living, have been depleted. Insecurity can come from a fear about the future

of one's language or culture, which is threatened with being swamped in a larger cultural pool. Or insecurity can come from the behaviour of specific individuals: not knowing whether the young men approaching one's car, stopped for a light, intend one harm; not knowing whether the person standing nearby in a Tel Aviv mall is about to explode a suicide bomb strapped to his chest; not knowing whether the crowd of Hindus marching down a Mumbai street protesting the latest predations by Pakistan will turn on Muslims they might find in their path; not knowing whether the knock on the door at 3:00 a.m. is the secret police.

If we look at security in this multifaceted way, we can see that individuals can in fact have a mixture of insecurities and securities at the same time. Individuals may have secure employment, but live in neighbourhoods where personal insecurity is high; or they may live in a community that is completely free from any concern about being overrun by the country next door, but nonetheless may be worried about the fact that they are of a different religious faith than the majority of their neighbours, who have shown a propensity to attack minorities. Or they may have no fear of their neighbours, but may worry that the state security forces will take exception to their union organizing. Or they may have no fear of any other member of the community, but may worry about the enmity of others across the border.

We can extrapolate these observations to different aggregates of individuals—families, groups, organizations, and even political communities. But with every aggregation, the complexity of the pattern of security and insecurity deepens. Often, supposedly secure units can hide deep insecurities of members of the unit.

For excellent discussions of security in international affairs, see David A. Baldwin, "The Concept of Security," *Review of International Studies* 23 (January 1997): 5–26.

freedom from control by others. The desire for an independent existence is manifested everywhere at a personal level, and usually gives rise to deeply seated social structures of dominance and control: parents over children, men over women, landowners over peasants, capital over labour, elites over masses, governments over peoples. But it is also manifest at the level of political community.

Definition

INDEPENDENCE: The state of being free from the control of others; the ability to make one's own decisions, not having to rely on anyone else. (The term comes from the Latin word *pendere*, meaning "to hang," so independence is not having to "hang" on others.) In the context of world politics, it is the ability of a political community to govern itself rather than be governed by others.

Consider how few communities have voluntarily decided to surrender their independence so that they could be ruled by others: the Scottish Parliament more or less voluntarily joined England in May 1707; in December 1845, Texans gave up the independence they had gained from Mexico in March 1836. In the contemporary era, those living in Puerto Rico and Bermuda have decided not to pursue independence. But these are the few exceptions to an otherwise virtually universal norm that people prefer to govern themselves. "What nation likes to be oppressed by a stronger power?" asks one of the Dead Sea scrolls, written about 2000 years ago.[5] The question is rhetorical, for much of world politics is about the intense struggle of people eager to escape the rule of others and establish their own independent existence.

Indeed, the histories of many communities revolve around the story of struggles for independence. And so intense is the desire for autonomy that individuals will willingly die rather than surrender their independence. Melos, a colony of Sparta, refused to join the Athenian Empire in the great war between Athens and Sparta and their respective allies. In 416 B.C., Athens demanded that the Melians either submit or be destroyed. As was usual in ancient Greece, Athenian representatives visited the *polis* of Melos to argue their case. In the ensuing debate, known to history as the Melian dialogue, the Athenians argued, "we want you to be spared for the good both of yourselves and of ourselves." The debate went on:

Melians: And how could it be just as good for us to be the slaves as for you to be the masters?

Athenians: You, by giving in, would save yourselves from disaster; we, by not destroying you, would be able to profit from you.

But in the end, the Melians decided to take their chances and fight, even though the Athenian forces were more powerful:

> Our decision, Athenians, is just the same as it was at first. We are not prepared to give up in a short moment the liberty which our city has enjoyed from its foundation for 700 years. We put our trust in the fortune that the gods will send ... and in the help of men—that is, of the Spartans; and so we shall try to save ourselves.

But the outcome was never in doubt: the militarily superior Athenians eventually forced the Melians to surrender. They killed every male and sold all the women and children into slavery.[6]

Comparable choices have been made by others. For example, when United States forces seized the Japanese island of Okinawa in June 1945 during the closing stages of World War II, many Japanese chose suicide rather than surrender. Hundreds of men and women jumped to their deaths off the cliffs at the southern end of the island, many throwing their children off first, ignoring the frantic pleas not to jump being shouted in Japanese through megaphones by those in U.S. Navy vessels below. The grim and piteous scene was captured on film by U.S. military photographers. There are few more compelling testaments to the power of the idea of independence than those grainy images of hundreds of Okinawans tumbling into the sea to the sound of the entreaties of American sailors below.

The Intersection of Interests and the Relevance of Power

What happens when the interests we just discussed are actively pursued by six billion individuals, whether individually, in groups, or in independent political communities? The interests and goals of individuals or groups can interact or intersect with one another in four possible ways. The first possibility is that interests may not intersect at all. They may be discrete interests, in the sense that there is no contact between the interests as they are being pursued. Second, interests may be different but compatible; these are called complementary interests. Third, interests may be convergent, with varying degrees of similarity that range from identical interests to similar interests. The final possibility is that interests, when they are pursued, may be conflicting.

When this framework is applied at the world level, we can get some sense of the huge harmonies and disharmonies that are produced by the intersections of interests as people seek their goals. Individuals, groups, organizations, and political communities all have their own conceptions of what their interests are—what they think is right and proper and just. Some of those interests are discrete: one can readily think of hundreds of examples where the pursuit of interests by some people does not affect the interests of vast numbers of others. Other interests are complementary or convergent: for example, much of the cooperation that we see between individuals, groups, organizations, and political communities is driven by the complementarity of interests of those many actors who crowd the global marketplace. Indeed, that cooperation makes the contemporary international political economy possible.

But a great deal of world politics is marked by conflicts of interest between individuals, groups, and political communities and their governments. Some of the disharmonies of interest are exceedingly deep. Consider two communities that claim that they own the same piece of territory: unless they agree to share it, there is simply no way that one can overcome that incompatibility. Or consider the huge disharmonies in interest that exist between those human beings whose lives are lived in deprivation and insecurity and those who live in luxury and security. Consider the disharmonies of interest about rules of the global game. Whether they are rules about funding terrorist organizations, disarmament, the control of weapons of mass destruction, the transborder flows of investments, the proper role of women in society, the application of human rights, or the flow of illegal drugs, there is considerable disagreement between individuals, groups, organizations, and political communities. This facet directs our attention to conflicts at the global level, their sources, and most importantly, their resolution.

When the interests of actors conflict, what determines whose interests prevail? Briefly put, **power** is the ability to prevail over others in a conflict of interests—or, to put it more crudely, the ability to get your way. Not everyone can get his or her own way, but some people are always able to exercise power over others and get to ensure that *their* interests, wants, desires, and definitions of the "good" prevail over those of others. Power has been described as the central concept of world politics—and for good reason, since it determines so much of the political world.[7]

> **Definition**
>
> **POWER:** The capacity of one actor to prevail in a conflict of interests with other actors, normally through force, sanction, coercion, or manipulation. Power resources are any of the things needed in order to exercise power.

Governance without Government: Anarchy and World Politics

Finally, world politics is about governance at a global level. Governance involves establishing rules for a community, making allocative decisions for the community as a whole, settling conflicts over the rules, and mediating disputes between individuals and groups. Governance also involves the exercise of authority, that fascinating human practice of submitting obediently to the orders of others without having to be forced, coerced, induced, or persuaded to do so.

The governance of political communities takes many different forms: tribal systems of governance by elders, the singular rule of absolute monarchies, or the highly institutionalized structures of the 20th-century bureaucratic states. But in most political communities, institutional systems of governance that we call the government, or the state, have evolved. While the degree of institutionalization varies widely, this form always involves a basic hierarchy, a division between the governors and the governed, between those entitled to command, and those obligated to obey. Generally, governments seek to establish laws, rules, policies, and day-to-day practices for the community. These rules not only cover the behaviour of individuals toward each other, but also govern the nature and operation of economic relationships within the community. Importantly, governments generally seek to impose these rules on the community as a whole, securing the obedience of the governed by legitimate authority if possible, but by brute force if necessary. Moreover, in many (but not all) communities, governments seek to monopolize the legitimate use of force, not only to make the task of ruling easier, but in many cases also to provide a safe and secure environment for the conduct of economic activity.

By contrast, governance at a global level occurs in the *absence* of government, for the world of world politics is an anarchical one. Coming to English from the Greek *anarchos*—without a chief or governor (*an + archos*)—the term **anarchy** describes a system of social, political, and economic relations without formal institutions of governance to define enforceable rules or exact obedience from the governed. In an anarchical condition, no hierarchy exists between governors and governed, nor is there any comparable entitlement to command or obligation to obey. In an anarchy, there is no institution with coercive powers (such as the state or the government) telling people what to do, defining what is right and wrong, or proscribing a whole range of forbidden acts.

Anarchy is an apt description for the setting of world politics. There is no government of the world—no institution with coercive powers to regulate the political relations among all six billion human beings, to make laws for all people that can be enforced over all the globe, or to arbitrate and settle disputes. In short, in world politics there is neither entitlement to command nor obligation to obey. In this way, politics at the world level differs substantially from politics within communities.

GLOBAL GOVERNANCE IN WORLD POLITICS

On the other hand, politics between political communities is similar to politics within communities precisely because it is marked by an effort to provide the structures of governance so that world politics is not marked by a chaotic and bloody war of all against all. **Global governance** is aimed at resolving the inevitable conflicts that arise from the effects of billions of individuals, organized in groups, pursuing their interests.

Five broad areas of global conflict can be identified: conflicts over independence; conflicts over power and dominance; conflicts over conceptions of rightness and justice; conflicts over wealth and its distribution; and conflicts over the environment.

Definition

GLOBAL GOVERNANCE: The process by which different actors—governments, organizations, firms, groups, and individuals—try to make common decisions about and for the global community.

Entrenching Independence

It was argued above that world politics is very much about the different political communities that people create—under a huge array of different names and forms, from the huge empires of antiquity to the compact *poleis* of Hellas, to the vassal relations of the feudal period, to the contemporary sovereign nation-state. The ideal of an independent political community has inspired uprisings, revolts, and wars—across the world and across the centuries, from the periodic revolts of Iberian tribes against their Roman overlords to the struggles of the East Timorese against Indonesian domination in the late 1990s (the most recent war of national liberation resulting in the creation of a sovereign nation-state in May 2002). This ideal continues to manifest itself in the large number of peoples who think of themselves as a national community, and who want to give their nation expression in a separate and sovereign state, be it Kurds in Turkey, Palestinians in the Middle East, or Québécois in Canada.

Once independence is achieved, maintaining it is often a struggle. It is thus not surprising that world politics has always been about the efforts of people to ensure that their communities are free from elimination, butchery, enslavement, absorption, exploitation, or domination by others. That desire to remain free has prompted numerous people to give up their lives in the cause of the independence of their communities: to put themselves in harm's way or even to commit suicide.

Less dramatically, but no less importantly, there is the ongoing struggle for autonomy and freedom from the impositions and importunities of the more powerful, a struggle that continues to inspire much of the politics of the contemporary era. Examples include the frustrations of Mexicans over American intrusions on their sovereignty in the hunt for narcotraffickers, the grumbling of the British over the disappearance of their pound, Austrian complaints about the effects of a single European currency on the already high unemployment rate, or the concern of Ukrainians over pressures from Moscow on the issue of the Russian minority in Crimea.

As William D. Coleman shows in the next chapter, the impact of **globalization**, and in particular the emergence of global financial markets, poses an even greater challenge to autonomy. Governments and peoples find their room for manoeuvre limited by the impact of the global economy, and the necessity of pursuing a course that will not attract the discipline of the market. The seemingly impersonal forces of the global market generate a chorus of concerns—voices of protest that range from the prime minister of Malaysia complaining about currency trading to antiglobalization protesters gathering at meetings of the World Trade Organization or the International Monetary Fund.

However, while globalization may threaten local autonomy, we can nonetheless see that the governing structures at the global level are explicitly designed to privilege and entrench that local autonomy and the national communities that value it so highly. The key institution here is the **United Nations (UN)**, a vast array of intergovernmental organizations, as Figure 16.1 shows. Created during World War II, the UN is an organization dedicated to the very idea of ensuring that the world is divided into separate sovereign states. Even though the preamble of the UN Charter begins with the lofty phrase "We the peoples of the United Nations," the use of the word "peoples" is entirely metaphorical, for only governments of states are admitted as members of the UN, and only governments of states that have been recognized as *sovereign* by existing UN members. Moreover, the UN is deeply dedicated to the idea that every state should retain the right to make its own decisions and decide its own fate, without interference by outsiders. Article 2.7 of the UN Charter makes it explicit: "Nothing contained in the present Charter shall authorize the United Nations to intervene in matters which are essentially within the domestic jurisdiction of any state." The UN's rules and procedures, its mission, and its institutional energies

have all been devoted to the maintenance of a system of separate sovereign nation-states.

Managing Conflict

The widespread desire for independence produces frequent struggles between political communities: some seek to dominate others, and others seek to avoid domination. Thomas Hobbes's description is still the most evocative of this dynamic:

> In all times, Kings, and Persons of Soveraigne authority, because of their Independency, are in continuall jealousies, and in the state and posture of Gladiators; having their weapons pointing, and their eyes fixed on one another; that is, their Forts, Garrisons, and Guns upon the Frontiers of their Kingdomes; and continuall Spyes upon their neighbours.[8]

To be sure, this does not describe the condition of every political community toward every other polity. However, even when neighbours do not have "weapons pointing" at each other, they invariably have them pointing at someone else. And the rest of Hobbes's description remains accurate. There are continual jealousies—conflicts, tiffs, annoyances—between governments and peoples; that is the day-to-day stuff of world politics. Frontiers are everywhere "fortified"; even if the front lines consist of agents who swipe passports through their computers, interrogate foreigners, and x-ray luggage, the coercive power of those "Persons of Soveraigne authority" are there to ensure that the frontiers are as impermeable as possible. And there are indeed spies everywhere.

More importantly, over the long stretch of history, those jealousies on occasion erupt into a struggle for dominance, an attempt to widen control, to achieve the security that can (but need not always) come with control. Those struggles for dominance tend to be periodic rather than omnipresent. Efforts to achieve dominance (or undermine the dominance of others) are more pronounced at some times than others. Thus, for example, the period between 1945 and 1989—the Cold War era—was marked by a deep rivalry between the United States and the Soviet Union, which saw the expenditure of trillions of dollars and rubles in an effort to prevail.

Figure 16.1 The United Nations System

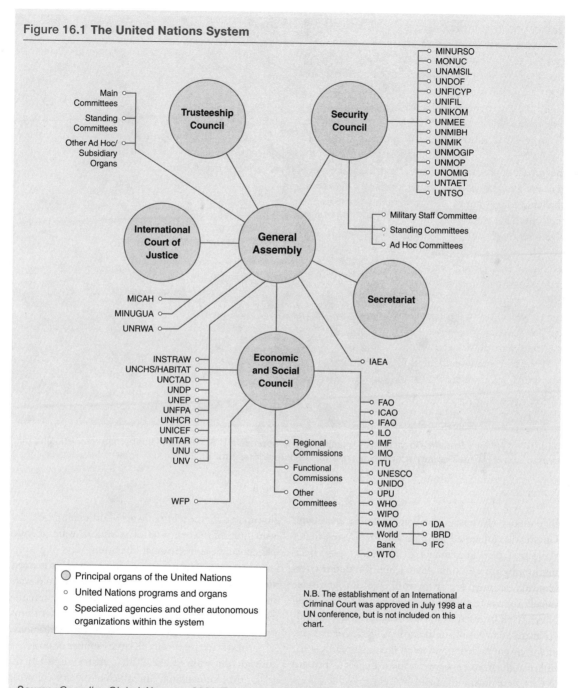

Principal organs of the United Nations

United Nations programs and organs

Specialized agencies and other autonomous organizations within the system

N.B. The establishment of an International Criminal Court was approved in July 1998 at a UN conference, but is not included on this chart.

Source: *Canadian Global Almanac, 2002* (Toronto: Macmillan Canada, 2002), pp. 262–263

The United Nations Security Council votes unanimously to approve a U.S. resolution supporting a fact-finding mission to look into Israeli military action in Jenin; at UN headquarters, April 19, 2002.

David Karp/CP Picture Archive

By contrast, the post–Cold War era—after the Soviet Union was disbanded in 1991 and the United States was left as the sole remaining superpower—has been marked by no comparable struggle for dominance. Instead, the only actors in world politics who have openly sought to upset the dominance of the United States have been transnational Islamist radicals, not countries. As a result, in the post-9/11 era, Americans and their enemies have adopted the posture of gladiators, but the frontiers between them are not as clearcut as they were during the Cold War era.

The persistence of the struggle for dominance, combined with the anarchical nature of world politics, also mean that war and the use of force are inevitable features of politics at a global level. The history of the world is dominated by the story of wars of different types: civil wars, guerrilla wars, wars of secession, wars of independence, wars of national liberation, wars of absorption, wars of attrition, wars of elimination, humanitarian wars, colonial wars, hot wars, cold wars, dirty wars, limited wars, general wars. Some wars are driven by desire for land, or for resources, or for dominance. Some are fought between political communities of various sizes; some affect a large number of people—indeed, the wars of the 20th century engulfed the majority of humankind. And much of the story of world politics is about the consequences of war, for every war that is fought, whether large or small, leaves long-lived traces, affecting all those who lived through the horror, terror, pain, and deprivation that go with war.

BOX 16.2

WAR AND THE USE OF FORCE IN CONTEMPORARY WORLD POLITICS

Recent Invasions

Iraqi invasion of Kuwait, 1990

American invasion of Panama, 1989

American invasion of Grenada, 1983

Israeli invasion of Lebanon, 1982

Argentinean invasion of Falkland Islands, 1982

Soviet invasion of Afghanistan, 1979

Tanzanian invasion of Uganda, 1979

Vietnamese invasion of Cambodia, 1978

Indonesian invasion of Timor, 1975

Recent Armed Humanitarian Interventions

East Timor, 1999

Kosovo, 1999

Location of Contemporary Civil Wars

Afghanistan

Burma

Colombia

Congo/Zaire

Russia/Chechnya

Rwanda

Sri Lanka

Sudan

Yugoslavia

Contemporary International Wars

Eritrea vs. Ethiopia

India vs. Pakistan

U.S. coalition vs. Afghanistan/Taliban

U.S. coalition vs. Iraq

Global politics is as much about the efforts of political communities to regulate, manage, and limit the destructiveness of war as it is about the efforts by some to use war and force as means of prevailing in conflicts of interest over others. A great deal of expense, energy, and effort are devoted to the prevention of war, whether by deterrence—that is, accumulating enough power to cause an enemy to calculate that it is not worth it to attack—or by the management of conflict through diplomacy or negotiation. Over the course of the 20th century, a number of international organizations were created in order to prevent war. The League of Nations, established after the end of World War I (1914–18), which claimed some 11 million lives, was designed to ensure that the global system would never again experience the destructiveness of such a war by putting in place a system of **collective security**, which involved all nations in the world agreeing that they would jointly attack any country that violated the Covenant of the League. In the end, however, the League proved to be an ineffective instrument of global governance in the interwar period: the struggle for dominance between the Axis powers (Germany, Italy, and Japan) and the other states in the international system eventually led to the second major war of the 20th century, even more destructive than the first. The United Nations was designed by the victors of World War II to correct the imperfections of the League, but the essential purpose of this global institution remained unchanged: to provide a mechanism for attempting to resolve conflicts between states before war breaks out—or to bring warring states to a condition of peace.

Thus, an important international mechanism for the achievement and maintenance of peace since 1945 has been **peacekeeping**, the practice of putting forces of a third party between warring parties who have come to a ceasefire, in order to encourage them to keep the peace. In the post–Cold War period, we have seen the transformation of peacekeeping into **peacemaking**, where the armed forces of a third party intervene in a war to bring peace to an area, as was done in Somalia in 1992, an intervention captured in the 2002 film *Black Hawk Down*. And after peace has been achieved, there is a third process, **peacebuilding**, which refers to the efforts of the international community to create the structures of a peaceful society, as was done in Bosnia after the Dayton Accords in 1995, in Kosovo after the defeat of Serbia in 1999, and after the ouster of Indonesia from East Timor in 1999–2000. While peacekeeping and peacemaking missions can be undertaken by any group of governments, the most common sponsor of these missions is the United Nations. Figure 16.2 shows the range of contemporary missions.

Figure 16.2 Ongoing UN Peacekeeping Missions, 2001

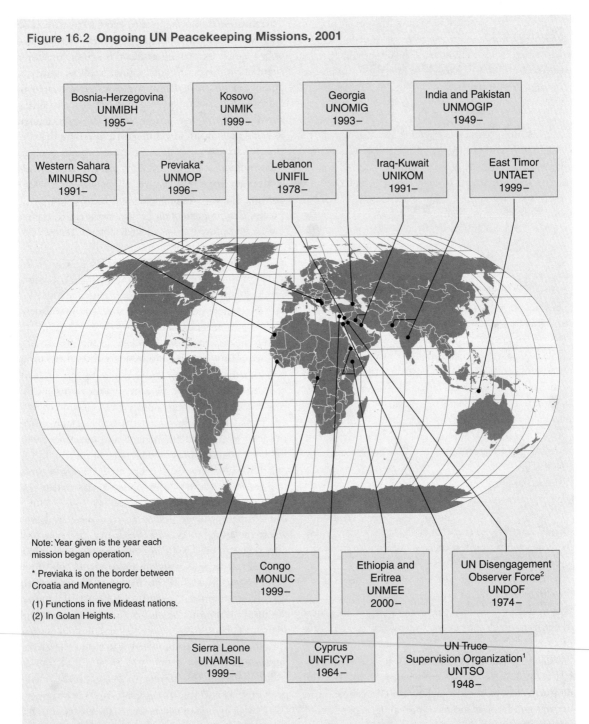

Bosnia-Herzegovina
UNMIBH
1995–

Kosovo
UNMIK
1999–

Georgia
UNOMIG
1993–

India and Pakistan
UNMOGIP
1949–

Western Sahara
MINURSO
1991–

Previaka*
UNMOP
1996–

Lebanon
UNIFIL
1978–

Iraq-Kuwait
UNIKOM
1991–

East Timor
UNTAET
1999–

Note: Year given is the year each mission began operation.

* Previaka is on the border between Croatia and Montenegro.

(1) Functions in five Mideast nations.
(2) In Golan Heights.

Congo
MONUC
1999–

Ethiopia and
Eritrea
UNMEE
2000–

UN Disengagement
Observer Force[2]
UNDOF
1974–

Sierra Leone
UNAMSIL
1999–

Cyprus
UNFICYP
1964–

UN Truce
Supervision Organization[1]
UNTSO
1948–

Source: *The World Almanac and Book of Facts, 2002* (New York: World Almanac Books, 2002), p. 874. Reprinted by permission of the United Nations.

Even if the institutional structures put in place to prevent war or maintain peace do not work—and in the years since 1945 there have been numerous wars that have cost millions of lives—the international community has always been keen to put in place rules and understandings to regulate the use of force. The various **Geneva Conventions** put in place over the course of the 20th century provide a comprehensive and detailed set of rules to try to ensure that warfare is conducted in a predictable and orderly way. And the rules of war are always being updated to take into account the most recent war: for example, after the Yugoslav civil war in the 1990s, rape was finally made illegal as a tool of war.

Seeking Justice

Everyone has a sense of justice, and this desire for justice creates considerable political conflict, for definitions of right and wrong—in other words, definitions of justice—are always deeply contested, regardless of the level of politics we examine. This is because individuals are prone to come to different conclusions about matters of morality, notions of goodness, and conceptions of righteous behaviour. Indeed, for Thomas Hobbes, that is why words such as *right, wrong, justice,* and *injustice* are entirely devoid of meaning unless and until there is a "common power"—a Leviathan, a supreme authority, or a government. Hobbes's formula is succinct: without government, "nothing can be Unjust. The notions of Right and Wrong, Justice and Injustice have there no place. Where there is no common Power, there is no Law: where no Law, no Injustice."[9] But with a common power, these words can be given meaning by defining *through law* what is right and what is wrong; with a common power, there is a means to insist that everyone abide by those laws.

In many political contexts, we do indeed have a Leviathan that makes laws defining wrong and right and possesses the coercive power to try to impose those definitions on all the people under its authority. But at the level of global politics, there is no institution comparable to local or national governments that is capable of deciding what is right and what is wrong and then imposing its definition of justice on everyone.

Yet the absence of government at the level of global politics in no way dampens the concerns for justice. People push hard to see justice done, and actors, organizations, and institutions at the international level are concerned with the standard of justice. Individuals and governments do not hesitate to express themselves on their views of right and wrong. This has been particularly true on issues such as **human rights** (including women's rights, children's rights, and the rights of Aboriginal peoples), the economic and sexual exploitation of children, nuclear proliferation and disarmament, environmental protections of all sorts, slavery, the use of child soldiers, and global poverty.

> **Definition**
>
> **HUMAN RIGHTS:** Rights pertaining to people simply because they are human beings, primarily including the prevention of discrimination or coercion on grounds of ethnicity, religion, gender, or opinion.

Moreover, while there is no global Leviathan, international organizations such as the United Nations have proved willing to try to articulate commonly held views of justice and rightness on a range of matters. The **International Court of Justice** (ICJ) seeks to develop and apply formal rules. Governments of countries bring disputes over what is just and unjust to the ICJ, and panels drawn from 15 judges (who are elected to the Court by the United Nations Security Council) hear cases and render their decisions based on the huge accumulated body of international law that has evolved over hundreds of years.

The ICJ deals only with governments of countries, but the international community also has institutionalized means for dealing with organizations and individuals. For example, those negotiating the Multilateral Agreement on Investment (MAI) in 1997 proposed that multinational corporations should have investment disputes with national governments submitted to panels of judges. Likewise, since 1950, individuals have had access to the European Court of Human Rights; its rulings are widely obeyed by governments of states, even when this means changing national laws.

In addition, the international community has developed means of dealing with individuals deemed to be international criminals. After World War II, the victorious powers established courts to try individuals accused of crimes against humanity. Following the civil wars in the former Yugoslavia and Rwanda in the 1990s, the United Nations established special international tribunals to try individuals accused of war crimes, including Slobodan Milosevic, the former president of

Yugoslavia, who was ousted from power and turned over by the new government to the special tribunal in The Hague and put on trial for genocide and **crimes against humanity**. There have been efforts to make such tribunals a permanent feature of the international political landscape: in 1999, a permanent **International Criminal Court** (ICC) was created to deal with individuals accused of a specific range of war crimes or crimes against humanity.

Definition

CRIME AGAINST HUMANITY: A wrongful act that is deemed to be not a violation of any particular nation's laws, but rather a violation against humankind as a whole.

It is true that the search for justice at a global level is constrained by the absence of a global Leviathan to define right and wrong and impose that definition on all actors. As a result, the underlying structure of the search for justice at the global level has not changed much since Thucydides was writing 2500 years ago. At the outset of the Melian dialogue, the Athenians claimed that they would use no "fine phrases" about rights in trying to persuade the Melians to surrender. Instead, they suggested that the Melians "look the facts in the face" and decide how to save their *polis* from destruction. "You know as well as we do," Thucydides had the Athenians say, "that, when these matters are discussed by practical people, the standard of justice depends on the equality of power to compel and that in fact the strong do what they have the power to do and the weak accept what they have to accept."[10]

And so it remains today: justice everywhere and at all levels, national and international, is heavily dependent on the "equality of power to compel." The powerful usually manage to evade the mechanisms that exist to enforce rules; the less powerful "accept what they have to accept." Power explains why Milosevic was put on trial in The Hague while other leaders who had given orders that also resulted in the deaths of thousands of human beings went free. Power explains why the governments of Cuba, Iraq, Myanmar, Nigeria, and North Korea—all small and relatively marginal actors in the international political economy—tend to be targets for international punishment while injus-

tices by countries that are more powerful tend to go purposely unnoticed or unchallenged.

However immature international law must be in an anarchical system, many people continue to be impelled to impose their standard of justice on others. This has been (and will likely continue to be) a source of tension between communities, and in particular between their governments. For there is little agreement on those issues. Hence "the standard of justice will depend on the equality of power to compel," just as Thucydides said it would some 2500 years ago.

Managing the Global Economy

Global governance is also about managing the global economy. In the absence of an overarching authority capable of economic regulation and management, it is left to the governments of the international system to seek mechanisms for overcoming the political problems that arise from the allocations of the marketplace. So global economic management is concerned not only with relations among industrialized countries, but also with the management of the basic division between the rich and the poor in the contemporary international system.

The first concentrated global efforts at economic management emerged toward the end of World War II, when the Allied governments met to plan the postwar international order, drawing on what they regarded as the lessons of the Great Depression of the 1930s. In the interwar era—that is, between 1919 and 1939—governments had tried to solve the economic problems that followed the crash of the New York stock market in October 1929 by offloading their economic problems to neighbouring countries, using what have become known as beggar-thy-neighbour policies: raising tariffs, restricting imports, and subsidizing exports. Moreover, many governments tried to correct their balance of payments deficits by abandoning the gold standard. By allowing their currencies to float, that is, to be no longer tied to gold, governments could engage in currency devaluations, making imports more expensive and exports more attractive to foreigners. However, this merely triggered competitive devaluations by other governments, deepening the cycle of depression.

In July 1944, the Allies met at Bretton Woods, a resort in New Hampshire, to find ways of avoiding these various problems. The United States government in particular sought to put in place a system for the conduct of international trade and the management of international finance that would provide stability and growth, which had been so lacking in the 1930s, while at the same time forcing nation-states to forfeit their independence.

The result was what John Gerard Ruggie has called the compromise of embedded liberalism. A tradeoff was involved: countries would agree to forego some of the benefits of pursuing their own economic policies without regard for others by cooperating with one another in liberalizing the system; on the other hand, countries would be free to pursue their own economic and social policies at home.[11] The key institutions to provide coordination and liberalization were to be the **World Bank**, the **International Monetary Fund (IMF)**, and the International Trade Organization (ITO). The World Bank and the IMF would regulate the international monetary system with fixed interest rates linked to gold and a limited pool of capital to ensure international liquidity; the ITO would seek to lower tariff barriers to trade. The ITO was never created: the United States Senate decided not to ratify it, and it was replaced with the General Agreement on Tariffs and Trade (GATT). And while the Bretton Woods system never worked precisely as those who met in 1944 had envisaged, it did produce the effects intended by the framers of the system. The European countries and Japan recovered, their economies increasingly robust and diversified. World trade grew. Confidence in the U.S. dollar remained strong.

Over time, however, the system grew unstable. By the end of the 1950s, such a quality of dollars had flowed out of the United States that it overwhelmed the capacity of the U.S. government to meet its commitment to convert dollars into gold. Through the 1960s, efforts by the United States and its major trading partners to correct this system created new organizations for multilateral management, such as the Group of Ten. But a number of deep underlying problems were not resolved. These included an increase in the gap between foreign dollar holdings and U.S. reserves of gold; a massive increase in financial transactions involving Japan and Europe; the rise of multinational corporations moving money around the international system; and the rise of a market in Eurodollars—U.S. dollars deposited in and traded by foreign banks (mostly but not necessarily in Europe, the name notwithstanding) without being converted to local currency, and hence not subject to domestic controls. By the early 1970s, these related elements of financial integration were creating monetary problems for the United States government, notably a continuing outflow of capital and a worsening trade balance.

The desire of a number of administrations in Washington to spend increasing sums on domestic social welfare programs while at the same time pursuing a costly war in Vietnam only exacerbated these economic problems. In the spring of 1971, there was a high demand for the dollar, causing a sharp decline in American gold reserves. This coincided with the announcement that the United States had experienced its first trade deficit. The response of the administration of President Richard Nixon was to abandon the Bretton Woods system. On August 15, 1971, the United States government unilaterally announced that it would no longer convert dollars into gold. In addition, Nixon imposed a 10-percent surcharge on all dutiable items in an attempt to bring American trade back into balance. These measures were known as the Nixon shocks.

These measures eventually led to a transformation of the world economy, as borrowing on international capital markets started to grow—from U.S.\$96.6 billion annually in the late 1970s to U.S.\$427.4 billion by the late 1980s. By 1993, borrowing amounted to U.S.\$818.6 billion a year, approximately 10 times what it was 15 years earlier. Over the past 20 years, world trade has also grown explosively. Much of that growth can be explained by the progressive liberalization of trade—the efforts to remove barriers to the transborder movement of goods and services. Liberalization aims to first lower and then eliminate altogether tariffs and duties. It seeks to replace discriminatory practices, such as trading preferences, with nondiscriminatory approaches, such as most-favoured-nation (MFN), in which all states are treated as though they were indeed the "most favoured." It seeks to eliminate dumping—the selling of goods in a foreign market at a price below that charged in a home market. It also seeks to eliminate

nontariff barriers, the various policies that governments put in place besides tariffs and duties to favour their goods and services over those of foreigners.

Definition

NONTARIFF BARRIER: Any measure or practice that places a barrier in the way of "free" commerce between nations, ranging from obvious measures, such as procurement policies that favour one's nationals, to not-so-obvious practices, such as the imposition of strict health and safety standards on imports in order to make the goods of other countries more expensive.

The key multilateral forum for the negotiated dismantling of barriers to trade has been at the GATT, in a series of multilateral negotiations called GATT Rounds: the Dillon Round (1961–62, named after the U.S. secretary of the treasury who initiated it, C. Douglas Dillon); the Kennedy Round (1963–67, named after President John F. Kennedy); the Tokyo Round (1973–79); and the Uruguay Round (1986–93), which resulted in the creation of the **World Trade Organization (WTO)**, the key global organization for the management of trade between and among nations. The WTO agreements provide a set of rules negotiated and signed by over 140 states to promote liberal trading practices and to reduce **protectionism.**

Definition

WORLD TRADE ORGANIZATION (WTO): An organization created during the Uruguay Round of GATT negotiations whose goal is to provide international trading rules to promote liberal trading practices and to reduce protectionism.

Definition

PROTECTIONISM: The use of various policy tools, such as subsidies, tariffs, and quotas, to protect goods and services produced within a country against competition from producers in other countries.

Today there is a dense web of international institutions for the management of the global political economy besides the WTO: the core international financial institutions include the World Bank and the International Monetary Fund, as well as a range of regional development banks. In addition to intergovernmental organizations, there are a number of essentially private groups who meet to organize economic affairs on a global scale. There are regional economic institutions, the most highly integrated of which is the European Union, a supranational polity that provides a common currency and a common market for the nations of Western Europe. There are also institutions designed to facilitate the discussion of global economic affairs. A major intergovernmental event is the annual summit meeting of the Group of Seven (G7), which developed from a meeting of major industrialized countries in 1975 and has met annually since then, expanding as the **Group of 8 (G8)** after the end of the Cold War to include Russia. An important nongovernmental venue for the discussion of global economic problems is the World Economic Forum, an annual meeting of leaders of governments, corporations, and international institutions, which used to take place at Davos in Switzerland until the events of 9/11 prompted the organizers to move it to New York City.

Managing the Global Environment

In 1968, Garrett Hardin, a biologist at the University of California, argued that people should give up their "freedom to breed" as a response to the global problems that he believed would come with population increases.[12] His argument about population was based on the idea of the commons, the land in medieval English villages that was set aside for common use, usually pasture, where all farmers could send their animals to graze. Hardin noted that the idea of a commons works well enough if the number of animals owned by farmers is less than the carrying capacity of the land. But what happens when that carrying capacity is reached? Hardin argued that the benefits to an individual farmer of adding one animal to the commons far outweigh the negative costs of overgrazing, since those costs are borne by all farmers using the land. Thus the rational farmer will add as many animals as possible. But, as Hardin pointed out, this conclusion is reached by all farmers. If they are all rational, they will all try to add animals, counting on the costs being borne by the collectivity. The result is that the commons is overloaded and overgrazed.

For Hardin, the tragedy of the commons was a tragedy in two senses. First, it was a tragedy that the commons suffered a disaster. But more importantly, Hardin was using the word in its literary sense. A tragedy is a form of drama in which the main character is brought to ruin or suffers extreme sorrow. But the essence of tragedy is the remorseless and inevitable way in which that calamity unfolds: the audience is gripped by an understanding that there is no way out for the central character, no escape from what they understand must be that character's fate. For Hardin, the tragedy of the commons described perfectly the dynamic of the global environment. All human beings and each political community to which they belong are like the farmer: they have every incentive to treat the "global commons" in a way that spreads the negative consequences of their treatment over the entire collectivity. This involves "taking out" of the commons (the way a grazing sheep takes out grass)— extracting nonrenewable resources (such as oil, gas, and minerals) or renewable resources (such as trees and fish) and decreasing biodiversity through development (such as urban growth). But it also means spreading the costs of what is "put into" the commons: the pollution, the effluents discharged into the water, and the noxious gases released into the air.

The tragedy of the commons arises from the fact that the threats posed by overpopulation, overexploitation, and pollution are virtually impossible to deal with in the absence of an authority to dictate the behaviour of individuals in such matters—and the capacity to enforce those decisions. By definition, the globe does not have such an apparatus. Appeals to morality or conscience have limited effects: without the prospect of punishment, there will always be those who follow their interests, exploiting or polluting, and shifting the burden to the collectivity. There is only one option: negotiation between the users of the commons with an eye to limiting use to the carrying capacity.

Global governance involves the attempts to grapple with this problem. But overcoming the tragedy has been and will no doubt continue to be almost impossible. Some argue that the solution is a global agreement on keeping "loadings" down to sustainable levels to ensure that the carrying capacity of the global ecosystem is not strained beyond repair. But, as we have seen in the case of the quarrels over global warming at the international conferences on the envi-

ronment at Kyoto, there is no particular incentive to agree to forego one's sovereign rights to exploit and develop—and pollute. Moreover, for some Southerners it is galling to be told that they must tailor their development plans to please rich Northerners, who burn more greenhouse gases per capita than countries of the South, and in whose interests the global system is structured in the first place. The logical and self-interested response of Southern nations will continue to be what it has been: to reject efforts by Northern states to negotiate a way out of the tragedy.

CONCLUSION

This chapter has painted a rather grim picture of politics at a global level. It has suggested that the global political realm is always marked by conflict, the pervasiveness of raw power as a determinant of political outcomes, the horror of war, the use of force, and the pain of poverty and deprivation—all consequences of the absence of government that could give justice a meaningful definition on a global scale.

At the same time, global politics is not unremittingly bleak. While conflict, war, deprivation, and environmental degradation are endemic and pervasive, the historical record suggests that there has also been both a desire and an ability to forge a sense of community at the global level—despite the obvious and clear divisions that have marked humankind. Such a compulsion has manifested itself in numerous ways: the efforts of the ancient Greeks from *poleis* with deep-seated enmities to fashion community; the attempts by merchants, traders, and producers to create security and predictability in order to lower risk and raise profit; the persistent propensity of governments to engage in global governance and establish "rules of the game"— and an equal willingness to abide by those rules a significant part of the time.

This desire to cooperate has resulted in the spread of peace over huge areas of the globe, allowing billions of people to live their lives free from the devastation of war; it has also permitted commerce to spread over virtually every part of the earth, with all the positive effects that the growth of wealth tends to bring. In short, there has always been a willingness to conceive of politics as extending beyond the confines of the political communities into which humans have always divided themselves.

DISCUSSION QUESTIONS

1. **What are some of the solutions that have been advanced to deal with the anarchical condition of world politics?**

2. **What is the role of the ideology of nationalism in maintaining divisions between peoples?**

3. **Why and how does war become "thinkable," and thus possible?**

4. **In what ways might the tragedy of the commons be overcome?**

WEB LINKS

Department of International Politics, University of Wales, Aberystwyth:

http://www.aber.ac.uk/~inpwww

The Canadian Forces College in Toronto:

http://www.cfc.dnd.ca/spotlight.en.html

Canadian Institute for Strategic Studies:

http://www.ciss.ca

International Alert:

http://www.international-alert.org

United Nations:

http://www.un.org

FURTHER READING

Bull, Hedley. *The Anarchical Society: A Study of Order in World Politics.* London: Macmillan, 1977.

Doyle, Michael W. *Ways of War and Peace: Realism, Liberalism, Socialism.* New York: W.W. Norton, 1997.

Morgenthau, Hans J. *Politics among Nations: The Struggle for Power and Peace.* New York: Alfred A. Knopf, 1948.

Sens, Allen, and Peter J. Stoett. *Global Politics.* 2nd ed. Toronto: ITP Nelson Canada, 2002.

ENDNOTES

1 Harold Lasswell, *Politics: Who Gets What, When, How* (New York: Meridian Books, 1958).

2 Kalevi J. Holsti, *Peace and War: Armed Conflicts and International Order, 1648–1989* (Cambridge: Cambridge University Press, 1991), p. 45.

3 Thucydides, *The Peloponnesian War*, trans. Rex Warner (Harmondsworth: Penguin, 1954), p. 80.

4 Thomas Hobbes, *Leviathan, or the Matter, Forme, & Power of a Common-Wealth Ecclesiasticall and Civill*, ed. C.B. Macpherson (Harmondsworth: Pelican, 1968 [1651]), p. 185. The echo should not be surprising: Hobbes's first published work was a translation of Thucydides into English, published in 1628.

5 Quoted in Hans J. Morgenthau, *Politics among Nations: The Struggle for Power and Peace*, 5th ed. (New York: Alfred A. Knopf, 1973 [1948]), p. 36.

6 Thucydides, *Peloponnesian War*, pp. 402, 407.

7 For an excellent discussion of the concept of power, see Steven Lukes, *Power: A Radical View* (London: Macmillan, 1974).

8 Hobbes, *Leviathan*, pp. 187–88.

9 Hobbes, *Leviathan*, p. 188.

10 Thucydides, *Peloponnesian War*, p. 402.

11 John Gerard Ruggie, "International Regimes, Transactions, and Change: Embedded Liberalism in the Postwar Economic Order," *International Organization* 36 (spring 1982), pp. 379–415.

12 Garrett Hardin, "The Tragedy of the Commons," *Science* 162 (December 13, 1968): 1243–48.

Chapter 17

The Politics of Globalization

William D. Coleman

CHAPTER OBJECTIVES

After you have completed this chapter, you should be able to

- define globalization and assess the degree to which globalization is taking place in the economic, cultural, and political domains
- assess how global and local politics are increasingly intertwined
- evaluate how the role of the nation-state might be changing as a result of globalization
- identify four challenges to democracy posed by globalization.

> *Definition*
>
> **GLOBALIZATION:** The growth of supraterritorial relations among people that creates a complex series of connections that tie together what people do, what they experience, and how they live across the globe.

INTRODUCTION

Over the past several decades, the processes now termed **globalization** have been steadily reshaping how many of us live and how we relate to others across the globe. They are reducing many limits on the interactions between individuals and communities once imposed by physical location. They are destabilizing existing centres of authority and security, such as nation-states, with new centres emerging at various levels of social life, from global down to local. The organization and scope of markets and the production and diffusion of cultural forms such as movies and literature and practices such as the choices of foods eaten have taken on even more global dimensions. The changes are potentially so profound that they may be altering some of the basic elements of the human condition.

One of the most basic of these elements is autonomy, that is, the capacity of individuals and communities to determine the conditions under which they live.[1] Over the past few years, protesters have gathered in the streets at meetings of major global institutions to register their worries about a loss of control over their lives. These worries extend, however, well beyond these protests. African political leaders note the increased marginalization of their economies and societies in the world system. Peasants throughout the developing countries see international trade rules as inevitably bringing an end to their way of life and the transnational biotechnology industry as stealing their traditional genetic resources. Ministers responsible for culture in countries outside the United States have formed a worldwide alliance in pursuit of the preservation of cultural diversity in the face of such

U.S. corporations as Disney and McDonald's. Fears about climate change and about the growing inability of communities to have any control over or say in how such change might affect their futures have become more widespread. Ethnic nationalist movements and religious fundamentalist communities have become more anxious and even violent as modernity is globalized in ways that threaten traditional practices.

Others speak about new possibilities. Changes in communications and information technology have created surprising openings in high-technology industries in developing countries, as the software sector in India illustrates. Aspects of culture such as music, literature, and films produced in one part of the world are increasingly accessible to large numbers of people in other parts, thanks to some of these same technologies. Attempts to establish an international system for the protection of human rights have helped some individuals and communities imagine autonomy in different ways, breathed new life into cosmopolitan thinking, and encouraged the growth of such notions as global justice and global citizenship.

In order to examine the politics of globalization, a politics highly centred on building, defending, and securing autonomy, this chapter is divided into three sections. The first section focuses on the meaning of globalization and explores the several dimensions of the concept. It shows how globalizing processes bring about new linkages between what happens globally and what occurs locally in our communities and in our daily lives. The second section builds on this definition by examining the kinds of changes to politics that have come about with globalization. These changes involve new forms of global governance (as was noted in the previous chapter), novel ways of life in local communities, changes in what nation-states can and cannot do, and new regional structures, such as the European Union and the **North American Free Trade Agreement (NAFTA)**. The final section investigates the relevance of these kinds of changes for democracy. Democracy is a form of governance that rose to prominence together with the nation-state as a political structure; most of the time, when we speak of democracy, we are referring to political practices in nation-states. If nation-states are ceding sovereign powers to new global centres of authority or are pooling these powers with other nation-states, what happens to democracy as we know it?

> **Definition**
>
> **THE NORTH AMERICAN FREE TRADE AGREEMENT (NAFTA):** An agreement ratified by the United States, Canada, and Mexico that contains rules to promote the freer movement of goods, capital, and services between these countries.

WHAT IS GLOBALIZATION?

Often in political science, we work with concepts that are highly charged with political meaning. On the one side, they are used in everyday political practices and discourse, while on the other scholars debate them and adapt them for the analysis of politics. Globalization has become one of these concepts. Political movements, the press, politicians, and public intellectuals writing in popular magazines or appearing on television refer to it often, if not incessantly. In these public usages, globalization takes on a number of different meanings. When many political and social movements say that they are against globalization (see Chapters 13 and 14), they usually mean that they are opposed to the liberalization of trade and that they fear the powerful role being played by **transnational corporations**. Sometimes they mean simply that they are opposed to capitalism becoming entrenched as the sole approach for organizing economic activity. Others use the term synonymously with Americanization. They see the growing economic and military dominance of the United States, whether through the spread of American movies and fast food outlets, or the global role taken on by U.S. multinational corporations such as Monsanto and Disney, or through the extensive reach of U.S. military power. Still others see globalization as another way of saying that capitalism is extending itself on a global scale (see Chapter 14).

> **Definition**
>
> **TRANSNATIONAL CORPORATIONS:** Business firms that are headquartered in one country, but that have plants or places of operation in other countries as well; also called multinational corporations.

Like other social scientists, political scientists examine carefully the way terms are used by various persons and organizations in society. They reflect upon these usages and seek to distil the core ideas and concerns implicit in them. Building on these core ideas and concerns, they develop an analytic definition of the phenomenon. This analytic definition then takes on a life apart from how the concept might be used by political actors in the broader society. It becomes a tool for analyzing politics.

Many social scientists have engaged in this careful process of reflection when it comes to globalization. After examining the competing definitions of globalization, political scientist Jan Aart Scholte suggests that globalization involves "the growth of 'supraterritorial relations' among people."[2] *Supraterritorial* refers to relations that are "above" territory or relatively unconstrained by one's physical location. John Tomlinson characterizes this "empirical condition" of supraterritoriality as one of "complex connectivity," a set of "connections that now bind our practices, our experiences and our political, economic and environmental fates together across the modern world."[3] Associated with this change in the character of social relationships for both authors is "deterritorialization." The relative importance of physical location as a basis for building social relationships is declining as supraterritorial ties grow in significance. In this respect, globalization is bringing far-reaching changes to the nature of social space: our social space is less and less defined by the physical space in which we live.

Following David Held and his colleagues, we can begin to assess the scope of these changes by looking at three properties of supraterritorial relations.[4] First, we can observe shifts in *extensity*, the degree to which cultural, political, and economic activities are stretching across new frontiers, creating a global space. For example, if we are interested in globalization of the American movie industry, we can ask whether U.S. movies are being shown in a larger number of countries and at an increased number of theatres than they were 20 years ago. If the answer is yes, we can argue that the propagation of U.S. movies is becoming more extensive over time. Second, we can assess *intensity*, changes in the magnitude and regularity of interconnectedness. To continue with our U.S. movie industry example, if we observe that American films are now showing every day in these coun-

tries and that they are displacing locally produced movies, then we can argue that the distribution of U.S. movies is becoming more intensive. Third, Held and his colleagues draw our attention to the property of *velocity*, changes in the speed of global interactions and processes. If, thanks to improvements in communications technology and in transportation, U.S. films spread quickly outside the United States, so much so that they are shown in foreign countries at virtually the same time that they are shown in the United States, we can say that the velocity of U.S. movie propagation is increasing.

BOX 17.1

PROPERTIES OF SUPRATERRITORIAL RELATIONS

Extensity: The extent to which cultural, political, and economic activities are stretching across a global space.

Intensity: The magnitude and regularity of the global connections that occur.

Velocity: The speed at which global connections occur.

Enmeshment: The degree to which what happens locally is tied to global events and the degree to which what happens globally is tied to local events.

Together these three properties contribute to the fourth, *enmeshment*—changes in the interdependence of the global and the local. Suppose we look at a small city in Sri Lanka. If U.S. movies are shown in this city now but were not shown 20 years ago, and if they appear regularly, displacing Sri Lankan films, and if they appear relatively quickly after they are first released in the United States, we can say that the people living in this small city are more enmeshed in global cultural processes today than they were two decades ago. What happens in this small city is more closely linked to what is happening globally in the movie industry.

Contrary, then, to what might have happened in the past, globalization is not just a matter of the rich and the famous travelling the globe. Rather, it involves changes to the lives of more people in all walks of life, living in an even more diverse range of local communities. Roland Robertson offers the concept of global unicity for understanding how these changes are linked to one another.[5] First of all, unicity comes from a global context of trading rules, including those related to the environment (see Chapter 16), cultural transmission, and corporate activities. All of these have an ever-increasing impact on how individuals and groups relate to one another in their local settings. Second, unicity arises from the creation of global frames of reference within which social actors increasingly understand who they are and how they should orient their activities. Accordingly, even acts of resistance, whether these be attempts to prevent massive depopulation of agricultural areas or to secure the traditional family in a strong religious community, are committed with an eye to what is happening globally. For example, demonstrations by farmers about agricultural policies are targeted at what is happening at negotiations on an Agreement on Agriculture at the **World Trade Organization (WTO)**. Religious fundamentalists make effective use of current communications technologies to send out their message about resisting secularization, thereby seeking to build alliances with other religious communities with similar concerns around the globe.

When we talk about globalization, therefore, we are referring to a complex phenomenon. It occurs in many aspects of our lives. We have spoken above about culture, using the examples of the distribution of movies and of religious fundamentalism. But there are countless examples in other domains. In the economy, foreign exchange markets now reach fully around the globe (that is, are more extensive) and involve trades of about a trillion dollars per day (that is, are more intensive). These trades take place almost instantly, thanks to computers (that is, they have higher velocity) and affect the lives of people in many localities, for example, when prices of imported and exported goods go up and down depending on the exchange rate (meaning that there is more enmeshment). Of course, associated with these economic activities is the growth of globally active, transnational banking companies. These transnational banks have expanded into new areas of finance, such as

Table 17.1	Global Over-the-Counter (OTC) Derivatives Markets, 1995–2000 (in U.S.$ Billions)					
	Notional Amounts, June 1995	Gross Market Values, June 1995	Notional Amounts, December 1998	Gross Market Values, December 1998	Notional Amounts, June 2002	Gross Market Values, June 2000
Foreign Exchange Contracts	13 095	1 048	18 011	786	15 494	578
Interest Rate Contracts	26 645	647	50 015	1 675	64 125	1 230
Equity-Linked Contracts	579	50	1 488	236	1 671	293
Commodity Contracts	318	28	415	43	584	80
Estimated Gaps in Reporting	6 893	432	10 388	492	12 163	400
Grand Total	47 530	2 205	80 317	3 231	94 037	2 581

Sources: Bank for International Settlements (BIS), *The Global Derivatives Market at end June 1998* (Basel: BIS, 1998): BIS, *The Global OTC Derivatives Market Continues to Grow* (Basel: BIS, 2000). Reprinted by permission of Bank for International Settlements (BIS).

derivatives. The value of the derivatives these banks buy and sell among themselves has grown from over U.S.$47 trillion per year in 1995 to over U.S.$94 trillion at the turn of the century (see Table 17.1).

In the social realm, migration to Canada now draws from all parts of the globe, not just Europe (more extensive). Canada has been admitting between 200 000 and 250 000 immigrants per year since the 1980s (more intensive). People can get here more quickly by airplane than in the past (higher velocity), and many of our cities are becoming much more culturally diverse (more enmeshment of the local and the global). In fact, as Figure 17.1 shows, Canada has become more diverse than most other developed countries.

In politics, the rules of the international trade agreements at the WTO now bind the activities of over 140 states, including China (more extensive). These rules affect a large range of policies (more intensive). Meetings on the interpretation and implementation of these rules go on almost constantly (higher velocity), and the economic fates of a larger number of workers and firms are affected by these rules (greater enmeshment of local production with global rules). The international agreement on trade, however, is just one of an increasing number of international treaties in the economic arena (see Figure 17.3 later in this chapter).

The arrival of international rules is not limited to the economic and social arenas. Other problems are supraterritorial as well, with one of the most obvious of these being environmental contamination. Figure 17.2 provides an example of one of these: global climate change in the form of global warming or the **greenhouse effect**.

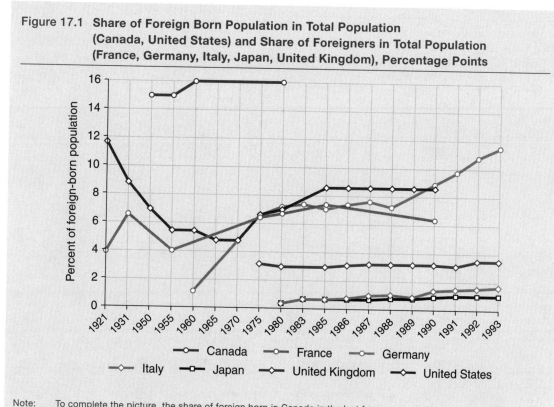

Figure 17.1 Share of Foreign Born Population in Total Population (Canada, United States) and Share of Foreigners in Total Population (France, Germany, Italy, Japan, United Kingdom), Percentage Points

Note: To complete the picture, the share of foreign born in Canada in the last four censuses was as follows: 1981—16.1 percent; 1986—15.6 percent; 1991—16.1 percent; 1996—17.2 percent.

Source: Michael Zürn, *Does International Governance Meet Demand? Theories of International Institutions in the Age of Denationalization* (Bremen, Germany: Institut für Interkulturelle und Internationale Studien, Universität Bremen, 1997), p. 72. Reprinted by permission of Michael Zürn, Universität Bremen.

This kind of problem is also becoming more extensive (affecting more parts of the world), more intensive (the pollution and dangers from it are becoming more regular and frequent), and has higher velocity (the temperature is changing much more rapidly than normal). There is also more enmeshment; for example, a problem such as the growing number of children with asthma in Canada is linked to the environmental mismanagement that is taking place in virtually every country in the world.

Definition

GREENHOUSE EFFECT: A warming of the surface and lower atmosphere of the earth caused by the increased presence of various pollutants that break down the ozone layer of gases that protects life from harmful rays from the sun. The process also leads to rising temperatures and climate change; it is also known as global warming.

These various dimensions of globalization are often linked. American movies are more easily distributed across the globe because global rules on trade and intellectual property make it more difficult for countries to block their entry. Religious fundamentalists in one part of the world now work with those in other parts of the world, since migration has brought a greater diversity of religions to a larger number of places. Foreign exchange markets are so active because so many more firms are trading goods and services and many more people are travelling to more and more areas of the world. Tourism has become an industry serving the ordinary people in many countries, not just the rich and the elite, as in the past. Accordingly, what happens in the local places in which we live is affected to a larger extent by global events. Conversely, local events, such as the difficulties with the baht, the currency of Thailand, in 1997, can have a global impact through financial markets,

Figure 17.2 Annual Deviations of Global Average Temperature from the 1961–1990 Average

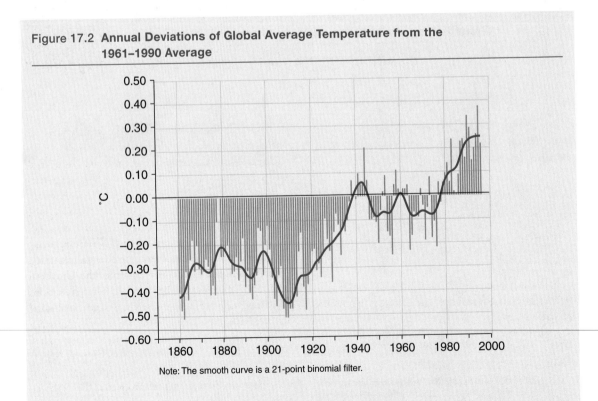

Note: The smooth curve is a 21-point binomial filter.

Source: Michael Zürn, *Does International Governance Meet Demand? Theories of International Institutions in the Age of Denationalization* (Bremen, Germany: Institut für Interkulturelle und Internationale Studien, Universität Bremen, 1997), p. 70. Reprinted by permission of Michael Zürn, Universität Bremen. Reproduced under Liscence Number Met0/IPR/2/2002/0026.

Globalization—a sneeze in a Third World country can cause panic around the world.

Reprinted with permission from The Globe and Mail

affecting the lives of millions of people around the globe, as happened in 1997–98. The cartoon on this page illustrates this process.

THE CHANGING POLITICS OF GLOBALIZATION

Globalization is changing how politics works at all levels of human governance: the global, the regional, the nation-state, the subnational, and the local. At the global level, an ever-increasing number of international organizations, more informal arrangements of principles and norms (called international regimes), and regularized coordination meetings of nation-states' governments have emerged. These cover a broad range of human activity, from how countries trade with one another, to how much equity capital banks must hold as a backup against failure, to how states treat refugees, to the way in which we label

food, and to how countries might jointly address global warming.

Some of these agreements are enforced quite stringently. For example, the WTO has a disputes settlement mechanism that is binding on its member states. If a country loses a dispute at the WTO, it must stop the offending activity and compensate the country involved. If it does not comply, the country lodging the complaint can impose a financial penalty on the offending country. Others have little effect. For example, the Universal Declaration on Human Rights of the United Nations (UN) has been ratified by many countries, including Canada. Such ratification, however, does not necessarily mean that these countries always respect human rights. For example, the UN Commission on Human Rights ruled in the late 1990s that Ontario's refusal to give people involved in workfare programs the right to unionize was, in fact, a violation of the right to freedom of association. The Mike Harris government simply ignored the ruling; there is no mechanism available to require either a provincial government or the federal government to comply with such a ruling.

BOX 17.2

LEVELS OF POLITICAL AUTHORITY, WITH EXAMPLES

Local: Vancouver City Council; Frankfurt City Council

Subnational: British Columbia Legislative Assembly; the Landestag (State Assembly) of Bavaria

National: Parliament of Canada; the Bundestag (federal Parliament in Germany)

Regional: Dispute settlement under the European Parliament or NAFTA

Global: Dispute Settlement Mechanism of the World Trade Organization

Perhaps the most significant examples of global governance come in the economic area. We have already had several opportunities to mention the World Trade Organization. There are other prominent examples as well. At the Bank for International Settlements in Basel, Switzerland, a host of nested committees and organizations has grown up since 1974 to define rules for the global banking sector and for financial markets. Many students will have heard of the **Group of 8 (G8)**, which includes Canada, France, Germany, Italy, Japan, Russia, the United Kingdom, and the United States. The heads of government from these countries meet once a year to discuss how they might coordinate their economic activities in ways to ensure that the global economy functions well. Their ministers of finance and the governors of their central banks (for example, of the Bank of Canada or the Federal Reserve System in the United States) meet twice a year to draw up more detailed procedures for assessing how their economies are performing and for coordinating their macroeconomic policies. The **International Monetary Fund (IMF)** has evolved into an organization that moves in to help countries when instabilities in the global financial system threaten to destroy their economies. Its partner organization, the **World Bank**, finances projects to assist in the development of poorer countries in the world (see Chapter 14). Many dispute the value of such organizations, however, arguing that they inevitably impose a neoliberal orthodoxy on developing countries that is highly inappropriate and harmful to the most disadvantaged.

Definition

GROUP OF 8 (G8): The countries of Canada, France, Germany, Italy, Japan, Russia, the United Kingdom, and the United States, the heads of which meet once a year to discuss ways to coordinate their economic activities to ensure that the global economy functions well.

These economic governance mechanisms coexist with other international institutions and regimes that seek to provide rules for other domains of social activity. The United Nations provides an umbrella for some of these. For example, the UN supported the drawing up of the Universal Declaration on Human Rights and set up an organization to promote the declaration: the United Nations High Commission on Human Rights. All UN members who sign the declaration are agreeing, in effect, to ensure those rights are respected within their borders. Many UN members have also signed a Convention on the Prevention and Punishment of Genocide, whereby they define what **genocide** means and commit themselves to act when genocides are being committed. In some instances, such as the mass killings in the former Yugoslavia and in Rwanda, the UN has set up binding international courts to try the perpetrators for their crimes of genocide. If the new **International Criminal Court** functions as many hope it will, the reach of binding international law will extend even further.

BOX 17.3

EXAMPLES OF GLOBAL GOVERNANCE INSTITUTIONS

Group of 8 (G8)

International Labour Organization (ILO)

International Monetary Fund (IMF)

Kyoto Protocol

United Nations High Commission on Human Rights

Universal Declaration of Human Rights

World Bank

World Meteorological Organization (WMO)

World Trade Organization (WTO)

Figure 17.3 **Development of the Number of New International Economic Treaties**

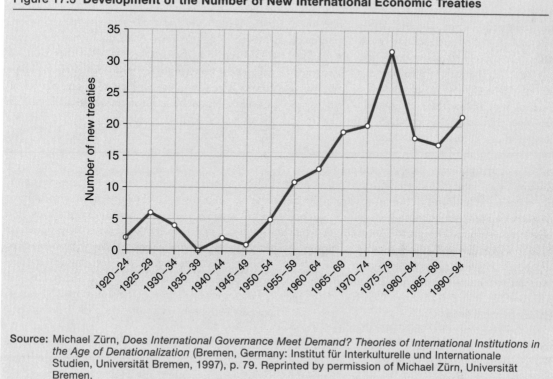

Source: Michael Zürn, *Does International Governance Meet Demand? Theories of International Institutions in the Age of Denationalization* (Bremen, Germany: Institut für Interkulturelle und Internationale Studien, Universität Bremen, 1997), p. 79. Reprinted by permission of Michael Zürn, Universität Bremen.

Politics at the local level is also changing with the progression of globalization. Three examples will illustrate here the kinds of changes taking place. First, let us consider Aboriginal peoples. The United Nations has been working on a covenant defining the rights and responsibilities of Indigenous peoples around the world. In becoming involved with the UN in this work, many Aboriginal communities find that their identities are changing. Rather than considering themselves only as Cree, or Haida, or Mohawk, or Sami (Scandinavia), or Torres Strait Islanders (Australia), or Maori (New Zealand), they now see themselves also as Indigenous peoples linked to one another. Because of the addition of a global component, their identity becomes more complex (see Chapter 3). The United Nations becomes a point of political reference for them when they find themselves unjustly treated. The Grand Council of the Crees in Northern Quebec followed this route when it was fighting the Quebec government's hydroelectric development in its territories.

Diaspora and transnational communities provide a second example. In Chapter 3, these were described as ethnic groups that experience dislocation in multiple states yet typically nurture narratives about their specific "homeland," held out as a place of possible return. For example, we might speak of part of a Tamil diaspora or transnational community living in Canada. Tamils are a minority ethnic group living in Sri Lanka and have been fighting the majority Sinhalese group for many years in pursuit of more political autonomy. The fierce fighting in their homeland has forced many to leave Sri Lanka for Canada, the United Kingdom, the United States, and other countries. Many of these emigrants remain attached to Sri Lanka and would like to return someday when political autonomy has become a reality or when the fighting has ended.

With the onset of contemporary transportation and communication technologies, these local, often marginalized communities can become global political actors. Members can travel back and forth to the homeland or to other states hosting their ethnic group more easily than before. Using the Internet, they can communicate with their relatives, friends, and political allies on a daily basis. They can import clothing and food more easily, thereby reproducing more aspects of the lives they were familiar with in their homeland. The international right of freedom of conscience gives them more room to practise their religion, with perhaps less fear of persecution or discrimination. With all of these changes, they can imagine their local group as part of a global community of Tamils—or Jains, or Chinese, or Serbians, or many others—more easily than in the past. Moreover, their local politics tend often to reflect politics in the homeland, and vice versa—their politics in the homeland are reproduced in local communities of these groups around the world. Accordingly, when Pakistan and India clash over Kashmir, dimensions of this same struggle may surface simultaneously in the Pakistani and Indian transnational communities living in Toronto, Hamilton, Vancouver, New York, London, Manchester, and Sydney.

A third example of changing local politics can be drawn from British Columbia. Forest companies in that province long used an approach to logging called clear-cutting. They simply went in and cut down every tree in a given tract of land. Local ecologists and Indigenous peoples' communities protested these practices as highly destructive of old-growth forests and as a threat to some endangered species. Gradually, international environmentalist movements, notably Greenpeace, joined these protests. Greenpeace is a transnational interest group with national branch organizations in many countries around the world. Angry at the effects of clear-cutting, members of several of its European branches organized a boycott of exports of British Columbia lumber products. These European boycotts proved to be quite effective and put immense pressure on the forest companies to change their practices. Visits to clear-cutting sites by such prominent ecologists as Robert F. Kennedy, Jr., added to the international dimension of this protest. Once again, local politics had global effects and led individual ecologists with local identities to couple these to an ecological identity that transcended national borders.

These changes in global governance on the one side, and in local politics on the other, raise difficult questions about whether nation-states are losing some of their powers to respond to the demands of their citizens. With the loss of such powers, some see nation-states as losing relevance. These questions are not easy to answer and have sparked some of the strongest debates in contemporary political science. These debates have shown us that there is no one-size-fits-all answer to this question. The impact of globalization on the United States may be somewhat less than it is on a middle power such as Canada and considerably less than it might be on developing countries such as Honduras or Ghana. What is clear is that for some policy problems, such as the rate of growth of the national economy or the quality of the environment within a state's boundaries, nation-states cannot find solutions unless they cooperate with other states and maybe even coordinate their policies with these states. Wolfgang Reinicke refers to this development as global public policy.[6] States no longer have sufficient power to act effectively on their own; they must "pool" their sovereignty with other states to accomplish their domestic objectives.

The rapid growth of formally binding international rules, such as those overseen by the World Trade Organization, or informally binding ones, such as those associated with the international regime for banking and financial markets, has clearly restricted many states' regulatory powers. If Canada provides a subsidy to Bombardier to help it export its small jet planes, it can be overruled by the World Trade Organization when a competitor like Brazil complains. For these reasons, some political scientists (for example, Stephen Clarkson) say that such rules are now part of an "external constitution" that is as binding on national governments as the "internal constitution" (see Chapter 6). International rules have also curbed other traditional areas of state regulation, such as **protectionism**—the practices of protecting intellectual property, erecting tariff barriers to trade, influencing the pricing of agricultural commodities, using state corporations to provide services such as telecommunications and electrical power, and giving their own citizens priority in the use of natural resources.

Globalization has also reshaped domestic politics by adding to the power of some parts of the government while reducing the power of other parts. As noted in Chapter 7, globalization tends to require a strengthening of central agencies, such as the offices serving the prime minister or the president and ministries of finance and trade. These agencies have to coordinate policymaking horizontally within states, and they must do it quickly and efficiently if they are to be effective in global policy discussions and negotiations. Conversely, departments whose mandates are heavily shaped by developments in global public policy—environment, culture, industry, labour—tend to lose influence and to become more subject to these central agencies. In many democracies, there are rising complaints about the increased powers of the head of government, be it the prime minister, or the chancellor, or the president, and of the finance minister, be it the secretary of the treasury (as in the United States), or the minister of finance (as in Canada, France, and Germany), or the chancellor of the exchequer (as in the United Kingdom).

As nation-states are drawn into multilevel governance arrangements to accomplish their domestic policy goals, the national identities of their citizens become more fluid (see Chapter 3). In the 18th and 19th centuries, when the nation-state was rising to become the dominant organizational form in the world, states invested considerable energy in constructing a national identity. In the United Kingdom, a "British" identity was forged out of the identities of peoples living in England and in the Celtic regions of Scotland and Wales. France melded the Celtic Bretons, the Provençal in the south, and the German-speaking Alsatians in the east into a single, universalistic French identity. Canada adopted a slightly different approach by building a political nationality composed of two supposedly complementary identities, those of English and French Canadians.

These national identities are now weakening and becoming part of more complex senses of citizenship. In the United Kingdom, a Scottish identity has strengthened over the past 20 years, as has a sense of being European. This idea is captured in the slogan of the Scottish nationalists, "An independent Scotland in a united Europe." Similar developments may be seen in France: the Breton language (Breizh) has resurfaced at the same time as discussions of European citizenship have gained importance. In Canada, the former French-Canadian identity has evolved into a Québécois one, which is much less complementary to the traditional English-Canadian identity. The latter identity has fractured with the onset of cultural pluralism, and the identities based in transnational and diaspora communities receive some limited legitimacy from a policy on multiculturalism. In all parts of Canada, Aboriginal peoples have asserted an identity based on their being the "first peoples" in North America and on their recognition as "peoples" by the United Nations. All of these developments mean that the traditional national identity constructed in the past three hundred years in many nation-states has declined in importance. Simultaneously, it has become coupled to new identities that transcend national borders or that are unique to ethnic minorities within those borders. Figure 17.1 illustrates the decline and growth of foreign-born population within the societies of seven highly developed countries.

GLOBALIZATION AND DEMOCRACY

If we are to understand the impact of globalization on democracy, we must first take note of the relationship between democracy and the nation-state. Liberal democracy emerged as a form of governance in tandem with the nation-state in Europe. The principles of democracy and the procedures developed based on those principles assumed the territorial integrity of the nation-state and the idea of sovereignty that was emerging in the system of states. Behind the concept, therefore, lie two crucial assumptions.

First, citizens are able to hold accountable all the political leaders who make decisions that affect the citizens' daily lives. For example, if citizens are concerned about air pollution, they can express these concerns to, and hold to account, all the political leaders governing the territories and firms that are the source of the air pollution. Second, citizens can bring about changes in the political factors that affect their daily lives by using democratic procedures to pressure or to change their political leaders. We refer to this aspect of democracy as popular sovereignty. For example, if citizens are unhappy about the quality of the air they breathe, they can choose new leaders who will have the necessary power and authority to respond to their concerns. These assumptions are important because globalization appears to be placing both of them into doubt.

BOX 17.4

KEY DIMENSIONS OF DEMOCRACY

Accountability: Citizens can make demands on and hold accountable the political leaders who make the decisions that affect the citizens in their everyday lives.

Popular sovereignty: Citizens can bring about changes in the political factors that affect their daily lives by using democratic processes to influence or to change their political leaders.

As noted above, liberal democracy was developed in tandem with the nation-state as a unit of territorial organization. Theorists of democracy assumed that the nation-state would be the principal, if not the only, body in a given territory with the powers to affect the daily lives of citizens inhabiting that territory. In the present era, this assumption no longer holds. Other organizations operating at the international level—be they the World Trade Organization, the International Monetary Fund, or various and numerous smaller (but no less vital) international regimes—have important impacts on our lives. As a result, there is a problem. How do we talk about democracy when the matters of concern to us are beyond our political reach? If we look at the notion of globalization as outlined in this chapter and at some of the effects of globalization discussed in other parts of this book, we can identify four challenges to democracy that come from globalization. Let us now look at each of these.

A Changing Demos or People within the Nation-State

Political scientists use the Greek term *demos* to refer to the idea of a people who have a sense of community and of common purpose. The demos (or sovereign people) within the nation-state has changed drastically over the past 150 years. Let us think back over 130 years to 1867, when the Dominion of Canada formally came into being. Who constituted the demos at that time, that is, who constituted the people who exercised some measure of democratic rights? First of all, it was men only. Women were not considered to be part of the people for the purpose of political decisions. And this group of men itself was a highly restricted one. It certainly did not include the men in First Nations communities. Nor did it include men who had lower incomes and little personal property. At the time of Confederation, only those men who possessed a certain amount of property and wealth actually exercised democratic rights. Historians estimate that about 13 percent of the male population of the Dominion had the vote in 1867.

So the Canadian demos has travelled a very long way from the small, relatively wealthy group of principally British and French men who exercised power in 1867. Women began to get the vote beginning in 1916 in Manitoba and ending in 1940 in Quebec. Chinese and Japanese Canadians lost their right to vote in the interwar period and regained it only in the late 1940s. Aboriginal people were finally able to vote freely in 1960. But as we have seen, the addition of women and First Nations peoples is not the only complicating factor to the Canadian political community. Since 1960, our political community has become much more heterogeneous in terms of visible minorities, religions, and more general cultural differences. If we add to these categories the **identity politics** associated with the second wave of the women's movement, the gay and lesbian movement, and various social movements interested in the environment and world peace, we have a much more complex political community than existed in the first half or so of the 20th century. And as we have argued above, globalization intensifies these complications because it enables the construction of identities that transcend borders.

Should we be worried about such developments? The problem is that the whole conception of democracy within the nation-state that we have had has involved the development of a common political identity as Canadians, or Americans, or French. Nation-states have worked to develop a common understanding of a shared history, a common political culture. They have sought to cultivate identification with common symbols, such as the Maple Leaf flag or "O Canada," or common practices, such as universal health care. They have stressed the institutions we have in common—Parliament, a public education system, modern hospitals, and so on. Behind these efforts to develop this sense of national community and identity are two qualities assumed to be important to democratic governance: trust and solidarity.

It is important, many argue, that citizens trust one another. If I have faith in my co-citizens that they will fulfil their duties, then I will fulfil mine. I will obey the laws and follow the general rules of my political community because I trust that others will do the same. Solidarity is also important. Citizens must believe that their compliance with laws, including the paying of taxes, is important, even if it does not bring them direct personal benefit. They must feel a sufficient sense of solidarity with their co-citizens that they are willing to help improve the situations of others, who are perhaps elderly or ill or disabled or temporarily without work.

The problem then is that the cultivation of trust and solidarity becomes ever more difficult the more different citizens become from one another. Differences based on gender or on religion or on ethnicity can be perceived to be so deep that women may not trust men, or that Muslims and Christians do not trust one another, or that immigrants from Sri Lanka may find it difficult to feel solidarity with immigrants from Jamaica. What steps can we take to improve solidarity and trust? We have adopted the Charter of Rights and Freedoms; other countries have similar charters. The UN also has covenants on political, civic, and human rights. Are these steps sufficient? Do we need to do more? If so, what should we be doing? If we want to preserve the principles of democracy within the nation-state, we are going to have to work much harder at trust and solidarity in this globalizing era.

Accountability

Working to achieve trust and solidarity may become difficult, however, because globalization is shrinking the areas of public policy in which citizens can hold their political leaders accountable. Democracy requires that citizens are able to hold accountable all the political leaders who make decisions affecting their daily lives. But such accountability is diminishing in certain key areas.

Take, for example, the changes in the value of our money: they are taking place very far away, and there is little that our political leaders can do about them. As the Canadian dollar fell in value in the late 1990s because of the East Asian economic crisis, our politicians did not take action; the fact of the matter is that there was virtually nothing they could do. Nevertheless, this change had a significant impact on the economic situation of thousands of Canadians.

Also in the economic realm, it is very difficult for a country such as Canada to have its own autonomous policy favouring economic growth and full employment. With the liberalization of capital movements, we lose important degrees of freedom in this area. The postwar economic order postulated that countries would have control over their own macroeconomic policies, so that they could promote full employment and provide a social safety net for those in need: the ill, the elderly, the disabled, the unemployed, and so on. Have Canadians and citizens in other countries asked that their health-care budgets, their education budgets, and other related social policies be cut or held constant while needs for such services increase? Probably not, and yet their politicians have gone ahead and done these kinds of things in response, in part, to externally imposed financial pressures. Such political outcomes indicate, in turn, a decline in accountability.

Another example that illustrates the problem can be drawn from developments in the area of the environment. Virtually everyone is familiar now with the fact that the size of the ozone layer that protects us from some of the harmful consequences of the sun's radiation is gradually diminishing. Over the past 20 years, there has been a steady decline in levels of ozone. Again, we have here a global problem that requires a set of global political decisions. It is also an area where accountability is low. Decisions about ozone depletion that are affecting us as Canadians are being made by governments and others who are well beyond our capacity to hold accountable. The possibility of a nuclear accident is in the same category. Think of the accident in Chernobyl in the Ukraine in the 1980s, when the radioactive fallout drifted over Western Europe and other parts of the globe with the winds. How could the citizens of Sweden, for example, hold any politicians to account for the radiation found in the vegetables growing in their backyard gardens?

While we are considering nuclear disasters, let us think of still another area of public policy, security. Since the end of World War II, there has been a steady growth in the number of countries that do research on, have a potential for, or possess nuclear weapons. These weapons are not only terrifying technologies—they are technologies whose use has global ramifications. If even a small nuclear war were to break out anywhere on the globe, the radioactive fallout and other disastrous consequences would have significant effects well beyond the territorial borders of the states involved. In February 1945, when the German city of Dresden was fire-bombed, the effects were felt principally in that city alone. If Pakistan and India were to begin dropping nuclear bombs on one another tomorrow, the radiation produced would have direct, immediate impact well beyond the territorial borders of those countries. Citizens of Sri Lanka or Iceland or Canada, however, have little capacity to affect such matters.

Popular Sovereignty

Can we as citizens bring about changes to our life circumstances through political action directed at the relevant decision-makers? The discussion above has already raised questions about this possibility. Many of the key decisions, it would appear, are being made either by other states or by international organizations. So it is difficult for citizens to have any impact on the kinds of political outputs that they might want to see in their lives.

As was argued in the previous chapter, leaders of nation-states are discussing policy options and reaching decisions in international organizations much more frequently than in the past. As the importance of these discussions has increased, it has brought about changes in the organization of government. Certain officials (prime ministers, ministers of finance and of trade) have grown in importance as the bureaucracies underneath them have grown. What is more, because these officials are making policy beyond the framework of the nation-state, and because they have to make decisions relatively quickly, the usual institutions for holding political leaders accountable do not work well. This kind of decision-making does not fit easily into cabinet government in a parliamentary system, nor does it provide much of a role for the parliament or legislature. In fact, in the United States, the president usually seeks fast-track authority from the Congress, so that he does not need to consult the elected representatives until the very end, when an international deal has already been struck. In short, as political decisions become globalized, citizens seem to be losing control over the persons making those decisions, even though the effects of these decisions might have a crucial impact on their

lives. Such a development is inconsistent with popular sovereignty, the idea that the people have the ultimate power and authority over their lives.

International Organizations and Democracy

In the face of these kinds of problems, a concern for the future of democracy brings us to focus more on the growing number of international organizations and on how they might be made to conform to democratic principles. International agreements affecting such policy areas as the environment and trade have increased significantly during the most recent period. Associated with many of these agreements is the development of international secretariats or committees that oversee the agreements and provide a site for ongoing decision-making. Other international organ-

Protest banner about lack of democracy at the WTO.

Reuters New Media Inc./Corbis/Magma

izations have developed without the signing of formal agreements.

It is important to recognize, however, that these international institutions are increasingly parts of systems of multilevel governance that include decision-making not only by regional organizations or national governments, but also by subnational governments in many instances. Democratic governance requires, therefore, that democratic principles be followed and that they inform policy processes at *all* levels of decision-making. Accountability at supranational levels becomes a hollow concept if accountability is lacking in regional, national, or subnational decision-making forums. In such systems of multilevel governance, legitimacy will be achieved only if democracy is entrenched throughout the system. For example, in a country with a federal system, such as Canada or the United States or Germany, it does not make sense to have a democratic federal government and dictatorships in the provinces or states. Similarly, there is no use in reforming international institutions if some of the problems in domestic governance that we have noted are not also addressed.

Six Criteria for Assessing Levels of Democracy in International Institutions

At this point, we are a considerable distance away from having institutions at the global level that conform to democratic principles. What we can do at this stage is to identify some criteria that might be used to assess democracy in existing institutions. Applying these criteria does not amount to the full realization of democratic principles. Rather, their application provides a start, a way of evaluating and possibly improving these institutions until they are replaced or supplemented by more democratic structures. These criteria extract key underlying principles of democracy that have emerged within nation-states, but they are applied in a way that does not tie them to political institutions, such as legislatures, that do not (yet) exist globally.[7]

Transparency

Can all interested observers inform themselves fully on the core questions and tradeoffs under consideration? Policies are often developed in locations or technical languages that remove them from the scrutiny of citizens. Transparency can be enhanced by such techniques as the posting of policy documents and other reports in technical and lay language on websites. The World Trade Organization has been adopting these kinds of practices more and more.

Openness to Direct Participation

Global governance becomes democratic only when political influence within processes of deliberation and decision-making is equally accessible or available to affected or concerned parties. Similarly, because the interests at stake in an issue area may change as that area develops, it is problematic to restrict access permanently to a specified set of actors. Evidence that an international institution is satisfying this criterion, therefore, will be found primarily when it lets citizens' organizations have some access to the policy process. Many of the antiglobalization movements argue that the WTO is closed off to civil society groups like their own.

Quality of Discourse

Democracy requires the existence of public arenas or spaces where open, informed debates can take place about possible policy options. Such public spaces are often absent at supranational levels. Accordingly, public spaces where debates can take place must be created for supranational governance arrangements. These debates must permit the "translation" of technical issues into language for a lay public, so that as many citizens as possible can inform themselves about the stakes involved and about the advantages and disadvantages of choosing one policy option over another. For example, if intellectual property rules at the WTO are to govern the length of the patents that transnational pharmaceutical companies can hold on their medicines, all countries and the WTO itself should have a "place" where citizens can debate the pros and cons of different lengths of time.

Representation

Representation is a formal means for articulating the interests of citizens at large by a smaller number of actors, a process that is required if bargaining, deliberation, or decisions are to be effective. Practices that are well established at the domestic level, such as the electing of representatives on the basis of majority voting in territorial constituencies, are often not applicable or not yet available at supranational levels. Although the idea may be simple, its application may be complex. All those potentially affected by policy-making in a given supranational institution should be represented in some way in the policy process. In the area of global finance in particular, representation is often a problem. Rules that have global effects are devised by specialists from a limited number of highly developed states. Citizens in developing countries have no voice or representation in these organizations.

Effectiveness

There is little value in having open, transparent, representative institutions if they cannot make decisions and implement them. Effectiveness refers to the ability of institutions to do these things and normally involves the creation of an executive-like grouping for making decisions and a bureaucracy for implementing them. This bureaucracy may, in fact, be located at the nation-state level, provided that participating governments have agreed upon rules for implementing decisions taken at a higher level. In the absence of effectiveness, the legitimacy of institutions may come into question, thereby undermining democracy. For example, if political leaders operating in open, transparent, and representative institutions cannot ever reach agreement on rules to reduce the pollution responsible for climate change, they are not effective, and the democratic institutions within which they are working may be questioned. Or if they can agree on the rules but have no bureaucracies with the needed expertise to implement their decisions, again decision-making is not effective, and again the legitimacy and value of democratic institutions might be questioned.

Fairness

Fairness refers to the idea that equals should be treated equally and unequals unequally. Political theorists talk about fairness in two ways. Procedural fairness refers to the types of considerations that have been discussed under the first four criteria above. Substantive fairness refers to the distribution of benefits from policy outcomes. Are some nation-states and some citizens systematically excluded from the distribution of benefits by given institutions? For example, if the WTO

becomes more open, more transparent, and more representative, and still the citizens of developing countries receive little benefit from stronger international trade rules, then the criterion of substantive fairness is being compromised.

CONCLUSION

If individual citizens wish to continue to preserve and build democracy in this globalizing era, they will need to be more demanding of their political leaders at the nation-state level. They must work to ensure that democratic principles are not marginalized by the growth of supranational decision-making. Further, they must resist closed-door decision-making at the international level. Individual citizens may need to join organizations that are active on the international level and that are seeking more democracy along the lines described in this chapter. Whatever the nation-state in which they find themselves governed, citizens may no longer have the luxury of limiting their political activity to within their own national borders. Too much that is important and crucial to their lives is now being decided elsewhere.

It took at least two centuries of struggle to realize some of the potential of democracy within the nation-state. Now that globalization has given rise to alternative centres of power and authority outside the control of the nation-states system, those who believe that democracy is important will need to add a new goal. Some of their energies will have to be directed at these new centres of power if they are to enjoy any potential control over the conditions under which they live.

DISCUSSION QUESTIONS

1. **Can you identify areas of the economy or of culture where there is greater extensiveness, intensity, and velocity in human social relationships? Give at least three examples and explain your answer.**

2. **Is globalization a welcome process or an unfortunate development? Explain.**

3. **Some scholars argue that globalization has been going on for five hundred years or more. Do you agree or disagree?**

4. What is the significance of the large antiglobalization protests that are taking place at meetings of world leaders and at meetings of such organizations as the WTO?

5. Give some examples of where nation-state governments have lost power as a result of globalization. Give some examples of where nation-state governments remain very powerful.

6. Take an international organization such as the United Nations or the World Trade Organization. Use the criteria presented in this chapter to assess where this organization is democratic and where it is lacking in democracy.

WEB LINKS

United Nations System:
http://www.unsystem.org

Rights and Democracy, a Canadian organization interested in globalization issues:
http://www.ichrdd.ca

Fred W. Riggs's Discussion of Globalization:
http://www2.hawaii.edu/~fredr/welcome.htm

Global Justice Agenda:
http://www.fpif.org/global/index.html

World Trade Organization:
http://www.wto.org

FURTHER READING

Giddens, Anthony. *Runaway World: How Globalization is Reshaping Our Lives.* London: Routledge, 2000.

Held, David. *Democracy and the Global Order.* Stanford: Stanford University Press, 1995.

Scholte, Jan Aart. *Globalization: A Critical Introduction.* Basingstoke: Macmillan, 2000.

ENDNOTES

1   David Held, *Democracy and the Global Order* (Stanford: Stanford University Press, 1995), p. 145.

2   Jan Aart Scholte, *Globalization: A Critical Introduction* (Basingstoke: Macmillan, 2000), p. 46.

3   John Tomlinson, *Globalization and Culture* (Chicago: University of Chicago Press, 1999), p. 2.

4   David Held, Anthony McGrew, David Goldblatt, and Jonathan Perraton, *Global Transformations* (Stanford: Stanford University Press, 1999).

5   Roland Robertson, *Globalization: Social Theory and Global Culture* (London: Sage, 1992), p. 26.

6   Wolfgang Reinicke, *Global Public Policy* (Washington, D.C.: Brookings Institution Press, 1998).

7   William D. Coleman and Tony Porter, "International Institutions, Globalisation and Democracy: Assessing the Challenges," *Global Society* 14(3) (2000), pp. 377–98.

Glossary

Aboriginal self-government A demand by Aboriginal or Indigenous groups that they be able to govern themselves, as they did before colonial rulers removed such power. (2)

Access to information The right of the public, usually enshrined in a law and subject to certain exceptions, to have access to government documents. Often used by journalists, interest groups, and opposition parties to reveal information in government files. (7)

Administration Usually used as a synonym for the bureaucracy, that branch of government that carries out the law; sometimes applied to the political executive, as in "the Bush administration." (7)

Administrative tribunals Boards or commissions established by the government to adjudicate certain disputes by applying laws to the facts; also called quasi-judicial tribunals. These tribunals are not proper courts presided over by judges. (10)

Affirmative action Policies that seek to overcome historical patterns of systemic discrimination against groups of individuals, primarily in employment practices; the giving of preferential treatment to targeted groups in such areas as employment, promotion, housing, or education to redress the effects of past discrimination. (3, 5, 8)

Agents of political socialization Those groups of people or institutions that convey political attitudes and values to others in society. (4)

Amending formula The procedure by which a constitution may be amended; in most states, it is a more onerous procedure than that which applies to the amendment of ordinary legislation. (6)

Anarchism A political ideology that sees no need to impose government order on a society because of the essential goodness of human beings; harmony will naturally prevail when free individuals participate equally in mutually beneficial decisions. (5)

Anarchy A system of social, political, and economic relations without formal institutions of governance to define enforceable rules or exact obedience from the governed; as such, it is more characteristic of world politics than of politics within communities. (16)

Aristocracy A system of government ruled by a few, namely "the best," which is commonly interpreted as the nobility. (2)

Authoritarian government A nondemocratic government that rules without public input, glorifies the leader, allows no dissent, strictly controls the mass media, relies on the police and military to root out opposition, and is dedicated to remaining in power at all costs. (2)

Authority The imposition of one's will on another by reason of legitimacy—because the subject regards the decision-maker as having a right to make such a binding decision. (1)

Autogolpe A self-coup by the leader of a country. (15)

Backbenchers Members of parliament who, if they are in the governing party, are not cabinet ministers or if they are in an opposition party are not among the important party critics. (9)

Bicameral legislature A legislature that has two separate houses, or chambers, each with its own set of members. (9)

Bill The formal text of a proposed law before it has been enacted into law. When it has completed all stages of the legislative process, it becomes a law and is known as a statute or an act. (9)

Bourgeoisie In Marxist theory, the ruling class in capitalist society consisting of those who own the means of production, such as factories or mines. This capitalist class rules over the proletariat or working people. (5)

Brokerage party A party that seeks power by appealing to a broad spectrum of the electorate, in an attempt to win enough parliamentary seats to form a government; it avoids clear and potentially divisive ideologies, preferring to attract voters from a wide range of perspectives and cleavages. Canada's Liberal and Progressive Conservative parties are prime examples of brokerage parties. (11)

Bureaucracy   The expert, permanent, nonpartisan, professional officials employed by the state to advise the political executive and to implement government policies. (2, 7, 13)

Cabinet   The group of people chosen by the prime minister or president to provide political direction to government departments; in Canada, cabinet members act collectively to make the key government decisions. (7)

Cabinet government   A system of government in which the major political decisions are made by the cabinet as a whole, as opposed to one in which the prime minister or president acts with considerable autonomy. (7)

Capitalism   An economic system based on the operation of market forces and the profit motive, free of government intervention. (5)

Caucus   A group composed of all members of a legislature that belong to a particular party or legislators who meet to further a specific policy interest. (9, 11)

Checks and balances   A constitutional system of power-sharing under which powers are assigned to different branches of government (especially executive, legislative, and judicial) so as to enable each branch to curb the unilateral exercise of power by the others. (6)

Citizenship   Legal membership in a political community, especially in a nation-state, entailing rights and responsibilities. (1)

Civil rights and liberties   Those legal and constitutional guarantees, such as freedom of speech, the right of *habeas corpus*, and nondiscrimination rights, that govern the conduct of the state, and some private power-holders, in relation to citizens and certain minority groups. (6)

Civil society   The array of social institutions and organizations that are independent of the state and in which citizens pursue their interests, express their beliefs, and live in communities. (2, 13, 14, 15)

Class   A concept that describes hierarchical groupings within societies that are based on social and economic factors such as income, occupation, education, and status. (4)

Class consciousness   An awareness of the divisions in society based on social and economic differences and a sense of identification with the appropriate division. (4)

Cleavage   Stable, long-term division among identifiable groups within an electorate. Examples include gender (men vs. women), religion (Protestants vs. Catholics), language (English vs. French), and region (East vs. West). A cleavage becomes politically significant only when it is effectively mobilized by a particular individual or group. (4, 11)

Closure   A term used to describe procedural rules that permit the majority to put an end to debate on a motion and require that a vote on the matter be held; also known as cloture, the guillotine, and time allocation in various countries. (9)

Coalition government   A government that occurs when two or more parties hold seats in cabinet supported by a combination of parties that forms a majority in the legislature. (9)

Coercion   The imposition of one's will on another by the use of penalty, force, or the threat of force. (1)

Collective security   A commitment by a number of states to join in an alliance to defend themselves militarily against any threat to the peace and jointly attack any aggressor. (16)

Colonialism   The ownership and administration of one territory and people by another as if the former were part of the latter. (14)

Common law   A system of law in which precedents from relevant cases in the past are applied to current cases. Judges are bound by precedent and should decide like cases alike. (10)

Communism   A political ideology based on eliminating exploitation through nearly total public ownership, full state control, and central planning of the economy. (2, 5)

Concurrent powers   Those fields of shared jurisdiction under a federal constitution in which both the national and the subnational governments may act and pass laws. (6)

Confidence (or no-confidence) vote   There are three types of such a vote. It may be an explicitly worded motion indicating that the legislature either has or does not have confidence in the government. It may be a vote on a matter that the government has previously declared to be a matter of confidence. It may also be a vote on important measures that are central to the government's plans, such as a vote on the whole budget. (9)

Conservatism   The ideology of defending the status quo against major social, economic, and political change. Today conservatism is often used to label anyone on the political right, especially those who want to conserve the free-market capitalist system against radical demands for progressive reforms. (5)

Constituency   A geographical electoral district or the group of people represented by a member of a legislature. (9)

Constitution   The body of fundamental laws, rules, and practices that defines the basic structures of government, allocates power among governmental institutions, and regulates the relationship between citizens and the state. (6)

Constitutional convention   An unwritten rule of constitutional conduct that fills in gaps in the written constitution and conditions the exercise of legal powers under the constitution. (6)

Constitutionalism   The idea that the constitution should limit the state by separating powers among different branches of government and protecting the rights of individuals and minorities through a bill of rights. (6)

Contentious politics   Protests that disrupt the normal activities of society, such as demonstrations or civil disobedience. (13)

Coup d'état   The overthrow of a political regime or leader by military force. (15)

Crime against humanity   A wrongful act that is deemed to be not a violation of any particular nation's laws, but rather a violation against humankind as a whole. (16)

Crown corporation   A corporation owned by the government that assumes a structure similar to that of a private company and that operates semi-independently of the cabinet. (7)

Cultural pluralism   The existence of many ethnic and cultural groups within a country. Such diversity is the starting point in arguing that all groups in a society can maintain their linguistic, cultural, and religious distinctiveness without being relegated to the economic or cultural margins; an example is the Canadian policy of multiculturalism. (3)

Decolonization   The process through which a population and territory formerly under colonial domination achieve formal political independence and becomes a sovereign state. (14)

Democracy   See Liberal democracy.

Democratic consolidation   The achievement of a situation in which none of the major political actors, parties, organized interests, forces, or institutions consider that there is any alternative to democratic processes to gain power, and in which no political institution or group has a claim to veto the action of democratically elected decision-makers. (15)

Democratic transition   The change from a nondemocratic to a democratic government, usually indicated by the existence of at least one free and fair election. (15)

Democratization   A group of transitions from nondemocratic to democratic regimes, involving the relaxation of authoritarian political control by political leaders, the expansion of political and civil liberties, and the creation of institutional mechanisms that open up a political system to greater representation and participation. (15)

Department of Finance   The department referred to as the government's chief economic advisor, responsible for overall economic management, raising revenue, preparing economic forecasts, and determining government expenditure levels. In Britain, it is called the Treasury. (7)

Dependency   A condition where countries in the South lack any degree of autonomy in their political, economic, and social development by virtue of their reliance on countries in the North for access to capital, technology, and markets. (14)

Deputy minister   The minister's chief policy advisor, the department's general manager, and a key participant in the collective management of the government; known in Britain as the permanent secretary. (7)

Devolution   The delegation of administrative or limited legislative powers by a central government to regional or local governments. (6)

Diaspora   An ethnic group that has experienced or currently experiences dislocation across multiple states, yet typically nurtures narratives and political projects about a specific "homeland" as a place of eventual return. (3, 17)

Dictatorship of the proletariat   A Marxist concept that refers to the interim period immediately after the proletariat (the working class) has triumphed in revolutionary class war over the bourgeoisie (capitalists). The rule of the proletariat is expected to later give way to the classless society when full communism is realized. (5)

Digital democracy   A broad term meant to encompass the application of technological innovation to politics and political participation; also called e-democracy or e-politics. (12)

Direct democracy   A political system in which citizens hold power directly rather than through elected or appointed representatives. (12)

Dominant conformity   A model of ethnic group integration that holds that all groups in a society should conform to the language and values of the dominant group. (3)

Dual executive   The executive in a political system such as that of Canada or Britain in which the head of state and head of government functions are divided.

The queen or king is the head of state and the prime minister is the head of government. (7)

Egalitarianism   The doctrine that advocates equal social and political rights for all citizens, regardless of sex, religion, ethnicity, etc. Reform-oriented liberals emphasize the need for an equality of opportunity, which guarantees to all the equal chance to compete for the social, economic, and political benefits available in society. Socialists often interpret egalitarianism to require an equality of condition, so that all goods and resources in a society would be distributed equally. (5)

Election   A mechanism by which the expressed preferences of citizens in democratic states are aggregated into a decision regarding who will govern. (12)

Electoral-professional party   A political party with a small membership (especially between campaigns), which relies heavily on corporate donors for its funding. Its primary goal is to form a government, not to advance a particular ideology. It invests heavily in capital-intensive campaign techniques, such as polling and slick television advertising. (11)

Elite   A small group of individuals who have significantly more power than other members of their community. They are either in a position to make authoritative decisions or have privileged access to decision-makers. (4)

Enumerated powers   Those areas of legislative authority in a federal state that are specifically listed in the constitution and assigned to one level of government or the other, or to both. (6)

Ethnic cleansing   The removal of one or more ethnic groups from a society, by means of expulsion, imprisonment, or killing. The term entered the political lexicon in reference to the former Yugoslavia; it was first used to describe the violent measures and policies designed to eliminate or dramatically reduce the Muslim and Croat populations in Serb-held territory. (3)

Executive   That branch of government that is responsible for running the country and that provides leadership and makes the major decisions. (7)

Executive Office of the President   Offices and agencies attached directly to the president of the United

States that provide advice on decisions and help develop and implement policies and programs. (7)

Extra-parliamentary wing That wing of a political party that consists of the members of local party associations and the permanent paid staff in the party headquarters; in other words, the party organization outside the legislature. The extra-parliamentary wing is less visible than the caucus, but much larger. In Canada, the extra-parliamentary wings of the major national parties are spread across over 300 separate constituency associations. (11)

Fascism The political system of the extreme right, based on the principles of the leader (dictator), a one-party state, nationalism, total control of social and economic activity, and arbitrary power, rather than constitutionalism. In 1922 in Italy, Benito Mussolini created the first fascist regime, emulated by Adolf Hitler in Germany. Today there are numerous neofascist movements advocating ultranationalist, racist, and anti-immigrant political positions. (2, 5)

Federalism A form of government in which the sovereign powers of the state are formally divided under the constitution between two levels of government, neither of which is subordinate to the other. (6)

Feminism A belief in the full equality of men and women and the insistence that all barriers to such equality be removed. (5)

Filibuster A device used by a member or group of members who take advantage of the procedural rules of a legislature that allow members to speak without a time limit in order to stall proceedings by speaking for extended periods of time. (9)

First-past-the-post (FPP) An electoral system that requires the winning candidate to receive more votes than any other in order to win the seat—that is, to receive a plurality of votes. (12)

Flexible amending formula A constitution whose provisions may be amended with relative ease. (6)

Foreign aid The administered transfer of resources from rich to poor countries, ostensibly to promote the latter's welfare and development. (14)

Franchise The right to vote in public elections. (12)

Fusion of powers In parliamentary systems, the joint exercise of legislative and executive powers by the prime minister and members of the cabinet who simultaneously hold office in both the legislative and executive branches of government. (6)

Geneva Conventions A comprehensive and detailed set of rules put in place over the course of the 20th century to try to ensure that warfare is conducted in a predictable and orderly way. (16)

Genocide The deliberate and systematic extermination of a national, ethnic, or religious group. The term was developed in response to the horrors of the Holocaust. (3, 17)

Global governance The process by which different actors—governments, organizations, firms, groups, and individuals—try to make common decisions about and for the global community. (2, 16)

Globalization The movement of goods, capital, ideas, and people across geopolitical boundaries today and in the past. Contemporary patterns of globalization involve a deepening constellation of economic, technological, and cultural changes that are worldwide in scope and that challenge the sovereignty of the state. Also, globalization is the growth of supraterritorial relations among people that creates a complex series of connections that tie together what people do, what they experience, and how they live across the globe. (2, 3, 8, 13, 16, 17)

Government The set of institutions that make and enforce collective public decisions for a society. (1, 2)

Greenhouse effect A warming of the surface and lower atmosphere of the earth caused by the increased presence of various pollutants that break down the ozone layer of gases that protects life from harmful rays from the sun. The process also leads to rising temperatures and climate change; it is also known as global warming. (17)

Group of 8 (G8) Canada, France, Germany, Italy, Japan, Russia, the United Kingdom, and the United States; the heads of these countries meet once a year to discuss how they might coordinate their economic activities in ways to ensure that the global economy functions well. (16, 17)

Head of government   The person in effective charge of the executive branch of government, namely the prime minister in a parliamentary system. (7)

Head of state   The person who symbolizes and represents the state but does not exercise effective political power, namely the monarch in a parliamentary system. (7)

Human Development Index (HDI)   A composite index measuring longevity, knowledge, and standard of living designed to give an indication of and a basis for comparing the quality of life in various countries. (1, 14)

Human rights   Rights pertaining to people simply because they are human beings, primarily including the prevention of discrimination or coercion on grounds of ethnicity, religion, gender, or opinion. (16)

Human security   A broadened concept of security focusing not just on national security and interstate war but on threats to the safety of individuals and groups. (14)

Identity politics   Political activity of particular groups for recognition of their status and identity, as well as of the ways their beliefs and value systems differ from those of others. (4, 17)

Ideological party   A political party whose primary goal is to promote a distinct ideology and/or policy approach. While most ideological parties would like to participate in government, winning power is a means to the end of implementing their policy goals, not an end in itself. Most mass-bureaucratic parties fit into this category. (11)

Ideology   A reasonably consistent system of political beliefs that aspires to explain the world, to justify certain power relationships, and to maintain or transform existing institutions; a fairly coherent set of beliefs that not only explains what may be wrong with society, but also provides a vision of what society should be like. (4, 5)

Imperialism   The domination of one country by another with the aim of controlling and/or exploiting the latter; this domination can be economic, political, social, or cultural. Imperialism literally means "empire building." (14)

Independence   The state of being free from the control of others; the ability to make one's own decisions, not having to rely on anyone else. In the context of world politics, it is the ability of a political community to govern itself rather than be governed by others. (16)

Influence   The imposition of one's will on another through persuasion and voluntary compliance. (1)

Initiative   A mechanism that allows citizens to petition the government to introduce or adopt specific pieces of legislation or force a referendum on an issue. (12)

Institutionalized group   A highly organized interest or pressure group that has a permanent, professional staff. (13)

Interest group   A group that brings together people with common interests and/or a common sense of identity to influence the political process. (13)

International Court of Justice   A branch of the United Nations consisting of 15 judges elected by the Security Council that hears disputes between governments of countries and renders decisions based on the accumulated body of international law. (16, 17)

International Criminal Court   A branch of the United Nations created on a permanent basis in 1999 to deal with individuals accused of a range of war crimes or crimes against humanity. (16, 17)

International law   A complex body of rules, derived principally from the treaties, covenants, and declarations signed by the governments of various countries. The resolutions of international organizations, the writings of academics, and rulings of domestic and international courts can also be sources of international law when the rules are not otherwise clear. (10)

International Monetary Fund (IMF)   A sister of the World Bank and a branch of the United Nations that regulates the international monetary system in order to stabilize national currencies and that makes loans to developing countries, subject to certain conditions. (14, 15, 16, 17)

Judicial activism A style of judges' decision-making that involves an active use of their discretion to create new policies. (10)

Judicial Committee of the Privy Council (JCPC) A British court that was the final court of appeal for Canada until 1949, when the Supreme Court of Canada took over this function. (10)

Judicial impartiality A state of mind in which judges preside over and decide cases with an open mind toward the parties and issues involved. (10)

Judicial independence A relationship between the courts and the other branches of government that allows judges to function without interference from other government officials. (10)

Judicial review A function of the courts in which judges examine actions of the government to determine whether they are authorized by law. This may also include a determination as to whether statutes and regulations are contrary to the constitution. (10)

Judiciary The term used to refer to all the judges in a country collectively. It can also mean the whole judicial branch of government, including juries and the courts' administrative staff. (10)

Laissez-faire Literally "to let be," this economic theory provides the intellectual foundation for the system of free-market capitalism. *Laissez-faire* rejects state ownership or control, advocates a free market, values individualism, and promotes free trade. (5)

Law A type of rule that has been formally approved by the legislature or the executive or declared by the courts and that people are obliged to obey. (10)

Left That part of the ideological spectrum that believes in equality in society and the intervention of government via such collectivist measures as taxation, regulation, redistribution, and public ownership to effect such equality. (5)

Legislature An institution with primary responsibility to enact laws. (9)

Legitimacy The degree to which citizens accept and tolerate the actions and decisions of social and political actors such as states, international organizations, and civil society groups themselves, usually based on the notion that the decision-makers have such a right. (12, 13)

Liberal democracy A form of government characterized by public participation and popular sovereignty, normally exercised in free and fair elections in which the franchise is universal, the ballot is secret, and political parties are free to organize. A liberal democracy is also marked by individual political freedoms and the absence of discrimination. Government decisions are made by majority rule but are subject to the protection of individual and minority rights. The mass media are not controlled by the government, the government observes the rule of law, and the judiciary operates independently. (2, 5)

Liberalism The ideology based on belief in the paramount value of individual liberty. Liberals assume that all humans are rational and can use their intelligence to decide how best to live life and maximize individual well-being; they also believe that they are free and equal by nature. (5)

List system The most commonly adopted form of proportional representation, employing relatively large electoral districts and a ballot that requires voters to choose from among party lists or candidates on party lists. (12)

Lobbyists Those professional, private sector firms and individuals that are paid by companies or groups to influence and access government. (13)

Maastricht Treaty A 1993 European treaty that created an economic and monetary union for the countries joined in the European Union, specifying that they have a single currency (the euro) and one common central bank (the European Central Bank); it also introduced a citizenship of the European Union. (3)

Majoritarian system An electoral system that requires the winning candidate to receive a majority of votes to win a seat. The majority is normally achieved through a second ballot or by an alternative voting system. (12)

Majority government A prime minister and cabinet of one party that have the support of over 50 percent of the seats in the legislature (or lower house in bicameral legislatures). (7, 9)

Mass-bureaucratic party A political party with a large membership, strict internal rules, and centralized power structures. While the leaders of mass-bureaucratic parties are formally accountable to the members, such accountability is not always evident in practice. The central offices of these parties tend to be large, with dedicated permanent staff. The parties depend on individual party members and on affiliated groups for the resources to keep those central offices running. (11)

Mass media The means of mass communication, especially radio, television, and newspapers, designed to reach large numbers of people. (4, 12)

Memorandum to Cabinet The key instrument by which proposals are brought forward by ministers for consideration by the cabinet. (7)

Merit system A system of hiring or promoting public servants on the basis of their merits (education, training, experience, and so on), rather than on party preference or other considerations. (7)

Ministerial responsibility The principle that cabinet ministers are individually responsible to the House of Commons to answer for everything that happens in their department. (7)

Minority government A prime minister and cabinet of one party that have the support of less than 50 percent of the seats in the legislature. (7, 9)

Modernization A paradigm that saw development as a process of progressive transformation, in which societies moved from "traditional" through a series of stages to "modern"; this paradigm emerged in the late 1950s and 1960s. (14)

Multiculturalism A policy sometimes adopted in a state characterized by cultural pluralism that encourages ethnic and cultural groups to maintain their customs and traditions, often with public financial assistance. (3)

Multination state A state that contains more than one nation. (3)

Multinational corporations See Transnational corporations.

Multiparty system A party system with three or more parties, none of which is large enough for one-party dominance or two-party alternation. New coalition governments must be constructed after each election and sometimes between elections. This system is usually associated with a highly proportional electoral system accurately that translates each party's share of the votes into its share of seats in the legislature. (11)

Nation A community of people, normally defined by a combination of ethnicity, language, and culture, with a subjective sense of belonging together. (2, 3)

Nationalism An ideology that holds that certain populations are nations, that the world is divided into nations, and that a nation should be self-determining (i.e., able to establish its own institutions, laws, and government and to determine its future). (3)

Neoconservatism A social ideology that advocates a traditional, hierarchical, patriarchal, authoritarian, and inequitable society; it usually overlaps with neoliberalism in economic terms. (5)

Neoliberalism An economic ideology that advocates an economic arena free of government regulation or restriction and free of government participation in the marketplace via public ownership, which usually overlaps with neoconservatism in social terms. (5)

New International Economic Order (NIEO) A set of proposals launched in 1974 for reform of the international economic order, with the goal of enhancing the self-reliance of the South and its influence over international institutions and events and achieving an increase in resource flows from the North to the South. (14)

No-confidence vote See Confidence vote.

Nongovernmental Organization (NGO) A non-profit organization outside of government, usually working across borders in fields such as peace, development, and human rights. (13)

Nontariff barrier Any measure or practice that places a barrier in the way of "free" commerce between states, ranging from obvious measures, such as procurement policies that favour one's nationals, to not-so-obvious practices, such as the imposition of strict health and safety standards on imports in order to make the goods of other countries more expensive. (16)

North American Free Trade Agreement (NAFTA) An agreement ratified by the United States, Canada, and Mexico that contains rules to promote the freer movement of goods, capital, and services between these countries. (17)

Oligarchy A system of government ruled by a few. (2)

One-party dominance A type of party system in which one large party consistently wins the largest share of the votes; consequently, that party is usually in government. It may form a majority or minority government on its own or it may be the senior partner in a series of coalition governments. A one-party dominant system should not be confused with a one-party system, in which opponents to the incumbent government are forbidden from seeking office. (11)

Opposition A term used in parliamentary systems to describe those members of the legislature who do not belong to the party or parties that form the government and cabinet. (9)

Organizational culture Beliefs about the way a group should be organized and how it should function. (13)

Pacted transition A regime transition that involves a set of agreements (or pacts) between the outgoing regime and the opposition as to the terms of the transition. Pacts usually include agreements on some of the following issues: election rules, exclusion of antisystem parties, prosecution for past human rights violations, and guarantees of representation levels under the new regime. (15)

Parliamentary wing That wing of a political party that includes the leader, the elected legislators, and the people who work in their offices. It is also called the caucus or the party in public office. (11)

Party discipline The practice that all members in a legislature belonging to the same political party should normally vote the same way, in accordance with their party's stand on the issue at hand. (9)

Party identification An individual's long-standing identification with a particular political party. (12)

Party system The sum total of the relevant parties in a given country at any one time. Relevant parties are those that enjoy representation in the legislature or that appear likely to win such representation in the near future. The core idea of a party system is that the parties are interdependent, and each affects the others. (11)

Patriotism A sense of pride in one's country. (4)

Peacebuilding An extension of peacekeeping that refers to the efforts of the international community to create the structures of a peaceful society, as was done in Bosnia in 1995, Kosovo in 1999, and East Timor in 1999–2000. (16)

Peacekeeping An undertaking by any group of governments, usually under the sponsorship of the United Nations, to put the forces of a third party between warring parties who have come to a ceasefire, in order to encourage them to keep the peace. (16)

Peacemaking An extension of peacekeeping that involves the armed forces of a third party intervening in a war to bring peace to an area, as was done in Somalia in 1992. (16)

Policy community A collection of groups and individuals (including both state bureaucrats and interest groups or social movement organizations) who influence each other in an effort to shape policy outcomes in their area of interest. See also Policy networks. (8, 13)

Policy cycle The various stages that are part of the policymaking process of governments, including some or all of the following: agenda-setting, problem definition, policy design, implementation, and evaluation. (8)

Policy networks The relationships that develop among those individuals and groups (including both government officials and members of the public) who have a common interest in a particular policy area. See also Policy community. (8)

Political action committee (PAC)   A political committee organized for the purpose of raising and spending money to elect and defeat a candidate, especially in the United States. (13)

Political alienation   A sense of detachment or resentment that arises in people who have little trust in political leaders and feel unable to influence political decisions that affect their own interests. (4)

Political culture   The collection of the understandings, values, attitudes, and principles of a community or society that relate to its political organization, processes, disputes, and public policies. Out of a society's political culture come important beliefs and values that structure the citizens' attitudes and expectations toward such basic political concepts as legitimacy, power, authority, and obedience. (4)

Political development   A concept that describes how well a society has developed politically, usually measured by the degree of state capacity to effectively carry out the legislative, executive, and judicial functions of government; the degree of political stability, or ability to resolve political conflicts in a peaceful manner; and the degree of governmental responsiveness to public demands and respect for fundamental rights. (14)

Political dissent   Any form of action taken to indicate a rejection of the existing order, such as peaceful protest, domestic violence, or terrorism. (15)

Political efficacy   The belief that we as individuals can have some influence upon the political decisions that affect our lives. (4)

Political participation   Actions taken by individuals and groups in an attempt to influence political decisions and decision-makers. (12)

Political party   An organization of members, mostly volunteers, who work together to achieve common goals. For most parties, the primary goal is to win seats in the national legislature; other goals vary among party organizations. Most, if not all, political parties have formal constitutions, internal bureaucracies, and at least some independent organizational and financial resources. (11)

Political patronage   The awarding of benefits to individuals or companies based on their support for the government political party. (10)

Political science   The systematic study of government and politics. (1)

Political socialization   The process through which attitudes toward and knowledge about political matters are passed on within a society. (4, 5)

Political trust   The belief that political leaders act in the best interests of society. (4)

Politics   That activity in which conflicting interests struggle for advantage or dominance in the making and execution of public policies. (1)

Power   The capacity of one actor to impose its will on another, to get its own way, to do or get what it wants; the capacity of one actor to prevail in a conflict of interests with other actors, normally through force, sanction, coercion, or manipulation. (1, 16)

Prime minister   The head of government in a parliamentary system who provides political leadership and makes the major decisions, usually in concert with a cabinet. (7)

Prime Minister's Office (PMO)   The office that provides political advice to and is staffed by close partisan advisers of the prime minister, and whose overriding concern is to safeguard the political fortunes of the prime minister. (7)

Private law   A branch of law dealing with relationships between private parties such as individuals, groups of people, and corporations; it includes laws governing contracts, property, and personal injury. (10)

Privatization   Transferring a government program, agency, or crown corporation to the private sector, for example, by selling shares in the corporation to the public at large or to a private firm. (7)

Privy Council Office (PCO)   The office that links the prime minister and cabinet to the world of administration and provides logistical and decision-making support to the government; it is made up of nonpartisan career public servants, (7)

Propaganda An organized attempt to spread beliefs through a communications campaign. It implies the use of exaggerated facts. (4)

Proportional representation (PR) An electoral system employing multimember districts that attempts to award legislative seats to parties in proportion to the share of votes earned. (12)

Protectionism The use of various policy tools, such as subsidies, tariffs, and quotas, to protect goods and services produced within a country against competition from producers in other countries. (16, 17)

Public law A branch of law involving governments and public authorities; it includes constitutional, administrative, and criminal law. (10)

Public opinion polling The use of survey interviews, often conducted over the telephone, with a representative, randomly selected sample of people, providing an accurate description of the attitudes, beliefs, and behaviour of the population from which the sample was drawn. (12)

Public policy A course of action or inaction that is selected by public officials, usually in response to a specific problem or set of problems. (8)

Question Period A set period of time in a parliament when members can put questions directly to the prime minister and other cabinet ministers. (9)

Race Historically, the term race was used to speak about differences between people that were supposedly biologically based. Today social scientists completely reject the idea that there are any significant biological differences between people that warrant the use of the term "race". While some suggest that the term should not be used at all, many contemporary social scientists use the term "race" in quotation to refer to differences that are socially constructed and historically specific, but have important consequences (e.g., racism is discrimination based on differentiating between groups). (3)

Rational voting A model that seeks to explain voting decisions by emphasizing the rational evaluation of alternatives (parties and candidates) and the retrospective assessment of the governing party, as opposed to less rational factors. (12)

Recall A mechanism that allows citizens to petition to remove their political representative before the next election. (12)

Referendum A mechanism that provides citizens with the ability to vote directly on pieces of legislation or constitutional changes. (12)

Representation by population The principle suggesting that the allocation of seats in assemblies should occur in a manner that encourages an equal division of the population across electoral districts, so that each vote is of equal weight. (12)

Representative democracy A political system in which citizens hold power indirectly by selecting representatives who render public decisions on their behalf in popular assemblies. (2, 12)

Residual powers Powers to pass laws in relation to any matters that the constitution does not expressly assign to any level of government; these powers typically belong either to the federal government or to the state or provincial governments. (6)

Responsible government A defining principle of Westminster-style parliamentary governments, which states that the cabinet must always have majority support in the legislature (or lower house in a bicameral parliament) for votes of confidence. (7, 9)

Right That part of the ideological spectrum that cherishes individualism and believes in leaving the private sector to operate with minimal government intervention. (5)

Rigid amending formula A constitution whose method of amendment is relatively onerous. (6)

Security The peace of mind that comes with a sense of safety, a freedom from threats of harm to all that one values; a sense of well-being that can have economic, environmental, social, linguistic, or cultural dimensions. It can be seen in terms of both individual and community safety. (16)

Self-determination A principle of international law that grants all peoples/nations the right to determine their political status and pursue their economic, social, and cultural development free from external domination or interference. (14)

Separation of powers The constitutional principle that holds that legislative, executive, and judicial powers should be allocated, in whole or in part, to separate branches of government as a safeguard against tyranny. (6)

Single executive The executive in a political system in which the head of state and head of government functions are combined and occupied by one person. In the United States, the position is filled by the president. (7)

Social movement An informal network of activists who seek to transform the values of society. (13)

Socialism The doctrine advocating economic equality of the classes and the use of government to serve the collective good of the whole society. Socialists value the collective good over the private interests of individuals and emphasize cooperation over competition. (5)

Sovereignty The final or ultimate power over a population and a piece of territory, commonly claimed by the government of a state. In other contexts, sovereignty can be said to reside in the people or in parliament; in all cases, however, it has probably been eroded by global forces. (2)

Speech from the Throne The document prepared by the prime minister and cabinet and read by the head of state at the opening of each session of Parliament; it outlines the government's legislative proposals for the session to follow. (7)

Stare decisis The principle of common law systems by which courts are bound to follow prior decisions that involved similar issues of law. A judgment by one member of a court binds other members, and lower courts are bound to follow the decisions of higher courts. (10)

State A human community that has the monopoly over the legitimate use of physical force within a given territory; a modern form of organizing political life that is characterized by a population, a piece of territory, and a sovereign government. The modern world is divided into nearly 200 such entities, each of which

has a government that claims the power to make the ultimate decisions over its population and territory. (2, 3)

State failure A situation in which the structure, authority, law, and political order have fallen apart and must be reconstituted in some form. (14, 15)

Subculture A cluster of people who share the same basic political values and attributes that are distinct from those of other groups in society and from the predominant values and attributes of society as a whole. (4)

Supranational A sphere of politics and political institutions that exists "above" the nation-state but usually "below" the global level. The only supranational polity in the world is the European Union. (16)

Supreme Court of Canada Canada's highest court and final court of appeal since 1949. (10)

Sustainable development An approach to development that makes environmental protection an integral part of the development process, in order to enhance the ability of current and future generations to meet their needs. (14)

Terrorism The threat or use of violence, usually directed at civilian populations in order to effect some form of political change. (12, 15)

Totalitarian government A special kind of authoritarian government—most notably Nazism, fascism, and Soviet communism—that is based on a single party and ideology; takes control of all aspects of political, social, economic, and intellectual life; and mobilizes its mass public into active support of the government. (2)

Transnational corporations Business firms that are headquartered in one country, but that have plants or places of operation in other countries as well; also called multinational corporations. (17)

Transnational group An interest group that organizes across the borders of nation-states with the goal of influencing governments, international organizations, or public opinion. (13)

Treasury Board   A cabinet committee that, along with its Secretariat, is often described as the manager of government. It acts as the employer of public servants for the purpose of collective bargaining and as the government's accountant to ensure that departmental budgets are respected. (7)

Two-party system   A party system in which two large parties alternate in government, while one or more smaller parties watch from the sidelines. On occasion, one of these smaller parties becomes large enough to deny a majority of parliamentary seats to the party that forms the government and its support becomes necessary to keep the government in power; this is a two-and-a-half-party system. In a two-party system, the dominant parties can alternate as single-party governments or as the senior partners in coalitions. (11)

Tyranny of the majority   Abuse of the minority by the majority through excessive use of power; it can occur in social settings (when, for example, members of an ethnic minority feel oppressed by the actions of the ruling majority) or in political settings (when, for example, members of a legislature feel influenced in their decision-making by the majority group in their riding). (5, 9)

Unicameral legislature   A legislature with only one house, or chamber, to which all members belong, such as provincial legislatures in Canada. (9)

United Nations (UN)   An international organization formed in 1945 as a successor to the League of Nations that has become the largest and most ambitious international governmental organization in world history, consisting of a vast array of organs and agencies. Its membership now includes almost every country in the world. Less than a world government, it attempts to promote peaceful relations among states and economic and human rights for all people. (2, 16)

Unwritten constitution   A constitution, such as that of the United Kingdom, whose subject matter is dispersed across a variety of statutes, court rulings, and constitutional conventions. (6)

Veto   The authorized power to block a decision or piece of legislation, especially of a president to reject a law passed by congress or of a province to reject a proposed constitutional amendment. (7)

Welfare state   A concept that stresses the role of government as a provider and protector of individual security and well-being through the implementation of interventionist economic policies and social programs. (5)

World Bank   Closely linked to the IMF, this bank is one of the world's largest sources of development assistance. Through loans, policy advice, and technical assistance, it aims to improve the living standards in the developing world. (14, 15, 16, 17)

World Trade Organization (WTO)   An organization created during the Uruguay Round of GATT negotiations whose goal is to provide international trading rules to promote liberal trading practices and to reduce protectionism. (2, 14, 15, 16, 17)

Written constitution   A constitution whose fundamental provisions have been reduced to a single document or limited set of documents. (6)

Index